Communications
in Computer and Information Science

1673

Editorial Board Members

Joaquim Filipe ⓘ
Polytechnic Institute of Setúbal, Setúbal, Portugal

Ashish Ghosh
Indian Statistical Institute, Kolkata, India

Raquel Oliveira Prates ⓘ
Federal University of Minas Gerais (UFMG), Belo Horizonte, Brazil

Lizhu Zhou
Tsinghua University, Beijing, China

More information about this series at https://link.springer.com/bookseries/7899

Ashwani Kumar · Iztok Fister Jr. · P. K. Gupta · Johan Debayle · Zuopeng Justin Zhang · Mohammed Usman (Eds.)

Artificial Intelligence and Data Science

First International Conference, ICAIDS 2021
Hyderabad, India, December 17–18, 2021
Revised Selected Papers

 Springer

Editors
Ashwani Kumar (iD)
Sreyas Institute of Engineering
and Technology
Hyderabad, India

P. K. Gupta (iD)
Jaypee University of Information Technology
Solan, India

Zuopeng Justin Zhang (iD)
University of North Florida
Jacksonville, FL, USA

Iztok Fister Jr. (iD)
University of Maribor
Maribor, Slovenia

Johan Debayle (iD)
LGF CNRS UMR 5307, MINES
Saint-Etienne, France

Mohammed Usman (iD)
King Khalid University
Abha, Saudi Arabia

ISSN 1865-0929   ISSN 1865-0937 (electronic)
Communications in Computer and Information Science
ISBN 978-3-031-21384-7   ISBN 978-3-031-21385-4 (eBook)
https://doi.org/10.1007/978-3-031-21385-4

This Springer imprint is published by the registered company Springer Nature Switzerland AG
The registered company address is: Gewerbestrasse 11, 6330 Cham, Switzerland

Preface

The First International Conference on Artificial Intelligence and Data Science (ICAIDS 2021) focused on the emerging trends, theories, development, applications, experiences, and evaluation of artificial intelligence with fellow students, researchers, and practitioners.

The conference is devoted to increasing the understanding of the role of technology, current issues, and how engineering has, day by day, evolved to prepare human-friendly technology. The conference aims to provide a platform for bringing forth significant research and literature across the field of artificial intelligence and data science for the welfare of society and to provide an overview of cutting-edge technologies. In the current era of computing, technologies like artificial intelligence, data science information processing, the Internet of Things, and data analytics have their own significance.

This volume contains the papers presented at the International Conference on Artificial Intelligence and Data Science (ICAIDS 2021) held during December 17–18, 2021, at Sreyas Institute of Engineering and Technology, Hyderabad, Telangana, India. The prime objective of this conference was to bring together researchers and developers from industry and academia to share new ideas, research results, and development experiences on artificial intelligence and data science for mutual benefits and knowledge sharing. As such, the conference had two main technical tracks: (i) artificial intelligence for intelligent applications and (ii) data science for emerging technologies.

The Technical Program Committee (TPC) of ICAIDS 2021 are highly thankful to the authors who demonstrated their interest in the form of paper submissions and helping with publicity throughout India and abroad. Therefore, we received a total of 195 papers, out of which 43 papers were accepted for presentation at the conference and publication in this Springer CCIS volume. All papers went through a rigorous single blind peer review process, with each paper receiving a minimum of four reviews. We are thankful to our reviewers for their timely efforts in filtering the high-quality research papers. Along with the paper presentations, ICAID 2021 featured four keynote addresses given by each of the conference chairs and two of the TPC chairs.

We would like to thank the Chief Patron, Patron, Convener, Organizing Chairs, Session Chairs, Advisory Board, Steering Committee, and Local Organizing Committee who made an invaluable contribution to the conference. We also acknowledge the contribution of EasyChair in enabling the efficient and effective management of paper submissions, reviews, and the preparation of the proceedings. We are thankful to our Technical Program Committee for their immense support and motivation towards making the ICAIDS 2021 a grand success.

We express our sincere gratitude to our publication partner, Springer, for believing in us and for their timely support and help. We hope that you find the book to be of value in the pursuit of academic and professional excellence.

December 2021

Ashwani Kumar
Iztok Fister Jr.
Pradeep K. Gupta
Johan Debayle
Danila Parygin
Mayank Singh
Zuopeng Justin Zhang
Mohammed Usman

Organization

Chief Patrons

Anantula Vinay Kumar Reddy   Sreyas Institute of Engineering and Technology, India

Chintala Ravindranath Yadav   Sreyas Institute of Engineering and Technology, India

Nirvetla Sharath Reddy   Sreyas Institute of Engineering and Technology, India

Hriday Reddy   Sreyas Institute of Engineering and Technology, Hyderabad, India.

Patron

S. Sai Satyanarayana Reddy   Sreyas Institute of Engineering and Technology, India

Steering Committee

Suresh Akella   Sreyas Institute of Engineering and Technology, India

J. Pandu Ranga Rao   Sreyas Institute of Engineering and Technology, India

General Chair

Ashwani Kumar   Sreyas Institute of Engineering and Technology, India

Technical Program Committee Chairs

Iztok Fister Jr.   University of Maribor, Slovenia

P. K. Gupta   Jaypee University of Information Technology, India

Johan Debayle   MINES Saint-Etienne, France

Danila Parygin   Volgograd State Technical University, Russia

Convener

V. Biksham   Sreyas Institute of Engineering and Technology,
                                    India

Organizing Chairs

S. Abdul Nabi   Sreyas Institute of Engineering and Technology,
                                    India
M. Jaya Ram   Sreyas Institute of Engineering and Technology,
                                    India
Venkata Achuta Rao   Sreyas Institute of Engineering and Technology,
                                    India
V. A. Sankar Ponnapalli   Sreyas Institute of Engineering and Technology,
                                    India
A. Hymavathi   Sreyas Institute of Engineering and Technology,
                                    India

Program Chair

Mayank Singh   JSS Academy of Technical Education, Noida,
                                    India

Conference Chairs

Zuopeng Justin Zhang   University of North Florida, USA
Mohammed Usman   King Khalid University, Saudi Arabia

Advisory Board

Meenakshi Arya   SRM Institute of Science and Technology, India
A. Govardhan   JNTUH, India
Deepa Garg   Bennett University, India
D. Vasumathi   JNTUH, India
Kamakshi Prasad   JNTUH, India
Ashok Chandra   Goa Institute of Management, India
Deepak Gupta   SVKM's NMIMS University, India
Shiva Prakash   JNU, India
Shirmohammad Tavangari   University of British Columbia, Canada

Technical Program Committee

Wasim Soliman   Andhra University, Syria
Fatima Faydhe Al-Azzawi   Middle Technical University, Iraq

Suryanarayana	Jawaharlal Nehru Technological University, India
Vijender Solanki	CMRIT Hyderabad, India
F. M. Javed Mehedi Shamrat	Daffodil International University, Bangladesh
Soumi Dutta	Institute of Engineering and Management, Kolkata, India
Rishav Singh	NIT Delhi, India
Deepak Gupta	Wichita State University, USA
Shiva Prakash	M. M. M. University of Technology, India
Ramjee Prasad	Aalborg University, Denmark
Mohd Wajid	Aligarh Muslim University, India
Deepak Dahiya	Majmaah University, Saudi Arabia
Deepa Garg	Bennett University, India
Walid Barhoumi	Université de Tunis El Manar, Tunisia
Kamarulafizam Ismail	Universiti Teknologi Malaysia, Malaysia
Kreangkri Ratchagit	King's Mongkut University of Technology Thonburi, Thailand
Rohit Thanki	Prognica Labs, Dubai, UAE
Pronaya Bhattacharya	Nirma University, India
Haci Mehmet Baskonus	Harran University, Turkey
Dac Nhuong	Haiphong University, Vietnam
Mitsunori Makino	Chuo University, Japan
Siva Somayaji	VIT University, India
Govind Suryawanshi	University of Pune, India
Inayathulla Mohammed	Malla Reddy Engineering College, India
Rahul Sharma	Tallinn University of Technology, Estonia

Contents

Artificial Intelligence

Comparative Analysis of Advanced Machine Learning Based Techniques
to Identify the Lung Cancer: A Review 3
   B. Samirana Acharya and K. Ramasubramanian

Classification and Identification of Objects in Images Using CNN 16
   Rajesh Kumar Chatterjee, Md. Amir Khusru Akhtar,
   and Dinesh K. Pradhan

An Appraisal of Cyber-Attacks and Countermeasures Using Machine
Learning Algorithms 27
   Akhilendranath Mummadi, B. Midhun Krishna Yadav,
   Rachamalla Sadhwika, and S. Shitharth

A Systematic Review on Autonomous Vehicle: Traffic Sign Detection
and Drowsiness Detection 41
   Panna Lal Boda and Y. Ramadevi

Crop Disease Auto-localization and Classification 52
   G. Deepank, Shivani Bisht, Aditya Verma, R. Tharun Raj, and R. Jyothi

Challenges in Crop Selection Using Machine Learning 66
   D. Lukshmi Padmaja, Surya Deepak G, G. K. Sriharsha,
   and Rohith Kumar K

Handcrafted Features for Human Gait Recognition: CASIA-A Dataset 77
   Veenu Rani, Munish Kumar, and Bhupinder Singh

Local Binary Pattern Symmetric Centre Feature Extraction Method
for Detection of Image Forgery 89
   M. Pavan Kalyan, D. Kishore, and Mahesh K. Singh

A Copy and Move Image Forged Classification by Using Hybrid Neural
Networks 101
   K. Sushma, V. Satyanarayana, and Mahesh K. Singh

Cardiac Surveillance System Using by the Modified Kalman Filter 112
   Sabbella Urmila, R. Anil Kumar, and Mahesh K. Singh

An Extensive Study on Parkinson's Disease Using Different Approaches
of Supervised Learning Algorithms 123
   V. Navya Sree and S. Srinivasa Rao

Adaptive Convolution Neural Networks for Facial Emotion Recognition 135
   P. V. S. Lakshmi, Haritha Akkineni, Ande Hanika, and Padmaja Grandhe

A Gravitational Search Algorithm Study on Text Summarization Using NLP ... 144
   Chatti Subbalakshmi, Piyush Kumar Pareek, and M. V. Narayana

Analysis of Deep Learning Methods for Prediction of Plant Diseases 160
   Subhashree Rath, Vaishali M. Deshmukh, Shree Raksha V.,
   Geetha Sree S., and Harshitha S.

ACHM: An Efficient Scheme for Vehicle Routing Using ACO and Hidden
Markov Model 169
   Righa Tandon and P.K Gupta

Detection of Leaf Disease Using Artificial Intelligence 181
   Sumit Bhardwaj, Devanshu Kumar Singh, Ria Singh, and Punit Gupta

Deep CNN Based Whale Optimization for Predicting the Rice Plant
Disease in Real Time 191
   S. Sai Satyanarayana Reddy, G. Sowmya, Vudara Bhaskar Reddy,
   Boodidha Deepak Kumar, and Ashwani Kumar

DCBC_DeepL: Detection and Counting of Blood Cells Employing Deep
Learning and YOLOv5 Model 203
   Md. Abdur Rahaman, Md. Mamun Ali, Md. Nazmul Hossen, Md. Nayer,
   Kawsar Ahmed, and Francis M. Bui

ML_SPS: Stroke Prediction System Employing Machine Learning
Approach 215
   Md. Sazzad Hossain, Mehedi Hassan Shovo, Md. Mamun Ali,
   Md. Nayer, Kawsar Ahmed, and Francis M. Bui

A System for Network Based Intrusion Avoidance Using Dedicated
Machine Learning and Artificial Intelligence-Based Model for Application
and Data Safety 227
   H. Manjunath and S. Saravana Kumar

AI-Based COVID Alert System on Embedded Platform 241
   Vipul Jethwa, Ruchi Gajjar, and Nagendra Gajjar

An Efficient Detection of Brain Stroke Using Machine Learning Robust
Classification 252
   Shaik Abdul Nabi and Revathi Durgam

Apple Leaf Diseases Detection System: A Review of the Different
Segmentation and Deep Learning Methods 263
  Anupam Bonkra, Ajit Noonia, and Amandeep Kaur

Underwater Image Restoration and Enhancement Based on Machine
and Deep Learning Algorithms 279
  Yogesh Kumar Gupta and Khushboo Saxena

Using Machine Learning for Inter-smell Detection: A Feasibility Study 291
  Ruchin Gupta and Sandeep Kumar Singh

An 8-Layered MLP Network for Detection of Cardiac Arrest at an Early
Stage of Disease 306
  N. Venkata Maha Lakshmi and Ranjeet Kumar Rout

Calculation Method of Economical Mode of Integrated Electrical Power
System 321
  Vladislav Kuchanskyy, Sree Lakshmi Gundebommu, S. Harivardhagini,
  Petro Vasko, Olena Rubanenko, and Iryna Hunko

Testing and Integration Method Utilization for Restricted Software
Development 336
  Ahmed J. Obaid, Azmi Shawkat Abdulbaqi, and Hayder Sabeeh Hadi

Brain MRI Noise Reduction Using Convolutional Autoencoder 348
  B. Nageshwar Rao and D. Lakshmi Sreenivasa Reddy

An Efficient Mobility Aware Scheduling Algorithm 363
  Pankaj Sharma and P. K. Gupta

Data Science

Cloud-Based E-Learning: Development of Conceptual Model for Adaptive
E-Learning Ecosystem Based on Cloud Computing Infrastructure 377
  Ashraf Alam

Performance of Secure Data Deduplication Framework in Cloud Services 392
  Rajesh Banala, Vicky Nair, and P. Nagaraj

A Comprehensive Study on Eucalyptus, Open Stack and Cloud Stack 404
  S. Saisree and S. Shitharth

Cloud Security by LZW Technique and Fast Searching by Genetic Data
Clustering 419
  Amit Kumar Jha and Megha Kamble

Document Summarization Model Using Modified Pagerank Algorithm 430
   S. Sai Satyanarayana Reddy, Chithram Deeven Kumar,
   Sreekanth Reddy Pisati, and Rama Devi Kolli

Architects Companion: Simulation of Visual Impairments for Architectural
Purposes 440
   Gaurish Garg, Aditya Makhija, Nikunj Madan, Vaibhav Vij,
   Gaurav Mathur, and Shivendra Shivani

Classification Models for Autism Spectrum Disorder 452
   Vincent Peter C. Magboo and Ma. Sheila A. Magboo

Life Prediction of Underwater Electroacoustic Sensor Using Data-Driven
Approach 465
   Vineeth P. Ramachandran, V. P. Pranavam, and Pramod Sreedharan

Smart Transportation and Evolutionary Algorithms: An Approach
to Understand Vehicular Ad-Hoc Network 476
   Rakesh Kumar Maram, V. A. Sankar Ponnapalli,
   and Harsha Vardan Maddiboyina

Blockchain and Climate Smart Agriculture Technologies in Agri-Food
Security System 490
   Viktoriia Vostriakova, M. Lakshmi Swarupa, Olena Rubanenko,
   and Sree Lakshmi Gundebommu

Using Symmetric Group to Generate Dynamic S-box 505
   Kareem Abbas Alghurabi, Ahmed J. Obaid, Heyam K. Alkhayyat,
   Yahya M. Abdulabbas, and Salah A. Albermany

Wolf Algorithm Based Routing and Adamic Adar Trust for Secured IOT
Network 518
   Shailendra Kumar Tiwari and Praveen Kumar Mannepalli

Using Convolution Networks to Remove Stripes Noise from Infrared
Cloud Images 530
   K. Chandana Sri, Y. Deepika, N. Radha, and Mahesh Kumar Singh

Correction to: Apple Leaf Diseases Detection System: A Review
of the Different Segmentation and Deep Learning Methods C1
   Anupam Bonkra, Ajit Noonia, and Amandeep Kaur

Author Index 541

Artificial Intelligence

Comparative Analysis of Advanced Machine Learning Based Techniques to Identify the Lung Cancer: A Review

B. Samirana Acharya and K. Ramasubramanian(⊠)

Koneru Laxmaiah Education Foundation, Hyderabad, India
{acharya501,ramasubramanian}@klh.edu.in

Abstract. Machine learning and deep learning have lately played a significant role in developing practical solutions in the field of medical care and treatment. Additionally, they enhance prediction precision in early and rapid illness diagnosis via the utilization of medical and audio-testing procedures. Given the shortage of qualified people in the medical field, physicians benefit from technology help, which allows them to visit more patients. Furthermore, it improves the efficiency with which pictures and one of the disease stages of lung cancer. Usually, cancer diseases are detected using a machine learning algorithm and the architecture of the Apache Spark design framework. T-BMSVM threshold technology supporting vector machine and SVM nonlinear binary classification using Radial Basis Function are used in conjunction with Multi-class WTA-SVM winner-take-all with threshold technology supporting vector machine T.BMSVM. RBF is used to investigate the categorization of nodules as malignant or benign and the presence of malignancies linked with the nodules. It is proposed that this article review analysis supports machine learning methods such as the Clinical Tree algorithm and Fuzzy C-Means Clustering (FCM). The and Cross-Validation with a small number of folds is used to improve various machine learning and deep learning approaches.

Keywords: Machine learning · Deep learning · Lung cancer

1 Introduction

Lung cancer kills over 2 million people each year, accounting for around one-quarter of all cancer mortality. Lung cancer identification at an early stage is crucial for effective therapy and patient survival. Because lung cancer screening detects tumors early, it is an effective technique for improving survival in high-risk individuals. Several significant clinical studies have shown the utility of Low-Dose Computed Tomography (LDCT) screening for lung cancer. The ELCAP (Early Lung Cancer Action Program) compared standard chest x-rays to LDCT (low-dose chest CT) in a lung cancer screening research with over 30,000 participants. Using LDCT and chest x-rays, the NLST (National Lung Screening Trial) compared over 50,000 former or current smokers who met various inclusion criteria. LDCT has been demonstrated to be more effective than chest x-rays in

A. Kumar et al. (Eds.): ICAIDS 2021, CCIS 1673, pp. 3–15, 2022.
https://doi.org/10.1007/978-3-031-21385-4_1

identifying most early lung cancers. Even though NLST was linked to a greater chance of survival following early lung cancer detection, the study included non-survivors. We hypothesized that risk factors linked with mortality in other non-screening cancers might be utilized to predict patient survival in the NLST cohort with LDCT-detected lung cancer. These include skeletal muscle loss, subcutaneous fat loss, CAC (Coronary Artery Calcification), and emphysema. The research aims to analyze the skeletal muscle area, subcutaneous fat attenuation, and coronary artery calcification of lung cancer survivors and non-survivors in the NLST (CACs).

In addition to significant health issues such as cancer and diabetes, respiratory problems wreak destruction on society. Because early diagnosis and treatment of respiratory infections are critical, respiratory audio combined with chest X-rays is very effective. The present research aims to assist medical practitioners by thoroughly examining chronic obstruction lung detection data using deep learning algorithms based on Convolutional Neural Networks. We investigated machine libraries' Chroma Constant-Q, Chroma CENS (Chroma Energy Normalized Variant), Chrome, Mel-Spectrogram, and MFCC (Mel-Frequency Cepstral Coefficients) functionalities. The severity of the ailment, such as moderate, severe, or acute, may also be interpreted by the assessment system. However, Healthcare claims data to determine cancer stage hampered the quality of oncology research and health outcomes. The consequences are minor. At present, a method for classifying lung cancer patients who develop early-stage vs. late-stage illness using linked cancer registration and Medicare claims data by

i.   Forecasting using ensemble machine learning,
ii. Developing a set of classification rules for the predicted likelihood, and
iii. Utilizing a more extensive collection of authoritative data claims.

They expected that measuring the severity of CA, emphysema, muscle mass, and fat attenuation in lung cancer patients included in the National Lung Screening Trial would assist in mortality prediction (NLST). The screening experiment identified all persons diagnosed with lung cancer after receiving regulatory approval from the Cancer Data Access System (CDAS). These themes were separated into two categories: survivors of the NLST experiment and non-survivors. The groups were matched on some factors, including age, gender, BMI, smoking history, stage of lung cancer, and survival time. In all groups, the low dose baseline CT (LDCT) was assessed in all patients with CAC, emphysema, muscle mass, and subcutaneous fat attenuation.

The health care industry is one of the most critical and self-sufficient in compared to other industries. Because of the money spent on the highest diagnostic, treatment, and service quality is one of the most significant and crucial industries. Depending on their subjectivity, clarity, and complexity, many medical instruments may be linked with a range of pictures and sounds. They may undergo significant changes after being reviewed by some interpreters/doctors. Until recently, the vast amount of medical data generated by various devices and kinds of technology was solely dependent on human cognition, capability, and ability to analyze and analyze it. The Chronic Obstructive Pulmonary Disease (COPD) is used to represent a group of lung diseases in which tiny air channels obstruct airflow from and into the lungs, making breathing difficult. As a result, the lungs cannot obtain enough oxygen and create harmful carbon dioxide.

Chronic bronchitis and emphysema are the multiple common causes of COPD. These two disorders often coexist, although they manifest differently in COPD patients. Bronchitis causes the airways to expand and constrict. Tobacco smoking, a genetic disease (alpha-1 antitrypsin deficiency), and pollution exposure are all known causes of COPD, and early or rapid COPD diagnosis is still a young area with plenty of room for advancement. Figure 1 depicts the use of machine learning methods for a variety of illnesses.

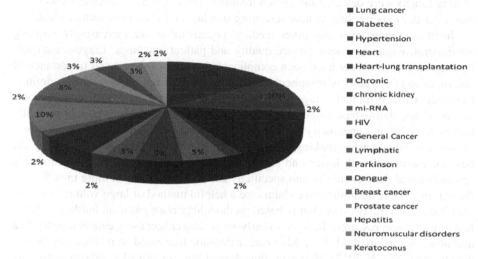

Fig. 1. Kinds of diseases percentages.

Lung function tests (pulmonary): To evaluate the patient's lungs to check whether they are working correctly and providing an appropriate quantity of oxygen while breathing. The most common test is.

Spirometry: Spirometry is a procedure that involves inhaling into a Spirometer, which records the amount of air exhaled.

X-ray imaging is a kind of imaging that employs the usage of X-rays. For example, chest X-rays may detect a variety of lung diseases, including emphysema. Emphysema is the most common cause of COPD.

CT scanning: CT scanning is seldom used unless in emergencies when more conventional methods are unavailable. A CT scan may show if the patient needs COPD surgery.

Arterial blood gas analysis: This test assesses the quantity of oxygen in a person's circulation.

In existing techniques have the following disadvantages:

- It is not advised for those who have underlying heart issues or have recently had cardiovascular surgery.
- Possible symptoms include shortness of breath, dizziness, and nausea.
- Radiation is administered to the patient through CT scans and X-rays, both of which endanger the patient's life.

Numerous machine learning and deep learning techniques and the advancement of artificial intelligence have been explored, tested, and deployed to determine whether they might help clinicians identify COPD more quickly and efficiently. COPD may be discovered through photographs or an internal audit performed by the respiratory organ's respiratory organ utilizing proper procedures. The stage of lung cancer diagnosis determines survival; those with the locally progressed disease had a 5-year relative survival rate of 55%, compared to 4% for those with metastases. Historically, the majority of lung tumors were detected late, when treatment options were restricted. However, it may alter due to better lung cancer screening standards for current or former smokers.

Insurance companies and other medical organizations are increasingly utilizing administrative data to assess service quality and patient outcomes. Large-scale quality assessments in cancer have been complicated because of the crucial importance of outcomes and the quality of treatment supplied by clinical stage experts. Using administrative data to determine the stage of a cancer patient presents some challenges. According to studies, claims-based algorithms have not produced instruments with consistently high sensitivity and specificity for identifying metastatic cancer, recurrence, or progression. While decision-making algorithms are based on ICD9 codes are among the best for associated with lower and chemotherapeutic agents, a published claims data research found that sensitivity and specificity cannot be obtained in more than 80% of the sample. While administrative claims are a helpful method of large volumes of data, the absence of a trustworthy claims-based methodology is a significant hurdle to inhabitants' lung cancer research. To forecast early-stage lung cancer using cancer registry data and observational methods from Medicare, a decision tree based on medical advice was constructed (NCCN 2017). However, this clinical tree performed poorly in sensitivity and specificity in recognizing people with early-stage cancer (Brooks, 2017).

2   Background of Cancer Stages with Machine Learning

2.1   Lung Cancer Detection in Related Works

Tan [12] investigated the possibility of integrating Adaboost with decision-making trees, often known as weak classifiers, and discovered a technique for predicting early lung cancer. Kim [13] proposed DT, a novel paradigm for detecting the development of lung cancer as a consequence of occupational exposures, in 2010. The framework was established in 2010. In 2014, Ziăba [14] proposed an updated SVM model to address data imbalance concerns. For raw data, the suggested methodology coupled the advantages of ensemble models with cost-sensitive SVMs. The improved SVM was then used to create an Oracle-based judging technique. Engchuan [15] described the AFS technique for multi-class data translation in a study released in 2015. The proposed model is very categorizable. Finally, Azzawi [16] pioneered microarray data to predict lung cancer using the GEP approach in 2016.

Two gene selection methods were also employed to discover essential lung cancer genes, and numerous GEP prediction methodologies were highly suggested. Petousis [17] demonstrated in 2016 how longitudinal data might be utilized to help with lung cancer monitoring decisions in a DBN population. In 2017, Lynch [18] proposed Linear

Regression, GBM, SVM, DT, and customized ensemble as supervised learning algorithms for identifying people with lung cancer in the SEER database. In 2019, Petousis [19] published a paper showing a revolutionary POMDP learning system that improved the specificity of lung cancer detection. Based on expert assessments, the NLST data were trained using a Bayesian Network, and then reverse strengthening learning was used to get the following function. ALzubi [20] introduced the WONN MLB ensemble for significant data on lung cancer in 2019. The required criteria for function selection were established using an integrated Newton-Raphsons MLMR to decrease classification time. By integrating defined criteria, the improved WONN Ensemble classification model was constructed to identify patients more correctly and with a reduced FPR.

2.2 Additional Methods

Lung cancer stages are essential when defined pharmaceutical applications are in place. So it is since the lung's cells are injured throughout the growth stages. Photographs of the diseased components may be taken in medical research, and early stages may be detected. Medical data, on the other hand, is organized, semi-structured, and unstructured. Eberendu et al. [21] provide an overview of unstructured data and how it may be utilized to do predictive testing. This section will highlight the importance and need of unstructured analytical data.

As a consequence, businesses are no longer disregarding unstructured data. Structured data is follows a specific structure or arrangement. Furthermore, data sets including both structured and unstructured data may be effectively handled when seen through the perspective of a complete data framework. These challenges and the direct connectivity between vast, large-scale datasets are addressed by machine learning and deep learning algorithms like the ones used in Ashfaq.

By using the Spark MLlib distributed machine learning framework, Apache-spark also assists with iterative machine learning challenges. As a result, while working with structured and unstructured data, machine learning and deep learning accelerate treatments. It is almost like having the best of both worlds. High-dimensional datasets are obtained throughout the machine learning process utilizing Spark-based models.

The work section describes the automated processes and physical technologies that are utilized to help with the diagnosis of respiratory illnesses. Physical technologies are like the Break Monitoring System sign at creating an intelligent breath analysis tool for COPD identification. A classification system that integrated ANN and Multi-Layer Perceptron background algorithms were used to predict major auditory events in patients with certain respiratory illnesses such as asthma and COPD. Because of its non-linear character, ANN outperforms commonly used regression and classification algorithms. Furthermore, equivalent analyses may be carried either by fine-tuning the classifier's parameters or using deep learning approaches. Peak event and reminder accuracies were 77.1 and 78.0%, respectively, whereas non-peak event and reminder accuracy were 83.9 and 83.2%. The average machine achieves an average performance of 81.0%. It was proposed to provide an integrated platform for accurate diagnosis and real-time monitoring of COPD patients. A framework for communicating chronic conditions has been created. A machine/device constantly monitors a patient's condition. In order to give an early and real-time classification approach for a COPD series, a hybrid classification system was designed for a tailored digital assistant employing machine learning methods like SVM, random forest, and a predicate approach. The gathered ion classifications were rated of high quality, with a score of 94%.

In addition, a computational approach for automatically deciphering stethoscope-recorded breathing sounds has been developed. This technology may be used for a variety of purposes, including telemedicine and self-screening. First, a single piece of sophisticated diagnostic equipment, three unique sounds are gathered from 60 people. Now, a deep CNN model with six convolutional layers, three max-pooling levels, and three fully-connected layers will be built. The data set is a frame-by-frame collection of 60 log-scaled Mel-Frequency Spectral feature strips separated as model inputs into 23 following frames using time-frequency transformation. Finally, the model was evaluated using a new dataset of 12 subjects, and the results were accurate and equivalent to the findings of five breathing experts on average.

Lung cancer is one of the most common malignancies in the world. To treat lung cancer, we will use a variety of approaches. The identification of pulmonary nodules in the given collection of images is shown and significantly outperforms CT scans using machine learning methods. Images are extracted using a deep neural network. The larger the nodule, the higher the risk of cancer, according to the detective technique. The characteristics are selectively entered into linear SVM and utilized to compare the test set to the class labels to increase classification accuracy, known as pattern recognition. The ROI segmentation compression approach is used to recover CT images. The ROI image is then divided into bands using a two-level DWT methodology in conjunction with SVM-based GLCM classification, which stimulates and enhances malignant or healthy categorization accuracy. A novel nodule-size approach based on ROI image segmentation will be developed to surpass existing algorithms for identifying cancer cells. The GLCM technique is used with the Otsu segmentation threshold to extract the feature, and the gray level matrix is utilized in this example. The observations were made in cancer nodules due to these features. Furthermore, they detect cancer stages earlier in order to reduce the severity of the illness.

The median filter is one way of removing salt and pepper noise from photos. Similarly, the absolute pixel values of the surrounding district's neighboring district are derived in numerical order. Water bucking, ROI removal and segmentation procedures, and a bottom line based on the Otsu threshold are all segmentation approaches. The overviews, as mentioned earlier, highlight the advantages of GLCM and SVM for grading lung cancer images. The CAD (Computer-assisted Design) technology is substantially different from prior color picture creation processes. The extraction feature returns model characteristics such as the NC and circularity ratios and cancer or normal cell combining rule prediction threshold. While feature extracts are more common than other processes, the rule-based classification does not provide the same results as SVM and GLCM. Other approaches, on the other hand, employ classification to begin cancer stages early. For example, after extracting typical properties such as area, perimeter, and excentricity, a better image utilizing Gabor filters and a mixture of harmonic and Gaussian functions followed by watershed segmentation are utilized to detect cancer stages.

Researchers classified stages I-III as early stages and stage IV as late stages to determine the primary outcome variable. Because of the discrepancy in clinical outcomes among stage IV patients, it is often the suggested categorization. The clinical tree methodology described in Algorithm 1 (Brooks, 2017) is a branch built from seven earlier decision trees formed on a single split sample [23].

Algorithm-1: Clinical Tree algorithm:

Step 1: For each data sample, write ix:
Step 2: If no lung disease treatment is available, the stage is considered early.
Step 3: Alternatively, if aside the fact cells lung cancer treatment is required, or advanced stage stereotactic cranial radiation;
Step 4: Otherwise, if lung resection procedure is performed, the phase is early.
Step 5: if radiation-k, then initial stage; otherwise, late phase;
Step 6: Otherwise, if small-cell chemotherapeutic drugs and platinum plates arc only used, the stage is late.
Step 7: Otherwise, if specific agents-y, advanced stages;
Step 8: Otherwise, it will be too late.

The super-learner run each of the eight algorithms three times, once for each of the factors C1, C122, and C123, and the clinical tree in Algorithm 1, which only utilizes C1 in de concept. Consequently, they investigate a convex combination of $K = 25$ approaches with a 26th approach for the super learner. The techniques were as follows:

1. A random forest with node sizes ranging from 250 to 500 trees.
2. A neural net with two units in the hidden layer.
3. Most considerable healthcare regression (GLM) terms.
4. Generalized models additions.
5. Lasso-penalized regression using inner cross-validation selections

$$\text{MSE} = \left(Y_i - Z_{k,i}\right)^2 \tag{1}$$

$$R^2 = 1 - \left(\sum_i \left(Y_i - Z_{k,i}\right)^2\right) / \left(\sum_i \left(Y_i - \overline{Y_i}\right)^2\right) \tag{2}$$

$$\text{RE} = \text{CVMSE}_k / \text{CV}MSE_{SL} \tag{3}$$

Algorithm-2: Fuzzy C-Means Clustering (FCM) Algorithm:

Step 1: For basis step n=1. Then K true for each k algorithm.
Step 2: Complete K+1 folds true for Cross Validation (CV), Find CV of Zk predicted values.
Step 3: Consider all data Di, find   Index with k algorithms using
Step 4: Minimize using by Choose   to predict:
Step 5: The last approximation of by , calculated using

---

3 Background of Cancer Stages with Machine Learning

COPD audio sample identification issues:

Previous analysis methods, particularly for non-CNNs, relied on somewhat resource-intensive, very complex analytical networks. It suggests that it will need high-quality processing capability, which may be expensive. Training and illness prediction may take a long time if infrastructure investment is not made. Furthermore, current techniques of identifying if a patient has COPD, such as a physician's manual diagnosis, need lengthy and frequent hospital visits. In many circumstances, the amount of respiratory audio samples accessible is unequalled in disease. Consequently, balancing the data set is always necessary since every network of unbalanced data training assists in predicting the sickness with the most significant sample size. The breathing audio recordings include much noise. It must be addressed in a variety of ways. Table 1 covers the most recent investigation on COPD illness prediction. Deep forms of education that are effective have particular qualities.

- Dataset selection: obtaining and keeping a clean data collection is crucial since the whole model is dependent on it. There must be no inconsistencies in the training data set.
- Algorithm selection: the research objective must be identified. Various algorithms might be tried to determine which ones get the closest to the objective.
- Feature extraction techniques: this is a crucial aspect of developing efficient models. It is advantageous to retain sufficient model fidelity and the best possible selection of attributes that contribute to the formation of duplicated data during each data analysis cycle.

Table 1. Related Studies Lung Cancer Prediction.

Author & Ref	Contributed year	Methods	Resolutions	Used Features	Identified issues	Performance measure
[9] Er O	2008		Two MultiLayer NN	Individual	Only two hidden layers	94
[11] Manoharan	2008	Back Propagation, RBF-NN	ANN for spirometric pulmonary	Spirometry Features	Huge database for training	96 and 100
[4] Amaral	2012	Bayesian, KNN, decision trees, ANN, and SVM	Oscillation measurements and Applied machine learning algorithms for identifying pulmonary disease	No features	No measure of severity mild, moderate or severe	KNN, SVM and ANN Accuracy, Sensitivity and specificity are 95, 87, 94

(continued)

Table 1. (*continued*)

Author & Ref	Contributed year	Methods	Resolutions	Used Features	Identified issues	Performance measure
[5] Asaithambi	2012	Adaptive Neuro-Fuzzy Inference System (ANFIS)	Adaptive Fuzzy	No features	No respiratory abnormalities detection	88
[7] Chamberlain	2016	Auto Encoder Denoising	Identify wheezes and crackles using Deep Learning	Audio recordings	No	Wheeze 86%
[3] Altan	2018	Deep Belief net	3Dspace quantization	Lung sound and COPD patients		Accuracy, Sensitivity and specificity are 96, 94, and 94
[6] Badnjevic	2018	ANN and FL	Expert Diagnostic System finds Asthma and pulmonary disease	symptom questionnaire	No justification the EDS	96 and 98%
[10] Fernandez	2018	Decision Tree	Early predictions of COPD	Discrete wavelet transform	Longer training time on audio	Accuracy, Sensitivity are 88, 78.1
[2] Altan	2019	Deep Belief net	COPD Detection with Lung Sounds using Deep Learning	No features	noise and less accuracy, Sensitivity and specificity	Accuracy, Sensitivity and specificity are 71, 68, and 74
[1] Ahmed	2020	Without and With Transfer Learning	a 3DCNN and CT images	soft kernel CT images	ideally using k-fold cross validation	69 and 79 and with test 59 and 70%
[8] Du R	2020	Deep CNN	Chronic Obstructive Pulmonary Disease	Spirometry	Small Dataset	Color, Grey and Binary with 88,89,86

4 Performance Analysis of Existing Techniques and Discussion

The super-learner method for early-stage prediction improves significantly on the clinical tree methodology, with R2 of 0.405 and MSE of 0.149 cross-validated. In contrast, the clinical tree had a relative efficiency of 0.30. Its positive inverted R2 implies that the mean probability is more significant than indicated by the clinical tree, and Fig. 2 shows the prediction of ML-based illnesses. Furthermore, though the super student surpassed the other students in MSE, as shown in Table 2, various algorithms used a variable set of C123 with 94–98% relative efficiency.

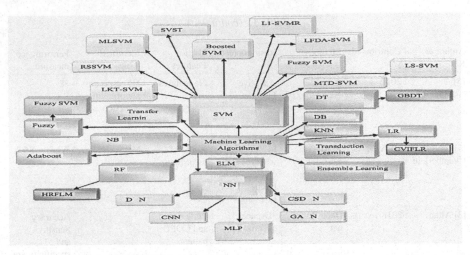

Fig. 2. Disease prediction using Machine Learning.

Deep learning frameworks and libraries:

The limits of previous technologies that have allowed deep learning to arise and how deep learning has progressed AI (Artificial Intelligence): It is hard for one person to witness and record all of the facts when a vehicle violates the speed limit. On the other hand, a machine can collect and translate a number plate image into a text representation. The most acceptable illustration of artificial intelligence is self-driving cars. AI enables machines to imitate intelligent human behavior. AI is created through researching how people think, learn, make choices, and cooperate to solve problems. AI applications include natural language, voice recognition, comprehension, and image processing. Deep learning was created in 2006 to overcome the limits of machine learning. First, the ML limitation is overcome by colossal input and output volumes, i.e., high dimensionality. The second discomfort that the conventional ML Model faces is one of its most serious weaknesses. It is a critical issue in complicated scenarios such as item or handwriting identification. AI categories in machine learning let computers learn without being explicitly instructed. (a) Supervised: Explain it using an example using a parameter (X) and corresponding output (Y), and comprehend how to translate inputs into outputs using an algorithm. (b) Unsupervised learning: the creation of a model with no previously categorized or labeled input. Based on its statistical qualities, this model may be used to classify incoming data. (c) Enhanced learning: learning via touch with the environment or space. Learning: Rather than what is openly taught to them, learners are enhanced by their outcomes. They choose activities depending on previous knowledge (utilization) and new opportunities (exploration).

The development of an algorithm to categorize lung cancer stages is required in order for researchers to use allocated data to analyze lung cancer treatment quality and patient health outcomes. Previous efforts at achieving 80% specificity and sensitivity at the same time failed. A previous study on the performance of the clinical tree algorithm (Brooks et al. 2017) corroborated our results of low performance. The main finding was that claim data could not be used to perform rigorous research on lung cancer patient

Table 2. Performance of algorithm

Name Algorithm	Cross-validation mean squared error	Cross-validation R^(2)	Relative Efficiency
Clinical Tree	0.501	−1.006	0.3
Elastic Net: C_(1)	0.195	0.219	0.76
Elastic Net: C_(12)	0.175	0.298	0.85
Elastic Net: C_(123)	0.151	0.395	0.98
GAM: C_(1)	0.195	0.219	0.76
GAM: C_(12)	0.175	0.299	0.85
GAM: C_(123)	0.151	0.396	0.98
GLM: C_(1)	0.195	0.219	0.76
GLM: C_(12)	0.176	0.297	0.85
GLM: C_(123)	0.152	0.392	0.98
Lasso: C_(1)	0.195	0.219	0.76
Lasso: C_(12)	0.175	0.298	0.85
Lasso: C_(123)	0.151	0.395	0.98
Neural Net: C_(1)	0.195	0.22	0.76
Neural Net: C_(12)	0.25	0	0.59
Neural Net: C_(123)	0.25	0	0.59
Random Forest: C_(1)	0.259	−0.035	0.57
Random Forest: C_(12)	0.175	0.3	0.85
Random Forest: C_(123)	0.152	0.393	0.98
Ridge: C_(1)	0.195	0.219	0.76
Ridge: C_(12)	0.175	0.298	0.85
Ridge: C_(123)	0.151	0.395	0.98
Super Learner	0.149	0.405	1
SVM: C_(1)	0.229	0.082	0.65
SVM: C_(12)	0.185	0.259	0.8
SVM: C_(123)	0.158	0.369	0.94

outcomes. Using a broader set of criteria and methods, we show that machine learning approaches may be used to identify patients who have had chemotherapy with 93%, 92%, and 93% accuracy. Simultaneously, the super learner achieved the best performance in cross-validated MSE with unique relative efficiency using various learning methods, including regression-based approaches. Defining prior 'enhancement thresholds,' but on the other side, would necessitate the use of more complex methods. In comparison to the following high-performance algorithm, based on the cross MSE, super learners assessed 1034 individuals as more like real positive people and 1034 individuals as more like real negative people, increasing their accuracy by 14% on average (GAM with C123). Improving that level may be therapeutic, but it is dependent on the context and methods.

5 Conclusion

The study described efforts to test a variety of lung cancer detection methods based on machine learning methods. In the study, machine learning algorithms were used to assess many recent publications explaining different diseases, and serious faults were uncovered using existing approaches. In addition, the study concentrated on various approaches to artificial intelligence and ML to identify various diseases to identify a gap in future clinical ML techniques for lung cancer prevention. For example, recognition to a deep learning assistance model based on CNN, doctors may detect COPD using respiratory sounds. To further the respiratory sound experiments Dataset, students may utilize Librosa's collection of tools such as Chroma CENS, Mel-Spectrogram, Chroma (Constant Q), Chroma, and MFCC.

Consequently, the analytics help medical diagnostics by providing reliable data early in the identification of lung cancer. Various of the traits seen in many datasets are the product of ongoing study. For both image recognition and analysis, some of them adopt a more straightforward design with image classification.

References

1. Ahmed, J., et al.: COPD classification in CT images using a 3D convolutional neural network. In: Maier-Hein, K., Palm, C. (eds.) Bildverarbeitung für Die Medizin 2020—Informatik Aktuell, pp. 39–45. Springer Vieweg, Wiesbaden (2020)
2. Altan, G., Kutlu, Y., Allahwardi, N.: Deep learning on computerized analysis of chronic obstructive pulmonary disease. IEEE J. Biomed. Health Inform. **24**(5), 1344–1350 (2019). https://doi.org/10.1109/JBHI.2019.2931395
3. Altan, G., Kutlu, Y., Pekmezci, A.Ö., Nural, S.: Deep learning with 3D-second order difference plot on respiratory sounds. Biomed. Signal Process. Control **45**, 58–69 (2018). https://doi.org/10.1016/j.bspc.2018.05.014
4. Amaral, J.L., Lopes, A.J., Jansen, J.M., Faria, A.C., Melo, P.L.: Machine learning algorithms and forced oscillation measurements applied to the automatic identification of chronic obstructive pulmonary disease. Comput. Methods Programs Biomed. **105**(3), 183–193 (2012). https://doi.org/10.1016/j.cmpb.2011.09.009
5. Asaithambi, M., Manoharan, S.C., Subramanian, S.: Classification of respiratory abnormalities using adaptive neuro-fuzzy inference system. In: Pan, J.-S., Chen, S.-M., Nguyen, N.T. (eds.) Intelligent Information and Database Systems, pp. 65–73. Springer, Berlin (2012)

6. Badnjevic, A., Gurbeta, L., Custovic, E.: An expert diagnostic system to automatically identify asthma and chronic obstructive pulmonary disease in clinical settings. Sci. Rep. **8**(1), 11645 (2018). https://doi.org/10.1038/s41598-018-30116-2

7. Chamberlain, D., Kodgule, R., Ganelin, D., Miglani, V., Fletcher. R.R.: Application of semi-supervised deep learning to lung sound analysis. In: 38th Annual International Conference of the IEEE Engineering in Medicine and Biology Society (EMBC), pp. 804–807. IEEE, Piscataway (2016)

8. Du, R., et al.: Identification of COPD from multi-view snapshots of 3D lung airway tree via deep CNN. IEEE Access **8**, 38907–38919 (2020). https://doi.org/10.1109/ACCESS.2020.2974617

9. Er, O., Temurtas, F.: A study on chronic obstructive pulmonary disease diagnosis using multi-layer neural networks. J. Med. Syst. **32**(5), 429–432 (2008). https://doi.org/10.1007/s10916-008-9148-6

10. Fernandez-Granero, M.A., Sanchez-Morillo, D., Leon-Jimenez, A.: An artificial intelligence approach to early predict symptom-based exacerbations of COPD. Biotechnol. Biotechnol. Equip. **32**(3), 778–784 (2018). https://doi.org/10.1080/13102818.2018.1437568

11. Manoharan, S., Veezhinathan, M., Ramakrishnan, S.: Comparison of two ANN methods for classification of spirometer data. Meas. Sci. Rev. **8**(3), 535 (2008). https://doi.org/10.2478/v10048-008-0014-y

12. Tan, C., Chen, H., Xia, C.: Early prediction of lung cancer based on the combination of trace element analysis in urine and an AdaBoost algorithm. J. Pharm. Biomed. Anal. **49**(3), 746–752 (2009)

13. Kim, T.-W., Koh, D.-H., Park, C.-Y.: Decision tree of occupational lung cancer using classification and regression analysis. Saf. Health Work **1**(2), 140–148 (2010)

14. Zięba, M., Tomczak, J.M., Lubicz, M., Świątek, J.: Boosted SVM for extracting rules from imbalanced data in application to prediction of the post-operative life expectancy in lung cancer patients. Appl. Soft Comput. **14**, 99–108 (2014)

15. Engchuan, W., Chan, J.H.: Pathway activity transformation for multi-class classification of lung cancer datasets. Neurocomputing **165**, 81–89 (2015)

16. Azzawi, H., Hou, J., Xiang, Y., Alanni, R.: Lung cancer prediction from microarray data by gene expression programming. IET Syst. Biol. **10**(5), 168–178 (2016)

17. Petousis, P., Han, S.X., Aberle, D., Bui, A.A.T.: Prediction of lung cancer incidence on the low-dose computed tomography arm of the national lung screening trial: a dynamic Bayesian network. Artif. Intell. Med. **72**, 42–55 (2016)

18. Lynch, C.M., et al.: Prediction of lung cancer patient survival via supervised machine learning classification techniques. Int. J. Med. Informatics **108**, 1–8 (2017)

19. Petousis, P., Winter, A., Speier, W., Aberle, D.R., Hsu, W., Bui, A.A.T.: Using sequential decision making to improve lung cancer screening performance. IEEE Access **7**, 119403–119419 (2019)

20. ALzubi, J.A., Bharathikannan, B., Tanwar, S., Manikandan, R., Khanna, A., Thaventhiran, C.: Boosted neural network ensemble classification for lung cancer disease diagnosis. Appl. Soft Comput. **80**, 579–591 (2019)

21. Eberendu, A.C., et al.: Unstructured data: an overview of the data of Big Data. Int J Emerg. Trends Tech. Comp. Sci. (2016). https://doi.org/10.14445/22312803/IJCTT

22. AshfaqKhan, M., et al.: A two-stage big data analytics framework with real-world applications using spark machine learning and long short-term memory network, Article, Chair of Computer Science 5: Infm Sys, 10. RWTH Aachen University, Aachen (2018)

23. Brooks, G.A., Landrum, M.B., Keating, N.L.: Inferring cancer stage from administrative data, March 2017. Report submitted to the Centers for Medicare and Medicaid Innovation

Classification and Identification of Objects in Images Using CNN

Rajesh Kumar Chatterjee[1]([⊠]), Md. Amir Khusru Akhtar[1],
and Dinesh K. Pradhan[2]

[1] Usha Martin University, Ranchi, India
rajchats2k2@gmail.com
[2] Dr. B. C. Roy Engineering College, Durgapur, India

Abstract. Convolution neural network also called as CNN is one of the deep learning technique. CNN in recent time has evolved as most popular tool to solve vision related use cases. In the field of computer vision, the challenge of classifying a given image and detecting an object in an image is extremely difficult and it has numerous real-world applications. In recent years, the use of CNN has increased dramatically in a variety of fields, including image classification, segmentation, and object recognition. Alex Nets, GoogLeNet, and ResNet50 are the most popular CNNs for object detection and from the different images. The performance of CNN depends directly on its hyperparameters. More you tune those parameters better you get the results. As a result, it's an important study on how to use CNN to improve object detection performance. Many strategies have been explored to optimise the hyperparameters of the CNN architecture. Gradient Descent, Back Propagation, Genetic Algorithm, Adam Optimization, and so on are some of them. The CNN architecture was trained using a variety of population-based search and evolutionary computing (EC) methodologies. Genetic algorithms, differential evolution, ant colony optimization, and particle swarm optimization, among other population-based techniques, have recently been utilised to train hyperparameters. In this literature, we will review the various aspects of CNN and its architecture followed by a detailed explanation of optimization strategies that aid in boosting accuracy.

Keywords: Computer vision · Convolutional neural network · Image classification · Object detection · Optimization technique

1 Introduction

The CNN is a part of the deep learning framework. The deep learning framework has kept evolving rapidly from the last decade and we found an increasing number of use cases across various industries and engineering fields. Starting from day to day life, valuable things like smartphones, smart sensing to, robotics deep learning has found their place. The core concept of deep learning is from an artificial neural network [1]. This works by creating multiple layers and abstracting

A. Kumar et al. (Eds.): ICAIDS 2021, CCIS 1673, pp. 16–26, 2022.
https://doi.org/10.1007/978-3-031-21385-4_2

the patters at each layer. Deep learning and convolutional neural networks have evolved significantly over the years, outperforming traditional machine learning approaches such as the Bayes method, SVM, and others. The availability of blue-massive data set and faster processing power has helped in solving many use cases starting from data analytics, computer vision, Natural language processing et al. Taheri et al. [2] has implemented an artificial bee colony (ABC) algorithm with a neural network and predicted blast-produced ground vibration. A homogeneous approach was conducted by Ghaleini et al. in [3], where ABC was acclimated to optimize control parameters of FNN to achieve a higher caliber of precision. Zhang et al. [4] used differential evolution (DE) to optimize FNN architecture and connected parameters (weights and biases) concurrently and claimed that the suggested algorithm could generate compact NNs with good generalization competency. Gupta et al. applied equilibrium optimizer with mutation strategy (EOMS) algorithm for solving numerical optimization and confirmed its efficacy over the existing results in [5]. CNN is found to be very useful tasks like image recognition and Object detection. The object detection can be sub categorized into face detection [6], pedestrian detection [7], skeleton detection [8]. As one of the core computer vision problem, it can provide useful information to gather more subtle understanding of images and videos which finds usefulness such as classifying image [9], analyzing human behaviour [10], face recognition [11], self driving [12,13].

The Object detection is about determining exactly where an object stays in an image (localizing object) and what kind of object it is (classifying object). As an example applications of image classification and object detection is in optical remote sensing images [14]. The pillar based approach to the fix imbalance issue caused by anchors.

In this chapter, we have written a review of different state-of-the-art Convolutional Neural Network(CNN) [15] based object detection models. We have described network architecture and training details by using various optimization methods of various models. The rest of the paper is segregated into the following agendas. The novelty of the proposed literature is discussed in Sect. 2. Background of the proposed study is assessed in Sect. 3. Section 4 embodies the computer vision variants. Different application areas are discussed in Sect. 5. Research challenges evaluated in Sect. 6 and the conclusion of the proposed study is discussed in Sect. 7.

2 Novelty

CNNs (Convolutional Neural Networks) are a type of deep learning technology that may be used to detect objects. The primary purpose of this research is to provide a basic understanding of CNN architecture. Also, how various optimization techniques can be utilised to train a CNN. Despite the fact that the present authors have varied perspectives on optimization, there is still a lot of work to be done in this field. For continuous improvement of existing solutions, scientists should choose and adopt novel optimization methodologies.

3   Background

Convolutional neural networks, or CNNs for short form is the backbone of many modern computer vision systems. CNN is a part of Artificial Neural Network popularly known as ANN and has been evolving since '50s. This is one of the powerful tool for many practical purposes.

3.1   Evolution of Computer Vision

The journey started in the late 50s when in 1959, David Hubel and Torsten Wiesel [16] described two different calls called complex and straightforward in our vision layer. Their study found that these cells are used in recognizing the pattern. The primary cells, which are simple in nature, answer different edges and bars visual orientations. In contrast, complex cells do the same thing, but while moving around scenes, they can respond. For example, simple cells may react only to the vertical bar at the bottom while complex cells may react to the bottom, top or middle. This exceptional property of complex cells is called spatial invariance. The author proposed that spatial invariance is achieved by summarizing the output of multiple simple cells. This is like keeping the same Vertical bar as the orientation while summing different receptive fields like bottom, middle, top, a particular point etc. Therefore, by collecting the knowledge gained with many simple cells, complex cells can respond well to Vertical bar occurring anywhere. This particular property of congregation of simple cells to develop a complex cell is present in each part of the human visual system. In the article [17], the author has proposed a model called recognition, taking inspiration from Hubel and Wiesel. The model includes "S-cell" and "C-cell". These are instead mathematical models and not biological models. The attempt was to capture "simple to complex" concept and capture in a computational model that can be used for visual pattern recognition.

The first modern CNN was actualized in 1990 using inspiration from neocognitron. In this paper [18], the author has proposed that the CNN model which sums up more specific features into progressively more complicated features can be successfully used for handwritten character recognition.

The dataset used was an MNIST dataset for handwritten digits with images of 0, 1, 2, 3, 4, 5, 6, 7, 8 and 9. These are all paired with their actual value between 0 to 9. This was able to work with an accuracy above 70 The progress on CNN continues between 1990 to 2000. In the paper [19], AlexNet has provided a state of the art CNN architecture with performance labelling pictures in the ImageNet challenge.

CNN has shown tremendous growth in the last couple of years and can describe the natural image. Only in 2017, a good 29 team out of 38 teams in ILSVRC achieved over 95% accuracy. We are at the point of solving 2D classification use cases. CNN in terms of computer vision shown tremendous development. It is great to see the new developments that will take place in future and can further provide technology advancement like self driving cars, robotics, radiology image interpretation etc.

3.2   CNN Architecture

In deep learning [20], CNN is one of the most sought models we use for computer vision-related activities. One typical example of CNN architecture is VGG16. Each layer of CNN is called a feature map. We have a 3D matrix of the varying value of pixels for different colour channels that shows the intensity. A feature map is a multi-channel image for an internal layer and its pixel can be seen as a specific feature. In the case of CNN, each node is connected to a smaller number of nodes from the previous layer, reducing the number of a potential number of learned weights. The authors have shown we can conduct of different transformations in their article [21–23] on feature maps. The different types of feature maps to use are filtering and pooling. The filtering operation, also called convolution, convolutes with learned weights to the values of a receptive field of neurons and takes a nonlinear function (such as sigmoid [24], ReLU) to obtain the final output. In the case of pooling operation, for example, max pooling, average pooling, L2-pooling, and local contrast normalization [25], these are used to summarizes the responses of an output that provides a better feature description. Each layer is operated with convolution and pooling. We construct a hierarchy of features and then apply a supervised model to create better features on each of the several fully connected layers and provide different learned features of various types. Once we are in the final layer, we apply the activation function to the final output. According to the tasks involved, the final layer with activation functions [21] to output a given conditional probability for each of the outputs. This can be optimized using an objective function like mean squared error, average value, cross-entropy loss using gradient descent, or metaheuristic method.

In the feature map, we can create conv using convoluting to 3*3 filter methods, and the feature map resolutions reduces with 2 stride max-pooling layers.

The network is trained with sufficient number of training data and the trained model then can be used to identify predict unseen image. The unseen image should be of the same size as the trained image data. If the image is of uneven size, we may either need to rescale or crop the image [21].

The benefits of CNN in computer vision as compared to traditional method is 1. The learning of features in hierarchy as we learn in each of the layers helps in learning high level different features which are different at each layer. This reduces in pixel level understanding and therefore we can focus more on meaningful feature and not on the pixels. As shown by the authors [26], the whole image can be learnt properly by different layers and also removes the dependency with hidden factors of input data through non-linear functions. 2. Unlike traditional models the deeper model like CNN provides more expressive capability by learning finer features. 3. The deep learning framework like CNN provides us with option to jointly optimize several related task together. 4) Benefitting from the large learning capacity of deep CNNs, some classical computer vision challenges can be recast as high-dimensional data transform problems and solved from a different viewpoint.

4   Computer Vision Variants

See Fig. 1.

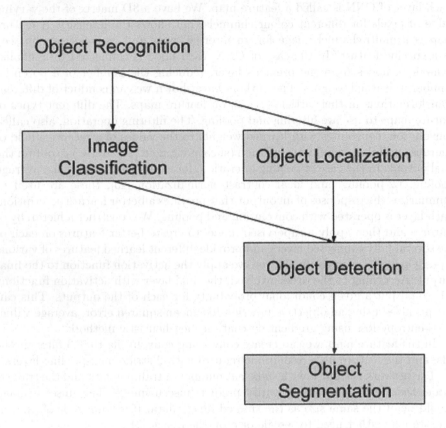

Fig. 1. Overview of object recognition computer vision tasks

4.1   Image Classification

Image classification [27] is the field of computer vision where we analyze a given image and ascertain in which class it belongs. Thereby, this process assigns maximum chance for a given class. Classifying an image [28] is a very important but complex task in computer vision. In order to achieve that we label each class and in neural network, we train the data with sufficient data to achieve high accuracy. The trained model then used to classify unseen image accurately. For example, we train the model with a set of cat and dig images so that the model can accurately predict a unseen image identify its class. Therefore, it is a process of analyzing images by a computer and accurately identifying the image.

This process is very natural for human as well as any living species while it gets so complicated when we do it using computers. In computers, we have individual pixels to represent an image as well as the image varies with angle, location, background, clarity et al. This creates the problem of two picture looking same but are treated differently by computers. It makes categorization even more challenging. Image classification [29] with deep learning is getting very popular for its effectiveness and often involves convolutional neural networks (CNN). In CNN, unlike typical ANN, the nodes in hidden layers don't always share their output with every other node in the next layer. Deep learning technique allows to identify and extract features from images reducing dependency on pixels. It learns the features by analysing lots of pictures. This reduces any bias and removes manual filtering.

4.2 Object Detection

Object Detection [24] is one of the prominent area in computer vision. This has multiple applications in tracking an object, captioning some Image, medical image and several other applications. This is a field where a given thing be it living or non living like human, animal, car, bicycle can be easily tracked in an image and a video. Typically it bounds an object with a bounding box in an image. Before deep learning, object detection takes multiple steps like detecting edges and features using methods like HOG, SIFT etc. and then these are compared with existing object templates. The Convolutional Neural Network [30] helps extracting feature automatically and helps in identifying an object by providing a bounding box. To interpret where the object is localized, we can do in multiple ways like bounding the object in box or by marking each pixel of the in the image which contains the object (called segmentation). In the deep learning time, multiple methods like YOLO, YOLOv2, YOLOv3, SSD, RetinaNet etc. that tries to combine detection and classification both the steps. Object detection is a growing field that sees various improvements over the year.

4.3 Image Classification with Localization

Image localization is one of core computer vision activity. This is to find exactly where an object is and finding a bounding box by creating proper co-ordinates. This is different from object detection in a way that we should classify and identify all the objects. Therefore localization is a subset of object detection where our task is to identify and followed by localize. Therefore this activity is divided into two different area first detect and then locate. In image classification, first we train the images using surpervised image followed by training bounding box around the object in the image. The term localization refers where the object lies in the image.

4.4 Semantic Segmentation

Image semantic segmentation is to analyze pixels and label each pixel or a group of label corresponding to a class. For example, if we have an image with a person riding bicycle along with having some background then the semantic segmentation will predict three class like person, bicycle and background. Semantic segmentation doesn't differentiate between instances of the same object and predicts the given object only. Therefore, if we have an image with more than one object of people riding bicycle then semantic segmentation will not identify different person and different bicycles. Semantic segmentation will identify objects as bicycle, person and background. This is very helpful in understanding what is in an image like one person is riding a bicycle in a road near a building where a car is parked. Convolutional neural network is very handy in semantic segmentation. There are many use case like in self-driving vehicles, medical image diagnostics etc.

4.5   Instance Segmentation

Unlike semantic segmentation, it is a prediction of each instance of object occurring in an image and also their segmentation mix of each pixel. Therefore it is a mix of both semantic segmentation along with object detection. It is different from semantic segmentation in the very nature that it provides uniquely assigned label to each of the instances of a given object in the image. In case of semantic segmentation, the pixels of each classes are given same pixel value and therefore it can identify each objects without differentiating each instance of each objects. Therefore if we have three cats in one image, instance segmentation will give different pixel value while semantic segmentation will give same pixel for all the three cats. This way we can identify three cats in instance segmentation and can identify as one cat object in case of semantic segmentation. Thus in instance Segmentation, we treat different objects of the similar class as separate entity.

5   Application Areas

CNN has been widely used and its popularity is increasing with time. It has been a great journey with many use cases coming up. It has wide applicability set across different domains. In [31], image super-resolution reconstruction is shown. Similarly in [32] used to mitigates current challenges of current models based on CNNs by integrating deep deconvolution network and proposal-wise prediction. The segmentation method detects detailed structures and handles objects in multiple scales naturally. Author has shown how Caffee [33] can be used for image classification development as well deployment for large scale industrial application, In this paper [34], author proposed a CNN model that grows each time and is called growing convolution neural network (GCNN). This is used for identification of plant leaf. The proposed GCNN peforms better than existing CNN model or features extraction using SVM classifiers. In the article [35], the author has shown how neural codes help in better image retrieval whereas in similar manner the article [36] describes how CNN can improve the retrieval performance of content-based image retrieval. [37] article proposes a three-stage cascading structure using CNN and is found to be effective in achieving strong perfomance in public datasets. Similarly in [38], face detection task can be improved with two networks first to gather list of region of interest and then take those as ROIs for classification purpose as face or non face. Author has use in the article [39] for pedestrian detection with low computational time wheareas in the article [40] author proposed a new sub category proposed CNN which uses joint detection and subcategory classification. Similarly in the paper [41], R-CNN framework of CNN is used to retrieve high quality pedestrian features for efficient and effective pedestrian detection even if the overall environments is not so simple. In this article [42], the author has proposed bimodality using deep network to take care of both audio and video. Similar in the article [42], combination of spatial and short-term motion features in the regularized fusion network shows better result than direct classification and fusion using the CNN.

6   Research Challenges

Deep learning and Computer vision has given a lot of promise for future as well as challenges. The current challenges that computer vision has been focused on are how automatically, we can extract features where focus is to automatically detect and extract feature. Richer the feature better the image processing task is. Similarly another challenge in creating an end to end model as CNN typically works in modular models as each model is created for a specific purpose like feature extraction, image alignment, classification etc. This will help in creating a model that can take care all or most of it. The other important challenge is to transfer the learning effectively like how feature and collection of features we learnt can be transferred to some other model. Next is how to create a model that can provide superior performance and the last one is to create a generalized model. In our current scope, we will work on improving performance followed by working on getting better features for future image processing.

7   Conclusion

CNN and computer vision are widely in use in different segments of industry including ecommerce, robotics, agriculture, industry automation etc. In the paper, we attempted to analytical review CNN techniques for object images operation. The computer vision task has been used multiple traditional application and industry related automation process. The expansion of hardware and rich data has lot of future work. Convolutional neural networks have proved to be the game changers for image recognition and object detection outputting on complex datasets and can be used in self driving cars, robotics etc. CNN is fast evolving and opens door for many use cases that can benefit science and engineering community in coming time. We looked at deep learning-based object detection methods in this paper. Our major goal was to talk about the many optimization strategies that can be used to train CNN to achieve the best accuracy. To begin, several optimization strategies that have already been used to tune the hyper-parameters in a CNN are described. Deep learning-based object detection systems have made incredible progress in recent years, thus it will continue to be a hot topic of research. In the future, we can create a CNN model by taking into account one or more existing models or by modifying existing models to solve object identification problems utilising population-based different optimization strategies.

References

1. LeCun, Y., Bengio, Y., Hinton, G.: Deep learning. Nature **521**(7553), 436–444 (2015)
2. Taheri, K., Hasanipanah, M., Golzar, S.B., Majid, M.Z.A.: A hybrid artificial bee colony algorithm-artificial neural network for forecasting the blast-produced ground vibration. Eng. Comput. **33**(3), 689–700 (2017)
3. Ghaleini, E.N., Koopialipoor, M., Momenzadeh, M., Sarafraz, M.E., Mohamad, E.T., Gordan, B.: A combination of artificial bee colony and neural network for approximating the safety factor of retaining walls. Eng. Comput. **35**(2), 647–658 (2019)
4. Zhang, L., Li, H.: A mixed-coding adaptive differential evolution for optimising the architecture and parameters of feedforward neural networks. Int. J. Sensor Netw. **29**(4), 262–274 (2019)
5. Gupta, S., Deep, K., Mirjalili, S.: An efficient equilibrium optimizer with mutation strategy for numerical optimization. Appl. Soft Comput. **96**, 106542 (2020)
6. Sung, K.-K., Poggio, T.: Example-based learning for view-based human face detection. IEEE Trans. Pattern Anal. Mach. Intell. **20**(1), 39–51 (1998)
7. Dollar, P., Wojek, C., Schiele, B., Perona, P.: Pedestrian detection: an evaluation of the state of the art. IEEE Trans. Pattern Anal. Mach. Intell. **34**(4), 743–761 (2012)
8. Kobatake, H., Yoshinaga, Y.: Detection of spicules on mammogram based on skeleton analysis. IEEE Trans. Med. Imaging **15**(3), 235–245 (1996)
9. Caffe | Proceedings of the 22nd ACM international conference on Multimedia
10. Cao, Z., Simon, T., Wei, S.E., Sheikh, Y.: Realtime multi-person 2D pose estimation using part affinity fields, pp. 7291–7299 (2017)
11. Yang, Z., Nevatia, R.: A multi-scale cascade fully convolutional network face detector. In: 2016 23rd International Conference on Pattern Recognition (ICPR), pp. 633–638, December 2016
12. Chen, C., Seff, A., Kornhauser, A., Xiao, J.: DeepDriving: Learning Affordance for Direct Perception in Autonomous Driving, pp. 2722–2730 (2015)
13. Chen, X., Ma, H., Wan, J., Li, B., Xia, T.: Multi-View 3D Object Detection Network for Autonomous Driving, pp. 1907–1915 (2017)
14. Li, K., Wan, G., Cheng, G., Meng, L., Han, J.: Object detection in optical remote sensing images: a survey and a new benchmark. ISPRS J. Photogramm. Remote. Sens. **159**, 296–307 (2020)
15. Dhillon, A., Verma, G.K.: Convolutional neural network: a review of models, methodologies and applications to object detection. Prog. Artif. Intell. **9**(2), 85–112 (2020)
16. Hubel, D.H., Wiesel, T.N.: Receptive fields, binocular interaction and functional architecture in the cat's visual cortex. J. Physiol. **160**(1), 106–154 (1962)

17. Fukushima, K., Miyake, S.: Neocognitron: a self-organizing neural network model for a mechanism of visual pattern recognition. In: Amari, S., Arbib, M.A. (eds.) Competition and Cooperation in Neural Nets, pp. 267–285. Springer, Heidelberg (1982). https://doi.org/10.1007/978-3-642-46466-9_18
18. LeCun, Y., Bottou, L., Bengio, Y., Haffner, P.: Gradient-based learning applied to document recognition. Proc. IEEE **86**(11), 2278–2324 (1998)
19. Krizhevsky, A., Sutskever, I., Hinton, G.E.: Imagenet classification with deep convolutional neural networks. In: Advances in Neural Information Processing Systems, vol. 25, pp. 1097–1105 (2012)
20. Kim, Y., Li, Y.: Human activity classification with transmission and reflection coefficients of on-body antennas through deep convolutional neural networks. IEEE Trans. Antennas Propag. **65**(5), 2764–2768 (2017)
21. Krizhevsky, A., Sutskever, I., Hinton, G.E.: Imagenet classification with deep convolutional neural networks. Commun. ACM **60**(6), 84–90 (2017)
22. Chatfield, K., Simonyan, K., Vedaldi, A., Zisserman, A.: Return of the devil in the details: delving deep into convolutional nets. arXiv preprint arXiv:1405.3531 (2014)
23. Oquab, M., Bottou, L., Laptev, I., Sivic, J.: Learning and transferring mid-level image representations using convolutional neural networks. In: Proceedings of the IEEE Conference on Computer Vision and Pattern Recognition, pp. 1717–1724 (2014)
24. Zhao, Z.-Q., Zheng, P., Shou-tao, X., Xindong, W.: Object detection with deep learning: a review. IEEE Trans. Neural Netw. Learn. Syst. **30**(11), 3212–3232 (2019)
25. Kavukcuoglu, K., Ranzato, M.A., Fergus, R., LeCun, Y.: Learning invariant features through topographic filter maps. In: 2009 IEEE Conference on Computer Vision and Pattern Recognition, pp. 1605–1612. IEEE (2009)
26. Girshick, R., Donahue, J., Darrell, T., Malik, J.: Rich feature hierarchies for accurate object detection and semantic segmentation. In: Proceedings of the IEEE Conference on Computer Vision and Pattern Recognition, pp. 580–587 (2014)
27. Shang, R., He, J., Wang, J., Kaiming, X., Jiao, L., Stolkin, R.: Dense connection and depthwise separable convolution based CNN for polarimetric SAR image classification. Knowl.-Based Syst. **194**, 105542 (2020)
28. Wen, S., et al.: Multilabel image classification via feature/label co-projection. IEEE Trans. Syst. Man Cybern. Syst. **51**(11), 7250–7259 (2020)
29. Chaganti, S.Y., Nanda, I., Pandi, K.R., Prudhvith, T.G., Kumar, N.: Image classification using SVM and CNN. In: 2020 International Conference on Computer Science, Engineering and Applications (ICCSEA), pp. 1–5. IEEE (2020)
30. Tang, C., Feng, Y., Yang, X., Zheng, C., Zhou, Y.: The object detection based on deep learning. In: 2017 4th International Conference on Information Science and Control Engineering (ICISCE), pp. 723–728. IEEE (2017)
31. Garcia Cardona, C.: Generalized convolutional representation for field data on graphs. Technical report, Los Alamos National Lab. (LANL), Los Alamos, NM (United States) (2017)
32. Noh, H., Hong, S., Han, B.: Learning deconvolution network for semantic segmentation. In: Proceedings of the IEEE International Conference on Computer Vision, pp. 1520–1528 (2015)
33. Jia, Y., et al.: Caffe: convolutional architecture for fast feature embedding. In: Proceedings of the 22nd ACM International Conference on Multimedia, pp. 675–678 (2014)

34. Zhao, Z.-Q., Xie, B.-J., Cheung, Y., Wu, X.: Plant leaf identification via a growing convolution neural network with progressive sample learning. In: Cremers, D., Reid, I., Saito, H., Yang, M.-H. (eds.) ACCV 2014. LNCS, vol. 9004, pp. 348–361. Springer, Cham (2015). https://doi.org/10.1007/978-3-319-16808-1_24

35. Babenko, A., Slesarev, A., Chigorin, A., Lempitsky, V.: Neural codes for image retrieval. In: Fleet, D., Pajdla, T., Schiele, B., Tuytelaars, T. (eds.) ECCV 2014. LNCS, vol. 8689, pp. 584–599. Springer, Cham (2014). https://doi.org/10.1007/978-3-319-10590-1_38

36. Wan, J., et al.: Deep learning for content-based image retrieval: a comprehensive study. In: Proceedings of the 22nd ACM International Conference on Multimedia, pp. 157–166 (2014)

37. Yang, Z., Nevatia, R.: A multi-scale cascade fully convolutional network face detector. In: 2016 23rd International Conference on Pattern Recognition (ICPR), pp. 633–638. IEEE (2016)

38. Mliki, H., Dammak, S., Fendri, E.: An improved multi-scale face detection using convolutional neural network. SIViP 14(7), 1345–1353 (2020). https://doi.org/10.1007/s11760-020-01680-w

39. Tomè, D., Monti, F., Baroffio, L., Bondi, L., Tagliasacchi, M., Tubaro, S.: Deep convolutional neural networks for pedestrian detection. Signal Process. Image Commun. 47, 482–489 (2016)

40. Xiang, Y., Choi, W., Lin, Y., Savarese, S.: Subcategory-aware convolutional neural networks for object proposals and detection. In: 2017 IEEE Winter Conference on Applications of Computer Vision (WACV), pp. 924–933. IEEE (2017)

41. Zhao, Z.-Q., Bian, H., Hu, D., Cheng, W., Glotin, H.: Pedestrian detection based on fast R-CNN and batch normalization. In: Huang, D.-S., Bevilacqua, V., Premaratne, P., Gupta, P. (eds.) ICIC 2017. LNCS, vol. 10361, pp. 735–746. Springer, Cham (2017). https://doi.org/10.1007/978-3-319-63309-1_65

42. Wu, Z., Wang, X., Jiang, Y.G., Ye, H., Xue, X.: Modeling spatial-temporal clues in a hybrid deep learning framework for video classification. In: Proceedings of the 23rd ACM International Conference on Multimedia, pp. 461–470 (2015)

An Appraisal of Cyber-Attacks and Countermeasures Using Machine Learning Algorithms

Akhilendranath Mummadi[1]([✉]), B. Midhun Krishna Yadav[1], Rachamalla Sadhwika[1], and S. Shitharth[2]

[1] Vardhaman College of Engineering, Hyderabad, India
akhil.mummadi9@gmail.com
[2] Kebri Dehar University, Kebri Dehar, Ethiopia

Abstract. In this computerized era, cyber-attacks have turned quite common. Every year, the number of cyber-attacks escalates, and so does the austerity of the harm. In today's digital environment, ensuring security against cyber-attacks has become important. Networking is becoming more sophisticated over time, and as the popularity of a successful technology grows, intrusion detection system security issues grow as well. There is a strong necessity for a solid defense in today's cyber world. New attacks and malware pose a great challenge to the security community. Various machine learning techniques are being used in many intrusion detection systems to counter such attacks. Machine learning can learn on its own with minimal human interaction. Hence, it is vital to call for further attention to security concerns and associated machine learning defensive strategies, which inspires this paper's complete survey. A thorough survey on diverse machine learning algorithms has been investigated in this paper to determine which algorithm is best suited for a specific attack; these techniques have been examined and compared in terms of their accuracy in detecting attacks.

Keywords: Machine learning · IDS - Intrusion Detection System · Security attacks · Detection methods

1 Introduction

Cyber Security is the technology developed to defend or protect one's personal computers, mobile devices, and network systems from information theft and hardware damage. Cyber security is one of the most pressing concerns among growing industries, as they must protect their devices and servers from a variety of attacks. Cyber security technologies are used in almost every aspect of our daily lives. Firewalls and intrusion detection systems protect servers. Among these, intrusion detection systems play a critical role; it analyzes traffic and detects abnormal behavior, alerting the system.

Machine learning belongs to the branch of AI which is used to develop a functioning model that is similar to the human brain [1]. The model can automate the data analysis process by gaining knowledge from the data, identifying patterns, and making a decision

A. Kumar et al. (Eds.): ICAIDS 2021, CCIS 1673, pp. 27–40, 2022.
https://doi.org/10.1007/978-3-031-21385-4_3

on its own with minimal human intervention. We can also use machine learning to implement cyber security, identify multiple attack patterns, and defend the system. Machine learning helps systems to scrutinize attack patterns, learn from previous attacks, and defend themself by responding to changing attack patterns. Machine learning has the potential to make cyber security more effective, proactive, and straightforward. Nevertheless, to be more effective, the model has to be as accurate and detect as many attacks as possible. We need an enormous amount of data to be more precise.

An intrusion detection system is a device or software developed to analyze and monitor the network or systems to defend the systems against different attacks or malicious activity [2]. There are three main detection methods in support of intrusion detection systems: misuse-based, anomaly-based, and hybrid. Misuse-based detection is a detection mechanism that inspects for a specific type of pattern such as hex values in viruses as those viruses are detected through their patterns. It treats new traffic as an attack that it fails to identify as secure.

The first intrusion detection system was appointed in 1980. In the last few years, many surveys on intrusion detection systems have been published. Attacks such as DDoS and sniffing made enormous adverse effects in the area of security. The initial reported DDoS attack occurred in 2000, where numerous computers are used to make requests repeatedly which ultimately impedes the site and avert it from reacting to requests from users [3]. Several researchers have analysed and developed an intrusion detection system that is competent with lofty detection rates and curtailed false alarm rates since it became pressure and a major concern for security analysts where the intrusion detection system demonstrated alarms even for unobjectionable circumstances. While sniffing, an attack happens using a packet sniffer. When the packets are not encrypted, the data within the network can be read easily using sniffers.

The Machine learning algorithms we focused on in this paper are:

Decision Tree: [4] Decision tree is a kind of tree data structure that is used in the supervised learning method. The learning process includes pruning, tree generation, and feature selection. The algorithm classifies the nodes by recursively splitting the dataset into subsets based on entropy and information gain of given attributes when training this model. The root node is chosen since it has low entropy and a high information gain. Random forest is an advanced version of the decision tree.

Clustering: [5] Clustering is an unsupervised learning method. This method does not necessitate any labelled data or prior classification knowledge. This algorithm groups data that are highly similar into the same clusters and the data that is less similar into different clusters. There are numerous strategies for clustering the data that are provided to the model, including connectivity models such as hierarchical clustering, in which the data points are grouped into clusters based on distances between them, and centroid models such as K-means, in which all clusters are represented by their mean vector. In distribution-based clustering, such as the Expectation-Maximization algorithm, clusters are based on Gaussian distributions. In density-based clustering like DBSCAN clusters are created based on high-density areas.

Artificial Neural Network: [6] ANN is a supervised learning model. This model mimics the functionality of the human brain. This is made up of layers of artificial neurons that are fully interconnected. The input data is used as the input for the first layer of neurons, and the output is used as the input for the second layer of neurons in the network. The Back Propagation algorithm is used to train these networks. Even if some layers are unresponsive, neural networks work. Due to its much processing and complex structure, it consumes a large amount of storage and training this model is laborious.

Support Vector Machine: [7] SVM is a supervised learning model. This model is used to find a maximum-margin separation hyperplane in the feature space between two classes. The hyperplane is positioned so that the distance between it and the closest data points in each class is as short as possible. The orientation of the hyperplane will change if support vectors are deleted, making it noise-sensitive near the hyperplane. Kernel functions are used to solve the non-linearity problem. A kernel function maps the current space dimensions to higher dimensions.

This literature paper concentrates and aims to elucidate on machine learning and intrusion detection, to understand the concept of intrusion detection system, demystify the security problems and decipher them using some befitting algorithms by involving machine learning, or to mitigate the effects of such issues. For this study, we have thoroughly researched survey papers published in 2016 [8], 2017 [28] and 2019 [9], which reveal the present progress. This paper delivers structured summarization of the challenges faced, about the intrusion detection system and methods to solve the security troubles to attain a quick conclusive knowledge for any researcher. This paper also presents a discussion on how frequently the attacks took place annually, the percentage of attacks, repercussions, or consequences faced, evaluating which countermeasure was desirable and productive for a specific attack. Kumar et al. proposed object detection using muti-box detector for small object [29–31]. The remaining paper is sorted out accordingly as follows: Sect. 2 interprets the concept of intrusion detection system using machine learning. Section 3 discusses security issues and attacks which formerly occurred and also which are happening in these current days. Section 4 formulates the techniques and enables favourable algorithms to unravel the attacks. Section 5 submits conclusions.

2 Machine Learning in Intrusion Detection System

2.1 History

The sole task of an intrusion detection system is to detect any abnormal/anomalous behavior in network traffic and to monitor network traffic by dissecting traffic flow. The first intrusion detection system was introduced around the 1980s, following the evolution of the Internet. Since then, the intrusion detection system has managed to evolve and advanced under a range of aspects. "Computer Security Threat Monitoring and Surveillance," a survey authored by James P Anderson, a colonist in information security and a follower of the Defense Science Board Task Force on Computer Security at the U.S. Department of Defense, is credited with introducing intrusion detection system. Indeed, there are some limitations towards the traditional intrusion detection system, which are as follows:

1. Noise can gravely reduce the competence of the intrusion detection system by generating an elevated false-alarm rate.
2. Steady updates in the software are required to be introduced for signature-based intrusion detection system to hang on with the threats.
3. Network-based intrusion detection system can only detect anomalies within the network which limits the attacks it can discover (Fig. 1).

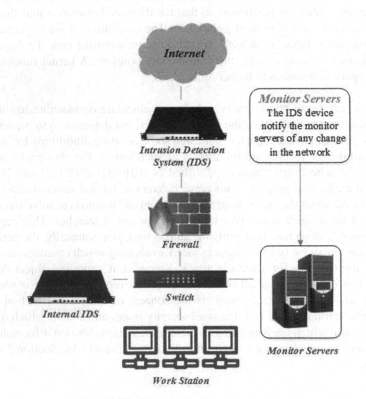

Fig. 1. Working of intrusion detection system

A firewall protects all outbound and inbound network traffic and monitors suspected intrusion attempts for given information such as IP address, port number, protocols used, and so on. Although firewalls can prevent malicious traffic, intrusion detection system detects breaches by correlating traffic to signatures of malicious threats or comparing system activities to a benchmark of known behaviour and notifying the network administrator if an intrusion attempt has been made. It can also prevent intrusions depending on the configuration.

2.2 Intrusion Detection System Detection Methods

The intrusion detection system detection methods can be predominantly classified as:

Misuse-Based Detection: Misuse-based detection is a detection mechanism that inspects for a specific type of pattern in viruses, such as hex values because viruses are identified by their patterns [10]. Misuse-based detection is only useful when the patterns are well known; however, if the patterns are unknown and encountered for the first time, the system does not alert.

Anomaly-Based Detection: When Misuse-based detection fails to detect unknown patterns, Anomaly-based detection plays a significant role [11]. Anomaly-based detection does not require the signature of the attack as it is much more dependent on the attack's behavior. Observing network occurrences and traffic is the fundamental basis of anomaly-based detection. The dilemma is that Anomaly-based detection generates false positive alarms. It considers new traffic being an attack that one fails to acknowledge as secure.

2.3 Type of Intrusion Detection System Alerts

Intrusion detection system raises four types of alerts i.e., true positive, false positive, true negative, false negative.

True Positive: A true positive is a condition in which intrusion detection system raises an alarm when there is a network anomaly.

False Positive: A false positive is a condition in which the intrusion detection system starts raising an alarm despite the absence of an anomaly.

True Negative: A true negative condition is one in which there is no network anomaly and the intrusion detection system does not raise any alarm.

False Negative: A false negative occurs when there is a network anomaly but the intrusion detection system does not raise an alarm.

2.4 Benchmarks or Datasets

A benchmark is a collection of datasets that represent real-world data science problems. It encompasses a variety of datasets of various sizes, phases of complexity, and problem domains. Machine learning is tasked with extracting significant information from large datasets. Benchmarks provide a portable baseline, they are reliable. Few datasets are:

DARPA 1998: MIT Lincoln Lab generated and regulated the DARPA 1998 dataset [12]. Researchers spent nine weeks compiling this dataset from raw TCP dump data.

KDD99: KDD99 was created to alleviate DARPA's issue of raw packets not being able to be applied to standard models [13]. This is the most widely used intrusion detection system benchmark. Its compilers mined DARPA1998 data for 41-dimensional characteristics. The four categories of features in KDD99 are host-based, time-based, and content.

NSL-KDD: This was developed to address the inadequacies of the KDD99 dataset [13]. It balances records from several classes, which eliminates the problem of categorization bias, it also eliminates duplicate and redundant records, resulting in a decreased number of records.

UNSW-NB15: This dataset was created by academics at the University of South Wales, who used a tool called Bro to extract 49-dimensional characteristics from network traffic captured by three virtual servers [14]. Flow features, basic features, content features, time features, extra features, and labelled features are among the features (Fig. 2).

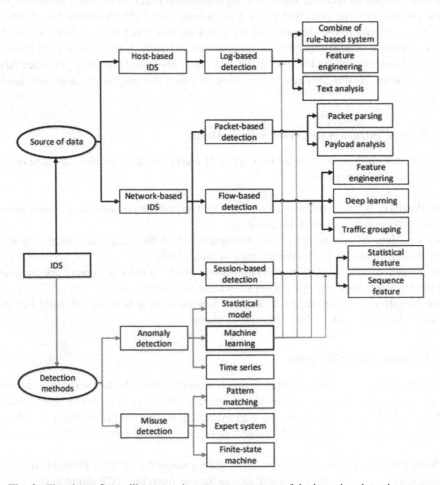

Fig. 2. The above figure illustrates the taxonomy system of the intrusion detection system.

2.5　Machine Learning Based Intrusion Detection System

Machine learning based intrusion detection models are generally based on different types include:

Packet Based Attack Detection: [15] Packets are used as an intrusion detection system data source in Packet Based Attack Detection. A packet consists of an IP header and

Payload. The source and destination addresses, ports, and other protocol information are contained in the IP header, whereas the payload is the data field. The header and payload of a packet together are examined in this method to determine whether it is an intrusion or not. Packet inspection can occur in different locations, such as routers and switches. Since this is a signature-based detection, it is unable to detect unknown attacks because it only compares known malicious data.

Flow-Based Attack Detection: [15] Flow-based attack detection, unlike packet-based detection, does not monitor a specific packet but instead monitors and analyses the network and traffic flow. It keeps a flow record of the number of packets transmitted in a stream and the time taken for the transmission. Because this is an anomaly-based detection, it can also detect unknown attacks, which may lead to a higher number of false alarms. It's perfect for detecting DoS attacks.

Session-Based Attack Detection: [15] A session is a channel of communication between two terminals, a client and a server. A session is divided into five tuples, i.e., client port, client internet protocol, server port, server internet protocol, protocol. Within a session, this method extracts a portion of the packets' header information and a portion of the payload information and stores it in the records. These records are used as the dataset for the model. This is an anomaly-based intrusion detection system between specific IP addresses and detects most of the trojans.

3 Common Security Attacks

SQL Injection: [16] In SQL injection SQL queries and commands are injected into modules to obtain sensitive data from the server database. The attack allows to spoof and tamper with the data in the database. When the website does not throw any error messages or information about the code, blind SQL injection is used by throwing true or false statements.

DoS: [17] DoS attacks work by bombarding the target with immense traffic or sending servers information that causes it to crash. DoS thwack typically targets eminent corporations such as banks, media, and e-commerce companies, as well as government organizations and trade organizations' web servers. DoS attack is launched in two ways: by flooding the systems or by crashing the services.

MITM: [18] MITM is an eavesdropping attack, where the intruder pretends to be a legitimate sender and receiver for both end-users. An attacker may tamper with the data and send malicious codes or malicious links to the victims, redirecting them to fake websites. The most common target for these attacks is session hijacking.

Malware: This is a software program designed to cause harm to the system and corrupt it [19]. In some cases, these affected systems may operate as zombies to attack a server while performing a DDOS attack. Malware takes different forms, such as viruses, trojans, spyware, and adware.

Sniffing Attack: Sniffing attacks compromise confidentiality and outlaw the CIA triad by capturing the network traffic with the help of a packet sniffer and gaining unauthorized access and also reading data which is in plain text form. Packet sniffers are the devices that are used to carry out this sniffing attack and seize network data packets as they pass through a network connection. Broadly, sniffing attacks are classified into 2 categories: Active and Passive Sniffing attacks.

Brute Force: A brute force attack is a cryptographic assault that succeeds by predicting all potential password combinations until the correct password is uncovered. The longer the password, the harder it is to crack. Aircrack-ng, John the Ripper, L0phtCrack, and RainbowCrack are all examples of brute force assault tools. Some common types of Brute Force attacks are hybrid, reverse, and credential stuffing.

DNS Spoofing: This attack takes advantage of DNS flaws to redirect traffic to fraudulent websites or servers [20]. This can be accomplished by inserting corrupted DNS into the DNS resolver cache. DNS spoofing can end up by dumping sensitive data of the victim and may lead him to malicious download sites. DNS spoofing is commonly used in phishing attacks, in which the attacker redirects the victim to his website, where he may enter any sensitive information.

Crypto-Jacking: Crypto-jacking is a type of cyberattack in which a hacker uses the computing power of a target to illegally mine cryptocurrency on the hacker's behalf. Crypto hackers are people who want the benefits of cryptocurrency mining without the concomitant high costs. Individual customers, industrial control systems can all be targets of crypto-jacking. File-based, browser-based are a few types.

DNS Tunneling: A method of [21] cyber-attack in which the attacker encodes the program or data into the DNS query and passes it. Attackers use DNS as a camouflage to avoid detection by firewalls.

File Inclusion: Using this attack, the attacker could easily run malicious code on the webserver and gain access to unauthorized files. This loophole exists whenever the validation mechanism is ineffective.

ATTACK TECHNIQUES

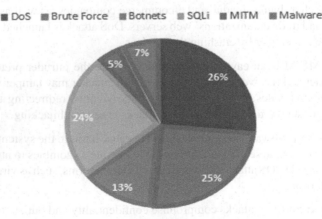

Fig. 3. Cyber-attacks rates over time.

The above Fig. 3 depicts that MITM attacks account for about 26% of all attacks. Brute force attacks account for 25% of all attacks. The SQLi attack, which reports for about 24% of all attacks, is the third most common. The botnet is responsible for 13% of all attacks. Other types of attacks, such as DoS and malware, account for 5% and 7% of all attacks, respectively.

4   Counter Measures

Machine learning based intrusion detection systems to tackle some of the common attacks:

SQL Injection: As proposed by Sonali, Mishra et al. [22] machine learning techniques such as Naive Bayes and Gradient Boosting methods can be used to detect SQL injection. Libinjection, the same tool used to create SQL injection payloads, can be used to create the dataset used to train the machine. Tokenization divides the text into tokens and distinguishes between plain text and SQL injections. By analysing the tokens and their count the attacks are detected

MITM: As suggested by Doreenda Nikoi Kotei et al. [18] MITM attacks can be detected by looking for semi-duplicate packets in network traffic or inspecting the transmission time of a packet. Wireshark is used to capture and store all of the legit and intentionally poisoned semi-duplicate packets. The model uses the stored packets as a data set to classify normal packets and MITM packets. The Random forest model is capable of accomplishing this.

DNS Spoofing: According to the idea of Yong Jin et al. [20]. A dataset containing the history of all DNS cache server logs is used to train a machine. The data is extracted from DNS query responses and the corresponding triggered DNS record from the cache, is used to feed the model. When a poisoned DNS record is inserted into the cache server, the machine detects it and analyses it using logs that have been stored.

DNS Tunneling: An DNS tunnelling detection system was proposed by Buczak et al. [23]. Which uses a classification method like a random forest to pin down the DNS tunnelling attack. The authors conveyed numerous facets including the estimated amount of answers provided in the response, the interlude between two successive packets, and their captured responses for a peculiar domain. To classify new and novel tunnelling, the proposed classifier was trained on such features. The random forest classifier is predominantly governed by rules, with a voting mechanism that fully reflects prophecy classes.

Malware: J. Kolter et al. [19] proposed a malware detection model based on machine learning and data mining algorithms. The model was effective at detecting both known and unknown malware. Based on the n-gram feature, the traces were encoded as a training sample. For prediction, the most relevant n-grams were preferred. Algorithms such as the support vector method, naive bayes, and decision tree were used during the evaluation.

Crypto-Jacking: The authors Ning R et al. [24] proposed CapsJack, an machine learning-based detection mechanism that has been effective in detecting in-browser malicious cryptocurrency mining activities. CapsNet is a prototype of a biological neural organization based on which CapsJack is developed. CapsJack makes use of system features such as memory, disc space, CPU utilization, and network utilization, implementing a host-based solution. This proposed mechanism was successful, with an 88% detection rate.

Botnet Attack: Mathur et al. [25] proposed a method for distinguishing botnet traffic from the regular traffic flow. CfsSubsetEval is a filtering method used to select the most relevant features. A model capable of making predictions was built using Random Committee classifiers, Logistic Regression, Randomized Filtered, Random SubSpace, and MultiClass. Logistic Regression and MultiClass Classifier achieved the highest accuracy of 98.5% of the algorithms mentioned above.

DoS: The goal [26] is to use the information gain approach to apply the feature selection strategy to the dataset. Determine the important characteristics of good outcomes. Multiple linear regression is carried out using the selected features. Fit charts and residual plots are then used to examine the dataset. Attributes that aren't important are removed, and regression is performed again. The difference between an actual label and a predicted label will be noticeable, and the updated attributes will be more effective in carrying out DoS attack detection.

Brute Force: Machine learning algorithms for brute force detection [27] include 5-NN, decision trees, and naive bayes. These were picked because they are quite simple to compute. K-NN builds learned hypotheses using the training data, and each sample must be distanced from all other samples. The branches of the C4.5 decision tree divide the samples into further branches based on the values of characteristics, and then Information Gain is used. The naive bayes algorithm determines the probability of an instance, but it's extremely complex to calculate; as a result, it's a slow classifier but a good learner (Table 1).

Table 1. List of a few cyber-attacks and their machine learning-based countermeasures

Types of attack	Description of the attack	Countermeasures using machine learning algorithms
SQL injection attacks	In SQL injection, SQL queries and commands are injected into modules to obtain sensitive data from the server database [16]	SQL injection can be detected by using Naive Bayes and gradient boosting trained with the payload dataset obtained from Libinjection [22]

(continued)

Table 1. (*continued*)

Types of attack	Description of the attack	Countermeasures using machine learning algorithms
Crypto-jacking	Crypto-jacking is a sort of cybercrime in which cybercriminals use people's equipment to mine for bitcoin without their permission	CapsNet is a prototype of a biological neural organization that makes use of system features implementing a host-based solution [24]
Denial of Service Attacks	DoS attacks work by bombarding the target with immense traffic that causes it to crash. DoS is launched by flooding the systems or by crashing the services [17]	Using the selected features, multiple linear regression is conducted. The dataset is next examined with fit charts and residual plots [20]
Identity Spoofing or IP Spoofing	This attack takes advantage of DNS flaws to redirect traffic to fraudulent websites or servers	A dataset containing the history of all DNS cache server logs is used to train a machine
MITM Attack	MITM is an eavesdropping attack, where the intruder pretends to be a legitimate sender and receiver for both end-users [18]	The Random Forest model is used to Identify the legitimate packets and MITM packets which is trained with intentionally poisoned semi-duplicated packets dataset [18]
DNS Tunnelling	DNS-Tunnelling is an attack in which the attacker encodes the program into the query to avoid detection by the firewall [21]	Numerous facets include the estimated number of answers provided in the response, the interlude between two successive packets, and their captured responses for a peculiar domain. To classify new and novel tunnelling, the proposed classifier was trained on such features [23]
Malware Threats	Malware is a software program designed to infect the device, steal the user credentials or personal data. The attacker can also control the behaviour of the device [19]	N-gram algorithm was used to counter the malware attack Based on the n-gram feature; the traces were encoded as a training sample [19]

The bar graph in Fig. 4 demonstrates the various types of attacks that have occurred as well as the detection accuracy of various machine learning algorithms. As can be seen, Naive Bayes surpasses the detection of SQL Injection with an accuracy of 97.6% [22], while Decision Tree detects malware with the best accuracy of 99% [19]. CNN detects

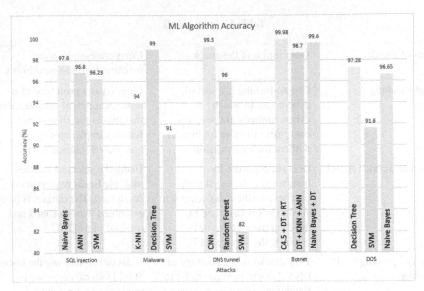

Fig. 4. The accuracy of various machine learning algorithms

DNS Tunneling with the maximum accuracy of 99.3% [23]. C4.5, Decision Tree, and RT have the best performance of 99.98% in detecting Botnet [25]. Decision Tree has the highest accuracy of 99% in detecting DOS [26].

5   Conclusion

On the whole, this paper presents a review of the literature on machine learning and intrusion detection system in Cyberspace. The importance of machine learning is discussed, as well as the various types of attacks that occur. Different machine learning algorithms are evaluated in terms of specific attacks that frequently occur. We also highlighted the fact about the accuracy of each algorithm based on comparative analysis. The taxonomy system of intrusion detection system, which has a source of data and detection methods, is explained in a very brief flowchart. Datasets are used to store information that is required by applications or other programs. The main objective of this study is to comprehend and interpret the most appropriate countermeasures for any given attack. It's worth noting that when comparing different models, not only the accuracy but also the complexity and time required to detect an attack should be considered.

In the future, we will enhance our work by presenting an intrusion detection system based on Convolutional Neural Network that can detect attacks like DDoS using the KDDCUP99 dataset which is converted into RGB or grayscale by adjusting the threshold setting values. The main aim is to improve the systematic approach for a stronger alert quality, which will greatly aid incident handling.

References

1. Angra, S., Ahuja, S.: Machine learning and its applications: a review. In: 2017 International Conference on Big Data Analytics and Computational Intelligence (ICBDAC), pp. 57–60 (2017). https://doi.org/10.1109/ICBDACI.2017.8070809
2. Tiwari, Mohit, Kumar, Raj, Bharti, Akash, Kishan, Jai: Intrusion detection system. Int. J. Tech. Res. Appl. **5**, 2320–8163 (2017)
3. Zeeshan Ahmad, Adnan Shahid Khan, Cheah Wai Shiang, Johari Abdullah, Farhan Ahmad: Network intrusion detection system: a systematic study of machine learning and deep learning approaches. Trans. Emerg. Telecommun. Technol. **32**(1), e4150 (2021). https://doi.org/10. 1002/ett.4150
4. Navada, A., Ansari, A.N., Patil, S., Sonkamble, B.A.: Overview of use of decision tree algorithms in machine learning. In: 2011 IEEE Control and System Graduate Research Colloquium, pp. 37–42 (2011). https://doi.org/10.1109/ICSGRC.2011.5991826
5. Selvarajan, Shitharth, Shaik, Masood, Ameerjohn, Sirajudeen, Kannan, Sangeetha: Mining of intrusion attack in SCADA network using clustering and genetically seeded flora-based optimal classification algorithm. IET Inf. Secur. **14**(1), 1–11 (2020). https://doi.org/10.1049/ iet-ifs.2019.0011
6. Hosameldin Ahmed, Asoke K. Nandi: Artificial Neural Networks (ANNs). In: Condition Monitoring with Vibration Signals: Compressive Sampling and Learning Algorithms for Rotating Machines, pp.239–258. IEEE (2019). https://doi.org/10.1002/9781119544678.ch12
7. Ghosh, S., Dasgupta, A., Swetapadma, A." A study on support vector machine based linear and non-linear pattern classification. In: 2019 International Conference on Intelligent Sustainable Systems (ICISS), pp. 24–28 (2019). https://doi.org/10.1109/ISS1.2019.8908018
8. Buczak, A.L., Guven, E.:. A survey of data mining and machine learning methods for cyber security intrusion detection. IEEE Commun. Surv. Tutor. **18**(2), 1 (2015). https://doi.org/10. 1109/COMST.2015.2494502
9. Shitharth, S., Sangeetha, Praveen Kumar: Integrated probability relevancy classification (IPRC) for IDS in SCADA. In: Design Framework for Wireless Network, Lecture notes in network and systems, vol. 82, Issue 1, pp. 41–64. Springer (2019).
10. Kulhare, R., Singh, D.: Survey paper on intrusion detection techniques. Int. J. Comput. Technol. **6**, 329–335 (2007). https://doi.org/10.24297/ijct.v6i2.3498
11. Zavrak, S., Iskefiyeli, M.: Anomaly-based intrusion detection from network flow features using variational autoencoder. IEEE Access. **8**, 108346–108358 (2020). https://doi.org/10. 1109/ACCESS.2020.3001350
12. Thomas, C., Sharma, V., Balakrishnan, N.: Usefulness of DARPA dataset for intrusion detection system evaluation. Proc. SPIE Int. Soc. Opt. Eng. **6973**, 8pp (2008)
13. Tavallaee, M., Bagheri, E., Lu, W., Ghorbani, A.: A detailed analysis of the KDD CUP 99 data set. In: Submitted to Second IEEE Symposium on Computational Intelligencefor Security and Defense Applications (CISDA) (2009)
14. Moustafa, N., Slay, J.: UNSW-NB15: a comprehensive data set for network intrusion detection systems (UNSW-NB15 network data set). In: Military Communications and Information Systems Conference (MilCIS). IEEE (2015)
15. Liu, H., Lang, B.: Machine learning and deep learning methods for intrusion detection systems: a survey. Appl. Sci. **9**, 4396 (2019). https://doi.org/10.3390/app9204396
16. Halfond, W.G., Viegas, J., Orso, A.: A classification of SQL-injection attacks and countermeasures. In: Proceedings of the IEEE International Symposium on Secure Software Engineering, vol. 1, pp. 13–15. IEEE (March 2006)
17. Schuba, C.L., et al.: Analysis of a denial-of-service attack on TCP. In: Proceedings 1997 IEEE Symposium on Security and Privacy (Cat. No. 97CB36097). IEEE (1997)

18. Kotei, D.N., Yeboah, J.A., Ansong, E.D.: The use of machine learning algorithms to detect man-in-the-middle (MITM) attack in user datagram protocol packet header. Res. J. Inform. Technol. (March 2020)
19. Kolter, J., Maloof, M.: Learning to detect malicious executables in the wild. In: Proceedings of KDD'04, pp 470–478 (2004)
20. Jin, Y., Tomoishi, M., Matsuura, S.: A detection method against DNS cache poisoning attacks using machine learning techniques: work in progress. In: 2019 IEEE 18th International Symposium on Network Computing and Applications (NCA), pp. 1–3 (2019). https://doi.org/10.1109/NCA.2019.8935025
21. Do, V.T., Engelstad, P., Feng, B., Do, T.V.: Detection of DNS tunneling in mobile networks using machine learning. In: International Conference on Information Science and Applications, pp. 221–230 (2017)
22. Mishra, S.: SQL injection detection using machine learning. *Master's Projects*. 727 (2019)
23. Buczak, L., Hanke, P.A., Cancro, G.J., Toma, M.K., Watkins, L.A., Chavis, J.S.: Detection of tunnels in PCAP data by random forests. In: Proceedings of the 11th Annual Cyber and Information Security Research Conference, CISRC 2016 (April 2016)
24. Ning, R., Wang, C., Xin, C., Li, J., Zhu, L., Wu, H.: CapJack: capture in-browser cryptojacking by deep capsule network through behavioral analysis. In: IEEE INFOCOM 2019 - IEEE Conference on Computer Communications, pp. 1873–1881 (2019). https://doi.org/10.1109/INFOCOM.2019.8737381
25. Mathur, L., Raheja, M., Chaudhary, P.: Botnet detection via mining of network traffic flow. Procedia Comput. Sci. **132**, 1668–1677 (2018). https://doi.org/10.1016/j.procs.2018.05.137
26. Sambangi, S., Gondi, L.: A machine learning approach for DDoS attack detection using multiple linear regression. In: Presented at the 14th International Conference on Interdisciplinary in Engineering-INTER-ENG 2020, Targu mures, Romania (2020)
27. Najafabadi, M.M., Khoshgoftaar, T., Kemp, C., Seliya, N.: Machine learning for detecting brute force attacks at the network level. In: Conference: 2014 IEEE International Conference of Bioinformatics and Bioengineering (BIBE) (2014)
28. Kumar, A.: Design of secure image fusion technique using cloud for privacy-preserving and copyright protection. Int. J. Cloud Appl. Comput. **9**(3), 22–36 (2019)
29. Kumar, A., Zhang, Z.J., Lyu, H.: Object detection in real time based on improved single shot multi-box detector algorithm. EURASIP J. Wirel. Commun. Netw. **2020**(1), 1–18 (2020). https://doi.org/10.1186/s13638-020-01826-x
30. Kumar, A.: A review on implementation of digital image watermarking techniques using LSB and DWT. In: The Third International Conference on Information and Communication Technology for Sustainable Development (ICT4SD 2018), held during August 30–31, 2018 at Hotel Vivanta by Taj, Goa, India (2018)
31. Shitharth, Prince Winston, D.: An enhanced optimization algorithm for intrusion detection in SCADA network. J. Comput. Secur., Elsevier, **70**, 16–26 (2017)

A Systematic Review on Autonomous Vehicle: Traffic Sign Detection and Drowsiness Detection

Panna Lal Boda[1] and Y. Ramadevi[2(✉)]

[1] Osmania University, Hyderabad, India
bpannalal555@gmail.com
[2] Chaitanya Bharathi Institute of Technology, Osmania University, Hyderabad, India
yrdcse.cbit@gmail.com

Abstract. The automatic detection of traffic signs is necessary for assisted driving, autonomous driving, and driving safety. Traffic sign play a significant task for advanced driver assistance systems (ADAS) also for autonomous driving vehicles and also driver drowsiness detection are an important part. Due to fatigue and drowsiness of the drivers, each day more number of fatalities and deaths are massively increases. In order to avoid these problems, developed a traffic signs detection and drowsiness detection based on machine learning and deep learning techniques. Histogram of Oriented Gradients (HOG), Adaptive Momentum Estimation (ADAM) optimizer features, Random Forest (RF), Region-based Convolutional Neural Network (R-CNN), Long Short Term Memory (LSTM), and Support Vector Machine (SVM) method are used. German Traffic Sign Detection Benchmarks (GTSDB) dataset is used for classification and detection and it consist of 164 classes grouped into 8 categories. The proposed methods achieve the better results in conditions of accuracy comparable performance with the state of the art.

Keywords: Autonomous vehicle · Convolutional Neural Network · Drowsiness detection · Deep Learning · Traffic sign detection

1 Introduction

Nowadays, detection of traffic sign is a fundamental and complex task for raising the autonomous vehicles, accidents may happen in this task due to the problem of critical visual perception. The major causes of road accidents are occurring due to driver errors and carelessness. The important key player in accident is driver sleepiness and carelessness. According to a research done by the National Sleep Foundation, roughly 20% of drivers' experience drowsiness while driving. This research presents a method for detecting driver tiredness in which the architecture detects the driver's tiredness and drowsiness. Deep learning (DL) algorithms are developed rapidly to focus on the problems of vision autonomous vehicle and the algorithm has different types of applications which are recognition on object, self-driving cars, and robotics so on [1]. The main aim of traffic signal is to recognize and detection easily with the help of colors and standard shapes. Recognition of traffic signs are generally divided into two types that is bounding box and specific traffic class classification with German Traffic Sign Recognition

© The Author(s), under exclusive license to Springer Nature Switzerland AG 2022
A. Kumar et al. (Eds.): ICAIDS 2021, CCIS 1673, pp. 41–51, 2022.
https://doi.org/10.1007/978-3-031-21385-4_4

Benchmark (GTSRB) dataset [2]. People's lifestyle is changed due to automobile and it improves the daily activities, also traffic accidents are associated with numerous negative effects [3]. The information of road is collected automatically with text-based traffic sign recognition and detection system. By using the global positioning system (GPS) the collected information are used to provide the location of road and this method divided into two categories 1) street scenes, 2) expressway and wild scenes [4]. For traffic sign recognition a CNN model is the popular algorithm and also has limitations it cannot capture some features in traffic sign such as direction, angle, pose so on [5].

Different architectures such as You Only Look Once (YOLO) and ROIs algorithm are used due to excellent performance on detection and low propagation latency and ROIs achieves better coverage of traffic sign instances [6]. Improved SSD algorithm with enhancement and feature fusion, called MF-SSD algorithm. Developed to enhance the performance of detection, improve the accuracy in detection low-level features into high-level features and small targets in efficiency detection of SSD [7]. Histogram of Oriented Gradient (HOG) features extraction and linear classifier SVM methods are proposed to detect the fatigue of oncoming driver [8]. Drowsiness can be detected automatically with an adaptable method and also with ordinary web cam would be valuable. For human alertness Eye Aspect Ratio (EAR) has already adopted successfully to detect the drowsiness in real-time with eye patterns. Advantage of this method is low computational cost, provide facial recognition landmark and blink detection [9]. There are lot of reliability issues and safety in autonomous driving cars it completely relies on human skills. To evaluate the level of driver drowsiness the combination of hybrid LSTM and CNN models is used. To detect the level of drowsiness the temporal information will be provide for LSTM, the accidents occur because of wheel movement, high speed of vehicle, road condition, and pedal acceleration [10].

The paper is organized as follows, the review of existing methods is discussed about autonomous vehicle in Sect. 1, and taxonomy of the method explained in Sect. 2, problem statement of the current paper explained in Sect. 3, comparison analysis of the paper Sect. 4, then the conclusion of this research is explained in Sect. 5.

2 Taxonomy on Autonomous Vehicle

Autonomous vehicle is also known as self-driving car or robotic car or driverless car, is a vehicle able to senses its surroundings and moves safely with small or no human input. At present this technology is the most important game changer and may have an impact on several industries and other conditions. Autonomous vehicle consists of two most important methods which are traffic sign recognition and drowsiness detection. Traffic Sign Recognition (TSR) method is used to identify the traffic signs present on the road and then driver drowsiness detection is used to records the behavior of driver at begin of trip (Fig. 1).

2.1 Traffic Sign Detection

Tadashi et al. [1] developed a Deep learning models based on the combination of Single Shot Multi box Detector (SSD) and Feature Pyramid Network (FPN) algorithm. Normal

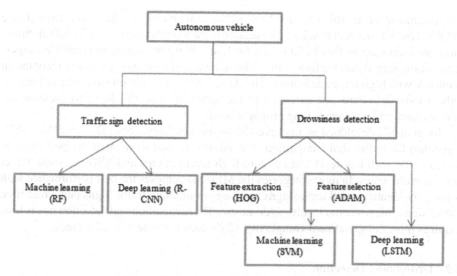

Fig. 1. Taxonomy of Autonomous vehicle

architecture is used for the classification of image with high-quality based on network layer. Combination of this model will provide more information about different hardware architecture and deep learning models. There is no problem with model and data load due to power consumption in hardware architecture. Development of new DL algorithm and architecture have memory limitation and low computation cost.

Serna and Ruichek [2] developed an architecture based on Region based Convolutional Neural Network (R-CNN) model to recognize the traffic sign. The method consists of three modules such as refinement and traffic sign detection, class classification or category. R-CNN model able to provide an exact prediction even in small traffic signs and distribution of feature is also same in large tragic sign. R-CNN model only focus on traffic signs detection and the GTSDB dataset is small and not available anymore.

Deng, and Wu, [4] developed a vertical-and-horizontal-text traffic sign recognition as well as detection method to identify the vertical and horizontal problem of text. The method uses the structural and position information in order to figure the text lines based on Chinese characters. The connection among the vertical and horizontal text lines is used to analyze and verify whether the overlap is vertical or horizontal. Stability of algorithm is less, analyzes the effects of the occlusion limited, and traffic sign recognition and detection has lighting conditions.

He et al. [5] proposed an automatic recognition algorithm with deep learning for the recognition of traffic sign based on visual inspection. To prevent projection distortion and image detection, a Histogram of Oriented Gradients (HOG) method is proposed. The overall gradient image is highly sensitive and the value of pixel image will be divided into two that is, gradient magnitude will be halved, and the whole image will become darker. CNN model cannot capture the traffic sign effectively such as direction, pose, and angel because the model has defect in max-pooling layer.

Avramović et al. [6] developed an architecture based on You Only Look Once (YOLO) model to detect baseline. For feature extraction three different YOLO architectures are used such as TinyYOLO, YOLOv4, and YOLOv3 it as high accuracy. Larger-scale traffic sign dataset achieves the detection on real-time based on high recognition accuracy with high image definition. The detection occurs only on small object because only low-level features are extracted in the initial layer so this leads to decrease the performance and also needs long propagation time.

Jin et al. [7] developed an improved Multi-Feature Single Shot Detector (MF-SSD) algorithm for traffic sign recognition. The method is used to enhance the performance on detection with low-level features into high level features and SSD has small target detection efficiency. In most categories the MF-SSD achieves the best performance with accurately identify small traffic signs and large or medium traffic signs and a real-time traffic sign achieves better results on domestic. The recognition and detection rate is less, requires more computational complexity, CNN does not detect small images.

2.2 Drowsiness Detection

Deng and Wu et al. [3] developed Multiple Convolutional Neural Network (MC-KCF) is a combination of KCF and CNN to detect the level of driver drowsiness and fatigue status. The method measures the angle of an opening eye to identify whether the eye is closed is not, also detect the yawning, and frequency of blinking. 68 key points are designed to detect the facial regions of driver's also with eyes and mouth features recognition. The recognition of eye closure is limited in CNN architecture and in real time the algorithm cannot track the object in real environment.

Bakheet et al. [8] developed a Histogram of Oriented Gradient (HOG) features to detect the driver drowsiness in vehicle. To predict the eye status, a simple probabilistic Naïve Bayes (NB) classifier is used and the data samples are modified between correlations. The input image of a drive is captured in the camera which is mounted in dashboard are initially preprocessed by using adaptive contrast-limited histogram equalization method. Computational cost is less; basic architecture is used in embedded system so it will decrease the operating and financial expenses.

Maior et al. [9] developed machine learning based Random Forest (RF), Support Vector Machine (SVM), and Multi-Layer Perceptron (MLP) classifier are used to recognize the driver drowsiness in vehicle. MPL classifier able to simplify the patterns using small training set and it is normally used in feedforward neural network, when a subject is alert this model does not provide any warning. There classification models use only images for the detection of driver drowsiness, costly, large, and advanced apparatus are needed.

Guo, and Markoni et al. [10] developed a Deep learning based on hybrid Long Short Term Memory (LSTM) and Convolutional Neural Network (CNN) methods for detecting the weakness and drowsiness of the drivers. The combination of LSTM and CNN model will extract the spatial features then by using haar-cascade feature are extracted and ada-boosting classifier are used to detect the face of the driver. CNN model provides a better accuracy; low computational cost and the evaluation will be done in one frame. CNN architecture is applied for whole images but the main drowsiness action lies on the face. Kumar et al. proposed object detection using muti-box detector for small object [13–15].

3 Vehicle-Focused Studies and Systems

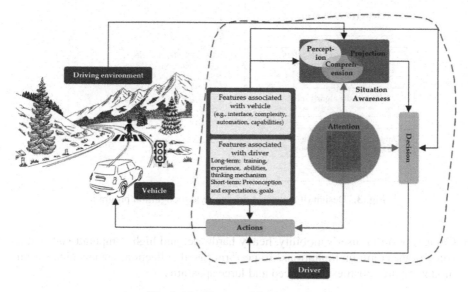

Fig. 2. Architecture driving process

    Understanding the driving style through vehicle-associated parameters is an important topic of traffic sign detection which helps in providing improved on-road safety and a greener environment. Moreover, knowledge of driving style is also mandatory for the development future of autonomous transportation systems [16, 17]. Recognition of driving style is a complex multidisciplinary topic influenced by several environmental (e.g., weather, season, time of the day, and lighting condition) and human (e.g., age, gender, and behavior) factors [11, 12]. Architecture driving process and flowchart of a generic driving style recognition program is shown in below.

4 Problem Statement

The problem statements of the study are as follows.

- Training set of the GTSDB dataset is relatively small and not available anymore then the features are very small to generate the traffic signs. Due to illumination changes the key components are not suitable for outside environments.
- The major action of drowsiness recognition lies on the face but, the CNN architecture is applied for the entire image. The entire frame does not evaluate in the image and it takes only one optical flow of image.

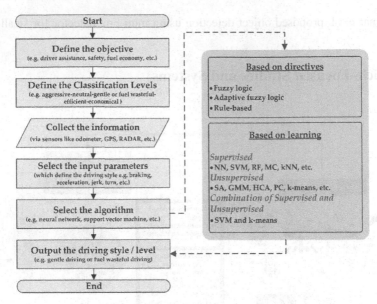

Fig. 3. Design of a generic driving style recognition program

- Camera position, user's mobility, heavy hardware, and high computational cost are some of the common limitations. To perform signal collection, the machine learning model requires costliest, advanced and large apparatus.

5   Comparative Analysis

Self-driving car also known as autonomous vehicle, without any human interference the vehicle will achieve the necessary function, able to drive itself and has the capacity to sense its surroundings. Compare to human-driven vehicle, the autonomous vehicle as advantages such as safety on the road-vehicle, reduce traffic congestion, decrease in the number of accident and it is very convenient transport for disability and aged people.

The performance of existing methods in terms of mAP value in Table 1 and Fig. 2. The proposed method's performance is better than the existing methods. The proposed deep learning and CNN methods present mAp values for 87.07% and 84.50% but The YOLO method presents a better mAP of 95.50%. The proposed Horizontal-text traffic sign recognition and SSD methods present Recall values for 0.782 and 88.10% but. The CNN method presents a better Recall value of 97.81%.

Table 1. Various encryption techniques in autonomous vehicle

Author	Database	Methodology	Advantage	Disadvantage	Results
Tadashi et al. [1]	LISA dataset	Developed a combination of deep learning models and different hardware architectures	The performance of both software and hardware fields are improved by generating the hardware accelerators. Statistical exploitation, data movement, and reuse of maximum data	In embedded system the requirement of hardware is less and limitations of memory and computational cost	Mean average precision on CPU = 87.07% Mean average precision on TPU = 88.50% Mean average precision on GPU = 88.31%
Serna, and Ruichek, [2]	GTSRB dataset	Developed a CNN architecture to identify the traffic sings	Compared to other methods CNN architecture provides a high-quality tradeoff between accuracy, computational time, and number of parameters more	GTSDB training sets is small and due to illumination changes, the color of key component is not suitable for outside environments	mAp = 84.5% Recall = 97.81%
Deng, and Wu, [3]	CelebA and YawDD datasets	Developed a MC-KCF algorithm and DriCare method to detect the fatigue status of drivers by using video images	The real-time system of DriCare has high operation speed, offer stable performance and also applicable in different circumstances	The recognition of eye closure is limited in CNN architecture In real time the algorithm cannot track the object in real environment	Accuracy = 95%
Guo, et al. [4]	Traffic Guide Panel Dataset	Developed a mixed vertical-and-horizontal-text traffic sign recognition also detection method for road level view	Cascaded color segmentation method is more efficient for exploring the full information of the color	Recognition method for text-based traffic signs is limited for locating characters	Precision = 0.697 Recall = 0.782 F1 = 0.731
He, et al. [5]	LISA dataset	Deep learning algorithm is developed based on CNN model to recognize the traffic sign	The gradients back propagation is facilitated, the blocks of downstream are simplified and the actual features are approximated CNN model ran faster, use less memory	Stability of algorithm is less, analyzes the effects of the occlusion limited	Accuracy = 97.08%

(continued)

Table 1. (*continued*)

Author	Database	Methodology	Advantage	Disadvantage	Results
Avramović et al. [6]	DFG traffic sign dataset	Developed You Only Look Once (YOLO) architecture to achieve real-time performance requirement	Multiple graphic cards are available so, several regions can be processed in parallel and in image the propagation of time is low	Computational cost is low, only small objects are detected in the initial layer and low-level features are extracted, this limitations will reduce the performance	mAP = 95.50%
Jin, et al. [7]	GTSRB dataset	Developed SSD algorithm to recognize and detect the road traffic sign	Small objects are detected by MF-SSD methods with respect to better efficiency and higher detection accuracy	Requires more computational complexity and recognition rate of these methods are limited	Recall = 88.1% Precision = 82.6% F1_measure = 85.8%
Bakheet, and Al-Hamadi, [8]	NTHU-DDD dataset	Developed a innovative framework for the detection of driver drowsiness	The framework has the ability to make real-time predictions about whether drivers are fatigued or drowsy	Physiological sensors are obtrusive and never used in a production vehicle and computational cost is less	Accuracy = 85.62%
Maior et al. [9]	DROZY dataset	Developed a ML model to detect the drowsiness based on eye patterns of people by using video strems	RBF requires only one parameter and has great flexibility ML-based technique is used to identify the early symptoms and also drowsiness patterns	To perform as signal collection it requires costly, large, advanced apparatus, infrared camera is needed and this model only use images frames	Accuracy = 94.9%
Guo, and Markoni, [10]	ACCN dataset	Developed a hybrid of LSTM and CNN models to detect the real time driver drowsiness detection	Computation is very fast so the evaluation will be done in one frame for each iteration	The frame of CNN architecture is very small in size so it will make a loss of rich face features and the vision will become poor	Accuracy = 84.85%

Table 2 and Fig. 3 provides the comparison of accuracy of various methods in autonomous vehicle. The proposed method performance is better than the existing methods. The deep learning method presents an accuracy value of 97.08% better accuracy than other methods. The SSD method presents a precision value of 82.60% and an F1 measure value of 85.80% better performance than other methods (Figs. 4 and 5; Table 3).

Table 2. Recall and mAP value comparison

Method	Dataset	mAp	Recall
Deep learning [1]	LISA	87.07%	–
CNN [2]	GTSRB	84.50%	97.81%
Horizontal-text traffic sign recognition [4]	Traffic Guide Panel	–	0.782
YOLO [6]	DFG traffic sign	95.50%	–
SSD [7]	GTSRB	–	88.10%

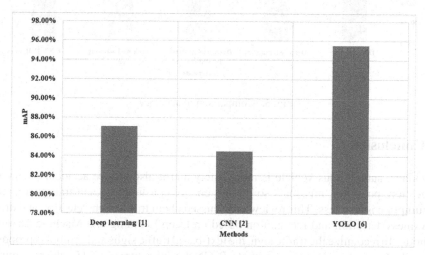

Fig. 4. Comparison of mAP value

Table 3. Comparison of accuracy and precision

Method	Dataset	Accuracy	Precision	F1_measure
DriCare [3]	YawDD	95%	–	–
Horizontal-text traffic sign recognition [4]	Traffic Guide Panel	–	0.697	0.731
Deep learning [5]	LISA	97.08%	–	–
SSD [7]	GTSRB	–	82.60%	85.80%
Detection of driver drowsiness [8]	NTHU-DDD	85.62%	–	–
Machine Learning [9]	DROZY	94.90%	–	–
CNN [10]	ACCN	84.85%		

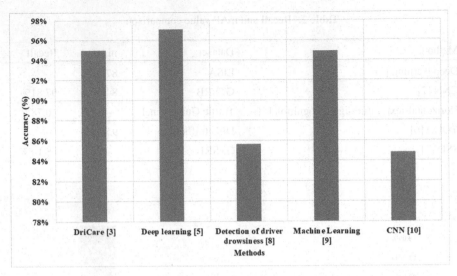

Fig. 5. Comparison of accuracy

6 Conclusion

Nowadays, autonomous vehicle is more safety and it also reduce accidents, transport congestion, pollution, mission's so on and energy consumption and transport energy consumption is also less. This review is discussed about traffic sign detection and driver drowsiness detection and recognition based on Deep Learning and Machine Learning methods. To recognize the traffic sign, the text-based traffic signs and symbol is proposed during the European urban environments. R-CNN architecture is used for the recognition of traffic sign with the help of colors, small class variations and shapes and it also achieves better accuracy with GTSDB dataset. The Feature Pyramid Network (FPN) and Single Shot Multi box Detector (SSD) methods are used for feature extraction. The approach of SSD is based on a feed-forward convolutional network, that produces scores and fixed-size of collections in bounding boxes then it will predict the box offsets and category of scores. FPN architecture combines semantically strong feature, low-resolution with semantically weak features, high-resolution via a top-down pathway, and connections of lateral. To handle the driver drowsiness, issue a hybrid LSTM and SVM methods is used to detect the face of the driver, to crop the mouth and eye regions there are five facial landmarks are regressed. LSTM properly adapt the changes for robustness problem and it also gives a learnable parameter and CNN model developed a low computational cost and gives better accuracy. The data utilized in this study was acquired in a lab setting; however, future research should examine evaluating the boundaries of this technology in real-world driving scenarios, which will include more demanding settings like as wearing sunglasses and driving in different lighting conditions. This research will eventually lead to the creation of an unobtrusive, reliable approach for long-term vigilance evaluation, an important step in managing driver tiredness and reducing motor vehicle crashes.

References

1. Tadashi, H., Koichi, K., Kenta, N., Yuki, H.: Driver status monitoring system in autonomous driving era. Omron Tech. **50**, 1–7 (2019)
2. Serna, C.G., Ruichek, Y.: Traffic signs detection and classification for European urban environments. IEEE Trans. Intell. Transp. Syst. **21**(10), 4388–4399 (2019)
3. Deng, W., Wu, R.: Real-time driver-drowsiness detection system using facial features. IEEE Access **7**, 118727–118738 (2019)
4. Guo, J., You, R., Huang, L.: Mixed vertical-and-horizontal-text traffic sign detection and recognition for street-level scene. IEEE Access **8**, 69413–69425 (2020)
5. He, S., Chen, L., Zhang, S., Guo, Z., Sun, P., Liu, H.: Automatic recognition of traffic signs based on visual inspection. IEEE Access, **9**, 43253–43261 (2021)
6. Avramović, A., Sluga, D., Tabernik, D., Skočaj, D., Stojnić, V., Ilc, N.: Neural-network-based traffic sign detection and recognition in high-definition images using region focusing and parallelization. IEEE Access **8**, 189855–189868 (2020)
7. Jin, Y., Fu, Y., Wang, W., Guo, J., Ren, C., Xiang, X.: Multi-feature fusion and enhancement single shot detector for traffic sign recognition. IEEE Access **8**, 38931–38940 (2020)
8. Bakheet, S., Al-Hamadi, A.: A framework for instantaneous driver drowsiness detection based on improved HOG Features and Naïve Bayesian Classification. Brain Sci. **11**(2), 240 (2021)
9. Maior, C.B.S., das Chagas Moura, M.J., Santana, J.M.M., Lins, I.D.: Real-time classification for autonomous drowsiness detection using eye aspect ratio. Expert Syst. Appl. **158**, 113505 (2020)
10. Guo, J.M., Markoni, H.: Driver drowsiness detection using hybrid convolutional neural network and long short-term memory. Multimed. Tools Appl. **78**(20), 29059–29087 (2019)
11. Li, G., Eben Li, S., Cheng, B.: Field operational test of advanced driver assistance systems in typical Chinese road conditions: the influence of driver gender, age and aggression. Int. J. Automot. Technol. **16**(5), 739–750 (2015). https://doi.org/10.1007/s12239-015-0075-5
12. Filev, D., Lu, J., Prakah-Asante, K., Tseng, F.: Real-time driving behavior identification based on driver-in-the-loop vehicle dynamics and control. In Proceedings of the IEEE International Conference on Systems, Man and Cybernetics, San Antonio, TX, USA, 11–14 October 2009, pp. 2020–2025 (2009)
13. Kumar, A.: Design of secure image fusion technique using cloud for privacy-preserving and copyright protection. Int. J. Cloud Appl. Comput. **9**(3), 22–36 (2019)
14. Kumar, A., Zhang, Z.J., Lyu, H.: Object detection in real time based on improved single shot multi-box detector algorithm. EURASIP J. Wirel. Commun. Netw. **2020**(1), 1–18 (2020). https://doi.org/10.1186/s13638-020-01826-x
15. Kumar, A.: A review on implementation of digital image watermarking techniques using LSB and DWT. In: The Third International Conference on Information and Communication Technology for Sustainable Development (ICT4SD 2018), held during August 30–31,2018 at Hotel Vivanta by Taj, Goa, India (2018)
16. Zheng, Y., Li, S.E., Wang, J., Cao, D., Li, K.: Stability and scalability of homogeneous vehicular platoon: study on the influence of information flow topologies. IEEE Trans. Intell. Transp. Syst. **2016**(17), 14–26 (2016)
17. Li, G., Li, S.E., Cheng, B., Green, P.: Estimation of driving style in naturalistic highway traffic using maneuver transition probabilities. Transp. Res. Part C Emerg. Technol. **2017**(74), 113–125 (2017)

Crop Disease Auto-localization
and Classification

G. Deepank[⊠], Shivani Bisht, Aditya Verma, R. Tharun Raj, and R. Jyothi

PES University, Bangalore 560085, Karnataka, India
deepankg@pesu.pes.edu, jyothir@pes.edu

Abstract. Plant disease detection plays an important role in the agriculture field, as different diseases affecting the growth of plants is inevitable. If suitable measures are not taken in time with respect to this aspect, then it harms the crop, resulting in substantial decrease in the quality of yield produced. This is where AI can be quite useful. It reduces human interference in monitoring big farms and aids in the detection of symptoms of diseases in time to find a solution. Computer vision, machine learning and deep learning algorithms are being used to process this data. In this paper, digital image processing and deep learning models (different architectures and algorithms) were used for classification (type of microorganism and disease) with localization and detection of the diseases (preconditions/symptoms) present in the plant crops. An attempt was made to carry out image segmentation in a novel way, using the DICOM format. The GradCAM algorithm was used to perform a detailed analysis of various deep learning algorithms to validate the accuracy with which each algorithm classifies the diseases. Furthermore, bounding box regression was performed to locate the disease symptoms on each image. Lastly, the whole process was automated by hosting it on a web application for an easier user experience.

Keywords: Deep learning · Classification · Localization · Crops · Image processing

1 Introduction

The agricultural sector is more than just a food source in these times. The world and the Indian economy are highly dependent on agricultural yields. Thus, in agriculture, detection, and diagnosis of various diseases in crops play a prominent role which can end up benefiting farmers and consumers alike. To detect any plant disease at an early stage and have an early diagnosis, automated disease detection techniques can be useful. For example, brown spot disease is a harmful disease found in rice crops. This disease can spread throughout the entire leaf and it can kill the whole crop in a short amount of time. The current method for plant disease detection and diagnosis is an observation made by experts through which detection and identification of plant diseases is done. For accomplishing this task, large teams of experts, with some amount of monitoring of the plants is required, which is expensive in an economical point of view. In many countries, some farmers, gardeners, and researchers do not have the ideas or the proper facilities

A. Kumar et al. (Eds.): ICAIDS 2021, CCIS 1673, pp. 52–65, 2022.
https://doi.org/10.1007/978-3-031-21385-4_5

and resources that they can consult the experts, due to which consulting experts costs a lot and is also very time consuming. In such circumstances, the proposed technique proves to be advantageous in monitoring a number of crops at once. The automated detection of diseases by just feeding the symptoms or just uploading a picture of the plant leaves makes it easier and cheaper. The method also supports machine vision ideologies to provide image based automatic process control, and inspection.

Plant disease detection and diagnosis done by the on-site way is a more effortful and time consuming task and it is less accurate and can be done only in limited locations and areas as resources are not spread out. If automated detection techniques are made use of, it will take less time, less effort, and return much more accurate results, which makes it more accessible to people with little or no access to such resources and expert advice. Processing images of disease affected crops can help in accurately identifying diseases, and also help to come up with possible solutions to the disease in the crop. Image processing can also be used for detecting the disease affected area.

2 Problem Statement

This project will facilitate the classification and identification of different crop diseases using various deep learning models (algorithms) and techniques. The evaluation, visualization, and analysis of the different implemented models are also carried out. Finally, the best model will be used for deploying into a web application. The dataset for the project will be created alongside, which will include labeling, classification, bounding box coordinates of areas of interest and augmenting of a corpus of image data. Localization allows us to find the area of interest i.e., the affected areas (pre-conditions) of the plant crop such as discoloration, spots, holes, etc. The proposed methodology also involves subjecting images to 'medical imaging' using the DICOM format. This technique allows us to capture issues that are not fully visible to agronomists by naked-eye observation. The obtained high spectral resolution gives us much more useful content to describe the analyzed area of concern of the affected crop.

3 Literature Review

Extensive research has been done in the area of detection and classification of rice crop diseases using machine learning. Some of the related works on this subject are presented below.

Singh and Misra [3] presented an algorithm for image segmentation technique which was to be used for automatic detection and classification of plant leaf diseases. In which an important aspect for disease detection in plant leaves was done by using a genetic algorithm, which gives a number of optimum solutions, not a single solution. So different image segmentation results could be obtained at the same time. In the image recognition and segmentation processes, mostly green colored pixels were masked. In this, a threshold value was computed to be used for these pixels. Then in the following way mostly green pixels were masked: if pixel intensity of the green component was less than the pre-computed threshold value, then zero value was assigned to the red, green and blue components of the pixel. In the infected clusters the masked cells were removed to obtain the useful segments.

Nagasubramanian et al. [15] deployed a modernistic three-dimensional deep convolutional neural network, which precisely assimilated hyperspectral information. Hyperspectral imaging was investigated with respect to disease detection and classification as discussed in [8]. They decided to work on charcoal rot as the disease, because apart from soybean, it affects important crops like corn, cotton etc. Moreover, there are limited chemical measures available, so resistance breeding was an important countermeasure as mentioned in [13]. The CNN model was developed such that it comprised 2 convolutional layers, associated with which there were 2 max-pooling layers and finally, 2 completely connected layers. Kernels of different sizes were considered to convolve the input, particularly 2 kernels of size $3 \times 3 \times 16$ were employed in the first layer and 4 kernels of the same size in the second layer. The activation function chosen for the output was Rectified Linear Unit (ReLU). Furthermore, a saliency map was plotted to highlight areas of the plant image that were most indicative of the presence of the disease. Thus, they concluded hyperspectral imaging techniques in combination with proper deep learning models can be used to identify specific features that distinguishes a healthy plant from an infected one, with sufficiently high accuracy.

Kumar et al. [10–12] proposed object detection using muti-box detector for small object. Yan Guo et al. [17] proposed the use of a region proposal network (RPN) in order to recognize and localize leaves in complex surroundings. The RPN is trained on a dataset consisting of leaf images in different environments and the images of the symptomatic leaves are returned. Different techniques were studied for feature extraction, such as using color and texture features to extract disease spots which was mentioned in a paper by Raza and colleagues [14]. The use of transfer learning for feature extraction and building a disease identification system was also studied as proposed by Couilbaly et al. [16]. These images are then segmented by making use of the Chan-Vese algorithm that performs iterative calculations to obtain specific leaf contours based on the minimum energy function and set zero level. These segmented images are then fed into a pre-trained transfer learning model to identify diseases in a simple white background. The correct rate percentage average of the proposed model is much better than traditional deep learning models like ResNet101. Although the model works with a reasonably good accuracy of 83.57%, since the Chan-Vese algorithm makes use of repetitive iterative calculations, the model works really slow when dealing with datasets of large sizes.

Kulkarni and Patil [4] aimed to discover a methodology for early and accurate plant diseases detection, by making use of many image processing techniques and neural networks. Their method offered results with a recognition rate of up to 91%. In the paper written by Bashir and Sharma [6], they mention performing disease detection in Malus domestica through algorithms like K-mean clustering, texture and color analysis.

Akhila and Deepan [5] proposed a deep-learning-based approach to detect plant leaf diseases in different plants using images of its leaves. They made use of three main detector models: Faster Region-based Convolutional Neural Network (Faster R-CNN), Region-based Fully Convolutional Network (R-FCN) and Single Shot Multibox Detector (SSD). This choice of models was inspired from the work of Ren S et al. [7]. In this paper, they attempted real time object detection using region proposal networks. The detector implemented by them captured images with the help of many camera devices and they were also collected from various online resources. In conclusion, their models were successful in discerning and recognizing different kinds of diseases in various plants. They also attempted to provide solutions relevant to the plant disease identified.

Ampatzidis et. al. [9] presented and reviewed robot based solutions and applications on plant pathology and management, and emerging agricultural technologies and development for the novel types of intra-urban agriculture [10–12]. With respect to agricultural productivity, Oerke [1] gave an overview on different types of crop losses as well as various methods of pest control developed over the course of the last hundred years. Barbedo [2] dove deep into the main factors that affect the effectiveness and design of deep neural networks applied to the field of plant pathology. Here he provided an in-depth analysis of the subject, in which advantages and shortcomings were highlighted.

4 Proposed Methodology

4.1 Dataset Preparation

A labeled dataset of rice crop diseases with bounding box coordinates was prepared initially. Various images of diseased rice crops were found and brought to one place. The images were then moved into folders with their respective disease name using python scripts. The images were then subjected to augmentation to expand the dataset size for training purposes. The images were subjected to different kinds of rotation, cropping and noise addition. For disease detection and localization of diseases, the dataset was annotated, along with the bounding box coordinates. Localized bounding boxes were manually created for all of the original as well as augmented images, using LabelImg. These coordinates were stored in XML files. Localization helps in finding areas of interest i.e., affected areas (pre-conditions) of plant crops like discoloration, spots, holes, etc. A CSV file containing the file paths of all the images, their respective disease labels and the bounding box coordinates of their areas of interest was created to be parsed and preprocessed later while creating the model.

4.2 Image Segmentation Using DICOM Format

This technique helps in capturing issues that are not visible to agronomists. High spectral resolution provides more informational content to describe the analyzed area of the object. Using the img2dcm command on Linux, all the images were subject to the DICOM segmentation and stored. The file paths of the newly created DICOM images were added alongside the file paths of the original images to the CSV file.

4.3 Feature Extraction

Feature extraction techniques are used to obtain features or characteristics that will help us in object detection and classification. OpenCV and NumPy libraries were used to perform feature extraction by resizing the dimensions of the images after having subjected them to normalization.

4.4 Transfer Learning

There are some pre-existing generally well performing convolutional models such as VGG16, Xception, Resnet50 etc., that can be leveraged for classification and identification. The models are trained on the ImageNet database which consists of images of regular objects. The weights that these models were trained on were used to perform classification for our dataset consisting of rice crop images by changing the dimensions of the final few layers.

4.5 Model Analysis

After the training, the dataset is split into train and test datasets which are used for validation. Next, the accuracy of the predicted images was validated and the results of the different models were presented. Using these results, the performance of different models were analyzed.

4.6 Grad-CAM: For Model Performance Analysis

Grad-CAM [5] is generally used to emphasize the most important areas from the point of view of the CNN model used for the classification. This makes the model more transparent. It uses the gradient information in the final layer to get an idea of the importance of the individual neurons for decision of interest. Grad-CAM was used to verify what the models learnt by highlighting the areas the model used to classify the image. This method is used to verify whether the classification of models is happening based on the features decided initially or some other co-incidental feature in the images.

4.7 Bounding Box Regression

The bounding box coordinates are in PascalVOC format. These coordinates are normalized based on image dimensions. This method reused the classification model used earlier as it was already pre-trained to do feature extraction. As a result, the model is aware of regions of interest. This speeds up our regression problem. The model loss and accuracy using IoU(intersection over union) metric was calculated. The model is trained for 400 epochs. And IoU of about 0.5 is obtained. To understand model performance a sample of high and low IoU images are visualized.

4.8 Model Deployment

After the different models are evaluated and compared, the model with the best measure of the defined metrics will be deployed as a small web application. While saving the model, its trained weights will be saved along with its layers. In the web app, a user can give their own image of a rice crop leaf as the input for classification. The features will be extracted from this image and the saved model will give the relevant output, which is the bounding box coordinates locating the disease symptoms on the image, as well as the identified disease of the plant. The possible solutions and preventive measures for the detected disease are also displayed for the users' convenience (Fig. 1).

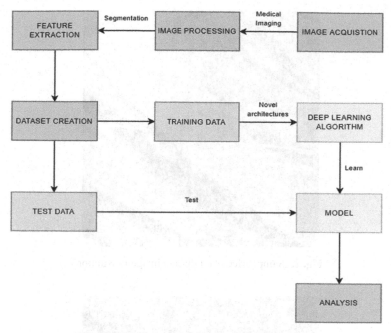

Fig. 1. Illustration of the proposed methodology

5 Implementation

5.1 Augmentation and Pre-processing

This was done using TensorFlow and Keras modules. To perform augmentation, the 'skimage' library in Python was used. Utilities like 'sk.transform.rotate' and 'sk.util.random_noise' were used to rotate the images by a random angle and to introduce some noise into the images, respectively. Along with the techniques mentioned, the images were also flipped, both horizontally and vertically to obtain a working dataset of 240 images. The pre-processing stage involved annotating the images and manually drawing localized bounding boxes around the infected areas using 'LabelImg'.

5.2 DICOM Segmentation

To recreate medical image segmentation the closest to a real-world equipment, the img2dcm unix command was used, which is based on the DICOM format. The img2dcm command was used to convert all the images to DICOM format. In this format, the symptoms were projected more prominently and this allowed us to test if the method helped increase the prediction and detection accuracy of the model and if it reduced the runtime and model training. The reason why the symptoms got projected clearly and saliently is still quite unknown. But the likely reason is mostly due to the visualization behaving like a lossless compression and this is most attributed to an inconsistency in between the color space indicated by the DICOM Photometric Interpretation and the actual color space indicated by the encapsulated Pixel Data JPEG stream (Figs. 2 and 3).

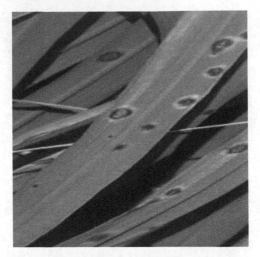

Fig. 2. Sample rice plant disease image illustration

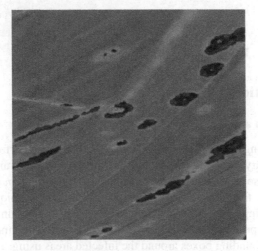

Fig. 3. Plant disease image after applying medical imaging

5.3 VGG16 Model

Used pre-existing models that were trained on the ImageNet database that consists of regular objects. Made use of the weights that the model was trained on, to perform classification for the dataset consisting of rice crop images by changing the dimensions of the final few layers. The layers from the input layer to the last max pooling layer (dimensions given by $7 \times 7 \times 512$) is called the feature extraction part of the model, while the rest of the network is called the classification part of the model.

After this, the model is loaded with the expected input image size of 224×224. The image object is converted to a NumPy array and the dimensions are increased and adjusted appropriately. The features can now be extracted with the predict method.

5.4 Resnet50 Model

A pretrained model trained on the ImageNet database and weights was loaded and used here. The last few layers of the model were modified to fit the logic of our problem statement. The layers from the input layer to the last max pooling layer (dimensions given by $7 \times 7 \times 2048$) is called the feature extraction part of the model, while the rest of the network is called the classification part of the model. After this, the model is loaded with the expected input image size of 224×224. The image object is converted to a NumPy array and the dimensions are increased and adjusted appropriately. The features can now be extracted with the predict method. The output feature vector was then flattened into a list of $7 \times 7 \times 2048$ which equals a total of 1,00,352 dimensions.

5.5 MobileNet V2 Model

The model is trained on the extensive ImageNet database and the corresponding weights. The dimensions of the last few layers which perform the classification are adjusted to enable the model to classify rice crop images instead of regular objects. The initial part of the network is left unchanged to make use of the pre-trained weights and perform feature extraction. Specifically, a sequential layer was added along with two dense layers and a dropout layer. The model was compiled using the RMSProp optimizer because it converges at a relatively faster rate. Model was tested on both the original images and the images subjected to DICOM segmentation and the results were compared.

5.6 Xception Model

The model was trained on the ImageNet database and weights. Similar to the other models, the initial layers aren't modified to allow the model to perform feature extraction. The last output layer which has dimensions of $2048 \times 3 \times 3$ is flattened to get 18432. A GlobalAveragePooling2D layer was added first and then a fully-connected layer was added to allow the model to perform classification. Model was tested on both the original images and the images subjected to DICOM segmentation and the results were compared.

5.7 Grad-CAM Analysis

This helps us in validating the performance of the CNN model. It's used to check what are the areas of interest that the model is looking into while performing the classification. Using the gradient information in the final layer, it obtains an understanding of the importance or relevance of individual neurons for decision of interest. Grad-CAM allows us to identify the important neurons in the network and a method to combine these neurons with their appropriate names to help provide graphical/textual information regarding the model decisions. If the model is looking at the wrong areas while performing classification, certain parameters can be adjusted to improve the accuracy of the model.

5.8 Bounding Box Regression

This was done using TensorFlow and Keras modules. All rows with "healthy leaf" category are dropped. This is because there are no coordinates annotated for this category. Dataset is split into train and test in the ratio of 80:20. The bounding box coordinates are normalized with respect to image dimensions. For calculating the model loss and accuracy for optimization, an IoU metric function was defined. It is used as the custom loss function while training. The saved neural network model (used earlier for classification) is modified and reused. The last layer was replaced with a linear activation layer. The model is compiled and trained using the Adam optimizer function for about 400 epochs. The model performance is then visualized by plotting a graph of epochs vs loss and epochs vs accuracy for both train and validation sets. To understand model performance, denormalization is done first and then both the misdetections and relatively better detections are visualized. The new regression model weights and architecture is then saved in a H5 file for later use during the deployment stage (Fig. 4).

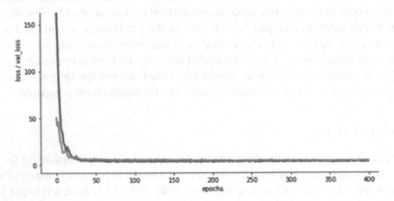

Fig. 4. Plot of loss/validation loss for localization

5.9 Deployment

From the analysis of different models done, the overall best performing model is chosen for model deployment. The VGG model, which gave the best performance overall, is saved along with its weights and architecture to an H5 file. Using the Flask microframework, this model is imported for use. Using the GUI, the user can then upload their own image file. Feature extraction is done on this image, and is fed to the imported VGG model. A predefined list with each index corresponding to a different disease in order of prediction is maintained. The VGG model then predicts the disease label in the form of a list of probable values, each value corresponding to the probability of a disease. The highest value from this list is chosen, and the corresponding disease of that value index is shown as output on the GUI.

6   Results and Discussion

6.1   Classification: Models Analysis and Evaluation

EDA of the whole dataset was done to figure out the intricate aspects of the final dataset. The dataset was then pre-processed with feature engineering to add some new columns and simplify the data, and prepped for model training. After feature engineering and extraction, the data was then fed into different neural networks and split into train and test batches of appropriate size.

The models used for this purpose were: VGG16, Resnet, Xception, and MobileNet. Table 1 below shows all the models performance in doing classification.

Table 1. Model accuracies of different models

Model	Train Accuracy (%)	Test Accuracy (%)
VGG16	98.96	93.75
Xception	94.79	93.75
MobileNet	98.44	91.67
ResNet50	97.92	91.67

From the above table it can be observed that all the selected models perform a remarkable job in classifying rice crop diseases. However, VGG16 and Xception have the best test accuracies, with VGG16 taking the edge in train accuracy. From this, the conclusion can be drawn that the VGG16 model seems to be the best performing model for the current working dataset.

To get a better overall understanding of the VGG16 model, the full confusion matrix was plotted, as shown in Table 2:

Table 2. Classification report of the VGG16 model

	precision	recall	f1-score	support
Bacterial leaf blight	0.94	0.94	0.94	16
Brown spot	0.82	0.90	0.86	10
Healthy leaf	1.00	1.00	1.00	11
Leaf smut	1.00	0.91	0.95	11
accuracy			0.94	48
macro avg	0.94	0.94	0.94	48
weighted avg	0.94	0.94	0.94	48

As seen in the confusion matrix in Table 2, the precision, recall and F1 scores of the whole model used, as well as these metrics for individual sub-datasets are shown. The column named "support" signifies the number of images of the particular disease label chosen for testing. Due to the predetermined 80–20 split on 240 images, it can be observed that a total of 48 images were used for testing the model.

6.2 Grad-CAM Visualization

After the model training, Grad-CAM visualization was done. This model was made to verify that the image classification models are looking at the right areas and symptoms while classifying the image. This was an important part of the analysis as it could be verified whether the models were using the right features and sections of images to classify them.

A heatmap of the classified image was made and superimposed on the image:

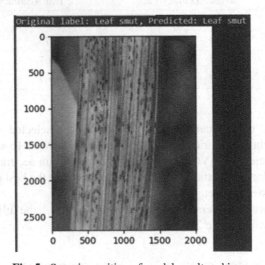

Fig. 5. Superimposition of model result and image

The yellow areas show where the classification model was "looking" when it made the classification. From Fig. 5, it can be seen that the yellow areas of the heatmap are over the smut-affected part of the leaf. This confirms that the model analyzed here (VGG16) is looking at the right areas of the different images for classification.

6.3 Bounding Box Regression

The bounding box coordinates used for localization of disease symptoms were fed into the best performing classification model (VGG16) and split into train and test batches to test out if the model can localize symptoms of the diseases in an unknown leaf (Fig. 6).

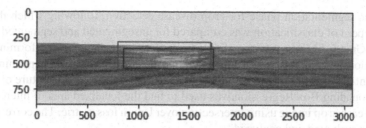

Fig. 6. Bounding box visualization in a sample image (Color figure online)

It is evident from the above image that our model is able to detect symptoms in plant crops satisfactorily. Here in the sampled bacterial leaf blight image, the 'blue box' represents groundtruth coordinates whereas the 'red box' depicts predicted coordinates. The degree of overlapping of the red and blue boxes signifies the closeness of the actual and predicted localized area of the disease. This is called IoU (Intersection over Union). After running our model for 400 epochs, an IoU score of 0.5 was achieved. While this is not entirely perfect, it appears sufficient for our application.

6.4 Medical Imaging as a Segmentation Technique

The use of DICOM for medical imaging as a segmentation process provided promising results. It achieved the same, if not, better accuracy in doing classification with localization. Using segmented images also gave a higher starting point in terms of model training. This was helpful as model training was relatively faster. Achieving higher accuracy in detecting plant diseases at smaller training times can be very effective in applications like ours where time is of utmost importance (Table 3).

Table 3. Comparison of time taken for DICOM segmented and unsegmented rice crop images

Models used	Training time for unsegmented image (in seconds)	Training time for segmented image (in seconds)
Xception	71	44
MobileNet	20	13

7 Conclusion and Future Work

The following section summarizes the various steps taken in implementing the project.

A complete working dataset was developed to perform model training. Different neural network architectures were used for identification, classification with localization like Resnet50, MobileNet, VGG16, and Xception networks. These different neural network models were then evaluated and analyzed. For novelty, medical imaging was used in the segmentation phase for crop disease detection, following which the accuracy and speed of classification was compared for unsegmented and segmented images. Then, the Grad-CAM was used to validate the performance of the best performing neural network model. Using this, it was confirmed that the classification was happening due to the relevant features in images, and not some other common external feature of images. Further, bounding Box Regression was used to find the localized area of interest of the disease in each crop image using Intersection over Union loss metric. The corresponding model was evaluated and analyzed.

Further work can involve including better coordinate features while labeling the localized areas of interest of a diseased leaf. This will help in optimization of the model. Some leaves have more than one area of interest, and instead of taking all diseased areas as one connected area, each area can be marked separately, and then use multiple bounding box regression for better accuracy.

Another future experimentation could involve adopting 'region proposals' strategy for finding areas of interest in crop disease detection like R-CNN, Fast-RCNN, Faster-RCNN etc. Also, mask R-CNN can be used which tries to detect and segment the locations and shapes of the infected areas. The improvement made by the Mask R-CNN is that the ROI Pooling layer is optimized into the ROI Align layer and a Mask branch is added while the final classification and positioning are carried out so that shapes of lesion spots can be accurately segmented on the leaf. The Mask R-CNN adds a third output through the Mask branch, i.e. The Mask R-CNN produces an output for each ROI.

References

1. Oerke, E.-C.: Crop losses to pests. J. Agric. Sci. **144**(1), 31–43 (2006)
2. Barbedo, J.G.A.: Factors influencing the use of deep learning for plant disease recognition. Biosyst. Eng. **172**, 84–91 (2018)
3. Singh, V., Misra, A.K.: Detection of plant leaf diseases using image segmentation and soft computing techniques. Inform. Process. Agric. **4**(1), 41–49, Elsevier, ISSN 2214–3173 (2017)
4. Kulkarni, A.H., Ashwin Patil, R.K.: Applying image processing techniques to detect plant diseases. Int. J. Mod. Eng. Res. **2**(5), 3661–3664 (2012)
5. Akila, M., Deepan, P.: Detection and classification of plant leaf diseases by using deep learning algorithm. Int. J. Eng. Res. Technol. ICONNECT. **6**(7) (2018)
6. Bashir, S., Sharma, N.: Remote area plant disease detection using image processing. IOSR J. Electron. Commun. Eng. **2**(6), 31–34. ISSN: 2278–2834 (2012)
7. Ren, S., He, K., Girshick, R., Sun, J. Faster R-CNN: towards real-time object detection with region proposal networks. IEEE Trans. Pattern Anal. Mach. Intell. **39**, 1137–1149 (2016)
8. Lowe, A., Harrison, N., French, A.P.: Hyperspectral image analysis techniques for the detection and classification of the early onset of plant disease and stress. Plant Methods. **13**, 80 (2017)
9. Ampatzidis, Y., De Bellis, L., Luvisi, A.: iPathology: robotic applications and management of plants and plant diseases. Sustainability. **9**(6), 1010 (2017)
10. Kumar, A.: Design of secure image fusion technique using cloud for privacy-preserving and copyright protection. Int. J. Cloud Appl. Comput. **9**(3), 22–36 (2019)
11. Kumar, A., Zhang, Z.J., Lyu, H.: Object detection in real time based on improved single shot multi-box detector algorithm. EURASIP J. Wirel. Commun. Netw. **2020**(1), 1–18 (2020). https://doi.org/10.1186/s13638-020-01826-x

12. Kumar, A.: A review on implementation of digital image watermarking techniques using LSB and DWT. In: The Third International Conference on Information and Communication Technology for Sustainable Development (ICT4SD 2018), held during August 30–31, 2018 at Hotel Vivanta by Taj, Goa, India (2018)

13. Romero Luna, M.P., Mueller, D., Mengistu, A., Singh, A.K., Hartman, G.L., Wise, K.A.: Advancing our understanding of charcoal rot in soybeans. J. Integr. Pest. Manag. **8**, 8 (2017)

14. Raza, M., Sharif, M., Yasmin, M., Khan, M.A., Saba, T., Fernandes, S.L.: Appearance based pedestrians' gender recognition by employing stacked auto encoders in deep learning. Future Gener. Comput. Syst. **88**, 28–39 (2018)

15. Nagasubramanian, K., Jones, S., Singh, A.K.: Plant disease identification using explainable 3D deep learning on hyperspectral images. Plant Methods. **15**, 98 (2019)

16. Coulibaly, S., Kamsu-Foguem, B., Kamissoko, D., Traore, D.: Deep neural networks with transfer learning in millet crop images. Comput. Ind. **108**, 115–120 (2019)

17. Yan, G., Zhang, J., Chengxin, Y., Hu, X., Zou, Y., Xue, Z., Wang, W: Plant disease identification based on deep learning algorithms in smart farming. Discrete Dyn. Nat. Soc. **2020**, 1–11 (2020)

Challenges in Crop Selection Using Machine Learning

D. Lakshmi Padmaja[1]($\boxtimes$), Surya Deepak G[1], G. K. Sriharsha[2], and Rohith Kumar K[3]

[1] Anurag University, Hyderabad, India
lakshmipadmajait@cvsr.ac.in
[2] Arizona State University, Tempe, AZ, USA
[3] KLU, Vijayawada, India

Abstract. Farming is one of the major sectors that influences a country's economic growth. In a country like India, the majority of the population is dependent on agriculture for their livelihood. Many new technologies, such as Machine Learning and Deep Learning, are being implemented into agriculture as it is easier for farmers to grow and maximize their yield. To increase productivity and quality, the farmers must know about the type of nutrients in the soil that is held. Farmers may not be having the utmost knowledge about all the nutrients which are available in the soil that play a vital role in the growth of the crop. An expert advisor is needed to reach every farmer which is very difficult. This paper aims to identify the right crop and also the necessary nutrients that are present in the soil and the nutrients that are required by the crop with the help of Machine learning techniques such as Support Vector Machines and Decision Trees for performing multiclass classification of different classes of crops.

Keywords: Feature Engineering · Hyperparameter tuning · SVM · Machine Learning

1 Introduction

India is a fast-developing country where agriculture is the backbone for the country's development at the early stages. Due to industrialization and globalization, this sector is facing hurdles. Apart from these challenges, the awareness and the necessity for cultivation needs to be instilled in the minds of the younger generation. Nowadays, technology plays a vital role in all the fields except for agriculture as we are using some old methodologies in agriculture [3, 4]. Identifying the condition of the soil, its chemical composition, and the nutrients that are essential for the crop to grow in a particular region is of utmost need and priority of farmers, a solution is proposed using Machine Learning to help the farmers and agricultural officers to know which crop is suitable to grow, and what are all the necessary adjustments which are to be made in the fertilizers so that the farmers can increase the productivity of the crops. We will be using different machine learning techniques like Hyper-parameter tuning, Support Vectors and Decision trees to decide the crop for best yield. In this paper, Sect. 1 describes Introduction, Sect. 2 Literature Survey or existing methods Sect. 3 Proposed Method and Experimental Results and in last Sect. 5 Conclusion.

A. Kumar et al. (Eds.): ICAIDS 2021, CCIS 1673, pp. 66–76, 2022.
https://doi.org/10.1007/978-3-031-21385-4_6

2 Literature Survey

The main reason we have chosen this idea of giving valuable insights about the soil is to support Crop Production in India, this paper illustrates how different parameters like the humidity, temperature, the amount of Nitrogen, phosphorus, Potassium can help the farmer or the officer to predict which kind of crop [1, 2] will be suitable and in what amount must the nutrients be present in the soil to give the maximum productivity. Minmax Scaling is used for scaling the data, so that all the features are present in the scale, and SVC classifier is used to classify the type of crop, which is most suitable as per the requirements which have been specified by the farmer [8, 9].

A survey is performed for crop yield prediction and identified which can be solved with the help of data mining techniques (Beulah, 2019) [15]. Recently, deep learning, which is a sub-branch of machine learning, has provided state-of-the-art results in many different domains, such as face recognition and image classification [16]. Another suggested improvement is that more data sources should be integrated. Finally, the publication indicated that the use of machine learning in farm management systems should be explored [5, 6, 16, 17]. If the models work as requested, software applications must be created that allow the farmer to make decisions based on the models. In the Wang et al. (2020) paper combined CNN and LSTM (CNN-LSTM) networks for the wheat yield prediction problem [17, 18]. The most applied deep learning algorithm is Convolutional Neural Networks (CNN), and the other widely used algorithms are Long-Short Term Memory (LSTM) and Deep Neural Networks (DNN) algorithms [19, 20].

3 Proposed Method

3.1 Data Collection

The Data required for this project is collected from the Kaggle repository, here we have 2 different kinds of data source files one is having details about all the fertilizers and the other is having the details about all the physical parameters or environmental factors like the temperature, humidity, pH value of the soil, etc., all of this raw data is collected and then preprocessed. Once the data is preprocessed and collected, the next step is feature Engineering. The flow of steps for the proposed approach is explained in Fig. 1 in detail.

3.2 Feature Engineering

After the collection of raw data and preprocessing it, we have to generate some statistical insights from the data, so here are few statistical plots which are required for analyzing the distribution of the data, as it plays a very vital role in finding the relationship and correlation among various in existing and raw features, here are few plots which display the statistical plots.

So from the above statistical plots made which are histograms, Quantile-Charts and Box-plots we can make observations that all the features are not present in one distribution, and according to the Quantile Charts we can observe that there are few features which are present under Gaussian Distribution and few are Distributed in some

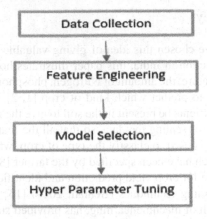

Data Collection

↓

Feature Engineering

↓

Model Selection

↓

Hyper Parameter Tuning

Fig. 1. Flow of proposed approach

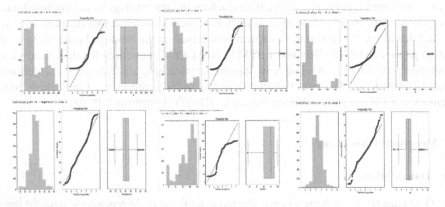

Fig. 2. Statistical plots for identifying outliers

other statistical Distribution, we have to transform all the features under one scale, and from the box-plots it is clearly visible that there are certain outliers, so outliers may play an important role and take a toll on the prediction accuracy of the data and we will be using the Interquartile Range for removal of outliers and making sure that the data is normally distributed (From Fig. 2).

After applying the Outlier Detection code and other transformations, there was a huge reduction in the total number of outliers, well outliers do play a very important role in case of linear model, so it becomes very important for removing the outliers as they may affect the performance of the model, here are the statistical models after removing of the outliers (From Fig. 3) [12–14].

After removal of outliers, we move on to the next step that is scaling all the features into a Gaussian Distribution (From Fig. 4), so we have two such features which are not perfectly skewed, so we can apply many transformations such as Log Transformation, Box-Cox Transformation, Square-Root transformation, here in this scenario, box-cox

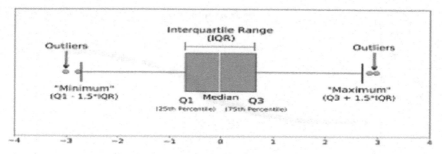

Fig. 3. Graph representation for outlier detection

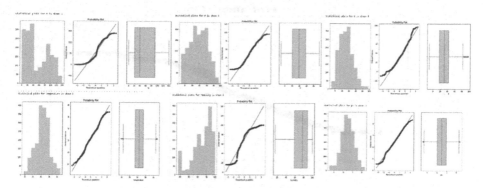

Fig. 4. Gaussian distribution of features after outlier removal

transformation worked the best (From Eq. (1)).

$$y_i^{(\lambda)} = \begin{cases} \frac{y_i^{\lambda}-1}{\lambda} & \text{if } \lambda \neq 0 \\ ln(y_i) & \text{if } \lambda = 0 \end{cases} \tag{1}$$

Here are the results after applying the box-cox transformation on the 2 features which were not skewed, after applying Box-Cox Transformation, we can observe that they become skewed and follow Gaussian Distribution (From Fig. 5).

After applying all kinds of transformations, the transformed data is visible as shown in Fig. 6.

We can clearly see after applying transformations we have made separate classes. Just by focusing on the last scatter image, we can clearly separate 3–4 classes with a decision boundary, by this we can think of a linear model which can separate them easily (From Fig. 6).

3.3 Model Selection

We have tried out many Machine Learning Algorithms like the Decision Tree, Random Forest Algorithm, Support Vector Classifier and many more, here is an outlook of how wide the Decision Tree was made in making the classifications (From Fig. 7).

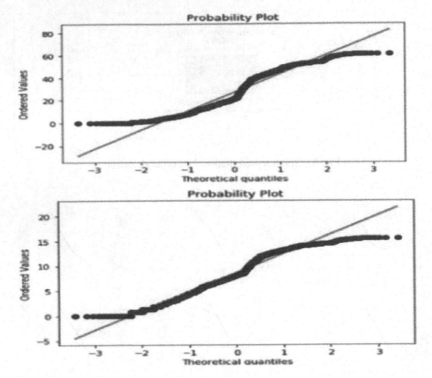

Fig. 5. Transformation of features

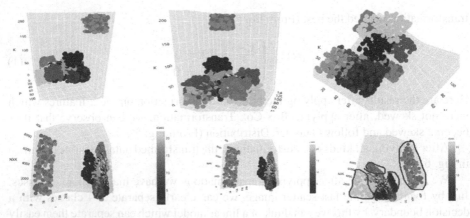

Fig. 6. Separation of classes after all transformations

We can observe how deep this tree is and this may sometimes lead to overfitting, we then switched to using the Support Vector Classifier using the kernel as poly, we first tried with only 3 features and this showed an amazing result, so we selected our model

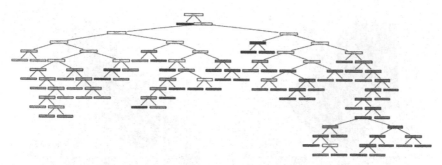

Fig. 7. Classification using decision tree (model)

as the Support Vector Classifier, here is a glimpse of how Support Vector Classifier separates classes (From Fig. 8) [7–11].

Fig. 8. Classification using Support Vector Classifier

Here are few more scatter charts wherein we have considered 3 labels from our dataset in order to visualize how Support Vector Classifier actually makes a praemunired to visualize all the 21 features in one plot is not possible, so that's the reason why we have selected 3–4 features and made a visualization as shown (From Fig. 9).

3.4 Hyperparameter Tuning

Now after selecting the model now, it's the time to optimize the parameters such that the model can make good predictions, and that is the main end goal, the model must not undergo overfittings as well as underfitting the model must perform well in all cases, for Tuning the hyperparameters We have used Randomized Search, it is the dictionary/collection of various models and their hyperparameters which have been used.

Once we have run the Randomized Search Cross Validation on the model, we recorded the performance of each model using the metric of "Accuracy", while training we have considered Accuracy, as this was not an unbalanced dataset, we did not focus

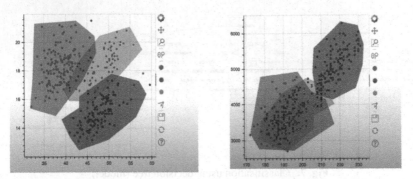

Fig. 9. Visualization graph after classification

much on other metrics, we focused on Accuracy and after finalizing the model, we tried to improve on the model's different metrics, here is the data frame of performances of different algorithms (Fig. 10) (From Table 1).

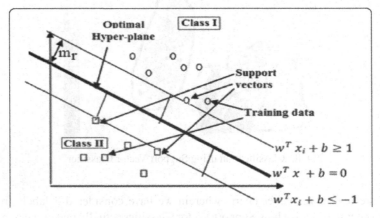

Fig. 10. Visualization of SVM classifier

3.5 Support Vector Machines (SVM)

SVM is a statistical learning-based solver. Statistical is a mathematics of uncertainty as it aims at gaining knowledge, making decisions from a set of data [8]. In the above figure a simple classification problem is given in two-dimensional input space. The two types of patterns indicate the presence of two different classes. We can draw a line separating the two classes and many such possibilities may exist. The second Hyperplane is the optimal line of separation because there is less error in prediction than the other two lines (OH). A line becomes a plane if we have three attributes' variables instead of two, and becomes a hyperplane if there are more than three attributes. Another name of OH is maximal margin hyperplane.

After hyperparameter tuning we observe that SVM did a very good job as compared to other models, and this would be true, as we have already seen visualizations of how SVC performed separations.

We can see that Decision Tree would overfit and would not present good result and that what is shown after the Tuning of Hyperparameters, so after the hyperparameter tuning phase we are good to go with SVC, as that produced very good results, lets visualize the predictions and confusion matrix score for SVC (Fig. 11).

After generating the classification report, we tested the model on a new set of data and the SVC model predicted it correctly as explained in Table 2, here is a glimpse of the random generated data [9].

After entering the values in the form and then predicting, the SVC suggested that the best crop to be grown is rice, and also it had given some suggestions based on the fertilizers which must be used [3, 4].

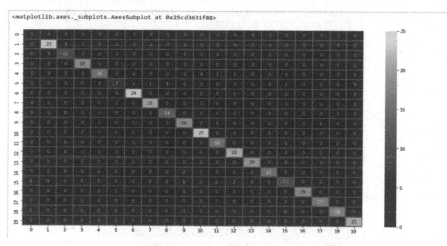

Fig. 11. Confusion matrix between predicted class and observed class

4   Experimental Results

We have used four different classifiers namely Random Forest, Logistic Regressor, Decision Tree and Support Vector Machine. As we can see in below Table 1 Support Vector Machine does a good job of separating the classes into different section with the use of different Optimal Hyperplanes. Score in the below table refers to the accuracy of the model.

The below Table 2 contains the confusion matrix for crop selection. It contains Precision, Recall and f1- Score for each class i.e., for each crop present in the dataset. There are two twenty two different crop used in the data set.

Table 1. Performance estimation using different classifiers

Sl No	Model Name	Estimator	Score
1	Random Forest	0.03	0.897321
2	Logistic	0.75	0.895875
3	Decision Tree	0.035	0.586482
4	Support Vector Machine	0.5	0.956793

Table 2. Precision, Recall and f1-score from the model

Sl No.	Precision	Recall	f1-Score	Support
1	0.33	0.33	0.33	3
2	1.00	0.92	0.96	25
3	1.00	1.00	1.00	11
4	1.00	1.00	1.00	19
5	1.00	0.94	0.97	17
6	1.00	0.78	0.88	9
7	1.00	1.00	1.00	24
8	0.88	1.00	0.93	21
9	0.93	1.00	0.97	14
10	0.86	1.00	0.93	19
11	1.00	1.00	1.00	25
12	0.94	1.00	1.00	16
13	0.92	1.00	0.97	22
14	1.00	1.00	0.96	22
15	1.00	1.00	1.00	20
16	1.00	1.00	1.00	20
17	1.00	0.89	0.94	18
18	1.00	0.73	0.85	15
19	1.00	1.00	1.00	19
20	1.00	1.00	1.00	17
21	0.90	0.95	0.92	19
22	1.00	1.00	1.00	21
Accuracy	-	-	0.96	354
Macro avg	0.94	0.93	0.93	354
Weighted avg	0.96	0.96	0.96	354

5 Conclusion

The proposed Machine Learning Model gives us predictions on which crop must be grown, what kind of fertilizers must be used and what must be most suitable ratio of combining different chemicals in order to obtain maximum productivity of that crop, there were 3 major steps which were done, Feature Engineering, Model Selection and Hyperparameter Tuning, Selecting the appropriate distribution for the dataset and making accurate classifications at the end. Based on results the best predicted crop is rice. We can extend this approach by using many more Feature Engineering techniques, many optimization techniques, by using various Machine Learning Algorithms. By using this concept, the user can know which crop is most suitable for growing/cultivating based on the given climatic conditions and also what all changes must be made in the chemical composition of the fertilizer so that the production of crop is more. Further this idea can be extended with the use of several Machine Learning techniques like Boosting and Bagging to increase the performance of the model. The general challenge of Intercorrelation of features can also be overcome by using different transformation like PCA and LDA.

References

1. Edwin, T.: Onion, tomato price spike: season not the only reason (November 13 2017). [Online]
2. Pudumalar, S., Ramanujam, E., Rajashree, R.H., Kavya, C., Kiruthika, T., Nisha, J.: Crop recommendation system for precision agriculture. In: 2016 Eighth International Conference on Advanced Computing (ICoAC), Chennai, pp. 32–36 (2017). https://doi.org/10.1109/ICoAC.2017.7951740
3. Kumar, R., Singh, M.P., Kumar, P., Singh, J.P.: Crop selection method to maximize crop yield rate using machine learning technique. In: 2015 International Conference on Smart Technologies and Management for Computing, Communication, Controls, Energy and Materials (ICSTM), Chennai, pp. 138–145 (2015). https://doi.org/10.1109/ICSTM.2015.7225403
4. Lekhaa, T.R.: Efficient crop yield and pesticide prediction for improving agricultural economy using data mining techniques. Int. J. Mod. Trends Eng. Sci. 3(10) (2016)
5. Viviliya, B., Vaidhehi, V.: The design of hybrid crop recommendation system using machine learning algorithms. Int. J. Innov. Technol. Explor. Eng. 9(2), 4305–4311 (2019)
6. Doshi, Z., Nadkarni, S., Agrawal, R., Shah, N.: Agro consultant: intelligent crop recommendation system using machine learning algorithms. In: 2018 Fourth International Conference on Computing Communication Control and Automation (ICCUBEA), Pune, India, pp. 1–6 (2018). https://doi.org/10.1109/ICCUBEA.2018.8697349
7. Padmaja, D.L., Vishnuvardhan, B.: Comparative study of feature subset selection methods for dimensionality reduction on scientific data. In: 2016 IEEE 6th International Conference on Advanced Computing (IACC), pp. 31–34 (2016)
8. Lakshmi Padmaja, D., Vishnuvardhan, B.: Classification performance improvement using random subset feature selection algorithm for data mining. Elsevier-Big Data Res. 12, 1–12 (2018). https://doi.org/10.1016/j.bdr.2018.02.007
9. Padmaja, D.L., Sriharsha, G.K., Nagalakshmi, N., Latha, T.A.: Analyzing the model performance using machine learning algorithms for plant disease detection. Solid State Technol. 63(5), 9015–9023 (2020)

10. Dhyaram, L.P., et al.: Ensemble methods for scientific data-a comparative study. In: Shamim Kaiser, M., Xie, J., Rathore, V.S. (eds.) Information and Communication Technology for Competitive Strategies (ICTCS 2020): Intelligent Strategies for ICT, pp. 587–595. Singapore, Springer Nature Singapore (July 2021). https://doi.org/10.1007/978-981-16-0882-7_51
11. Rakesh Kumar, Singh, M.P., et al.: Crop prediction using machine learning. Int. J. Future Gen. Commun. Net. 13(3), 1896–1901 (2020)
12. Padmaja, D.L., Vishnuvardhan, B.: Variance-based feature selection for enhanced classification performance. In: Information Systems Design and Intelligent Applications, vol. 862, pp. 543–550 (31 December 2018). https://doi.org/10.1007/978-981-13-3329-3_51
13. Lakshmi Padmaja, D., Vishnuvardhan, B.: Evaluating the influence of parameter values on the performance of random subset feature selection algorithm on scientific data. Elsevier-DKE. 117, 174–182 (2018). https://doi.org/10.1016/j.datak.2018.07.008
14. Lakshmi Padmaja, D., Vishnuvardhan, B.: Comparative study of feature subset selection methods for dimensionality reduction on scientific data. In: IEEE Conference 27–28 February 2016. IACC (2016). https://doi.org/10.1109/IACC.2016.16
15. Beulah, R.: A survey on different data mining techniques for crop yield prediction. Int. J. Compute. Sci. Eng. 7(1), 738–744 (2019). https://doi.org/10.26438/ijcse/v7i1.738744
16. Brownlee, J.: Deep learning for computer vision: image classification, object detection, and face recognition in python. In: Machine Learning Mastery (2019)
17. Maimaitijiang, M., Sagan, V., Sidike, P., Hartling, S., Esposito, F., Fritschi, F.B.: Soybean yield prediction from UAV using multimodal data fusion and deep learning. Remote Sens. Environ. 237, 111599 (2020)
18. Tedesco-Oliveira, D., da Silva, R.P., Maldonado Jr, W., Zerbato, C.: Convolutional neural networks in predicting cotton yield from images of commercial fields. Comput. Electron. Agric. 171, 105307 (2020)
19. Bhojani, S.H., Bhatt, N.: Wheat crop yield prediction using new activation functions in neural network. Neural Comput. Appl. 32(17), 13941–13951 (2020). https://doi.org/10.1007/s00521-020-04797-8
20. Wang, X., Huang, J., Feng, Q., Yin, D.: Winter wheat yield prediction at county, level and uncertainty analysis in main wheat-producing regions of china with deep learning approaches. Remote Sens. 12(11), 1744 (2020)

Handcrafted Features for Human Gait Recognition: CASIA-A Dataset

Veenu Rani[1], Munish Kumar[1]($\boxtimes$), and Bhupinder Singh[2]

[1] Department of Computational Sciences, Maharaja Ranjit Singh Punjab Technical University, Bathinda, Punjab, India
munishcse@gmail.com
[2] IT Enabled Services, Maharaja Ranjit Singh Punjab Technical University, Bathinda, Punjab, India

Abstract. Human Gait Recognition has become a burning research area because of its promising application in security enhancement. There are numerous state-of-the-art feature detectors and classifiers available for gait recognition. In this article, three popular feature descriptor algorithms that are Scale Invariant Feature Transform (SIFT), Speeded Up Robust Feature (SURF) and Shi-Tomasi edge corner detector are used for extracting the unique features of the gait images. At first, the experiment is done by using a single feature descriptor then a combination of these three is applied. Various classifiers like Decision Tree, Random Forest, MLP are used to make the class membership based on features. Maximum accuracy of 76.12%, by applying the Decision Tree classifier, 80.11% by Random Forest, and 74.25% by applying MLP has been achieved for the CASIA-A dataset. In this article authors have computed recognition rate, false-positive rate (FPR) and root mean squared error (RMSE) in all cases to compare the performance of features and classifiers considered in this article. The experimental results depict that a combination of these three feature descriptors is performing better than other existing state-of-the art-work.

Keywords: MLP · LPP · SIFT · SURF · Shi-Tomasi

1 Introduction

Identification of individuals by his/her physical behaviors has become an area of great interest for researchers owing to continuously increasing the number of criminal activities. There are a lot of biometric traits to identify the individual based on physiological (iris, face, finger, etc.) and behavioral (voice, signature, gait, etc.) traits as shown in Fig. 1. From the last two decades, gait recognition has become a promising area in the biometric field because it offers the highest level of security without involving human cooperation. As there are many other human identification methods available but most of the methods are based on the subject involvement. Gait recognition is getting popular day by day because each human being has a unique walking style and is used in the forensic and healthcare informatics domain. If there is any disorder in the human body

A. Kumar et al. (Eds.): ICAIDS 2021, CCIS 1673, pp. 77–88, 2022.
https://doi.org/10.1007/978-3-031-21385-4_7

then that can also be recognized using his/her gait because any abnormality in any organ of the human body affects the gait of individuals [1]. Using the gait of a person, not only the identity of a human can be revealed but other factors like age, sex, emotions can also be identified [2]. Automatic gait recognition is becoming popular because it can work on low-resolution images [3]. As there are many advantages that gait recognition provides, it also has some weak points like speed variation, carrying condition, multi-view angles, etc. that reduce the performance of gait signature formation.

In general two approaches are used for gait recognition: The model-based approach and the Model-free approach. In a model-based approach, the whole human body structure is used to extract silhouettes from videos. The model-based approach works on high-resolution videos. On the other hand, a model-free or appearance-based approach uses the whole motion pattern of the human body and can work on low-resolution videos. Model-based approaches use a combination of static and dynamic human body information. Gait recognition system consists of various phases namely, data acquisition, feature extraction, classification, and recognition. The accuracy of gait recognition systems depends upon data acquisition methods. In the data acquisition phase, gait data is collected by various devices like cameras, sensors, accelerometers and wave radar. After data acquisition, a database of gait patterns with labels is created, which is pre-processed by removing background noise, and a silhouette is extracted. Then feature selectors and classifiers are used to obtain an efficient gait recognition system. Three feature descriptors SIFT, SURF and Shi-Tomasi are considered to extract the unique properties for gait recognition. SIFT is a robust descriptor used to extract the dynamic behavior of gait patterns. While SURF is a local feature descriptor used for image registration and 3D reconstruction and Shi-Tomasi is a corner detection algorithm. After applying feature descriptors, three classifiers namely Decision Tree, Random Forest and MLP have been used to make the class membership based on the extracted features. The remainder of the article is organized as follows: Sect. 2 depicts the related work done in this field. In Sect. 3 methodology of the proposed work and a brief description of features descriptors and classifiers have been discussed. In Sect. 4 obtained experimental results have been shown. Section 5 summarize this article by discussing the conclusion and future discussion.

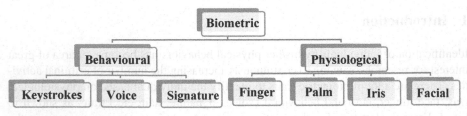

Fig. 1. Types of Biometrics

2 Related Work

A lot of work has been done by researchers in this research area for example Yazdi *et al.*[4] have proposed a leg gesture separation algorithm to identify human gait. This algorithm works in five stages, in the first stage background noise is removed, then the movement of the lower body is recorded which is invariant to many covariates like clothing, carrying, surface, etc. After that Energy Halation Image (EHI) dataset is created, then authors have applied Eigen Space dimensionality reducer to reduce the features, and in the last stage, Neuro-Fuzzy Combiner Classifier (NFCC) is applied to obtain a high precision rate. HumanID Challenge dataset (HGCD) is used for experimentation with 122 objects, which is the largest dataset for gait recognition. The authors have reported a 99.8% recognition rate in their method. Tafazzoli *et al.* [5] have proposed an improved human gait recognition system using feature selection. Authors have used Genetic Algorithms (GAs) to discard background noise and to select subsets of features. Authors have used the CASIA dataset for experimental work, their experimental result shows an 82.9% accuracy rate. Chaitanya and Sekhar [6] proposed a gait recognition model in which they have used residual convolution neural network (RCNN) for classification. Their proposed method works in three steps, data collection, pre-processing and matching phase. Data has been collected through tiny sensors embedded within smartphones. Authors have used three datasets CASIA-A, CASIA-B and OU-ISIR for experimental work. They have reported 99.9%, 97.9% and 98.15% accuracy rate respectively. Khan *et al.* [7] have used Motion Trajectory Analysis for gait recognition. In their proposed method, dense trajectories are constructed based on human motion, extracted from videos. Then these features are recycled to create a codebook using the GMM model, in the third step Fisher Vector encoding is used to encode local descriptors and in the last SVM is used to solve the classification problem. Two datasets are used in this method which is TUM GAID and CASIA-A (20 subjects). Their accuracy rate is high compared to others. Cheheb *et al.* [8] have used Gait Energy Images (GEI) and Autoencoders for feature extraction to identify human gait. In this article, the authors have first extracted binary silhouettes from videos then they have used autoencoders to extract features and the last classification is performed. They have used the CASIA B dataset for experiment work and achieved a 98.81% accuracy rate. Mohammed & Eesee [9] have used Neural Network Multi-Layer Perceptron in their approach to identifying gait patterns. In this article Gait Energy Image (GEI), human body width and height features are extracted for human gait identification. MLP is used for classification with 10 fold cross-validation. The author has reported 90% accuracy. Guo *et al.* [10] have used the Gabor filter to extract gait features from Gait Energy Image (GEI), which is the average silhouette of a gait cycle. Gabor filter is capable of extracting features from different directions and scales. After extracting features authors have used LDA to reduce the dimensions. Then they have applied an improved version of Extreme Learning Machine (ELM) and Particle Swarm Optimization (PSO) algorithms to classify the reduced feature. Authors have reported 98.24% and 98.66% accuracy rate on CASIA-A and CASIA- B datasets from multiple cross-view angles respectively. Nardo *et al.* [11] have proposed a deep learning approach for human gait recognition with a single knee electro goniometer. In their approach, they have collected data from 23 healthy subjects and implemented MLP and their experimental result shows that MLP provides suitable results for classification.

Si *et al.* [12] have presented remote identity verification using gait analysis. In this method authors have used Ground Reaction Force (GRF) signals for capturing data, then features are extracted and SVM classifier is applied on captured data, in the last Fuzzy Association Rule (FAR) for data analysis is applied. Correlation between low level features and high level features is captured by FAR. The authors have achieved 95.2% accuracy. Khan *et al.* [13] have presented an article on Human Gait Analysis for Osteoarthritis prediction. They have used deep learning methods for feature extraction, their proposed method works in various steps. In the first step, two pre-trained CNN models, named AlexNet and VGG 16 are used to extract features from the public gait dataset and in the second step, the most favorable features are selected using Euclidean and Geometric Mean maximization approach. In the last step, the Canonical Correlation Analyzer is used to aggregate robust features and the fitness function (FKNN) classifier is used for classification. Authors have used two different angles of the CASIA-B dataset for experimental work and reported 96% accuracy.

3 Methodology of the Proposed System

To achieve the highest accuracy rate in the proposed system the following methodology is planned. It consists of various phases like feature extraction, feature selection, and classification algorithms. CASIA-A dataset is considered for the experimental work. CASIA stands for Chinese Academy of Sciences, it is a standard gait dataset that contains 19139 images [14]. In this dataset images of 20 persons are captured. Each person has 12 images with 3 different directions (45°, 90° and parallel to view plane). For the proposed work SURF, SIFT, and Shi-Tomasi feature descriptors are used to extract features. LPP is used to reduce the size of a feature vector. Then three classifiers Decision Tree, Random Forest and MLP are applied to classify the dataset into various classes. True Positive Rate (TPR), False Positive Rate (FPR) and recognition accuracy parameters are calculated and compared in this proposed method. This study reveals that SIFT, SURF and Shi-Tomasi individually can't perform well. This proposed method aims to improve the accuracy rate of gait recognition by using hybrid techniques. The implementation of the proposed system is shown in Fig. 2.

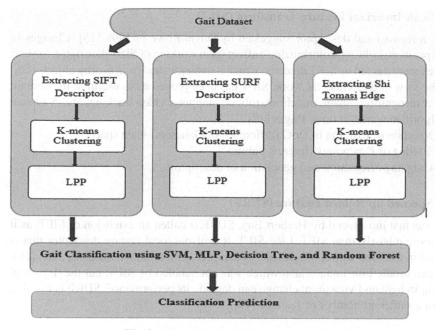

Fig. 2. Block diagram of the proposed system

Algorithm

Step 1: In this proposed method authors have used the CASIA-A dataset.

Step 2: Features descriptors are extracted using SURF, SIFT, and Shi-Tomasi from each gait sample

Step 3: After features descriptors from each image, K-means clustering is performed to make clusters.

Step 4: LPP is used as a dimensionality reduction algorithm to preserve the local structure of images.

Step 5: Result from these three features descriptors: SURF, SIFT, Shi-Tomasi are collected and stored into database storage.

Step 6: The proposed system is trained using a combination of SIFT, SURF, and Shi Tomasi.

Step 7: Query image is given as input and these three feature descriptors are used to obtain features from the queried image.

Step 8: In the last step Random Forest, Decision Tree, and MLP classifiers are used to find out the most similar image with the input image and returned to the user as result.

3.1 Feature Extraction Techniques

Feature extraction plays an important role in machine learning which extracts features from an image and makes it possible to differentiate between the image samples. The performance of gait recognition systems gets affected by feature extraction techniques. Three feature extraction algorithms SIFT, SURF, and Shi-Tomasi are used for the experiment work in this article.

3.1.1 Scale Invariant Feature Transform (SIFT)

SIFT is a robust local descriptor suggested by David Lowe in 1999 [15]. Changes in camera position, lighting, coloring don't affect upon working of SIFT descriptor. Several attributes are extracted by SIFT detector, which is distinguished from nearby objects [16]. From the view of experimental work, SIFT has been proved most useful in the domain of object recognition, image matching, robotic mapping, video tracking, etc. A typical SIFT algorithm works in three stages [17].

1. Detection of extrema in DoG (difference of Gaussian) scale space.
2. Filtering of Key points (Interest points).
3. Assigning orientation and generation of descriptors.

3.1.2 Speeded up Robust Feature (SURF)

SURF was first introduced by Herbert Bay. SURF is called an extension of SIFT, as it works more robustly than SIFT. Like SIFT, it is also a local feature descriptor that is also used in machine learning tasks like object recognition, image matching, etc. [18]. SURF can handle blur images also which was not handled by SIFT, but the impact of changing in light and viewpoint change can degrade its performance. SURF is not able to return a sufficient number of features [19].

3.1.3 Shi-Tomasi

In machine learning, corner detection has a great role to extract different kinds of features from an object. Shi-Tomasi is the most popular corner detection algorithm, developed by Jianbo Shi in 1994 [20]. Shi-Tomasi algorithm works similar to Harris corner detector. The major difference between both is the Selection criteria. Shi-Tomasi is an improvement over the Harris corner detector, it works successfully where Harris corner fails. Image noise and rotation do not affect the working of the Harris Corner Detector. Shi-Tomasi also works similarly but it calculates corner points differently. In this algorithm, some threshold value is defined, if the value of R exceeds that value then selected points are regarded as corner points. In Harris corner algorithms each pixel is calculated but Shi-Tomasi avoids this. Shi-Tomasi also works on two eigenvalues but its working criteria are different from the Harris corner detection algorithm. Results of the Shi-Tomasi algorithm are more stable than the Harris corner algorithm [21].

3.2 K-means Clustering Algorithm

K-means clustering algorithm is used for segmentation developed by Hartigan in 1975, it is simple and has low computational complexity and a Lazy learning algorithm. K-means simply groups similar data points and discover underlying patterns [22]. A cluster is a collection of data points aggregated together because of certain similarities. It is applied in those areas where one data belongs to only one class or cluster.

3.3 Locality Preserving Projection (LPP)

LPP was first introduced by Leonid Kantorovich in the mid-19th century in the field of manufacturing. In machine learning, two methods are mostly used for dimensionality reduction, PCA and LPP. LPP is mostly used to reduce dimensionality and to preserve the structure of data for neighborhood graphs [23]. LPP is an unsupervised linear reduction method that is used to preserve the local structure of any image and provides more accuracy than a global structure preserver (PCA) [24]. LPP transforms the high dimensional space into a low dimensional space by using a matrix in the place of nonlinear mapping [25]. LPP performs its work in three steps [15] shown in Fig. 3.

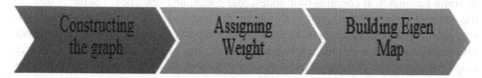

Fig. 3. LPP's Working Steps

3.4 Classifiers

Classification helps in deciding on how many objects of a class belong to another class. The Gait dataset is divided into different classes based on extracted features, these classes are assigned with a label. In this article, MLP, Random Forest, Decision Tree classifiers are used for the experiment.

3.4.1 Multi-layer Perceptron (MLP)

MLP is a feed-forward neural network that has three layers, an input layer, an output layer, and a hidden layer. Layers are fully connected to the next one. Each layer has been assigned some weight, which is forwarded to the next layer while performing calculations. A threshold value is required for the activation of inputs. MLP can discriminate non-linear separable data which was not covered by standard linear perceptron [26]. Jalmi [27] has used MLP for testing and training datasets for human gait recognition and achieved 80% accuracy.

3.4.2 Random Forest

More than one decision tree is collaborated to achieve more accuracy in Random Forest [28]. It is a multi-class classifier that is used when an object is fragmented into subparts. As a random forest is a collection of decision trees that is delicate to train a dataset, minor changes in the dataset can alter the structure of the decision tree, because this random forest uses a bag of words. Random Forest works in two steps.

- In the first step, the dataset is trained by inserting randomness into decision trees and then the result of each decision tree is combined to make a single classifier.
- In the second step, a test pattern is performed at each level until a leaf node is encountered.

Random Forest reduces correlation among decision trees. Gupta *et al.* [29] used a random forest classifier in their method to identify gait patterns and achieved 80.54% accuracy, which is higher than other classifiers.

3.4.3 Decision Tree

A Decision tree is a supervised learning method in which data is classified according to some parameter. It contains root nodes, leaf nodes, and branches. Testing is done at the internal node and the result is shown on the leaf node. Problems are divided into sub-problems and sub-problems are further into sub-parts. Nodes are divided into further levels until no result is obtained. When data doesn't offer benefit while splitting it directly stops the execution. Decision Tree is similar to human decision making so it is easy to understand.

4   Experimental Results

In this section, experimental results have been discussed which have been obtained by using the above-discussed parameters. We have used the CASIA-A data set for experiment work which consists of 19139 images with three different angles. We implemented our proposed method by taking 70% images as training data and 30% as testing data. In this article, an 80.11% accuracy rate has been reported by using a combination of SURF, SIFT, and Shi-Tomasi feature descriptors, which provides better performance than other existing methods. Accuracy rate and other measuring factors are shown in tabular as well as graphical form. As Table 1 shows the recognition accuracy rate of 74.25% by using a combination of SIFT, SURF, Shi-Tomasi, and MLP classifiers. In a similar way Tables 2 and 3 depicts the results of the Random Forest classifier and Decision Tree classifier, respectively.

Table 1. Recognition Results using MLP

Evaluation Parameter	Feature Extraction Techniques			
	SIFT	SURF	Shi-Tomasi	SIFT + SURF + Shi-Tomasi
Accuracy	55.20%	62.07%	63.15%	74.25%
FPR (False Positive Rate)	0.14%	0.13%	0.06%	0.08%
RMSE (Root Mean Squared Error)	16.72%	11.56%	9.12%	5.24%

Table 2. Recognition Results using Random Forest Classifier

Evaluation Parameter	Feature Extraction Techniques			
	SIFT	SURF	Shi-Tomasi	SIFT + SURF + Shi-Tomasi
Accuracy	58.13%	57.93%	59.83%	80.11%
FPR (False Positive Rate)	0.20%	0.22%	0.26%	0.11%
RMSE (Root Mean Squared Error)	17.16%	20.26%	20.02%	7.92%

Table 3. Recognition Results using Decision Tree Classifier

Evaluation Parameter	Feature Extraction Techniques			
	SIFT	SURF	Shi-Tomasi	SIFT + SURF + Shi-Tomasi
Accuracy	55.84%	75.79%	68.36%	76.12%
FPR (False Positive Rate)	0.29%	0.22%	0.16%	0.03%
RMSE (Root Mean Squared Error)	23.18%	16.09%	14.06%	7.69%

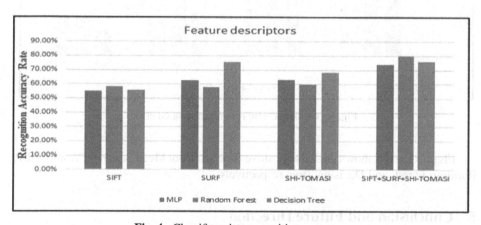

Fig. 4. Classifier wise recognition accuracy

Figure 4 shows the recognition accuracy rate of MLP, Random forest, show, and Decision tree classifiers. It is clear from the graph that a Random forest classifier with the combination of SIFT, SURF, and Shi-Tomasi can achieve more accuracy rate than the other two classifiers.

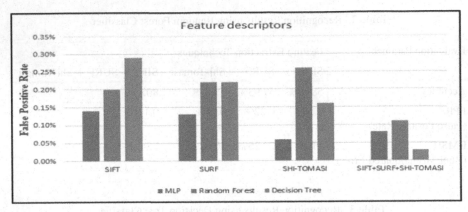

Fig. 5. Classifier wise False Positive Rate

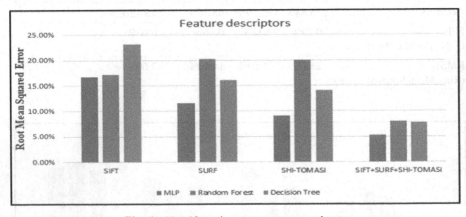

Fig. 6. Classifier wise root mean squared error

Figures 5 and 6 shows the False Positive Rate and Root Mean Squared Error of MLP, Random Forest, and Decision Tree, respectively.

5 Conclusion and Future Direction

Recognition of individuals based on gait pattern is a very challenging task for computer vision application due to changes in image capturing angles, different affecting covariates, footwear, etc. Gait recognition is mostly used to identify an individual without his/her knowing. In this article, three feature descriptors and detectors are used that make gait recognition easier. For experimental work, CASIA-A standard dataset has been used, which is widely used for gait recognition purposes. Authors first extract features using SIFT, SURF, and Shi-Tomasi, then three classifiers Random Forest, Decision Tree, and MLP are used for classification. To make clusters K-means clustering has been applied. LPP has been used to reduce dimensionality. The authors have achieved 80.11% accuracy by using combinations of the above-discussed descriptors and classifiers. Which shows improvement over other existing state-of-art-work. The future aim of our study is to perform this methodology on our own created dataset to achieve higher accuracy. The method proposed in this article can be useful to recognize individuals in a crowded area, in the forensic domain, etc.

References

1. Jun, K., LeeD, W., Lee, K., Lee, S., Kim, M.S.: Feature extraction using an RNN autoencoder for skeleton-based abnormal gait recognition. IEEE Access **8**, 19196–19207 (2020). https://doi.org/10.1109/ACCESS.2020.2967845
2. K, S., Wahid, F.F., G, R.: Statistical features from frame aggregation and differences for human gait recognition. Multimedia Tools and Applications **80**(12), 18345–18364 (2021). https://doi.org/10.1007/s11042-021-10655-z
3. Singh, J.P., Jain, S., Arora, S., Singh, U.P.: Vision-Based Gait Recognition: A Survey. IEEE Access **6**, 70497–70527 (2018). https://doi.org/10.1109/access.2018.2879896
4. Yazdi, H.S., Fariman, H.J., Roohi, J.: Gait recognition based on invariant leg classification using a neuro-fuzzy algorithm as the fusion method. ISRN Artificial Intelligence, 289721 (2012). https://doi.org/10.5402/2012/289721
5. Tafazzoli, F., Bebis, G., Louis, S., Hussain, M.: Improving Human Gait Recognition Using Feature Selection. In: Bebis, G., et al. (eds.) ISVC 2014. LNCS, vol. 8888, pp. 830–840. Springer, Cham (2014). https://doi.org/10.1007/978-3-319-14364-4_80
6. Chaitanya, G. K., Sekhar, K. R. A human gait recognition against information theft in smartphone using residual convolutional neural network. Int. J. Adv. Comput. Sci. Appl. **11**(5) (2020). https://doi.org/10.14569/ijacsa.2020.0110544
7. Khan, M.A., et al.: Human gait analysis for osteoarthritis prediction: a framework of deep learning and kernel extreme *RVol**learning machine. Complex & Intelligent Systems. 1–19 (2021). https://doi.org/10.1007/s40747-020-00244-2
8. Cheheb, I., Al-Maadeed, N., Al-Madeed S., Bouridane, A.: Investigating the use of autoencoders for gait-based person recognition. In: 2018 NASA/ESA Conference on Adaptive Hardware and Systems, AHS 2018, pp. 148–151 (2018). https://doi.org/10.1109/AHS.2018.8541447
9. Mohammed, F. G., Eesee, W. K.: Human gait recognition using neural network multi-layer perceptron. J. Mech. Cont. Math. Sci. **14**(3), pp. 234–244 (2019). https://doi.org/10.26782/jmcms.2019.06.00018
10. Guo, H., et al.: Gait recognition based on the feature extraction of gabor filter and linear discriminant analysis and improved local coupled extreme learning machine. Math. Probl. Eng. **2020**, 1–9 (2020). https://doi.org/10.1155/2020/5393058
11. Nardo, D.F., Morbidoni, C., Cucchiarelli, A., Fioretti, S.: Recognition of gait phases with a single knee electrogoniometer: A deep learning approach. Electronics **9**(2), 355 (2020). https://doi.org/10.3390/electronics9020355
12. Si, W., Zhang, J., Li, Y.D., Tan, W., Shao, Y.F., Yang, G.L.: Remote identity verification using gait analysis and face recognition. Wirel. Commun. Mob. Comput. **2020**, 1 (2020). https://doi.org/10.1155/2020/8815461
13. Khan, M.H., Li, F., Farid, M.S., Grzegorzek, M.: Gait recognition using motion trajectory analysis. In: Kurzynski, M., Wozniak, M., Burduk, R. (eds.) CORES 2017. AISC, vol. 578, pp. 73–82. Springer, Cham (2018). https://doi.org/10.1007/978-3-319-59162-9_8

14. Hu, M., Wang, Y., Zhang, Z., Zhang, D., Little, J.J.: Incremental learning for video-based gait recognition with LBP flow. IEEE Trans. Cybernet. **43**(1), 77–89 (2013). https://doi.org/10.1109/TSMCB.2012.2199310

15. Bansal, M., Kumar, M., Kumar, M.: 2D object recognition: a comparative analysis of SIFT, SURF and ORB feature descriptors. Multim. Tools Appl. **80**(12), 18839–18857 (2021). https://doi.org/10.1007/s11042-021-10646-0

16. Chhabra, P., Garg, N.K., Kumar, M.: Content-based image retrieval system using ORB and SIFT features. Neural Comput. Appl. **32**(7), 2725–2733 (2018). https://doi.org/10.1007/s00521-018-3677-9

17. Huang, M., Mu, Z., Zeng, H., Huang, H.: A Novel approach for interest point detection via laplacian-of-bilateral filter. J. Sens. **2015**, 1–9 (2015). https://doi.org/10.1155/2015/685154

18. Saini, A., Singh, H.: Enhanced human identity and gender recognition from gait sequences using SVM and MDA. Int. J. Comput. Appl. **119**(2), 6–9 (2015). https://doi.org/10.5120/21037-3358

19. Htun KZ., & Zaw SMM. (2018). Human identification system based on statistical gait features. In: 2018 IEEE/ACIS 17th International Conference on Computer and Information Science (ICIS). doi:https://doi.org/10.1109/icis.2018.8466396

20. Kadhim, H. A., Araheemah, W. A.: A method to improve corner detectors (Harris, Shi-Tomasi & FAST) using adaptive contrast enhancement filter. Period. Eng. Nat. Sci. **8**(1), 508–515 (2020). https://doi.org/10.21533/pen.v8i1.1158.g532

21. Pribyl, B., Chalmers, A., Zemck, P.: Feature point detection under extreme lighting conditions. In: Proceedings—SCCG 2012: 28th Spring Conference on Computer Graphics, pp. 143–150 (2012). https://doi.org/10.1145/2448531.2448550

22. Kumar, M., Chhabra, P., Garg, N.K.: An efficient content based image retrieval system using BayesNet and K-NN. Multimedia Tools and Applications **77**(16), 21557–21570 (2018). https://doi.org/10.1007/s11042-017-5587-8

23. Long, T.: Locality preserving projection via deep neural network. In: 2019 International Joint Conference on Neural Networks (IJCNN), July, pp. 1–8 (2019).

24. Strukova, O. V., Myasnikov, E. V. The choice of methods for the construction of PCA-based features and the selection of SVM parameters for person identification by gait. *J. Phys.: Conf. Ser.* **1368**(3) (2019). https://doi.org/10.1088/1742-6596/1368/3/032001

25. Tang, Y., Rose, R.: A study of using locality preserving projections for feature extraction in speech recognition. In: ICASSP, IEEE International Conference on Acoustics, Speech and Signal Processing—Proceedings, May, pp. 1569–1572 (2008). https://doi.org/10.1109/ICASSP.2008.4517923

26. Naik, S., Virani, H.G.: Human gait recognition using BPN and MLP. Int. J. Innov. Res. Sci. Technol. **1**(11), 440–446 (2015)

27. Jalmi, S. K.: MLP based gait recognition technique. Int. J. Eng. Res. Technol. **10**, 8 (2021)

28. Kececi, A., Yildirak, A., Ozyazici, K., Ayluctarhan, G., Agbulut, O., Zincir, I.: Implementation of machine learning algorithms for gait recognition. Engineering Science and Technology, an International Journal **23**(4), 931–937 (2020). https://doi.org/10.1016/j.jestch.2020.01.005

29. Gupta, A., Jadhav, A., Jadhav, S., Thengade, A.: Human gait analysis based on decision tree, random forest and KNN algorithms. In: Iyer, B., Rajurkar, A.M., Gudivada, V. (eds.) Applied Computer Vision and Image Processing. AISC, vol. 1155, pp. 283–289. Springer, Singapore (2020). https://doi.org/10.1007/978-981-15-4029-5_28

Local Binary Pattern Symmetric Centre Feature Extraction Method for Detection of Image Forgery

M. Pavan Kalyan[1], D. Kishore[1], and Mahesh K. Singh[2]([✉])

[1] Department of ECE, Aditya College of Engineering and Technology, Surampalem, India
[2] Aditya Engineering College, Surampalem, India
mahesh.singh@accendere.co.in

Abstract. A new method for extracting the image from the copy-move forging was created by changing the Gabor filter and the Local Binary-Pattern Center Symmetric (LBP-CS) is given in this article. In this article the LBP- CS is a mod-ification of the local binary pattern which is free of the illumination and rotational effect differences, which is commonly used as a feature extractor for the core detecting stage. This method is used to find Center Symmetric Local Binary Pat-tern values for every Gabor picture (sub-bands) from the previous stage, based on the Gabor filter in different scales and orientations in the input image. This article contains information about the mechanism to detect a forgery in the copy-move and a flowchart of the system proposed. The input image is pre-processed and the Gabor Filter and LBP-CS function is extracted with various scales and guide-lines. There are five different types of passive image forgery detection methods. Pixel-based techniques draw attention to the pixels in a digital image. Copy-move processes include things like splicing, resampling, and statistical approaches. The similitude of the original and the forgery image was calculated using Euclidean distance in the next step. In the last study, the output of the method proposed is compared to the excising function extraction method.

Keywords: Classification · Copy-move forgery · Feature extraction · Gabor filter · Image forgery

1 Introduction

Digital cameras and smartphones have become communication tools daily as a result of technological advances [1]. Today there are a lot of pictures posted on the internet. The authenticity of these images is still doubtful and these images can be manipulated by different software tools. With digital software like Photoshop, 3D Max, the production of fake images is currently simple [2]. It can lead to serious problems with authenticity and confidence, particularly for certain applications, such as the presentation of evidence in the court and the press, in the digital images.

Computer tools for image editing, such as Adobe Photoshop, Vegas Pro, Mobil Edit Pro, and some other complicated computer technologies are available worldwide and are thus used to create false pictures [3]. Various techniques for forgery detection have

A. Kumar et al. (Eds.): ICAIDS 2021, CCIS 1673, pp. 89–100, 2022.
https://doi.org/10.1007/978-3-031-21385-4_8

been developed and commonly used in the various applications for which copy-move classifying is the most prominently used technology. The method is to copy and paste part of the picture into the same picture. The image sampling and processing generates a two-domain imaging process, including a pixel-based and a transformed system [4]. Various image processing techniques such as preprocessing, extraction of features, comparison of similarities, and classification are used for the identification of forged images [5]. This article develops an effective method for classifying the forgery images based on a copy-move detection technique. The main aims of this research are to identify the classification picture and divide the picture into classification or authentication. This is done by the use of such algorithms and classification machine learning algorithms. The key process is texture extraction and for classification it is important. The texture section contains input picture data [6]. The texture characteristics are significant and the digital image has a lower material. The texture characteristic is extracted for blocks and pattern formation. For processing the forged and original image, this block and pattern are based on a feature removal technique [7].

A classification detection attempts to disturb the color-shade irregularities in lighting changes in images. To accomplish estimators for the image regions to distinguish texture and edge-based features by consolidating data from material science and statistics. The identification of classification images plays a major role in forensics to make the image real. Figure 1 shows image classification detection techniques divided into two methods [8].

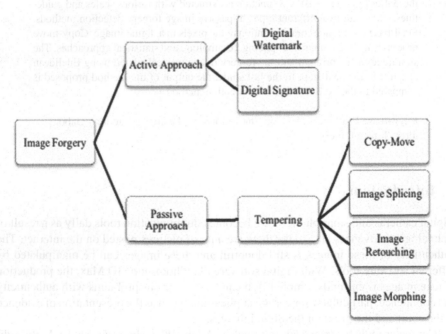

Fig. 1. Different techniques used for image forgery

The active approach involves pre-processing activities such as an embedded water-mark or digital image signatures that are generated during image production [9]. Signature and digital watermarking are two remarkable image forgery safety techniques. This identifies the picture that is manipulated, provides protection, and extracts the relevant data in the picture. Watermarking is a technique for the identification of forgery as a sensitive image or integrated material, but the imagery devices currently in place don't use watermarking or a signature module [10]. SURF and PCA provide effective results but do not provide an efficient result for the extraction of texture. This method is suitable for a limited amount of classification detections, however. This method contains some faulty results in a high processing time and less recognition rate when selecting features and the region of the coefficient block [11].

PCA analysis is mainly demerited by the delay in the dimension reduction analysis. The input picture noise value is equal to the higher intensity value of the original image so that the forged image area is not exact [12]. These extraction techniques in low-quality images are difficult to detect. High-level features from the images are difficult to remove. The proposed approach minimizes these types of limitations. For the extraction of texture, a new function technique is used and the Hybrid Neural Network has classified the forgery images in the Decision Tree presented in this article [13]. The proposed method is designed to detect the classification by incorporating techniques of extraction such as the Gabor filter and LBP-SC. The proposed methods are very attractive according to the performance findings [14]. The papers are presented in the following manner in Sect. 1 discussed the introduction of a local binary pattern. Section 2 discussed the previous work related to the local binary pattern. The copy-move forgery detection process is discussed in Sect. 3. Section 4 discussed the result for the detection of local binary patterns for the detection of image forgery. The conclusion is discussed in Sect. 5.

2 Related Works

This article discusses various strategies involved in detecting forgery by copy-moving. The related work on optimization strategies for a better classification based on copy-move classification is shown. There was a comparative study and analysis of the detection and classification of forgery based on optimization techniques [1, 15]. In addition, the Support Vector Machine Classifiers are evaluated to boost the classification accuracy and the hybrid combination of the Extreme Learning Machine with the Fuzzy network. In addition, several neural networks for effective imaging training in the classification process were discussed based on copy-move classification detection [2].

Suggested a Copy-Rotate-Move (CRM) system with Zernike moments to minimize compression, darkening, and white additive of JPEG [3]. In addition, also in rotating areas, this approach can identify forgery since Zernike moments are logarithmically invariant. However, the disadvantage of this technique is that its scaling and manipulation based on affine transformation are still weak. The identification of forged pictures is mentioned [4, 16]. For forgery detection the image of the input is used to achieve the authentic output using the forged image, the block-based matching algorithm is created. The k-mean method of clusters is used to identify the factor of similarity and segregate input data in different clusters [5]. A feature extraction process extracts the clustered data for identification of the image features and forged data. The performance parameter values provide an efficient result and characterize the output image for high accuracy to correct the class. Compared with other current methods, the time complexity is increased by 50% [6].

Here, a technique has been suggested to automatically estimate the threshold. The threshold is used to compare the similarity of the function vectors [7, 17]. An example of forgery detection is shown for copy transfer. In real-time technology and computerized areas, digital image plays a critical role. New advanced technology with digital cameras, PCs, and software tools has simplified the adjustments and manipulation of images [18–21]. Additional research is needed to strengthen classification detection with new algorithms and image processing techniques. Recently, few scholars worked and studied the issues of identification of a forged image and could not detect a comparison between the basic data of image manipulation and the original image [8]. To achieve efficient performance, the machine learning, and optimization algorithm. This study focuses on digital forensic images and their forms and focuses on the identification of copy-move forgeries. An ANT colony optimization for the detection of image classification is established [9].

For identification and classification by point and block features, feature extraction by SIFT and SURF is used [10]. This method separates the picture into blocks that do not overlap. At this stage, the element focuses are expelled from every block and matched to each block to differentiate the images of the classification [11]. The experimental results show that the forgery images tested for accuracy, precision, and reminder are identified, which show successful results in comparison with other approaches. A splicing detection method has been developed to segment camera response [12]. This approach is based on the uniformity of camera characteristics search in an input picture for different locations. The CRF is assessed for each area using local planar irradiance statistical invariants (LPIPs). For classification of the original and spliced file, CRF and intensity functionality are evaluated and forwarded to the SVM. The experimental results are assessed with 363 uncompressed, 183 authentic, and 180 spliced images, which achieve effectively, 70 percent accuracy and 70% repetition results [13].

Digital image fraud detection has become a hot study topic in recent years because of the increasing number of incidents involving picture alteration. The most frequent way of altering an image is copy-paste forgery, which may easily be done by the average person using online software programs [7]. Recently, the detection of forgeries has been a major concern. Copy-paste frauds can be detected using frequency transforms and spatial-structure characteristics on three different benchmark datasets, namely CASIA v1.0, CASIA v2.0, and the COVERAGE dataset. The accuracy, precision, and F1-score of the following datasets were tested in MATLAB to verify the feature's efficacy in forgery detection. Calibration of the threshold is done by utilizing the F1 score, and the ROC curves are used to present findings [16].

3   Methodology for Copy Move Forgery Detection

Copy-move forgery techniques are image editing tools available to forge digital images simply. A new function extraction algorithm is used to remove the textures and identify the classified images with the copying movement forgery detection system. A key point-based detection system with forgery extraction techniques, which extracts the key point from smooth regions and textures for effective classification, is featured in this article. The flow chart for the system suggested is shown in Fig. 2. The image input is initially re-dimensioned and converted to a grey image. Wiener filter reprocessing is used to minimize noise, to improve contrast and image quality. By integration of Gabor filter and image textures recovery LBP-SC, the texture features are extracted and key points extracted from the image.

Figure 3 described the picture of the input that is resized by 256 x 256. The picture is read and transformed into a grey picture. With the filtering, the input image is prepro-cessed to eliminate the noise. Gabor and LBP-SC are used to extract the corresponding features from the input files. The resemblance corresponds to the distance between the Euclidean. The images are listed as forgery and authentication by HNN-DT. Some per-formance measurements, such as precision measurement, sensitivity, and specificities, estimate the performance assessment of the proposed system.

3.1 Local Binary Pattern Centre Symmetric (LBM–CS) Approach

Gabor filter is used to extract the texture part after pre-processing by the LBP-CS operator and to extract a function from regional blocks. For the identification of copy-move forgery, LBP-CS is mainly used for the disassembly of the patter areas of the segments. The LBP-CS proposed to resolve LBP's high dimensionality. It used linearization to each pixel pair that is symmetrical to the center, free of illumination variances and rotational effects, as a central pixel. The new features include a certain asset that includes lighting shift tolerance, flat-picture robustness, and computer simplicity. LBP-CS also provides less performance in comparison with LBP compared with function vectors. This approach takes less time.

Local binary pattern generates 256 separate binary patterns in an image with a P*Q value, whereas LBP-CS only produces 8 binary patterns. Robustness is also achieved in flat image regions by thresholding the variations in grey levels with the small 'N' value.

$$LBPCS(P, Q) = \sum_{i=0}^{\frac{T}{2}-1} d\left(t_i - t_i\left(\frac{T}{2}\right)\right)2^i \tag{1}$$

Where,

$$c(p) = \begin{cases} 1 & p > N \\ 0 & other\ wise \end{cases} \tag{2}$$

The LBP-CS is used to detect the forgeries in the copy-move mode. The copied image should be rotated to insert the forgery image into the image.

The distance function was optimized for this proposed scheme by using the Bat algorithm to calculate efficiencies of similarity to increase the classification detection precision. The parameter for example Precision (p), Accuracy (ACC), Specificity (Spec), and Sensitivity (Sen.) are utilized (Table 1).

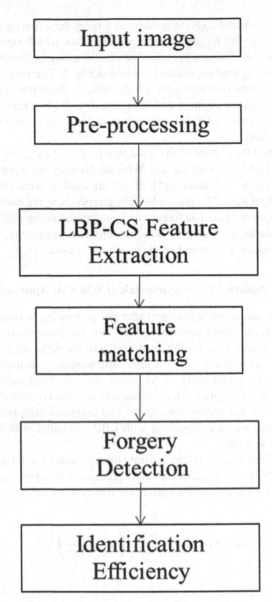

Fig. 2. Copy moves forgery detection technique

4   Result Analysis for Detection of Image Forgery

Performance assessment of the approach proposed in this method used WINDOWS environment, the local binary pattern has been simulated with the MATLAB Tool. This only implements the feature extraction method and supplies the classification to the HNN-DT to increase the precision of the classification. The local binary pattern proposal with the Gabor filter and center start function extraction trains the system. Let the neural network in motion is an error permissible or not acceptable? Add a covered assault compare the secret node with the node of weight to calculate the output of the method proposed to stop symmetric local binary patterns and are compared to HNN-DT with SURF and PCA. The database is taken as a randomly resized, input image that is preprocessed through it. To classify an image, classification HNN-DT is used. A collection of data is divided into 5 sets. In each set, there are 200 pictures, 150 original pictures, and 50 fragments were taken shown in Fig. 3.

Fig. 3. (a). Input image was taken for processing (b). Detection of Forgery Image copy and move

The output of the local binary pattern for detection of the image forgery method proposed with LBP-CS extraction for each input set is shown in Table 2. To estimate the precision, accuracy, and sensitivity of each collection, the proposed approach is assessed by output measurements that include fake negative, false positive, true positive, true negative. Table 3 discussed the performance analysis using the SVM classifier of the Existing copy and move forgery detection method.

Figure 4 demonstrates the accuracy comparison between SVM and LBP-SC for each collection and current techniques. It is obvious that in contrast to other technologies the LBP-SC proposed achieves efficient efficiency. The best classification accuracy is the effective classification of the classified picture.

Figure 5 and Fig. 6 show the results of the simulation for each collection and classifier specificity and sensitivity output. In comparison with existing schemes such as SVM

Table 1. The important formula used for copy-move forgery detection

S. No	Calculated parameter	Formulation
1	Accuracy	$Accuracy(Acc) = \frac{(T_p+T_n)}{(T_p+F_n+T_n+F_p)}$
2	Specificity	$Specificity(Spc) = \frac{(T_n)}{(T_n+F_p)}$
3	Precision	$Precision(p) = \frac{(T_p)}{(T_p+F_p)}$
4	Sensitivity	$Sensitivity(Sen.) = \frac{(T_p)}{(T_p+F_n)}$

Table 2. Performance analysis using LBP-SC Method (Proposed)

Input set image	No. of authentic image	No. of forged image	Tp	Tn	Fp	Fn	Spc (%)	Sens (%)	Acc (%)
Set_1	200	200	195	188	12	5	94.0	97.5	95.8
Set_2	200	200	189	177	23	11	88.5	94.5	91.5
Set_3	200	200	197	183	17	3	91.5	98.5	95.0
Set_4	200	200	185	180	20	15	90.0	92.5	91.3
Set_5	200	200	179	189	11	21	94.5	89.5	92.0
Set_6	200	200	183	182	18	17	91.0	91.5	91.3
Set_7	200	200	184	180	20	16	90.0	92.0	91.0
Set_8	200	200	190	189	11	10	94.5	95.0	94.8
Set_9	200	200	181	182	18	19	91.0	90.5	90.8
Set_10	200	200	194	190	10	6	95.0	97.0	96.0
Average	200	200	187.7	184	16	12.3	92.0	93.9	92.9

the efficiency of the proposed LBP-SC. The results obtained indicate that the proposed LBP-SC results show better image classification because of high LBP-SC training times and effective pre-processing and functional extraction relative to other approaches. The results show better results.

From the above description, it is shown a comparative overall study of all image forgery detection classifiers. Due to the efficient classification accuracy, the proposed approach shows efficient results in all performance metrics and achieves low computational speed and complexity. The experimental results show that SVM is efficient for the identification of the fake image by extracting features LBP-CS. The overall performance for image classification indicates better results.

Table 3. Performance analysis using SVM classifier (Existing)

Input set image	No. of authentic image	No. of forged image	Tp	Tn	Fp	Fn	Spc (%)	Sens (%)	Acc (%)
Set_1	200	200	180	176	24	20	88.0	90.0	89.0
Set_2	200	200	175	160	40	25	80.0	87.5	83.8
Set_3	200	200	180	172	28	20	86.0	90.0	88.0
Set_4	200	200	186	165	35	14	82.5	93.0	87.8
Set_5	200	200	176	156	44	24	78.0	88.0	83.0
Set_6	200	200	189	170	30	11	85.0	94.5	89.8
Set_7	200	200	170	158	42	30	79.0	85.0	82.0
Set_8	200	200	168	154	46	32	77.0	84.0	80.5
Set_9	200	200	159	156	44	41	78.0	79.5	78.8
Set_10	200	200	180	171	29	20	85.5	90.0	87.8
Average	200	200	176.3	163.8	36.2	23.7	81.9	88.2	85.0

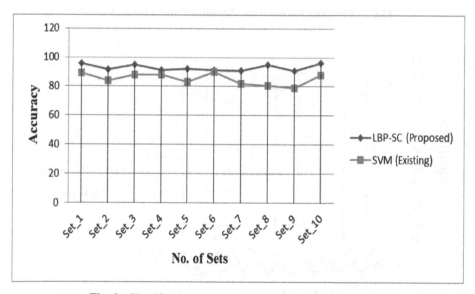

Fig. 4. Classification result for 'Accuracy' result for each set

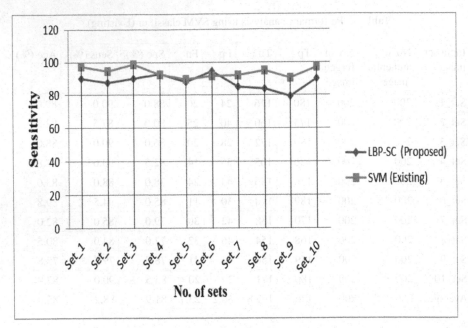

Fig. 5. Classification result for 'Sensitivity' result for each set

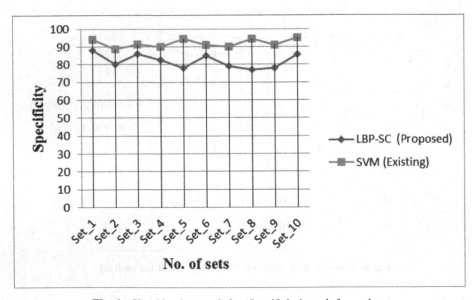

Fig. 6. Classification result for 'Specificity' result for each set

5 Conclusion

This article compares the methods for extracting characteristics to detect the forgery image detection effectively. The LBP-CS features are primarily used for texture extraction, and the output is compared with the existing SVM model. The image is pre-processed by Wiener filter, Gabor filter, and LBP-CS extraction features, similar to the SVM classification used for forgery image detection. The experimental results demonstrate the efficient accuracy of classification performance. The proposed approach shows that the fabric image can be efficiently detected for real-time use. One of the growing problems in digital imaging forensics is copy movement detection forgery. This dilemma was addressed by several techniques. The key problem is to detect the picture forged without disrupting the other methods in dealing with these techniques. Computing time is the problem facing today's technology; it has become an essential issue among large databases. In future work related to copying and moving it is the emphasis of this research on sensing primarily to recognize the classified image, although it is very different from other images and to ensure that the images are genuine and integral.

References

1. Uliyan, D.M., Jalab, H.A., Wahab, A.W.A.: Copy move image forgery detection using Hessian and center symmetric local binary pattern. In 2015 IEEE Conference on Open Systems (ICOS), pp. 7–11 (2015)
2. Davarzani, R., Mozaffari, S., Yaghmaie, K.: Perceptual image hashing using center-symmetric local binary patterns. Multimedia Tools and Applications 75(8), 4639–4667 (2015). https://doi.org/10.1007/s11042-015-2496-6
3. Park, J.Y., Kang, T.A., Moon, Y.H., Eom, I.K.: Copy-move forgery detection using scale invariant feature and reduced local binary pattern histogram. Symmetry 12(4), 492 (2020)
4. Tuncer, T., Kaya, M.: A novel image watermarking method based on center symmetric local binary pattern with minimum distortion. Optik 185, 972–984 (2019)
5. Singh, M.K., Singh, A.K., Singh, N.: Multimedia analysis for disguised voice and classification efficiency. Multimedia Tools and Applications 78(20), 29395–29411 (2018). https://doi.org/10.1007/s11042-018-6718-6
6. Soni, B., Das, P. K., Thounaojam, D. M.: Copy-move tampering detection based on local binary pattern histogram Fourier feature. In Proceedings of the 7th International Conference on Computer and Communication Technology, pp. 78–83 (2017)
7. Singh, M.K., Singh, A.K., Singh, N.: Disguised voice with fast and slow speech and its acoustic analysis. Int. J. Pure Appl. Math 11(14), 241–246 (2018)
8. Dey, A., Pal, P., Chowdhuri, P., Singh, P. K., Jana, B.: Center-symmetric local binary pattern-based image authentication using local and global features vector. In Computational Intelligence in Pattern Recognition, pp. 489–501. Springer, Singapore (2020)
9. Singh, M. K., Singh, A. K., Singh, N.: Acoustic comparison of electronics disguised voice using different semitones. Int. J. Eng. Technol. (2018).
10. Chalamalasetty, S. P., Giduturi, S. R.: Research perception towards copy-move image forgery detection: challenges and future directions. Int. J. Image Grap. 2150054 (2021).
11. Singh, M., Nandan, D., Kumar, S.: Statistical analysis of lower and raised pitch voice signal and its efficiency calculation. Trait. Sig. 36(5), 455–461 (2019)
12. Singh, M.K., Singh, A.K., Singh, N.: Multimedia utilization of non-computerized disguised voice and acoustic similarity measurement. Multimedia Tools and Applications 79(47–48), 35537–35552 (2019). https://doi.org/10.1007/s11042-019-08329-y

13. Brogan, J.: Advancing Biometrics and Image Forensics Through Vision and Learning Systems. The University of Notre Dame, Dame (2019)
14. Kanchana, V., Nath, S., Singh, M. K. (2021). A study of internet of things oriented smart medical systems. In: Materials Today: Proceedings
15. Balaji, V.N., Srinivas, P.B., Singh, M.K.: Neuromorphic advancements architecture design and its implementations technique. In: Materials Today: Proceedings (2021)
16. Jalilian, E., Uhl, A.: Enhanced segmentation-CNN-based finger-vein recognition by joint training with automatically generated and manual labels. In: 2019 IEEE 5th International Conference on Identity. Security, and Behavior Analysis (ISBA), pp. 1–8. IEEE, New York (2019)
17. Punyavathi, G., Neeladri, M., Singh, M.K.: Vehicle tracking and detection techniques using IoT. In: Materials Today: Proceedings (2021)
18. Kumar, A.: Design of secure image fusion technique using cloud for privacy-preserving and copyright protection. Int. J. Cloud Appl. Comput. **9**(3), 22–36 (2019)
19. Kumar, A., Zhang, Z.J., Lyu, H.: Object detection in real time based on improved single shot multi-box detector algorithm. EURASIP J. Wirel. Commun. Netw. **2020**(1), 1–18 (2020). https://doi.org/10.1186/s13638-020-01826-x
20. Kumar, A.: A review on implementation of digital image watermarking techniques using LSB and DWT. In: the Third International Conference on Information and Communication Technology for Sustainable Development (ICT4SD 2018), 30–31 Aug 2018, Hotel Vivanta by Taj, GOA, India
21. Walia, S., Kumar, K.: Pragmatical investigation of frequency-domain and spatial-structure-based image forgery detection methods. Int. J. Comput. Intell. IoT **1**, 2 (2018)

A Copy and Move Image Forged Classification by Using Hybrid Neural Networks

K. Sushma[✉], V. Satyanarayana, and Mahesh K. Singh

Department of ECE, Aditya Engineering College, Surampalem, AP, India
sushmakoppula9@gmail.com, vasece_vella@aec.edu.in,
mahesh.singh@accendere.co.in

Abstract. Hybrid Neural networks decision tree (HNN-DT) based algorithm was discussed in this article to achieve an efficient detection of image classification for both copy move and spliced picture classification. The effects of the HNN-DT are shown to be stronger than the other techniques. However, to those criteria, it does not achieve an optimal classification result. It is implemented and effective for easy training and image checking for the skilled classification of classification pictures. This framework covers image processing techniques such as pre-processing, extraction of features, and similarity for effective grading. The Wiener Filter Pre-processing is demonstrated by the speeded-up robust features (SURF) and principal components analysis (PCA) function extraction method for extracting the corresponding classification characteristics. It then moves to identify the corresponding similarities between the original and the classified images by Manhattan distance. The last section discusses the classification of forged images, such as the neural network and decision tree.

Keywords: Classification · Manhattan distance · Neural network · PCA · SURF

1 Introduction

Digital forensics recently got a lot of attention due to its ability to preserve details on the picture of classification [1]. Accessibility of several software tools for editing and changing information, to reduce authenticity by modifying the original content of the image. It is necessary to ensure the originality and safety of images used to detect the forgery as one of the challenges of government and NGOs. Real-time device forgery detection is an excellent way to enhance the image's authenticity [2, 3]. It is possible to detect whether the image is fake or original that cannot be analyzed by the eyes of human beings in numerous real-time applications including Digital Image Processing (DIP), Computer Vision (CV), biomedical, forensics, journalism, scientific journals, multimedia safety, surveillance systems, etc. Many methods were previously developed to detect forgery images and automated detection was also developed to verify forgery images' originality and integrity [4]. Yet, the picture of forgery does not detect those limitations that trigger. The previous chapter briefly explains and analyses the current approach focused on the detection of copy-moving forgery. It indicates that better detection results than other techniques are obtained. However, in terms of certain

A. Kumar et al. (Eds.): ICAIDS 2021, CCIS 1673, pp. 101–111, 2022.
https://doi.org/10.1007/978-3-031-21385-4_9

criteria, it does not achieve effective classification results and it causes more processing time [6].

In certain instances, fast copy-move classification detection complexes cannot detect small copied regions, and regions of normal or original replication should not be detected as well [5]. When detection is harder with more noise and a lower level of contrast, the introduction of algorithms leads to the worst results. The copy-move example is shown in Fig. 1.

(a)   (b)

Fig. 1. Example of (a). Original Image (b). Copy-move forged image

The implementation of the severe learning machine leads to inefficient image classification to increased convergence time and local minima issues. For large data and even large datasets, HNN-DT is applicable [7]. A new system for training and evaluating pictures for the skilled classification of forgery images is implemented to solve these problems. An HNN-DT system for classifying the classified images is built in this article [8].

The neural network is chosen because less formal mathematical training is needed and it can detect non-linear complications and potential classified image complications. The neural network offers several training courses for forgery image classification [9, 19]. To produce effective performance, the hybrid neural network combined with the decision tree is introduced. This approach uses image processing techniques such as pre-processing, extraction of functionalities, and similarity for efficient classification. The work in this chapter explains in detail the "HNN-DT" for classifying images of classification [10, 18]. The improved SURF algorithm is used to remove the texture of the image by combining PCA, Manhattan's distance is used as a measure of similarity between images forgery. Then the HNN-DT classification for the classification of and authentication of the image. The performance tests are assessed to distinguish forgery images effectively and to equate them with other techniques [11, 20]. Kumar et al. [21–23] proposed an object detection method for blind people.

2 Related Works to Copy-Move Forgery

Digital image forgery is a new area of study and has received considerable attention. Researchers are focused on protecting the authenticity of photographs and videos [1]. Because of increasing alterations to photographs, image forensics has identified these forgeries to prevent illegal problems. Numerous methods are used to identify forged images, but the emphasis on accuracy and time complexity still has to be increased. Few techniques are excellent in situations where the copied component is blurred, loaded with noise, or cut [2, 11]. Few methods are good because of efficient rotation and scaling, and others are more complicated but effective in computational complexity. Further research is required to improve the detection of classification using image processing techniques and numerous algorithms [3]. Recently, only a handful of scholars have worked and studied the issues of forging and not being able to detect comparison with the original image with the fundamental information of manipulation images. For efficient outcomes, machine learning and optimization algorithms are used. This survey focuses on copy-move classification and digital forensics and their forms [4].

The "DCT" is used to restrict the functional vector elements and the generalized Bedford legislation is also used to set the picture [12]. The method uses element-by-element equity between the feature vectors and does not use Euclidean distance or cross connectivity and instead uses the picture tested for the threshold value. Experimental findings show that the copied and pasted regions can be recognized in different circumstances and achieve higher accuracy ratios with minimal false-negative rates than current algorithms. The demonstration function that is invariant to noise or blur is discussed [3, 13]. These extracted features are invariant in a few geometric modifications, including scaling and rotation which can be attached before pasting to the copied field. The function "(Fourier Mellon Transform FMT)" is used to reflect and count bloom filters to improve time complexity. Test results showed that the JPEG compression of the FMT function block is stronger [4].

A robust copy-move forgery detection system is suggested. DCT coefficients and division quantization are used for quantization. It was added to each picture that was sub-blocks that were not overlapping [5]. SVD is used to minimize the block size of each block derived by using its highest singular value. The feature vectors are lexicographically sorted and forged blocks of the picture are determined by the similarity of the shift frequency threshold. The experimental results show that the forging copy-move process is strongly resistant to Gaussian compression, AWGN, and JPEG [6]. The copy-move classification based on video processing to discern the forging region of the video is analyzed [8]. This technique was used for the elimination of noise and the classification of the forged region using different pre-processing procedures. For editing videos and duplication motions, the video editing program is used [7]. The relationship between video frames is designed as particular segments so that the copied and pasted frames from another region are easily recognized. In the extraction step, the SIFT algorithm forms the edges. The test results show competent noise reduction processes to improve the quality of the picture. For temporal images with efficient rating precision, this approach works efficiently [8, 14].

Classification is proposed by using DCT and IDCT technologies based on the method of row and column reduction. The new technique reduces time, expense, and picture competence computational complexity [15]. The image input is initially separated into rows and columns in the grids. With the support of lines and segments, in which DCT is connected with every line and column and has been modified into different parts with different estimates. Finally, from the point of view of confinement, the copied picture is handled [16]. The proposed detection is used for deep learning forgery CNN-based Copy-move. First, the parameters obtained from Image Net were forwarded by small copy-shifting training samples to the training model and then slightly modified to classify the test image using the training model [17]. The experimental results show that the proposed strategy performs well for the identification of fabricated images, although the signal of tampering is very low and the precision results for classification are high [9].

3   Methodology for Hybrid Copy-Move Detection Approach

The main goal of imaging forgery detection is to develop techniques to assess the validity and credibility of digitally based image processing with the help of automated detection technologies. In this study, forgery-based movement detection techniques are used to identify the classification images. Copy-move forgery is the act of copying and pasting the same image from part to part. This section contains the neural network and decision tree to characterize the picture of classification. The flowcharts for copy-move forgery detection using the HNN-DT method are shown in Fig. 2.

Figure 2 shows the flow diagram for the proposed HNN-DT. The input image is pre-processed, extracted with features and similarities to be classified efficiently. At first, the Wiener filter pre-processes the image to remove the noise and enhance the image quality. By using the PCA, the function vector from the pre-processed image is extracted by SURF. The similarity of the Manhattan distance vectors to identify the exact correspondence of the original image. HNN-DT trains the matched image to classify the classified image.

Pre-processing is the way background noise is reduced and visual contrast improves. It often involves the method of resizing images and converting RGB to grey to improve picture functions by eradicating undesirable distortions. Pre-processing is mostly used to increase background image contrast and to blur the degradation function to make the extraction of the element more accurate. Kalman filter is used to smooth the picture with variance adjustment so that the additive noise is reduced by white noise.

The Kalman filter has two approaches: the original signal and the noise characteristics of the given input picture and the linearly time-invariant filter such that the output is linked to the original signal. The process model describes the state's development from time 't-1 to time t as:

$$y_t = Ky_{t-1} + Cu_{t-1} + v_{t-1}(1)$$ (1)

Where 'K' is denoted as transition matrix driven by input image with previous state vector 'y_{t-1}'. 'C' is the control input matrix that is applied on the control vector 'u_{t-1}'.v_{t-1} is the process of noise vector supposed to be Gaussian with zero-mean. The process model is combined with the measuring model describing the relation between

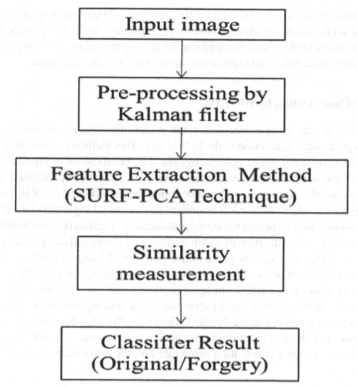

Fig. 2. The proposed method for copy-move forgery detection using the HNN-DT method

the state and the measurement in the current phase 'k'.

$$z_k = Hy_k \mid n_k \qquad (2)$$

Here 'z_k' is denoted as measurement vectors. 'H' is the measurement matrix and 'n_k' is measured as noise vectors.

Feature extraction is the method by which the related functionality is extracted, including some input image information. The detection of block-based copy-move forgery is used as a key point for the detection of forgery. The high entropy elements in each block are extracted to increase the complexity of the imported algorithms and to locate the marked points in the input image. SURF is a robust vector detection algorithm with invariant scales. SURF was not less computationally complex than SIFT, and its use of integrated images as an approximation of second-order Gaussian derivatives was effectively inferable. The SURF algorithm is used by constructing pyramids, screening, and estimating the difference between every layer and Gaussians. SURF also creates a 2:1 un-sampled stack for higher levels such as a pyramid that produces the same resolution output images.

PCA is a method of finding data patterns that express its similarities and differences in the method. PCA Since PCA is a powerful tool to analyze data, trends in data are difficult for high dimensions to recognize. The principal advantage of using PCA is that when patterns are detected, the data is then compressed without loss of information and reduced without loss of information. It is commonly used as an application for pattern recognition such as face recognition, image creation, Data models, similarities and differences are defined and high-dimensional data patterns are found.

3.1 Image Classification by HNN-DT

The match will be sent to the image classification classifier. The productive results have now given a great deal of attention to the hybrid mix. This method is commonly used for classification purposes in image processing. For the classification of the fake image in this hybrid segment, the Neural Network and Decision Tree are implemented. For large data sets, the classification accuracy must be improved; an updated ANN is proposed to identify the forgery image as an ANN boundary decision-making method are discussed.

The classifier based on neural networks and decisions tree has become a more important approach for the classification of multisource data. Having difficulty finding features such as forms, edges and regions is the major problem of image classification. Neural networks and classification are however able to automatically pick the functions. The neural network plays a key role in image processing and can handle a wide range of data sets to infer both complex and hidden non-linear connections between dependent and independent variables (image blocks). However, the vast complexity of the network structure and the computational cost is affected, so that the exact outcome can be achieved with a high classification error rate and the noisy data are combined in a decision tree.

4   Result in Analysis Using HNN-DT Method

Some performance metrics for precision, sensitivity, specificity for estimating HNN-DT performance are used to assess the performance of the proposed process. The performance metrics are compared and measured for each package. 100 images have been trained in this simulation and 50 images have been reviewed. We took 5 sets each containing 2 images in the inputs and 2 classifying images for this simulation. The picture for the pre-processing and extraction of functions shown in Fig. 2 is taken. MATLAB simulation is used to measure the similarity of Manhattan's distance and demonstrates effective similitude between 0–1 ranges as a better similitude. The HNN-DT classifier is used to differentiate between the original picture and the image forgery.

Specificity (Spc): It indicates that the forgery picture is not classified even though the real Condition is missing.

$$Specificity(Spc) = \frac{(T_n)}{(T_n + F_p)} (3) \tag{3}$$

Accuracy (Acc): the Classifier Measures to Create the Correct Classification of the Inaccurate Image.

$$Accuracy(Acc) = \frac{(T_p + T_n)}{(T_p + F_n + T_n + F_p)} (4) \tag{4}$$

Sensitivity (Sen.): It signifies the optimistic classification image categorization still the real situation is resent.

$$\text{Sensitivity(Sen.)} = \frac{(T_p)}{(T_p + F_n)} (5) \tag{5}$$

The performance analysis of HNN-DT proposed and existing methods including SVM for parameter measurements obtained in the confusion matrix was compared to Table 1 and Table 2. Each collection of images is included in databases, including true positive, real negative, false positive, false negative, and for accuracy estimates, sensitivities, and specificity.

Table 1. Performance analysis using HNN-DT Classifier (**Proposed**)

Input set image	No. of authentic image	No of forged image	Tp	Tn	Fp	Fn	Spc (%)	Sens (%)	Acc (%)
Set_1	100	100	89	95	5	11	95.0	89.0	92.0
Set_2	100	100	92	86	14	8	86.0	92.0	89.0
Set_3	100	100	94	84	16	6	84.0	94.0	89.0
Set_4	100	100	95	92	8	5	92.0	95.0	93.5
Set_5	100	100	92	90	10	8	90.0	92.0	91.0
Set_6	100	100	84	91	9	16	91.0	84.0	87.5
Set_7	100	100	90	89	11	10	89.0	90.0	89.5
Set_8	100	100	82	93	7	18	93.0	82.0	87.5
Set_9	100	100	86	82	18	14	82.0	86.0	84.0
Set_10	100	100	93	86	14	7	86.0	93.0	89.5
Average	100	100	90	89	11	10	89.0	90.0	89.5

Figures 3 and 4 shows the results of the simulation for each collection and classifier specificity and sensitivity output. In comparison with existing schemes such as SVM the efficiency of the proposed HNN-DT. The results obtained indicate that the proposed HNN-DT results show better image classification because of high NN training times and effective pre-processing and functional extraction relative to other approaches. The results show better results.

The accuracy of each set is shown in Fig. 5. For all classifiers, the results of the simulation are assessed and determined to measure the output of the proposed method for each collection. From the graphics, it is obvious that better accuracy than current methods like SVM is achieved with a proposed HNN-DT. The test results show that the suggested HNN-DT results in the assessment of all performance metrics are efficient in comparison to existing methods that lead to accurate classification of classification and original images. In different applications, the identification of the classifying image

Table 2. Performance analysis using SVM classifier **(Existing)**

Input set image	No. of authentic image	No. of forged image	Tp	Tn	Fp	Fn	Spc (%)	Sens (%)	Acc (%)
Set_1	100	100	80	82	18	20	82.0	80.0	81.0
Set_2	100	100	75	81	19	25	81.0	75.0	78.0
Set_3	100	100	79	72	28	21	72.0	79.0	75.5
Set_4	100	100	82	81	19	18	81.0	82.0	81.5
Set_5	100	100	83	84	16	17	84.0	83.0	83.5
Set_6	100	100	78	74	26	22	74.0	78.0	76.0
Set_7	100	100	76	68	32	24	68.0	76.0	72.0
Set_8	100	100	72	81	19	28	81.0	72.0	76.5
Set_9	100	100	80	75	25	20	75.0	80.0	77.5
Set_10	100	100	76	74	26	24	74.0	76.0	75.0
Average	100	100	78.1	77.2	22.8	21.9	77.2	78.1	77.7

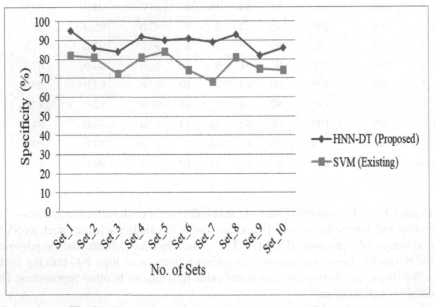

Fig. 3. Classification result for 'Specificity' result for each set

remains a challenge. This proposed method can be used to detect forgery images in different fields in real-time applications.

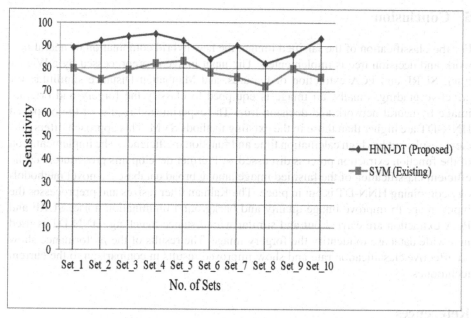

Fig. 4. Classification result for 'Sensitivity' result for each set

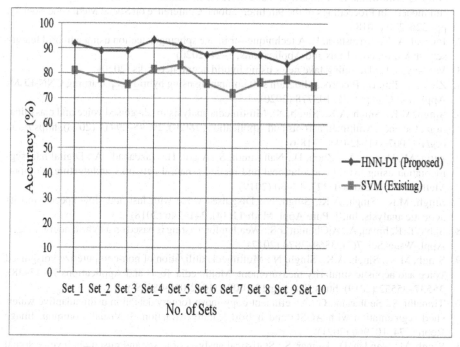

Fig. 5. Classification result for 'Accuracy' result for each set

5 Conclusion

For the classification of the falsified image, the new hybrid combination of neural network and decision tree is implemented. The input image is preprocessed by a Wiener filter, SURF and PCA extraction of features, and Manhattan Distance similitude for effective grading. Finally, an image is equipped to classify the forgery and original image by neural network and decision tree. The experimental results of the proposed HNN-DT are higher than those in the existing methods SVM. This approach offers efficient results but has high calculation time and function inefficiency. The implementation of the function extraction process discussed will further develop this procedure. For the efficient classification of the falsified image among broad databases, a novel methodology combining HNN-DT is put in place. The Kalman filter resizes and preprocesses the input image to improve image quality and background illumination noise, SURF and PCA extraction are carried out and similar with distance matching. HNN-DT is used in a wide database to identify the forgery image. The results of the performance show an effective classification rate and show improved results in comparison to the current techniques.

References

1. Ajao, O., Bhowmik, D., Zargari, S.: Fake news identification on Twitter with hybrid cnn and rnn models. In Proceedings of the 9th International Conference on Social Media and Society, pp. 226–230 (2018)
2. Jaiswal, A. K., Srivastava, R. A technique for image splicing detection using a hybrid feature set. In: Multimedia Tools and Applications, 1–24 (2020)
3. Vardanyan, E.: Detecting fake news using hybrid neural networks (2020)
4. Zhou, S., Tan, B.: Electrocardiogram soft computing using hybrid deep learning CNN-ELM. Appl. Soft Comput. **86**, 105778 (2020)
5. Singh, M.K., Singh, A.K., Singh, N.: Multimedia analysis for disguised voice and classification efficiency. Multimedia Tools and Applications **78**(20), 29395–29411 (2018). https://doi.org/10.1007/s11042-018-6718-6
6. Attia, M., Hossny, M., Zhou, H., Nahavandi, S., Asadi, H., Yazdabadi, A.: Digital hair segmentation using hybrid convolutional and recurrent neural networks architecture. Comput. Methods Prog. Biomed. **177**, 17–30 (2019)
7. Singh, M.K., Singh, A.K., Singh, N.: Disguised voice with fast and slow speech and its acoustic analysis. Int. J. Pure Appl. Math **11**(14), 241–246 (2018)
8. Saba, T., Rehman, A., AlGhamdi, J.S.: Weather forecasting is based on a hybrid neural model. Appl. Water Sci. **7**(7), 3869–3874 (2017)
9. Singh, M.K., Singh, A.K., Singh, N.: Multimedia utilization of non-computerized disguised voice and acoustic similarity measurement. Multimedia Tools and Applications **79**(47–48), 35537–35552 (2019). https://doi.org/10.1007/s11042-019-08329-y
10. Tinnathi, S., Sudhavani, G.: An efficient copy-move forgery detection using adaptive watershed segmentation with AGSO and hybrid feature extraction. J. Visual Commun. Image Repres. **74**, 102966 (2021)
11. Singh, M., Nandan, D., Kumar, S.: Statistical analysis of lower and raised pitch voice signal and its efficiency calculation. Traitement Sig. **36**(5), 455–461 (2019)
12. Jang, K., Kim, N., An, Y.K.: Deep learning-based autonomous concrete crack evaluation through hybrid image scanning. Struct. Health Monitor. **18**(5–6), 1722–1737 (2019)

13. Singh, M. K., Singh, A. K., Singh, N.: Acoustic comparison of electronics disguised voice using different semitones. Int. J. Eng. Technol. **7**, 98 (2018)
14. Punyavathi, G., Neeladri, M., Singh, M.K.: Vehicle tracking and detection techniques using IoT. In: Materials Today: Proceedings (2021)
15. Veerendra, G., Swaroop, R., Dattu, D.S., Jyothi, C.A., Singh, M.K.: Detecting plant Diseases, quantifying and classifying digital image processing techniques. In: Materials Today: Proceedings (2021)
16. Padma, U., Jagadish, S., Singh, M.K.: Recognition of plant's leaf infection by image processing approach. In: Materials Today: Proceedings (2021)
17. Satya, P.M., Jagadish, S., Satyanarayana, V., Singh, M.K.: Stripe noise removal from remote sensing images. In: 2021 6th International Conference on Signal Processing. Computing and Control (ISPCC), pp. 233–236. IEEE, New York (2021)
18. Nandini, A., Kumar, R.A., Singh, M.K.: Circuits based on the memristor for fundamental operations. In: 2021 6th International Conference on Signal Processing. Computing and Control (ISPCC), pp. 251–255. IEEE, New York (2021)
19. Anushka, R.L., Jagadish, S., Satyanarayana, V., Singh, M.K.: Lens less cameras for face detection and verification. In: 2021 6th International Conference on Signal Processing. Computing and Control (ISPCC), pp. 242–246. IEEE, New York (2021)
20. Van Niekerk, J.L.: Degradation estimation of high energy steam piping using hybrid recurrent neural networks. Doctoral dissertation, University of Pretoria (2018)
21. Kumar, A.: Design of secure image fusion technique using cloud for privacy-preserving and copyright protection. Int. J. Cloud Appl. Comput. **9**(3), 22–36 (2019)
22. Kumar, A., Zhang, Z.J., Lyu, H.: Object detection in real time based on improved single shot multi-box detector algorithm. EURASIP J. Wirel. Commun. Netw. **2020**(1), 1–18 (2020). https://doi.org/10.1186/s13638-020-01826-x
23. Kumar, A.: A review on implementation of digital image watermarking techniques using LSB and DWT. In: The Third International Conference on Information and Communication Technology for Sustainable Development (ICT4SD 2018), held during August 30–31, 2018 at Hotel Vivanta by Taj, Goa, India

Cardiac Surveillance System Using
by the Modified Kalman Filter

Sabbella Urmila[1], R. Anil Kumar[1], and Mahesh K. Singh[2]([✉])

[1] Aditya College of Engineering and Technology, Surampalem, India
anilkumar.relangi@acet.ac.in
[2] Department of ECE, Aditya Engineering College, Surampalem, India
mahesh.singh@accendere.co.in

Abstract. High-speed, reliable cardiac surveillance system that can detect cardiac arrest even before 24 h is the major goal of this study. The detection is based on the Kalman filter algorithm and advanced fast Fourier transform (FFT) compressor algorithm. A number of cardiac arrest techniques have been documented in contemporary literature. Irregular ventricular fibrillation or cardiovascular disorders are the main reason for abrupt cardiac failure. The suggested enhanced heart monitoring device continuously records electrocardiogram (ECG) readings. The preprocessing block boosts and filters the ECG signal in order to avoid interference with the power line and high frequency overlaps. The digital analog converter transforms a digital sample of the analogue ECG signal and uses the Kalman filter as an advance processing method for future ECG samples 24 h a day. FFT algorithm proposed to analyze the cardiac symptoms and their diagnosis, using the ECG test signal and the ECG reference signals similarity and dissimilarity approaches (Kalman predicted ECG Samples). After the irregularity is recognized, the warning feedback is sent to the receiver.

Keywords: ECG Signal · Kalman filter · FFT · Cardiac surveillance · IIR filter

1 Introduction

People were not concerned about their health recently because of changes in lifestyle. However, the cardiac rhythms and the danger of rapid cardiovascular arrest are particularly essential [1]. Much of the deaths result from cardiovascular disease, in particular owing to abrupt cardiac arrest. The success of the restaurant primarily hinges on the patient's first aid. Sudden heart arrest can happen everywhere and anybody, even fatally. All are common with ventricular tachycardia, ventricular heart readiness, heart disease, myocardial infarction, and valve dysfunction. A number of kinds of heart arrhythmia are present [2]. These include extremely serious ventricular tachycardia and bready cardiac, which cause fast heart death. A typical ECG cycle shows the roles of atria and ventricular depolarization or depolarization at all heartbeats. Figure 1 shows the ECG wave patterns known as the waves P, Q, R, S and T [3, 4].

© The Author(s), under exclusive license to Springer Nature Switzerland AG 2022
A. Kumar et al. (Eds.): ICAIDS 2021, CCIS 1673, pp. 112–122, 2022.
https://doi.org/10.1007/978-3-031-21385-4_10

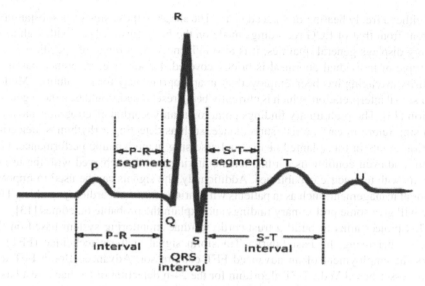

Fig. 1. ECG Waveform

The R-R period indicates 60 to 100 ppm under normal rest conditions. The R-R stage denotes the stage of arterial depolarization and the transition via electric impulses from the SA node to the AV node [5]. This P-R stage is the transit period when electrical drives from a sinus node to an AV node, whilst the AV-node, histogram packet, branch bundle, and purinc fibers are all concerned with the P-R segment [6]. The QRS is the right and left ventricular depolarization. The QRS complex shows the high amplitude of the P wave, because the QRS complex has large muscles relative to atria, which is an important parameter for ventricular clinical assessment. The modification of QRS amplitude is diagnostic of heart rhythmic [7]. The ST segment is the depolarizing ventricle, T is a repolarizing ventricle, and ST is the interval between J and T and U and T. The ST is the hemisphere. It is rarely regarded as a wave of low amplitude [8].

One of the most serious challenges in current health-care delivery is the utilization of increased information, telecommunications, and implant technology for cardiac risk classification and management. Sudden cardiac death is the main cause of overall car-diovascular mortality, accounting for almost 60% of all coronary heart disease fatalities each year [6]. Although statistical analysis has identified many high-risk patient groups with acceptable sensitivity and specificity, assessing the acute risk of individuals remains unattainable. Implants with telemetric capabilities, such as cardiac pacemakers, allow for continuous, permanent monitoring. As a result, developments in technology have made it possible to design a new systematic technique for diagnosing high-risk indi-viduals, commencing proper therapeutic therapy, and preventing sudden death. The first results from heart transplant patients, patients who have had a myocardial infarction, and patients with coronary artery disease make it possible to evaluate currently available technology and highlight the promise of cardiac telemonitoring as a new profession [8].

Ventricular intramyocardial electrograms are obtained by inserting electrodes directly into the heart, either intraventricularly or primordially, and can be obtained from either a freely beating or a paced heart. The shape of these signals is substantially different from that of ECG recordings made on the body surface [12]. Although morphology displays general qualities, it is also influenced by a range of specific factors. This topic of individual appraisal is briefly covered. Personalized reference based on similarity averaging has been employed as an appropriate way for its solution. Model-based signal interpretation, which is currently being researched, could be a more general solution [13]. The preliminary findings point to intramyocardial electrograms having a promising future in cardiac risk surveillance, such as detecting arrhythmias, detecting rejection events in transplanted hearts, and assessing hemodynamic performance. Permanent and even continuous cardiac telemonitoring may be achieved with the use of implants with telemetric capabilities. Additionally, the signals can be used to improve treatment management, such as in patients with various forms of cardiomyopathies. This study will give some preliminary findings and explain the probable outcomes [13].

This project aims to build a trustworthy cardiac monitoring system based on the Kalman filter using the Fast Fourier Transform signal analysis technique (FFT). It allows the employment of an advanced FFT compressor, Advanced Booth FFT and a compressor-based Vedic FFT algorithm for the 24-h detection of cardiac arrest based on Kalman's predictive techniques and estimates [9]. The suggested monitoring system includes both analogue and digital circuitry. In order to improve the signal intensity and filtering noise, ECG signals are recorded by functioning blocks on the suggested systems and pre-processing blocks processed. A sample is transferred from the analogue to the digital converter [10]. This digital sample is constantly processed by a Kalman filter to forecast ECG samples 24 h a day. The principal purpose of this study, with the aid of a Kalman predictor with a single FFT-like similarity and differences in the QRS peak detection algorithm, is to detect cardiac arrest 24 h before it occurs, while increasing the velocity of FFT-calculation by using the Advance Booth and the Vedic Compressor-based algorithm [11].

2 Literature Review

The 1990 study explored different interference disruptions damaging the ECG signals. To monitor electrical activity of the heart muscle the ECG electrode standard used to attach the patient's chest (ECG) [12]. The normal ECG cycle depicts the function of the auricular and ventricular agent to depolarize and re-polarize every heartbeat. The wave pattern peaks & troughs in waves P, Q, R, S and T are shown in one ECG signal cycle. The existing aberrant ECG wave patterns such cardio-beat, bradycardia, tachycardia and ectopic beats is required in order to discover and diagnose the problem. However, the EKG bio-signal is recorded as a non-stationary analogue signal and external noise can easily be disrupted. Some of them are base drift, power line interference, low frequency and excessive signal overlap. An adaptive filter strategy was developed in 2015 to the ECG noise signal 10 cancellations [13].

This technique has the disadvantage of having a low stability for the IIR filter. A method suggested removing noise from the ECG recorded signal via the gamma filtering approach. In order to tackle the issues with adaptive filters, significant properties of IIR and FIR filters have been incorporated. In general, the signal of the cardiovascular bio-signal frequency is broad, while white broadband is the noise of these signals [14].

The superpose of signal-to-noise frequency means that typical processes such as FIR low-pass filters, for instance, cannot be used to reconstruct a high-quality signal [16]. Due to the low stability of existing filter structures, the least averaged square algorithm and recursive lower than square algorithms, all different existing filtering methods such as the IIR, gamma filters and adaptive filters are used to reduce the ECG interference signal. Chetan S Patil & Shailaja Gaikwad proposed the ECG monitoring system for the testing and diagnosis of cardiac arrhythmia [17].

Triple lead sensor modules record the ECG signal. The main issues in this capture are the mistakes generated by the power line interference and the high frequency aliasing signal. So, the prediction of original ECG is absolutely required to diagnose rhythmic condition. Kumar et al. [18–20] proposed an object detection method for blind people. The discredited transform wavelet is therefore used to recover the original signal from the received ECG data, eliminating any interference signal noise with good precision [21]. The signal is analyzed by the Pan-Tomkins algorithm to detect the cardiac rhythm. The disadvantage of this strategy is lower because of the clever and discreet wavelet transformation [1]. The technique was investigated for the detection of ventricular tachycardia, ventricular fibrillation and ventricular brad cards in hospitals. For the detection of heart arrest, a fluffy architecture was presented. But, as an input to the floating system to identify heart disease signs, two parameters, for example the median period (T) and the QRS pulse width are used. Naser Safavian et al. strengthened the TSK fuzzy cardiac rhythm system [2].

The fuzzy systems are educated according to the R-to-R peak to QRS composite amplitude input interval data. The membership triangle function is used to convert the narrow input points to the fuse input points. Optimization rules and membership functions are used to detect various cardiac arrhythmias [3]. Fuzzy's downside is that the detection of abnormalities was not originally characterized by ECG input data from the temporal domain. Built in 2015 for sudden heart attack a computer based on a timeline analysis of the machine learning system based on cardiac variability data. Standard and cardiac ECG samples are taken from the MIT-BIH database and the machine uses the closest neighbor and flouted classification methods to train on diverse cardiac rhythms [4]. The drawbacks of this approach include a minimum number of samples in order to evaluate cardiac arrhythmias, significant computer complexity and an inefficient noise deletion [8]. An ECG was used to detect various cardiac rhythms in a collective information manner. Various ECG cardiac samples from the medical MIT-BIH 12 database are studied in these works and cardiac arrest detection strategies such as multi-collector sensor training in back propagation, supporting vector machines, and the neural function network radial basis are assessed. These categorization approaches combine and compare performance in single and complete groups. All these algorithms in the categorization are combined to one model and heart rhythms are analyzed. Elias Ebrahim Zadeh et al. (2014), with non-linear analysis of neural network technology time and frequency, established a new approach for detecting sudden heart arrest from a heart rate variability data. The system was trained on the basis of the Multilayer and K Neural Network (MLP) to forecast Sudden Cardiac Arrest (SCA) [5].

There is a high possibility that many people will develop cardiac arrhythmia, which is a potentially deadly heart condition that alters the heartbeat. Present diagnostic techniques for diagnosing arrhythmias tend to be only partially effective due to limitations in their application, which can be based on both time and space. With the help of wireless sensor network technology, this study has developed an arrhythmia real-time continuous detection system [7]. The ambulatory wireless ECG sensor can provide long-term real-time surveillance due to its low resource and power consumption [8]. Small and easy to use, the AWES allows patients to continue about their daily routines without interruption (indoors or outdoors). The RECAD platform has four subsystems: the AWES, the local access server, the remote access server, and the remote surveillance server, among others. Each subsystem can be programmed to operate in a variety of modes depending on the circumstances. Real-time ECG analysis can be ensured through the use of lossless signal compression and an application layer protocol specialized for ECG analysis in real time [9].

This approach uses the adaptive IIR filter to remove noise interference, albeit its stability is weak. Therefore, the lack of uniqueness of the ECG input signal is a highly critical issue in medical research. It has been conducted cardiovascular variability measures and Lab VIEW arrhythmia (2015). The ECG parameters are received in real time for pre-processing amplification function. The DAQ board then filters and provides a data acquisition board, which plays a communication role between the analogue frontend and the computer [6]. This digitized input is checked in Lab VIEW technology on the basis of the set user threshold value of the standard or anomalous QRS amplifier level. Calls are a high time consumption, a high system complexity and equipment that is not user friendly. Strom consumption is important for computer use, and irregularity identification is wrong [7].

3 Methodology for Cardiac Surveillance

Costly clinical care and constant monitoring are continuously required in many cardiac patients. The quality of patient treatment is improved through real-time monitoring technology. Even modest alterations can be immediately identified and handled in the vital signs of the patient. For cardiac patients and seniors, patient vigilance is very important. Deaths of cardiovascular diseases have been mostly caused in the last two decades by advancements in emergency treatment and heart surgery. As a result, myocardial infarction and fibrillation have been increasing in patients. However, these individuals require continuous monitoring to begin therapy during the crucial time. Cardiac rhythm is a common cardiac beat condition that unexpectedly ceases heart action, leading to unpredictable heart attack. The main reason for cardiac arrest is hard or irregular ventricular fibrillation. A thorough discussion of analogue and digital circuit output. Figure 2 illustrates the operating flow schedule of the proposed cardiac surveillance system. The patient's ECG signal is enhanced and translated into the digital signal using the integrated circuit ADS1298. The digital signal is supplied as an entry of the Kalman filter in the SOC-based FPGA Module. The Kalman filter is utilised for removing the noise signal and foreseeing the future ECG signal. The heart symptoms of this Kalman filtered output signal are determined with an FFT technique. Warning notes are given to numerous recipients in case of heart issues.

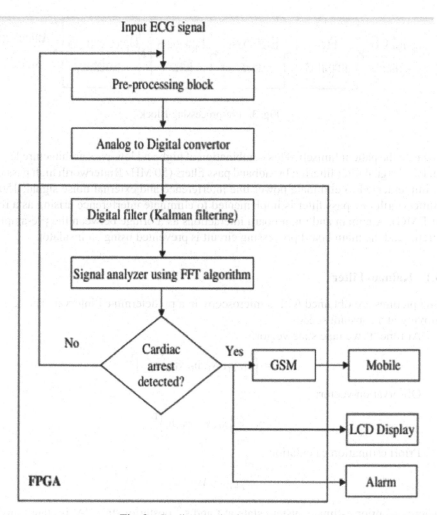

Fig. 2. Cardiac monitoring system

A ECG sensor module provides the patient with an analogue real-time ECG signal. A RA (right arm), LA (left arm) and LL (left leg) in the patient's body are supplied to an ECG signal, which is transferred to a pre-processing block. Shows the pre-processing block schematic for the cardiac monitoring system. Because this block is the initial stage in the system, it is separated from the main panel which is stored near the patient to prevent attenuation of the signal and to prevent noise depression. Moreover, a coaxial cable connects the pre-processing block with the central board. This analogue circuit receipts and preamplifiers the ECG input signal depicted in Fig. 3.

Figure 3 depicts the block utilized to pre-treat the weak ECG signal. This block has a high input impedance, a high gain, low noise and a high common reflectivity mode. This ensures that an amplifier satisfies the high degree of low signal amplification. The active filter after the preamplifier is used to control different noises because of conditions or

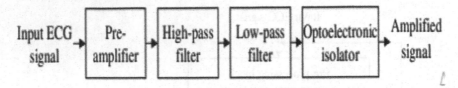

Fig. 3. Pre-processing Block

because the patient himself. This combination of high and low-pass architecture leads to an EGG signal filter filtering broadband pass filters (50 MHz Butterworth high pass filter is implemented to eliminate power line interference and external noise signal; 150 Hz Butterworth low pass filter is implemented to eliminate interference arising as a result of EMG). A human and main board interactions as a bridge between the pre-amplifier circuit and the main board processing circuit is prevented using an insulator.

3.1 Kalman Filter

The pictures are obtained with a microscopy in a predetermined interval. The cells are moving at a constant speed.

At time 't' we take state vector:

$$s_t = \left[x_t, y_t, w_t, h_t, v_{t,x}, v_{t,y} \right]^T \tag{1}$$

Observation vector:

$$o_t = \left[x_t, y_t, w_t, h_t \right]^T \tag{2}$$

Priori estimation calculation

$$s_{\tilde{i}+1} = As_{\hat{i}} + w \tag{3}$$

where 's_t' prior estimate system state at t and $s_t^\wedge$ posterior state, 'A' is state transistor matrix, 'W' is process noise.

3.2 Kalman Gain

$$K_{t+1} = p_{\tilde{i}+1} H^T \left(H p_{\tilde{i}+1} H^T + R \right)^{-1} \tag{4}$$

Here 'H' is observation matrix, 'R' is measurement noise covariance

Posteriori estimation:

$$S_{\hat{i}+1} = s_{\tilde{i}+1} + k_{t+1}(o_{t+1} - Hs_{\tilde{i}+1}) \tag{5}$$

where 'O_{t+1}' is observed at 't + 1' and 'V' is measurement noise

4 Results: Implementation Results of Kalman Filter

Signals such as square waves, sinusoidal waves, pulses and cardiac ECG signals serve as standard testing inputs. Table 1 shows the output frequencies and the efficiency of different input frequencies. In Table 1 shown a ratio of ECG output and ECE input is used to compute the profit. The pretreatment block has an increase of around 41 dB. The cardiac patient surveillance system will bring a new technique to future ECG signal prediction and FFT heart arrest detection 24 h ahead, enable doctoral analysis and treatment to be performed in a critical period to save the lives of patients in the cardiac system. This technique incorporates both analogue and digital circuitry. SOC offers FPGA with the platform stage in both hardware and software architecture. In order to comprehend the features of the cardiovascular system and its architecture such as the pre-processed block, Kalman digital filter, signal analyses and SMS warnings are described in detail. SOC system utilized for sophisticated and easily performed hardware operations. Furthermore, the hardware and the system simultaneous process allow a wide range of applications for further biological signals and tests. In medical research, the Kalman filter is crucial to evaluate cardiac arrest for future ECG samples and Fast Fourier transformation (FFT). The primary feature for the examination of the FFT signals is to calculate the FFT frequency spectrum. In order to boost the speed and performance of simple FFT computations, the advanced booth FFT algorithm is further described based on the compressor.

Table 1. Pre-processing block implementation result

Types of signals	Gain (dB)	Output Signal (mV)	Input Signal (mV)	Frequency (Hz)
Pulse	52.31	32.45	0.5	40
Sine Wave	52.46	36.16	0.3	50
Square Wave	52.12	29.56	0.8	30
ECG 1	54.23	31.44	4.5	0.5
ECG 2	52.12	33.82	4.6	5
ECG 3	53.80	35.56	5.2	8
ECG 4	51.24	32.45	4.2	6
ECG 5	52.19	30.48	5.6	10

The modified Kalman filter will be used to forecast the forthcoming ECG signal and to assess the credibility of the Kalman output. The medium error in the Kalman output is also measured. 10 standard patients and 10 cardiac patients receive the input signal for the planned future ECG signal. A description of Kalman's Digital Filter Results of Normal Patients and Heart Patients is presented in Fig. 4 which evaluated the hardware description and the accompanying simulation results of Verilog.

The Kalman filter will anticipate the forthcoming ECG signal 24 h a day in the early stage, depending on weight and signal growth. The system template 1 and 2, and

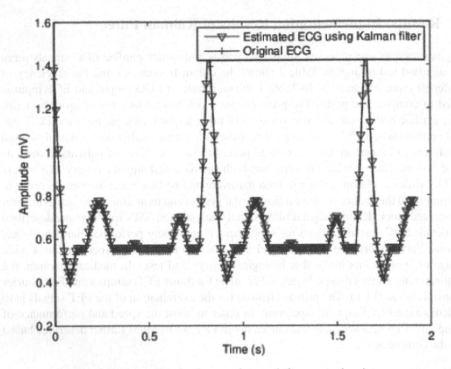

Fig. 4. Kalman filter implementation result for a normal patient.

the sample based on Eq. 3, have been derived. Equation 4 from equation error shall be used to compute the co-variance. The prediction model determines the Kalman gain and estimates the ECG sample with Eq. 5. The error covariance is updated and the orthogonal rule of Eq. 3 shall be applied to determine MSE. The filter increases the Kalman gain when the maximum MSE has been achieved and estimates the true sample to control the Kalman filter MSE. This process repeats until MSE has made a minimum error. Figure 4 shows the initial EKG input signal by the plus symbol and the symbol of the reverse triangle is shown 24 h beforehand. In the initial stages of the prediction and estimation of the future 24 h ECG signal the Kalman filter constantly receives the ECG samples on the basis of the Kalman algorithm. The recuperated signal is checked using the original ECG signal to detect the mean square error zero.

5   Conclusion

The research has developed an integrated System-on-Chip (SOC) cardiovascular surveillance system. The ECG Vital Signals are collected by the ECG sensors and amplified by a preprocessing device and translated as an input for SOC-based FPGA processor into digital equivalent. This suggests an improved Kalman filter to anticipate future ECG data, from the recorded ECG signal in real time and the Plain FFT algorithm to analyze signal is utilized in the cardiac arrest detection in a gold hour. A compressor-based Advanced Booth FFT algorithm and a compressor-based Vedic FFT algorithm are developed and implemented to further improve FFT computing speed and performance of FFT signal processing. The key advantage of this research is that before cardiac arrest is recognized using the suggested modified Kalman filter and FFT signal analysis technique, enabling treatment in the critical time to save life of the patient and therefore improve hospital healthcare.

References

1. Peters, A.E., Keeley, E.C.: Trends and predictors of participation in cardiac rehabilitation following acute myocardial infarction: data from the behavioral risk factor surveillance system. J. Am. Heart Assoc. **7**(1), e007664 (2017)
2. Palanivel Rajan, S., Sukanesh, R.: Experimental studies on intelligent, wearable and automated wireless mobile tele-alert system for continuous cardiac surveillance. J. Appl. Res. Technol. **11**(1), 133–143 (2013)
3. Brovko, O., Wiberg, D.M., Arena, L., Bellville, J.W.: The extended Kalman filter as a pulmonary blood flow estimator. Automatica **17**(1), 213–220 (1981)
4. Li, Q., Mark, R.G., Clifford, G.D.: Robust heart rate estimation from multiple asynchronous noisy sources using signal quality indices and a Kalman filter. Physiol. Measur. **29**(1), 15 (2007)
5. Zhang, Q., et al.: Cuff-less blood pressure measurement using pulse arrival time and a Kalman filter. J. Micromech. Microeng. **27**(2), 024002 (2017)
6. Singh, M.K., Singh, A.K., Singh, N.: Multimedia analysis for disguised voice and classification efficiency. Multimedia Tools and Applications **78**(20), 29395–29411 (2018). https://doi.org/10.1007/s11042-018-6718-6
7. Shamsollahi, M.B.: ECG denoising and compression using a modified extended Kalman filter structure. IEEE Trans. Biomed. Eng. **55**(9), 2240–2248 (2008)
8. Singh, M. K., Singh, N., Singh, A. K. (2019, March). speaker's voice characteristics and similarity measurement using Euclidean distances. In 2019 International Conference on Signal Processing and Communication (ICSC), pp. 317–322. IEEE, New York (2019)
9. Punyavathi, G., Neeladri, M., Singh, M. K.: Vehicle tracking and detection techniques using IoT. In: Materials Today: Proceedings (2021)
10. Veerendra, G., Swaroop, R., Dattu, D. S., Jyothi, C. A., Singh, M. K.: Detecting plant Diseases, quantifying and classifying digital image processing techniques. In: Materials Today: Proceedings (2021)
11. Padma, U., Jagadish, S., Singh, M. K.: Recognition of plant's leaf infection by image processing approach. Materials Today: Proceedings (2021)
12. Satya, P.M., Jagadish, S., Satyanarayana, V., Singh, M.K.: Stripe noise removal from remote sensing images. In: 2021 6th International Conference on Signal Processing. Computing and Control (ISPCC), pp. 233–236. IEEE, New York (2021)
13. Nandini, A., Kumar, R.A., Singh, M.K.: Circuits based on the memristor for fundamental operations. In: 2021 6th International Conference on Signal Processing. Computing and Control (ISPCC), pp. 251–255. IEEE, New York (2021)
14. Singh, M.K., Singh, A.K., Singh, N.: Disguised voice with fast and slow speech and its acoustic analysis. Int. J. Pure Appl. Math **11**(14), 241–246 (2018)
15. Sasilatha, T.: Investigations on cardiac monitoring system using modified Kalman filter. (2017)
16. Liu, Y., Wang, L., Qiu, Z., Chen, X.: A dynamic force reconstruction method based on modified Kalman filter using acceleration responses under multi-source uncertain samples. Mech. Syst. Sig. Process. **159**, 107761 (2021)

17. Singh, M.K., Singh, A.K., Singh, N.: Multimedia utilization of non-computerized disguised voice and acoustic similarity measurement. Multimedia Tools and Applications **79**(47–48), 35537–35552 (2019). https://doi.org/10.1007/s11042-019-08329-y
18. Kumar, A.: Design of secure image fusion technique using cloud for privacy-preserving and copyright protection. Int. J. Cloud Appl. Comput. **9**(3), 22–36 (2019)
19. Kumar, A., Zhang, Z.J., Lyu, H.: Object detection in real time based on improved single shot multi-box detector algorithm. EURASIP J. Wirel. Commun. Netw. **2020**(1), 1–18 (2020). https://doi.org/10.1186/s13638-020-01826-x
20. Kumar, A.: A review on implementation of digital image watermarking techniques using LSB and DWT. In: The Third International Conference on Information and Communication Technology for Sustainable Development (ICT4SD 2018), held during August 30–31, 2018 at Hotel Vivanta by Taj, Goa, India
21. Sostric, D., Mester, G., Dorner, S.: ECG simulation and integration of Kalman filter in cardio pediatric cases. Interdiscip. Descrip. Complex Syst. **17**(3-B), 615–628 (2019)

An Extensive Study on Parkinson's Disease Using Different Approaches of Supervised Learning Algorithms

V. Navya Sree$^{(\boxtimes)}$ and S. Srinivasa Rao

Department of Computer Science and Engineering, Koneru Lakshmaiah Education Foundation, Vaddeswaram, AP, India
navya.sree@gmail.com, srinu1479cse@kluniversity.in

Abstract. A medication called "Dopamine" is in charge of controlling human mobility. In this absence, information may not be sent to brain cells, resulting in brain cell injury. Lack of sleep is a significant symptom of "Parkinson's Disease." The impact of this disease on the nervous system grows in tandem with people's increasingly stressful lives. This is especially true in locations where health care falls short of the bare minimum. As a result, a healthcare system is required to identify the signs of this disease at an early stage to improve human life. This research has investigated many systems built to identify Parkinson's illness using various prominent ML and DL algorithms to save human lives. Although the majority of the systems have improved their accuracy, this paper still finds a few flaws. This survey will aid future studies in identifying the most critical characteristics and mechanisms for classifying the condition.

Keywords: Parkinson's disease · Feature Extraction · Health Care · Voice Analysis · Classification · Evaluation Metrics

1 Introduction

It is a little depressing to learn that the survey conducted by medical groups will touch roughly 10 million people worldwide by 2020. The majority of those present are either middle-aged or elderly. Stress causes neurons to stop producing dopamine, which causes brain cells to die and the nervous system to deteriorate. The loss of one's voice is a prominent symptom of this disease. The total categorization of machine learning algorithms is shown in Fig. 1.

If a model performs better compared to a previous experience with a comparable situation, it is considered learning. It is termed supervised learning when a machine learns with some help from the data, such as labels or tags. In this case, the model must precisely specify the facts or forecast the outcomes. The system may learn from the data and apply its understanding to fresh information with the help of the labels. Classification [16] uses an algorithm to categorize test findings properly. It detects specific elements in the collection and attempts to conclude their identity or characterization. This can be

A. Kumar et al. (Eds.): ICAIDS 2021, CCIS 1673, pp. 123–134, 2022.
https://doi.org/10.1007/978-3-031-21385-4_11

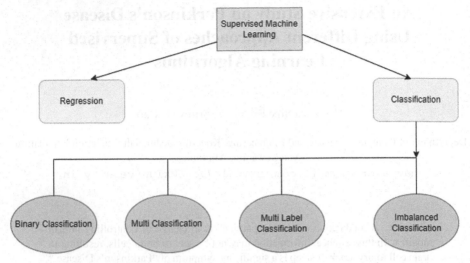

Fig. 1. Classification of Supervised Machine Learning Algorithms

done on both labeled and unlabeled data [17] because the procedure is usually used to find data points that belong to the same category. The classes have been predefined in the system, and their goal is to classify newly entered data into the appropriate target category. As a result, it must be specified and distinguished from its class whenever new data is introduced to the model.

System cannot presume that the data is accurate. Similarly, a system that categorizes input data into two groups is said to be binary categorized. As the name implies, the data is classed as yes or no, correct or erroneous, and so on. This form of categorization can be used in various real-time applications, such as determining whether a patient is sick or not, whether a message is spam or not, and so on. This topic explains the fundamentals of data classification. There is no constraint that data for a category must be limited to only two classes; there may be many attributes with various qualities. Then there is the issue of differentiating. Multiclass classification solves these issues and accurately categorizes data regardless of the number of classes. As previously said, the labeled data [19] is usually fed, and the classes are predefined. Nonetheless, using the technique of choice, the built model must precisely classify the new data into the appropriate class.

System may encounter situations where a specific type of data can be classified into two or more categories and is difficult to categorize. This form of data could be multi-labeled [18], as it is derived from textual data classification. The goal of this technique is to predict hidden qualities and link them to the defined classes. The primary difference between the multiclass and multi-label classification algorithms is that multiclass confines data to a single class. In contrast, multi-label encompasses information that falls into multiple categories due to comparable qualities. This technique can be seen in movie genres and news articles. Model training is an essential step in making the produced system exact. When a model is trained incorrectly, it has difficulty categorizing specific data points [20] due to the system's lack of expertise with them. An imbalanced categorized model is one example of this type of model. This issue causes a slew of errors since the system generates misleading reports and, in the worst-case scenario, results in a biased system. This is commonly found in fraud detection, spam filtering, and other similar applications.

2 Literature Survey

In [1] Zehra et al. devised a medical interpretation for Parkinson's disease, a dangerous disease that damages a person's brain cells that control communication motions. The cells that produce dopamine, a chemical that aids in brain cell communication, are damaged by this condition. The main goal of this study work is to detect this condition at an early stage so that appropriate safeguards can be taken before it worsens. Based on the voice signals of healthy persons and PD patients as a comparison study, the created system consists of a property extraction mechanism and a classifying module. Develop a system using a recursive approach; the developed feature selection phase consisted of various modules that focused on extracting the key attributes and deleting extraneous features. The scientists claim that using coordination and dependency trees (RTs), ANN, and SVM distribution mechanisms, they reached 93.84% accuracy in predicting PD patients compared to traditional technologies.

In [2] Wu Wang et al. focused on accurately detecting PD at an early stage, which is critical for slowing its progression and providing patients with the option of receiving treatment. The initial motor stage in Parkinson's disease should be closely monitored to a certain extent. A ground-breaking DL technique has been created to determine whether a person has PD or is not reliant on pre-motor functions. Various signs were studied in this study to detect Parkinson's disease in its early stages, including Accelerated Eye Mobility and sensory loss, Cerebrospinal fluid statistics, and dopaminergic imaging indicators. Due to the limited amount of data available, the proposed intense learning model was compared with twelve machine intelligence and ensemble learning methodologies. To detect PDs, a boosting mechanism for detecting attributes was also employed. The data was gathered from healthy people and people in the early stages of Parkinson's disease to construct a more accurate model with a 96.45% accuracy rate.

In [3] Sajal et al. explained, a patient with PD does not have to have similar symptoms, and diagnosing them at a specific stage is difficult. In this study, the developers worked on rest tremors and vocal signals acquired by mobile phones equipped with the essential sensors for voice recording. The data of the sick people are collected first, and then the healthy people construct a practical machine learning framework to achieve better results. After that, newly diagnosed PD patients were gathered, and the requisite training algorithms were chosen. Based on the models' majority vote, people with Parkinson's disease are directed to an appropriate neurologist for assessment. The application may enhance the framework by learning the most recent data after receiving comments from patients following a neurologist evaluation. Furthermore, the system constantly requires newly discovered patients to supply new data to track their illness' progression. The proposed method outperformed the competition by achieving the most fantastic accuracy of 99.8%.

In [4] Magesh et al. explained a detailed study on Parkinson's disease, its horrors, and how it affects those who suffer from it. They also noted that this condition could be more critical in degenerative brain disorders after Alzheimer's. In addition to regular research on the subject, the studies were carried out on images of relevant scans of PD sufferers and healthy people. Deeper frameworks for the experimental picture data and its features have been proposed by the researchers here. They have embraced another methodology known as the LIME algorithm and the chosen system, visually depicting the respective qualities. The researchers find that their constructed framework has produced significant results in various performance measurements carried out over the obtained data, with 95.2% accuracy, 97.5% sensitivity, and 90.0% specificity. The researchers mentioned that they employed the LIME algorithm to accurately identify between photos of patients with PD and those without PD to make this model more dominant in performance.

In [5] Maarten et al., focused not just on Parkinson's disease but also on PSP, a severe neurological degenerative condition. The researchers have emphasized the significance of such issues due to their negative consequences and limited acknowledgement and awareness. The data were acquired from patients with PSP, PD, and other healthy people using an innovative wearable sensor that captured the information while they performed subjective mobility activities. As previously indicated, this sensor stores its data in the form of an array, which will be fed into the constructed ML machine. The experiment was carried out by creating the LR and RF machine learning frameworks. The application decides the array's sophistication; for testing purposes, a high specificity is necessary, meaning that a larger collection is preferable; nevertheless, for disease surveillance, a finer granularity may suffice. The proposed framework demonstrated a sensitivity of 86% and a specificity of 90% for PSP from PD, and 90% and 97% sensitivity and specificity for PSP from HC, respectively.

In [6] Y. Oliver et al., described the difficulty of guiding patients with PD by directly sending them to the appropriate physician, such as incorrect clinical visits. As a result, the researchers devised a model that could create the required data through various activities led by doctors and utilizing the built-in sensors of mobile phones. The information was gathered when patients with Parkinson's disease and other healthy people completed mobility tasks directed by their doctors. In exchange, the mobile phones collect these characteristics and prepare to test the suggested machine learning architecture. The researchers created this system in two steps: a two-step properties selection stage and a genetic approach based on popular algorithms that combine two separate penalty calculation algorithms, respectively. To use data, the constructed model was able to identify between the sick and the healthy and explain their severity. Compared to the 97.3% accuracy of research as a base, the constructed framework has a lower accuracy of 96%.

In [7] Aich et al., revealed why people with Parkinson's disease have different mobility functions due to the action of dopamine hormone in the brain. Finally, getting precise information based on fluctuation qualities using self-reported data from patients with PD is difficult. As a result, concerning some wearable devices, it is critical to building an actual mechanism that can detect the level of diagnosis, which can be referred to as an "On/ Off" stage. The researchers also warned that data acquired from the home environment would be inaccurate and of limited utility. Wearable devices have been built as a result of technological breakthroughs so that the data collected from them can be directly fed into the developed ML framework and analyzed. The created framework incorporates several machine learning methods, including RF, SVM, KNN, and NB, to develop statistical features from data supplied by wearable devices. With RF algorithms, the system performed better, reaching 96.72% perfection, 97.35% recall, and 96.92% precision.

In [8] Ana et al., described the severity of Parkinson's disease and the difficulties in dealing with those who suffer from it. They claimed that PD symptoms manifest themselves in a person's mobile actions, beginning with vision problems. The disease's effect on the hormone dopamine generated in the brain causes poor motor performance. The experiment's main purpose in this research is to detect the disease at an early stage when vision loss is visible. The investigation involves gathering diverse data from sensory signals associated with the early symptom. The devised technique uses a biomarker to represent data gathered from the patient's sensory organs to mark these qualities. The system may classify the data into three categories: patients with a diagnosis, PD patients with medication deficiency, and healthy people. When RF was compared to other ML techniques, including SVM, MLP, J48, NB, and genetic algorithm, it produced the best results with 99.22% accuracy. Both accuracy calculations and statistical analysis were used in the evaluations.

In [9] Raval et al., illustrated how critical it became to design a machine that could correctly identify patients with PD and other healthy participants. For advanced Parkinson's disease diagnosis, this needs the adoption of a machine teaching approach. Examining current computational intelligence methodologies in the field of study used for PD detection is a prerequisite for developing a fully reliable model. Many current models either focus on a single modality or superficially investigate numerous sensations. This study intends to create a comparative study using several criteria that affect patients with PD in the early stages, such as speech, movement acts, and so on. Many machine learning models, including LR, SVM, DT, KNN, SGD, and GNB, were utilized to convert text and speech into machine-readable information. Other advanced modules, such as RF, AB, and HV that use a combination of typical ML approaches, were also used. They claimed that RF detection of the tremor had a 99.79% accuracy rate, which is the highest.

In [10] Franz et al., focused on people with advanced Parkinson's disease who regularly experience unstable muscle movements. Consistent and reliable monitoring of these oscillations is an unmet demand. We used DL to identify movement information on a single IMU sensor normally worn at an individual's wrist in unstructured circumstances, and the data were acquired from those recordings. Subjects were observed for validation reasons by a movement abnormality specialist, and their physical status was assessed every minute. The experiment was conducted by collecting data from thousands of minutes of IMU sensor recordings from 30 people, together with detailed information on their various actions during certain motions. The researcher demonstrated a three-class balanced accuracy of 65.4% on the initially unobserved information from the participants using CNN techniques with a 1-min window as input. This translates to ratio of sensitivity/ specificity of 0.64/0.89, 0.67/0.67, and 0.64/ 0.89 in detecting the stage of movement state at Off, On, and DYSKINTIC, respectively.

In [11] Haq et al., focused on Parkinson's disease, one of the most pressing challenges in medicine, according to the authors, is the accurate and timely identification of Parkinson's disease. Various solutions to this problem have been proposed in this study.

Existing methods, on the other hand, are ineffective and fail to detect PD consistently. To address the drawbacks of previous approaches, this study suggests a machine learning strategy for PD detection. As a response, the researchers devised a combinatorial design that might aid in selecting objective features for model training and development utilizing the ACO and Relief algorithms in genetic modelling. In order to achieve the best performance in differentiating, the researchers used SVM in both learning and testing the model over the selected criteria. In addition, a higher level of validation technique is used to test the complete dataset with a limited range of testing sets to improve the built system's performance. The researchers claim that their experiment was conducted on a real-time dataset and that they could attain 99.50% accuracy by outperforming traditional algorithms.

In [12] E.Balaji et al., found that when neurologists evaluate PD and grade the severity rating using the UPDRS, they take into account a variety of clinical presentations of the patient. This form of evaluation is arbitrary and ineffective because it is primarily reliant on the doctors' ability. As a result, this study proposes a gait categorization system based on machine learning that can assist doctors in identifying the stages of Parkinson's disease. The gait sequence is an essential indicator for determining whether a person is healthy or has Parkinson's disease. As a result, we obtain the fundamental feature map using the VGRF gait dataset and statistical approaches. The SW test is then performed to confirm the data's standard dispersion, and the prominent indicators are chosen using a similarity characteristic selection approach based on geographic and statistical characteristics of gait behaviour. For statistical analysis that predicts the severity of PD, four machine learning algorithms, DT, SVM, EC, and BC, were developed. The researchers claim that their suggested method accurately rates PD severity using the H&Y scale with 99.4% accuracy using DT and SVM.

In [13] Chakraborty, described that Parkinson's disease is caused by the slow loss of dopamine-producing neurons in the brain. According to the author, with the rapid expansion in the world's elderly population, this disease will be observed in large numbers, posing a significant financial burden on the government. Because no therapy for this illness has yet been discovered, it is recommended to identify the disease at an early stage. The study gathered 906 medical scanned copies from people with Parkinson's disease, non-PD patients, and disciplined patients. The researchers used the property's extraction techniques to create 107 variation traits for each copy. The proposed model is based on a two-level properties identification framework that performs computation based on a coordinated analysis and a heuristic properties eradication approach that eliminates all extraneous features and selects the top 20 most important ones. ML approaches (ANN (MLP), XG boost, RF, and SVM) were also applied to this data and a contrast study to determine the best performing algorithm. Finally, with 95.3% accuracy, ANN's MLP beat all others.

In [14] M.Marimuthu et al., stated that PD has recently become one of the most common persistent global geriatric illnesses. Motor-related aspects identify the condition, which is caused by the absence of dopamine production by neurons. However, other non-motor related early indicators occur far sooner than may be recognized and predict the various stages of sickness. Early disease detection can help us stop the disease from advancing; people will be easier to deal with. The study even says that traditional strategies used to solve this problem could not reliably forecast the likelihood of developing PD at an earlier stage, but that advances in technology and the use of machine learning techniques could. This study aims to identify PD early on by gathering data and using XGB, DT, LR, and SVM classifiers in a classification technique. The results showed that XGB had the highest level of correctness, with a score of 94.87%.

In [15] Moon et al., explained that both PD and ET illnesses have comparable symptoms, and both diseases are linked to motor dysfunctionality. Due to these qualities, it may be difficult to distinguish between the disease and the symptoms, which may lead to erroneous judgement. Using a wearable sensor that gathers mobility data, this study tries to distinguish between PD and ET diseases. An experiment was conducted using supervised activities, and calculations were made based on the data collected on balance and gait limitations. ML techniques such as NN, SVM, KNN, DT, RF, and gradient boosting were used, and the results were compared to the same LR result with F1 scores. The NN architecture gets a higher score of 61% than the other approaches. Finally, the study shows how machine intelligence approaches may be used to classify various motion illnesses based on the equilibrium and stride aspects of intelligent technologies. Additional research using a well-balanced set of data is required for the therapeutic use of machine learning algorithms to find PD and ET.

2.1 Observations

The proposed paper has illustrated the mechanisms, their merits and demerits in Table 1.

Table 1. Comparative Study on the Developed Models

S.No	Author Name	Algorithms worked	Advantages	Disadvantages / Future Works.	Accuracy Obtained
1	Zehra	RT, ANN, SVM, FS – CART	Derived higher performance	In a larger study, DL techniques must be preferred	93.84%
2	Wu Wang	DEEP1, DEEP2, DEEP3, LOGIS, LOGIS_PEN, BOOST_GLM, RF, DIS, KNN, SVM, TREE	Greater detection capacity of the model	Cannot prove DL performed well over ML is considered data is more minor	96.45%
3	Sajal	KNN, SVM, and NB	The voting-based framework for choosing suitable algorithms was developed	Picture processing-based calculation of symptoms can be suggested for future work	99.8%

(*continued*)

Table 1. (*continued*)

S.No	Author Name	Algorithms worked	Advantages	Disadvantages / Future Works.	Accuracy Obtained
4	Magesh	SPECT, DaTSCAN and LIME	With larger real-time data early diagnosis performed	No clinical validation &testing of its performance in real-time	95.2%
5	Maarten	LR and RF	Innovative approach Adequate performance in classification	Dealing with complex data through sensors is quite difficult	90%
6	Y. Oliver	MDS- UPDRS, Binary classification	Distinguishes the diseased, and healthy with their severity	The processing time may be greater	97.3%
7	Aich	RF, SVM, KNN, and NB	Shows the level of a Medication to a PD patient	The research was developed over very little data	96.72%
8	Ana	RF, SVM, MLP, J48, NB, and genetic algorithm	Detection at early stages Showed the highest accuracy	The model might have over fitting of data	99.2%
9	Raval	LR, SVM, DT, KNN, SGD, GNB, RF, AB and HV	The comparative study acts as a guide for future experimentation	Bagging, Boosting, Voting, and the dataset size is less	99.79%
10	Franz	CNN	Have shown a 3 class balanced accuracy on the information	Advanced DL techniques might show greater accuracy	65.4%
11	Haq	ACO, Relief, and SVM K-cross validation	They are focused more on testing to achieve the perfection of the model	Other disease identification and their recovery purposes not addressed	99.5%
12	E.Balaji	Rating by H & Y scale	Better prediction rates	Time consumption is more to predict the values	99.4%

(*continued*)

Table 1. (*continued*)

S.No	Author Name	Algorithms worked	Advantages	Disadvantages / Future Works.	Accuracy Obtained
13	Chakraborty	ANN (MLP), XG Boost, RF and SVM	To minimize the dimensional reduction issues best features were selected	DL, RL, etc., could be opted in further studies for better system	95.3%
14	M.Marimuthu	LR, SVM, DT, and XGB	The model retrieved greater overall performance	In the future, AI can also be included to attain greater systems' performance	94.87%
15	Moon	NN, SVM, KNN, DT, RF, GB and LR	The model could clearly distinguish between PD and ET diseases	In further, a model based on relationships among data can be developed	62%

Figure 2 shows that most of the systems attained 99% accuracy, yet most of the systems still had flaws.

3   Research Gaps Identified

This article has outlined a few flaws that can be solved in a future study in order to produce a good and accurate system by filling in the gaps: a. although many attributes exist for prediction purposes, incorporating them into the system will be complicated and time-consuming. As a result of further research, the system may be able to build an efficient approach to eliminate the associated features and have a significant impact on the prediction process. b. To assist with the complex decision-making process, the system can further identify the deep learning algorithm to create an accurate system that predicts disease in less time and prescribes medication. c. In addition, when working with customized layers, the system can hyper-tune the parameters to fit the layer values without training best and obtaining the layers to suit the application. Based on these gaps identified, the overall architecture of the system is designed as shown in Fig. 3.

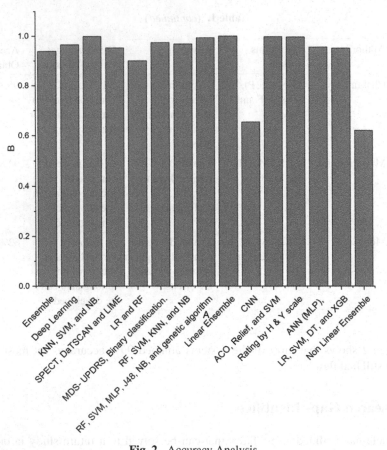

Fig. 2. Accuracy Analysis

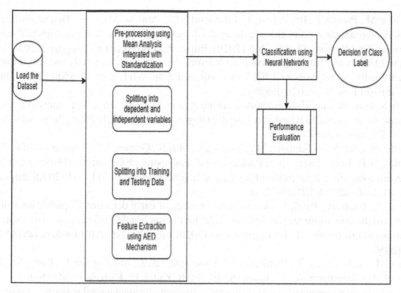

Fig. 3. Proposed architecture for identification of PD's disease

4 Conclusion

The ML techniques cannot predict the Parkinson's disease at an early stage because they are good at handling the static attributes but most of the attributes in this dataset are time series dependent, so it's better to involve deep learning techniques. The disease also consists of motor and non-motor symptoms, which need a good model with accurate and fast learning environment to classify and take decisions. A model which can detect the Parkinson's disease at an early stage with variable learning capability can help the old people because the symptoms of this disease vary from person to person. The model should also be able to find the both linear and non-linear relations between features and should hold back only the important symptoms that can easily predict the disease based on the homogeneity of the node.

References

1. Karapinar Senturk, Z.: Early diagnosis of Parkinson's disease using machine learning algorithms. Med. Hypotheses **138**, 109603 (2020). https://doi.org/10.1016/j.mehy.2020.109603
2. Wang, W., Lee, J., Harrou, F., Sun, Y.: Early detection of Parkinson's disease using deep learning and machine learning. IEEE Access **8**, 147635–147646 (2020). https://doi.org/10.1109/access.2020.3016062
3. Sajal, M.S.R., Ehsan, M.T., Vaidyanathan, R., Wang, S., Aziz, T., Mamun, K.A.A.: Telemonitoring Parkinson's disease using machine learning by combining tremor and voice analysis. Brain Informatics **7**(1), 1–11 (2020). https://doi.org/10.1186/s40708-020-00113-1
4. Magesh, P.R., Myloth, R.D., Tom, R.J.: An explainable machine learning model for early detection of Parkinson's disease using LIME on DaTSCAN imagery. Comput. Biol. Med. **126**, 104041 (2020). https://doi.org/10.1016/j.compbiomed.2020.104041

5. De Vos, M., Prince, J., Buchanan, T., FitzGerald, J.J., Antoniades, C.A.: Discriminating progressive supranuclear palsy from Parkinson's disease using wearable technology and machine learning. Gait Posture **77**, 257–263 (2020). https://doi.org/10.1016/j.gaitpost.2020.02.007

6. Chen, O.Y., et al.: Building a machine-learning framework to remotely assess parkinson's disease using smartphones. IEEE Trans. Biomed. Eng. **67**(12), 3491–3500 (2020). https://doi.org/10.1109/tbme.2020.2988942

7. Aich, S., et al.: A supervised machine learning approach to detect the on/off state in Parkinson's disease using wearable based gait signals. Diagnostics **10**(6), 421 (2020). https://doi.org/10.3390/diagnostics10060421

8. de Oliveira, A.P.S., de Santana, M.A., Andrade, M.K.S., Gomes, J.C., Rodrigues, M.C.A., dos Santos, W.P.: Early diagnosis of Parkinson's disease using EEG, machine learning and partial directed coherence. Research on Biomedical Engineering **36**(3), 311–331 (2020). https://doi.org/10.1007/s42600-020-00072-w

9. Raval, S., Balar, R., Patel, V.: A comparative study of early detection of parkinson's disease using machine learning techniques. In: 2020 4th International Conference on Trends in Electronics and Informatics (ICOEI), pp. 48184 (2020). https://doi.org/10.1109/icoei48184.2020.9142956

10. Pfister, F. M. J., Um, T. T., Pichler, D. C., Goschenhofer, J., Abedinpour, K., Lang, M., Endo, S., Ceballos-Baumann, A. O., Hirche, S., Bischl, B., Kulić, D., Fietzek, U. M.: High-resolution motor state detection in Parkinson's disease using convolutional neural networks. Scient. Rep. **10**, 1 (2020). https://doi.org/10.1038/s41598-020-61789-3

11. Ul Haq, A., Li, J., Memon, M.H., khan, J., Ali, Z., Abbas, S. Z., & Nazir, S.: Recognition of Parkinson's disease using a hybrid feature selection approach. Journal of Intelligent & Fuzzy Systems **39**(1), 1319–1339 (2020). https://doi.org/10.3233/JIFS-200075

12. Balaji, E., Brindha, D., Balakrishnan, R: Supervised machine learning-based gait classification system for early detection and stage classification of Parkinson's disease. Appl. Soft Comput. **94**, 106494 (2020). https://doi.org/10.1016/j.asoc.2020.106494

13. Chakraborty, S., Aich, S., Kim, H.-C.: 3D Textural, morphological and statistical analysis of voxel of interests in 3T MRI scans for the detection of Parkinson's disease using artificial neural networks. Healthcare **8**(1), 34 (2020). https://doi.org/10.3390/healthcare8010034

14. Marimuthu M., Vidhya G., Dhaynithi J., Mohanraj G., Basker N., Theetchenya S., Vidyabharathi D.: Detection of Parkinson's disease using machine learning approach. Ann. Rom. Soc. Cell Biol. 2544–2550 (2021). https://www.annalsofrscb.ro/index.php/journal/article/view/4792

15. Moon, S., Song, H.-J., Sharma, V. D., Lyons, K. E., Pahwa, R., Akinwuntan, A. E., Devos, H.: Classification of Parkinson's disease and essential tremor based on balance and gait characteristics from wearable motion sensors via machine learning techniques: a data-driven approach. J. NeuroEng. Rehab. **17**, 1 (2020) https://doi.org/10.1186/s12984-020-00756-5

16. Mittal, V., Sharma, R.K.: Machine learning approach for classification of Parkinson disease using acoustic features. Journal of Reliable Intelligent Environments **7**(3), 233–239 (2021). https://doi.org/10.1007/s40860-021-00141-6

17. Nahar, N., Ara, F., Neloy, M.A.I., Biswas, A., Hossain, M.S., Andersson, K.: Feature selection based machine learning to improve prediction of Parkinson disease. In: Mahmud, M., Kaiser, M.S., Vassanelli, S., Dai, Q., Zhong, N. (eds.) BI 2021. LNCS (LNAI), vol. 12960, pp. 496–508. Springer, Cham (2021). https://doi.org/10.1007/978-3-030-86993-9_44

18. Nagasubramanian, G., Sankayya, M.: Multi-Variate vocal data analysis for Detection of Parkinson disease using Deep Learning. Neural Comput. Appl. **33**(10), 4849–4864 (2020). https://doi.org/10.1007/s00521-020-05233-7

19. A. Parziale, R. Senatore, A. Della Cioppa, A. Marcelli: Cartesian genetic programming for diagnosis of Parkinson disease through handwriting analysis: Performance vs. interpretability issues. Artif. Intell. Med. **111**, 101984 (2021). https://doi.org/10.1016/j.artmed.2020.101984

Adaptive Convolution Neural Networks for Facial Emotion Recognition

P. V. S. Lakshmi[1]([⊠]), Haritha Akkineni[1], Ande Hanika[2], and Padmaja Grandhe[3]

[1] Prasad V. Potluri, Siddhartha Institute of Technology, Vijayawada, India
[2] Cognizant Solutions, Hyderabad, India
[3] Potti Sriramulu Chalavadhi Mallikarjuna Rao College of Engineering and Technology, Vijayawada, India
padmajagrande@gmail.com

Abstract. Joy, sorrow, astonishment, worry, rage, contempt, and neutral are the seven primary emotions that may be easily classified in human facial expressions. The activation of several sets of face muscles expresses our facial emotions. These seemingly tiny yet complex signals in our expressions frequently convey a wealth of information about our mental state. A simple and low-cost approach termed face expression identification, the system can measure the effects of content and services on the audience/users. Retailers could use these indicators to gauge customer interest, for example. Using extra information regarding patients' emotional states during therapy, healthcare providers can give better service. In order to continuously deliver desired material, entertainment producers can track audience involvement during events. The proposed paper uses the AdaBoost classifier as the output layer in the neural network and trains the model to identify the different emotions from the facial expressions captured.

Keywords: AdaBoost · Neural networks · Tensor · OpenCV · Emotion classifier · HAAR

1 Introduction

Facial expressions recognition using traditional image processing approaches is complicated because real-time capturing videos are scenarios of uncontrolled conditions where kernel filters for pre-processing, HoG for feature extractions makes the system more complex in terms of cost and time. This problem can be solved with the help of an automatic process supported by tensors. Tensors are the fundamental data structures in the Tensor Flow programming language. Tensors are the connecting edges in the Data Flow Graph, a flow diagram. The term "tensor" refers to a multidimensional array or list. The three parameters that define a tensor are as shown in Table 1.

Keras is centred on the concept of a model. A Sequence, which is a linear stack of layers, is the most common sort of model. Make a series and add layers to it in the order system want the computation to be completed. Compile the model using the underlying framework to optimize the computations to be done by the proposed model once it has

A. Kumar et al. (Eds.): ICAIDS 2021, CCIS 1673, pp. 135–143, 2022.
https://doi.org/10.1007/978-3-031-21385-4_12

been defined. The system can define the loss function and optimizer in this section. The model must then be fitted to data once it has been created. Filtering can be done by shooting off the complete model training regime or one batch of data at a time. Memory is where all of the computation takes place. Once the model has been trained, the system may make predictions based on new data.

Table 1. Tensor parameter descriptor

S.No	Parameter Name	Description
1	Rank	A rank is a unit of dimensional within a tensor. It specifies how many dimensions the Tensor has. A tensor's rank can be defined as the order or number of dimensions of a tensor definable
2	Shape	The Tensor's shape is determined by the number of rows and columns combined
3	Type	The data type associated with Tensor's elements is described by type

The sigmoid function determines the activation of inputs multiplied by their weights in a neural network. Assume our neural network had two columns of input data (features) and one hidden node (neuron). Each characteristic would be multiplied by the associated weight value before being combined and processed via the sigmoid (just like logistic regression).

2 Literature Survey

[1] Zhou et al., with advancing the usage of technologies, detecting facade expressions is trending and leads a far way for development. This paper has developed an automatic face expression detection method by presenting a unique end-to-end network incorporating an attention system. The researchers have proposed this model with 4 phases to meet every detailed issue of the system. Initially, the inputted information generates the patterns, and the knowledge is observed. Then, to understand the critical knowledge and access it in depth, the exclusive attributes are processed to retrieve the best results. Later, this data is induced into an alternative method that develops precisely based on the elite attributes by generating higher results. Finally, the data is distinguished and is explained by the developed model and retrieve higher efficient results. They considered four datasets, has numerous tagged frames with seven distinguished expressions with varied age groups.

[2] X. Sun et al. Proposed research that has undergone façade look detection with NN concepts. However, they have neglected the upcoming issues regarding information transfer loss at the multiple layers of the network. This research suggested a powerful differentiation methodology with the help of converting the attribute's quantity from one stage to another for variation in the information. This model observes the properties from the induced group of pictures through ROI, which usually serves as the initial layer for the proposed systems' methodology. This model was marked over the picture frame before it was induced in the system. Practically, an attention model will be set up

initially for the developed model to forego the ROI analysis and to take out the advanced properties from the information. Later, another tool increases the dimension of the issue by extending the stages. A single-stage was used to expand the levels of this project.

[3] Agrawal, A et al. Introduced the advancing methodologies in the neural grid algorithms for face detection issues had paved the way for increasing the concerns and the solutions proposed, irrespective of the grid system. A grid system in general needs to be elementary and adequate. Many advanced grid systems from the well-known notion of CNN were already in use like a tool that identifies and investigates a particular object from the frame. The tool that explains a particular object in an image expands the horizons of an issue and reduces the complex amplitudes of the developed problems. However, these technologies have not solved the issues regarding the parameters like the window magnitude and the bunch of filters for enhancing the efficiency of the model's distribution. Considering these issues, the authors stated that their developed grid systems have greater efficiency than traditional ones.

[4] Sun, K. et al. stated about the influence and complexities of face detection and how the standard technologies have performed their methodologies by defining the developer's properties of the picture frame. On a large end, defining each frame, understanding, and implementing the pattern outline would be difficult and can neglect the feature composition of the frame leading to information catastrophe. A FERFC grid system was developed that uses the LBP method over the original frames to solve the problem. Usually, the basic steps involve data cleanse and move on to later stages here, by using LBP to extract the compositions of the images relying on the standard ones. Finally, CNN comes into the picture and is used to accomplish the outcomes. The researchers have stated that their system has generated higher efficiency over simple workout samples and is precise.

[5] Liang et al. quoted that, despite accurate facial depiction being critical for final identification efficiency, typical handmade presentations highlight superficial features. It is unclear yet if the CNN model can recover decent attributes. Furthermore, sharing ratings along an entire image is ineffective for organized facial images. In dealing with such complications, an advanced technique that primarily focuses on the area over a frame and acts along was introduced to better notice the textures of a picture frame. At first, a developer-defined GSF method with some filters is used. Furthermore, using distinctive regional spots with various lenses, the resulting feature is divided into distinguished patches that can record relatively deep characteristics. The subsequent CNN tiers are then graded basic elements to collect elevated characteristics. The authors explained that their method could be used on a single frame without the need for facial feature data.

[6] Wei, Q et al., the researcher workers, have explained the significant growth of the façade aspect recognition and how the CNN method's inclined usage involves this problem. Because the CNN inadequacy in visual perception direction introduces ambient disturbances when it receives expression profile, concluding decreased recognition efficiency. A conspicuous extracting features model, which includes the enlarged inception stage, the DOG module, and the cross-identifier protuberance prediction segment, is suggested to imitate the focus strategy in the human processing network. Later, a predominant FER technology for each human was included in the developed grid network. Using the knowledge on the previously obtained protuberance maps and several

level depth properties in CNN, the detection efficiency increased by gaining the rapidly focused and fully deep characters information.

3 Proposed Methodology

By anticipating the expressions of both still visuals and real-time video, we will overcome the shortcomings of current systems. This paper aims to build a vision-based system that can recognize facial expressions in video sequences. The reason for opting for a vision-based system is that it allows for a more straightforward and intuitive exchange of information between a human and a computer. This paper considers five basic human expressions, and the model has been trained to detect facial expressions in animated images. The architecture of the proposed system is illustrated in Fig. 1.

3.1 Image Pre-processing

Because both the input and output images are intensity images, pre-processing is a common term for processes involving images at the most basic level of abstraction. The majority of the pre-processing processes that are used are demonstrated in Fig. 2.

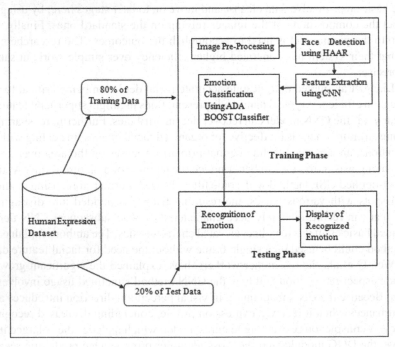

Fig. 1. Architecture of facial emotion recognition system

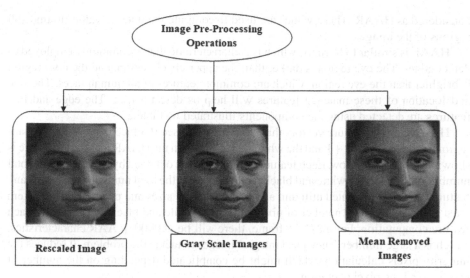

Fig. 2. Results obtained after pre-processing operations

3.2 Face Detection Using HAAR

Facial features extraction is the process of finding certain regions, points, landmarks, or curves/contours in a 2-D image or 3-D range image. The resulting registered picture produces a numerical feature vector in this feature extraction stage. The following are some of the most common traits that can be extracted are Mouth, Cheekbones, Eye-lids, Eye, a suggestion for a nose, which is illustrated in Fig. 3.

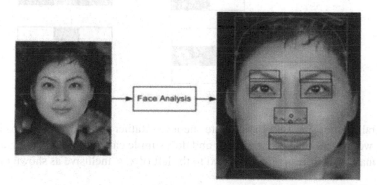

Fig. 3. Process of feature detection

HAAR is a popular algorithm to detect the faces in the images by analyzing the properties of edges and lines. The advantage of HAAR lies in its detection of pixel intensities where, there is a sudden change in the value occurs. The pixels with value 1 are treated as dark and with value 0 as light. The difference between these values is considered as HAAR. These values are used to compute the integral values to find sub regions of the image.

HAAR is similar to Kernels, which is a characteristic that is commonly employed to detect edges. The eye region is darker than the upper check region, and the nose region is brighter than the eye region, which are common features of all human faces. The size and location of these matched features will help us detect a face. The edge and line features are detected using the components illustrated in Table 2.

Here are a few Feature vectors that can be used to see if a face is present. The dark region is represented by +1 and the white region by −1 in the HAAR feature. An image is shown in a 24X24 window. Each feature is a single value obtained by subtracting the total number of pixels in the white and black rectangles from the total number of pixels. Many features are now computed utilizing all potential kernel sizes and positions. The system must calculate the total number of pixels under the white and black rectangles for each feature computation. For a 24X24 frame, there will be 160000 + AAR characteristics, which is a large number. They used integral images to tackle the problem. It reduces the integrity pixels calculation, which might be complicated depending on the number of pixels, to a four-pixel operation.

Table 2. Components of edge and line feature extractors

S.No	Feature	Component-1	Component-2
1	Edge		
2	Line		

Integral images are used to compute the area. Rather than adding all pixel values together, we will take the corner values and do a simple calculation. The integral image at x, y is made up of the pixels above and to the left of x, y, inclusive as shown in Eq. (1)

$$f(A, B) = \sum_{i=1}^{n} f(A_{new}, B_{new}) \tag{1}$$

3.3 AdaBoost Classifier

Adaboost is used to remove HAAR's superfluous feature [9, 10]. Only a few of these characteristics can be combined to build a useful classifier. The most difficult part is locating these characteristics. Both the features and the classifier are trained using an AdaBoost variation. The second characteristic is used to detect the nasal bridge, although it does not affect the upper lips, which have a continuous feature. As a result, the system may quickly get rid of it. The system can use Adaboost to figure out which 160000 + features are relevant. After all of the traits have been identified, a weighted value is assigned to each one, then utilized to decide whether or not a given window is a face. The computation of the neurons is shown in Eq. (2).

$$ADA(X) = ADA\_F1(X) + ADA\_F2(X) + DA\_FN(X) \qquad (2)$$

Weak classifiers always return a binary result, such as 0 or 1. The value will be one if the feature is present. Otherwise, it will be 0. A 25-strong classifier, 2500 classifiers are often employed to construct. Selected features are deemed acceptable if they outperform random guessing, which means they must detect more than half of the situations. The Adaboost can classify the emotions as illustrated in Fig. 4.

Fig. 4. Classification of emotions

3.4 Pseudo Code for Neural Networks

Begin
    face_model ← conv2d().
    eye_model ← face_model.output.
    eye_model ← GlobalAveragePooling2D()(eye_model).
    eye_model ← Dense(4096,activation = 'relu')(eye_model).
    eye_model ← Dense(4096,activation = 'relu')(eye_model).
    eye_model ← Dense(1024,activation = 'relu')(eye_model).
    eye_model ← Dense(num_classes,activation = 'softmax')(eye_model).
    return eye_model.
    End

4 Experimental Results

Different emotions are recognized, with their corresponding confidence levels and are illustrated in this section.

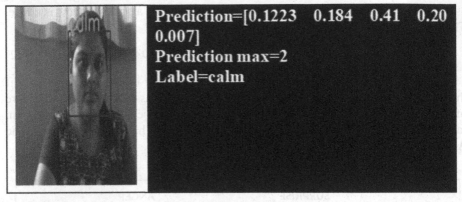

Fig. 5. Prediction of calm emotion

Figure 5 shows the prediction values for five emotions, with the highest value regarding emotion prediction. Because the forecast value for calm is the highest in this scenario, the label calm is returned.

Fig. 6. Prediction of happy emotion

Figure 6 shows the prediction values for five emotions, with the highest value regarding emotion prediction. Because the forecast value for happy is the highest in this scenario, the label happy is returned.

5 Conclusion and Future Work

When a model incorrectly predicts an emotion, the correct label is often the second most likely emotion. This research describes a robust face recognition model based on mapping behaviour and physiological biometric characteristics. The physiological qualities of the human face are linked to geometrical structures that are rebuilt as the recognition system's base matching template and are associated with varied expressions such as joy, sorrow, worry, rage, astonishment, and contempt. The behaviour part of this system, as a property foundation, relates the attitude behind diverse expressions. The property bases of algorithmic genetic genes are classified into two categories: revealed and hidden. More research might be done in matching to geometric parameters in facial expressions. In future work, a transfer learning model in which the last layers of the neural network can be customized to identify more emotions than proposed in the paper. It also helps in detecting stress identification based on facial expressions alone.

References

1. Li, J., Jin, K., Zhou, D., Kubota, N., Ju, Z.: Attention mechanism-based CNN for facial expression recognition. Neurocomputing **411**, 340–350 (2020). https://doi.org/10.1016/j.neucom.2020.06.014
2. Sun, X., Zheng, S., Fu, H.: ROI-attention vectorized CNN model for static facial expression recognition. IEEE Access **8**, 7183–7194 (2020). https://doi.org/10.1109/ACCESS.2020.2964298
3. Agrawal, A., Mittal, N.: Using CNN for facial expression recognition: a study of the effects of kernel size and number of filters on accuracy. Vis. Comput. **36**(2), 405–412 (2019). https://doi.org/10.1007/s00371-019-01630-9
4. Sun, K., et al.: The facial expression recognition method based on image fusion and CNN. Integr. Ferroelectr. **217**(1), 198–213 (2021). https://doi.org/10.1080/10584587.2021.1911313
5. Liang, X., et al.: Patch attention layer of embedding handcrafted features in CNN for facial expression recognition. Sensors **21**(3), 833 (2021). https://doi.org/10.3390/s21030833
6. Wei, Q.: Saliency maps-based convolutional neural networks for facial expression recognition. IEEE Access **9**, 76224–76234 (2021). https://doi.org/10.1109/access.2021.3082694
7. Nandi, A., Xhafa, F., Subirats, L., Fort, S.: Real-time emotion classification using EEG data stream in e-learning contexts. Sensors. **21**(5), 1589 (2021). https://doi.org/10.3390/s21051589
8. Huang, C., Trabelsi, A., Qin, X., Farruque, N., Mou, L., Zaïane, O.: Seq2Emo: A sequence to multi-label emotion classification model. In: Proceedings of the 2021 Conference of the North American Chapter of the Association for Computational Linguistics: Human Language Technologies (2021). https://doi.org/10.18653/v1/2021.naacl-main.375
9. Grandhe, P., Reddy, D. E., Vasumathi, D.: An adaptive cluster based image search and retrieve for interactive ROI to MRI image filtering, segmentation , and registration (2016).
10. Grandhe, P., Reddy, E.S., Devara, V.: Adaptive analysis and reconstruction of 3D DICOM images using enhancement based SBIR algorithm over MRI. Biomed. Res. **29**(4), 644–653 (2018)

A Gravitational Search Algorithm Study on Text Summarization Using NLP

Chatti Subbalakshmi[1]([⊠]), Piyush Kumar Pareek[2], and M. V. Narayana[1]

[1] Department of Computer Science and Engineering, Guru Nanak Institutions Technical Campus, Hyderabad, India
subbalakshmichatti@gmail.com
[2] Nitte Meenakshi Institute of Technology, Bengaluru, India
piyush.kumar@nmit.ac.in

Abstract. Over the last decade, the amount of data available on the internet has grown exponentially. As a result, there is a need for a resolution that converts this massive atomic data into valuable information that a brain could comprehend arises. Text Summarization (TS) is the procedure of generating a synopsis of a particular document that comprises only the most critical info from the novel; the objective is to obtain a concise synopsis of the important points in the document. Text summarization is one such technique that is frequently used in research to aid in the management of massive amounts of data. Automated summarization is a well-known technique for distilling the main points of a document. It works by preserving significant information in the text by creating a condensed version of it. Extractive and Abstractive methods of text summarization are available. Extractive summarization methods alleviate some of the concern of summarization by extracting a subset of relevant sentences from the original text. The objective of abstractive method of multiple records is to create condensed form of the record while retaining essential info. While there are numerous methods available, investigators studying in NLP using Gravitational Search Algorithm are predominantly focus on extractive methods. The inferences of sentences are determined in terms of linguistic and statistical characteristics. Finally, this paper compiles the new and pertinent study in the area of TS for further research and examination. It will be important because it will provide a new path for forthcoming scholars concerned in this domain.

Keywords: Abstractive · Extractive · Text summarization

1 Introduction

Due to the massive amount of data that is being generated digitally, it is critical to develop a procedure for quickly condensing lengthy texts while maintaining their main idea [1]. Summarization also assists in reduce the required reading time, expediting the information exploration, and obtaining the maximum volume of information on a single

A. Kumar et al. (Eds.): ICAIDS 2021, CCIS 1673, pp. 144–159, 2022.
https://doi.org/10.1007/978-3-031-21385-4_13

subject [2, 3]. The primary goal of automated TS is to reduce the size of reference text while retaining its knowledge and meaning. Numerous definitions of TS are available. For instance, [4] determined the report as text created from one or even more records that disseminate appropriate information in the first text and length should not exceed half of primary texts and is typically considerably shorter.

Recent years, content extraction has been developed into an enthralling investigation topic, owing to vast amount of current subject matter on the network [5]. Content extraction is an elementary area of discovering information aimed at locating fascinating examples of literary information. The examination and extraction of these data models from the massive data sets is regarded as a necessary technique [6, 7]. Numerous survey studies have been prompted to employ a variety of content digging methodologies for unstructured datasets. Additionally, the blend of the exploration challenges and philosophies of the published papers will aid text mining researchers in pursuing their future studies. According to [8], TS is defined as synopsis and accurate account of the important matters of a text. In [9], TS is a method of displaying the most powerful information from a source in a condensed format or by providing multiple references to information in response to specific requirements.

Text Summarization is the technique of producing a precise brief of a document which comprises of critical evidence from the primary document; aim is to obtain short brief of the document's important points [10]. The goal of abstractive method of multiple documents is to create a condensed form of the record by retaining essential info. Because of vast quantity of data available today, value of TS has increased.

Text summarization is a relatively new area of study that has gained considerable attention; as research continues, we hope to see an advancement that would address by offering a system for briefing long texts in a concise manner. This paper presents an extensive survey of TS strategies in this article to emphasize their utility in dealing with large amounts of data and to assist researchers in implementing them. The Fig. 1 illustrates the number of articles published in TS area from 1999 to 2019.

The following sections comprise this paper: Sect. 1 introduced and organized this article for the domain of text summarization. The following section discusses the various methods of text summarization. Section 3 discusses and reviews related works, as well as the techniques employed. Section 4 summarizes the metrics used in the evaluation process. Section 5 concludes.

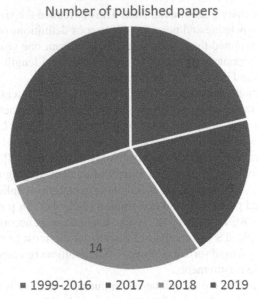

Fig. 1. Number of published articles

2 Classification of Text Summarization

Text summarization techniques can be broadly classified into the following categories, as illustrated in Fig. 2.

On the Basis of Input Type:
There are two types – Single Document methods (SDM) and Multi Document methods (MDM). In SDM, the input is brief in length. There would be only one document provided for Summarization. This technique was used in the initial stages of TS. In MDM, since the input length on a particular subject is excessive, numerous documents are given as input to TS technique. It is more tough than SDTS because the summary of multiple documents must be combined into a single document. The problem with this is that the themes of various documents may vary. A good summary technique frequently shortens the major themes by preserving legibility, comprehensiveness, and not omitting important sentences.

On the Basis of Output Form:
It includes extractive TS methods (ETSM) and abstractive TS methods (ATSM). In ETMS, Sentences are retrieved from the entire text and condensed to convey the same meaning as the entire text. Nowadays, the most of the TS techniques are extractive in nature. ATSM involves construction of sentences/ phrases which are not included in the text but convey the identical meaning as the complete text. This process is more

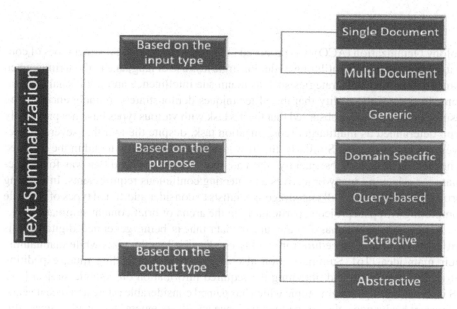

Fig. 2. Text summarization classification

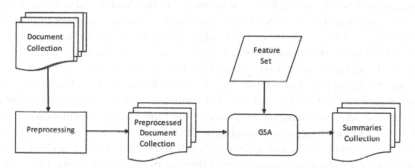

Fig. 3. Proposed gravitational search system framework

enthralling, but requires framework to construct phrases or statements that convey the identical gist.

On the Basis of Intent:

There are 3 types – Generic TS (GTS), Domain Specific TS (DSTS) and Query based TS (QTS). Generic Text Summarization is a technique in which no conclusions are derived about the meaning of text to be briefed. It generates a comprehensive brief of the entire documents, images, or videos. In DSTS, the model makes use of domain specific knowledge, such as scientific or medical documents. This improves precision and results in a more meaningful, succinct, and simple to understand summary of the entire text. QTS method takes a query as input and generates a text summary by choosing phrases and sentences that are highly related to the query.

3   Related Works

Colony Optimization (ACO) was proposed [15]. Regrettably, three distinct types of content synopsis endeavors utilizing SI demonstrate less use of language in the writing when compared to other TS strategies such as manmade intelligence and traditional calculations, in spite of the reality that the SI techniques demonstrate genuinely encouraging results. However, it was observed that the TS task with various types have not previously been determined as multitarget reorganization task, despite the fact that several objectives can be considered. Similarly, the SI was not used previously to aid in the repeated synopsis's approach. Subsequently, alternate model was suggested that was found adequate for achieving many objectives and meeting continuous requirements. In the long term, this examination will encourage specialists to consider additional types of SI while completing synopsis projects, particularly in the arena of brief content summary.

As a result of the massive amount of data that is being generated digitally, it is critical to develop a procedure for quickly condensing lengthy texts while maintaining their main idea [16]. Summarization also aids in reducing reading time, expediting information retrieval, and obtaining the required information on a single subject [17]. TS is an enthralling studying topic which has gained considerable interest in recent years. As research advances, they hope to experience an advancement that would impact this by offering a concise way for summarizing lengthy texts [16].

The eruption of info available via the networks, virtual media, and info technologies emphasizes the importance of TS, all the more so given the large volumes of data being dispersed as a result of transfer of knowledge among its users, making it difficult to distinguish between correct and incorrect information. To overcome the data explosion issues, a tool capable of summarizing these large amounts of data has become necessary. The summarization procedure reduces the time and effort needed to identify the prominent and significant statements. In general, a summary can be defined as subject matter composed of at least one sentence that conveys the most critical information contained in the first text while trying to remain concise [18].

This article demonstrates a program for content assessment that utilizes fuzzy ideologies and a variety of obtained data to discover the important info in examined texts; resulting descriptions of texts are compared to reference work prepared by domain experts. In this method, manuscripts are summarized by finding the correlation to decrease the dimensionality and fuzzy standards used for TS. Thus, the planned system for TS using a limited number of distorted rules could benefit the development of forthcoming expert schemes capable of evaluating written work [19].

Automatic summarization, linking, and evaluation strategies are significant since more and more classical datum are collected and made accessible via a assortment of virtual libraries (VLs), virtual learning conditions (VLCs), and social media). In r recent times, NLP and IE systems have been suggested for determining the comparability of free writings with minimal computational overhead [20].

Grammatical feature labelling is the process of determining an appropriate semantic label or syntactic taxonomy for a term based on context. Aspect of Speech tagging represents a paradigm shift in the majority of Natural Language Processing (NLP) applications, including info summarizing, question answering, data mining, and data retrieval.

[15] proposes a labelling strategy for the Arabic dialectal based on Bee Colony calculations. The problem is represented graphically, and an unique procedure is proposed for assigning scores to potential sentence labels, at which point honey bees determine the optimal arrangement. The proposed model is evaluated using the KALIMAT corpus, which contains 18 million words. The proposed methodology achieved 98.2 percent precision, compared to 97.4, 94.6 and 98.2 percent for HM Model, Rule Based strategies, and hybrid respectively. Additionally, the proposed methodology determined each tag presented in the corpus, whereas referenced procedures are only capable of recognizing three labels. Additional optimization techniques are available [21–26].

Text summarization generates concise versions of input documents while retaining significant info. It is a necessary duty that can be linked to real-world operations. Several strategies for addressing the content summarization problem have been proposed [27, 28]. Extractive and abstractive principles underpin text summarization systems. Extractive summarization generates synopses by selecting noteworthy phrases or gestures from the source material, whereas abstractive summarization rewords and rebuilds statements to create the brief. They concentrate on abstractive summarization because it is increasingly adaptable and thus allows for the creation of increasingly distinct summaries [29].

Current neural schemes are used to generate an overview that are typically either statement extractive, in which a large number of statements are chosen as the brief, or abstractive, in which the brief is created from a seq2seq prototype. They introduce a neuronic system for individual file summary in this work [30], which is reliant on combined extraction and pressure. They describe the summarization challenges as a development of local choices, similar to later fruitful extractive models. This model extracts statements from the document and then decides which compression option to apply to each sentence from a set of available options. They evaluate this configuration of distinct compression rules using linguistic reviews; moreover, the recommended model is quantified and can be applied to any available compression sources. Extractive brief compression of oracle was constructed to facilitate study, that represent weakness across the suggested scheme's decision pattern, and then study these components concurrently under this observation. The Daily Mail and NY Times sets of data illustrate that this model satisfies ROUGE's requirement for innovative execution in substance determination. Additionally, manual evaluations proved that the recommended system's yield is largely unchanged.

In [31], SummCoder is an unsupervised system for extractive TS from a single record. After pre-processing, SummCoder converts the statements to constant length sequences by using STM. To generate the summary, sentences are selected based on three variables: Sentence Position Admissible, Statement Content Relevance, and Statement Novelty. After computing all of the scores, a final result and relative result are computed. Ultimately, the summary can be created in two ways: first, by decreasing order of relative rank, and second, by prevalence in the input text.

In [32], describes the EdgeSumm system, which is a single record and graphical extractive arrangement. Pre-processing and lemmatization are carried out in the proposed method. Following that, a graph with nouns words as nodes and non-noun phrases as edges is constructed for text representation. The nodes "S#" and "E#" denote the beginning and end of the sentence, respectively. Weights are assigned to nodes based on their occurrence frequency. When sentences are chosen, it is assumed that each noun represents a distinct subject. To begin, it looks for the most frequently occurring phrases or words and generates a list of the vertices and edges that were selected. To select the source and target nodes, the score must exceed the average of all vertices, and source and target vertices must be nominated to choose an edge. If the brief created by the system surpasses the user-defined boundary, the candidate summary's statements are rated and ranked ascending. Following that, K-Means' algorithm is used to combine identical statements together, and statements with the highest class in every cluster are chosen to produce finished brief.

In [33], suggested a Summarization technique based on PacSumm. It utilizes ranking methods based on graphs, in which statements serve as vertices and edges serve as con nections among them. BERT were used to map the sentences. There are two jobs for training BERT: the first is masked language patterning, which involves allocating a token to the statement in light of the LHS and RHS sentences, and the second is sentence forecasting, which involves predicting the connection among two statements. Five negative samples are used to calibrate BERT for every positive sample. Following the discovery of all sentence representations, a pair wise dot product is used to generate an un-normalized matrix. Selected sentences will be made using this matrix.

In [34], advocated for the use of a Weighted Compression Model to extract critical information from text. This is accomplished in the proposed model by incrementally erasing Elementary Discourse Units from the sentence (EDUs). To begin, a non-negative weight is assigned to each term. Weights are determined using Gillick & Favre and McDonald's extractive models. The following step is to pick and choose which EDUs to delete. Using tree syntax, we generate a set of EDUs. The list has been omitted of EDUs that, if removed, would result in a sentence being grammatically incorrect. Others are discarded, weight and sorting of "important" EDUs are computed. To generate the brief, EDUs are chosen based on the proportion of length of summary and weight/cost.

In [35], TS using Latent Semantic Study was suggested. It is an algebraic quantitative technique for discovering hidden logical relationships among phrases and sentences. A text representation is accomplished by creating an input array in which rows correspond to the phrases and columns correspond to the statements. The cubicles indicate value of TF-IDF of words. Singular Value Decomposition (SVD) is employed to show the correlation between words and sentences. SVD's output enables the cross method to be used to select sentences. The longest vectored sentences are chosen.

For clustering sentences, [36] proposed using Fuzzy Evolutionary Optimization Modeling (FEOM). Consider a set of 'n' entities that will be clustered based on their distances. Then, three evolutionary operators will be used: select, hybrid, and mutate, up to end condition (Nmax $= 200$) is not satisfied. Three control parameters affect the crossover and mutation probabilities, pc and pm, respectively: The Coefficient of distribution, Comparative Distance and Average Evaluation impact. Following that, the most appropriate statements are chosen.

In [37], considers the framework of Recurrent Neural Networks (RNNs). Because the sentences in our dataset are randomly ordered, there is no immediate definition for individual statement based on the neighboring statements. A collection of these characteristics is used to provide context for each word, both locally and globally, as described below.

a) Abstract ROGUE: It is a feature that is used for summarization. It manipulates the defined pattern of a paper by utilizing the vague, a pre-existing description. Abstract ROUGE's concept is that statements which contain strong subjective briefs are more probable to contain strong highlights synopsis.
b) Numerical Count: It is computed by calculating the number of occurrences of numerical characters in statement, as statements incorporating numbers does not make a contribution to a balanced synopsis.
c) Title Count: In the summary, continuous phrases in text that correspond to those words in headline are assigned greater weight.
d) Author-defined or author-used keywords are given greater weight in the brief when they appear in the text.
e) Length of Sentence: It include the phrase's length as an attribute to capture the instinct that brief phrases are highly improbable to be effective descriptions since they do not convey as much information as longer phrases.

In [38], suggests that a CNN can be incorporated to perform automated text summarization by ranking statements. It extracts characters from statements contained within a word and then assign levels without requiring any manual work on the part of humans. It accepts word embeddings as input. Its ranks are generated in conjunction with the outcome for these words. The 'word2vec' component is exploited to accomplish this. Selecting statements based on model's previous ranks by using linear programming. ILP aims to solve problems in which an optimization function should be greatly reduced or maximized while adhering to certain constraints, with the restriction that the variables used be integers. The CNN model is fed the output of the preceding module word. This prototype is capable of learning the features of the statements and assigning them a rating. A matrix is the final input created by concatenating variables of the words in sentences. The pre-trained phrase vectors are developed using word2vec. Each sentence has multiple feature maps. Filters are applied to the statement matrix to create each feature map.

In [39], investigated the features of compound sentences. He used a supervised training system to weight various characteristics in order to determine the likelihood of a sentence being meaningful. After analyzing the feature vectors of sentences, a supervised classification classifier is used. Candidate sentences are reranked in particular, taking into account the fixed length of the ultimate summaries. Finally, best statements were extracted from the final summaries. Statement Characters is a general name used by the writer to indicate that definite words are significantly assigned more weightage and significant than other phrases in a statement or file depending on the occurrence, position, and, if applicable, a quote. Additional features considered for Extractive Summarization include the following:

1) Content Features: We combine three features of statements, namely fundamental phrases, sign conditions, and high recurrence phrases, as well as depictions of Unigram and Bigram, based on content bearing words.

2) Event Features: It comprised of an event's name and associated event elements.
3) Relevance Features: Significant characteristics are incorporated to manipulate inter-sentence relationships. A basic SVM requires the calculation of the mentioned maximization problem for labeled examples. The SVM classifier predicts that a hyper plane has been used to differentiate between positive and negative research examples.

Dohare in [41] develops the Linguistic Abstractive Summarization (SAS) pipeline. SAS generates a Conceptual Definition Representation (CDR) graph of the source story, from which it extracts a truncated graph and finally generates abridged sentences. They devised a comprehensive method for generating an CDR story graph through the use of Meta Vertices and coreference resolution. They extracted the summary graph below using an unsupervised novel algorithm that is dependent on how individuals brief a text. Three critical steps comprise the pipe. Converting the document to CDR is the first step. The second step is deriving an CDR brief from AMR file. The third step is to generate content from sub graph that was extracted.

In [42], briefs are created in repositories of text documents. Moreover, these data are uncommon in other domains, as are the models trained on them. Recently, single pair advancement has been achieved in a series of sequences. They focus exclusively on areas with only text and recommend endways creations that build a neural system to generate unrestricted summaries. The Average Sum includes two distinguishing characteristics: An auto encoder component that understands the description of every survey and ensures that resulting synopsis is not a linguistic field. A summary component that is trained to create meeting synopses that are identical to the input. The commonly method is to summarize exclusive documents on the magnitude through supervised readings of numerous pairs. The proposed model is unappealing due to its disregard for consideration or guidelines. The prototype does not provide a good resolution to a sig nificant crisis for the summarization of a single document.

According to Padma Kumar and Saran, [43], the vector group sentences detect clusters of identical statements and choose specimen for each cluster to form a synopsis. The converter is groomed to state sentence root. They combine Sentence Embedding with RNN via LSTM, in which they determine sentence embedding using a repetitive NN with short-term memory. When constituting statements at a greater level of vector, aim is typically to integrate statements explicitly or implicitly so that the closest sentences to the concept are adjacent in the feature space. Given that sentences which create a pattern in feature space will be comparatively near to one another, it is adequate to retain one specimen from one such set for the purpose of creating a summary.

Schumann [44] provides an uncontrollable method called VAE for logically summarizing sentences. It is renowned for its adaptable numerical learning, that requires a large input quantity. This method is trained to consider potential attributes for input recreation. Explicitly disclosing the discharge length during training has the effect of influencing VAE not to use that in creation and be used while evaluation. By directing the decipherer to generate a concise output seq, the input sentence is resulted in a one or two words. This system employs RNNs as encoders and decoders to process text data. The attributes μ and σ are constructed from previous concealed coding condition, whereas the state of first cell is initialized to be z. A bidding algorithm is employed that is both forward and backward in nature. They demonstrate, using various aggregated data, while simple statements cannot create a consistent base. ROUGE facts are produced instead of constructing a complete statement. The summary test confirms that optimizing the decipherer to generate concise results in more features displayed in a few phrases. Linear regression tests revealed that the latest variable contains the input sentence length.

According to Zhang et al., [45], the scheme of briefing the conversation should consider the perspective of multiple speakers, each of whom has a distinct role, purpose, and language style. Conversation of every speaker is briefed in tete-a-tete, by modelling customer words independently while integration is retained. SuTaT is composed of two unselected summary modules and a conditional production module. The goal is to create a summary of the customer and data negotiator. The proposal is analogous to tete- a-tete. Representative replies are dependent on customer requests. Rentable models with a pleasing appearance outperform unsupervised output models. SuTaT-LSTM outperforms other unorganized abstract fundamentals equipped with LSTM enciphers and decipherers.

According to [46], the briefs are primarily created on organized prototypes found in ordered texts. In comparison to newscast, podcasts are usually stretched, interactive, chattier, and forthcoming about promotional content, which makes the Podcast briefing a significant concern. Two straightforward frameworks for model comparisons: 1) Summarize the text using the first signs. Principle 2: As a summary, use the text's final tokens. The purpose of fundamental quantities is to indicate that conclusion of podcast may comprise critical content facts. We discuss numerous suggestions for future research based on this paper's basic analysis: (1) A summary based on a lengthy narrative structure: A heuristic's simple structure is not synonymous with a lengthy narrative structure. (2) Podcasts are communicative, interactive, and all encompassing. The ability to leverage existing research to aid in the summarization of podcasts remains scarce.

(3) Multidisciplinary podcast evaluation: We presume that cross disciplinary analysis is critical for comprehending podcasts.

In [47], huge amount of power is generated by applying a system with denoising scheme. This article is divided into three parts: (1) To summarize using vital sentences and train method to forecast them. (2) Idea model and denoising system is used for training. TED employs a decipherer convertor with multiple lines. (3) They employ Sentence Piece tokenization in place of traditional word tokenization. It is configured in the network converter's default configuration.

In [48], SEQ3 comprises of two sets of encoder decoders. Phrases are used as an unintelligible sequence of attributes. The first and last patterns are respectively embedded and recreated sentences, whereas the intermediate seq is a condensed statement. The Embedded layer utilizes bidirectional RNN to embed source sequences in coded projects. To summarize, we employ an RNN decoder for their ground services and input feeds. While the compressor comprises of compiling program functions, its encoder is responsible for embedding abbreviated words.

In [49], Author anticipated a Genetic Algorithms used by extractive based Text Summarization technique. DAG concept was introduced in the document where each edge was represented by the weight based on the explanation of schema. Readability factor, cohesion factor, topic relation factors were used as an objective function. Genetic Algo rithm make use the objective functions firstly, to select the important sentences from the entire text for easy understanding. Secondly, the cohesion factor is used to calculate the related sentences. Lastly, in topic relation factor the highest preferences are to be given for the sentences that are related to input query. Based on the calculation of all these factors the genetic algorithm increases the fitness functions.

In [50], multi document summarization technique was proposed by the author to reduce the associated information from multiple documents which minimizes the time and increases the efficiency. The cluster based, topic based and lexical chain based approaches were used in this paper. Lex Rank prevent the irrelevant sentence to main document to maximization the score of sentences. The sentences that include noisy data are given lower score as they do not contain the similarity of clusters. Initially, summary of the document is collected and metadata is generated for particular document. The graphs are constructed using meta data where related sentences can be identified in the document and they are represented as a node. Thereby considering previous meta data the suitable weights are given for each edge in a graph.

In [51], discusses in detail about 3 single document techniques and 2 multi-document techniques. In [52], Extractive text summarization utilized a model named word vector embedding. This paper consists of 4 major problems while obtaining the data. First, identifying the most significant sentence from the document. Second, removing the irrelevant data from the record. Third, reducing the information and lastly, obtaining the related data together which can be reduced and structured. Word vector embedding is utilized to overcome these problems. Extractive summarization utilized the NN (Neural network) system. DUC2002 datasets were verified and the outcomes were precise than the previous outcomes.

In [53], consists of 2 methods of Summarization namely, Extractive and Abstractive methods. As mentioned in [53] the Extractive method chooses the important sentences and summary is derived from it by retaining the consistency between the sentences and the theme of the report. The Abstractive method the summary is generated by phrases/sentence that might be present in the file. This technique is little difficult than the extractive method used previously. The detection of similar words got failed through word embedding and one hot vector systems. This was fixed in the papers [54, 55] were skip gram model was utilized were input sentences and contextual data's can be projected with the use of CSG.

A query-oriented method was used to construct summary by using query as an input. Most of the Semantic data do not utilize the queries so it is not efficient. The author in [56] suggested a search engine to get knowledge on the particular topic in the report. The document information was used by page rank algorithm to generate the summary. Addition to this China search engine was introduced to get past information of the topic that need to be summarized. Using these models, a precise summary can generate by having a knowledge on previous data collected.

According to [57] the precise outcome of the summarization cannot be obtained only with the meaning of word. Hence knowledge is required on specific area. Coreference resolution algorithm utilized to get rid of the difficulty by giving the precise outcome.

In [58], proposed the significance of summarization and categorizing the product studies. Support vector machine and NB were used as hybrid classifiers which increases the accuracy by increasing the count of the classifiers. Seq2seq model was used to get higher accuracy while summarizing the online products. Using this model precise summary can be obtained by customers on specific product.

4 Gravitational Search Algorithm Assessment Metrics

Following the creation of a summary, the critical step is evaluation. There are two ways to evaluate the summary: automatically or manually. Because it is simple, quick, and scalable, automatic assessment is viable choice than human assessment. The following methods are used to assess text summarization:

Algorithm 1 Schematic representation of the suggested approach.

1: Input: Documents are gathered together.
2: Preparation of the Materials Completion of sentences and recognition of stop words in the text
3. X c is the third character (N)

4: for i=1 to N, use the function () to generate random initialization solutions.

f(S i)=Score(S i)+P(S i)+D(S i)+T(S i)+KW(S i)   -(1)
5- Calculate-fitness (S i) f(S i));()-calculate-fitness (S i) f(S i) f(S i);()-calculate-fitness-function-using

f(S i)=Score(S i)+P(S i)+D(S i)+T(S i)+KW(S i)

6: for end
7: Repeat Steps 3 through 6 until the fitness function provides the same results.
8: Create a summary of the content by extracting the set percentage of the document.

External Assessment
Summary is assessed on the basis of how well it aids in the successful completion of other tasks, such as formation classification, question answering, and so on. For instance, reading comprehension provides an overview of a subject and assists in the resolution of multiple questions.

Internal Assessment
This section compares the brief generated by computer to the one created by a human. This assessment is based on the superiority of the text, its co-selection, and its content. The most widely used and popular essential technique of summary assessment is the ROUGE score, which falls under the category of content-based assessment.

$$ROUGE - N = \frac{\sum_{S \in summ_{human}} \sum_{N-gram \in S} Count_{match}(N - gram)}{\sum_{S \in summ_{human}} \sum_{N-gram \in S} Count(N - gram)} \qquad (2)$$

ROUGE is an automated system summary appraisal scheme that computes a score on the basis of resemblance of computer and human-generated summaries. Five different methods can be used to determine the ROUGE score:

ROUGE-N: This assesses recall using a related sequence of phrases in both summaries referred to as n gram, 'n' - is the length.

ROUGE-L: It calculates the proportion of length of the Lengthiest Common Subseq shared by the two briefs to the reference length. This ratio should be lesser than F

Table 1. Summarization conferences and their collections

Conference	#Documents	Source genre
MUC-1	10 messages	Military reports
MUC-2	105 messages	Military reports
MUC-3	1300 messages	News reports
MUC-4	1500 messages	News reports
MUC-5	1200–1600 documents	News reports
MUC-6	100 articles	News reports
MUC-7	100 articles	News reports
DUC 2001	30 sets of 10 documents each	Newswire/paper stories
DUC 2002	30 sets of 10 documents each	Newswire/paper stories
DUC 2003	30 TDT clusters-298 doc, 30 TREC clusters-326 doc, 30 TREC Novelty clusters-734 doc	Newswire/paper stories
DUC 2004	50 and 24 clusters of 10 documents each	English/Arabic newswire
DUC 2005	50 DUC topics and each topic 25–50 documents	English news
DUC 2006	50 DUC topics and each topic 25–50 documents	English news
DUC 2007	45 DUC topics and each topic 25–50 documents	English news
TAC-08	48 topics contains 20 documents per topic	English news/blog
TAC-09	44 topics contains 20 documents per topic	English news
TAC-10	46 topics contains 20 documents per topic	English news
TAC-11	44 topics contains 20 documents per topic	English news

score. **ROUGE-W:** It is identical to ROUGE-L except for the weights, i.e., commonly occurring successive phrases.

ROUGE-S: This function determines the level of skip bigram that exists among two summarizes.

ROUGE-SU: It is weighted unigram variant of ROUGE-S.

5   Conclusion

This article discussed in detail several noteworthy works in the area of TS. Due to the exponential growth of data on the internet, retrieving the most critical data in the form of a theoretical brief may be beneficial for specific users. Due to massive amount of data implemented in digitized world, it is necessary to discover a system to condense texts and offer concise briefs. Summarizing texts is still under investigation in a number of studies and requires additional research and development. Due to the explosion of data on the internet, some researchers will find it beneficial to extract the most critical data as a semantic summary. This article has gained the reader's attention to most recent and significant data issues and the importance of text summarization in this paper, and we demonstrated the usability of text data while retaining the original texts.

References

1. Marie-Sainte, S.L., Alalyani, N.: Firefly algorithm-based feature selection for Arabictext classification. J. King Saud Univ.-Comput. Inf. Sci. (2018)
2. Abualigah, L.M., Khader, A.T., Al-Betar, M.A.: Multi-objectives-based text clustering technique using K-mean algorithm. In: 2016 7th International Conference on Computer Science and Information Technology (CSIT), pp. 1–6. IEEE (2016)
3. Azmi, A.M., Altmami, N.I.: An abstractive Arabic text summarizer with user-controlled granularity. Inf. Process. Manag. **54**(6), 903–921 (2018)
4. Radev, D.R., Hovy, E., McKeown, K.: Introduction to the special issue on summarization. Comput. Linguist. **28**(4), 399–408 (2002)
5. Qaroush, A., Farha, I.A., Ghanem, W., Washaha, M., Maali, E.: An efficient single document Arabic text summarization using a combination of statistical and semantic features.J. King Saud Univ.-Comput. Inf. Sci. (2019)
6. Xu, J., Durrett, G.: Neural extractive text summarization with syntactic compression. arXiv preprint arXiv:1902.00863 (2019)
7. Abualigah, L.M.Q.: Feature Selection and Enhanced Krill Herd Algorithm for text Document Clustering. Studies in computational intelligence (2019)
8. Saggion, H.: Automatic summarization: an overview. Revue française de linguistique appliquée **13**(1), 63–81 (2008)
9. Al-Abdallah, R.Z., Al-Taani, A.T.: Arabic text summarization using firefly algorithm. In: 2019 Amity International Conference on Artificial Intelligence (AICAI), pp. 61–65. IEEE (2019)
10. Carreras, X., Màrquez, L.: Introduction to the CoNLL-2004 shared task: semantic role labeling. In: Proceedings of the Eighth Conference on Computational Natural Language Learning (CoNLL-2004) at HLT-NAACL 2004, pp. 89–97 (2004)
11. Abualigah, L.M., Khader, A.T., Hanandeh, E.S.: Hybrid clustering analysis using improved krill herd algorithm. Appl. Intell. (2018)
12. Abualigah, L.M., Khader, A.T., Al-Betar, M.A., Alomari, O.A.: Text feature selection with a robust weight scheme and dynamic dimension reduction to text document clustering. Expert Syst. Appl. **84**, 24–36 (2017)
13. Abualigah, L.M., Khader, A.T., AlBetar, M.A., Hanandeh, E.S.: Unsupervised text feature selection technique based on particle swarm optimization algorithm for improving the text clustering. In: EAI International Conference on Computer Science and Engineering (2017)
14. Abualigah, L.M., Khader, A.T., Al-Betar, M.A., Alyasseri, Z.A.A., Alomari, O.A., Hanandeh, E.S.: Feature selection with β-hill climbing search for text clustering application. In: 2017 Palestinian International Conference on Information and Communication Technology (PICICT), pp. 22–27. IEEE (2017)
15. Alhasan, A., Al-Taani, A.T.: POS tagging for arabic text using bee colony algorithm. Procedia Comput. Sci. **142**, 158–165 (2018)
16. Mosa, M.A., Anwar, A.S., Hamouda, A.: A survey of multiple types of text summariza tion with their satellite contents based on swarm intelligence optimization algorithms. Knowl. Based Syst. **163**, 518–532 (2019)
17. Barzilay, R., Elhadad, M.: Using lexical chains for text summarization. Adv. Autom. Text Summ., 111–121 (1999)
18. Ibrahim, A., Elghazaly, T.: Improve the automatic summarization of Arabic text depending on Rhetorical Structure Theory. In: 2013 12th Mexican International Conference on Artificial Intelligence, pp. 223–227. IEEE (2013)
19. Goularte, F.B., Nassar, S.M., Fileto, R., Saggion, H.: A text summarization method based on fuzzy rules and applicable to automated assessment. Expert Syst. Appl. **115**, 264–275 (2019)

20. Nallapati, R., Zhai, F., Zhou, B.: Summarunner: a recurrent neural network based sequence model for extractive summarization of documents. In: Thirty-First AAAI Conference on Artificial Intelligence (2017)
21. Abualigah, L.M.Q., Hanandeh, E.S.: Applying genetic algorithms to information retrieval using vector space model. Int. J. Comput. Sci., Eng. Appl. **5**(1), 19 (2015)
22. Abualigah, L.M., Khader, A.T.: Unsupervised text feature selection technique based on hybrid particle swarm optimization algorithm with genetic operators for the text clustering. J. Supercomput. **73**(11), 4773–4795 (2017)
23. Abualigah, L.M., Khader, A.T., Hanandeh, E.S.: A new feature selection method to im prove the document clustering using particle swarm optimization algorithm. J. Comput. Sci. (2017)
24. L.M. Abualigah, A.T. Khader, E.S. Hanandeh,
25. A combination of objective functions and hybrid krill herd algorithm for text document clustering analysis. Eng. Appl. Artif. Intell. (2018)
26. Abualigah, L.M., Khader, A.T., Hanandeh, E.S.: A novel weighting scheme applied to improve the text document clustering techniques. In: Innovative Computing Optimization and Its Applications: Modelling and Simulations, pp. 305–320. Springer, Cham (2018)
27. Abualigah, L.M., Khader, A.T., Hanandeh, E.S., Gandomi, A.H.: A novel hybridization strategy for krill herd algorithm applied to clustering techniques. Appl. Soft Comput. **60**, 423–435 (2017)
28. Ionescu, B., Müller, H., Villegas, M., de Herrera, A.G.S., Eickhoff, C., Andrearczyk, V., …Ling, Y.: Overview of Image CLEF 2018: challenges, datasets and evaluation. In: International Conference of the Cross-Language Evaluation Forum for European Languages, pp. 309–334. Springer, Cham (2018)
29. Al-Sai, Z.A., Abualigah, L.M.: Big data and E-government: a review. In: 2017 8th International Conference on Information Technology (ICIT), pp. 580–587. IEEE (2017)
30. Zhang, H., Gong, Y., Yan, Y., Duan, N., Xu, J., Wang, J., … Zhou, M.: Pretraining- based natural language generation for text summarization. arXiv preprint arXiv:1902.09243 (2019)
31. Karpagam, K., Saradha, A.: A framework for intelligent question answering system using semantic context-specific document clustering and Wordnet. Sadhana **44**(3), 62 (2019)
32. Joshi, A., Fidalgo, E., Alegre, E., Fernández-Robles, L.: SummCoder: An unsupervised framework for extractive text summarization based on deep auto-encoders. Expert Syst. Appl. **129**, 200–215 (2019)
33. El-Kassas, W.S., Salama, C.R., Rafea, A.A., Mohamed, H.K.: EdgeSumm: Graph-based framework for automatic text summarization. Inf. Process. Manage. **57**(6), 102264 (2020)
34. Zheng, H., Lapata, M.: Sentence centrality revisited for unsupervised summarization. arXiv preprint arXiv:1906.03508 (2019)
35. Vanet ik, N., Litvak, M., Churkin, E., Last, M.: An unsupervised constrained optimization approach to compressive summarization. Inf. Sci. **509**, 22–35 (2020)
36. Ozsoy, M.G., Alpaslan, F.N., Cicekli, I.: Text summarization using latent semantic analysis. J. Inf. Sci. **37**(4), 405–417 (2011)
37. Song, W., Choi, L.C., Park, S.C., Ding, X.F.: Fuzzy evolutionary optimization modeling and its applications to unsupervised categorization and extractive summarization. Expert Syst. Appl. **38**(8), 9112–9121 (2011)
38. Collins, E., Augenstein, I., & Riedel, S.: A supervised approach to extractive summarisation of scientific papers. arXiv preprint arXiv:1706.03946 (2017)
39. Charitha, S., Chittaragi, N.B., Koolagudi, S.G.: Extractive document summarization using a supervised learning approach. In: 2018 IEEE Distributed Computing, VLSI, Electrical Circuits and Robotics (DISCOVER), pp. 1–6. IEEE (2018 August)
40. Wong, K. F., Wu, M., Li, W.: Extractive summarization using supervised and semi-supervised learning. In: Proceedings of the 22nd international conference on computational linguistics (Coling 2008), pp. 985–992 (2008, August)

41. Dohare, S., Gupta, V., Karnick, H.: Unsupervised semantic abstractive summarization. In: Proceedings of ACL 2018, Student Research Workshop, pp. 74–83 (2018, July)
42. Chu, E., Liu, P.: MeanSum: a neural model for unsupervised multidocument abstractive summarization. In: International Conference on Machine Learning (pp. 1223–1232) (2019, May)
43. Padmakumar, A., Saran, A.: Unsupervised text summarization using sentenceembeddings, pp. 1–9. Technical Report, University of Texas at Austin (2016)
44. Schumann, R.: Unsupervised abstractive sentence summarization using length controlled variational autoencoder. arXiv preprint arXiv:1809.05233 (2018)
45. Zhang, X., Zhang, R., Zaheer, M., Ahmed, A.: Unsupervised Abstractive Dialogue Summarization for Tete-a-Tetes. arXiv preprint arXiv:2009.06851 (2020)
46. Zheng, C., Wang, H.J., Zhang, K., Fan, L.: A Baseline Analysis for Podcast Abstractive Summarization. arXiv preprint arXiv:2008.10648 (2020)
47. Yang, Z., Zhu, C., Gmyr, R., Zeng, M., Huang, X., Darve, E.: TED: A Pretrained Unsupervised Summarization Model with Theme Modeling and Denoising. arXiv preprint arXiv:2001. 00725 (2020)
48. Baziotis, Christos, et al.: SEQ^3: Differentiable Sequence-to-Sequence-to-Sequence Autoencoder for Unsupervised Abstractive Sentence Compression. arXiv preprint arXiv:1904.03651 (2019)
49. Chatterjee, N., Mittal, A., Goyal, S.: Single Document Extractive Text Summarization Using Genetic Algorithms (2012)
50. Tandel, A., Modi, B., Gupta, P., Wagle, S., Khedkar, S.: Multi-document text summarization - A survey. In: 2016 International Conference on Data Mining and Advanced Computing (SAPIENCE)
51. Modi, S., Oza, R.: Review on Abstractive Text Summarization Techniques (ATST) for single and multi-documents. In: 2018 International Conference on Computing, Power and Communication Technologies
52. Jain, A., Bhatia, D., Thakur, M.K.: Extractive Text Summarization using Word Vector Embedding (2017)
53. Raphal, N., Duwarah, H., Daniel, P.: Survey on abstractive text summarization. In: 2018 International Conference on Communication and Signal Processing (ICCSP)
54. Mikolov, T., Sutskever, I., Chen, K., Corrado, G., Dean, J.: Distributed representations of words and phrases and their compositionality arXiv:1310.4546v1 (2013)
55. Mikolov, T., Chen, K., Corrado, G., Dean, J.: Efficient estimation of word representations in vector space. arXiv:1301.3781v3 (2013)
56. Wei, Y., Zhizhuo, Y.: Query based summarization using topic background knowledge. In: 2017 13th International Conference on Natural Computation, Fuzzy Systems and Knowledge Discovery (ICNC-FSKD)
57. Shi, Z.: The Design and Implementation of Domain-specific Text Summarization System based on Co-reference Resolution Algorithm. In: 2010 Seventh International Conference on Fuzzy Systems and Knowledge Discovery
58. Pawar, P., Tandel, S., Bore, S., Patil, N.: Online Product Review Summarization. In: 2017 International Conference on Innovations in Information, Embedded and Communication Systems (ICIIEC)

Analysis of Deep Learning Methods
for Prediction of Plant Diseases

Subhashree Rath, Vaishali M. Deshmukh, Shree Raksha V.$^{(\boxtimes)}$, Geetha Sree S.,
and Harshitha S.

Department of Computer Science and Engineering, New Horizon College of Engineering,
Bangalore, India
raksha.honey2000@gmail.com

Abstract. Agriculture being the important aspect of India's economy and also a major source of crop production. A huge number of India's population depends on yield production for their livelihood. We are living in an era where problem regarding agriculture is a major issue now a days. The major problem in the crop growth is we have to take care of the health of the plants and the crops. Agriculture is one sector that has a significant influence on human lives and economic condition. Agriculture goods are lost due to poor management. Plant leaves which are the most vulnerable are the first to develop illness signs. From the beginning of their life cycle through the moment they are ready to be harvested, crops must be checked for illnesses. The devices used to predict illness have shown to be faster, cheaper, and more accurate than farmers' conventional approach of manual observation. Disease signs can be noticed on the leaves, stems, and fruits in the majority of instances. Due to the various factors the productivity of the crop is affected. The factors include change in climatic conditions, pest attacks or various diseases a plant suffers from. An automatic detection is designed to detect disease symptoms at an early or growing stage. The paper exposes a methodology for detecting the diseases in leaves with deep learning and image processing techniques.

Keywords: Plant leaf disease detection · Image processing · Deep learning · Convolutional Neural Network (CNN) · Accuracy · Symptoms

1 Introduction

The occurrence of disease in plants has negative impact in production. When a disease occurs on crops, the country's economy is affected. The early detection is an effective method to prevent or to control diseases in plants, which would lead to loss of crop production with increase. The identification of the plant diseases has been a challenging issue in the recent years. In plants, symptoms of diseases are visible easily in areas like stem, fruit and leaves of a plant. The leaves being the sensitive part of the plant, diseases or symptoms are being observed on the leaves. So, the plant's leaves are considered for as the primary route for detection of diseases. The perception of leaf diseases is the main motive to control the loss occurs in agriculture. Various plant leaves bear variety

© The Author(s), under exclusive license to Springer Nature Switzerland AG 2022
A. Kumar et al. (Eds.): ICAIDS 2021, CCIS 1673, pp. 160–168, 2022.
https://doi.org/10.1007/978-3-031-21385-4_14

of diseases. The major types are generally based on bacteria, fungal and viral and the most common diseases are Bacterial Blight, Downy Mildew, Anphracnose.

The main approach involved for identification is through naked eye of experts. But this requires periodic and continuous observation. When there is huge farm to be cultivated, this method could be expensive and practically impossible. Furthermore, in some non-development areas contacting the experts is quite hard and time consuming and moreover all the farmers are not exposed of non-native leaf diseases. The technique of detecting diseases automatically is an important aspect that has been proven to benefit large scale crop production and thus detect diseases automatically through the symptoms on the leaves. Therefore, detection of leaf diseases through automatic approach involving image processing and deep learning techniques has proven to provide much better accuracy. Comparatively naked eye detection is time consuming as well as less accurate.

There are many cases where farmers do not have a fully compact knowledge about the crops and the disease that can get affected to the crops. This paper can be effectively used by farmers thereby increasing the yield rather than visiting the expert and getting their advice. The main objective is not only to detect the disease using image processing technologies. It also directs the user directly to an e-commerce website where the user can purchase the medicine for the detected disease by comparing the rates and use appropriately according to the directions given. The purpose of this study is to develop a feature-based method that attempts to overcome the limits of earlier work in terms of accuracy and portability, with the goal of providing high accuracy and portability to user's mobile devices.

This method of automated technique has been introduced to over come difficulties faced by manual system. For obtaining the features of the leaf the image captured through high resolution digital camera or mobile camera is taken as the input. The process consists of various steps like identification, classification and extraction of features (Fig. 1).

In the recent times, (CNN) Convolutional Neural Networks, In deep learning it a type of technique which has become a preferred method. This method is the common popular technique used for recognition of images and also, possesses a ability in classification and processing of image. This paper aims at providing reviews based on existing papers and in the recent study review using deep learning techniques and image processing of diseased leaf recognition. The rest of the paper is designed as follows:

2 Related Works

In the Research produced by Prasanna Mohanty [1] "Deep Learning plant detection on image base". In the paper the authors proposed a system to detect the plant disease using training dataset using the Convolutional Neural Networks method. The model was designed based on 14 different species of diseased and healthy plants. The model attained an accuracy of 99.35%. According to Malvika Rajanet al. [2] "Using Artificial Neural Network detection of diseased leaf" introduced an approach to identify the diseases in a diseased leaf. The accuracy carried using the ANN model is 80%.

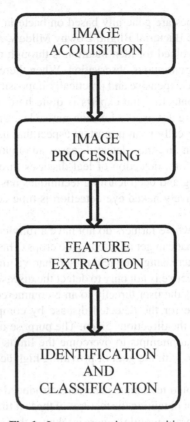

Fig. 1. Image processing recognition

In the paper by S. Arivazhagan et al. [3] "Detection of unhealthy plant leaves using texture features" the process involved four steps i.e., the RGB image is taken as the input, detection of green pixels followed by segmentation, at last for the feature classification a classifier is used. The accuracy was observed to be around 89%. Kulkarni et al. [4] proposed a system for early detection of diseases in plants accurately. "Detect plant disease by image processing". The paper was mainly based on ANN and Gabor filter. The ANN is used for classification followed by Gabor filter for extraction of features, which give better results with an accuracy rate up to 91%.

Jyopsna Bankar et al. [5] in the paper, "CNN based inception V3 approach for classification of animals", had proposed a system that uses inception model to classify different species. The capability of the approach gave a result of 92%. In paper, "Using CNN and GAN in detection of diseases in plants" by Emaneul Corts et al. [6] involved an approach known as Genrative Adversial Network, however did not improve the accuracy rate above 85% (Table 1 and Fig. 2).

Table 1. Accuracy rate

Author	Accuracy
Prasanna Mohanty	99.35%
Malvika Rajan	80%
S. Arivazhagan	89%
Kulkarni	91%
Jyopsna Bankar	92%
Emaneul Corts	85%

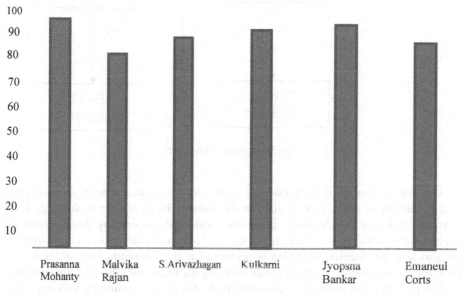

Fig. 2. Accuracy graph

3 Methodology

The concept of deep learning was first used for recognition of plant images based on vein patterns. The approach has three to six layer CNN that classified different plant species like soyabean, red bean and other varieties. However, the approach attained precision of 93% and above all over the results are amazing which are noted in the related work, however the diversification in the dataset were finite. Involvement of large scale data required better approaches like CNN. There are many research papers that summarize the research about plant disease recognition by deep learning, due to the lack of exposure in few techniques involved for visualization could not be implemented along with deep learning. The most common approaches that were used for classification are KNN and K-Means (Fig. 3).

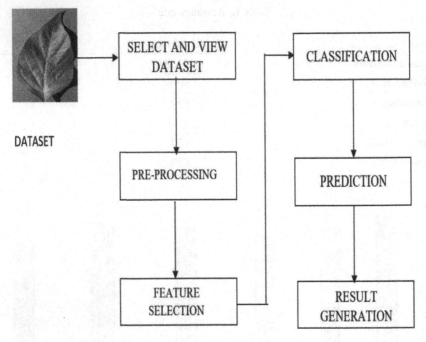

Fig. 3. System architecture

The implementation in deep learning approach/tech in categorize of diseases gives a fresh thought in terms of research for the authors. However, the technology lacks transparency hence the classifiers generally considered without any details about the mechanism used for classification. It is always not only necessary to attain high accuracy but also how the diseased detection is performed at the symptoms seen in the leaves. Therefore many researchers have started evolving the techniques used for visualization.

For example, the method to visualize plant disease symptoms by saliency maps was introduced by Brahe et al., The author (Brahe,) brought up a fresh approach for the vision that involved identifying spots of diseased leaves and comparing it with the already existing methods. This new approach attained a much better visualization effect.

3.1 Deep Learning Architecture for Detection of Leaf Disease

In this section a detail analysis for identification and classification of diseased leaves we are also going to analyze the modifications and improvement that was bought up for attaining better results in terms of identification of disease and the accuracy.

Each disease exhibits up its own features Lee et al., used a different approach i.e., considering the spots and individual lesions then taking the whole part the leaf. Through this approach many disease a single leaf were identified and data of the leaf image is divided in multiple sub images.

C. Bi, J. Wang et al., experimented 15 different species and discovered 79 different leaf diseases using the GoogLeNet. The accuracy obtained by using the spot and single lesion was 95% which is comparatively higher while considering the whole image (81%). However, Lee et al., proposed a new idea of targeting the name of the disease than the name of crop. But this new view was the failure as the new data of the crop could not been identified.

The Mean shift algorithm was used by Jiang et al., to corporate four different types of disease spots. Initially, extracted the shape feature by artificial calculation and then extracted the color feature using CNN. In the end, SVM was used for the classification and identification of the diseases. With detailed analysis it was observed that the accuracy rate of 93% was obtained when the CNN segmentation algorithm is used, without the use of segmentation algorithm the precision was 83% accuracy rate. The combination of CNN along with SVM had an accuracy of 96.8%.

Huang, brought a algorithm on a neural structure for a kind off leaf diseased image based on the study having dataset of balanced and imbalanced. The accuracy was 97%

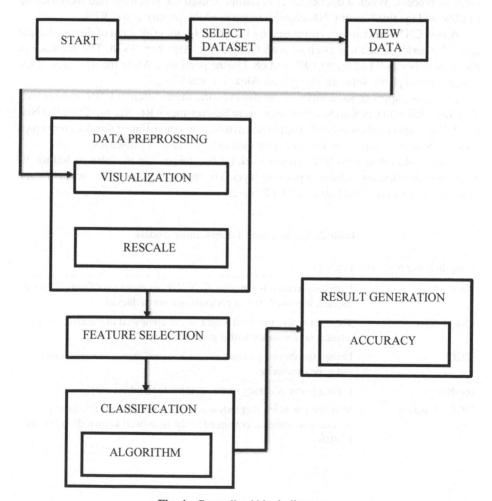

Fig. 4. Generalized block diagram

and 99% respectively. However, there was no improvement in the balance of images, the accuracy shrinks down to 95%.

Among Long., took two different kind of training dataset using Alex Net, the training set one from ImageNet and the other from scratch to shownen out the camellia disease. The results conveyed that there could be significant improvement and performance with a better accuracy. Xu et al., proposed a model on with Convolutional Neural Network. The ideology was mainly used for recognition for diseases in corn leaf. On an average the recognition of accuracy was 93.45% (Fig. 4).

3.2 Modified/New Deep Learning Architecture for the Detection of Leaf Disease

Dechant et al., used many CNN classifiers for the research of high-resolution pictures. From the research survey it is observed that the accuracy rate is 89.9% when CNN classify were in process. When a double layer classifier is used the precision rate increased up to 96% and the third layer CNN classifiers are used the precision was 97%.

A new CNN structure was proposed by Liu et al., for identification of diseased apple leaf. The performance was contrast with Google Net, Alex Net, SVM. The accuracy of these models was 93.69%, 90.19% and 68.73% respectively. While the accuracy of the Cascaded Inception Network along with Alex Net was 97.62%.

Icon et al., approached a different method i.e., the three different CNN architecture. The three different CNN architecture used were ResNet-mc-3, ResNet-mc-2 and ResNet-mc-1. This experiment was carried out in an environment consisting of five different crops (corn, wheat, rice, rapeseed and barley) which suffered from 17 diseases.

Chen et al., introduced VGG frame work for two inspection modules including the activation function and adding a pooling layer. The major crop used here was corn and reached the accuracy level up to 92% (Table 2).

Table 2. Comparison of deep leaning models

Deep learning methods	Features
AlexNet	Popularly known for modern fist CNN. To avoid over fitting drop out method was used. Better performance was achieved
GoogLeNet	The parameters involved were few are compared to AlexNet but gave a better performance with a good accuracy
VGG	Larege number of parameter were involved, hence the model turned out to be expensive
ResNet	Gave a better accuracy results compared to others
VGG-Inception	VGG nd inception methods was a cascaded version. The testing accuracy was higher comaperd to the other well known deep learning models

4   Conclusion

The paper discusses about the similar concepts of deep learning, over view done about the recent research in plant disease recognition. It has proven that the method used in deep learning and capable of giving out an expected and better results compared to the other techniques. We have also discussed how important is it to collect a dataset with high resolution and choosing an appropriate method for identification as well as classification of the diseased leaves. Most of the deep learning technologies that are proposed has given a positive response and also brought an light to the areas of improvement with the future scope. Therefore, human life is completely dependent upon crop production, the decrease will affect the country's economy. Hence, there is a need for appropriate technique that can automatically detect diseases in plant leaves at an early stage.

References

1. Kaur, S., Pandey, S., Goel, S.: Plant disease identification and classification through leaf images – A survey. Arch. Comput. Methods Eng.. https://doi.org/10.1007/s11831-018-9255-6
2. Bauer, A., et al.: Deep neural networks based recognition of plant diseases by leaf image classification (2019). https://doi.org/10.1038/s41438-019-0151-5Dec
3. Smys, S., Basar, A., Wang H.: CNN based flood management system with IoT sensors and cloud data. J. Artif. Intell. 2(04), 194–200 (2020)
4. Suma, V.: Community based network reconstruction for an evolutionary algorithm framework. J. Artif. Intell. 3(01), 53–61 (2021)
5. Sungheetha, A., Sharma, R.: Real time monitoring and fire detection using internet of things and cloud based drones. J. Soft Comput. Parad. (JSCP) 2(03), 168–174 (2020)
6. Raiesh, G., Saroia, B., Dhivya, M., Gurulakshmi, A.B.: DBscan algorithm-based colon cancer detection and stratification analysis. In: 2020 Proceedings of the 4th International Conference on IoT in Social, Mobile, Analytics and Cloud, ISMAC 2020, Conference Paper Scopus. Roy, A., Basak, K., Ekbal, A., Bhattacharyya, P.: A deep ensemble framework for fake news detection and classification. ArXiv, abs/1811.04670 (2018)
7. Gopal, M.K., Amirthavalli, M.: Applying machine learning techniques to predict the maintainability of open source software. Int. J. Eng. Adv. Technol. 8 (2019)
8. Nithya, B., Ilango, V.: Predictive analytics in health care using machine learning tools and techniques. In: Proceedings of the 2017 International Conference on Intelligent Computing and Control Systems. ICICCS 2017 (2017)
9. Wang, J., Chen, L., Zhang, J., Yuan, Y., Li, M., Zeng, W.: CNN transfer learning for automatic image-based classification of crop disease. In: Image and Graphics Technologies and Applications, pp. 319–329. Springer, Beijing, China (2018)
10. Ferentinos, K.P.: Deep learning models for plant disease detection and diagnosis. Comput. Electron. Agricult. 145, 311–318 (2018)
11. Wang, G., Sun, Y., Wang, J.: Automatic image-based plant disease severity estimation using deep learning. Comput. Intell. Neurosci. 2017, 1–8 (2017)
12. Deshmukh, V.M., Shukla, S.: Content-Restricted Boltzmann Machines for Diet Recommendation (2021). https://doi.org/10.1007/978-981-16-4486-3_12
13. Kumar, R.S., Ramesh, C.: A study on prediction of rainfall using datamining technique. https://doi.org/10.1109/INVENTIVE.2016.7830208
14. Anidha, M., Premalatha, K.: Integrated Cox model for survival analysis and biomarker discovery with a feature ranking technique based on z-score transformation in non-small cell lung cancer patients. Biomed. Res. 28(5), 1975–1983 (2017) [Impact Factor:0.226, SJR:0.16]

15. Gopal, M.K., Amirthavalli, M.: Applying machine learning techniques to predict the maintainability of open-source software. Int. J. Eng. Adv. Technol. **8** (2019)

16. Raiesh, G., Saroia, B., Dhivya, M., Gurulakshmi, A.B.: DB-scan algorithm based colon cancer detection and stratification analysis 2020 Proceedings of the 4th International Conference on IoT in Social, Mobile, Analytics and Cloud, ISMAC 2020, Conference Paper Scopus. Roy, A., Basak, K., Ekbal, A., Bhattacharyya, P.: A deep ensemble framework for fake news detection and classification. ArXiv, abs/1811.04670 (2018). Liu, Y., Sun, P., Highsmith, M.R., Wergeles, N.M., Sartwell, J., Raedeke, A., Mitchell, M., Hagy, H., Gilbert, A.D., Lubinski, B., et al.: Performance comparison of deep learning techniques for recognizing birds in aerial images. In: 2018 IEEE Third International Conference on Data Science in Cyberspace (DSC), pp. 317–324 (2018)

17. Rebinth, A., Kumar, S.M., Kumanan, T., Varaprasad, G.: Glaucoma image classification using entropy feature and maximum likelihood classifier. Journal of Physics: Conference Series, 1964, Scopus (2021)

18. Susmitha, A., Dash, L., Alamuru, S.: Recognition and extraction of rain drops in an image using hough transform, 2020,109, book chapter, scorpus.

19. Veerasamy, V., Wahab, N.I.A., Othman, M.L., Padmanaban, S., Sekar, K., Ramachandran, R., Hizam, H., Vinayagam, A., Islam, M.Z.: LSTM recurrent neural network classifier for high impedance fault detection in solar PV integrated power system. In: 2021 IEEE Access 9 Article Scopus.

20. Rebinth, A., Kumar, S.M., Rebinth, A., Kumar, S.M.: Lecture notes in networks and systems, 134, conference paper, scopus (2021)

21. Ramkumar, M., Ganesh Babu, C., Vinoth Kumar, K., Hepsiba, D., Manjunathan, A., Sarath Kumar, R.: ECG cardiac arrhythmias classification using DWT, ICA and MLP neural networks. Journal of Physics: Conference Series,1831, conference paper, scopus (2021)

22. Boobalan, S., Venkatesh Kumar, P., Vinoth Kumar, K., Palai, G.: Three ways chip to chip communication via a single photonic structure: a future paragon of 3D photonics to optical VLSI. IETE Journal of Research, Article, Scopus (2021)

23. Kunhan, J.P., Chandrappa, P.S., Ravikumar, C.R., Hanumantharayappa, N., Naik, R., Pothu, R., Boddula, R., Al Otaibi, A.: Study of cobalt doped gdalo3 for electrochemical application. Current Analytical Chemistry, 17, Scopus (2021)

24. Suganthi, S.T., Vinayagam, A., Veerasamy, V., Deepa, A., Abouhawwash, M., Thirumeni, M.: Detection and classification of multiple power quality disturbances in Microgrid network using probabilistic based intelligent classifier. Sustain. Energy Technol. Assess., 47, Article, Scopus (2021)

25. Rath, S., Deshmukh, V.M., Manzoor, R., Singh, S., Singh, S.J.: IoT and machine learning based flood alert and human detection system. In: 2022 4th International Conference on Smart Systems and Inventive Technology (ICSSIT), pp. 132–137. https://doi.org/10.1109/ICSSIT 53264.2022.9716441

26. Swaminathan, A., Aswin Vellaichamy, S., Dr. Kalaivani, S., Varun, C.: Multiple plant leaf disease classification using DenseNet121 architecture. IJEET **12** (2021). https://doi.org/10.34218/IJEET.12.5.2021.005

27. Durmuş, H., Güneş, E.O., Kırcı, M.: Disease detection on the leaves of the tomato plants by using deep learning. In: 2017 6th International Conference on Agro-Geoinformatics, pp. 1–5. IEEE (2017)

28. Rath, S., Kumar, S., Guntupalli, V.S.K., Sourabh, S.M., Riyaz, S.: Deep learning methods for bird species detection. In: 2022 Second International Conference on Artificial Intelligence and Smart Energy (ICAIS), pp. 234–239. https://doi.org/10.1109/ICAIS53314.2022.9742798

ACHM: An Efficient Scheme for Vehicle Routing Using ACO and Hidden Markov Model

Righa Tandon[1]($\boxtimes$) and P.K Gupta[2]

[1] Department of Computer Science and Engineering, Chitkara University Institute of Engineering and Technology, Chitkara University, Punjab 140401, India
`righa.tandon@chitkara.edu.in`
[2] Department of Computer Science and Engineering, Jaypee University of Information Technology, Solan 173 234, HP, India
`pkgupta@ieee.org`

Abstract. With the recent advancement in the field of Internet of Vehicles (IoV), there is a surge in the number of connected vehicles on the road. Various technological breakthroughs have revived the field of dynamic vehicular routing. Though, there are many schemes that focus on resolving the vehicular routing issue, but very few have focused on the dynamic aspect related to it. In this paper, we have focused on the dynamic aspect of vehicular routing. This is done by implementing Ant Colony Optimization (ACO) along with Hidden Markov Model (HMM). The vehicles are considered as ants and they release pheromones while travelling in the network. These pheromone values are fed to HMM where-after a HMM state sequence is formed. This helps in finding the best possible path for the vehicles to travel. This scheme has reduced the average travel time of vehicles on road by using pheromone values and HMM state sequences. The computational overhead of vehicle routing is also minimized. Further, the performance of the proposed scheme has been evaluated and compared with other existing schemes.

Keywords: Ant colony optimization · Hidden Markov Model · IoV · Pheromones · Vehicle routing

1 Introduction

Intelligent Transportation System (ITS) is a sophisticated technology that seeks to deliver distinctive services to the automobiles and also reduce traffic related problems. This in-turn allows the consumers to be more aware and guides them in making safer, more efficient, and smart use of transportation services. The Internet of Vehicles (IoV) is a new idea in ITS that aims to improve transportation related issues by incorporating it with the Internet of Things (IoT) [13]. IoV has been the most prominent in transportation networks due to a variety of unique characteristics such as complex topological structures, massive network

A. Kumar et al. (Eds.): ICAIDS 2021, CCIS 1673, pp. 169–180, 2022.
https://doi.org/10.1007/978-3-031-21385-4_15

size, dependable internet access, connectivity with personal computers, and fast computing capability, among others [18].

With the rapid development in IoV, vehicles form an important and promising aspect for ITS. With the help of IoV and advanced technologies, vehicles communicate with other vehicles, infrastructure and wireless sensors. Further, vehicles share their current location, speed, state of current traffic, etc. for avoiding accidents, and reducing traffic congestion in certain areas [3]. General architecture of a vehicular network is shown in Fig. 1.

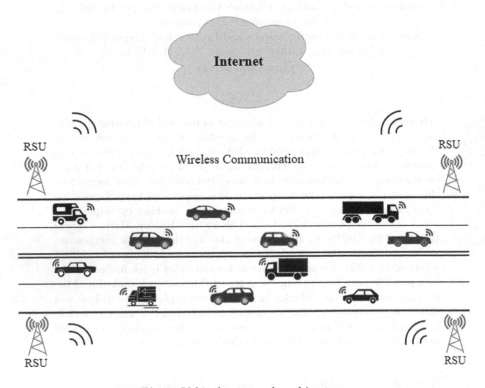

Fig. 1. Vehicular network architecture

In recent years, many vehicles are connected with IoV that results in enhancing traffic efficiency, minimizing traffic congestion, and improving safety [20]. When large number of vehicles are connected, most critical issue that may arise is traffic routing [16]. This happens due to the slow down of traffic flow on roads with increased number of vehicles. This further increases the travel time of vehicles on road, more fuel consumption, increased vehicles collision rate, etc. The lack of infrastructure on roads and traffic management plays a major role in critical traffic congestion issue. Many optimized solutions have been proposed for solving this critical issue but they are limited to the vehicles with same source and destination [11,12].

In this paper, we focus on dynamic vehicle routing in order to solve traffic routing problem on roads. ACO along with HMM is implemented in this paper to find the efficient path for connected vehicles from source to destination. This not only tackles the above mentioned drawback, but also provides a more practical solution for solving the issue. This routing path helps in reducing the average travel time of vehicles on road. Further, the computational overhead is minimized using this routing path for vehicles. The key points of this paper are summarised as follows:

- Proposes a model for vehicle routing.
- Selects efficient and best route using ACO-HMM for vehicles.

Further, this paper is categorized into various sections where, Sect. 2 discusses the related work for vehicle routing. Section 3 discusses about methodology that includes proposed system model and ACHM routing scheme for finding the efficient path. Section 4 represents the performance evaluation of the proposed work. Finally, Sect. 5 concludes the paper.

2   Related Work

In the past, various works have been done related to routing of vehicles on the road. This section summarises the various studies about different schemes for vehicle routing.

2.1   HMM Based Schemes

In [26], a prediction scheme has been proposed which is based on HMM. This scheme helps in predicting the best route for a vehicle while driving very efficiently in less amount of time without knowing the vehicles' starting and ending locations. HMM along with the viterbi algorithm can possibly predict future routes of a vehicle. In [24], a predictive routing scheme that is based on HMM has been proposed for enhancing transmission performance by considering vehicle behaviour. In this scheme, vehicle's past paths have been considered for predicting the future paths of vehicle using HMM. This helps in finding the shortest path for data packet transmission. Furthermore, it achieves better delivery ratio, less time-delay and congestion overhead. In [7], topological route selection is used which is based on markov process chain. This helps in finding the route from source to destination in effective and efficient manner. This process uses cognitive mechanism for selecting the routing movement of the vehicles. Route selection is basically based on individual's population choice and will fed on markov chain process to find the best route for different vehicles. In [2], HMM has been used to predict the future path of vehicle in two phases. In first phase, information of vehicle has been predicted using HMM, and in second phase, future path of the vehicle has been predicted using transition probability of HMM with viterbi algorithm.

In [15], vehicular navigation system has been implemented for finding navigation paths using HMM and radio frequency identification. Navigation path is accurately predicted here. This system helps is overcoming timing and various information loss issues by providing correct sequence of observations in markov process in less time. In [6], HMM based mechanism scheme has been proposed for vehicular environment. Authors have used trust model for transmission over the channel. Vehicles can communicate in less time using this scheme. In [27], a self-adaptive algorithm has been used for vehicular network. Heuristic function is used in this algorithm to find the optimal path for vehicle routing. This helps in achieving the better performance of the network. In [4], a routing scheme has been proposed which can prevent DoS attack. This scheme can also speculate the vehicle's future behavior. In [14], HMM model has been used in vehicular environment for fault tolerant communication among vehicles. This also helps in reducing link failures during communication. In [8], a novel model has been proposed in for routing problem in vehicular environment. It also enhances the performance of the overall mobility model in vehicular network.

In [25], a cooperative caching scheme has been proposed for addressing the issue during routing of vehicles. Authors have implemented a HMM model for predicting vehicular behavior to reach its destination.

2.2 Routing Schemes

In [16], multiple ACO-based method has been proposed that helps in finding the shortest path for vehicle routing. This scheme further reduces the travel time of vehicles and increases vehicle throughout. In [5], a framework has been proposed for simulating traffic system on the road. This framework is effective and efficient when compared with existing frameworks in respect to vehicle routing on roads. In [23], a system model has been proposed based on ACO and tabu search for vehicle routing. This model helps in reducing traffic congestion by minimizing the travel time of vehicles on road. In [19], an optimized solution has been proposed that reduces the average waiting time of vehicles and helps in enhancing the efficiency when compared to existing solutions. In [21], a framework has been proposed which broadcasts the message related to current traffic conditions among all the vehicles. This further reduces the travel time of vehicles on road. In [22], a routing has been proposed that is based on artificial intelligence and SDN controllers. This helps in better routing and mobility prediction. This routing technique further helps in reducing transmission delay and enhancing its performance. In [9], a decision based routing scheme has been proposed. This scheme is based on self organising wireless communication. Further enhanced greedy algorithm has been used for optimising the vehicular network. This results in reduced time delay and enhancement of transmission performance in the network. In [17], a routing protocol for VANET has been proposed which results in effective and efficient network resource utilisation. This protocol enhances the overall performance of the network. It reduces end-to-end delay which further enhances the performance of the network.

3   System Model

In this paper, a system model is proposed in which multiple intersections have been considered for an independent area. These areas are termed as local area maps and consist of various independent routes for traffic movement. Each area consists of Roadside units (RSUs), wireless sensors and vehicular traffic. When a vehicle enters an independent area, it will load the local area map in order to find the best route to reach its destination. The best route is determined by implementing the ACHM scheme that hybrids ACO with HMM. In this scheme, the vehicles are considered as ants which release pheromones as they move on the road. These pheromones form set of HMM state sequences where after probabilities are calculated. This helps in identifying the traffic density on a specific route so as to find the best possible routes in the current area for the vehicle. The system model representing a single intersection is shown in Fig. 1. The various notations used in this paper are shown in Table 1.

Table 1. Notations

Notation	Illustration
$\varphi_{(a,b)}$	Pheromone value while moving from region 'a' to 'b'
$Avg_{(\omega_{dp})}$	Average pheromone density
V_N	Vehicle node
$Avg_{(\omega_{(ss)})}$	Average pheromone density of start state
$Avg_{(\omega_{(obs,ms)})}$	Average pheromone density observed
$Avg_{(\omega_{(ps)})}$	Average pheromone density of the previous state
$Avg_{(\omega_{(trans_{ps \to ns})})}$	Average pheromone density when transition is made
$Avg_{(\omega_{(obs,ns)})}$	Average pheromone density observed for the next state

3.1   ACHM Vehicle Routing

In the proposed ACHM vehicle routing, ants are represented as vehicles that release pheromones $(\varphi_{(a,b)})$ while travelling from area 'a' to area 'b'. For every area, the average pheromone density $(Avg_{(\omega_{dp})})$ is calculated. This depicts the vehicular traffic density for that area. By using these values, HMM state sequences are formed. Based on the state sequences, the starting, transition, and emission probabilities are calculated.

Each transition in an area is recorded and helps in forming a HMM sequence. We are considering an example having two states 0 and 1 and two observations X and Y. Probabilities are assigned to each transition in the state by the $Avg_{(\omega_{dp})}$. The probabilities considered in this case are:

Starting probabilities:
State 0: 0.30
State 1: 0.70

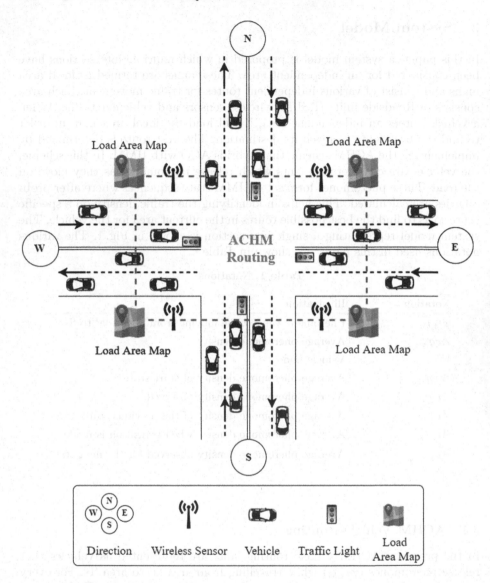

Fig. 2. System Model

Transition probabilities:

0 to 0: 0.25   0 to 1: 0.75

1 to 0: 0.40   1 to 1: 0.60

Emission probabilities:

X→ 0 : 0.35   X→ 1 : 0.65

Y→ 0 : 0.45   Y→ 1 : 0.55

The path that is selected for area 'a' using above probabilities is calculated as:

$$Avg_{(\omega_{(ss)})} * Avg_{(\omega_{(obs,ns)})} \tag{1}$$

where, $Avg_{(\omega_{(ss)})}$ is the average pheromone density of start state.
$Avg_{(\omega_{(obs,ns)})}$ is the average pheromone density observed for the next state.
Path 0 : 0.3 * 0.35 = 0.105
Path 1 : 0.7 * 0.65 = 0.455
For the observation corresponding to area 'b', the probabilities of the paths are calculated as:

$$Avg_{(\omega_{(ps)})} * Avg_{(\omega_{(trans_{ps \to ns})})} * Avg_{(\omega_{(obs,ns)})} \tag{2}$$

where, $Avg_{(\omega_{(ps)})}$ is the average pheromone density of the previous state.
$Avg_{(\omega_{(trans_{ps \to ns})})}$ is the average pheromone density of the next state when transition is made. $Avg_{(\omega_{(obs,ns)})}$ is the average pheromone density observed for the next state.
Path 00 : 0.105 * 0.25 * 0.45 = 0.0118
Path 01 : 0.105 * 0.75 * 0.55 = 0.0433
Path 10 : 0.455 * 0.40 * 0.45 = 0.0819
Path 11 : 0.455 * 0.60 * 0.55 = 0.1502

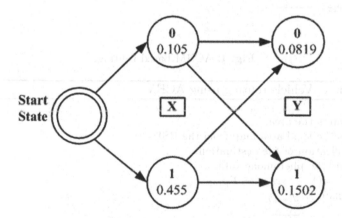

Fig. 3. Transition states probabilities

After calculating the probabilities of each path, we choose the path that has a lower probability and the other paths are discarded. This is because, higher probability value depicts higher pheromone value and hence, higher traffic density. For the case considered above, the probability 0.0118 of Path 00 and probability 0.0433 of Path 01 are the lowest as shown in Fig. 3. If we consider another region, the probabilities calculated for the paths are 100, 101, 110 and 111. Likewise, the probabilities for more regions will be calculated and the path can be determined.

Figure 4 represents the process of vehicle routing based on ACHM scheme. When a vehicle enters an area, it loads the local area map from the RSU. It then identifies the destination it wants to travel to. The RSU then updates the pheromone values $\varphi_{(a,b)}$. Average pheromone density is calculated using which HMM state sequences are formed. These sequences are then used in calculating various probabilities that determine the best route for the vehicle. Once the vehicle is routed, the pheromone values are again updated. The complete process of vehicle routing for proposed scheme is given in Algorithm 1.

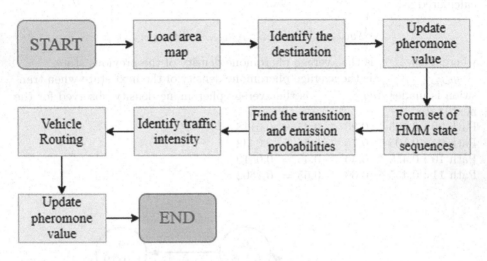

Fig. 4. ACHM based routing.

Algorithm 1. Vehicle routing using ACHM

START
1. V_N enters the area.
2. Loads the local area map from the RSU.
3. Identification of the destination.
4. Update the pheromone values:
$$\varphi_{(a,b)} = (1 - \lambda)\varphi_{(a,b)} + \Upsilon\varphi_{(a,b)}$$
5. Calculate $Avg_{(\omega_{dp})}$:
$$Avg_{(\omega_{dp})} = \frac{\sum(\omega_{dp})}{V_N}$$
6. Formation of HMM state sequences.
7. Calculate the probabilities using HMM state sequences.
8. Route the vehicle.
9. Re-update the pheromone values.
END

---

4   Performance Evaluation

The performance of the vehicular networks is determined by various key factors such as the travel time of vehicles in the network and the efficiency and speed of the routing algorithms. In this section, the effectiveness of our proposed ACHM scheme is evaluated on the basis of average travel time and computational overhead. The proposed scheme has incorporated ACO and HMM for efficient vehicle routing. The average travel time of vehicles has been reduced by using the pheromone values and HMM state sequence. The computational overhead of finding the effective and efficient path has also been minimized in the proposed scheme.

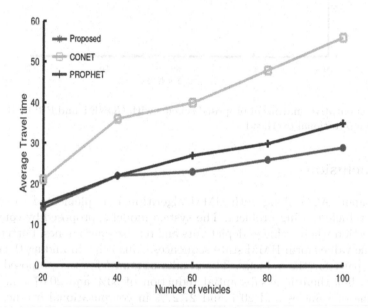

Fig. 5. Comparative analysis of proposed scheme with CONET and PROPHET on the basis of average travel time.

When the proposed scheme is compared with CONET [1] and PROPHET [10] for 100 vehicles, there is reduction of 93% and 20.67% in the average travel time of vehicles respectively and is shown in Fig. 5. The computational overhead of the proposed scheme is shown in Fig. 6. The performance comparison is also made with CONET [1] and PROPHET [10]. From the results, it is found that there is a substantial reduction of 20% and 27.27% respectively.

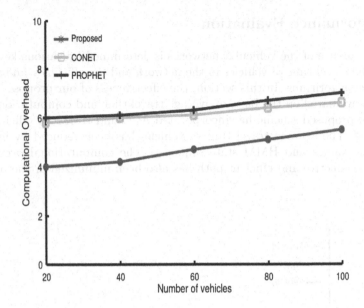

Fig. 6. Comparative analysis of proposed scheme with CONET and PROPHET on the basis of computational overhead

5   Conclusion

In this paper, ACO along with HMM algorithm is implemented to solve the dynamic vehicle routing problem. The system model is proposed by considering an intersection where vehicles depict ants and release pheromones. Further, these pheromone values form HMM state sequences. This helps in finding the efficient and best path for the vehicles. The results obtained for the proposed scheme represent that there is a substantial reduction of 93% and 20.67% in average travel time of vehicles and 20% and 27.27% in computational overhead while comparing it with CONET and PROPHET respectively. In future, we will try to incorporate other optimization techniques along with the proposed scheme in order to solve the routing problem and get better results.

References

1. Ahmed, S.H., Bouk, S.H., Yaqub, M.A., Kim, D., Gerla, M.: CONET: controlled data packets propagation in vehicular named data networks. In: 2016 13th IEEE Annual Consumer Communications & Networking Conference (CCNC), pp. 620–625. IEEE (2016)
2. Akabane, A.T., Pazzi, R.W., Madeira, E.R., Villas, L.A.: Modeling and prediction of vehicle routes based on hidden Markov model. In: 2017 IEEE 86th Vehicular Technology Conference (VTC-Fall), pp. 1–5. IEEE (2017)
3. Alouache, L., Nguyen, N., Aliouat, M., Chelouah, R.: Survey on IOV routing protocols: security and network architecture. Int. J. Commun Syst **32**(2), e3849 (2019)

4. Bouali, T., Sedjelmaci, H., Senouci, S.M.: A distributed prevention scheme from malicious nodes in VANETS' routing protocols. In: 2016 IEEE Wireless Communications and Networking Conference, pp. 1–6. IEEE (2016)
5. Bui, K.H.N., Jung, J.J.: ACO-based decision making for connected vehicles in IoT system. IEEE Trans. Industr. Inf. **15**(10), 5648–5655 (2019)
6. Chaurasia, B.K., Tomar, R.S., Verma, S.: Using trust for lightweight communication in VANETS. Int. J. AI Soft Comput. **5**(2), 105–116 (2015)
7. Cheng, T., Manley, E., Haworth, J.: Markov chain topological route selection. In: 2013 International Conference of GeoComputation, pp. 1–6 (2013)
8. Danquah, W.M., Altilar, T.D.: HYBRIST mobility model-a novel hybrid mobility model for VANET simulations. arXiv preprint arXiv:1406.0256 (2014)
9. Gao, H., Liu, C., Li, Y., Yang, X.: V2VR: reliable hybrid-network-oriented V2V data transmission and routing considering RSUs and connectivity probability. IEEE Trans. Intell. Transp. Syst. **22**(6), 3533–3546 (2020)
10. Han, S.D., Chung, Y.W.: An improved prophet routing protocol in delay tolerant network. Sci. World J. **2015**, 623090 (2015)
11. Jovanović, A., Nikolić, M., Teodorović, D.: Area-wide urban traffic control: a bee colony optimization approach. Trans. Res. Part C Emerg. Technol. **77**, 329–350 (2017)
12. Kumar, P.M., Manogaran, G., Sundarasekar, R., Chilamkurti, N., Varatharajan, R., et al.: Ant colony optimization algorithm with internet of vehicles for intelligent traffic control system. Comput. Netw. **144**, 154–162 (2018)
13. Kumar, S., Singh, J.: Internet of vehicles over VANETS: smart and secure communication using IoT. Scalable Comput. Pract. Experience **21**(3), 425–440 (2020)
14. Kumar, V., Kumar, K.P., Amudhavel, J., Inbavalli, P., Jaiganesh, S., Kumar, S.S.: A hidden Markov model for fault tolerant communication in VANETS. In: Proceedings of the 2015 International Conference on Advanced Research in Computer Science Engineering & Technology (ICARCSET 2015), pp. 1–5 (2015)
15. Malekian, R., Kavishe, A., Maharaj, B.T., Gupta, P.K., Singh, G., Waschefort, H.: Smart vehicle navigation system using hidden Markov model and RFID technology. Wireless Pers. Commun. **90**(4), 1717–1742 (2016)
16. Nguyen, T.II., Jung, J.J.: Multiple ACO-based method for solving dynamic MSMD traffic routing problem in connected vehicles. Neural Comput. Appl. **33**(12), 6405–6414 (2021)
17. Sadakale, R., Ramesh, N., Patil, R.: TAD-HOC routing protocol for efficient VANET and infrastructure-oriented communication network. J. Eng. **2020**, 1–12 (2020)
18. Sharma, S., Kaushik, B.: A survey on internet of vehicles: applications, security issues and solutions. Veh. Commun. **20**, 100182 (2019)
19. Tandon, R., Gupta, P.K.: Optimizing smart parking system by using fog computing. In: Singh, M., Gupta, P.K., Tyagi, V., Flusser, J., Ören, T., Kashyap, R. (eds.) ICACDS 2019. CCIS, vol. 1046, pp. 724–737. Springer, Singapore (2019). https://doi.org/10.1007/978-981-13-9942-8_67
20. Tandon, R., Gupta, P.: SP-EnCu: a novel security and privacy-preserving scheme with enhanced cuckoo filter for vehicular networks. In: Machine Learning and Information Processing, pp. 533–543 (2021)
21. Tandon, R., Gupta, P.K.: SV2VCS: a secure vehicle-to-vehicle communication scheme based on lightweight authentication and concurrent data collection trees. J. Ambient Intell. Human. Comput. **12**(10), 9791–9807 (2021). https://doi.org/10.1007/s12652-020-02721-5

22. Tang, Y., Cheng, N., Wu, W., Wang, M., Dai, Y., Shen, X.: Delay-minimization routing for heterogeneous VANETS with machine learning based mobility prediction. IEEE Trans. Veh. Technol. **68**(4), 3967–3979 (2019)
23. Verma, A., Tandon, R., Gupta, P.: TrafC-AnTabu: AnTabu routing algorithm for congestion control and traffic lights management using fuzzy model. Internet Technol. Lett. **4**(6), 1–6 (2021)
24. Yao, L., Wang, J., Wang, X., Chen, A., Wang, Y.: V2X routing in a VANET based on the hidden Markov model. IEEE Trans. Intell. Transp. Syst. **19**(3), 889–899 (2017)
25. Yao, L., Wang, Y., Wang, X., Wu, G.: Cooperative caching in vehicular content centric network based on social attributes and mobility. IEEE Trans. Mobile Comput. **20**(2), 391–402 (2019)
26. Ye, N., Wang, Z.Q., Malekian, R.: Lin: a method for driving route predictions based on hidden Markov model. Math. Probl. Eng. **2015**, 1–12 (2015)
27. Zhang, D., Zhang, T., Liu, X.: Novel self-adaptive routing service algorithm for application in VANET. Appl. Intell. **49**(5), 1866–1879 (2019)

Detection of Leaf Disease Using Artificial Intelligence

Sumit Bhardwaj[1], Devanshu Kumar Singh[1], Ria Singh[1], and Punit Gupta[2]([✉]) [iD]

[1] ASET, AMITY University Noida, Noida, UP, India
[2] Department of Computer and Communication Engineering, Manipal University Jaipur, Jaipur, India
punitg07@gmail.com

Abstract. In current generation with technological evolvement in various field its has made possible to implement intelligence in the field of health, education, irrigation and many more. The techniques using AI and ML has make it possible to help society and design applications for social welfare. The Convolution Neural Network (CNN) has recently become popular in agricultural applications, such as predicting healthy plants and detecting illnesses. This work forwards a self-build CNN for detection of leaf diseases. The model is trained over a dataset of 1456 images and validated over a dataset of 365 images which are preprocessed (resized) in order to decrease the computation complexity. The best training accuracy that is achieved is 99.96%, and the best validation accuracy is 90.96%. The plots of accuracy vs epoch and loss vs epoch are reported accordingly.

Keywords: AI · Leaf · Farming · Convolution Neural Network

1 Introduction

Since long agriculture has been the source of livelihood for majority of our country. Our food industry is ever on the rise and has been increasing its market presence constantly. The Indian food and grocery market was able to contribute to more than half of the worlds sales. Even though India ranked amongst the highest in the world hunger index, still we have not learnt and are wasting a huge portion of the crops we grow. Fruits and vegetables, especially being perishable, are ruined due to loss of proper storage or transport facilities. Cereals, pulses, and oil seeds are not far behind as all of these have reported major losses in produced crops. This gap between the farmers and the market has only resulted in losses for both the parties.

Modern day farmers have resorted to pesticides- chemical potions- to fight off incest's and other dangers to their fields. These often sprayed across the crops are carriers of many diseases and health adversary's unknown by the uninformed farmer. They have caused short as well as term effects on our health known as acute effects and long-term effects known as chronic effects on our health which can last for even decades after exposure. The disastrous aftereffects of these chemicals to the environment are widely known and witnessed and are a major red flag. Infants and pre-teens are seen to be

A. Kumar et al. (Eds.): ICAIDS 2021, CCIS 1673, pp. 181–190, 2022.
https://doi.org/10.1007/978-3-031-21385-4_16

more vulnerable to these pesticidal diseases than adults which is even more concerning regarding the already high infant mortality rate in India. In these times a solution in the form of natural pesticides can be applied with a lot of people already using Neem as it doesn't cause any health hazards.

In today's world, with increasing diseases for humankind, there is also an increase in diseases for the crops that we consume. But for some reason, we tend to neglect the health of crops which in turn affects us and this generates a negative feedback loop that is very difficult to get out of. As we know, with advancement in technology, and with the help of techniques in Artificial Intelligence, it has made it possible for us to diagnose these diseases more accurately and remotely, which we have further discussed in our research paper.

It is necessary to study and take into consideration the approach that were developed in previous works [2] also study their results in order to pave the way for a new approach.

R.S. Latha [1] in their research model with the help of deep learning, proposed an idea of detecting and classifying diseases in a tea leaf. The most critical processes in this model were disease detection and health monitoring that are essential for sustainable agriculture. In their research work, the convolutional neural network model was used in their research work with 2 fully connected layers, an input layer and four convolution layers. These convolutional layers basically draw out given input image and to classify the given name the output layer comes into work and categories them into 8 different classes which are Grey blight, Brown blight, Gray blight, normal leaf, Red scalp, Algae leaf spot, Bud blight and White spot.

Anushka Rao [3], in her study, introduced a novel hybrid approach Achieved in three phases, in the primary, image conversion and enhancement were included, which helped them to control the noise-related issues and low- illumination. The secondary phase, a combined features removal methods thrived and dependent on image moments, Gabor filter, GLCM, and Curvelet. In the end they trained a Neuro-Fuzzy Logic classifier with the extracted features. MATLAB was used for implementing the approach, considering Plant Village Database for analysis. Fatma MARZOUGUI [4], In his research model used pre-trained weights as a starting point and compared the proposed approach with several artisanal shallow structure approaches based on machine learning. They create data for experimentation using images of both healthy and unhealthy leaves. They applied the data augmentation technique; the model is based on Python's TensorFlow library. There exist various work [7–9, 13, 14] with similar work for detection diseases in tomato, grapes and grapes leaf's which has be caried out using machine learning models. In this work similar work has be show cases. Kumar et al. proposed object detection using muti-box detector for small object [10–12].

2 Methodology

The architecture of the network constitutes of multiple convolution layers followed by pooling layers. In order to prevent overfitting of the model over the dataset, dropout layers have also been used before moving onto the next set of convolution and pooling. Moving further the network consists of a flatten layer followed by a dense layer and then a dropout layer and finally a dense layer that gives the output. Data that is fed to the model must be preprocessed in order to further reduce the computation and make the whole training process more time efficient. The training process is made time efficient as on resizing the input data (input images), the reduced the sample size of the images enables the model to reduce the time that it takes learn (Figs. 1, 2, 3).

Fig. 1. Proposed methodology

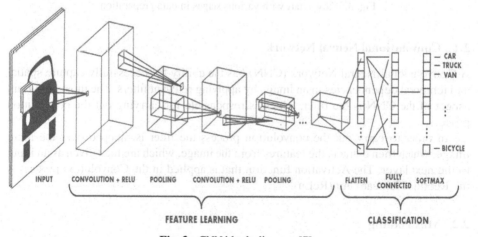

Fig. 2. CNN block diagram [7]

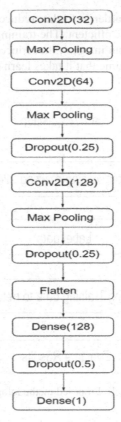

Fig. 3. Flow chart with various stages in data preparation

2.1 Convolutional Neural Network

A Convolutional Neural Network (CNN) has the ability to successfully capture spatial and temporal dependencies in an image by applying relevant filters. The most important aspect of the CNN is the filter, which is responsible for carrying out the convolution process.

In order to carry out the convolution process the filter is mapped over the input image, which then extracts the features from the image, which are then given as an input to the next layer. The Activation function that is applied in the Convolution process is the Rectified Linear Unit (ReLu).

2.2 Max Pooling

Generally, the layer that comes after the convolutional layer is the Max Pooling layer. Although many networks for example the architecture of VGG16 feed the features extracted from a CNN layer to another CNN layer to make the process of feature extraction more comprehensive, but this turns out to be computationally more demanding.

The purpose of the Max Pooling layer is to extract the most relevant features from an image using feature maps. It essentially down samples the image making the network computationally less demanding along with the output containing the most prominent features, as the max pooling layer calculates the maximum or largest value in each patch of feature map.

2.3 Dropout

The Dropout layer is used turn a specified percentage of units (neurons) that are chosen randomly off by setting their input to zero in order to reduce overfitting.

2.4 Flatten

The Flatten layer is used to simply vectorizes the input that it receives.

2.5 Dense

Dense is a fully connected layer of a specified number of units (neurons) that applies the activation function of choice.

2.6 Feature Extraction

The features of the images are extracted using the Convolution Neural Network (CNN) architecture. Each image that is given as an input has 3 color channels and is resized into a 224 × 224 pixel image prior to it being used as an input to the CNN layer in order for the feature extraction process to start and also because this standardization process will reduce the complexity of the network. The complete CNN architecture as mentioned above comprises of Convolution layers followed by Max Pooling layers and Dense (fully connected) layers along with Dropout layers to perform the feature extraction process. Among these, the number of filters used in the Convolutional layers is 32, 64 and 128.

The activation function applied transforms the weighted sum of the input to its higher or lower value, essentially 0 or 1. Among the various activation functions, we applied the Rectified Linear Unit (ReLu) due to its computational efficiency. The Rectified Linear Unit activation function also has some of its modified forms which are Leaky ReLu, parameteric ReLu and RReLu (Randomized Rectified Linear Unit).

The output of the last Convolution layer is fed to the Flatten layer that converts the input into vectorized form. This is a necessary step before feeding the input into the Dense layer. The first Dense layer consists of 128 units (neurons) activated with the ReLu activation function. The second Dense layer which is also the output layer consists of just 1 unit (neuron), and is activated with the Sigmoid activation function which gives the output either 0 or 1 depending upon the probability that is calculated by the network. If the probability is greater than 0.5, the image is labeled to be of class 1 which means the corresponding leaf is not healthy. And the output of 0 means that the leaf is healthy.

3 Result

The complete dataset is divided into 80% for the training process and 20% for validation and testing process. The samples that are chosen for segregation of dataset into training set and validation set are chosen randomly. From Table 1 we can say that the validation accuracy is best at 100 epochs with a figure of 90.96%. Comparison of the model at different number of epochs is shown in tabulated form.

Table 1. Comparison of accuracy and loss of the model

No. of epochs	Training accuracy (%)	Validation accuracy (%)
10	86.88	84.93
20	97.27	89.59
47	99.90	90.14
62	99.96	87.67
100	99.51	90.96

These results were obtained by making a few changes in the initial model which included Batch Normalization after every dropout layer. Below are the results of the model that failed.

Figure 4 and 5 explains the accuracy and the loss respectively of the model that failed in the training process and the training process was terminated at the 6th epoch due to the activation of the early stopping callback that itself terminated the training process when the training accuracy saturated.

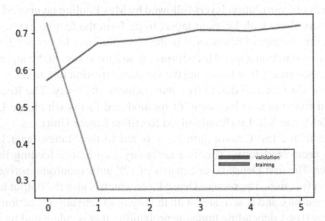

Fig. 4. Plots of accuracy of model with Batch Normalization

Figures 6 and 7 depict the loss and accuracy respectively of the model without Batch Normalization which is also the model that was successful. Although from Table 1 we

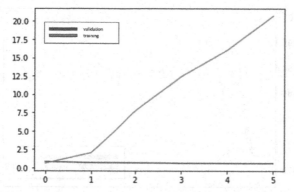

Fig. 5. Plots of loss with Batch Normalization

can see that the training accuracy was the maximum at 62nd epoch with a value of 99.96%, the training process was still not terminated because the model accuracy was fluctuating to a very small degree when as the number of epochs progressed which quite clear from the plots.

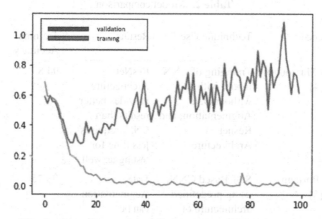

Fig. 6. Plots of loss of model without Batch Normalization

3.1 Performance Comparison

According to the Table 2, we see that Fatma et al. [4] used training of CNN model with and without Data Augmentation along with ResNet to arrive at a training accuracy of 94.8% and a validation accuracy OF 98.96%. Utpal Barman et al. [5] used self-based CNN using predefined architecture of CNN to attain a training accuracy of 98.75% and a validation accuracy of 96.75%. Shyamtanu Bhomwik et al. [2] applied image preprocessing and CNN based training to obtain training and validation accuracies of 95.66% and 96.78% respectively. Using image preprocessing, image recognition algorithm based on Neural

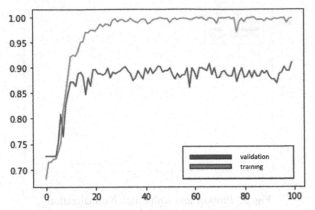

Fig. 7. Plots of accuracy of model without Batch Normalization

Network, and ReLu algorithm, Monu Bhagat et al. [6] arrived at a training accuracy of 98.4% and a validation accuracy of 96.78%.

Table 2. Model comparison

S.No	Reference	Technique Used	Results	Training Accuracy	Validation Accuracy
1	Fatma Marzougui et al. [4]	Trainging of CNN model with and without Data Augmentation, and Resnet Architecture	ResNet Architecture provides better results than CNN, requires less time for testing as well	94.8	98.96
2	Utpal Barman et al. [5]	Self-Based CNN, using predefined architecture of CNN	Data Augmentation can be implemented to improve the performance of CNN	98.75	96.75
3	Shyamtanu Bhomwik et al. [2]	Image Acquisition, Image Preprocessing, CNN based Training	A model which detects tea leaf disease with minimum computational complexity and minimum resource	95.66	95.94

(continued)

Table 2. (*continued*)

S.No	Reference	Technique Used	Results	Training Accuracy	Validation Accuracy
4	Monu Bhagat et al. [6]	Image preprocessing, Image Recognition algorithm based on neural network	Using ReLu along with ConvNet provides better accuracy than standard CNN application	98.4	96.78
5	Sumit/Devanshu et al	Image preprocessing, Self-Based CNN, using predefined architecture of CNN with ReLu and Dropouts	Using ReLu and multiple ConvNets, E58a model which detects leaf disease with significant accuracy	99.96	90.96

4 Conclusion

In our research paper, we have applied image preprocessing, self-based CNN and predefined architecture of CNN along with ReLu and Dropouts to obtain a maximum training accuracy of 99.96% and a maximum validation accuracy of 90.96%. The input data fed to the neural network was preprocessed in order to make the training process faster. Since the input images were resized, the model took more number of epochs to train. It was evident from the plots of accuracy and loss that network is more stable at the beginning of the training process and has already reached a significant training and validation accuracy. In future the work will be extended to various other datasets of leaf's and various other ML models can be tested to achieve better accuracy.

References

1. Latha, R.S., et al.:Automatic detection of tea leaf diseases using deep convolution neural network. In: 2021 International Conference on Computer Communication and Informatics (ICCCI), pp. 1–6 (2021)
2. Bhowmik, S., Talukdar, A.K., Kumar Sarma, K.: Detection of disease in tea leaves using convolution neural network. In: 2020 Advanced Communication Technologies and Signal Processing (ACTS), pp. 1–6 (2020)
3. Rao, A., Kulkarni, S.B.: A hybrid approach for plant leaf disease detection and classification using digital image processing methods. Int. J. Electr. Eng. & Educ. (October 2020)
4. Marzougui, F., Elleuch, M., Kherallah, M.: A deep CNN approach for plant disease detection. In: 2020 21st International Arab Conference on Information Technology (ACIT), pp. 1–6 (2020)

5. Barman, U., Sahu, D., Barman, G.G., Das, J.:Comparative assessment of deep learning to detect the leaf diseases of potato based on data augmentation. In: 2020 International Conference on Computational Performance Evaluation (ComPE), pp. 682–687 (2020)
6. Bhagat, M., Kumar, D., Mahmood, R., Pati, B., Kumar, M.: Bell pepper leaf disease classification using CNN. In: 2nd International Conference on Data, Engineering and Applications (IDEA), pp. 1–5 (2020)
7. https://towardsdatascience.com/convolutional-neural-networks-explained-9cc5188c4939. Accessed 2nd Jan 2022
8. Rothe, P.R., Kshirsagar, R.V.: Cotton leaf disease identification using pattern recognition techniques. In: 2015 International conference on pervasive computing (ICPC), pp. 1–6. IEEE (2015)
9. Wu, Q., Chen, Y., Meng, J.: DCGAN-based data augmentation for tomato leaf disease identification. IEEE Access 8, 98716–98728 (2020)
10. Kumar, A.: Design of secure image fusion technique using cloud for privacy-preserving and copyright protection. Int. J. Cloud Appl. Comput. (IJCAC) 9(3), 22–36 (2019)
11. Kumar, A., Zhang, Z.J., Lyu, H.: Object detection in real time based on improved single shot multi-box detector algorithm. EURASIP J. Wirel. Commun. Netw. 2020(1), 1–18 (2020). https://doi.org/10.1186/s13638-020-01826-x
12. Kumar, A.: " Review on implementation of digital image watermarking techniques using LSB and DWT. In: The Third International Conference on Information and Communication Technology for Sustainable Development (ICT4SD 2018), held during August 30–31, 2018 at Hotel Vivanta by Taj, GOA, INDIA
13. Sethy, P.K., Barpanda, N.K., Rath, A.K., Behera, S.K.: Deep feature based rice leaf disease identification using support vector machine. Comput. Electron. Agric. 175, 105527 (2020)
14. Liu, B., Ding, Z., Tian, L., He, D., Li, S., Wang, H.: Grape leaf disease identification using improved deep convolutional neural networks. Front. Plant Sci. 11, 1082 (2020)

Deep CNN Based Whale Optimization for Predicting the Rice Plant Disease in Real Time

S. Sai Satyanarayana Reddy[1]([✉]) [iD], G. Sowmya[2], Vudara Bhaskar Reddy[2], Boodidha Deepak Kumar[3], and Ashwani Kumar[3]

[1] Sreyas Institute of Engineering and Technology, Hyderabad 500068, India
saisn90@gmail.com

[2] Department of Computer Science and Engineering, Sreyas Institute of Engineering and Technology, Hyderabad 500068, India

[3] Department of CSE (AIML), Sreyas Institute of Engineering and Technology, Hyderabad 500068, India

Abstract. Plant diseases have a devastating impact on the security of food production, and they cause significant reductions in both the quality and quantity of agricultural products. To reduce this threat, various approaches such as machine learning and deep learning are presented. Therefore, automated recognition and detection of plant diseases is highly preferred in the field of agricultural industry. Most preferred systems utilize a greater number of training parameters but the classification accuracy is low. This paper proposes a deep CNN classifier for disease prediction in rice plant which is optimized by the whale optimization. The performance of the proposed whale based deep-CNN is analyzed using measures such as Accuracy, Sensitivity and Specificity. Based on training percentage Accuracy, Sensitivity and Specificity is 95.60%, 9557, 96.58 and 84%, 81.50, 88.73% for the K-Fold analysis. The accuracy is high when the training percentage is increased thus shows the improved performance outcome when compared with the existing conventional methods.

Keywords: Whale optimization · Deep CNN · Plant disease prediction

1 Introduction

Plant disease diagnosis entails a large amount of intricacy, which is accomplished through optical inspection of symptoms on plant leaves. Even plant pathologists and skilled agronomists frequently failed to diagnose particular diseases because of this complication and the enormous number of cultivated plants and their existing Phyto pathology issues, leading to incorrect conclusions and treatments. Agronomists who are asked to undertake such diagnoses through optical observation of infected plant leaves [4, 6, 7] would benefit from the development of an automated computational system for the diagnosis and detection of plant diseases. The plants may be suffered from certain type of infection based on the origin of the sickness, which complicates proper disease detection

© The Author(s), under exclusive license to Springer Nature Switzerland AG 2022
A. Kumar et al. (Eds.): ICAIDS 2021, CCIS 1673, pp. 191–202, 2022.
https://doi.org/10.1007/978-3-031-21385-4_17

using computer vision tools and approaches [5, 8, 9]. Furthermore, most approaches fail to successfully separate the leaf and accompanying lesion picture from its backdrop under complicated background settings, resulting in unsatisfactory disease recognition result.

As a result, due to the intricacy of sick leaf photos, automatic recognition of plant disease images remains a difficult task. Deep learning approaches, notably convolutional neural networks (CNNs), have recently risen to the top of the priority list for overcoming several obstacles [10]. In both big and small-scale challenges, CNN is the most used classifier for image recognition. It has demonstrated exceptional image processing and classification capabilities [1, 11–13]. For 3D CNN-based approaches, an active learning framework was presented to improve classification accuracy to the target level. Conventional methods are outperformed by CNN-based techniques. While 3D CNN outperformed 2D CNN, SVM was the most effective of the traditional approaches [14]. A CNN-based architecture that was tested on datasets such as Leaf Snap, Foliage, and Flavia released LeafNet [15]. By utilizing some parameters [16] investigated and assessed various CNN architectures. They looked on CNN for two computer-assisted diagnostic software programme. [17] created a model that uses deep CNN [2] to recognize 13 different plant diseases.

This paper proposes a rice plant disease prediction technique using whale optimization based deep CNN classifier. Although there are numerous existing techniques to detect the plant diseases is reviewed in the literature segment but they achieve low accuracy. Due to proposed deterministic structure and have greater learning capability, it allows the system to perform accurately predict the disease and classification. The major benefaction is as follows:

- In order to increase the quality of input images preprocessing is applied which is helpful for further processing.
- Due to its good investigation capability whale optimization is introduced for different applications.
- The optimization reduces the local trapping and it enhance the confluence and speed.

The residue of the paper is structured as follows: Sect. 2 reveals the various conventional methods reviews. Section 3 provides the proposed method with optimized classifier. Section 4 provides result and discussion of the proposed work and finally the outcome is concluded in Sect. 5.

2 Motivation

In this section, we enumerate the various existing techniques ascendance and drawbacks for the plant disease prediction. Moreover, the challenges involved in predicting the plant disease were also discussed.

2.1 Literature Review

Junde Chen, *et al.* [1] developed an Inception model by Visual Geometry Group for deep convolutional network, named INC-VGGNet. Its main intention is to countdown the width of feature maps for that purpose global pooling layer is utilized by replacing the fully connected layers. Although, this technique is not planned to be applicable in mobile devices to predict the plant disease in computerized manner.

Aditya Khamparia, *et al.* [2] integrating the attributes of convolutional neural networks and autoencoders that develops Convolutional encoder network. It involves two cases, in the size of 3 × 3 filter, the accuracy reaches high when the epochs are slightly increased. The 2 × 2 filter size model achieves good performance, but the accuracy tends to decrease after crossing 70 epochs, even though the loss begins to increase.

Koushik Nagasubramanian, *et al.* [3] employed an emerging technique for predicting the plant disease named Hyperspectral imaging. They arrange a 3D deep convolutional neural network which explicitly integrates the hyperspectral data. By the utilization of deep learning model, it helps to achieve high accuracy and it provides physiological insight into the sample predictions.

Konstantinos P. Ferentinos [4] developed convolutional neural network to detect and analyze the plant disease through deep learning techniques using the samples of healthy and diseased plants. Based on its high level of performance, it is well suited for automatic detection of plant diseases in leaves images.

Punam Bedi and Pushkar Gole [18] hybridized the convolutional neural network and auto encoder to analyze the bacterial plant disease in leaves. The training parameters required to detect the disease is in small amount so the training period of the model is minimum.

2.2 Challenges

- Due to the intricacy of the disease affected leaf images, the automatic detection of infectious leaf images is an even more demanding task [1].
- Various methods break down to effectively separate the infected leaves and their related ulcer figure from its surrounding due to their complicated environment [1].
- The deep convolutional neural network used to classify the plant species with high accuracy. Even though, it experienced few misclassifications by the reason of a smaller number of datasets [2].

3 Proposed Plant Disease Prediction Using Whale Optimization Dependent Deep CNN Classifier

This part enumerates the process involves in disease prediction and the proposed whale optimization dependent deep CNN classifier. Where the input data are extracted from the repository and the collected data fed forward to the preprocessing stage. Here, the input data get modified based on machine format. The color, shape and size be remolded and is adapted for further processing. The preprocessed data will be trained using deep CNN classifier in which the trained features are optimized by the whale optimization method. The outcome will be done based on the classifier which predicts the occurrence of disease (Fig. 1).

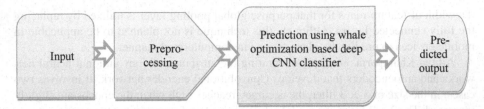

Fig. 1. Block diagram for the proposed plant disease prediction model

3.1 Image Pre-processing

In image pre-processing, the images are subjected to improvise the data which do not elaborate the content of the image information but it reduces the entropy even it is an important statistical scale. The main intention of the pre-processing is to repress the needless malformation and to improve the particular image quality which is associated with future processing. Depending on the size of the pixel neighborhood, it is categorized into four different processes for analyzing the new pixel luster.

3.2 Plant Disease Prediction Using Optimized Deep CNN Classifier

This section explains the architecture of optimized deep CNN classifier which helps to predict the rice plant disease. Whale optimization is utilized for optimal tuning of the classifier to accurately predicting the plant diseases.

3.2.1 Architecture of Deep CNN Classifier

Convolutional based Neural Network involves effectively processing the provided input which is motivated by its optical layer. This process is done by transferring the given sample image into simpler form, without affecting the major features for the identification. In Primary convolutional layer, to modify the input images into low level convoluted features that is to shape the edges of images some filters are included. When the filters get overlapped, the convolution can be view of as the matrix multiplication in between the kernel (filters) with each subgroups of sample input image. Then the pooling layer which helps in eliminating the dimensions of features obtained from primary convolution and it choose the particular features for further training the model. The required number of convolution and pooling layers is based on the intricacy of the data, if the number of layers reaches high, the computation process is increased. The terminal layer involves one or more fully connected layers and the output layer.Kumar *et al.* proposed an object detection method using SSMD algorithm [20–27].

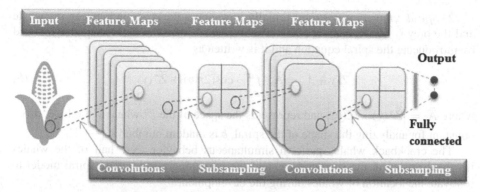

Fig. 2. Architecture of Deep Convolutional based Neural Network

3.2.2 Whale Optimization algorithm for optimal tuning of the classifier

The mathematical model of surrounding the prey, Spiral bubble web food conspire and exploring for prey is required initially and the whale optimization is then developed.

i) Surrounding the prey

The crookback whales analyze the location of prey and forming a barrier. The WOA consider that the initial finest solution is the aimed prey or it reaches nearer to the best solution until the unknown search space. The behavior of forming a barrier around the prey is formulated as,

$$\vec{A} = \left| \vec{B} \cdot \vec{Z}^*(y) - \vec{Z}(y) \right| \tag{1}$$

$$\vec{Z}(y + 1) = \vec{Z}^*(y) - \vec{C} \cdot \vec{A} \tag{2}$$

The initial iteration is represented by y, the coefficient vectors are $\vec{C}$ and $\vec{B}$, Z^* is the updated best position vector and $\vec{Z}$ is the position vector. In each iteration Z^* get renovated if there is a possible solution.

The $\vec{C}$ and $\vec{B}$ vectors are evaluated as,

$$\vec{C} = 2\vec{d} \cdot \vec{s} \cdot \vec{d} \tag{3}$$

$$\vec{B} = 2 \cdot \vec{s} \tag{4}$$

where $\vec{s}$ represents the random vector

ii) Bubble web offencing method (swindling phase)

Encircle the prey and renovate its position are the two processes in the bubble web offencing method and these techniques are formulated as follows,

1) Shrivel the surrounding mechanism: The value of $\vec{d}$ can be reduced in Eq. (3) from 2 to 0 in the range between $[-d, d]$ to obtain this behavior. The updated position of the exploring agent can be placed anywhere between the own position of the agent and also the position of present finest agent.

2) Spiral renovating position: Initially it evaluates the space in between the whale and the prey is (Z, X) *and* (Z*, X*). The movement whale in helix-shaped is reduced by introducing the spiral equation and it is written as,

$$\vec{Z}(y+1) = \vec{A}' \cdot f^{ab} \cdot \cos(2\pi b) + \vec{Z}^*(y) \qquad (5)$$

where $\vec{A}' = \left| \vec{Z}^*(y) - \vec{Z}(y) \right|$ and represents the space of the jth whale to the food, a is a constant for analyzing the shape of the spiral, b is random number in $[-1,1]$.

The crookback whales perform simultaneous behavior were half of the whales involved in shrivel the surroundings and the remaining takes part in spiral model to renovate the location of whales during the development.

$$\vec{Z}(y+1) = \begin{cases} \vec{Z}^*(y) - \vec{Z}(y) & \text{if } i < 0.5 \\ \vec{A}' \cdot f^{ab} \cdot \cos(2\pi b) + \vec{Z}^*(y) & \text{if } i \geq 0.5 \end{cases} \qquad (6)$$

where i is a random number in $[0,1]$.

The mathematical model of exploring the prey in random manner is evaluated as,

iii) Exploring for prey (scrutiny phase)

The exploring agent position get renovated in the scrutiny phase which is based on a random selection. This implementation and $\left| \vec{C} \right| > 1$ brings scrutiny and perform the global search is modelled as,

$$\vec{A} = \left| \vec{B} \cdot \vec{Z}_r - \vec{Z} \right| \qquad (7)$$

$$\vec{Z}(y+1) = \vec{Z}_r - \vec{C} \cdot \vec{A} \qquad (8)$$

where $\vec{Z}_r$ is the random vector selected from the present population.

4   Results and Discussion

This section demonstrates the results and discussion of the whale optimization dependent deep-CNN classifier for accurate prediction of rice plant diseases. The performance analysis is based on the Accuracy, Sensitivity and Specificity with the basis of training percentage and K-Fold values. Moreover, the comparative analysis is performed with the conventional methods in order to vindicate the performance of the proposed method.

4.1   Experimental Setup

The proposed whale optimization based deep-CNN for detecting the disease in rice plant is implemented using MATLAB r2021 tool running in Windows 10, Operating system with 8GB RAM.

4.2 Comparative Methods

The methods utilized for the comparison includes Artificial Neural Network (ANN) [20], Support Vector Machine (SVM) [28] and Convolutional Neural Network (CNN) [29] which are compared with the developed whale based deep-CNN method.

4.3 Performance Measures

The measures used for the discussion in the conventional methods SVM, ANN and CNN with the proposed whale based deep-CNN model are Accuracy, Sensitivity and the Specificity.

4.4 Analysis Based on Comparative Methods

The performance evaluation of the conventional method in predicting the rice plant disease is depends on the Sensitivity, Specificity and Accuracy to describe the significance of the newly developed whale based deep Convolutional NN model.

i) Analysis based on training percentage

The comparative analysis of the methods in rice plant disease is illustrated in Fig. 2. The analysis performed in methods such as SVM, ANN, CNN and the proposed whale based deep-CNN for the prediction of diseases in rice plant. The results obtained from the conventional methods SVM, ANN and CNN are 84.62%,86.47% and 93.69% and the proposed method whale based deep-CNN achieves 95.60% these indicates the accuracy rate of the method with the training percentage of 90. The sensitivity of the conventional methods SVM, ANN and CNN are 80.90%, 84.29% and 91.79% and the proposed method whale based deep-CNN achieves 93.29% with the training percentage of 80. The analysis of specificity in the conventional methods SVM, ANN and CNN with training percentage of 70 are 87.71%, 89.26% and 93.50% and the proposed method whale based deep-CNN achieves 94.54% respectively.

i) Evaluation based on K-Fold:

The comparative estimation of the methods in rice plant disease is illustrated in Fig. 3. The analysis performed in methods such as SVM, ANN, CNN and the proposed whale dependent deep-CNN for the prediction of diseases in rice plant. The results obtained from the conventional methods SVM, ANN and CNN are 79%, 81% and 83%and the proposed method whale based deep-CNN achieves 84%these indicates the accuracy rate of the method with the K-Fold value 10. The sensitivity of the conventional methods SVM, ANN and CNN are 77.36%,78.39% and 79.85%and the proposed method whale based deep-CNN achieves 81.01%with the K-Fold value 9. The analysis of specificity in the conventional methods SVM, ANN and CNN with the K-Fold value 8 are 85.17%,86.25% and 87.22%and the proposed method whale based deep-CNN achieves 88.14% respectively (Fig. 4).

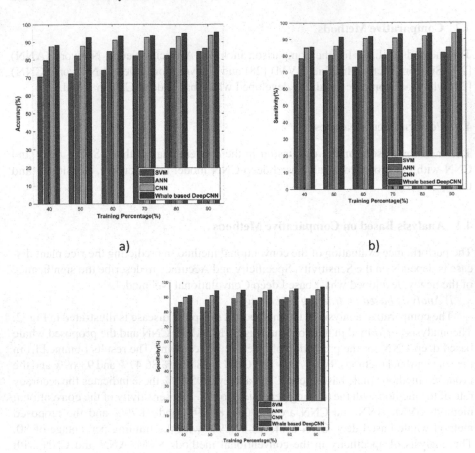

Fig. 3. Comparative evaluation of developed whale dependent deep-CNN using training pe centage based on performance metric a) Accuracy b) Sensitivity and c) Specificity

4.5 Comparative Discussion

This section presents the discussion of the methods employed for the disease prediction in rice plant. The discussion depicts the performance evaluation of the methods accuracy, sensitivity and specificity. Table 1 shows the comparative discussion of the methods with the training percentage of 90 and K-Fold value be 10.

Comparative discussion of conventional methods with the proposed whale based deep-CNN by using the training percentage 90 and K-Fold value be10 is sown in Table1. The comparative analysis performed in methods such as SVM, ANN, CNN and the proposed whale based deep-CNN for the prediction of diseases in rice plant. The results obtained from the conventional methods SVM, ANN and CNN are 84.62%,86.47% and

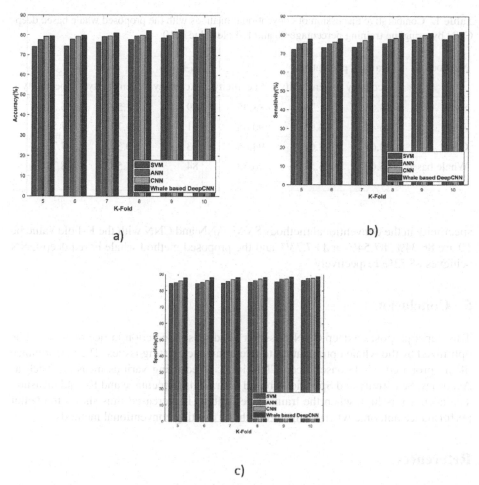

Fig. 4. Comparative analysis of proposed whale based deep-CNN using K-Fold values based on a) Accuracy b) Sensitivity and c) Specificity

93.69% and the proposed method whale based deep-CNN achieves 95.60% these indicates the accuracy rate of the method with the training percentage of 90. The sensitivity of the conventional methods SVM, ANN and CNN are 81.70%, 84.85% and 93.67% and the proposed method whale based deep-CNN achieves 95.57% with the training percentage of 90. The analysis of specificity in the conventional methods SVM, ANN and CNN with training percentage of 90 are 88.65%, 90.65% and 94.66% and the proposed method whale based deep-CNN achieves 96.58% respectively. The results obtained from the conventional methods SVM, ANN and CNN are 79%, 81% and 83% and the proposed method whale based deep-CNN achieves 84% these indicates the accuracy rate of the method with the K-Fold value be 10. The sensitivity of the conventional methods SVM, ANN and CNN are 77.59%, 79.79% and 80.32% and the proposed method whale based deep-CNN achieves 81.50% with the K-Fold value be 10. The analysis of

Table 1. Comparative discussion of conventional methods with the proposed whale based deep-CNN by using the training percentage 90 and K-Fold value be10

Methods	Training percentage			K-Fold		
	Accuracy	Sensitivity	Specificity	Accuracy	Sensitivity	Specificity
SVM	84.62	81.70	88.65	79	77.59	86.34
ANN	86.47	84.85	90.65	81	79.79	87.54
CNN	93.69	93.67	94.66	83	80.32	87.73
Whale based deep-CNN	95.60	95.57	96.58	84	81.50	88.73

specificity in the conventional methods SVM, ANN and CNN with the K-Fold value be 10 are 86.34%, 87.54% and 87.73% and the proposed method whale based deep-CNN achieves 88.73% respectively.

5   Conclusion

This paper proposes a deep CNN classifier for disease prediction in rice plant which is optimized by the whale optimization to overcome the existing issues. The performance of the proposed whale based deep-CNN is analyzed using various measures such as Accuracy, Sensitivity and Specificity based on training percentage and K-Fold measure. The accuracy is high when the training percentage is increased thus shows the better performance outcome when compared with the existing conventional methods.

References

1. Chen, J., Chen, J., Zhang, D., Sun, Y., Nanehkaran, Y.A.: Using deep transfer learning for image-based plant disease identification. Comput. Electron. Agric. **173**, 105393 (2020)
2. Khamparia, A., Saini, G., Gupta, D., Khanna, A., Tiwari, S., de Albuquerque, V.H.C.: Seasonal crops disease prediction and classification using deep convolutional encoder network. Circuits Syst. Signal Process. **39**(2), 818–836 (2020)
3. Nagasubramanian, K., Jones, S., Singh, A.K., Sarkar, S., Singh, A., Ganapathysubramanian, B.: Plant disease identification using explainable 3D deep learning on hyperspectral images. Plant Methods **15**(1), 1–10 (2019)
4. Ferentinos, K.P.: Deep learning models for plant disease detection and diagnosis. Comput. Electron. Agric. **145**, 311–318 (2018)
5. Vishnoi, V.K., Kumar, K., Kumar, B.: Plant disease detection using computational intelligence and image processing. J. Plant Dis. Prot. **128**(1), 19–53 (2020). https://doi.org/10.1007/s41 348-020-00368-0
6. Mohanty, S.P., Hughes, D.P., Salathe, M.: Using deep learning for image-based plant disease detection. Front. Plant Sci. **7** (2016)
7. Yang, X., Guo, T.: Machine learning in plant disease research. Europ. J. BioMed. Res., 6–9 (2017)

8. Kulkarni, A., Patil, A.: Applying image processing technique to detect plant diseases. Int J. Modern Eng. Res. IJMER **2**(5), 3661–3664 (2012)
9. Nagasai, S., Rani, S.J.: Plant disease identification using segmentation techniques. Plant Dis. **4**(9), 411–413 (2015)
10. Barbedo, J.G.: Factors influencing the use of deep learning for plant disease recognition. Biosys. Eng. **172**, 84–91 (2018)
11. Kamilaris, A., Prenafeta-Boldú, F.X.: Deep learning in agriculture: a survey. Comput. Electron. Agricul. **147**, 70–90 (2018)
12. Kussul, N., Lavreniuk, M., Skakun, S., Shelestov, A.: Deep learning classification of land cover and crop types using remote sensing data. IEEE Geosci. Remote Sens. Lett. **14**(5), 778–782 (2017)
13. Yalcin, H.: Plant phenology recognition using deep learning: Deep-Pheno. In: 2017 6th International Conference on Agro-Geoinformatics, pp. 1–5. IEEE (2017)
14. Gupta, D., Ahlawat, A.: Usability feature selection via MBBAT: a novel approach. J. Comput. Sci. **23**, 195–203 (2017)
15. Barre, P., Stover, B.C., Muller, K.F., Steinhage, V.: LeafNet: a computer vision system for automatic plant species identification. Ecol. Inform. **40**, 50–56 (2017)
16. Shin, H.C., et al.: Deep convolutional neural networks for computer-aided detection: CNN architectures, dataset characteristics and transfer learning. IEEE Trans. Med. Imaging **35**(5), 1285–1298 (2016)
17. Sladojevic, S., Arsenovic, M., Anderla, A., Culibrk, D., Stefanovic, D.: Deep neural networks-based recognition of plant diseases by leaf image classification. Comput. Intell. Neurosci (2016)
18. Bedi, P., Gole, P.: Plant disease detection using hybrid model based on convolutional autoencoder and convolutional neural network. Artif. Intell. Agric. **5**, 90–101 (2021)
19. Kaur, P., Pannu, H.S., Malhi, A.K.: Plant disease recognition using fractional-order Zernike moments and SVM classifier. Neural Comput. Appl. **31**(12), 8749–8768 (2019)
20. Sai Satyanarayana Reddy, S., Kumar, A.: Edge detection and enhancement of color images based on bilateral filtering method using K-Means clustering algorithm. In: Tuba, M., Akashe, S., Joshi, A. (eds.) ICT Systems and Sustainability. Advances in Intelligent Systems and Computing, vol. 1077. Springer, Singapore (2020)
21. Kumar, A., Reddy, S.S.S. (eds.): Advancements in Security and Privacy Initiatives for Multimedia Images. IGI Global, Hershey, PA (2021). https://doi.org/10.4018/978-1-7998-2795-5
22. Kumar, A., Srivastava, S.: Object detection system based on convolution neural networks using single shot multi-box detector. Procedia Comput. Sci. **171**, 2610–2617 (2020)
23. Kumar, A., Zhang, Z.J., Lyu, H.: Object detection in real time based on improved single shot multi-box detector algorithm. EURASIP J. Wirel. Commun. Netw. **2020**(1), 1–18 (2020). https://doi.org/10.1186/s13638-020-01826-x
24. Fatima, S.A., et al.: Object recognition and detection in remote sensing images: a comparative study. In: 2020 International Conference on Artificial Intelligence and Signal Processing (AISP). IEEE (2020)
25. Kumar, A., Ghrera, S.P., Tyagi, V.: Modified buyer seller watermarking protocol based on discrete wavelet transform and principal component analysis (2015)
26. Kumar, A.: Design of secure image fusion technique using cloud for privacy-preserving and copyright protection. Int. J. Cloud Appl. Comput. (IJCAC) **9**(3), 22–36 (2019)
27. Kumar, A., Ghrera, S.P., Tyagi, V.: Implementation of wavelet based modified buyer-seller watermarking protocol (BSWP) (2014)

28. Agatonovic-Kustrin, S., Beresford, R.: Basic concepts of artificial neural network (ANN) modeling and its application in pharmaceutical research. J. Pharm. Biomed. Anal. **22**(5), 717–727 (2000)
29. Dutta, A., Batabyal, T., Basu, M., Acton, S.T.: An efficient convolutional neural network for coronary heart disease prediction. Expert Syst. Appl. **159**, 113408 (2020)

DCBC_DeepL: Detection and Counting of Blood Cells Employing Deep Learning and YOLOv5 Model

Md. Abdur Rahaman[1], Md. Mamun Ali[1], Md. Nazmul Hossen[2],
Md. Nayer[3], Kawsar Ahmed[2,4(✉)], and Francis M. Bui[4]

[1] Department of Software Engineering, DIU, Sukrabad, Dhaka 1207, Bangladesh
[2] Group of Biophotomatix, Department of ICT, MBSTU, Tangail 1902, Bangladesh
kawsar.ict@mbstu.ac.bd
[3] Department of CSE, BIT Patna, B.I.T. Patna Campus, Samanpura 800014,
Bihar, India
[4] Department of ECE, USASK, 57 Campus 9 Drive, Saskatoon,
SK S7N 5A9, Canada

Abstract. Blood cell identification and counting is critical for doctors and physicians nowadays in order to diagnose and treat a variety of disorders. Platelet identification and counting are frequently performed in the context of many types of sickness such as COVID-19 and others. However, it is frequently costly and time intensive. Additionally, it is not widely available. From this vantage point, it is necessary to develop an efficient technical model capable of detecting and counting three fundamental types of blood cells: platelets, red blood cells, and white blood cells. Thus, this study proposes a deep learning-based model based on the YOLOv5 model with a precision of 0.799. The model consists of thre different layers such as backbone, neck and output layer The model is extremely capable of detecting and counting individual blood cells. Doctors, physicians, and other professionals will be able to detect and count blood cells using real-time images. It will significantly minimise the cost and time associated with detecting and counting blood cells by utilizing real-time blood images.

Keywords: Deep learning · Platelets · Red blood cell · White blood cell · YOLOv5

1 Introduction

Blood cell counting, according to medical authorities, is more significant approach to apply in clinical diagnosis and aids in the evaluation of health issues. It is known to all of us that human blood has three kinds of blood cells. Red blood cells (RBC), white blood cells (WBC), and platelets are the three kinds of blood cells found in the human body [1,2]. RBC is also known as erythrocytes in medical science, and it is the most common form of blood cells, which is responsible for 40–45% of entire blood cells [3]. RBCs are the mostly available forms of blood cell and perform the most important functions such as, the circulatory system transports oxygen from the lungs and bodily capillaries to the various tissues of the body via blood flow and hemolytic anemia, thalassemia, enzymopathies, various membranopathies, and sickle cell anemia are all disorders that require RBC counts [4,5]. In addition to that, hemoglobin is one of the most important element of blood which belongs to RBC. Maintaining hemoglobin rate is very crucial for human body. Platelets, also described as thrombocytes, are large blood cells that aids in the preventing of bleeding. WBCs make up only 1% of total blood cells and are also known as leukocytes, which are responsible for immune system that defends the body from infection and sickness.

When there are so many blood cells in blood, manually estimating them with a tool such as hemocytometer is extremely inaccurate and time intensive, and case validity is highly dependent on clinical laboratory skills, which is not efficient enough [6]. As a result, automated counting technology will aid in the production of flawless and precise detection and count of blood cells. Computer vision and deep learning can play a vital to solve such a problem to identify and estimate the blood cells from cell images. For object detection and picture classification applications, deep learning approaches grow more emphatic and accurate. As an outcome of this technique, it uses a severe field of medical science [7]. From this perspective, the research aims to propose a deep learning-based computer vision technique employing the newest variant of YOLO, which is a deep learning based model.

2   Related Work

Generally, there are two types of processes, which are used for automatic blood cell identification and estimation such as machine learning and image processing approach. In recent times, a number of research works have been conducted to identify and estimate blood cells from images. Alam and Islam proposed an automated object detection and count blood cells using machine learning from smear images [6]. YOLO comes in a variety of versions, each of which specifies that the model is comprehensible. Hough transform approach is used by Acharjee and Chakrabartty to count RBCs and determine two types of shapes, which are biconcave and oval [5]. Habibzadeh and Jannesari proposed a differential estimation of WBC, where they employed traditional classifications and deep learning approaches to perform feature extraction and recognise WBCs, and offer five different categories of WBC [8].

In the year 2020, Qiu et al. developed an algorithm that performs sickle RBC classification tests, mapping of RBC, cell clustering, and classification automatically [9]. This article explains how to identify and estimate distinct types of blood cells employing real time blood smear image using deep learning. To work, a method does not need to cluster into two individual clustering or grayscale transformation. This is a completely automatic, precise, and time-saving method.

Suryani et. al. approached to Identify the sickness of leukemia in particular Acute leukemia (ALL) and acute myeloid leukemia (AML) type M3 using morphological parameters and image processing. They did not hit the expected outcome for low amount of data [10]. Chadha et. al. proposed image processing, an automation approach for estimation of red blood cells has been developed through the Hough transformation was used to extract text features utilizing morphology, thresholding segmentation, and cell counting. More data make more accurate results but there is no information about dataset [11]. Navea et. al. suggested to utilize an image processing software to identify and estimate red and white blood cells in urine samples was made possible with 94.99% average results. Execution time consuming is more effective for a machine [12]. Safca et. al. provided a method for classifying blood cells into two categories: normal and pathological. The entire program is built on MATLAB image processing algorithms. They proposed blood cells detecting while blood cells counting is more vital role for a laboratorian [13].

From afforementioned discussion, it is found that more efficient system is required to recognize and estimate blood cells from real blood images for medical advancements. From this point of view, the study focuses on finding an effective model to identify and estimate blood cells and YOLOv5 is selected for its high efficiency and stability. So, we apply YOLOv5 on an open access dataset to build a highly efficient model. Our contribution in this study is mentioned as following:

– At first, we collected a large number of blood cell images, it was annotated to fit for the applied model.
– Secondly, to detect blood cells, we employed multiple efficient preprocessing techniques to allow images to accurately fit by YOLOv5 model.
– Finding the best fit parameter for the proposed model to get the highest performance from the proposed model.
– Proposed a well performed deep learning based YOLOv5 model, which is the latest version of YOLO series.

The remaining of this study work is arranged as follows: Sect. 3 presents the Materials and Methods with dataset description employed in this study. The tools and evaluation results with discussion are presented in Sect. 4. We present conclusions and future direction of this work has been added in the conclusion section.

3   Materials and Methods

Python (Version 3.8.5) has been employed to conduct the study and build the model. Google colab was used as python programming environment for analyzing the data and build the model. In this study, the most latest iteration of the YOLO entity recognition technological advances was employed to recognize blood cells. In terms of computer vision, it concentrates on algorithmic implementation, data labeling, and data collection. The overall workflow and research methodology is illustrated in Fig. 1.

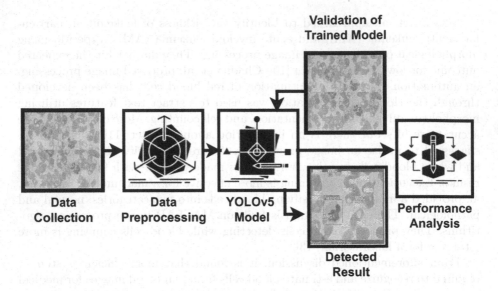

Fig. 1. Workflow of the study

3.1 Dataset

A image dataset was collected with blood cell images, which is freely available, was used in this study [14]. It featured a total of 366 annotated smear photos, but there were significant evidence problems in the collected samples, and some of the photo labelling were incorrect. Many RBCs, for instance, are labeled as Plateletels and others as well. As a consequence, the error was corrected by proper placement. Our dataset contains three types of blood cells: RBCs, WBCs, and Platelets. The data samples were split into three parts such as training (50%), testing (30%), and to validate the prediction 20% of samples are taken as validation set. All the images of the dataset was manually labelled for recognition of cells efficiently. The next step was to convert the XML sample to TXT sample.

3.2 YOLOv5 Architectural Model to Identify Object

The most recent and latest variant of YOLO approach [15] is YOLOv5. YOLOv5 also has different version such as YOLOv5m, YOLOv5s, YOLOv5l, and YOLOv5x. In this study, YOLOv5m has been employed since this model has the highest object detection accuracy from different types of images and videos and can identify 140 frames per which is its maximum speeds of object identification. As opposed to the YOLOv5 entity recognition system network is mediocre, YOLOv5 is 90% more accurate compare to YOLOv4, for real time object detection YOLOv5 model is compatible. Thus, the advantages of the YOLOv5 [15] network are its high object identification accuracy, lightweight features, as well as fast detection speeds. On account of the accuracy performance

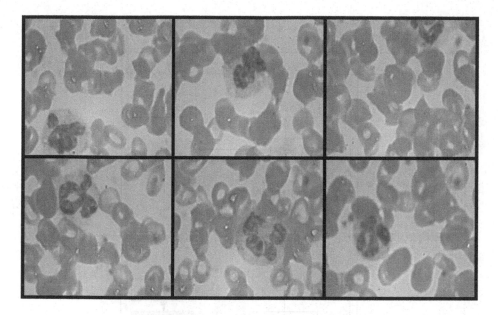

Fig. 2. Sample of collected data

of live entity recognition and lightweight exhibition of blood cell detection models are fundamental activity to the efficiency and accuracy of the targeted blood cells detection found on YOLOv5 architecture. Here, many kinds of YOLOv5 versions are available respectively which has been proposed in different adding differnt advance features [15]. YOLOv5 modules at first perform feature extraction which is the main advantage of YOLOv5 and the convolution kernels alter among all the versions.

Backbone: The backbone, as depicted in Fig. 2, is the first part of YOLOv5 network architecture. Backbone is built up by numerous components like focus and csp structure. The slicing operation and turning into a feature mapping are the most significant operations in the focus structure. Using the YOLOv5 structure as an instance, the real picture, whose size is $608 \times 608 \times 3$, is fed into the focus level, and the slicing approach begins to generate a mapped feature, whose size is $304 \times 304 \times 12$, which is then changed to a $304 \times 304 \times 32$ mapped feature based on a technique which is mostly known as convolution operation of 32 convolution kernels. Then leaky relu modified the feature map. Backbone is made up of CBL (Convolution (CONV), Batch Normalization (BN), and Leaky-ReLU). Batch normalization and leaky relu are the active functions of this primary module, which is made up of convolutional layers. In YOLO, this active feature is mostly employed equipment. In YOLOv5, CSPX is the final part of the backbone [16], and two forms of CSP structures are used. CSP1 X is utilized in the backbone network, while CSP2 X is utilized in the neck network.

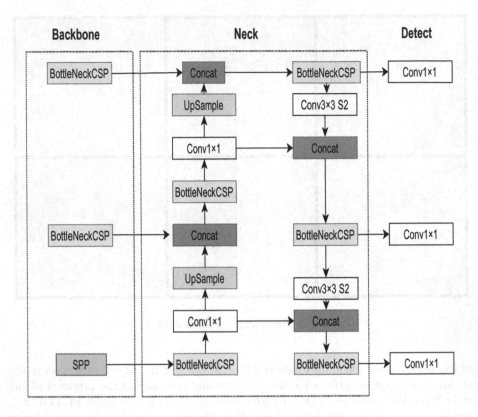

Fig. 3. YOLOv5 network architecture

The primary element in CBL is residual units (RES), which are utilized to make network architecture deeper. As a foundational element of CBL, the immediate superposition of tensors to adding another layer was accomplished.

Neck: The neck is the second part of the YOLOv5 network. Feature Pyramid Network (FPN) and Path Aggregation Network structure are used in the neck (Fig. 3). To increase the ability of network feature integration, the CSP2 architecture created by CSPnet is employed in the portion of Neck of YOLOv5 [17]. It plays a vital role in the object detection by YOLO model [18].

Detect: The last element of the YOLOv5 network infrastructure is the head, also known as the predictor. Based on the supplied picture dimensions and boxes, the head estimates the category or object size using neck characteristics (large, moderate, tiny) [19]. YOLOv5 can detect large, medium, and small items, whereas previous versions of YOLO were unable to do so. To identify little objects, the targeted shaped area must be smaller than 32 pixels × 32 pixels. 96

pixels for moderate objects, on the contrary. Lastly, the point of impact must be greater than 96 pixels × 96 pixels in order to recognize big items. [20].

3.3 Performance Evaluation

The most important task in machine learning and deep learning is to evaluate the performance of an applied models and compare their result to find the best possible classifier or model. For evaluating the applied model, three performance evaluation metrics are considered in this study such as precision, recall, and mean average precision (mAP). The performance of these performance evaluation metrics are calculated using following equations [21–24].

$$Precision = \frac{TP}{TP + FP} \tag{1}$$

$$Recall = \frac{TP}{TP + FN} \tag{2}$$

$$mAP = \frac{1}{N} \sum_{N}^{i-1} Api \tag{3}$$

True positive *(TP)* refers to the perfect identification of a real item in a picture. False positive *(FP)* object recognition occurs when the system finds an entity that does not exist in the picture. A false negative *(FN)* is an item that is present in the frame but is not recognized by the system. The intersection over union (IoU) approach in object recognition analyzes the overlapping area between the predicted bounding box and the actual entity's corresponding ground truth box. Identification can be classified as correct or wrong by evaluating the IoU to a predefined threshold.

4   Results and Discussion

At first the dataset was annotated to fit the dataset to YOLOv5 since YOLO architecture need annotated dataset. Then the dataset was preprocessed as necessary for better detection of blood cells. After processing the data, the deep learning model YOLOv5, latest version of YOLO, is applied on the processed dataset. For training the models, 100 epochs were employed to the model to conduct this study for the detection and count blood cells.

4.1 Performance Analysis of Applied Models

The result of all performance measures for all classes are shown in Table 1, which was obtained using model YOLOv5 on the processed dataset. The tables show each of the 3 categories as well as the whole validation data. The table displays that the applied model gained 0.799 precision value for whole dataset, where

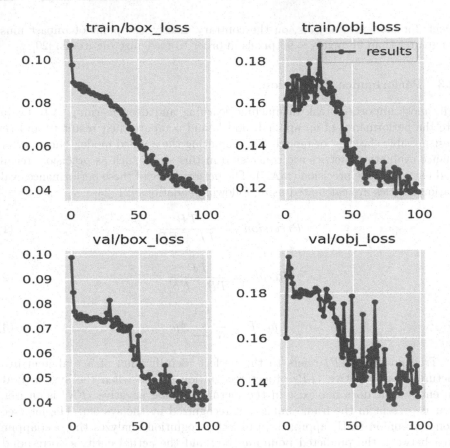

Fig. 4. YOLOv5 network architecture

0.967, 0.796, and 0.633 for Platelets, RBC and WBC respectively. In terms of recall, the model showed 100% performance for the detection of Platelets, where 0.803 for entire dataset. Overall performance indicates that the applied model's performance is satisfactory to identify and estimate blood cells employing real time blood image data (Fig. 4).

4.2 Validation of the Applied Model

The YOLOv5 framework is first trained to train, and then it is evaluated to determine the effectiveness of the developed application. The trained model's projected outcome and efficiency were then verified using % of the complete dataset, and the validating outcome is shown in Fig. 2 (Fig. 5).

Figure 2 depicts the expected outcome of the employed framework, YOLOv5, as evaluated by 20% of the entire photos. The figure depicts the identified blood cells as well as their accuracy. Figure 2 shows that the maximum accuracy for recognizing platelets is 90%, with 70% for RBCs and 80% for WBCs in the first

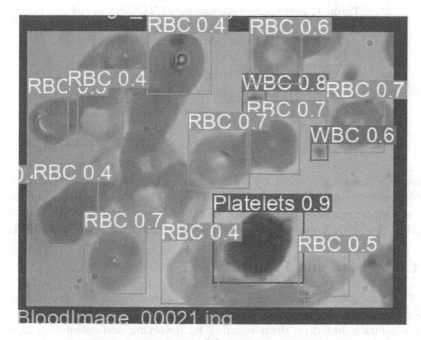

(a)

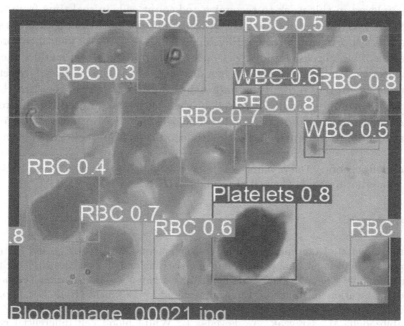

(b)

Fig. 5. Validated outcome of the proposed model

Table 1. Performance comparison of YOLOv5 model

Class	Detected cells	Precision	Recall	mAP@ 0.5	mAP@ 0.5:0.95
All	1246	0.799	0.803	0.824	0.428
Platelets	80	0.967	1	0.995	0.652
RBC	1076	0.796	0.654	0.775	0.41
WBC	90	0.633	0.756	0.701	0.221

picture. The maximum accuracy for recognizing platelets in the second picture is 80%, with 80% for RBCs and 60% for WBCs. Figure 3 shows that the models used are extremely able to recognize blood cells automatically. As a result, it describes the model's capacity to recognize and identify specific blood cells.

5   Conclusion and Future Work

Blood cell identification and estimation is a critical chore for certain types of patients at times, and it is highly expensive. The purpose of this project was to build a solution based on deep learning for detecting and estimation of blood cells such as RBC, WBC, and Platelets. Two versions of the YOLOv5 model were employed in this work to recognise and count cells in real time from blood pictures. It was discovered that YOLOv5m performs better than YOLOv5s since it gained 0.799 precision in value. Physicians will be capable of identification and estimation of blood cells employing the proposed approach. It will reduce the cost of diagnostics. Thus far, the study has discovered that the proposed system, is capable of accurately recognising and estimating blood cells in real-time blood pictures. The number of images used in this study was limited. In future, we will add more images and upgraded technologies to develop more effective and accurate model to recognize and estimate blood cells from real time cell images.

Acknowledgement. The research was financially supported by the Natural Sciences and Engineering Research Council of Canada (NSERC).

References

1. Cruz, D., et al.: Determination of blood components (WBCs, RBCs, and Platelets) count in microscopic images using image processing and analysis. In: 2017 IEEE 9th International Conference on Humanoid, Nanotechnology, Information Technology, Communication and Control, Environment and Management (HNICEM), pp. 1–7. IEEE, December 2017
2. Habibzadeh, M., Krzyżak, A., Fevens, T.: White blood cell differential counts using convolutional neural networks for low resolution images. In: Rutkowski, L., Korytkowski, M., Scherer, R., Tadeusiewicz, R., Zadeh, L.A., Zurada, J.M. (eds.) ICAISC 2013. LNCS (LNAI), vol. 7895, pp. 263–274. Springer, Heidelberg (2013). https://doi.org/10.1007/978-3-642-38610-7_25

3. American Society of Hematology. https://www.hematology.org/education/patients/blood-basics. Accessed 30 Dec 2021
4. Acharya, V., Kumar, P.: Identification and red blood cell automated counting from blood smear images using computer-aided system. Med. Biol. Eng. Comput. **56**(3), 483–489 (2018)
5. Acharjee, S., Chakrabartty, S., Alam, M.I., Dey, N., Santhi, V., Ashour, A.S.: A semiautomated approach using GUI for the detection of red blood cells. In: 2016 International Conference on Electrical, Electronics, and Optimization Techniques (ICEEOT), pp. 525–529. IEEE, March 2016
6. Alam, M.M., Islam, M.T.: Machine learning approach of automatic identification and counting of blood cells. Healthc. Technol. Lett. **6**(4), 103–108 (2019)
7. Islam, M.T., Aowal, M.A., Minhaz, A.T., Ashraf, K.: Abnormality detection and localization in chest x-rays using deep convolutional neural networks. arXiv preprint arXiv:1705.09850 (2017)
8. Habibzadeh, M., Jannesari, M., Rezaei, Z., Baharvand, H., Totonchi, M.: Automatic white blood cell classification using pre-trained deep learning models: ResNet and inception. In: Tenth International Conference on Machine Vision (ICMV 2017), vol. 10696, p. 1069612. International Society for Optics and Photonics, April 2018
9. Xu, M., Papageorgiou, D.P., Abidi, S.Z., Dao, M., Zhao, H., Karniadakis, G.E.: A deep convolutional neural network for classification of red blood cells in sickle cell anemia. PLoS Comput. Biol. **13**(10), e1005746 (2017)
10. Suryani, E., Wiharto, W., Polvonov, N.: Identification and counting white blood cells and red blood cells using image processing case study of leukemia. arXiv preprint arXiv:1511.04934 (2015)
11. Chadha, G.K., Srivastava, A., Singh, A., Gupta, R., Singla, D.: An automated method for counting red blood cells using image processing. Procedia Comput. Sci. **167**, 769–778 (2020)
12. Navea, R.F., Dupo, V., Bacudio, L.: Red blood cells and white blood cells detection differentiation and counting using image processing. In: DLSU Research Congress, March 2015
13. Safca, N., Popescu, D., Ichim, L., Elkhatib, H., Chenaru, O.: Image processing techniques to identify red blood cells. In: 2018 22nd International Conference on System Theory, Control and Computing (ICSTCC), pp. 93–98. IEEE, October 2018
14. Blood Cell Data. https://github.com/akshaylamba/all_CELL_data. Accessed 15 Dec 2021
15. Yan, B., Fan, P., Lei, X., Liu, Z., Yang, F.: A real-time apple targets detection method for picking robot based on improved YOLOv5. Remote Sens. **13**(9), 1619 (2021)
16. Liu, S., Qi, L., Qin, H., Shi, J. and Jia, J.: Path aggregation network for instance segmentation. In: Proceedings of the IEEE Conference on Computer Vision and Pattern Recognition, pp. 8759–8768 (2018)
17. Rezatofighi, H., Tsoi, N., Gwak, J., Sadeghian, A., Reid, I., Savarese, S.: Generalized intersection over union: a metric and a loss for bounding box regression. In: Proceedings of the IEEE/CVF Conference on Computer Vision and Pattern Recognition, pp. 658–666 (2019)
18. Rahaman, M.A., Ali, M.M., Ahmed, K., Bui, F.M., Mahmud, S.H.: Performance analysis between YOLOv5s and YOLOv5m model to detect and count blood cells: deep learning approach. In: Proceedings of the 2nd International Conference on Computing Advancements, pp. 316–322, March 2022

19. Ontor, M.Z.H., Ali, M.M., Hossain, S.S., Nayer, M., Ahmed, K., Bui, F.M.: YOLO_CC: deep learning based approach for early stage detection of cervical cancer from cervix images using YOLOv5s model. In: 2022 Second International Conference on Advances in Electrical, Computing, Communication and Sustainable Technologies (ICAECT), pp. 1–5. IEEE, April 2022

20. YOLOv5 New Version - Improvements and Evaluation, Roboflow Blog (2021). https://blog.roboflow.com/yolov5-improvements-and-evaluation/. Accessed 05 Apr 2021

21. Malta, A., Mendes, M., Farinha, T.: Augmented reality maintenance assistant using YOLOv5. Appl. Sci. **11**(11), 4758 (2021)

22. Hemu, A.A., Mim, R.B., Ali, M.M., Nayer, M., Ahmed, K., Bui, F.M.: Identification of significant risk factors and impact for ASD prediction among children using machine learning approach. In: 2022 Second International Conference on Advances in Electrical, Computing, Communication and Sustainable Technologies (ICAECT), pp. 1–6. IEEE, April 2022

23. Ali, M.M., Ahmed, K., Bui, F.M., Paul, B.K., Ibrahim, S.M., Quinn, J.M., Moni, M.A.: Machine learning-based statistical analysis for early stage detection of cervical cancer. Comput. Biol. Med. **139**, 104985 (2021)

24. Ali, M.M., Paul, B.K., Ahmed, K., Bui, F.M., Quinn, J.M., Moni, M.A.: Heart disease prediction using supervised machine learning algorithms: performance analysis and comparison. Comput. Biol. Med. **136**, 104672 (2021)

ML_SPS: Stroke Prediction System Employing Machine Learning Approach

Md. Sazzad Hossain[1], Mehedi Hassan Shovo[1], Md. Mamun Ali[2], Md. Nayer[3], Kawsar Ahmed[4,5(✉)], and Francis M. Bui[5]

[1] Department of Computer Science and Engineering, Daffodil International University, Sukrabad Dhaka-1207, Bangladesh
[2] Department of Software Engineering, Daffodil International University, Sukrabad Dhaka-1207, Bangladesh
[3] Department of Computer Science and Engineering, B.I.T. Patna Campus, Samanpura, BIT Patna, Bihar 800014, India
[4] Group of Bio-Photomatix, Department of Information and Communication Technology, Mawlana Bhashani Science and Technology University, Tangail 1902, Bangladesh
kawsar.ict@mbstu.ac.bd
[5] Department of Electrical and Computer Engineering, University of Saskatchewan, 57 Campus 9 Drive, Saskatoon, SK S7N 5A9, Canada

Abstract. Stroke is a dangerous health issue that happens when bleeding valves in the brain get damaged. and blood supply to the brain is cut off. As a result of these factors, numerous body parts may cease to function. Stroke is currently a significant risk factor for mortality, as per World Health Organization (WHO). It may be preferable to mitigate the severity of stroke by detecting it early. In recent years, data science has been critical to the growth of research in the medical field. Various machine learning techniques are built employing a patient's physical and physiological reporting data to forecast the risk of stroke. In this article, we use five machine learning approaches to find the best effective model that can predict the risk of stroke, including Decision Tree (DT), XGBoost, Light Gradient Boosting Machine (LGBM), Random Forest (RF), and K-nearest Neighbors learning. Kaggle was used to collect the dataset. Random forest produces acceptable findings with an accuracy of roughly 96%, which might be included in actual clinical information. The machine learning approach can aid in the prediction of many diseases like a stroke in the early stages.

Keywords: Machine learning · Precision-Recall curve · Random forest · Roc curve · Stroke prediction

1 Introduction

When oxygenation to certain portions of the brain is stopped or diminished, tissues in those parts of the brain do not receive the oxygenated blood they require,

© The Author(s), under exclusive license to Springer Nature Switzerland AG 2022
A. Kumar et al. (Eds.): ICAIDS 2021, CCIS 1673, pp. 215–226, 2022.
https://doi.org/10.1007/978-3-031-21385-4_19

resulting in demise. The tissues in some portions of the brain are deprived of nutrients and oxygenation when blood flow to those parts of the brain is stopped or limited [1]. They have depleted their oxygen supply and are beginning to expire. A stroke is a clinical condition. It is a serious health issue that necessitates immediate clinical intervention. Late To be successful, you must first identify the problem and then manage it effectively, avoid future harm to the brain's affected area, and a slew of other problems in various regions of the body. Strokes affect 15 million people each year, as per the World Health Organization, one person who dies every 4 to 5 min in the afflicted community. According to the Centers for Disease Control and Prevention, stroke is the sixth largest cause of deaths in the United States, and the second most common cause worldwide [2].

Stroke is a nosocomial illness that affects about 11% of the people. Ischemic and hemorrhagic strokes are the two types of strokes. A biochemical stroke is hampered by clots, whereas an internal bleeding happens when a weakened blood vessel explodes and bleeds into the nervous system. Although a balanced lifestyle, quitting smoking, maintaining BMI and sugar level can prevent stroke. Permanent damage or death can prevent by predicting stroke in primary level. Now Machine learning techniques are used to detect stroke in initial stage and also used to detect type of algorithm. However, stroke can be prevented if it can be predicted earlier and taken proper steps. From that continuity, the study aims to propose an efficient model, which will enable people and physicians to predict stroke in early stage deploying machine learning techniques.

2 Literature Review

Machine learning was previously exploited by a group of scientists to forecast stroke. String manipulation and a deep learning approach were exploited by Govindarajan et al. to identify stroke updates in 507 patients [1]. They investigated a number of different machine learning techniques for training, including Artificial Neural Networks, and explored that the SGD approach gave the best efficiency, with a 95% success rate. The ability to forecast the occurrence of a stroke was investigated by Amini et al. [3]. In 807 healthy and sick adults, they discovered 50 important factors for stroke, hypertension, heart disease, nicotine, dyslipidemia, and heavy drinking. They utilised two methods: the c4.5 decision tree algorithm, which was 95% accurate, and the K-nearest neighbour strategy, which was also 95% accurate. Cheng discussed his work in predicting ischemic strokes. In their work citeb4, researchers employed 82 ischemic stroke incidence data sets, two ANN models, and accuracy rates of 79 and 95% [4].

Sung et al. carried out study in order to create a stroke maximum intensity [5]. Researchers studied 3577 people whom have suffered an acute myocardial stroke. To develop the forecasting analytics, researchers used a range of data mining algorithms, notably regression analysis. With a 95% confidence level, its forecasting surpassed the k-nearest neighbor technique. Monteiro et al. utilized machine learning to identify an ischemic stroke's functional outcomes [6].They tested their method on a person who has been suffering for three months after being hospitalized. Researchers obtained an AUC of higher than 90%.

Cheon et al. carried a study on 15,099 participants to determine stroke death rate frequency [7]. They applied Deep Neural Network technique on gathered medical datasets where they got AUC 83%. Singh and Choudhury introduce new approach for predicting stroke [8]. They used artificial intelligence technique on cardiovascular health study dataset. They also applied feature extraction method in conjunction. Chin et al. create a CNN-based technique for automated approach for detecting primary ischemic stroke [9]. They used lengthening image pre-processing technique to enlarge their collected image which was 256 photos in the collection. Their model achieves 90% accuracy rate. Adam et al. did study to classify an ischemic stroke using the k-nearest neighbor methodology and the decision tree algorithm [10]. The decision tree approach was more effective in classifying strokes which gained a 90% accuracy.

Kansadub et al. applied Naive Bayes, decision trees and neural networks to see the stroke danger [11]. Author found decision trees, naive Bayes generate are more reliable prediction. In this study, researchers applied eight machine learning algorithms to classify ischemic stroke and stroke hemorrhage [12]. They used CT scan images of stroke patients. Their result shows among eight algorithm, highest level of accuracy (95.97%) obtain by Random Forest along with precision, recall respectively 94.39% and 96.12%.

From the above mentioned discussion it is clear that more advance technology needs to be developed to avoid the existing limitations and build some more accurate and upgraded technology. From this perspective, the study aims to find out the best performing classifier to build more advance model to predict stroke in early stage. Our contributions are as follows:

- At first we collected an opens source data to train and test all target models to find the best performing classification algorithm.
- Then, we applied different preprocessing techniques to make the more suitable for better understanding to the ML classifiers.
- Then the best performing classification algorithms are found out to propose for the more advance technology to predict stroke in early stage.
- Finally, the best classification algorithm for predicting stroke is proposed in this study comparing with several classifiers.

The rest of this study is arranged as follows: Sect. 3 presents the Materials and Methods with dataset description utilized in this study. The tools and experimental results with discussion are presented in Sect. 4. We represented conclusions and future direction of this work has been added in the conclusion section.

3   Materials and Methods

As previously discussion, it is clear that still there is an scope to build an effective machine learning based model to predict stroke in early stage. To conduct

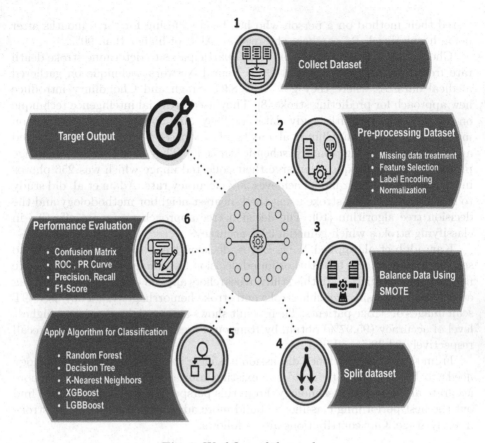

Fig. 1. Workflow of the study

this study is that we used a publicly available dataset to test multiple machine learning models. The majority of researchers employed a substantial technique to predict stroke disease in prior studies. We did, however, compare the results to previous research using five different models. The following section summarises the findings and comparisons.

The Fig. 1 illustrates the research methodology and workflow for building an efficient machine learning based system which is able to predict stroke for a patient with higher accuracy. The proposed model can be applied to build more advance technology which will be able to predict stroke based on some information or attributes of a patient.

3.1 Data Description

To implement and build our model among a few considered different datasets we used a dataset of Kaggle [13]. The dataset contains 12 features with 5110 instances, where 2994 are Female and 2115 are Male patient and 1 instance was others where gender was not mentioned. About 50% of the patients in this dataset reside in urban areas and others in rural areas. Among all the individuals 249 patients have stroke and the remaining haven't any chances of stroke. Of all the patients, 276 had a previous experience of heart disease and 17% had a stroke. Although this dataset isn't a balanced dataset, it gives a satisfactory result. The details of the dataset along with feature information is mentioned in the Table 1.

Table 1. Data Description

Attribute	Data Type	Description
ID	Numerical	Every patient has a unique id
Gender	Categorical	Tells patients gender
Age	Numerical	Describe patients age
Hypertension	Binary	Whether the patients are hypertensive or not
Heart disease	Binary	Whether patients experience heart disease or not
Ever married	Binary	Describe married status
Work type	Categorical	Tells working category
Residence type	Categorical	Represent living area
Average glucose level	Numerical	It tells the level of average glucose
BMI	Numerical	Show patients Body Mass Index value
Smoking status	Categorical	Tells the patients smoking scenario
Stroke	Binary	Tells the previous stoke

3.2   Data Preprocessing

The raw data is sometimes inconsistent and inefficient to produce better results in machine learning. So, for better training and testing performance, data preprocessing is a fundamental tasks to be performed to prepare data for better analytical result [5]. In the preprocessing stage, at first missing values are handled using mean and mode statistical methods. Then, label encoding is performed for categorical features. Then the dataset was balanced using Synthetic Minority Oversampling Technique (SMOTE) since the dataset was imbalanced. There were 5110 instances where 249 patients had stroke and rest of the patients are free of risks. It indicates that the dataset is imbalance and it was balanced using SMOTE.

3.3   Supervised Machine Learning Algorithm

Random Forest (RF): RF is one kind of supervised learning approach for solving both of classification and regression related issues [6]. Mainly, RF classification algorithm is developed based on several decision trees. Random Forest randomly select features and use bagging and booting technique to build each tree. This uncorrelated forest has higher accuracy than individual tree. It exploits the majority vote for categorization and the mean for prediction to generate decision trees from various samples [7]. For categorization difficulties, it produces superior results. Random forest's adaptability is one of its most appealing features. Random forests have the best accuracy within all existing classification techniques, and it may be utilized including both regression and classification applications. The random forest method can also deal with large datasets with hundreds of parameters [8,9]. For avoiding overfitting issues, RF palys a vital role.

XGBoost (XGB): XGBoost is a free and open source variant of gradient-boosted decision trees that is optimized for strength and stability. It is an ensemble type of classification algorithm but it also can be used regression related tasks. It is capable of parallelization [16]. On classification, regression, and predictive modeling issues, XGBoost dominates structured or tabular datasets because of its high flexibility and versatility. It contains automated handling missing values, followed by a block structure to facilitate parallelization of tree building, and finally a method of ongoing training so that additional boosting may previously fitted model on fresh data.

K-Nearest Neighbors (KNN): KNN classifier is a one kind of supervised machine learning which is simple and powerful recognition algorithm to solve classification and regression problems. It's a non-parametric algorithm and most popular for pattern recognition [17]. KNN is trained using the labelled data which is already available. KNN approach is well suited to applications that need extensive domain expertise. K refers to the number instances which can be considered as neighbor for an raw data point. The prediction methodology of KNN has been depicted Fig. 2.

Light Gradient Boosting Machine (LGBM): Light Gradient Boosting Machine (LGBM) is one kind of ensemble learning classification algorithm. LGBM depends on decision tree algorithms that is speedy, distributed and high efficient gradient boosting framework. It focuses on accuracy of results and handle massive volumes of data, especially when extreme precision is required [18]. LGBM employs two methods: gradient-based one-side sampling and exclusive feature bundling. These two models work jointly to enable the system operate effectively.

Best Parameter for All the Applied Algorithms: Table 2 represents parameter for all the applied algorithms those are found after hyper tuning all the applied parameters. These settings are the best fit for all the applied algorithms in this study.

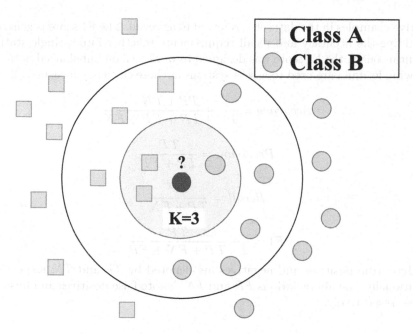

Fig. 2. Prediction methods of KNN

Table 2. Best Parameter for All the Applied Algorithms

Classifier	Best Param
Random Forest	'max_depth': 100, 'max_features': 'auto', 'min_samples_leaf': 1, 'n_estimators': 200
LGBM classifier	'learning_rate': 0.1, 'max_depth': 10, 'min_child_samples': 5, 'num_iterations': 300, 'num_leaves': 80, 'reg_alpha': 0
XGB classifier	'n_estimators': 300, 'colsample_bytree': 0.5, 'gamma': 0.25, 'learning_rate': 0.1, 'max_depth': 7, 'reg_lambda': 10, 'scale_pos_weight': 5, 'subsample': 0.8
Decision Tree	'criterion': 'gini', 'max_depth': 10, 'min_samples_leaf': 50
K-Nearest Neighbors	'leaf_size': 3, 'n_neighbors': 13, 'p': 1

3.4 Performance Evaluation Metrics

Four assessment criteria are used to evaluate all of the applicable classification techniques: accuracy, precision, recall, and f1-score. Accuracy is defined as the ratio of accurately categorized occurrences to total anticipated instances. Precision is the proportion of positive class forecasts that are truly positive class forecasts. The number of right positive class predictions made out of all correct positive examples in the dataset is referred to as recall. The F1 score is generated by adding the accuracy and recall requirements together into a single statistic. Simultaneously, the F1 score was designed to work well on imbalanced data. The following formula are used to assess systems in these efficiency measures [21–23].

$$Accuracy = \frac{TP + TN}{TP + TN + FP + FN} \tag{1}$$

$$Precision = \frac{TP}{TP + FP} \tag{2}$$

$$Recall = \frac{TP}{TP + FN} \tag{3}$$

$$F1 = \frac{2 \times TP}{2 \times TP + FN + FP} \tag{4}$$

Here, true positives and negatives are denoted by TP and TN, respectively. Additionally, the abbreviations FP and FN denote false positives and false negatives, respectively.

4   Experimental Results

Python (version 3.8.5) was used to examine the data and perform supervised machine learning techniques in this work. Five supervised machine classifiers were applied in this study such decision tree, random forest, xgboost, LGBM, and K-Nearest Neighbor. Then, analysing their performance, best fit classifiers were selected.

Table 3. Performance Comparison among applied classifiers

Algorithm	Accuracy	Precision	Recall	F1-score
Random Forest	95.84	0.96	0.96	0.96
LGBBoost	95.63	0.96	0.96	0.96
Decision Tree	93.68	0.94	0.94	0.94
K-nearest Neighbors	91.47	0.92	0.92	0.92
XGBoost	89.61	0.90	0.90	0.90

Table 3 represents the performance results of all the applied algorithms. From the table it is found that XGBoost performs lower than any other classifiers, where Random Forest and LGBM performed the best with 95.84% and 95.63% accuracy and 0.96 precision, recall and f1 score for both. Since, Random Forest gained better accuracy compare to LGBM, it is highly recommended to employ for stroke prediction.

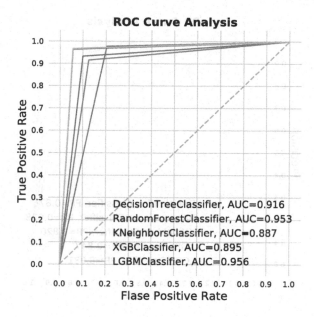

Fig. 3. Comparison of ROC curve among all the applied algorithms

Figure 4 depicts the ROC curve of all the applied classification algorithms. It is visualized that K-Nearest Neighbor covers the lowest area under ROC curve where LGBM covers the most area in terms of both area under ROC with 0.956 values. Random Forest also provides closer result to LGBM which is 0.953 in value.

Figure 5 illustrates the ROC curve of all the applied classification algorithms. It is visualized that K-Nearest Neighbor covers the lowest area under ROC curve with 0.820 in value where LGBM covers the most area in terms of both area under ROC with 0.931 values. Random Forest also provides closer result to LGBM which is 0.928 in value. Here it is found that Random forest and LGBM both are performing satisfactorily.

Table 4 represents the comparative performances of our proposed system with the existing systems. It is found here that our proposed systems performs better than all the mentioned systems. From this point of view it can be said our proposed system is highly capable of predicting stroke possibility providing patient systems. Most importantly, patients and physicians both can use this system for better decision making and treatment regarding stroke.

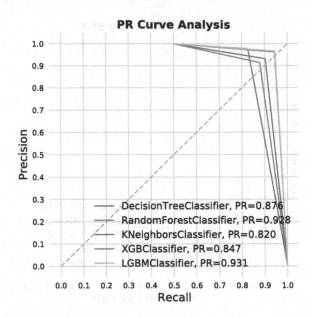

Fig. 4. Comparison of Precision-Recall curve among all the applied algorithms

Table 4. Performance comparison among proposed system and existing systems

Author	Method	Accuracy (%)
Tahia Tazin ea al. [19]	Logistic Regression	87
Sailasva et al. [20]	Decision Tree	66
Cheon et al. [5]	DNN	83
Chin et al. [9]	CNN	90
Proposed System	Random Forest	96

5   Conclusion

Stroke is a clinical emergency that must be treated as soon as possible to avoid further consequences. The development of an effective machine learning-based solution that can help in the earlier detection and reduction of stroke's catastrophic consequences. This article examines the use of multiple machine learning approaches for accurately guessing strokes based on a collection of vital indicators. With a classification accuracy of 95.84% for random forest and 95.64% for LGBM classification algorithm exceeds the other strategies evaluated. When cross-validation metrics are employed to predict brain strokes, the study discovered that both the Random forest and LGBM methods exceed other approaches. In the future, the framework models might be expanded by employing a greater population and machine learning algorithms as AdaBoost, SVM, and Bagging. This improves the app's dependability as well as its visual appeal. The suggested approach would allow doctors and clinicians to predict strokes and take appropriate action for patients.

Acknowledgement. The study was supported by funding from the Natural Sciences and Engineering Research Council of Canada (NSERC).

References

1. Govindarajan, P., Soundarapandian, R.K., Gandomi, A.H., Patan, R., Jayaraman, P., Manikandan, R.: Classification of stroke disease using machine learning algorithms. Neural Comput. Appl. **32**(3), 817–828 (2020)
2. Reza, S.M., Rahman, M.M., Mamun, S.A.: A new approach for road networks-a vehicle xml device collaboration with big data. In: Proceedings of the International Conference on Electrical Engineering and Information and Communication Technology, pp. 1–5. Mirpur, Dhaka (2014)
3. Amini, L., Azarpazhouh, R., Farzadfar, M.T., et al.: Prediction and control of stroke by data mining. Int. J. Prev. Med. **4**(2), S245–S249 (2013)
4. Cheng, C.A., Lin, Y.C., Chiu, H.W.: Prediction of the prognosis of ischemic stroke patients after intravenous thrombolysis using artificial neural networks. Stud. Health Technol. Inf. **202**, 115–118 (2014)
5. Sung, S.-F., et al.: Developing a stroke severity index based on administrative data was feasible using data mining techniques. J. Clin. Epidemiol. **68**(11), 1292–1300 (2015)
6. Monteiro, M., et al.: Using machine learning to improve the prediction of functional outcome in ischemic stroke patients. IEEE/ACM Trans. Comput. Biol. Bioinf. **15**(6), 1953–1959 (2018)
7. Cheon, S., Kim, J., Lim, J.: -e use of deep learning to predict stroke patient mortality. Int. J. Environ. Res. Public Health **16**(11), 1876 (2019)
8. Singh M.S., Choudhary, P.: Stroke prediction using artificial intelligence. In: Proceedings of the 2017 8th Annual Industrial Automation And Electromechanical Engineering Conference (IEMECON), pp. 158–161. Bangkok, Thailand (2017)
9. Chin, C.-L., et al.: An automated early ischemic stroke detection system using CNN deep learning algorithm. In: Proceedings of the 2017 IEEE 8th International Conference on Awareness Science and Technology (iCAST), pp. 368–372. Taichung, Taiwan (2017)
10. Adam, S.Y., Yousif, A., Bashir, M.B.: Classification of ischemic stroke using machine learning algorithms. Int. J. Comput. Appl. **149**(10), 26–31 (2016)
11. Kansadub, T., -ammaboosadee, S., Kiattisin, S., Jalayondeja, C.: Stroke risk prediction model based on demographic data. In: Proceedings of the 2015 8th Biomedical Engineering International Conference (BMEiCON), pp. 1–3. Pattaya, Thailand (2015)
12. Badriyah, T., Sakinah, N., Syarif, I., Syarif, D.R.: Machine learning algorithm for stroke disease classification. In: 2020 International Conference on Electrical, Communication, and Computer Engineering (ICECCE), pp. 1–5. IEEE (2020)
13. Stroke Dataset. https://www.kaggle.com/fedesoriano/stroke-prediction-dataset. Accessed 30 Dec 2021
14. Ali, M.M., Paul, B.K., Ahmed, K., Bui, F.M., Quinn, J.M., Moni, M.A.: Heart disease prediction using supervised machine learning algorithms: performance analysis and comparison. Comput. Biol. Med. **136**, 104672 (2021)

15. Ali, M.M., et al.: Machine learning-based statistical analysis for early stage detection of cervical cancer. Comput. Biol. Med. **139**, 104985 (2021)
16. Ramraj, S., Uzir, N., Sunil, R., Banerjee, S.: Experimenting XGBoost algorithm for prediction and classification of different datasets. Int. J. Control Theory Appl. **9**, 651–662 (2016)
17. Suguna, N., Thanushkodi, K.: An improved k-nearest neighbor classification using genetic algorithm. Int. J. Comput. Sci. Issues **7**(2), 18–21 (2010)
18. Ahamed, B.S., Arya, S.: LGBM classifier based technique for predicting type-2 diabetes. Eur. J. Mol. Clin. Med. **8**(3), 454–467 (2021)
19. Tazin, T., Alam, M.N., Dola, N.N., Bari, M.S., Bourouis, S., Khan, M.M.: Stroke disease detection and prediction using robust learning approaches. J. Healthcare Eng. **2021**, 1–12 (2021)
20. Sailasya, G., Kumari, G.L.A.: Analyzing the performance of stroke prediction using ML classification algorithms. Int. J. Adv. Comput. Sci. Appl. **12**(6), 539–545 (2021)
21. Hemu, A.A., Mim, R.B., Ali, M.M., Nayer, M., Ahmed, K., Bui, F.M.: Identification of significant risk factors and impact for ASD prediction among children using machine learning approach. In: 2022 Second International Conference on Advances in Electrical, Computing, Communication and Sustainable Technologies (ICAECT), pp. 1–6. IEEE (2022)
22. Rahaman, M.A., Ali, M.M., Ahmed, K., Bui, F.M., Mahmud, S.H.: Performance analysis between YOLOv5s and YOLOv5m model to detect and count blood cells: deep learning approach. In: Proceedings of the 2nd International Conference on Computing Advancements, pp. 316–322 (2022)
23. Ontor, M.Z.H., Ali, M.M., Hossain, S.S., Nayer, M., Ahmed, K., Bui, F.M.: YOLO_CC: deep Learning based approach for early stage detection of cervical cancer from cervix images using YOLOv5s model. In: 2022 Second International Conference on Advances in Electrical, Computing, Communication and Sustainable Technologies (ICAECT), pp. 1–5. IEEE (2022)

A System for Network Based Intrusion Avoidance Using Dedicated Machine Learning and Artificial Intelligence-Based Model for Application and Data Safety

H. Manjunath$^{(\boxtimes)}$ and S. Saravana Kumar

Department of Computer and Engineering, CMR University, Bangalore, India
manjunath.19cphd@cmr.edu.in, saravanakumarmithun@gmail.com

Abstract. The influx in usage of internet has led to decent amount of risk happening on target application systems and servers which are part of the ecosystem. Detecting the unwanted events which might be triggered by security loophole or improper deciphering the messages is the most common phenomenon in the current practice. Such unfavorable events are called intrusion and detecting such intrusions are called as Intrusion detection. Our proposed system supports dynamic facets and handles multiple events with message queues. It is an intelligent system to handle the incoming events in a better way due to proposed tagging mechanism. This also handles the categorization of the intrusion detected values such that from the next occurrence of such events will be handled gracefully without making much utilization of computation and re-iteration of the events under observation. The whole categorized event handling ensures that there is no data loss due to threshold and latency issues which are commonly observed in current systems. This system ensures faster mode to reach the conclusion by making dynamic decision system development and feedback looping, for better grouping of the detected intrusions to take appropriate actions when needed. Such grouping helps to dynamically identify the threats observed through this system without manual intervention and allows the system to take actions based on the patterns observed using brute force methodologies. This provides a dedicated space for IT management to adopt much better guidelines to keep app, app gateway, servers, etc. safe.

Keywords: Intrusion · Tagging · Message queue · Classification · Categorization

1 Introduction

Information technology and network communication systems handle a wide range of sensitive user information that is subject to both external and internal intruder attacks [1]. These assaults can be automated or human, and their obfuscation techniques are growing more complex, resulting in undiscovered information breaches. For example, a 553 million loss was created by Facebook, a $350 million loss was created by the Yahoo data breach, and a $70 million loss was caused by the Bitcoin breach [2]. Cyber-attacks are

© The Author(s), under exclusive license to Springer Nature Switzerland AG 2022
A. Kumar et al. (Eds.): ICAIDS 2021, CCIS 1673, pp. 227–240, 2022.
https://doi.org/10.1007/978-3-031-21385-4_20

constantly changing with increasingly sophisticated algorithms as physical components, application software, and networks are advancing, notably the recent achievements in the field of Internet of Things [3]. Cyber-attacks pose major security risks, necessitating the development of a new, adaptable, and more reliable intrusion detection system (IDS). These systems are proactive intrusion detection technologies for detecting and classifying breaches of security policies, intrusions, and attacks in real time at the host and network level framework [4]. The main aim of IDS system is to furnish a systematic approach and methodology to detect/identify/categorize the unusual access of information which might be inbound or outbound in nature from network system under observation. The Intrusion which is commonly seen, is broadly classified into 4 types as mentioned below,

1 An IDS that monitors network for unwanted traffic is known as a Network Intrusion Detection System (NIDS). It frequently needs abandoned network ingress to review every traffic, including the unicast traffic. It also keeps track of traffic without interfering with it.
2 An intrusion detection system that tracks suspicious behavior on the computer infrastructure on which it is installed and analyses traffic is known as a Host Intrusion Detection System (HIDS). It allows you to monitor your critical security systems in real time.
3 An IDS that is typically installed on the web server used for monitoring and analyzing the protocol utilized by the computer system is known as Protocol Based Intrusion Detection System (PIDS). It's the system or the agent which resides at server's fore end for observing and analyzing communication within the connected devices and system they're protecting.
4 An IDS that focuses on the computer system's application protocol or protocols for monitoring and analyzing is referred to as Application Protocol-based Intrusion Detection System (APIDS).
5 An IDS can be categorized into two categories: hybrid IDS and misuse or anomaly IDS. The Hybrid IDS combines network traffic anomaly detection (NETAD) and packet header anomaly detection (PHAD), which are anomaly-based IDSs.

Based on the above types of possible intrusions observed, this paper focus on handling multivariate intrusions happening on different network systems which are in term connected to multiple application hosted on multiple app servers. In any given applications servers, the intrusion may happen on OS, Application data, malicious data getting pushed, data injection on SQL type data sources etc. To handle such events through centralized system we need to have dedicated mechanism which will provide a sophisticated way to bifurcate between intrusion and safe messages. This is need of the hour due to gigantic explosion in internet usage is observed in last couple of years and it will continue to grow in exponential terms in coming days.

2   Literature Survey

Apache Spark Big Data tools are utilized to uphold the speed and performance of intrusion perception in a Colossal Data setting because they are 100 times faster than Hadoop

[5]. Using SVM on KDD datasets, the feature selection, which takes a long time to compute, can be minimized the decision retrieval from Intrusion Detection System (IDS). This system is developed to deliver the fundamental detection strategies for securing systems in networks that are either directly or indirectly connected to the Internet. When compared to either complete feature or entropy, the framework RST-SVM approach output has a higher accuracy [6]. Two-fold feature selection and hyper parameter optimization approaches of the innovative attack detection system are used to protect against typical attacks [7]. It's a very efficient generic defensive Artificial Intelligence system that detects typical attack flows, thanks to training technique and a revolutionary feature selection and innovative feature store which categorizes the type of intrusion detected for future iterative information generation.

In a network, a NIDS is a strategy for identifying malicious or unwanted packets. This technique uses real-time traffic monitoring to check whether there's anything unusual going on within the network. The need for the essential tasks to be processed out concurrently in present-time is increasing due to typical big data challenges such as large volume of data, complexity associated within the data and time taken to process the huge volume of data. Also, lack of sophisticated processing facilities, and the network size expand [8]. For training and testing, the benchmarking dataset NSL-KDD is taken into consideration. Data pretreatment, feature normalization, and feature selection procedures are required to enhance the algorithm's ability for right prediction and coordinate for a well processed training with minimal resources and time.

Routers, network defense, and systems have been modified for detecting and reporting malicious network communication signals using IDS [9]. For testing and determining the best features, the decision tree classifier model can be utilized. For evaluating and determining the best features, the SVM classifier is utilized. For evaluating and determining the best features, the Bayes classifier is utilized [10]. For faster processing of count of the unique events/elements in the feature store we are using Flajolet–Martin technique to handle skewness and unique retrieval problem. Using the algorithms such as k-means clustering algorithm [11] etc., IDS experiments have been accomplished. For integrating relationship among objects a scene modelling concept hybrid Boltzman Machine was suggested. To showcase better in various scene reasoning activities Boltzman Machine was further made to use three paths between objects for communication [12]. The deep learning approach was confirmed has a better option by making use of data set KDD Cup99 in Recurrent Neural Network through the application of Long Short Term Memory architecture [13]. Host based obstructions finding system for Windows XP platform developed in order to fulfil the role of detector for finding intrusions in systems [14].

The KDD 99 dataset is primary aspect for many an experiment, but in proposed system we have developed our own random datasets which generates random events varying all sorts of events which might be malicious, righteous, abnormal events etc. This dataset has malicious events and abnormal events generated at sporadic time frame with respect to data set. This dataset is many a times used for Intrusion Detection Systems. The optimal discriminating plane technique [15] was used for training Artificial Neural Network by mapping an Nth dimensional pattern into a pattern of two dimensional, along with aforementioned techniques. The Echo state Neural Network [16] has the topology of highly associated and repeating nonlinear Processing Elements (PEs) which operates as the "pool of wealthy dynamics" by captivating data from the previous incoming and outgoing sequence. This method was used to try and detect intrusion. Abundant algorithms developed throughout the research were employed in intrusion detection process for data gathering via Knowledge Discovery and Data Mining (KDD).

3 Proposed Work/Methodology

Capturing messages/Event and classifications/Tagging. The overall process should follow the capturing of all events/trackers coming into centralized system via network traffic. These events are categorized based on type of events. Each event is added with specification/classification tag based on type of event. These specifications help in identifying the type of request/response to be made towards those messages from the target app systems. Each event is treated as messages and needs to be moved into intelligent systems to get further rectification and signature validation before we input them to target applications. To ensure each event gets into next downstream consumption we need to enable the message queuing system to ensure we do not lose any events/messages.

The Tagging can be considered as grouping of eventually used message stream based on homogeneous nature and many other factors depending on the type of source or publishers of the messages which is under generation of the request. Also, this is mainly dependent on target consumption groups of these message events. Tagged features are very much essential in classifications of downstream relations in later stages (Fig. 1).

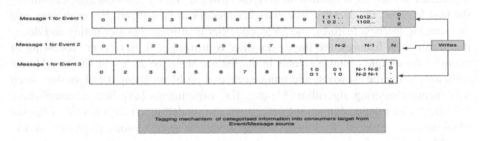

Fig. 1. Tagging consideration of incoming messages/events

In the above representation diagram, ideally the new data streams are processed to fetch the values. These values are written into event values as needed for downstream consumptions. The values are often grouped based on type of the messages aggregated from the homogenous metadata and data messages.

Tagging is process in which a specific value is assigned to similar sets of incoming messages/events. These helps in faster identifications and faster retrieval in later stages for any processing and insight generation. One main purpose of tagging is to avoid duplicated processing and having a unique set processed at once for better ML and AI Engines to work upon (Fig. 2).

An example of incoming message is discussed below. The incoming message which in-turn treated for events are broadly classified in the below format for metadata. This metadata categorizes the eventually tagging methods (Table 1).

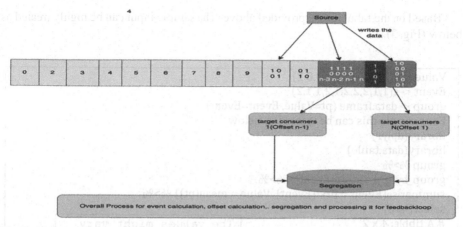

Fig. 2. Next level processing from tagged events which increases the offset calculation performance

Table 1. Message/event description Meta data

Base-Offset: int-64
Batch-Length: int-32
Partition-Leader-Epoch: int-32
Crc-bit: int-32
Attributes-value: int16
bits 0 ~ 2: None
0: no-compression required
1: gzip
2: snappy
Bit-3: TimestampTypeValue
Bit-4: isTransactional (0 means Source not from transactional Batch)
Bit-5: is-Control-Batch (0 means Source not from Control Batch)
Bit-6 ~ end: IdealMessageValue
Last-Offset-Delta: int3-2
Arrival-Timestamp: int-64
max-Timestamp: int-64
Source-Id: int-64
Source-Epoch: int16
Base-Sequence: int-32
records: Actual Value

Based on the tabular data provided above. The sample input can be highly treated as below (Fig. 3).

```
Value <- c(2,3,5,4,5,6,1,4,0,3)
Event <- c(1,1,2,2,2,1,2,1,1,2)
group <- data.frame (pt=Value, Event=Event)
For example this can be treated as below
library(dplyr)
library(data.table)
group %>%
group_by(grp = rleid(Event)) %>%
summarise(Event = first(Event), Value = mean(pt)) %>%
select(-grp)
# A tibble: 4 x 2
# Event Value
# <dbl> <dbl>
#1   1  2.5
#2   2  4
```

```
The values might vary
depending the size,
tagging percentage,
frequency.
```

Fig. 3. Grouping of categorical event messages for tagging

Message/Events distribution for feature extraction and classification. The categorized events which have tagged information attached to it are now located in message queue. This will be distributed to downstream consumptions for specific validation process based on category they are into. These categories are treated based on type of requests coming in like OS based, Database based, API based etc. This process enables to handle the dedicated stream of categorized events that are being treated as needed. As shown in Fig. 4, the categorized events will be fed into Pattern recognition model which is based on machine leaning models and also fed parallel into AI based system which is a feedback classifier.

As shown in Fig. 4 the ML model for pattern recognition has mechanism to select the features based on the features mentioned below,

a. **Type of event.** This gives us the event type. This is taken from tagging mechanism we introduced in first step.
b. **Occurrence of event and source of the event.** This provides the occurrence system of the event with its Mac, IP address and client type like OS, Browser, DNS etc. This also provides the information like what made the event occurrence to appear.
c. **Durability of the event.** Calculate the durability and its possible duration of event to stay in the system
d. **Generated time of the event.** Provides the timestamp of the event generated time
e. **Target app of the event to be fed.** Provides the target app for which the event is meant.
f. **Frequency of event.** This needs to be calculated based on a, b and d.
g. **Any previous occurrences of the same event.** Calculate and provide the list of hex-map of previous occurrences of the similar event.

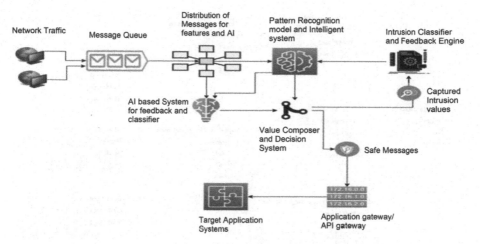

Fig. 4. Architecture diagram of the ML model for pattern recognition

h. **Repetition pattern type flag.** How the repetition is happening based on the occurrence, its source and its combination which needs to be calculated.
i. **False alarm count.** Any False alarm captured for similar event and its ratio with respect to overall percentage of False alarm needs to be calculated.
j. **Intrusion chances percentage value.** Provide probability of chances of intrusion if captured already

The ML model keeps getting the event loop mechanism updated by Intrusion classifier and feedback engine. This feedback events are fed to ML model to optimize the patterns propositions and improvements on every subsequent runs.

The event tagged from source to target systems for AI/ML engines is provided below with detailed entity-relation of attributes (Fig. 5).

Classifier and feedback loop: The ML model keeps providing the inputs to Classifier engine. The feedback loop is providing the regular stream of inputs to this engine. This engine specifies on how to categories the next subsequent inputs for downstream consumption and provides an intelligent mechanism to handle them as explained below.

Each feedback event and new events are treated into equal type sized and non-overlapping subsets. The model training using the K-1 folds and provide a deterministic approach to predicate the performance of that model utilizing the fold that has been taken away from consideration in this iteration. Perform this iterative mode by taking away the 1st iteration element in second and hence forth till n-1th element/event which is fed to this engine.

Also, some time due to inefficient information and improper tagged values we will get to see False Positive and False Negative. A False Negative is when a negative test result is incorrect that is rightly opposite of False Positive which is an activity identified by an IDS as an attack, but the event is acceptable behavior.

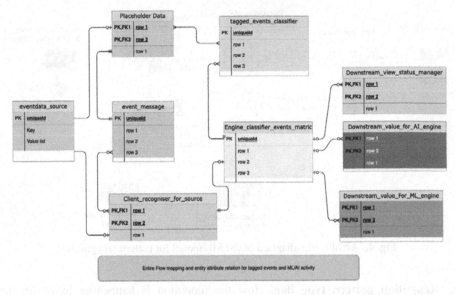

Fig. 5. Entity mapping for attributed for tagged events to be used for AI/ML engines

3.1 Calculations

To calculate the Event's specification, we have to calculate the ML models approach of figuring out the events distribution processing in ML engine which has been calculated by the presumed delta from the previous run of value Kji which is the event-k based on the feature of Nij.

The value Kji and Nij are essentially needed to be reciprocated into improvement terms. The improvement can be observed provided further enhancement can be seen on the faster grouping mechanism of any given event K with respect to all the events n_{ik}.

$$K_{ji} = \frac{\sum_j tag\ Event\ k\ on\ feature\ of\ n_{ij}}{\sum_{k\ \in\ all\ Events}\ n_{ik}}$$

where,

Kji is the instance of the K event in j message

n_{ik} And n_{ij} are the entire message stream.

The scoring improvement of the source and target events under consideration can be calculated for cumulative differences which further provides serial list of Nij with the given time frame. The value Nij is difference between source and target delta HashMap value and also difference in time delta. Measure event and measure event proportionality are calculated as shown below,

$$n_{ij} = W_j C_j - W_{sorce(i)} - W_{(target)} - time\ delta$$

where,

W is the MOD of events under processing.

For Event measure improvisation, the given events durability can be measured as below,

$$Measure\_Event = X_n\left(\frac{n+1}{2}\right)$$

where,

Xn is the length of the entire stream where n is duration of the event.

The proportionality of the given event in a message event can be calculated as (Fig. 6),

$$Measure\_Event\_Proportionality = \frac{X_{n/2} + X\left(\frac{n+1}{2}\right)}{2(X_{n-1})}$$

3.2 Flow Chart

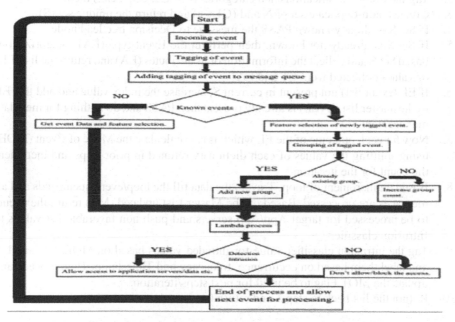

Fig. 6. Control flow diagram

4 Algorithm to Generate the Insights Sequence and Validate Using SVM

Generate the decision tree from the data set/inputs fed to algorithm and validate the tree to classify the occurrence of the event using SVM. The data set used is called event data (ED) Input:

(1) Event type (ET)
(2) Event attribute (EA)
(3) Mode _ of _ event (MOE)
(4) Repetition _ model _ type _ value (RMV) Boolean Flag Output: decision tree validated by SVM

Method:

1. Create Nodes/Events N
2. Tag the event classifications and categories (C1, C2, C3... etc.) them.
3. Create a non-duplicate set of N and (C1...n) and return the unique set (S)
4. If Set S is already known PASS the message to Decision tree lead node.
5. If Set S is already not known, then perform the Event type (EA) categorization-based Set S and collect the information of its attributes (EA) and return the list (EL) of values collected from ET and EA
6. If EL (event list) not present in current S, increase the index value and add this EL to the master list. If (EL) is already present then PASS and do nothing for metadata management.
7. Now for each outcome of the EL which is new calculate the Mode of Event (MOE) using splitting the values of each dictionary retuned in prior steps and increment the count for the iteration
8. Based on increment of loop, Travers the data till the loop/event queue ends and all messages are processed. Based on the Master List updated (ML) return the events to be processed for target App/App servers and push non favorable list values to Intrusion classifier
9. Tag the intrusion classifier value for intruded values based on MOE, ET, and EA and label them based on occurrence, frequency and Timestamp. Then proceed and update the MOT Flag to be used for next steps/iteration.
10. Return the list back to step 1 and return 0

Overall, the SVM acts as placeholder here in this approach to provide the essence of the insight generated from the proposed algorithm. This basically improves overall efficiency in feature extraction for downstream consumption.

5 Results and Discussion

The sample data under study is generated from multiple cloud logs and artificially generated using python packages which is used to simulate the randomness of the event occurrences. The same is provided below (Fig. 7).

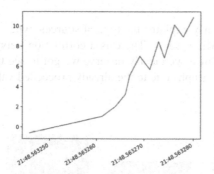

(myenv) Desktop ›
(myenv) Desktop › head -100 Cloud_source_log.csv
0,tcp,ftp_data,SF,491,0,0,0,0,0,0,0,0,0,0,0,0,0,0,0,0,2,2,0,0,0,0,1,0,0,150,25,0.17,0.03,0.17,0,0,0,0.05,0,normal,20
0,udp,other,SF,146,0,0,0,0,0,0,0,0,0,0,0,0,0,0,0,0,13,1,0,0,0,0,0.08,0.15,0,255,1,0,0.6,0.88,0,0,0,0,0,normal,15
0,tcp,private,S0,0,0,0,0,0,0,0,0,0,0,0,0,0,0,0,0,123,6,1,1,0,0,0.05,0.07,0,255,26,0.1,0.05,0,0,1,1,0,0,neptune,19
0,tcp,http,SF,232,8153,0,0,0,0,1,0,0,0,0,0,0,0,0,0,0,5,5,0.2,0.2,0,0,1,0,0,30,255,1,0,0.03,0.04,0,0.03,0.01,0,0.01,normal,21
0,tcp,http,SF,199,420,0,0,0,0,1,0,0,0,0,0,0,0,0,0,30,32,0,0,0,0,1,0,0,09,255,255,1,0,0,0,0,0,0,normal,21
0,tcp,private,REJ,0,0,0,0,0,0,0,0,0,0,0,0,0,0,0,0,121,19,0,0,1,1,0.16,0.06,0,255,19,0.07,0.07,0,0,0,0,1,1,neptune,21
0,tcp,private,S0,0,0,0,0,0,0,0,0,0,0,0,0,0,0,0,0,166,9,1,1,0,0,0.05,0.06,0,255,9,0.04,0.05,0,0,1,1,0,0,neptune,21
0,tcp,private,S0,0,0,0,0,0,0,0,0,0,0,0,0,0,0,0,0,117,16,1,1,0,0,0.14,0.06,0,255,15,0.06,0.07,0,0,1,1,0,0,neptune,21
0,tcp,remote_job,S0,0,0,0,0,0,0,0,0,0,0,0,0,0,0,0,0,270,23,1,1,0,0,0.09,0.05,0,255,23,0.09,0.05,0,0,1,1,0,0,neptune,21
0,tcp,private,S0,0,0,0,0,0,0,0,0,0,0,0,0,0,0,0,0,133,8,1,1,0,0,0.06,0.06,0,255,13,0.05,0.06,0,0,1,1,0,0,neptune,21
0,tcp,private,REJ,0,0,0,0,0,0,0,0,0,0,0,0,0,0,0,0,205,12,0,0,1,1,0.06,0.06,0,255,12,0.05,0.07,0,0,0,0,1,1,neptune,21
0,tcp,private,S0,0,0,0,0,0,0,0,0,0,0,0,0,0,0,0,0,199,3,1,1,0,0.02,0.06,0,255,13,0.05,0.07,0,0,1,1,0,0,neptune,21
0,tcp,http,SF,287,2251,0,0,0,0,1,0,0,0,0,0,0,0,0,3,7,0,0,0,1,0,0.43,8,219,1,0,0.12,0.03,0,0,0,0,normal,21
0,tcp,ftp_data,SF,334,0,0,0,0,0,1,0,0,0,0,0,0,0,0,2,2,0,0,0,1,0,0,2,20,1,0.1,0.2,0,0,0,warezclient,15

Fig. 7. Sample dataset

A simple display of time taken for grouped vent classification for tagging extraction is provided in the graph below (Figs. 8 and 9).

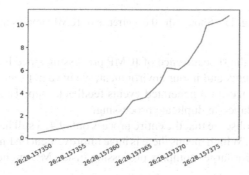

Fig. 8. Display of time taken for grouped vent classification

Fig. 9. Display of improved time taken for grouped vent classification

If we closely observe the improvement in the tagging, it increases more with redundancy. The homogenous data event which is generated will improve the performance of

ML and AI engines by 20% because the training will be happening on distributed and parallel way simultaneously. It is also observed that more the similarity in the events better will be the grouping functionality, lesser the time better will be the overall performance, lesser the duration better the capability and finally more the duration linear processing time will be taken.

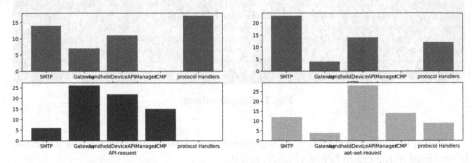

Fig. 10. Show's 4 execution runs on a subset of the data sets.

Figure 10 graph clearly explains the type of sources, type of request and its values which got tagged for ML models. There is a correlation between the same types of sources in all graphs. But if we clearly observe we got to see that the ICMP source is reducing to 0(zero) in 2 graphs due to the already proceeded value in the previous run.

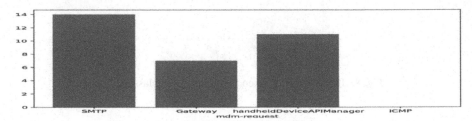

Fig. 11. Show's the 0 occurrence of ICMP processing

Figure 11 shows the 0 occurrence of ICMP processing since ICMP generates most common message events and in our environment, we have not seen the message events running more than once for a generated events feedback loop. This explains the faster processing and avoidance in duplicate processing.

From Fig. 12 we observe that the entire process out of 4, 3 still had runs but 1 process didn't even have runs. Which means there is huge improvement on linear data processing. This is best suitable for larger complex processing inside ML engine capacity.

6   Conclusion

The papers shed the light on new ways to orchestrate the intrusions detection systems and also explains the facilitation of the collected intrusions to be categorized for further

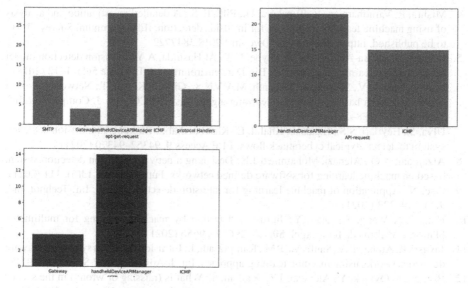

Fig. 12. Shows subsequent multiple runs

feedback loop to be handled in better way for source of the intrusion occurrence and specific treatment of the same in our target system. This handles the propagation of such valid request for downstream consumption for regular process. We have proposed an algorithm to generate the decision tree from the data set/inputs fed to algorithm and validate the tree to classify the occurrence of the event using SVM. Current system doesn't have the dynamic tagging and event queuing for event related to both intrusion and non-intrusion generating network sources. Also, the current system doesn't have the full capacity to event loop the feedback mechanism needed for intelligent engine to take much better dynamic decision. The proposed system also handles the categorization of the intrusion detected values such that from next time right way of handling can be done at the source level itself. Overall, the proposed system will provide 15% to 20% improvement on overall performance based on the performance of current system, whereas the current system takes on an average 40 intrusions per hour per network, but the proposed system intuitively handles 56 intrusions per hour per network on a single node machine running the entire algorithm.

References

1. Mukherjee, B., Heberlein, L.T., Levitt, K.N.: Network intrusion detection. IEEE Netw. **8**(3), 26–41 (1994)
2. Larson, D.: Distributed denial of service attacks–holding back the flood. Netw. Secur. **3**, 5–7 (2016)
3. Venkatraman, S., Alazab, M.: Use of data visualisation for zero-day Malware detection. Secur. Commun. Netw. (2018), Dec. 2018, Art. no. 1728303. [Online]. Available: https://doi.org/10.1155/2018/1728303

4. Mishra, P., Varadharajan, V., Tupakula, U., Pilli, E. S.: A detailed investigation and analysis of using machine learning techniques for intrusion detection, IEEE Commun. Surveys Tuts., to be published. https://doi.org/10.1109/comst.2018.2847722

5. Othman, S.M., Ba-Alwi, F.M., Alsohybe, N.T., Al-Hashida, A.Y.: Intrusion detection model using machine learning algorithm on Big Data environment. J. Big Data 5(1), 1–12 (2018)

6. Das, V., Pathak, V., Sharma, S., Srikanth, M.V.V.N.S., Gireesh Kumar, T.: Network intrusion detection system based on machine learning algorithms. AIRCC's Int. J. Comput. Sci. Inf. Technol. 2(6), 138–151 (2010)

7. Ulya, S., Heydari, S.S., Elgazzar, Khalid, El-Khatib, Khalil.: Building an intrusion detection system to detect atypical cyberattack flows. EEE Access 9, 94352–94370 (2021)

8. Alzahrani, A.O., Alenazi, Mohammed J.F.: Designing a network intrusion detection system based on machine learning for software defined networks. Futur. Internet 13(5), 111 (2021)

9. Pise, N.: Application of machine learning for intrusion detection system. Inf. Technol. Ind. 9(1), 314–323 (2021)

10. Hsu, C.Y., Wang, S., Qiao, Y.: Intrusion detection by machine learning for multimedia platform. Multimed. Tools Appl. 80(19), 29643–29656 (2021)

11. Jayasri, P., Atchaya, A., Sanfeeya, P.M., Ramprasath, J.: Intrusion detection system in software defined networks using machine learning approach. Int. J. Adv. Eng. Res. Sci. 8(4), (2021)

12. Bozcan, I., Oymak, Y., Alemdar, I.Z., Kalkan, S.: What is (missing or wrong) in the scene? A hybrid deep Boltzmann machine for contextualized scene modeling. In: 2018 IEEE International Conference on Robotics and Automation (ICRA), pp. 1–6 (2018)

13. Kim, J.J., Kim, H.L., Thu, T., Kim, H.: Long short term memory recurrent neural network classifier for intrusion detection. In: Proceedings of International Conference on Platform Technology and Service (PlatCon), pp. 1–5 (2016)

14. Ali, F.A.B.H., Len, Y.Y.: Development of host based intrusion detection system for log files. In: Proceedings of 2011 IEEE Symposium on Business, Engineering and Industrial Applications (ISBEIA), pp. 281–285 (2011)

15. Deng, L.: Deep learning: methods and applications, found. Trends Signal Process 7(3–4), 197–387 (2014)

16. Javaid, A.Q., Niyaz, W.S., Alam, M.A.: Deep learning approach for network intrusion detection system. In: Proceedings of the 9th EAI International Conference on Bio-inspired Information and Communications Technologies (BIONETICS), pp. 21–26 (2016)

AI-Based COVID Alert System on Embedded Platform

Vipul Jethwa[✉] , Ruchi Gajjar , and Nagendra Gajjar

Nirma University, Ahmedabad, GJ 382481, India
vipuljethwa09@gmail.com, {ruchi.gajjar,
nagendra.gajjar}@nirmauni.ac.in

Abstract. Corona Virus Disease (COVID-19) has hit the world hard and almost every country has faced its consequences may be the population and number of people affected or economically. Crowd management is incredibly tough for big surroundings and continuous watching manually is troublesome to execute. Vaccinated people are also getting affected by the virus so it is advisable to take Public Health & Social Measures (PHSM) such as wearing a proper mask, sanitization and keeping social distancing in crowded places. The proposed paper presents a machine learning based real-time Covid alert and prevention system to ensure Covid appropriate behavior in public places and social gatherings. There are three modules under this system: (i) Real-time Face mask detection, where persons with masks, improper masks or no mask are detected and classified; (ii) Real-time people counting for ensuring a limit on public meetings and social gatherings and (iii) Real-time social distance monitoring. All these modules are integrated and deployed on embedded hardware, NVidia's Jetson Nano. The implementation results are presented and analysis of the detection is done in real-time on the edge-AI platform.

Keywords: COVID-19 · Embedded Hardware · Machine learning · Mask detection · Social distancing

1 Introduction

Corona Virus disease 2019 (COVID-19) has affected the whole world. In recent years the fast-spreading of COVID-19 has forced the World Health Organization (WHO) to declare COVID-19 as a worldwide pandemic. In line with [1], quite 5 million cases were infected by the pandemic in a very short span of a few months, across 188 countries. The virus spreads through shut contact and overcrowded areas while there is primarily through droplets of saliva or discharge from the nose when an infected person coughs or sneezes [2]. Delta (B.1.617.2) variation is turned into two times as contagious as in advance variations and can motive extra extreme illness. Omicron (B.1.1.529) variation would possibly unfold extra effortlessly than different variations.

In order to control the spread of the virus, WHO has provided a set of guidelines like covering face, sanitization, avoiding social gatherings and maintaining social distancing

© The Author(s), under exclusive license to Springer Nature Switzerland AG 2022
A. Kumar et al. (Eds.): ICAIDS 2021, CCIS 1673, pp. 241–251, 2022.
https://doi.org/10.1007/978-3-031-21385-4_21

[22]. However, it becomes difficult to monitor people in large crowded places to ensure that the said guidelines are not violated. Some countries have enforced mandatory mask policies publicly areas. Crowd management is very difficult for a large environment and continuous monitoring manually is difficult to execute. The aim of this work is to develop a machine learning-based system that can be implemented in real-life situations like social gatherings like classrooms, cinemas halls, bus stops where people can be monitored for Covid appropriate behavior in order to prevent the spread of the virus. As the pandemic continues to evolve, PHSMs should be regularly reviewed and there are few things that we cannot avoid like working, travelling, functions and gatherings as they are intrinsic part of humanity but we have evolved and we have computing power that can be used to develop applications that can help to solve or minimize the problem. WHO recommends for use of the COVID-19 vaccine but still we do not have any cure for it.

The capabilities of machine learning and specifically Convolutional Neural Networks (CNN) in pattern discrimination and analysis has led to its deployment in a variety of applications like object detection, classification, etc. CNN offers several article discovery calculations that depend upon image handling. R-CNN, Fast R-CNN, Faster R-CNN, YOLO and SSD square measure some item discovery calculations were dependent on CNN [3]. To contribute to this pandemic era, we have developed a deep learning-based real-time system that can be deployed on embedded hardware. This paper's contribution is summarized as follows:

- A vigorous machine learning-based framework is proposed which can identify human face masks effectively and order them dependent on their wearing condition: "MASK ON", "MASK NOT PROPER" and "NAKED FACE".
- The second framework is to detect and count the number of people present in the real-time video feed.
- The last structure of the proposed model is a social distancing module that works continuously to distinguish the distance between the individuals and produce an alert if the distance is compromised.
- For real-time use, all the frameworks are deployed on embedded hardware Jetson Nano board from NVidia.

The rest of the paper is organized as follows: Sect. 2 presents the literature survey and describes the related work done in face mask detection. Section 3 describes the proposed approach for real-time face mask detection, people counting and social distancing. The implementation results are presented and analyzed in Sects. 4 and 5 presents the conclusion.

2 Related Works

Previously loads of work has been done using YOLO (You Only Look Once) for object detection. YOLO rule has numerous versions of it and also YOLO network will be compacted or many layers might be more thereto. Hence, this section focuses on the assorted approaches followed for investigating individuals or object victimization in the YOLO network. A couple of the antecedently used methodologies reported in the literature are listed below (Table 1).

Table 1. Comparison to related works.

Sr no.	Author	Application	Used Approach	Details	Outcomes
1	[4]	Mask Detection	YOLO Tiny V4	Results obtained using the YOLO variant in the proposed dataset	Precision 78%
2	[5]	Vehicle Detection	O-YOLO V2	The O-YOLO-v2 models provide higher detection accuracy and meet video detection requirements	Precision 94%
3	[6]	Mask Detection	Res-Net 50, YOLO V2	Using this model face mask detected	Precision 81%
4	[7]	Mask Detection	PCA	Unmasked faces give better recognition rates in PCA-based face recognition systems	Mask Accuracy 72% Non-Mask Accuracy 95%
5	[8]	Masking faces	GAN	GAN-Based Network for detecting of Masked Face	Evaluation parameters unavailable
6	[9]	Mask Detection	MAFA &LLE-CNN	The dataset MAFA and LLE-CNNs for masked face detection	Precision 74%
7	[10]	People Counting	PC-YOLO	YOLOPC, a YOLO-based real-time number counting approach using boundary selection	Confidence 64%
8	[11]	Traffic Counting	YOLO	Detector to generate the bounding box for vehicle counting	Accuracy 100%

(continued)

Table 1. (*continued*)

Sr no.	Author	Application	Used Approach	Details	Outcomes
9	[12]	Object detection	YOLO-compact v1	YOLO-compact network has a high performance with a fairly small size	Accuracy 86.85%
10	[13]	Object detection	CPU Based YOLO	Object detection model to run on Non-GPU computers	Precision 31.05%
11	[14]	Mask Detection	YOLO v5L,v5s	Used on Nvidia Jetson Xavier and Nano	mAP 92.49, mAP 86.43
12	[15]	Mask Detection	Knowledge Distillation	Uses Knowledge distillation	Accuracy 90.13%

Existing distributed work in this domain of mask detection investigates face mask detection. In Kumar et al. [4] The authors proposed novel dataset classes with covers, without covers, covers mistakenly, and cover a region that guides in accomplishing exact and dependable YOLO v4 as the identification accomplishing mAP of 71.69 proposes YOLO-PC that outflanks YOLO because it re-trains YOLO organization, that empowers it to acknowledge boxes and attain higher than traditional certainty esteem. The limit determination in YOLO-PC makes the checking a lot of centred on and its outcome precise additionally, quickly. All in all, this strategy is viable and it's, in addition, able to understand individuals and disrespect them within the checking live feed from the camera. YOLO-PC contains a wide scope of uses because it will facilitate the advancement of diverse elements of the shrewd urban areas. In [16] a proficient YOLO-compact network structure is presented in this approach. It is proposed for real-time detection of the object of only one category. Various experiments with the layers and networks of YOLOv3 were performed and then merged to obtain a YOLO-compact network that is even lesser in size compared to YOLO tiny. The tests were performed on the pedestrians crossing. Approach even ties to tune with convolution matrixes and instead of using 5 × 5 matrix it uses 1 × 3 + 3 × 1 + 3 × 3 type of matrix. 86.85% accuracy is obtained using YOLO-compact which is even 37% better than YOLOv3 [16] So, the above arrangement of changing the layers of the network resulted in a compact network along with better output capabilities for a single category detection.

In Loey et al. [6] For picture recognition, authors have utilized the YOLO v2 based ResNet-50 model to deliver high-performance results. The proposed model improves recognition execution by acquainting mean IoU with gauging the best number of anchor boxes. To prepare and approve their detector in a managed state, they plan another dataset dependent on two public concealed face datasets. M. Loey et al.[6] selected three face mask datasets for study. The three datasets are RealWorld Masked Face Dataset (RMFD), Simulated Masked Face Dataset (SMFD), and Labeled Faces in the Wild (LFW). The

SVM classifier achieved 99.64% test accuracy with RMFD. Achieved 99.49% with SMFD and 100% test accuracy with LFW. In Nagrath et al. [18] authors have used single shot multibox detector and MobileNetV2 for the detection purpose.

It can be observed from the presented survey, that YOLO and its related versions have been employed for mask detection or object detection, but not much work has been reported for a system that is an integration of social distance check along with people counting. Also, the works reported by been presenting simulation results and hardly there are any systems that have been deployed on the embedded platform for real-time detection. This work overcomes the said limitations and presents a complete system for real-time face mask detection along with an alert for social distance as well as the limit of the count of people.

3 Proposed Approach

This work is mainly focused to help organizations and authorities maintain crowds under COVID situations where proper implementations of COVID -19 regulations has to be followed. So the approach has been divided into 3 modules: Mask detection, people counting and social distancing. All the modules use the YOLO algorithm but are individually tuned for the specific module. All the modules are deployed on NVidia's Jetson Nano and work in real-time and present the detected output on the video feed.

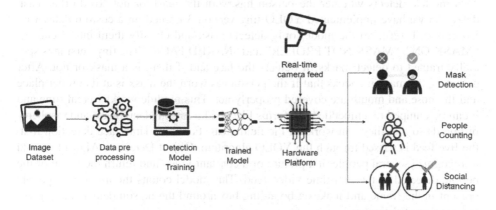

Fig. 1. Proposed real-time COVID alert system block diagram

Figure 1 shows the block diagram of the whole system the first block is the dataset. For mask detection the model is trained on the images of 3 classes having a proper mask, no mask and improper mask for the people detection which uses Microsoft COCO (Common Objects in context) dataset for mask detection [19]. For people counting is uses YOLO and the training is done on the object dataset available on Kaggle [19]. After getting ready the dataset images were separated into classes and all the images were resized. The third step is training for which each image was fed to a neural network with annotation and trained weights were derived from the training and finally, these weights were used for inference purposes on the embedded hardware. The real-time video was recorded from a webcam and we can accurately detect masks and count the number of people, if they are very close to each other an "ALERT" bounding is also generated over the person.

3.1 Model

This work uses YOLO as the backend, behind all the modules. The YOLO network is the combination of 52 along with skip connections and 3 prediction heads for classification. The convolutional layer uses 1×1 and 3×3 windows for feature extraction and is 5×5 in size. Some convolutional layers are grouped into a set to extract features from an image. Hence, we can assume that a certain group of layers would extract eyes, hands such kind features from an image. YOLOv3 is better at recognizing objects since it utilizes a 13×13 layer for detecting big sized objects, 52×52 for tiny objects and 26×26 for medium-sized objects. Instead of having softmax in the output layer YOLOV3 does the multi-label classification of objects. YOLO v3 Tiny is a lightweight version of YOLO v3, with less execution time as reduction in convolutional layers there is a tradeoff of accuracy due to the changes.

3.2 The Real-Time Mask Detection and People Counting

This module detects whether the person has worn the mask or not. To do this mask detection we have implemented YOLO tiny version 3 trained on a custom dataset by Bruggisser F [20]. So the model only detects mask and classify them into 3 classes. "MASK ON", "MASK NOT PROPER" and "NAKED FACE". The tiny version is specially trained to detect masks, It detects the face and if there is a mask or not. After detecting the mask it checks that if the person has worn the mask is at its proper place and the nose and mouth are covered properly not. This module works in real-time and it can be dumped on embedded platforms like Nvidia Jetson Nano board and raspberry pi boards so that they can work on the field areas. For Real-Time face detection first, the live feed is passed through the YOLO algorithm. Object Detection Algorithm used to recognize several people in a picture or a constant video and return the count of the people detected in the real-time video feed. This model counts the number of people present in the frame and makes a bounding box around the person detected and gives the number of the count.

3.3 The Real-Time Social Distancing Module

The Real-time Social distancing module also uses YOLO Version 3 and uses Microsoft Common Objects in Context dataset for object detection [19]. The input frames undergo through the algorithm and it detects whether the distance between the groups is a safe distance or whether it is overcrowded by computing the Euclidean distances between all pairs of the centroids. If the overcrowded image or people standing nearby is detected it makes a red rectangle over the area and denoted the object as "ALERT". This way the module works in real-time and gives the output for the distance between people.

YOLO treats object detection as a regression problem, taking a given input image and at the same time learning bounding box coordinates and corresponding category label chances that the detected object is a part of the object on which we have trained the model. It gives back the person prediction chance, bounding box coordinates for the detection, and therefore the centroid of the person.

NMS (Non-maxima suppression) is additionally used to scale back overlapping bounding boxes to solely one bounding box, therefore representing truth detection of the item. Having overlapping boxes isn't precisely sensible and ideal, particularly if we'd like to count the quantity and the count of objects in a picture. Euclidean distance is then computed between all pairs of the returned centroids. Simply, a centroid is the centre of a bounding box. Supported these pairwise distances, we check if any 2 people standing close to each other are area units less than/close to 'N' pixels apart.

4 Experimental Results and Discussion

4.1 Embedded Hardware

To deploy the trained CNN AI-Based Covid alert model, NVIDIA Jetson Nano is used as an inference engine. It features an NVIDIA Maxwell GPU with 128 NVIDIA CUDA Cores, Quad-core ARM-based application processors CortexA57, 4 GB 64-bit LPDDR4, and other peripherals [21]. Figure 2 shows the hardware setup for the experimentation. We connected to a power supply and peripherals like keyboard and mouse, USB webcam and HDMI monitor are connected.

[a]   [b]

Fig. 2. Experimental setup

4.2 Results for Real-Time Mask Detection

As shown in Fig. 3a it is the output of the mask detection module, the real-time video is captured by the webcam and the output is generated by the algorithm we can analyze the image that the algorithm has detected 3 people. The image also shows the confidence value of the detected mask for each individual. Here person 1 has not worn the mask so his face is bound with a red rectangle and class as "NAKED FACE". Person 2 in middle has worn the proper mask so it is classified with the green box as "MASK ON", Person

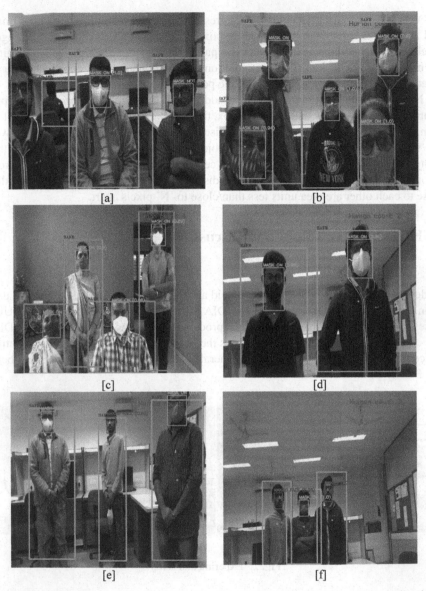

Fig. 3. Real-time test results (**a**) and (**b**) are Results of Mask detection, (**c**) and (**d**) are Results of People Counting, (**e**) and (**f**) are Results of Social Distancing results

3 is in the middle who has worn the mask but his nose and face are not covered properly so it makes an orange bounding box over the face and classifies it as "MASK NOT PROPER". It can be observed that the mask-wearing conditions are precisely detected and classified with an accuracy of nearly 98%. Figure 3b shows masks of all the people present in the frame with corresponding probability score and green bounding box for "MASK ON".

4.3 Results for Real-Time People Counting

This module is the second module of the proposed work, which is also a real-time module, fetched the video from the webcam available and creates green bounding boxes over the people detected in the frame. This module uses the YOLO V3 model to detect the number of people in the frame. The people counting is efficiently implemented providing an accuracy of around 98%. As shown in Fig. 3c there are 4 people in the frame and the module output is shown on the top right corner. Similarly, for Fig. 3d the count is 2.

4.4 Results for Real-Time Social Distancing Alert

The Social distancing module calculates the Euclidian distance between the centroid of the rectangular bounding boxes. This way real-time distancing modules works and generates an alert signal by creating a red bounding box over the person available in the frame which is nearby of the other person. Figure 3e–f is a snippet from the module output where the person is bounded by a rectangular bounding box and a green centroid is visible in the image. And if the distance of the centroid is less than the threshold then "ALERT" is created and shown by Fig. 3f. And if the distance is more than the limit "SAFE" is printed over the bounding box that can be seen in Fig. 3e. The social distancing alert system is accurate enough and detects the violation of social distance with an accuracy of around 87%, which is appreciable in real-time analysis.

5   Conclusion and Future Scope

This paper presents a machine learning-based system to prevent the spread of Covid. The proposed system is an amalgamation of three modules that detects the face mask, counts the number of people and check social distancing in real-time. The system is deployed and tested on the embedded hardware platform, Nvidia's Jetson Nano. The proposed models achieved an accuracy of around 98% for mask detection, 98% for people counting and nearly 87% for social distance alert. The system is robust against actual real-life scenarios and works efficiently under varied lighting conditions and locations. Recently latest versions of YOLO and many other models have been developed that can be trained as tiny models for single object detection which can be implemented as the future scope. Along with the software models, the current market is leveraging adaptable edge hardware devices to accelerate the code, work can be done on Adaptive Compute Acceleration Platform (ACAP) a heterogeneous compute platform or on FPGA acceleration that will help to achieve dramatic performance improvements for real-time feed and extend the capabilities of existing models with power efficiency.

References

1. WHO Coronavirus (COVID-19) Dashboard. In: Covid19.who.int. https://covid19.who.int/, last accessed 1 Dec 2021
2. In: Covid19.who.int. https://covid19.who.int/measures, last accessed 1 Mar 2021
3. Kaarmukilan, S, Poddar, S.K.:A FPGA based deep learning models for object detection and recognition comparison of object detection comparison of object detection models using FPGA. 2020 Fourth International Conference on Computing Methodologies and Communication (ICCMC). https://doi.org/10.1109/iccmc48092.2020.iccmc-00088 (2020)
4. Kumar, A., Kalia, A., Verma, K., Sharma A, Kaushal M.:Scaling up face masks detection with YOLO on a novel dataset. Optik **239**, 166744. https://doi.org/10.1016/j.ijleo.2021.166744 (2021).
5. Han, X., Chang, J., Wang, K.: Real-time object detection based on YOLO-v2 for tiny vehicle object. Procedia Comput. Sci. **183**, 61–72. https://doi.org/10.1016/j.procs.2021.02.031(2021)
6. Loey, M., Manogaran, G., Taha, M., Khalifa, N.: Fighting against COVID-19: a novel deep learning model based on YOLO-v2 with ResNet-50 for medical face mask detection. Sustain. Cities Soc. **65**, 102600. https://doi.org/10.1016/j.scs.2020.102600 (2021)
7. Ejaz, M., Islam, M., Sifatullah, M., Sarker, A.: Implementation of principal component analysis on masked and non-masked face recognition. In: 2019 1st International Conference on Advances in Science, Engineering and Robotics Technology (ICASERT). https://doi.org/10.1109/icasert.2019.8934543 (2019)
8. Ud Din, N., Javed, K., Bae, S., Yi, J.: A novel GAN-based network for unmasking of masked face. IEEE Access **8**, 44276–44287 (2020). https://doi.org/10.1109/access.2020.2977386
9. Ge, S., Li, J., Ye, Q., Luo, Z.: Detecting masked faces in the wild with LLE-CNNs. In: 2017 IEEE Conference on Computer Vision and Pattern Recognition (CVPR). https://doi.org/10.1109/cvpr.2017.53 (2017)
10. Ren, P., Wang, L., Fang, W., Song, S., Djahel, S.: A novel squeeze YOLO-based real-time people counting approach. Int. J. Bio-Inspired Comput. **16**, 94 (2020). https://doi.org/10.1504/ijbic.2020.109674
11. Lin, J., Sun, M.: A YOLO-based traffic counting system. In: 2018 Conference on Technologies and Applications of Artificial Intelligence (TAAI). https://doi.org/10.1109/taai.2018.00027 (2018)
12. Li Z, Wang, J.: An improved algorithm for deep learning YOLO network based on Xilinx ZYNQ FPGA. In: 2020 International Conference on Culture-oriented Science & Technology (ICCST). https://doi.org/10.1109/iccst50977.2020.00092 (2020)
13. Ullah, M., Ullah, M.: CPU based YOLO: A real time object detection algorithm. In: 2020 IEEE Region 10 Symposium (TENSYMP). https://doi.org/10.1109/tensymp50017.2020.9230778 (2020)
14. Stavan, R., Monil, J., Ruchi, G.: Real-time face mask detection system on edge using deep learning and hardware accelerators. In: 2nd International Conference on Communication, Computing & Industry 4.0-2021, CMR Institute of Technology, Bengaluru, 16–17 December 2021 (2021)
15. Ambika, L., Priyansh, J., Ruchi, G., Manish, P.: Face mask detection for preventing the spread of Covid-19 using knowledge distillation. In: IEEE International Conference on Computational Performance Evaluation (ComPE), North Eastern Hill University, Shillong, 1–3 December 2021 (2021)
16. Lu, Y., Zhang, L., Xie, W.: YOLO-compact: an efficient YOLO network for single category real-time object detection. 2020 Chinese Control and Decision Conference (CCDC). https://doi.org/10.1109/ccdc49329.2020.9164580 (2020)

17. Loey, M., Manogaran, G., Taha, M., Khalifa, N.: A hybrid deep transfer learning model with machine learning methods for face mask detection in the era of the COVID-19 pandemic. Measurement **167**, 108288. https://doi.org/10.1016/j.measurement.2020.108288 (2021)
18. Nagrath, P., Jain, R., Madan, A., Arora, R., Kataria, P., Hemanth, J.: SSDMNV2: a real time DNN-based face mask detection system using single shot multibox detector and MobileNetV2. Sustain. Cities Soc. **66**, 102692. https://doi.org/10.1016/j.scs.2020.102692 (2021).
19. COCO 2017 Dataset. In: Kaggle.com. https://www.kaggle.com/awsaf49/coco-2017-dataset, last accessed 7 July 2021
20. Bruggisser F Google DriveDrive.google.com https://drive.google.com/drive/folders/1aA XDTl5kMPKAHE08WKGP2PifIdc21-ZG?usp=sharing, last accessed 1 Oct 2021
21. Jetson Nano. In: NVIDIA Developer. https://developer.nvidia.com/embedded/jetson-nano, last accessed 30 July 2021
22. https://www.worldbank.org/en/who-we-are/news/coronavirus-covid19, last accessed 14 Dec 2021

An Efficient Detection of Brain Stroke Using Machine Learning Robust Classification

Shaik Abdul Nabi[1]([⊠]) and Revathi Durgam[2]

[1] Sreyas Institute of Engineering and Technology, Hyderabad, India
dr.nabi@sreyas.ac.in
[2] School of Computer Science and Engineering (SCOPE), VIT AP, Amaravati, India

Abstract. Machine Learning (ML) approaches became increasingly popular in solving many real world problems. They are used widely in healthcare industry for disease diagnosis. From the literature, it is found that feature selection is the area of the research that contributes to improving prediction accuracy. Towards this end, we proposed a feature importance algorithm known as Information Gain based Feature Importance (IGFI). It considers informatioin gain metric that makes use of entroy in order to know importance of features. After finding importance of features, decision is made to choose best features. The IGFI algorithm is capable of impacting brain stroke prediction models positively. It is used in the process of detecting brain stroke. The training is given to ML classifiers using the selected features only. This could reduce search space leading saving time and memory resources. In addition to this, the proposed algorithm also improves accuracy of prediction models. The highest accuracy is exhibited by Random Forest with 95.97% while least performance is shown by GaussianNB. The second highest performance is shown by XGBoost with 95.58%. From the results it is understood that the RF method outperform other ML based prediction models. It can be used in clinical decision support systems in healthcare units. In future, we build hybrid prediction models for improving prediction performance further..

Keywords: Brain stroke detection · Feature selection · Machine learning · Supervised machine learning models

1 Introduction

With the advancements in Artificial Intelligence (AI), there are many ML models that are used to serve the applications in the real world. In fact, they are widely used to solve problems in the real world. Supervised learning models are aplenty and they have different approaches in prediction or classification. However, their performance largely depends on the quality of training data. This is the significant weakness of those models that provide deteriorated performance when there is inadequate training quality. Therefore, it is indispensable to have mechanisms to improve quality of training data. One approach is to identify redundant and irrelevant features and removing them. In this paper, we focused on finding importance of features and considering the features that are best for brain stroke prediction.

© The Author(s), under exclusive license to Springer Nature Switzerland AG 2022
A. Kumar et al. (Eds.): ICAIDS 2021, CCIS 1673, pp. 252–262, 2022.
https://doi.org/10.1007/978-3-031-21385-4_22

The Machine Learning method observes developing a prediction model it will be used to get the solution to a given Problem Statement. To understand the process of e-learning let's imagine that you have been given a problem that needs to be solved using Machine Learning method.

All data and models obtained during the Data Test are used to create a Machine Learning Model. This can be done by dividing the data into two parts, First one is training data and second is test data. Training data can be used to construct and evaluate the model.

Many researchers contributed towards the brain stroke detections. But it is observe that the existing prediction models work attheir best only when training data has adequate quality. Otherwise, they tend to provide mediocre performance which is the problem to be addressed.

Our contributions in this paper are as follows.

- Proposed a feature importance algorithm known as Information Gain based Feature Importance (IGFI). It considers informatioin gain metric that makes use of entropy in order to know importance of features.
- Evaluated many supervised ML models with the propoed feature selection algorithm.
- Implemented a porotype using Python data science platform to know the performance of different prediction models in presence of feature importance method.

The organization of the paper is structured as follows. Section 2 reviews literature on different methods for brain stroke detection. Section 3 provides the details of the proposed framework and algorithm. Section 4 presents experimental results while Sect. 5 concludes the work with possible future scope of the research.

2   Related Work

This section reviews literature on brain stroke prediction research using ML techniques. Many researchers contributed towards brain stroke detection using ML techniques. Ieracitanoa *et al.* [1] used EEG recordings in order to make an automated detection of brain stroke using ML methods. Pradeepa *et al.* [2] used social media data and analysed it to find risk factors in brain stroke. Chia-Feng *et al.* [3] used advancements in machine learning for detection of risks in different healthcare problems. Wenbing *et al.* [4] investigated on the health issues such as hypertension and its outcomes using ML based predictions. Helge *et al.* [5] used machine learning approaches on CT scans to understand posterior circulation stroke probabilities. Asit *et al.* [6] focused on automatic classification of brain stroke using RF and expectation maximization. Andreas [7] used MRI imagery and deep learning for brain pathology segmentation. Similar kind of work is carried out by Zeynettin *et al.* [8] using MRI. Sanjay *et al.* [9] made an extensive review of different ML algorithms used for brain stroke. Shim *et al.* [10] used graphical data in order to predict patterns of brain problems rapidly. They combined ML approaches and feature engineering. Kassania *et al.* [11] investigated on the possible feature selection that helps in efficient prediction to solve real world problems. Yasheng *et al.* [12] used brain CT scans to investigated on the neurological disorders using ML approaches. Javeria *et al.*

[13] focused on features fusion and ML for solving healthcare problems. Iqtidar *et al.* [14] investigated on healthcare industry and the need for using ML techniques. Aditya *et al.* [15] proposed an integrated approach towards stroke prediction using ML methods.

Christian *et al.* [16] explored ML approaches for solving certain speech problems automatically. Hang *et al.* [17] used Internet of Things (IoT) based approach towards detection of brain diseases. Ramachandran *et al.* [18] studied on sleep apnea kind of problems using machine learning. Hamidreza *et al.* [19] explored predictive analytics to estimate possible stroke and its related medications. Asit *et al.* [20] decision tree algorithm used to clean noise data [21] focused on detection of ischemic stroke using MRI and Delaunay Triangulation. Other methods found in the literature are classification [22], neighbourhood-level impact based approach [23], Embolic Stroke Prediction [24], Prediction of NIH stroke scale [25] and detection of ischemic stroke from radiology reports [26, 27] Hybrid machine learning approach scenario on genetic algorithms to improve characteristic features. [28] used pso approach for feature selection to improve prediction accuracy. Kumar et al. [29, 30] proposed an object detection method for blind people.

From the literature, it is found that the existing prediction models work at their best only when training data has adequate quality. Otherwise, they tend to provide mediocre performance which is the problem to be addressed.

3   Proposed Framework

We proposed a ML based framework and an algorithm for improving performance of prediction models using brain stroke prediction case study. The framework shown in Fig. 1 takes brain stroke dataset as input. It does pre-processing in order to divide the data into 80% training and 20% testing. The training data is subjected to feature selection using the proposed algorithm named Information Gain based Feature Importance (IGFI).

The IGFI algorithm returns best features that contributes to prediction of brain stroke. ML algorithms are trained with the selected features of the dataset in order to gain knowledge model known as brain stroke detection model. This model takes knowledge from prediction models and also takes testing data to detect probability of brain stroke.

As stated in Algorithm 1, an algorithm is defined to have efficient feature selection method that can find contributing features. This could leverage prediction performance of supervised learning models. The algorithm takes dataset as input and produces features that have importance so as to have its impact on ML models.

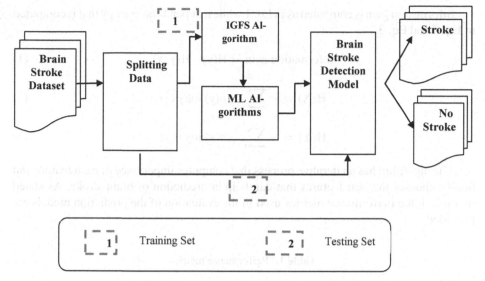

Fig. 1. Proposed framework for brain stroke detection

Algorithm: Information Gain based Feature Importance (IGFI)

Input: Brain stroke dataset **D**

Output: Important features **F**

1. Start
2. Initialize a feature map M
3. **F**←ExtractAllFeatures(**D**)

   Compute Information Gain
4. For each *f* in **F**
5. **gain**←FindInformaitonGain(*f*,**F**)
6. **M**←Insert(*f*, **gain**)
7. End For

   Find Important Features
8. For eachfeature*f* in **F**
9. **gain**←Get(*f*,**M**)
10. IF **gain**<**th** THEN
11.   Remove the feature*f* from **F**
12.   End If
13. End For
14. Return **F**
15. End

Information gain is computed as in Eq. 1 while it depends on entropy that is computed in Eq. 2 and Eq. 3.

$$\text{Information gain} = H(y) - H(y/x) \tag{1}$$

$$H(X) = -\sum_{y \in Y} p(y) \log p(x) \tag{2}$$

$$H(Y) = -\sum_{y \in Y} p(y) \log p(y) \tag{3}$$

The algorithm has an iterative process that computes importance of each feature and finally chooses the best features that can help in prediction of brain stroke. As stated in Table 1, the performance metrics used in the evaluation of the prediction models are provided.

Table 1. Performance metrics

Metric	Formula	Value range	Best value
Precision (p)	$\frac{TP}{TP+FP}$	[0; 1]	1
Recall (r)	$\frac{TP}{TP+FN}$	[0; 1]	1
Accuracy	$\frac{TP+TN}{TP+TN+FP+FN}$	[0; 1]	1
F1-Score	$2 * \frac{p*r}{p+r}$	[0; 1]	1

4 Experimental Results

A prototype is built using Python data science platform to evaluate the proposed framework, feature selection method and underlying ML models.

As stated in Fig. 2, the BMI effect on stroke probability is provided. The data analysis implied the significance of considering BMI for detecting brain stroke.

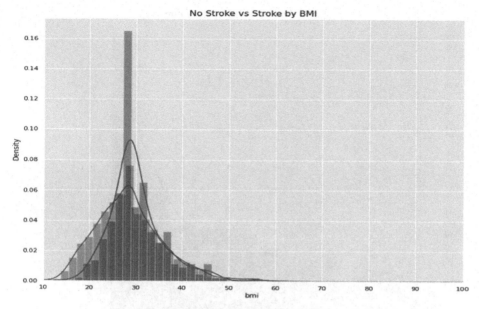

Fig. 2. Effect of BMI on brain stroke

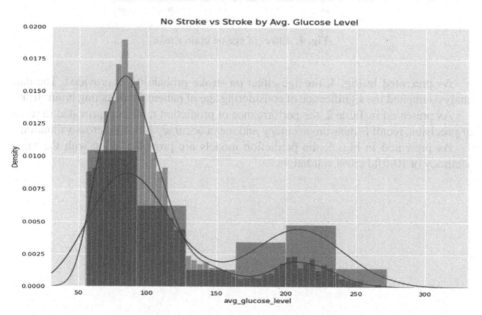

Fig. 3. Effect of average glucose level on brain stroke

As stated in Fig. 3, the average glucose level effect on stroke probability is provided. The data analysis implied the significance of considering average glucose level of patient for detecting brain stroke.

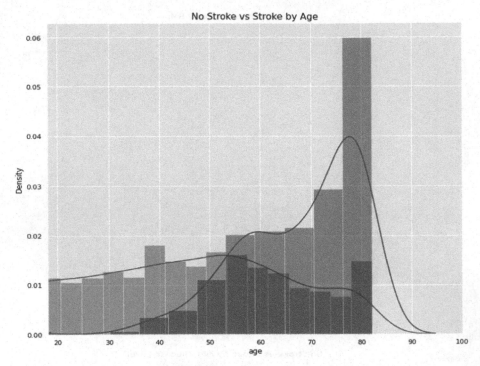

Fig. 4. Effect of age on brain stroke

As presented in Fig. 4, the age effect on stroke probability is provided. The data analysis implied the significance of considering age of patient for detecting brain stroke.

As presented in Table 2, the performance of prediction models is provided in terms of precision, recall F-measure accuracy and mean accuracy of k-fold cross validation.

As presented in Fig. 5, the prediction models are provided along with the mean accuracy of 10-fold cross validation.

Table 2. Performance evaluation of different brain stroke prediction models

Brain stroke prediction model	Precision	Recall	F-measure	Accuracy	K-fold validation mean accuracy (%)
Logistic Regression	0.15	0.72	0.72	0.77201	79.45
SVM	0.11	0.41	0.18	0.79843	88.36
KNeighbors	0.12	0.33	0.18	0.83659	90.77
GaussianNB	0.06	0.96	0.11	0.19275	57.33
BernoulliNB	0.10	0.83	0.18	0.60567	72.94
Decision tree	0.07	0.13	0.09	0.86007	90.39
Random forest	0.10	0.09	0.09	0.906066	95.97
XGBoost	0.15	0.09	0.11	0.92465	95.58

Different prediction models are provided in horizontal axis. Vertical axis shows the mean accuracy obtained from k-fold cross validation. It is observed from the results that each prediction model has shown different level of accuracy. The rationale behind this is that each prediction model has its own internal approach in discriminating samples.

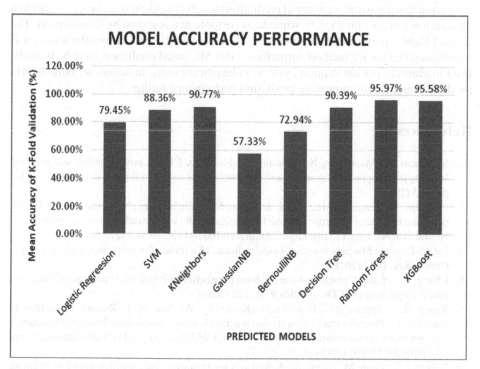

Fig. 5. Performance of brain stroke prediction models

Logistic regression model has shown accuracy 79.45% while SVM exhibited accuracy better than logistic regression with 88.3%. The least accuracy is shown by GaussianNB with 57.33% while BernoulliNB is better than GaussianNB with 72.94%. Decision Tree accuracy is 90.39% while KNeighbors shows better accuracy than Decision Tree with 90.77%.

The highest accuracy is exhibited by Random Forest with 95.97% while least performance is shown by GaussianNB. The second highest performance is shown by XGBoost with 95.58%. From the results it is understood that the RF method outperform other ML based prediction models. It can be used in clinical decision support systems in healthcare units.

5 Conclusion and Future Work

In this paper, we proposed a feature importance algorithm known as Information Gain based Feature Importance (IGFI). It considers informatioin gain metric that makes use of entroy in order to know importance of features. After finding importance of features, decision is made to choose best features. The IGFI algorithm is capable of impacting brain stroke prediction models positively. It is used in the process of detecting brain stroke. The training is given to ML classifiers using the selected features only. This could reduce search space leading saving time and memory resources. In addition to this, the proposed algorithm also improves accuracy of prediction models. The highest accuracy is exhibited by Random Forest with 95.97% while least performance is shown by GaussianNB. The second highest performance is shown by XGBoost with 95.58%. From the results it is understood that the RF method outperform other ML based prediction models. It can be used in clinical decision support systems in healthcare units. In future, we build hybrid prediction models for improving prediction performance further.

References

1. Ieracitano, C., Mammone, N., Hussain, A., Morabito, F.C.: A novel multi-modal machine learning based approach for automatic classification of eeg recordings in dementia. Elsevier, p, 1–35 (2019)
2. Pradeepa, S., Manjula, K.R., Vimal, S., Khan, M.S., Chilamkurti, N., Luhach, A.K.: DRFS: detecting risk factor of stroke disease from social media using machine learning techniques. Neural Process. Lett. (2020). https://doi.org/10.1007/s11063-020-10279-8
3. Lu, C.-F., et al.: Machine learning-based radiomics for molecular subtyping of gliomas. Clin. Cancer Res. 1–34 (2018)
4. Chang, W., et al.: A machine-learning-based prediction method for hypertension outcomes based on medical data. Diagnostics **9**(4), 178 (2019)
5. Kniep, H.C., Sporns, P.B., Broocks, G., Kemmling, A., Nawabi, J., Rusche, T., Fiehler, J., Hanning, U.: Posterior circulation stroke: machine learning-based detection of early ischemic changes in acute non-contrast CT scans. J. Neurol. **267**(9), 2632–2641 (2020). https://doi.org/10.1007/s00415-020-09859-4
6. Subudhi, A., Dash, M., Sabut, S.: Automated segmentation and classification of brain stroke using expectation-maximization and random forest classifier. Biocybernetics Biomed. Eng. **40**(1), 1–13 (2019)

7. Holzinger, A.: Machine learning for health informatics. In: Holzinger, A. (ed.) Machine Learning for Health Informatics. LNCS (LNAI), vol. 9605, pp. 1–24. Springer, Cham (2016). https://doi.org/10.1007/978-3-319-50478-0_1

8. Akkus, Z., Galimzianova, A., Hoogi, A., Rubin, D.L., Erickson, B.J.: Deep learning for brain MRI segmentation: state of the art and future directions. J. Digit. Imaging 30(4), 449–459 (2017). https://doi.org/10.1007/s10278-017-9983-4

9. Sirsat, M.S., Fermé, E., Câmara, J.: Machine learning for brain stroke: a review. J. Stroke Cerebrovasc. Dis. 29(10), 1–17 (2020)

10. Shim, V.B., et al.: Rapid prediction of brain injury pattern in mTBI by combining FE analysis with a machine-learning based approach. IEEE Access 8, 179457–179465 (2020)

11. Kassania, S.H., Kassanib, P.H., Wesolowskic, M.J., Schneidera, K.A., Detersa, R.: Automatic detection of coronavirus disease (COVID-19) in X-ray and CT images: a machine learning based approach. Biocybernetics Biomed. Eng. 41(3), 867–879 (2021)

12. Chen, Y., et al.: Automated quantification of cerebral edema following hemispheric infarction: application of a machine-learning algorithm to evaluate CSF shifts on serial head CTs. NeuroImage: Clin. 12, 673–680 (2016)

13. Amin, J., Sharif, M., Raza, M. Yasmin, M.: Detection of brain tumor based on features fusion and machine learning. J. Ambient Intell. Humanized Comput. 117 (2018). https://doi.org/10.1007/s12652-018-1092-9

14. Newaz, A.I., Sikder, A.K., Rahman, M.A., Uluagac, A.S.: HealthGuard: a machine learning-based security framework for smart healthcare systems. In: IEEE 2019 6th International Conference on Social Networks Analysis, Management and Security (SNAMS), Granada, Spain, 22-25 October 2019, pp. 389–396 (2019)

15. Khosla, A., Cao, Y., Lin, C.C.-Y., Chiu, H.-K., Hu, J., Lee, H.: An integrated machine learning approach to stroke prediction. In: Proceedings of the 16th ACM SIGKDD International Conference on Knowledge Discovery and Data Mining, KDD '10, 25–28 July 2010, pp. 1–9 (2010)

16. Kohlschein, C., Schmitt, M., Schuller, B., Jeschke, S., Werner, C.J.: A machine learning based system for the automatic evaluation of aphasia speech. In: IEEE 19th International Conference on e-Health Networking, Applications and Services (Healthcom), 1215 October 2017, pp. 1–6 (2017)

17. Chen, H., Khan, S., Kou, B., Nazir, S., Liu, W., Hussain, A.: A smart machine learning model for the detection of brain hemorrhage diagnosis based internet of things in smart cities. Complexity 2020, 1–10 (2020)

18. Ramachandran, A., Karuppiah, A.: A survey on recent advances in machine learning based sleep apnea detection systems. Healthcare 9(7), 914 (2021)

19. Saber, H., Somai, M., Rajah, G.B., Scalzo, F., Liebeskind, D.S.: Predictive analytics and machine learning in stroke and neurovascular medicine. Neurol. Res. 41, 1–10 (2019)

20. Abdul, S., Rasool, S., Premchand, P.: Detection and extraction of videos using decision trees. Int. J. Adv. Comput. Sci. Appl. 2(12) (2011).https://doi.org/10.14569/IJACSA.2011.021222

21. Subudhi, A., Acharya, U.R., Dash, M., Jena, S., Sabut, S.: Automated approach for detection of ischemic stroke using delaunay triangulation in brain MRI images. Comput. Biol. Med. 103, 1–35 (2018)

22. Ho, K.C., Speier, W., Zhang, H., Scalzo, F., El-Saden, S., Arnold, C.W.: A machine learning approach for classifying ischemic stroke onset time from imaging. IEEE Trans. Med. Imaging 38, 1 (2019)

23. Ji, J., Hu, L., Liu, B., et al.: Identifying and assessing the impact of key neighborhood-level determinants on geographic variation in stroke: a machine learning and multilevel modeling approach. BMC Public Health 20, 1666 (2020). https://doi.org/10.1186/s12889-020-09766-3

24. Kamel, H., et al.: Machine learning prediction of stroke mechanism in embolic strokes of undetermined source. Stroke 51, 1–8 (2020)

25. Yu, J., Park, S., Lee, H., Pyo, C.-S., Lee, Y.S.: An elderly health monitoring system using machine learning and in-depth analysis techniques on the NIH stroke scale. Mathematics **8**(7), 1–16 (2020)
26. Ong, C.J.: Machine learning and natural language processing methods to identify ischemic stroke, acuity and location from radiology reports. PLoS ONE **15**(6), 1–16 (2020)
27. Durgam, R., Devarakonda, N., Nayyar, A., Eluri, R.: Improved genetic algorithm using machine learning approaches to feature modelled for microarray gene data. In: Ranganathan, G., Fernando, X., Shi, F., El Allioui, Y. (eds.) Soft Computing for Security Applications. AISC, vol. 1397, pp. 859–872. Springer, Singapore (2022). https://doi.org/10.1007/978-981-16-5301-8_60
28. Nabi, S.A., Laxmi, K.R.:Prediction accuracy model aiming to improve prediction accuracy in congenital heart anomaly detection using hybrid feature selection with modified particle swarm optimization approach. In: Journal of Physics: Conference Series, Vol. 1998, 3rd International Conference on Smart and Intelligent Learning for Information Optimization (CONSILIO 2021), Hyderabad, India, 9–10 July 2021
29. Kumar, A.: Design of secure image fusion technique using cloud for privacy-preserving and copyright protection. Int. J. Cloud Appl. Comput. (IJCAC) **9**(3), 22–36 (2019)
30. Kumar, A., Zhang, Z.J., Lyu, H.: Object detection in real time based on improved single shot multi-box detector algorithm. EURASIP J. Wirel. Commun. Netw. **2020**(1), 1–18 (2020). https://doi.org/10.1186/s13638-020-01826-x

Apple Leaf Diseases Detection System: A Review of the Different Segmentation and Deep Learning Methods

Anupam Bonkra[1](✉), Ajit Noonia[1], and Amandeep Kaur[2]

[1] Amity School of Engineering and Technology, Amity University Rajasthan, Jaipur, India
anupambonkra@gmail.com

[2] Chitkara University Institute of Engineering and Technology, Chitkara University, Punjab, India
amandeep@chitkara.edu.in

Abstract. These are various critical aspects that limiting apple quality and productivity, the leaf disease one of them. The usual examination process of leaf disease takes a lot of time to diagnose problems, a majority of farmers lose the ideal time to protect as well as cure diseases. Apple crop is one of the most essential crops on which the global economy lies. Therefore, apple leaf diseases detection is the most important topic of image processing. The most important goal is to figure out how to effectively depict damaged leaf images. Due to climate changes, different types of diseases have been developed. Marssonia left blotch, powdery mildew, fire blight, apple scab, black rot, and frogeye leaf spot are categories of apple leave diseases and different datasets. The manual way to find diseases on leaves are difficult to detect, error rate, and time consuming. The deep learning and segmentation techniques are very helpful for the detection of apple leaf diseases. In this paper, different DL techniques are reviewed and compared with other methods. In advanced techniques, different segmentation and detection techniques of plant leaf disease detection are explained and compared for the analysis.

Keywords: Apple leave disease · Categories of apple leaves · Deep learning methods · Segmentation

1 Introduction

Various diseases have a significant influence on the growth of crops as well as crops around the world. A production drop resulted in a global recession inside the agricultural business. Apple trees are grown throughout the globe, and apples are amongst the most commonly consumed fruits. During 2018, the globe generated a total of 86 million metric tons of apples, with consumption and production rising steadily since that day [1]. Unfortunately, as compared to the productive capacity of apples, the overall average production of apples is insufficient. Environmental variables, insufficient post-harvest technology, less emphasis upon fundamental research, insufficient availability of high-quality vegetative propagation to producers, as well as social-economic limitations are

---

The original version of this chapter was revised: The affiliation of the Author Amandeep Kaur has been changed to "Chitkara University Institute of Engineering and Technology, Chitkara University, Punjab, India". The correction to this chapter is available at https://doi.org/10.1007/978-3-031-21385-4_44

© The Author(s), under exclusive license to Springer Nature Switzerland AG 2022, corrected publication 2023
A. Kumar et al. (Eds.): ICAIDS 2021, CCIS 1673, pp. 263–278, 2022.
https://doi.org/10.1007/978-3-031-21385-4_23

among the key causes of poor apple output. Apple trees are susceptible to a range of disorders caused by insects as well as germs which including bacteria, known for their high ingestion. The major leaves diseases of the apple plant are fire blight, rust, anthracnose, scab, cedar, powdery mildew, etc. The use of chemicals to properly care for plants is indeed an essential part. Producers can benefit from early detection of these kinds of abnormalities in foliage as well as take appropriate measures to avoid future liabilities [2]. Producers that rely solely on traditional methods for identifying disease symptoms miss out on the best time to avoid illness because all these methods take too much time. There are various autonomous processes in place to identify such threats in a reasonable timeframe.Apple leaves have different categories of diseases in INDIA such as apple scab, rot, blotch, etc. Leaves include necessary data which can be used to determine species of plants. Leaves, Floral parts, and fruits are commonly used to identify plants.As fruits and flowers only exist for a limited moment, these are not appropriate for plant disease detection. Leaves are present for a long period as well as in greater quantities. Therefore, leaves are the best alternative for automated plant classification. Plant classification has recently become a serious concern for several experts, including gardeners, foresters, and agronomists, due to industrialization as well as the degradation of forests. The classification of plants is critical for understanding plant genetic relationships as well as explaining plant evolution. Plant identification, also for horticulturists, is a challenging undertaking because of the number of different species. As a result, researchers have been looked into automatic deep learning-based segmentation and categorization of leaves in plants imagery with cluttered backgrounds.

In this study, various exiting methods of apple leaves disease detection are surveyed in Sect. 2. The different categories of apple leave diseases are discussed in Sect. 3. The apple plant leave datasets are explained in Sect. 4. In Sect. 5, different segmentation and deep learning techniques of apple leaves are explained with architectures. The detection methods with exsiting result analysis with various DL methods are discussed in Sect. 6. Lastly, this paper is concluded in Sect. 7.

2 Related Work

The literature of existing technique is reviewed in this section. Srinidhi et al., (2021) [3] proposed a framework for the detection of apple leaves diseases. The framework was based on deep CNNs models (DenseNet and EfficientNet). The proposed framework was classified into six phases, the first phase was the image gathering phase, the second phase was a pre-processing phase, the third phase was segmentation, the fourth phase was augmentation phase, the fifth phase was feature extraction, and the last phase was classification phase. The classifiers were used to categorize the different four classes: the first class was healthy (normal class), the second was rust class, the third was a scab, and the last class was multiple diseases. The blurring, flipping, and Canny edge detector were used to enhance the results of classification. The DenseNet had achieved an accuracy of 99.75% and EfficientNetB7 had attained 99.8% accuracy. Khan, et al., (2021) [4] designed a deep learning based methodology for the detection and classification of apple diseases. The dataset building phase of the research entails data gathering and data categorization. Then, using the supplied data, convolutional neural network architecture for automated illness categorization of apples was built. Convolutional networks were used end-to-end training techniques that automatically extract the features as well as training the complicated characteristics using image files, and proving them appropriate for a wide range of applications such as object recognition, classification task, and segments. To establish the properties of the proposed learning algorithm, the authors were used transfer learning. To avoid overfitting, data augmentation approaches such as translation, rotation, reflections, and magnification were used. On the provided dataset, the presented CNN model achieved statistically significant improvements, with an accuracy of roughly 97.18%. Bansal, et al., (2021) [5] designed a methodology for the detection of apple leaves disease. The methodology was based on the deep CNN (Convolutional neural network) model. The multiple pre-trained classifiers were used for the efficient results of the classification. The pre-trained classifiers such as EfficientNetB7, EFFI-CIENTNET Noisy Student, and DenseNet121 were used in the proposed framework. The apple leaf diseases were classified into different classes such as healthy leave class, cedar rust class, apple scab class, and several other diseases. For the efficient results of the datasets, data augmentation methods were used. During dataset validation, 96.25% of accuracy had achieved. During the classification of disease, 90% of accuracy had attained. Sun, H., et al., (2021) [6] used the advance learning for the detection of apple leaf disease. The authors had used the data annotation and data augmentation technologies for efficient results. A database of apple leaf illnesses named Appledisease5 was created, which was made up of simple and complicated background scans. Furthermore, by recreating the general convolution, a fundamental unit named Mobile End AppleNet block was presented to boost recognition performance and minimize model complexity. Conversely, the Apple-Inception unit was created by using GoogleNet's Convolutional Neural Network model as well as substituting every convolution layer inside Inception with Mobile End AppleNet blocks. Furthermore, the Mobile End AppleNet module, as well as the Apple-Inception module, were used to create a novel apple leaf disease detection model called mobile end AppleNet based SSD algorithm. The findings of the investigation demonstrate that mobile end AppleNet based SSD algorithm could identify five common apple leaf illnesses with an accuracy of 83.12% mAP as well as a speed was 12.53 FPS, demonstrating that the unique mobile end AppleNet based SSD system could accurately and efficiently identify five common apple leaf diseases on portable devices. Chao, et al., (2020) [7] designed a technique based on convolutionary neural network for the detection of apple leaf disease. The CNN was used to enhance the identification accuracy and efficiency of the apple leaf disease. By gathering scans of normal and diseased apple orchard leaves both from the cultivating areas and laboratories and then creating a dataset that contains 5 common apple leaves diseases and normal leaves. The convolutionary neural network for apple leaf disease identification suggested in this research incorporates DenseNet as well as Xception, but instead of just completely linked layers, it uses average global pooling. The SVM (Support Vector Machine) was used to categorize the apple leaf diseases after extracting the features with the suggested convolutional neural network. Numerous convolutionary neural networks including the proposed deep convolutionary neural network, have been trained to recognize apple leaf diseases. The appropriate network outperforms VGG-16, Inception-v3, DenseNet-201, MobileNet, VGG-INCEP, and Xception in identifying leaves diseases, with an overall accuracy of 98.82%. Zhong, et al., (2020) [8] designed a framework for the identification of apple leaves diseases. The framework was based on deep learning. The densenet-121 was implemented in the deep model. The main objective of the model was to attain multi-class identification and evaluate the function loss. The different methods of regression were implemented. The proposed model had attained an accuracy of 93% and efficiently identifies the apple plat leaves diseases. The various existing techniques for the detection of apple leaf disease are depicted with problem definition, dataset, and performance metrics are shown in Table 1.

Table 1. Various existing methods used for apple leave detection diseases

Author's year	Proposed techniques	Gap/problem definition	Dataset	Performance metrics
Srinidhi et al., (2021) [3]	Deep CNNs models (DenseNet and EfficientNet) based approach	More data is required for the training of CNN based model	Plant village dataset	Accuracy
Khan, et al., (2021) [4]	Convolutional neural network-based algorithm	Need to use data augmentation techniques	Collected samples	Accuracy
Bansal, et al., (2021) [5]	Deep CNN based algorithm	Limited dataset No detection of Foliar diseases	Collection of 3642 images	Accuracy Precision Recall F1-score
Sun, H., et al., (2021) [6]	Light-weighted real-time CNN model	Complex background and illumination effects degrade the overall performance of the model	Appledisease5	Accuracy Speed
Chao, et al., (2020) [7]	Xception deep model-based framework	Insufficient results on complex background images	Samples of 2970 images	Accuracy
Zhong, et al., (2020) [8]	Deep densenet-121 model	Data imbalance issues	AI challenger-plant-disease-recognition	Accuracy Precision Fi-score Sensitivity

Table 2. Several classifications of existing methods

Author's year	Classification techniques	Results	Drawbacks	Enhancement
Srinidhi et al., (2021) [3]	DenseNet and EfficientNetB7	Accuracy = 99.8% and 99.7%	Limited class classification	More data will be used and classified into multiple classes
Khan, et al., (2021) [4]	CNN	Accuracy = 97.18%	Over fitting problem	CNN will be enhanced with data augmentation techniques for the efficient results
Bansal, et al., (2021) [5]	EfficientNetB7, EFFICIENTNET Student, and DenseNet121	Accuracy = 90%	Limited classes of diseases are detected	Dataset will be increased and classification technique will be enhanced for the more class classification of the disease
Sun, H., et al., (2021) [6]	Mobile end AppleNet based SSD	Accuracy = 83.12%	Inaccurate results of classification	Classification will be improved by another classifier
Chao, et al., (2020) [7]	VGG-16, Inception-v3, DenseNet-201, MobileNet, VGG-INCEP, and Xception	Accuracy = 98.82%	Overfitting issues Computational complexity	Transfer learning will be implemented for effective results
Zhong, et al., (2020) [8]	DenseNet	Accuracy = 93% Precision = 92% F1-score = 92% Sensitivity = 92%	Inefficient classification results	A hybrid technique will be used for the better classification

In Table 2, classification techniques of the existing methods with results are depicted. The drawbacks of the existing methods with future enhancement are also presented in Table 2.

3 Categories of Apple Leave Disease

The different types of apple leave diseases are presented in below with definition and diagrammatical presentation.

3.1 Marssonia Leaf Blotch

This type of disease manifests itself as deep green circular patches mostly on top side of the leaves, followed by 5–10 mm brownish leaf spots that darken over time (Fig. 1).

Fig. 1. Marssonia Leaf Blotch [9]

3.2 Powdery Mildew

When the buds grow to new leaves and stems, this type of disease emerges. On the underside of the leaves, little spots of grey or white chalky aggregates appear. The leaves become longer and thinner than typical leaves, with a curled border [10] (Fig. 2).

Fig. 2. Powdery Mildew [10]

3.3 Fire Blight

In spring and summer months, leaf dots emerge mostly on leaves. On young shoots, the infection has to be the most destructive, although it can started spreading to all portions of the plant above surface [11] (Fig. 3).

Fig. 3. Fire blight [11]

3.4 Apple Scab

Mostly in spring, tiny scratches on the bases of the leaves surfaces are the first signs of this dangerous fungal infection generated by Venturia inaequalis. It grows across to the leaves tips and finally goes towards the fruit, in which it appears as tiny black scabs [12] (Fig. 4).

Fig. 4. Apple scab [12]

3.5 Black Rot and Frogeye Leaf Spot

Physalospora obtusa is the infection due to which, black rot and frogeye leaf spot are caused. The cause of both diseases is same fungus but it spreads at different stages [13] (Fig. 5).

Fig. 5. Black rot and forgeye leaf spot [13]

4 Dataset Description: Apple Leaf Diseases

4.1 ALDD (Apple Leaf Disease Dataset) [14]

Apple leaf disease composition varies based on the season as well as many other conditions like temperature, temperature, and brightness. Monsoon rains, for instance, promote the growth as well as spreading of microorganisms, culminating in the development as well as the extension of diseased patches on damaged leaves. By consideration of the above, ALDD scans are acquired in a variety of weather patterns for much more detailed implementations. There are a variety of 2029 scans of infected apple leaves that correlate to five different groups. The different classes of apple leaves are presented in Table 3.

Table 3. Different classes of apple leave diseases [14]

Categories of apple leaves	Mosaic	Alternaria leaf spot	Rust	Brown spot	Grey spot
Leave images					

4.2 Plant Pathology Challenge 2020 Dataset [15]

This dataset is generated by the Kaggle community for the competition of Plant pathology challenges. The competition is the part of Computer vision and pattern recognition workshop. There are 3651 images in this dataset consist multiple categories of diseases such as scab, cedar, rust, etc. There are some complex infected leaves images and some disease-free images. Some images of leaves from the plant pathology challenge 2020 dataset are shown in Fig. 6.

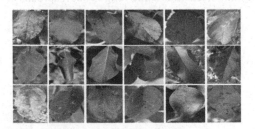

Fig. 6. Leave samples [15]

5   Various Segmentation and Deep Learning Detection Methods

In several visual comprehension technologies, image segmentation is a vital part. It entails dividing an image into several sections or units. There are several areas where segmentation plays a vital role such as tumour detection in medical field, text detection, vehicles detection etc. There is various type of image segmentation techniques has existed, some are based on machine learning and some are based on advance deep learning. Following are the deep learning based segmentation techniques of the apple leaf disease detection. Deep learning methods have advanced significantly in the recent two decades, providing enormous prospects for application in a variety of sectors and services. There are several types of deep learning techniques such as YOLO, Transfer Learning with CNN, and Inception–V4.

5.1 Vgg-16 Network

Simonyan and A. Zisserman were created the VGG16, which is a CNN model. It was among the most well-known designs entered in the 2014 ILSVRC challenge. On the Imagenet database, the VGG model obtains a top-five prediction performance of 92.7%. The region connects sixteen levels in aggregate. Numerous 3 × 3 operator filtrations were implemented next to each other in VGG16, eliminating massive operator filtering that was utilized in traditional approaches. The artificial network's capacity is boosted by using many levels of neurons. The artificial network's thickness is boosted by using many levels of neurons. This allows the neural net to recognize and grasp more complicated issues and characteristics. Vgg16 has 3 × 3 dimensional activation functions, 2 × 2 dimensional ordinary layers, and a fully linked layer upon layer. The neural network's starting dimension is 64. After every max pooling, the neuronal network's size increases. Each of the other two completely activation functions contains 256 stations, whereas the network structure only has two. The ReLU objective function is used in the initial multiple convolutional layers, while the nonlinear activation neural network is used in the output layer. After each 256 connection hidden layers, dropping is implemented. The channel's activation function used in VGG16 is 0.0001. Employing categorization inter as the covariance matrix, the optimizer Adam was employed. VGG16's descriptive complexity is advantageous for prediction performance [16]. The basic architecture of VGG-16 is shown in Fig. 7.

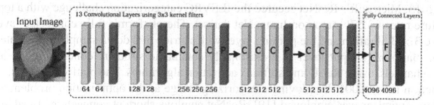

Fig. 7. The basic architecture of VGG-16 network [16]

5.2 Fully Convolutional Neural Network (FCNN)

FCNN's have gained popularity as a result of significantly increased frame segmentation effectiveness. Fully Convolution Neural Network is kind of deep learning technique for processing information which is grid pattern like as pictures. The organization's activation functions, together with classifiers, aid in retrieving temporal and spatial characteristics from frames [17]. A weight-sharing mechanism is used in the levels, which significantly reduces computing time. Convolutional neural networks are essentially backpropagation computational models with additional restrictions such as terminals in almost the same filtration system are only linked to small sections of something like the frame to maintain geographic distribution, and individual strengths are distributed to significantly reduce the number of hyperparameters.

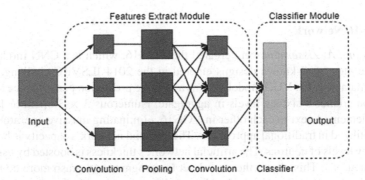

Fig. 8. Baisc architecture of fully CNN algorithm [5]

A CNN is made up of three layers: the first layer is feature map to subsequent development, the second layer is subsampling (max-pooling) layer to downward sampling the frame, minimize dimensions, and reducing computation complexity, the last third layer is the convolutional layer that provides categorization functions to the structure [18]. The architecture of convolutional neural network is presented in above Fig. 8.

5.3 ResNet50 Network

Resnet is the residual network. ResNet50 is a type of image categorization algorithm. In 2015, Microsoft's ResNet secured the ILSVRC categorization challenge with a top 5 failure rate of 3.57% upon on ImageNet dataset. The platform's fully connected layers have 3 × 3 filtration and the pooling layer with a stride of 2 down sample immediately. The platform's output layer is a reasonably obtainable structure containing 256 and two channels, using ReLU and softmax activation algorithms. The platform's activation function is 0.000001. Employing categorizing bridge as the optimization problem, the Adam optimizer was employed [19]. ResNet employs shortcut connections to address the issues of degraded precision and disappearing elevation that plague DNN (deep neural networks). These links enable the customers to pass across levels that it deems unimportant during development. There are multiple types of ResNet34, ResNet50, ResNetV2, ResNetxt. There are fifty layers in ResNet50 that are used for the detection and classification of apple leave images.

5.4 Mask RCNN

Mask RCNN is the Regional convolutional neural network. Mask RCNN is a class of deep CNN designed to handle the issue of semantic segmentation in computer vision.

The working of Mask RCNN is divided into two phases. The first phase is feature extraction and candidate region detection. In the second phase, a mask on the detected region is produced. The regression of box and classification is also included in this phase. The basic architecture is shown in Fig. 4. The mask R-CNN is divided into different modules: The first module included Resnet-FPN. **(i) ResNet-Feature Pyramid Network (ResNet-FPN):** The ResNet-FPN serves as the foundation for Mask R-CNN, which combines ResNet and the FPN abbreviated as feature pyramid network. ResNet is a deep neural network that can obtain information from pictures. The initial several layers collect minimal information, followed by greater functions in subsequent levels. The developers of Mask R-CNN presented the FPN as an enhancement to enhance the extracted features, that can effectively depict the image inside the feature space at several dimensions [20]. By adding a layer to the typical extraction of features pyramid, the FPN enhances the extracting efficiency. The 2nd pyramid can feed strong attributes with the first pyramid into the bottom layer, allowing them to fully incorporate details across differing stages. **(ii) Region Proposal Network (RPN):** The RPN module may choose a huge number of locations from attributes mapping that includes artifacts that used a sliding window. Links, which have been the rectangles, which surround the artifacts, seem to be the specified locations. Throughout fact, there must be approximately 200 K anchoring with various shapes and sizes, and dimensions, both of which will encompass the image's features to the best of its ability. The anchoring, which is most likely to involve the items will be selected by the RPN forecast, as well as the frames will be resized to accommodate them. When various anchoring in a location overlapped excessively, the RPN forecast will preserve one with the greatest foreground rating while discarding the others (Fig. 9).

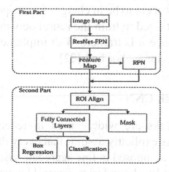

Fig. 9. Architecture of mask-RCNN[20]

5.5 Yolo

YOLO uses a regression process to immediately compute the dimensions of bounding boxes as well as the likelihood of every class, significantly improving the velocity of target identification. YOLO segmented the image into 7*7 grids at the initial stage. If the target ground truth (GT) is included with in grid, it's also in control of image identification. The grid predicts B boundaries and associated confidence ratings, and also C dependent conditional probabilities [21]. Whenever the grid incorporates objectives, confidence score indicates the correctness of the expected boundaries. If several boundaries include the same item, the non-maximal suppressing procedure is used to determine which one is the most prominent and has the largest confidence interval. The basic architecture of YOLO model is presented in Fig. 10.

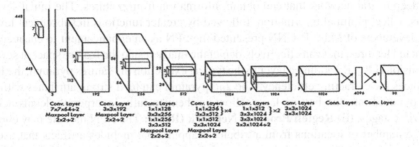

Fig. 10. Architecture of YOLO model [21]

5.6 SSD (Single Shot Multibox Detector)

SSD is the single shot multibox detector. During learning, SSD utilizes a pairing phase to connect the relevant anchoring container also with neighboring pixels of each object's ground-truth value of the image. In essence, the anchoring boxes with the greatest overlapping including an element seem to be in charge of anticipating the element's location and class. This attribute is utilized to train the neural network as well as to forecast the identified items' positions once it is trained. With implementation, zoom level and an aspect ratio are assigned to each anchor box [22].

5.7 Transfer Learning with CNN

Convolutional neural networks are widely used in recent image processing high-dimensional data. Most layers explicitly assume that every data they receive is a bitmap. Initially convolution layer is composed in fine aggregate visuals and find ways to recognise decreased characteristics like boundaries. Several layers are effective in controlling an object's temporal and spatial correlations. Filtrations are used to do this. These layers, contrast traditional feed-forward folds, feature a substantially smaller set of variables and use a weight-sharing mechanism to save calculation time [23]. The employment of similar pre-trained algorithms is essential rather than engaging through to the complicated process of classification algorithms from start when embarking on a comparable image recognition challenge. Transferring learning refers to the process of emigrated through one present and training system to a web application through recycling the different network parameters. The basic architecture of transfer learning with CNN is shown in Fig. 11.

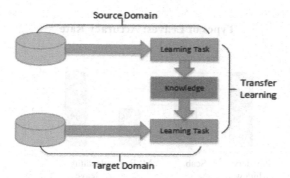

Fig. 11. Architecture of transfer learning CNN [5]

5.8 Inception-V4

Shallow Convolutional Neural Network (CNN) architectures are essential for one of the most advanced breakthroughs in image segmentation. Inception has become one of the architectures that display satisfactory accuracy at a reasonable cost of processing. The Inception deep network design is also known as Inception-v1. The Inception-v1 framework with the theory of residual blocks is resulting in Inception-v2. Then, in subsequent versions, the decomposition concept is incorporated, as well as the framework is dubbed Inception ResNet V1, Inception-v1, Inception ResNet V2, Inception-v3, and Inception-v4 [23].

6 Existing Result Analysis

The existing techniques of apple leave disease detection had attained effective results. In this section, the results of CNN-based ResNet [4] existing technique for different classes of apple leave disease detection are compared. The technique was used for the detection of leaf diseases. The powdery mildew, scab, MLB (Marssonia Leaf Blotch), and healthy leaves are compared. The comparison is based on accuracy parameters.

The graphs presented that MLB (Marssonia Leaf Blotch) disease is hard to detect. The Comparison of different classes of apple leaves detection through the existing CNN-based ResNet technique is depicted in Fig. 12. The comparison of different existing CNN-based techniques of apple leaves disease detection is presented in Fig. 13. The existing methods based on deep learning such as DenseNet [3], EfficientNetB7 [3], CNN [4], DenseNet121 [5], SSD [6], VGG-16 [7], Inception [7], DNN [8] are compared based on their accuracy. The comparative analysis of existing methods presented that SSD [6] had attained the lowest accuracy as compared to other methods. The DenseNet [3] and EfficientB7 [3] had attained maximum accuracy.

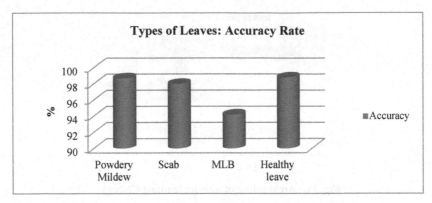

Fig. 12. Parameter 1: comparison analysis with accuracy rate (%) [4]

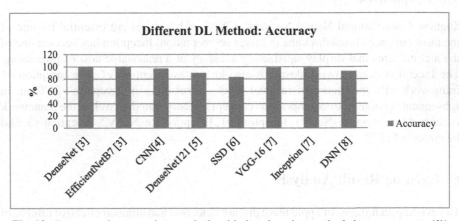

Fig. 13. Parameter 2: comparison analysis with deep learning methods in accuracy rate (%)

7   Conclusion and Future Scope

Existing classification techniques of apple leave disease detection are compared. There are different datasets of apple plant leave such as ALDD (Apple leaf disease dataset), Plant Pathology challenge 2020 dataset, etc. These datasets contained multiple types of leaves and were helpful for the training and testing of advanced techniques. The basic architectures of the detection and segmentation techniques are depicted in this paper. For the segmentation and classification of leaf images with many difficulties as well as a difficult backgrounds, the Mask R-CNN model and the Vgg-16 model are implemented. The comparison analysis of different apple leaves diseases through CNN-based ResNet presented that Marssonia leaf blotch disease is difficult to detect. CNN-based techniques provided high accuracy and are easy to implement, so for the analysis of apple leaf disease detection techniques different existing CNN-based techniques are compared. The DenseNet [3] and EfficientNetB7 [3] CNN-based techniques have attained maximum accuracy from other existing techniques. More research needs to be done using other deep learning techniques as well as a larger amount of data to see for better outcomes can be achieved. Aside from the method's improvement, greater image quality and good equipment too can help for efficiency.

References

1. Liu, B., Zhang, Y., He, D., Li, Y.: Identification of apple leaf diseases based on deep convolutional neural networks. Symmetry **10**(1), 11 (2018)
2. Fang, T., Chen, P., Zhang, J., Wang, B.: Identification of apple leaf diseases based on convolutional neural network. In International Conference on Intelligent Computing, August, pp. 553–564. Springer, Cham (2019)
3. Srinidhi, V.V., Sahay, A., Deeba, K.: Plant pathology disease detection in apple leaves using deep convolutional neural networks: Apple leaves disease detection using Efficient-Net and DenseNet. In: 2021 5th International Conference on Computing Methodologies and Communication (ICCMC), April, pp. 1119–1127. IEEE (2021)
4. Khan, A.I., Quadri, S.M.K., Banday, S.: Deep learning for apple diseases: classification and identification. Int. J. Comput. Intell. Stud. **10**(1), 1–12 (2021)
5. Bansal, P., Kumar, R., Kumar, S.: Disease detection in apple leaves using deep convolutional neural network. Agriculture **11**(7), 617 (2021)
6. Sun, H., Xu, H., Liu, B., He, D., He, J., Zhang, H., Geng, N.: MEAN-SSD: a novel real-time detector for apple leaf diseases using improved light-weight convolutional neural networks. Comput. Electron. Agric. **189**, 106379 (2021)
7. Chao, X., Sun, G., Zhao, H., Li, M., He, D.: Identification of apple tree leaf diseases based on deep learning models. Symmetry **12**(7), 1065 (2020)
8. Zhong, Y., Zhao, M.: Research on deep learning in apple leaf disease recognition. Comput. Electron. Agric. **168**, 105146 (2020)
9. Shuaibu, M., Lee, W.S., Schueller, J., Gader, P., Hong, Y.K., Kim, S.: Unsupervised hyperspectral band selection for apple Marssonina blotch detection. Comput. Electron. Agric. **148**, 45–53 (2018)
10. Chandel, A.K., Khot, L.R., Sallato, B.: Apple powdery mildew infestation detection and mapping using high-resolution visible and multispectral aerial imaging technique. Sci. Hortic. **287**, 110228 (2021)
11. Jarolmasjed, S., et al.: High-throughput phenotyping of fire blight disease symptoms using sensing techniques in apple. Front. Plant Sci. **10**, 576 (2019)
12. Kodors, S., Lacis, G., Sokolova, O., Zhukovs, V., Apeinans, I., Bartulsons, T.: Apple scab detection using CNN and transfer learning (2021)
13. Abbasi, P.A., Ali, S., Braun, G., Bevis, E., Fillmore, S.: Reducing apple scab and frogeye or black rot infections with salicylic acid or its analogue on field-established apple trees. Can. J. Plant Path. **41**(3), 345–354 (2019)
14. Jiang, P., Chen, Y., Liu, B., He, D., Liang, C.: Real-time detection of apple leaf diseases using deep learning approach based on improved convolutional neural networks. IEEE Access **7**, 59069–59080 (2019)
15. Thapa, R., Snavely, N., Belongie, S., Khan, A.: The plant pathology 2020 challenge dataset to classify foliar disease of apples. arXiv preprint. arXiv:2004.11958 (2020)
16. Yan, Q., Yang, B., Wang, W., Wang, B., Chen, P., Zhang, J.: Apple leaf diseases recognition based on an improved convolutional neural network. Sensors **20**(12), 3535 (2020)
17. Long, J., Shelhamer, E., Darrell, T. Fully convolutional networks for semantic segmentation. In: Proceedings of the IEEE Conference on Computer Vision and Pattern Recognition, pp. 3431–3440 (2015)

18. Baranwal, S., Khandelwal, S., Arora, A.: Deep learning convolutional neural network for apple leaves disease detection. In: Proceedings of International Conference on Sustainable Computing in Science, Technology and Management (SUSCOM), February, Amity University Rajasthan, Jaipur, India (2019)
19. Noon, S.K., Amjad, M., Qureshi, M.A., Mannan, A.: Use of deep learning techniques for identification of plant leaf stresses: A review. Sustain. Comput.: Inform. Syst. 100443 (2020)
20. Yang, K., Zhong, W., Li, F.: Leaf segmentation and classification with a complicated background using deep learning. Agronomy **10**(11), 1721 (2020)
21. Mathew, M.P., Mahesh, T.Y.: Determining the region of apple leaf affected by disease using YOLO V3. In: 2021 International Conference on Communication, Control and Information Sciences (ICCISc), June, vol. 1, pp. 1–4. IEEE (2021)
22. Liu, W., Anguelov, D., Erhan, D., Szegedy, C., Reed, S., Fu, C.Y., Berg, A.C.: Ssd: single shot multibox detector. In: European Conference on Computer Vision, October, pp. 21–37. Springer, Cham (2016)
23. Hussain, M., Bird, J.J., Faria, D.R.: A study on cnn transfer learning for image classification. In: UK Workshop on Computational Intelligence, September, pp. 191–202. Springer, Cham (2018)

Underwater Image Restoration and Enhancement Based on Machine and Deep Learning Algorithms

Yogesh Kumar Gupta$^{(\boxtimes)}$ and Khushboo Saxena

Department of Computer Science, Banasthali Vidyapith, Banasthali, India
gyogesh@banasthali.in

Abstract. Underwater image processing is the key research of the last decade. Due to attenuation and scattering of light into beneath of ocean, it is impossible to find capture image. Therefore image processing keeps into picture. To automate process and find relevant information, there is a need of good quality image. There are many of the applications, where need of processed image due to unclear of original images. In the artificial intelligence the image processing is also one of the important research domains. The machine learning (ML), deep learning (DL) approaches based image processing like image enhancement, denoising, encryption, fusion etc. are emerging trend of the research. Under-water imagery is an important carrier and presentation of under-water information, which plays a vital role in the exploration, exploitation and utilization of marine resources. This paper studied about under-water image restoration and enhancement based on machine and deep learning algorithms, it also suggest an approach to restore and enhance image.

Keywords: Artificial Intelligence · Deep learning · Denoising · Encryption · Fusion · Image · Machine · Restoration

1 Introduction

Computer vision assumes a significant part in logical examination, asset investigation, and other under-water applications. In any case, it experiences the extreme shading twisting, which is brought about by the dispersing and retention of light in the water. As we probably are aware, the learning-based strategy would require a combined informational index for preparing. An under-water picture age strategy is additionally proposed in this article to get the informational collection comprising of shading mutilated pictures and relating ground truth [1]. Nonetheless, because of the limits of target imaging climate and gear, the nature of under-water pictures is consistently poor, with debasement wonders like low difference, obscured subtleties and shading deviation, which truly confine the improvement of related fields. Accordingly, how to upgrade and recuperate debased under-water pictures through after creation calculations has gotten expanding consideration from researchers. As of late, with the fast advancement of DL innovation,

A. Kumar et al. (Eds.): ICAIDS 2021, CCIS 1673, pp. 279–290, 2022.
https://doi.org/10.1007/978-3-031-21385-4_24

incredible advancement has been made in under-water picture enhancement and reconstruction dependent on DL [2]. Blind decrease of dot clamor has turned into a longstanding inexplicable issue in a few imaging applications, for example, clinical ultrasound imaging, manufactured opening radar (SAR) imaging, and under-water sonar imaging, and so forth The undesirable commotion could prompt adverse consequences on the dependable discovery and acknowledgment of objects of interest. According to a factual perspective, dot commotion could be thought to be multiplicative, fundamentally unique in relation to the normal added substance Gaussian clamor. The reason for this review is to indiscriminately diminish the dot commotion under non-ideal imaging conditions. The multiplicative connection between dormant sharp picture and irregular clamor will be first changed over into an added substance form through a logarithmic change [3]. Under-water pictures experience the ill effects of extreme shading projects, low differentiation and haziness, which are brought about by dispersing and retention when light engenders through water. Notwithstanding, existing DL techniques treat the reconstruction cycle in general and don't completely consider the under-water actual twisting interaction. Accordingly, they can't enough handle both assimilation and dispersing, prompting helpless reconstruction results. To resolve this issue, propose an original two-stage network for under-water picture reconstruction, what isolates the reconstruction interaction into two sections viz. Flat and vertical twisting reconstruction [4]. As land assets have constantly diminished, sea investigation by people has consistently developed. Under-water imaging is one of the most natural intends to mirror the inner states of the sea. Notwithstanding, because of the intricate imaging climate of the sea and light dissipating in the ocean, under-water pictures show serious corruption, making it hard to recognize viable data (Fig. 1).

Fig. 1. Sample of under-water picture (google)

In this manner, under-water imaging should be upgraded. Contrasted and conventional techniques (for example histogram evening out technique) and demonstrating strategies, DL has been very much applied in the field of PC vision. The central issues are the procurement of the preparation set and the speculation capacity of the convolution model. Since the model-based strategy frequently needs to quantify earlier information physically ahead of time, it will cause inescapable mistakes; and direct speculation of the neural organization will likewise cause picture obscuring [5]. The proposed network is isolated into two sections viz. Channel-wise shading highlight extraction module and thick remaining element extraction module. Additionally, to prepare the proposed network for under-water picture enhancement, another manufactured under-water picture information base is proposed. Existing engineered under-water information base pictures are portrayed by light dispersing and shading lessening twists. In any case, object haziness impact is overlooked. We, then again, presented the obscuring impact alongside the light dispersing and shading constriction mutilations [7] (Fig. 2).

Fig. 2. Under-water meeting (news)

Under-water picture enhancement has been drawing in much consideration because of its importance in marine designing and oceanic advanced mechanics. Various under-water picture enhancement calculations have been proposed over the most recent couple of years. In any case, these calculations are chiefly assessed utilizing either engineered datasets or hardly any chose genuine pictures. It is accordingly indistinct how these calculations would perform on pictures obtained in the wild and how we could check the advancement in the field. To overcome this issue, we present the principal thorough perceptual review and investigation of under-water picture enhancement utilizing enormous scope certifiable pictures [8]. Under-water picture handling is a knowledge research field that can possibly assist designers with bettering investigate the underwater climate. Under-water picture handling has been utilized in a wide assortment of fields, like under-water minute identification, territory checking, mine location, media transmission links, and independent under-water vehicles. In any case, under-water picture experiences solid retention, dissipating, shading mutilation, and commotion from the counterfeit light sources, causing picture obscure, murkiness, and a somewhat blue or greenish tone. Thusly, the enhancement of under-water picture can be partitioned into two strategies: 1) under-water picture dehazing and 2) under-water picture shading reconstruction [9].

2 Literature Survey

J. Lu et al., [1] presents, an under-water picture shading reconstruction organization (UICRN) is proposed to acquire the genuine shade of the picture by assessing the principle boundaries of the under-water imaging model. Initial, an encoder neural organization is applied to remove highlights from the info under-water picture. Second, three free decoders are utilized to appraise the immediate light transmission map, backscattered light transmission guide, and veiling light. Third, the misfortune capacities and the preparation methodology are intended to task on the exhibition of restoration. The technique joins the intrinsic optical properties and obvious optical properties with structure data to create the combined informational collection. In excess of 20 000 sets of underwater pictures are created dependent on the technique. At long last, the UICRN strategy is quantitatively assessed through different trials, for example, shading diagram testing in the South China Ocean and normal under-water picture assessment. It shows that the UICRN technique is cutthroat with past best in class strategies in shading reconstruction and vigor. H. Wang et al., [2] propose a further developed MSCNN under-water picture defogging strategy, which consolidates Retinex and CLAHE for brilliance leveling and differentiation enhancement of under-water pictures, making the technique more invaluable for complex circumstances like low enlightenment, lopsided light and clear Rayleigh dissipating marvels in under-water conditions, and lead target examination and correlation of the recuperated pictures to demonstrate the adequacy of this calculation in under-water defogging and shading revision. The adequacy of the calculation for under-water defogging and shading rectification is exhibited by target investigation and examination of the recuperated pictures.

Y. Lu et al., [3] To advance imaging execution, we presented the component pyramid organization (FPN) and atrous spatial pyramid pooling (ASPP), adding to an all the more remarkable deep visually impaired DeSPeckling Organization (named as DSPNet). Specifically, DSPNet is basically made out of two subnetworks, i.e., Log-NENet (i.e., commotion assessment network in logarithmic space) and Log-DNNet (i.e., denoising network in logarithmic area). Log-NENet and Log-DNNet are, separately, proposed to assess commotion level guide and diminish irregular clamor in logarithmic space. Y. Lin et al., [4] In the principal stage, a model-based organization is proposed to deal with flat mutilation by straightforwardly installing the under-water actual model into the organization. The weakening coefficient, as a component portrayal in describing water type data, is first assessed to direct the precise assessment of the boundaries in the actual model. For the subsequent stage, to handle vertical mutilation and reproduce the reasonable under-water picture, we set forth an original lessening coefficient earlier consideration block to adaptively recalibrate the RGB channel-wise element guides of the picture experiencing the upward twisting. Trials on both manufactured dataset and true under-water pictures show that our technique can viably handle dissipating and assimilation contrasted and a few best in class strategies.

Z. Wang et al., [5] this task plan a twofold U-Net for under-water picture enhancement with solid speculation capacity, in blend with demonstrating and DL techniques. The dark picture of the info picture is handled with the consideration instrument ahead of time, and the important conveyance data is gotten utilizing a U-Net. Then, at that point, the information picture is handled with the data yield from each layer of the past U-Net. The eventual outcome is gotten by isolating the two U-Net outcomes by pixels. The proposed network is prepared utilizing a combined preparing set created by CycleGAN. Through quantitative and subjective examination, our strategy is ended up being more powerful than the techniques in late works in the field of under-water picture enhancement. E. Silva et al., [6] The quick development of computational and sensor limits permits the improvement of picture reconstruction strategies that can be applied to under-water pictures. Because of its serious level of assimilation, water turns into a significant test for automated discernment applications. An essential issue for some under-water robot applications is the prerequisite of a profundity map. One of the difficulties to getting monocular under-water profundity picture is the absence of huge picture sets to approve the technique, or in any event, preparing a learning-based strategy. For the assessment, a few strategies have been proposed in the best in class either dependent on an actual model and on a DL approach.

A. Dudhane et al., [7] The proposed network is approved for under-water picture reconstruction task on genuine under-water pictures. Exploratory investigation shows that the proposed network is predominant than the current cutting edge approaches for under-water picture restoration. C. Li et al., [8] presents an Under-water Picture Enhancement Benchmark (UIEB) including 950 certifiable under-water pictures, 890 of which have the relating reference pictures. We treat the rest 60 under-water pictures which can't acquire agreeable reference pictures as trying information. Utilizing this dataset, we direct an extensive investigation of the best in class under-water picture enhancement calculations subjectively and quantitatively.

M. Han et al., [9] This task presents the justification for under-water picture corruption, studies the best in class knowledge calculations like DL techniques in under-water picture dehazing and restoration, shows the exhibition of under-water picture dehazing and shading reconstruction with various strategies, presents an under-water picture shading assessment metric, and gives an outline of the major under-water picture applications. At long last, we sum up the use of under-water picture handling. S. Yang et al., [10] Because of the intricacy of the under-water climate, under-water pictures caught by optical cameras ordinarily experience the ill effects of fog and shading contortion. In light of the likeness between the under-water imaging model and the air model, the dehazing calculation is generally embraced for under-water picture enhancement. As a vital factor of the dehazing model, foundation light straightforwardly influences the nature of picture enhancement. This task proposes a clever foundation light assessment strategy which can upgrade the under-water picture. Also, it tends to be applied in 30-60m profundity with counterfeit light.

C. He et al., [11] Under-water pictures will be misshaped because of the impact of disturbance, and pictures will seem mathematical mutilation since the light is refracted by the choppiness, which makes undertaking of picture acknowledgment troublesome. P. Liu et al., [12] presents the misfortune capacity and preparing mode are improved. A multi-term misfortune task is shaped with mean squared blunder misfortune and a proposed edge contrast misfortune. A nonconcurrent preparing mode is additionally proposed to task on the presentation of the multi-term misfortune work. At last, the effect of clump standardization is talked about. As per the under-water picture enhancement tests and a similar examination, the shading rectification and detail enhancement execution of the proposed strategies are better than that of past DL models and customary techniques.

P. Liu et al., [13] Distinctive scaling boundaries are allocated to these alternate routes to separate and associate broadened and muddled components adaptively. Because of the extraordinary plan of MACB, the proposed calculation can upgrade the blend of different levels includes and give various scopes of picture setting for super-goal remaking. These misfortunes push our recreated picture to the objective picture. P. Liu et al., [14] The proposed model has better solidness to finish the remaking of super-goal pictures for × 4 scale factor. The worked on lingering organization and perceptual misfortune task are applied in the proposed calculation which exhibits a better presentation over best in class reconstruction quality.

J. Deng et al., [15] In thistask, polynomial insertion which is a MLtechnique was used to reestablish the multi-shaft sonar picture. Shading data is one of the most significant for multi-pillar sonar picture, particularly for the portrayal of submarine geology, accordingly in this task, a procedure for shading picture reconstruction was used. The trial result shows that the proposed technique can recuperate the most pieces of multi-shaft picture. E. Tusa et al., [16] The point of this review is the advancement of a dream framework for coral identifications dependent on managed machine learning. To accomplish this, we utilize a bank of Gabor Wavelet channels to extricate surface component descriptors, we use learning classifiers, from OpenCV library, to separate coral from non-coral reef. We think about: running time, exactness, explicitness and affectability of nine distinctive learning classifiers. We select Choice Trees calculation since it shows the quickest and the most reliable exhibition [17]. In the mean time, the proposed remaking network has a quicker preparing and intermingling speed contrasted and other super-goal strategies. The proposed approach is assessed on standard datasets and gets further developed execution than past works that dependent on deep convolutional neural organizations [18]. Other than the heap of MACB, the skip associations with personality planning are utilized to additional total the elements of two explicit layers in the proposed network. Besides, to surmise photograph sensible regular pictures, a perceptual misfortune task is proposed to regulate the remaking, which comprises of four pieces of misfortune: include misfortune, style misfortune, complete variety misfortune, and pixel misfortune [19]. S. Wu et al. develop picture acknowledgment under-water, this task proposes an picture reconstruction strategy utilizing under-water twisted picture arrangement through DL method. Considering the intricacy of elements movement, picture grouping is more possible to acknowledge undertaking of restoration, which contains sufficient data of water choppiness [20].

3 Challenges

Under-water picture reconstruction is a difficult issue because of the numerous distortions. Degradation in the data is mostly because of the followings-

- light scattering effect

  Light dispersing and shading change are two significant wellsprings of bending for under-water photography. Light dissipating is brought about by light occurrence on objects reflected and avoided on different occasions by particles present in the water prior to arriving at the camera (Fig. 3).

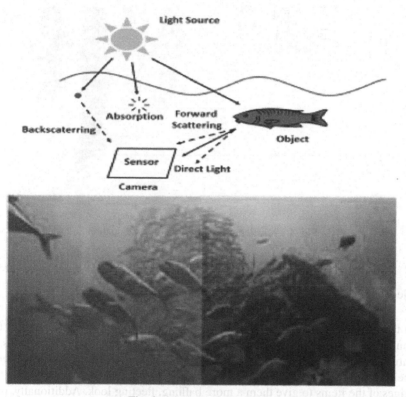

Fig. 3. Light scattering effect

- wavelength dependent color attenuation

  Under-water pictures experience the ill effects of shading mutilation and low differentiation, since light is weakened while it proliferates through water. Lessening under water differs with frequency, dissimilar to earthbound pictures where weakening is thought to be frightfully uniform. The weakening depends both on the water body and the 3D construction of the scene, making shading reconstruction troublesome. Dissimilar to existing single under-water picture enhancement procedures, our strategy considers numerous otherworldly profiles of various water types. By assessing only two extra worldwide boundaries: the lessening proportions of the blue-red and blue-green shading channels, the issue is diminished to single picture dehazing, where all shading channels have similar constriction coefficients. Since the water type is obscure, we assess various boundaries out of a current library of water types. Each type prompts an alternate reestablished picture and the best outcome is consequently picked dependent on shading dissemination (Fig. 4).

Fig. 4. Wavelength dependent color attenuation

- object blurriness effect

Since the light is assimilated and dissipated, under-water pictures have numerous twists like underexposure, fogginess, and shading cast. An obscured foundation carries more accentuation to the primary subject of your photograph. Lettering looks particularly compelling against obscure foundation. Obscure impact can assist you with relaxing the edges of the items to give them a more baffling, fleeting look. Additionally, picture obscuring can make a feeling of speed and elements (Fig. 5).

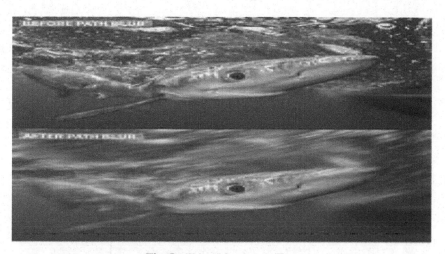

Fig. 5. Object blurriness effect

Mark Removal

A trait of these huge informational collections is an enormous number of factors that require a great deal of figuring assets to process. Mark removal is a course of dimensionality decrease by which an underlying arrangement of crude information is diminished to more sensible gatherings for handling.

Evaluation

Three principle measurements used to assess an arrangement model are exactness, accuracy, and review. Precision is characterized as the level of right expectations for the test information. It tends to be determined effectively by partitioning the quantity of right expectations by the quantity of all out forecasts. DL is a subset of ML where fake neural nets, calculations roused by the human mind, gain from a lot of information. DL permits machines to take care of mind boggling issues in any event, when utilizing an informational index that is extremely different, unstructured and between associated.

4 Methodology

The dark medium Earlier and Convolution Neural Organization Calculation will be utilized to quantify transmission and apply the dehazing system to make an enhanced under-water picture. Here under-water picture recuperation calculation utilizing dim medium earlier with DL is proposed (Fig. 6).

(i) Hazy Picture: In under-water photography, shading change and haze are two well-springs of bending. This rot is brought about by the straightforward dissemination and impression of light by light streaming in water with various frequencies. So the photos are dark and have a blue tone.

(ii) Color Correction: The motivation behind the shading amendment technique is to gauge shading channels and to make tone, brilliance and splendor of under-water

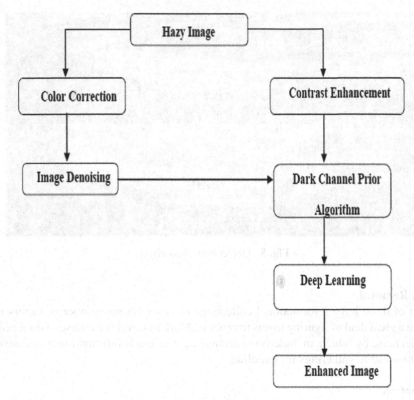

Fig. 6. Strategy

pictures. To begin with, shading remuneration for each shading medium is make up for to diminish the energy brought about by the focal sensory system.

(iii) Picture Denoising: Under-water photography systems and advancement procedures that further develop the under-water personality improvement measure. The proposed strategy won't just eliminate the clamor and task on the BSNR, yet will likewise improve seeing impact.

(iv) Dark medium Prior: Dark medium Earlier used to eliminate mass dehazed from under-water film. As indicated by significant perceptions - the greater part of the neighborhood spots in under-water pictures have tiny pixels in something like one shading channel.

(v) Contrast Enhancement: Under-water pictures might vary altogether from rectification because of the assimilation and appropriation of light in the under-water climate. Along these lines, relative enhancements are made in the RGB space. By utilizing this technique, the impacts of scattering and retention are decreased.

(vi) Convolution Neural Network: In deep learning, the Regular Neural Organization (CNN, or Connet) is a kind of deep neural organization. CNNs are normal kinds of multi-facet perceptrons. Multi-facet perceptrons generally allude to completely associated networks, that is, every neuron in a solitary layer is associated with every one of the neurons in the following layer. The "full association" of these organizations is not exactly loaded with information.

5 Result

Expected outcomes of our proposed methodology can be:

1. It will be able to generate haze free images by compute the complexity of haze.
2. It will be able to report the problem of imperfect visibility.
3. It will be able to articulate a hybrid method to enhancement and restoration.
4. It will be able to expand the quality of an image to compact with low contrast.
5. It will be able to equate the usefulness of suggested algorithm with conventional methods.

6 Conclusion

The under-water vision attributes, some new picture handling methods are proposed to manage the low difference and the weakly illuminated problems. A deep learning method is proposed to picture reconstruction and enhancement. The under-water vision is in low quality, and the objects are always overlapped and shaded. The proposed strategy is suitable for under-water picture reconstruction and enhancement. In future we develop python or MATLAB based model to under-water picture reconstruction and enhancement with the picture performance improvement. The future works is based on the implementation of machine and deep learning algorithm for image restoration and optimize the results. The implementation technique will be carried out either MATLAB 9.4 form or Python Spyder IDE 3.7 variant. There will be upgrade in exactness and other huge boundaries utilizing proposed approach.

References

1. Lu, J., Yuan, F., Yang, W., Cheng, E.: An imaging information estimation network for underwater picture color restoration. IEEE J. Ocean. Eng.
2. Wang, H., Chen, X., Xu, B., Du, S., Li, Y.: An improved MSCNN method for under-water picture defogging. In: 2021 IEEE International Conference on Artificial Intelligence and Industrial Design , pp. 296–302 (2021)
3. Lu, Y., M. Yang, Y., Liu, R.W.: DSPNet: deep learning-enabled blind reduction of speckle noise. In: 2020 25th International Conference on Pattern Recognition (ICPR), pp. 3475–3482 (2021)
4. Lin, Y., Shen, L., Wang, Z., Wang, K., Zhang, X.: Attenuation coefficient guided two-stage network for under-water picture restoration. IEEE Signal Process. Lett. **28**, 199–203 (2021)
5. Wang, Z., Xue, X., Ma, L., Fan, X.: Under-water picture enhancement based on dual U-net. In: 2020 8th International Conference on Digital Home (ICDH), pp. 141–146 (2020)
6. Silva Vaz, E., de Toledo, E.F., Drews, P.L.J.: Under-water depth estimation based on water classification using monocular picture. In: 2020 Latin American Robotics Symposium (LARS), 2020 Brazilian Symposium on Robotics (SBR), pp. 1–6 (2020)

7. Dudhane, A., Hambarde, P., Patil, P., Murala, S.: Deep under-water picture restoration and beyond. IEEE Signal Process. **27**, 675–679 (2020)
8. Li, C., et al.: An under-water picture enhancement benchmark dataset and beyond. IEEE Trans. Picture Process. **29**, 4376–4389 (2020)
9. Han, M., Lyu, Z., Qiu, T., Xu, M.: A review on intelligence Dehazing and color restoration for under-water pictures. IEEE Trans. Syst. Man Cybern. Syst. **50**(5), 1820–1832 (2020)
10. Yang, S., Chen, Z., Feng, Z., Ma, X.: Under-water picture enhancement using scene depth-based adaptive background light estimation and dark medium prior algorithms. IEEE Access **7**, 165318–165327 (2019)
11. He, C., Zhang, Z: Restoration of under-water distorted picture sequence based on generative adversarial network. In: 2019 IEEE 8th Joint International Information Technology and Artificial Intelligence Conference (ITAIC), pp. 866–870 (2019)
12. Liu, P., Wang, G., Qi, H., Zhang, C., Zheng, H., Yu, Z.: Under-water picture enhancement with a deep residual framework. IEEE Access **7**, 94614–94629 (2019)
13. Liu, P., Hong, Y., Liu, Y.: A novel multi-scale adaptive convolutional network for single picture super-resolution. IEEE Access **7**, 45191–45200 (2019)
14. Liu, P., Hong, Y., Liu, Y.: Dual discriminator generative adversarial network for single picture super-resolution. In: 2018 IEEE 9th International Conference on Software Engineering and Service Science (ICSESS), pp. 1–8 (2018)
15. Deng, J., Ma, Z: Multi-beam sonar picture restoration using polynomian. OCEANS 2017 - Aberdeen, pp. 1–4 (2017)
16. Tusa, E., Reynolds, A., Lane, D.M., Robertson, N.M., Villegas, H., Bosnjak, A.: Implementation of a fast coral detector using a supervised machine learning and Gabor Wavelet feature descriptors. IEEE Systems for a Changing Ocean (SSCO) **2014**, 1–6 (2014)
17. Yang, X., Li, H., Fan, Y.-L., Chen, R.: Single image haze removal via region detection net. IEEE Trans. Multimedia **21**(10), 2545–2560 (2019). https://doi.org/10.1109/TMM.2019.290 8375
18. Barbosa, W.V., Amaral, H.G.B., Rocha, T.L., Nascimento, E.R.: Visual-quality-driven learning for underwater vision enhancement. In: 2018 25th IEEE International Conference on Image Processing (ICIP), pp. 3933–3937 (2018). https://doi.org/10.1109/ICIP.2018.8451356
19. Protas, E., Bratti, J., Gaya, J., Drews, P., Botelho, S.: Understading image reconstruction convolutional neural nets with net inversion. In: 2017 16th IEEE International Conference on ML and Applications (ICMLA), pp. 215–220 (2017). https://doi.org/10.1109/ICMLA.2017. 0-156
20. Shengcong, W., et al.: A two-stage underwater enhancement network based on structure decomposition and characteristics of underwater imaging. IEEE J. Ocean. Eng. **46**(4), 1213–1227 (2021). https://doi.org/10.1109/JOE.2021.3064093

Using Machine Learning for Inter-smell Detection: A Feasibility Study

Ruchin Gupta[1,2]([✉]) and Sandeep Kumar Singh[1,2]

[1] Jaypee Institute of Information Technology, Noida, India
skg11in@yahoo.co.in
[2] KIET Group of Institutions, Delhi-NCR, Ghaziabad, India

Abstract. Code smells may degrade code quality owing to the unnoticed introduction of side effects. Various approaches for identifying code smells have been developed since the term "code smell" was coined. Furthermore, the available literature suggests that code smells may be connected, and there is theory concerning smell interactions such as collocated, coupled smells, inter smell and so on. Machine learning has proven to be one of the most effective ways for detecting code smell. However, the capability of machine learning to detect such code smell relations has yet to be demonstrated. This paper proposes a new novel classification of smell interactions and investigates the feasibility of machine learning techniques to detect four inter-smells by employing seven widely used machine learning algorithms on four publicly available datasets and employing commonly used performance measures such as recall, accuracy, precision, and Matthews coefficient (MCC). A low MCC value (0.5) for all four inter-smells indicates a poor inter-smell relationship and contradicts the facts provided in the literature. As a result, machine learning may not be a viable option for inter-smell detection.

Keywords: Code smell · Inter-smell · Machine learning · Smell relation · Matthews coefficient (MCC)

1 Introduction

The term "code smell" pertains to a variety of unintended consequences in the code that may indicate more serious issues. The source code is disintegrated by code smell. Refactoring the code is a viable solution in this situation. Refactoring is a technique for enhancing the structure of code while maintaining its functionality [1]. Since than there have been various attempts to categorize them into different groups. Initially Martin Fowler gave a list which contained 22 code smells [1] as given in Table 1. Bloaters, Object Orientation Abusers, Change Preventers, The Dispensables, Couplers, Encapsulators, and Others have been added to the list of classifications [2]. Later Rasool et al. [3] came up with another classification, with an objective to improve the understanding of smells, by putting 22 code smells in to five unique groups.

Existing literature [4–10] showcases that a good amount of work has been done to detect several code smells using a variety of techniques. Smell detection has been

A. Kumar et al. (Eds.): ICAIDS 2021, CCIS 1673, pp. 291–305, 2022.
https://doi.org/10.1007/978-3-031-21385-4_25

mostly focused on individual smells rather than interactions of smells, according to the literature. The literature survey on smell interactions shows that there does not exist a proper method to detect smell interaction and a little knowledge is available about possible scenarios of smell interactions. Also, literature study shows that code smells do not appear in the code alone [1, 11] and come up with other code smells [12–16]. Palomba [17] investigated co-occurrences of 13 different code smells and found 6 pairs of code smells that regularly co-occurred. When two or more code smells have a relationship or dependencies, inter smell relations occur [18].

Inter-smell relations were first presented by Pietrzak and Walter [19] to help more precise recognition of code smells. The plain-support inter-smell example relation that they offer is as follows: "...*smell B is supported by smell A if the existence of A implies the existence of B with sufficient certainty. As a result, B is a companion smell of A, and program entities (classes, methods, expressions, and so on) that are burdened with A are likewise burdened with B*". Arcelli Fontana [20] have studied relationships among 14 different types of code smells using PCA (principal component analysis) and correlation and detected many new code smell relations.

Table 1. Martin Fowler's list of 22 code smells [1]

1. Alternative Classes with Different Interfaces	12. Long method
	13. Long Parameter List
	14. Message Chains
2. Comments	15. Middle Man
3. Data Class	16. Parallel Inheritance Hierarchies
4. Data Clumps	
5. Divergent Change	17. Primitive Obsession
6. Duplicated Code	18. Refused Bequest
7. Feature Envy	19. Shotgun Surgery
8. Inappropriate Intimacy	20. Speculative Generality
	21. Switch Statements
9. Incomplete Library Class	22. Temporary Field
10. Large Class	
11. Lazy Class	

To broaden and to better utilize the concept of inter-smell relations to detect or to help in the detection of other code smells using the knowledge of known code smells, to the best of our knowledge, we are the first to formally define a new term *Inter smell detection* and a classification scheme for smell interactions. Inter smell detection means to detect another code smell using a different or same code smell. For example, using long method code smells in java projects to detect long method code smells in C++ projects. Despite this, there appears to be no publication in the literature describing inter smell detection using machine learning techniques [9]. We are the first to use machine learning to investigate inter-smell detection, to the best of our understanding. According to the research articles [8, 9, 21–24], machine learning has been a very successful approach for detecting code smells, thus we choose to examine it for inter smell detection.

The structure of the paper is outlined below. The related work in the context of smell interaction is discussed in Sect. 2. The concept of inter-smell interactions, as well as a novel classification system for smell interactions, are introduced in Sect. 3. The detection methods and experiment used in the study are described in Sect. 4. The outcomes of the experiments are discussed in Sect. 5. The conclusion and future scope are presented in Sect. 6.

2 Related Work

This section discusses relevant research on smell interactions. However, we were able to locate only a few studies that discussed smell interaction in terms of smell relation and smell co-occurrences. Table 2 shows the relevant work, including the types of smell interactions mentioned in the research report, the smell relations discovered, the projects done, and the accompanying reference.

Pietrzak and Walter [19] defined several type of relations such as Mutual support, Plain support, Aggregate support, Rejection, Inclusion, Transitive support to determine different relations among code smells. They investigated 830 classes of Apache Tomcat 5.5.4 project and found six unique code smell relations as shown in Table 2. Yamashita et al. [25] analyzed 1 industrial and 2 open source systems and detected 15 code smells. They discovered inter smell linkages for coupled and collocated odors using PCA with orthogonal rotation. They discovered that coupled and collocated smells minimize false negatives. As significant smell relations, they got God Class and Feature Envy, Data Class and Feature Envy.

Another study conducted by Yamashita [26] discovered that contextual elements like domain and surroundings can have a significant impact on the presence, co-presence, and coupling of smells, implying that such variables should be taken into account while doing smell analysis. To detect 15 code smells, they employed one industrial system and two open-source software. They discovered 15 different inter-smell patterns using Principal Component Analysis (PCA). Palomba et al. [14] used association rule mining at the class level to evaluate co-occurrences of 13 different code smells over 395 releases of 30 software projects and determined the strength of the association rule using support and confidence metrics. They detected six pairings of code smells that co-occurred based on metrics.

Lozano et al. [16] used a number of releases of 3 open source projects: Log4j, Jmol, JFreechart and analyzed smell relations using 6 different metrics and relating them with relations given by Pietrzak and Walter [19]. This study discovered a correlation between three bad smells: Feature Envy, Long Method, and God Class. The strongest association was between Feature Envy and Long Method, followed by a weak link between Long Method and God Class and a weak link between Feature Envy and God Class. Palomba et al. [17] used 395 releases from 30 software projects to conduct a large-scale investigation on the co-occurrences of code smells. They looked at over 13 code smells and discovered that 59% of classes were influenced by more than one code smell, with six pairs of code smells appearing frequently.

Table 2. List of smell relations

SI. No	Smell interaction	Smell relations	Projects	Reference
1	Inter smell relation	Data Class and Feature Envy, Large Class for Feature Envy, Inappropriate Intimacy and Data Class, Inappropriate Intimacy and Data Class and feature envy	Apache Tomcat 5.5.4	[19]
2	Inter smell relation	God Class and Feature Envy, Data Class and Feature Envy	Ebehandling, ElasticSearch (Version 1.2.1), Apache Mahout (Version 0.7)	[25]
3	Inter smell relation	15 inter smell patterns	Ebehandling, ElasticSearch, Apache Mahout	[26]
4	Code Smell Co-occurrences	Complex Class and Message Chains, Long Method and Long Parameter List, Long Method And Feature Envy, Spaghetti Code and Long Method, Inappropriate Intimacy and Feature Envy, Refused Bequest and Message Chains	30 open-source systems	[14]
5	Relation between smells	Feature Envy and Long Method, Long Method and God Class, and between Feature Envy and God Class	Log4j, Jmol, JFreechart	[16]
6	Code Smell Co-occurrences	6 code smell pairs	395 releases of 30 open-source systems	[17]

3   Proposed Classification for Smell Interactions

Collocated smells, inter-smells, and coupled smells are all terms used in the literature to describe smell interactions or smell relations. Collocated smells occur when two or more smells are present in the same artifact. If two smells exist in artifacts (classes) that are coupled, they are said to be coupled. When the operation of one artifact (class) necessitates the presence of another artifact, two artifacts (classes) are connected. Inter-smell relationships (sometimes called inter smells) can exist within a project as well as between two or more projects (we refer here as cross projects).

Nonetheless, regardless of whether a part of code shows a code smell or not relies upon the developer [27]. A code smell may be domain [28–32] and context [10] dependent. A domain can be a language or a specific application or a context. A developer's perspective, a software quality issue, and a design concern could be the context. If the language domain is Java, code smells in Java code represent a domain. It's because each language has its own set of characteristics. As a result, we've developed a new classification scheme for smell interactions, as shown in Fig. 1.

Projects can be classified as belonging to the same or different domains. Smell interactions can occur within a project, across projects, or across a set of projects. Smell interactions discovered in an artifact are referred to as collocated smells. Coupled smells are smell interactions between different artifacts in a project.

When projects come from various domains, there are two options. Smell interaction between projects for the same code smell (or different code smells) is feasible. For instance, suppose there are two projects: one in Java and the other in C#. If long method smells in Java projects are known, this information could be utilized to anticipate long method smells in C# projects in some way. It's possible because a code smell frequently depicts symptoms. Also smell interaction between projects for different code smells is feasible since code smells may be related and the literature already has shown relations between some code smells. For example, let us assume that long method code smell is known in Java projects then this knowledge can be utilized to find some other related code smell (such as feature envy) in C# projects.

Smell interactions in projects belonging to the same domain have been studied according to the literature [12–16]. Several code smells may appear in one artifact of a project. Also, code smells may be found between different projects. For instance, suppose that long method code smell is known in some Java project then this knowledge may be utilized to find long method code smells in some other different Java project since long method code smell exist due to some symptoms (such as size and cohesion) in the code [33]. Also, artifacts in projects may be coupled, so in such case one code smell present in one artifact may induce some other code smell(s) in other artifact(s). The other case is having a set of projects. For example, let us assume that there are several Java projects available with the knowledge of some code smells present in these projects, then this knowledge may be utilized to detect those same code smells in some other set of Java projects as done by paper [24].

In this article, we looked the smell interactions (inter-smells) among a collection of different types of projects that all belong to the same domain which falls in the category of within a group of different projects under same domain in the proposed classification shown in Fig. 1.

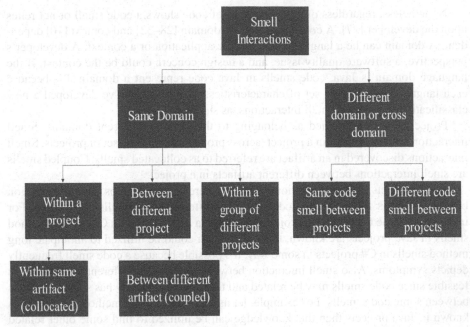

Fig. 1. Proposed classification for smell interactions (inter smell)

4   Experimentation Methodology

The methodology employed in the experiment, as well as the datasets used in the study, are discussed in this section.

4.1 Methodology

Machine learning approaches demand training and testing data for a specific problem. In machine learning, the training and testing data are usually from the same source and contain the same set of features. A dataset is divided into training and testing datasets when using machine learning to detect code smells, and a machine learning model is trained on the training dataset before being tested on the testing dataset.

Accuracy, precision, recall, and the F-measure are common performance measures used to evaluate machine learning models. As a result, the same code smell is associated with both the training and testing datasets.

In our investigated machine learning model for inter-smell detection, we use two datasets for two different code smells, as shown in Fig. 2. A machine learning model is trained on one dataset, then the trained machine learning model is tested on a different dataset. As a result, it is possible to anticipate code smell on a different dataset. The performance of the machine learning model is then assessed. As a result, inter-smell identification based on machine learning necessitates two datasets rather than the usual one.

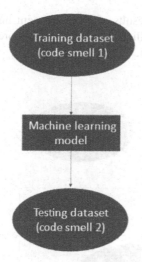

Fig. 2. Machine learning for inter-smell detection

We've provided an appropriate methodology depicted in Fig. 3. The methodology depicted in Fig. 3 has five basic steps. Dataset preparation is a vital element in the methodology that has not been significantly addressed previously. The steps of the adopted methodology are outlined below.

Step 1: Obtaining publicly available datasets or creating a dataset for experimentation is the initial step.

Step 2: In Step 2, the dataset is cleaned and examined. The dataset is first examined to ensure that it contains valid data and that no values are missing or duplicated. The dataset is then cleaned by looking for missing values.

Step 3: Preparation for the experiment is the third step. The experimentation setup includes downloading and installing relevant software, discovering, and selecting appropriate libraries and library functions, and determining how to use (along with their values) standard machine learning parameters.

Step 4: We experiment with a range of traditional machine learning algorithms in this step.

The seven popular and commonly used [8] machine learning models (Random forest, Decision tree, Logistic regression, Naïve bayes, Multilayer perceptron, Support vector machine, K-neighbour classifier) were applied on 4 datasets to detect 4 different inter code smells: long method to feature envy, data class to god class, god class to data class and feature envy to long method. Long method to feature envy means that a machine learning model is trained on the long method dataset first, and then used to predict labels for the feature envy dataset using the trained machine learning model. As a result, the long method dataset serves as a training dataset, while the feature envy dataset serves as a testing dataset. Other inter smells may be recognized in the same way. On a standalone personal computer system, all seven machine learning algorithms were implemented in python [34] using Keras [35].

Step 5: Step 5 combines the results of all experiment instances in terms of precision, recall, accuracy, Matthews coefficient (MCC), and F-score, and produces a summary for further analysis and conclusion.

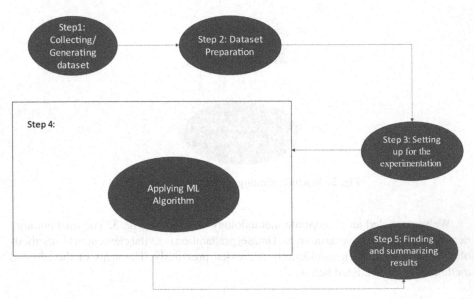

Fig. 3. Experimental methodology

4.2 Datasets Used in the Study

We used four datasets from Arcelli Fontana et al. [24] to test four different code smells: long method, feature envy, data class, and god class. To create the datasets, the authors [24] chose 74 different Java open source systems. The datasets were downloaded and processed to learn more about the various features utilized in them, as well as other statistical parameters including feature maximum and minimum values, number of samples in the datasets, and duplicate and missing values. The lengthy method and feature envy datasets had the same and exact number of features, while the god class and data class datasets had the same and exact number of features, according to the analysis. Each dataset had one-third stinky samples and two-thirds non-smelly samples, according to data analysis (Table 3). Due to a suitable mix of smelly and non-smelly objects, these datasets were well balanced. Because a balanced dataset increases the performance of a machine learning algorithm, Arcelli Fontana may have utilized one.

According to our observations, each downloaded dataset contained multiple missing values. Table 4 shows the number of missing values, % of missing values, and the name of the feature with the matching number of missing values for each downloaded dataset. Around 0.002% of the values in each dataset were missing. The mean value approach was chosen to compute missing data because it is a basic and commonly used method of imputation in the literature. Appendix A details the list of features used in the datasets. Appendix B shows the rules used to detect the code smells.

Table 3. Description of the dataset

Code smell dataset	No of features	No of +ve samples (smelly)	No of –ve samples (non-smelly)	No of samples
God class	62	140	280	420
Data class				
Long method	83			
Feature envy				

Table 4. Missing values in datasets

Sl No.	Code smell dataset	No. of missing values	% of missing values	Name of feature with number of missing values
1	Data class	75	0.0028%	NMO_type -19, NIM_type -19, NOC_type -9, WOC_type -28
2	God class	76	0.0029%	NMO_type -20, NIM_type -20, NOC_type -8, WOC_type -28
3	Long method	92	0.0026%	NOC_type-3, WOC_type-31 NIM_type-29, NMO_type-29
4	Feature envy	92	0.0026%	NOC_type-3, WOC_type-31 NIM_type-29, NMO_type-29

5   Results and Discussion

Table 5 shows the results of the experiment. The stacked bar for the results in Table 5 is shown in Fig. 4 because it makes it easier to compare all the values at once. The F-measure, precision, accuracy, recall and Matthews correlation coefficient have all been used to calculate the performance of machine learning methods. In a recent study, for binary classifications, Matthews correlation coefficient (MCC) has been preferred over accuracy and F-measure [36] since MCC is a one-of-a-kind binary classification rate that is high when a predictor accurately predicts correctly most of the positive and negative samples simultaneously [37, 38]. MCC has a minimum value −1 and maximum value + 1. When perfect classification occurs, the MCC value is 1; when perfect misclassification occurs, the MCC value is −1. As a result, we only use the MCC performance measure to draw conclusions. The values in red in Table 1 represent precision and recall values of zero. When a value isn't defined, the symbol #### is used. The symbol has also showed F-measure in blue color when it is not defined. The F-measure is undefined when both precision and recall are zero.

The MCC value for feature envy to long method spans from 0 to 0.46, while the MCC value for feature envy to long method ranges from 0.28 to 0.48. MCC values for God class to data class vary from −0.28 to −0.46 and MCC values for data class to God class range from −0.28 to −0.47. Because MCC uses a contingency matrix to calculate the Pearson correlation coefficient. As a result, it has the same meaning as the Pearson correlation coefficient [39]. The Pearson correlation coefficient (r) is a number that ranges from −1 to 1. A significant correlation is defined as a r > 0.7 value.

The MCC score for all four inter smells is significantly lower than 0.70, indicating a bad smell interaction between long method and feature envy, God class and data class, and vice versa. This is a direct contradiction to the facts found in the literature. The inter connectedness between feature envy and long method was before discovered by [14, 16, 20]. Fontana et al. [12] prior have additionally demonstrated a used relation between god class and data class.

Table 5. Machine learning results for inter-smells

Sl No.	Machine Algorithm/ Code smell	Long method to Feature Envy					God Class to Data Class					Feature Envy to Long method					Data Class to God Class				
		Accuracy	Precision	Recall	Matthew coeff	F-measure	Accuracy	Precision	Recall	Matthew coeff	F-measure	Accuracy	Precision	Recall	Matthew coeff	F-measure	Accuracy	Precision	Recall	Matthew coeff	F-measure
1	Random Forest	0.76	0.55	0.70	0.45	0.62	0.40	0.00	0.00	-0.42	####	0.76	0.60	0.65	0.46	0.62	0.39	0.00	0.00	-0.44	####
2	Decision Tree (C4.5)	0.76	0.55	0.69	0.45	0.61	0.42	0.00	0.00	-0.40	####	0.76	0.60	0.65	0.46	0.62	0.39	0.00	0.00	-0.44	####
3	Logistic Regression	0.74	0.51	0.78	0.46	0.62	0.37	0.00	0.00	-0.46	####	0.73	0.55	0.61	0.38	0.58	0.33	0.00	0.00	-0.50	####
4	Naïve Bayes	0.77	0.57	0.70	0.47	0.63	0.42	0.00	0.00	-0.41	####	0.85	0.88	0.61	0.65	0.72	0.06	0.02	0.04	-0.87	0.03
5	Multilayer Perceptron	0.73	0.00	0.00	0.00	####	0.38	0.03	0.04	-0.42	0.03	0.70	0.52	0.46	0.28	0.49	0.55	0.00	0.00	-0.28	####
6	K nearset neighbour	0.69	0.42	0.35	0.18	0.38	0.48	0.01	0.07	-0.28	0.02	0.76	0.60	0.65	0.46	0.62	0.45	0.08	0.74	-0.31	0.14
7	Support Vector Machine	0.75	0.54	0.65	0.41	0.59	0.40	0.00	0.00	-0.42	####	0.77	0.63	0.65	0.48	0.64	0.36	0.00	0.00	-0.47	####
8	Average	0.74	0.45	0.55	0.35	####	0.41	0.01	0.02	-0.40	####	0.76	0.63	0.61	0.45	0.61	0.36	0.01	0.11	-0.47	####

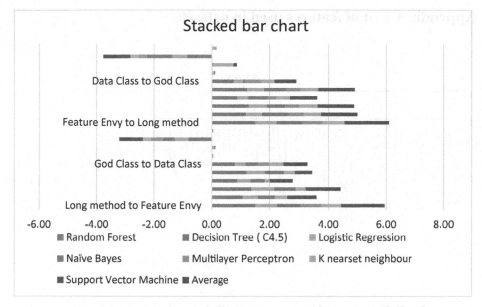

Fig. 4. Stacked bar for Machine learning results for inter-smell detection

6 Conclusion and Future Scope

We have proposed a new classification scheme for smell interactions and assess the utility of seven common machine learning algorithms in detecting four different inter-smell interactions in this study. Experiments were carried on 4 public datasets under the category of same domain and its subcategory within a group of different projects (one of the categories of the proposed classification scheme) to detect 4 inter smells using seven machine learning algorithms. The experimental results revealed a low MCC (<0.5) in the majority of machine learning algorithms, indicating insufficient smell interactions contradicting the facts in the literature. As a result, machine learning methods may not be suitable for detecting inter-smells. However, a more thorough investigation of additional datasets and code smells may be required to firmly establish the reality. Deep learning could be used to test its suitability for detecting inter-smells in the future due to its capability to discover patterns autonomously. Another option could be to modify or tune the parameters of machine learning models, as well as to analyze the results. In future, further we intend to investigate other categories of the proposed classification scheme also.

Appendix A List of features used in datasets

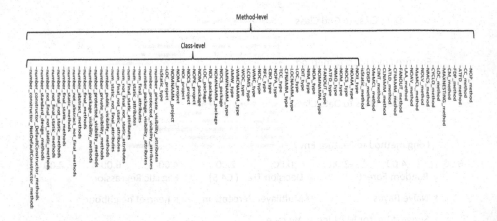

Appendix B Rules used for code smell detection

Code smell	Rules / Guidelines
God class	• They have large and complex methods.
	• They are large.
	• They expose several methods.
	• They usually have access to many attributes from large no of classes.
Data class	• They should not have complex methods.
	• They can expose small number of non-accessor simple methods,
	• Their attributes must be either public or exposed through accessor methods.
Long method	• They are complex.
	• They usually access many attributes, a large no. of class members, Large no of used variables including ancestor's attributes.
	• They are large.
	• They contain many parameters.
Feature envy	• They have access to many foreign attributes than local ones.
	• They primarily use the attributes of few foreign classes.

References

1. Fowler, M.: Refactoring: improving the design of existing code. In: Wells, D., Williams, L. (eds.) XP/Agile Universe 2002. LNCS, vol. 2418, pp. 256–256. Springer, Heidelberg (2002). https://doi.org/10.1007/3-540-45672-4_31

2. Mäntylä, M., Vanhanen, J., Lassenius, C.: A taxonomy and an initial empirical study of bad smells in Code. IEEE Int. Conf. Softw. Maintenance, ICSM 381–384 (2003). https://doi.org/10.1109/icsm.2003.1235447

3. Rasool, G., Arshad, Z.: A lightweight approach for detection of code smells. Arab. J. Sci. Eng. **42**(2), 483–506 (2016). https://doi.org/10.1007/s13369-016-2238-8

4. AlShaaby, A., Aljamaan, H., Alshayeb, M.: Bad smell detection using machine learning techniques: a systematic literature review. Arab. J. Sci. Eng. **45**(4), 2341–2369 (2020). https://doi.org/10.1007/s13369-019-04311-w

5. AbuHassan, A., Alshayeb, M., Ghouti, L.: Software smell detection techniques: A systematic literature review. J. Softw. Evol. Process. 1–48 (2020). https://doi.org/10.1002/smr.2320

6. Alkharabsheh, K., Crespo, Y., Manso, E., Taboada, J.A.: Software Design Smell Detection: a systematic mapping study. Software Qual. J. **27**(3), 1069–1148 (2018). https://doi.org/10.1007/s11219-018-9424-8

7. Zaidi, M.A., ColomoPalacios, R.: Code smells enabled by artificial intelligence: a systematic mapping. In: Misra, S., et al. (eds.) ICCSA 2019. LNCS, vol. 11622, pp. 418–427. Springer, Cham (2019). https://doi.org/10.1007/978-3-030-24305-0_31

8. Azeem, M.I., Palomba, F., Shi, L., Wang, Q.: Machine learning techniques for code smell detection: a systematic literature review and meta-analysis. Inf. Softw. Technol. **108**, 115–138 (2019). https://doi.org/10.1016/j.infsof.2018.12.009

9. Caram, F.L., Rodrigues, B.R.D.O., Campanelli, A.S., Parreiras, F.S.: Machine learning techniques for code smells detection: a systematic mapping study. Int. J. Softw. Eng. Knowl. Eng. **29**, 285–316 (2019). https://doi.org/10.1142/S021819401950013X

10. Sharma, T., Spinellis, D.: A survey on software smells. J. Syst. Softw. **138**, 158–173 (2018). https://doi.org/10.1016/j.jss.2017.12.034

11. Wettel, R., Lanza, M.: Visually localizing design problems with disharmony maps. SOFTVIS 2008 - Proc. 4th ACM Symp. Softw. Vis. 155–164 (2008). https://doi.org/10.1145/1409720.1409745

12. Fontana, F.A., Ferme, V., Zanoni, M.: Towards assessing software architecture quality by exploiting code smell relations. Proc. - 2nd Int. Work. Softw. Archit. Metrics, SAM 2015. 1–7 (2015). https://doi.org/10.1109/SAM.2015.8

13. Abbes, M., Khomh, F., Guéhéneuc, Y.G., Antoniol, G.: An empirical study of the impact of two antipatterns, Blob and Spaghetti Code, on program comprehension. Proc. Eur. Conf. Softw. Maint. Reengineering, CSMR. 181–190 (2011). https://doi.org/10.1109/CSMR.2011.24

14. Palomba, F., Oliveto, R., De Lucia, A.: Investigating code smell co-occurrences using association rule learning: A replicated study. MaLTeSQuE 2017 - IEEE Int. Work. Mach. Learn. Tech. Softw. Qual. Eval. co-located with SANER 2017 8–13 (2017). https://doi.org/10.1109/MALTESQUE.2017.7882010

15. Ma, W., Chen, L., Zhou, Y., Xu, B., Zhou, X.: Are anti-patterns coupled? An empirical study. Proc. - 2015 IEEE Int. Conf. Softw. Qual. Reliab. Secur. QRS 2015 242–251 (2015). https://doi.org/10.1109/QRS.2015.43

16. Lozano, A., Mens, K., Portugal, J.: Analyzing code evolution to uncover relations between bad smells. 2015 IEEE 2nd Int. Work. Patterns Promot. Anti-Patterns Prev. PPAP 2015 - Proc. 1–4 (2015). https://doi.org/10.1109/PPAP.2015.7076847

17. Palomba, F., Bavota, G., Di Penta, M., Fasano, F., Oliveto, R., De Lucia, A.: A large-scale empirical study on the lifecycle of code smell co-occurrences. Inf. Softw. Technol. **99**, 1 (2018). https://doi.org/10.1016/j.infsof.2018.02.004

18. Martins, J., Bezerra, C.I.M., Uchôa, A.: Analyzing the impact of inter-smell relations on software maintainability. PervasiveHealth Pervasive Comput. Technol. Healthc. (2019). https://doi.org/10.1145/3330204.3330254

19. Pietrzak, B., Walter, B.: Leveraging code smell detection with inter-smell relations. In: Abrahamsson, P., Marchesi, M., Succi, G. (eds.) XP 2006. LNCS, vol. 4044, pp. 75–84. Springer, Heidelberg (2006). https://doi.org/10.1007/11774129_8

20. Walter, B., Fontana, F.A., Ferme, V.: Code smells and their collocations: A large-scale experiment on open-source systems. J. Syst. Softw. **144**, 1–21 (2018). https://doi.org/10.1016/j.jss.2018.05.057

21. De Stefano, M., Pecorelli, F., Palomba, F., De Lucia, A.: Comparing within-and cross-project machine learning algorithms for code smell detection. MaLTESQuE 2021 - Proc. 5th Int. Work. Mach. Learn. Tech. Softw. Qual. Evol. co-located with ESEC/FSE 2021 1–6 (2021). https://doi.org/10.1145/3472674.3473978

22. Kaur, A., Jain, S., Goel, S., Dhiman, G.: A Review on Machine-learning Based Code Smell Detection Techniques in Object-oriented Software System(s). Recent Adv. Electr. Electron. Eng. (Formerly Recent Patents Electr. Electron. Eng. **14**, 290–303 (2020). https://doi.org/10.2174/2352096513999200922125839

23. Fontana, F.A., Zanoni, M., Marino, A., Mäntylä, M. V.: Code smell detection: Towards a machine learning-based approach. IEEE Int. Conf. Softw. Maintenance, ICSM 396–399 (2013). https://doi.org/10.1109/ICSM.2013.56

24. Arcelli, F., Mäntylä, M.V., Zanoni, M., Marino, A.: Comparing and experimenting machine learning techniques for code smell detection. Empir. Softw. Eng. **21**(3), 1143–1191 (2015). https://doi.org/10.1007/s10664-015-9378-4

25. Yamashita, A., Zanoni, M., Fontana, F.A., Walter, B.: Inter-smell relations in industrial and open source systems: A replication and comparative analysis. 2015 IEEE 31st Int. Conf. Softw. Maint. Evol. ICSME 2015 - Proc. 121–130 (2015). https://doi.org/10.1109/ICSM.2015.7332458

26. Yamashita, A., Zanoni, M., Fontana, F.A., Walter, B.: Exploratory study on the landscape of inter-smell relations in industrial and open source systems (2014)

27. Mäntylä, M. V., Vanhanen, J., Lassenius, C.: Bad smells - humans as code critics. IEEE Int. Conf. Softw. Maintenance, ICSM 399–408 (2004). https://doi.org/10.1109/icsm.2004.1357825

28. Pereira dos Reis, J., Brito e Abreu, F., Figueiredo Carneiro, G.: Code smells incidence: does it depend on the application domain? Glauco de F. Carneiro. Proc. 10th Int. Conf. Qual. Inf. Commun. Technol. 172–177 (2016). https://doi.org/10.1109/QUATIC.2016.37

29. Linares-Vásquez, M., Klock, S., McMillan, C., Sabané, A., Poshyvanyk, D., Guéhéneuc, Y.G.: Domain matters: Bringing further evidence of the relationships among anti-patterns, application domains, and quality-related metrics in Java mobile apps. 22nd Int. Conf. Progr. Comprehension, ICPC 2014 - Proc. 232–243 (2014). https://doi.org/10.1145/2597008.2597144

30. Fontana, F.A., Ferme, V., Marino, A., Walter, B., Martenka, P.: Investigating the impact of code smells on system's quality: An empirical study on systems of different application domains. IEEE Int. Conf. Softw. Maintenance, ICSM. 260–269 (2013). https://doi.org/10.1109/ICSM.2013.37

31. Guo, Y., Seaman, C., Zazworka, N., Shull, F.: Domain-specific tailoring of code smells: An empirical study. In: Proceedings - International Conference on Software Engineering, pp. 167–170 (2010). https://doi.org/10.1145/1810295.1810321

32. Delchev, M., Harun, M.F.: Investigation of code smells in different software domains. Full-scale Softw. Eng. FsSE 31–36 (2015)

33. Charalampidou, S., Ampatzoglou, A., Avgeriou, P.: Size and cohesion metrics as indicators of the long method bad smell: An empirical study. ACM Int. Conf. Proceeding Ser. 2015-Octob (2015). https://doi.org/10.1145/2810146.2810155

34. Python Software Foundation: Welcome to Python.org. https://www.python.org/. Last Accessed 04 Aug 2021

35. Keras: the Python deep learning API. https://keras.io/. Last Accessed 16 Feb 2022
36. Chicco, D., Jurman, G.: The advantages of the Matthews correlation coefficient (MCC) over F1 score and accuracy in binary classification evaluation. BMC Genomics **21**, 1–13 (2020). https://doi.org/10.1186/s12864-019-6413-7
37. Chicco, D.: Ten quick tips for machine learning in computational biology. BioData Min. **10** (2017). https://doi.org/10.1186/S13040-017-0155-3
38. Jurman, G., Riccadonna, S., Furlanello, C.: A comparison of MCC and CEN error measures in multi-class prediction. PLoS One. **7** (2012). https://doi.org/10.1371/journal.pone.0041882
39. Powers, D.M.W.: Evaluation: from precision, recall and F-measure to ROC, informedness, markedness and correlation (2020)

An 8-Layered MLP Network for Detection of Cardiac Arrest at an Early Stage of Disease

N. Venkata Maha Lakshmi[(✉)] and Ranjeet Kumar Rout

Computer Science and Engineering, National Institute of Technology, Srinagar, Hazratbal, Srinagar 190006, Jammu and Kashmir, India
mahalakshminit@gmail.com, ranjeetkumarrout@nitsri.net

Abstract. Automation of the health care industry is grabbing more attention from patients and doctors to save a person's life by early prediction of diseases. Due to changing food habits irrespective of age and gender, many people suffer from chronological diseases. One major disease that needs attention from time to time is "Heart Attacks". Today, all the automated systems implemented either traditional or ensemble machine learning algorithms to build the model. Just a handful of these systems, such as Random Forest, an ensemble mechanism and SVC algorithms, have been harmed by overfitting. As a result, the suggested method uses a "Multi-Layer Perceptron" neural network algorithm to combat overfitting by creating a precise amount of valid labels associated with the training model. The proposed System aids specialists in forecasting a user's cardiac arrest at an initial stage by examining just the 7 most significant variables rather than all of the attributes mentioned in the dataset. The model has a precision of "97.02%", which was designed to demonstrate the state of the art.

Keywords: Attribute selection · Meta classifier · Genetic greedy approach using CSF · 8- layered architecture · Multi-layer perceptron · Random forest

1 Introduction

Learning model is a supervised machine learning technique that creates a link between a set of inputs and the dataset's class labels using a mapping function. Different kinds of classification algorithms are shown in Fig. 1. The proposed System used the J48 Algorithm to generate a tree based entropy as a decision parameter in a Tree-based classifier to determine if a person is suffering from a cardiac arrest or not. J48 is the best decision tree method among all tree classifiers since it assesses all potential subgroups and builds a forest, as illustrated in Fig. 2. The internal nodes represent attributes like exang, old peak and others, whereas branches represent the test conditions to produce an outcome for the next level, and external nodes represent class labels predicted by that particular path with corresponding frequency ratios. In a probability classifier, the independence of features is taken into consideration among the different attributes to predict the class label. The probability is calculated using Bayesian probability, which is well-known for producing accurate results based on decision rules. During the prediction

© The Author(s), under exclusive license to Springer Nature Switzerland AG 2022
A. Kumar et al. (Eds.): ICAIDS 2021, CCIS 1673, pp. 306–320, 2022.
https://doi.org/10.1007/978-3-031-21385-4_26

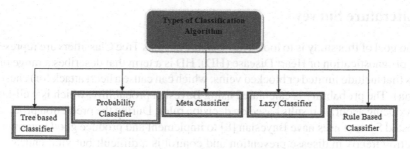

Fig. 1. Categories of classification algorithm

process, the suggested System uses nave Bayesian [8] to implement and produce good outcomes.

In Meta Classifier, the proposed algorithm uses an ensemble algorithm known as "Ada Boost", which identifies the weak classifiers and combines them to generate an accurate classifier to predict the model. Most vulnerable learners do produce by the decision trees and are popularly known as "Stumps". The main advantage of these Meta classifiers is that they invest more time evaluating complex relations that are difficult to predict the records and less time on the documents that can easily predict the class labels. The trees are constructed by choosing one feature at a time with an associated threshold value. The splitting of trees starts based on this threshold value to generate feature subsets. However, working on every possible feature with different values of threshold values makes this algorithm a complicated time consuming one.

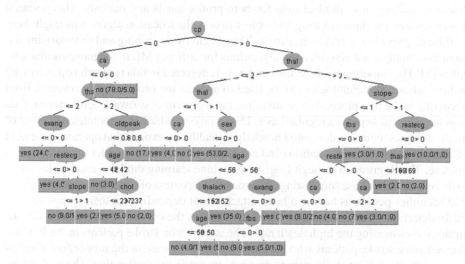

Fig. 2. Tree generation using J48 classification algorithm

2 Literature Survey

[1] The goal of this study is to look at how Data Analysis Tree Classifiers are represented in the prognostication of Heart Disease (HD). HD is a term that describes a range of disorders that include limited or blocked veins, which can cause a heart attack (or) chest pain (angina). The probability is calculated using Bayesian probability, which is well-known for producing accurate results based on decision rules. During the prediction process, the suggested System uses nave Bayesian [8] to implement and produce good outcomes [2]. Predicting trends in disease prevention and control is a difficult but vital endeavour in medicine. The System introduces a machine learning system that uses many approaches to assess the possibility of heart sickness in this study. For a performance overview and a better understanding of the algorithm that provides more significant outcomes, five distant algorithms were chosen [3]. This study illustrates how today technology may be uses in medical research to create incredible results. It was in response to a well-known national piece that highlighted the issue by focusing on cardinal diseases. There are a variety of data analysis methods and procedures that necessitate suitable data collection; then, depending on the newly collected datasets, we can apply specialized machine learning algorithms to predict whether the patient will be impacted by cardinal disease. The techniques of deep - learning (ML) classification were employed in a wide range of methods [4]. The most crucial aspect of health is recognizing the disease. When a problem is detected before the usual or scheduled period, it is feasible to save human lives. Medical professionals can benefit from machine learning categorization algorithms since they can provide accurate and rapid disease diagnoses. Because of the challenges in identifying heart disease, it is currently one of the world's most astounding and severe diseases, making now an ideal time for both professionals and patients. This research discusses how machine learning and object fusion classification algorithms might help healthcare providers detect heart illness. They begin by describing and summarising the most commonly used classification algorithms for utilizing ML to diagnose cardiac diseases [5]. The importance of cardinal sickness is depicted in this research paper, as well as how advanced technologies can be used to address the problem and prevent it from occurring in the first place. As a result of the rapid growth of software development, data is generated and kept on a regular basis. Data analysis, which incorporates a number of methodologies, converts data into knowledge. Healthcare experts that operate in the field of cardiac disease have limitations and are unable to accurately predict the risk of heart disease. The Regression through Logistics machine learning model is used in this study to increase heart disease forecasting efficiency in the context of a medical services dataset that identifies people as having a heart attack or not depending on their symptoms [6]. Early detection of cardiac arrest in stroke patients in the context of data analysis is one strategy for lowering the high death rate. The statistics on stroke patients in the ICU are skewed since stroke patients who have had a heart attack are in the proportion. Predicting a heart attack from stroke patient data gets increasingly challenging. The researchers choose to construct arbitrary least sampling, grouping, and off sampling approaches to change the unbalanced data, simply the UCO method, which provides completely balanced information that is useful in training ML methods for cardiac arrest forecasting models. Extensive trials are carried out using the Medical Records Mart for Critical Care III database to validate the UCO methodology. The algorithm UCO, abbreviated UCO

(120), with an under-sampling value of 120, performs well in assisting ML classifiers in extracting features [7]. In this paper, to select prominent features of the heart disease imperialist competitive algorithm with meta-heuristic approach is suggested. It shows a more optimal response for feature selection toward genetic in compare with other optimization algorithms [8]. Proposed an efficient and accurate system to diagnosis heart disease and the system is based on machine learning techniques. The system is developed based on classification algorithms includes Support vector machine, Logistic regression, Artificial neural network, K-nearest neighbor, Naïve bays, and Decision tree while standard features selection algorithms have been used such as Relief, Minimal redundancy maximal relevance, Least absolute shrinkage selection operator and Local learning for removing irrelevant and redundant features. We also proposed novel fast conditional mutual information feature selection algorithm to solve feature selection problem [9]. Developed HD classification system by using machine learning classification techniques and the performance of the system was 77% in terms of accuracy. Cleveland dataset was utilized with the method of global evolutionary and with features selection method [10]. In another study, developed a diagnosis system using multi-layer Perceptron and support vector machine (SVM) algorithms for HD classification and achieved accuracy 80.41%. Humar et al. [11] designed HD classification system by utilizing a neural network with the integration of Fuzzy logic. The classification system achieved 87.4% accuracy [12]. Developed an ANN ensemble based diagnosis system for HD along with statistical measuring system enterprise miner (5.2) and obtained the accuracy of 89.01%, sensitivity 80.09%, and specificity 95.91% [13]. Designed a ML based HD diagnosis system. ANN-DBP algorithm along with FS algorithm and performance was good. [14] proposed an expert medical diagnosis system for HD identification. In development of the system the predictive model of machine learning, such as navies bays (NB), Decision Tree (DT), and Artificial Neural Network were used. The 86.12% accuracy was achieved by NB, ANN accuracy 88.12% and DT classifier achieved 80.4% accuracy.

3   Materials and Discussion

The System is now working on a heart disease dataset, and the UCI repository has made a Hungarian dataset with 52 attributes available. Later, a simplified dataset of 303 instances with 13 attributes and 1 class label is released on various open source platforms. The dataset for the proposed system came from the Kaggle open-source data repository for Machine Learning [7]. To clean and transform the data, the system used the popular data mining programme "WEKA" to apply several data analysis algorithms. For the business analyst, the WEKA tool is a decent GUI tool for both visualization and experimental running (Table 1).

Table 1. Comparative study on previous models

S. No.	Author	Algorithms used	Advantages	Disadvantages
1	Kumar, N. K. [1]	Random Forest, Decision Tree, Logistic Regression, SVM and KNN	Rather than focussing on improving the model's accuracy, they concentrated on time restrictions	For larger data sets and for tracing real-time data, deep learning algorithms are preferred
2	Motorway, P. [2]	Random Forest, Naïve Bayes, Support Vector Machine, Hoeffding Decision Tree, and Logistic Model Tree	Increased accuracy	This Paper concentrated only on gaining accuracy by using boosting algorithm It can show lesser results if more attributes are added
3	Barik S. [3]	K-nearest neighbor, decision tree classifier, and random forest classifier	A comparison of different machine learning models to determine which is the most accurate	DL techniques can be used for bigger datasets
4	Diwakar, M. [4]	Decision tree, Boosting with SVM, Modified K-means, naïve Bayes, KNN, ANN, SVM	The specific feature extracting models were used	The System Stated that results might vary when different datasets are used. No guarantee for the model that leads here can also show greater results for other datasets
5	Saw, M., Saxena [5]	Logistic Regression	Multiple attributes were considered for better evaluation	Choosing random data with knowing its effectiveness can lead to choosing the least valued data in some cases
6	Wang, M. [6]	Oversampling and under-sampling algorithm	The usage of 3 different algorithms detects the patients that are prone to cardinal disease	This algorithm was only trained with positive values through k - means operation

3.1 Exploratory Data Analysis

The remaining properties, with the exception of the class label, are all numerical. As a result, the System computed the mean and standard deviation (Table 2).

3.2 Observations Made from Analysis

Data normalization and transformation are the most important and time-saving stage in creating a precise model. The suggested system observes the following points and choose the right approach to clean the data to fill in the missing values with statistical measurements depends on the type of attributes.

a. The mode is used to process the age, chol, and thalach properties.
b. The median is used to fill trestbps, old peak, and CA. The other features are cleaned by calculating the attribute's mean value.

3.3 Attributes Selection Mechanisms

To identify the informative attributes that can improve the quality of the model either during training (or) validation, the proposed System implements the genetic algorithm, which is integrated as a part of sub-set feature selection and compares with the traditional approaches like correlation matrix, wrapper methods. The classification of the feature selection mechanism is shown in Fig. 3.

Correlation Matrix is the simplest method to reduce the data by finding the relation between the attributes using Pearson's coefficient. The computation of the Pearson coefficient is measured as shown in (1)

$$
Pearson\_Coeff = \frac{(\sum_{i=0}^{n} X[i] - \mu(X)) * (\sum_{i=0}^{n} Y[i] - \mu(Y))}{\sqrt[2]{(\sum_{i=0}^{n} X[i] - \mu(X))^2 * (\sum_{i=0}^{n} Y[i] - \mu(Y))^2}}
\tag{1}
$$

where, X[i]: Sample value of the ith distribution
$\mu(X)$: Mean value of the particular sample value in the dataset
Y[i]: Class label value of the ith distribution
$\mu(Y)$: Mean value of the class labels.

In the correlation, it is found that very few attributes are related; say, the first attribute age is slightly correlated with trestbps, chol, FBS, old peak and CA. The result obtained is shown in Fig. 4.

(a) **Principal Component Analysis:** Since there is no clear information about the data, that can be reduced. The proposed System tries to implement the principle component analysis based on the Eigen Vectors. Given a square matrix, P and vector, V then a scalar coefficient (β), known as Eigenvalue, is computed that which satisfies (2)

$$
PV = \beta V
\tag{2}
$$

The principal component to reduce the dimensionality space it considers all the features initially. Then it reduces the N-dimensions by combining the different possible

Table 2. Meta data about heart disease dataset

S. No.	Name	Description	Possible values	Min	Max	Mean	Standard deviation
1	Age	It represents the age of the person. It ranges from 29 to 77	41 different values	29	77	54.366	9.082
2	Sex	It represents the gender of the person	{0, 1} 0: female 1: male	0	1	0.683	0.466
3	CP	It represents the chest pain based on the location, cause and relief	{0, 1, 2, 3} 0: All condiions are satisfied 1: Any two conditions are satisfied 2. At least one condition is satisfied 3. None of the conditions are satisfied	0	3	0.967	1.032
4	trestbps	It measures the level of blood pressure in resting mode in mmHg units	49 different values	94	200	131.64	17.538
5	Chol	It measures cholesterol in mg/DL	152 different values	126	564	246.26	51.83
6	Fbs	It measures sugar levels in the blood during fasting	{0, 1} 0:True 1:False	0	1	0.149	0.356
7	restecg	It represents ECG state in resting mode	{0, 1, 2} 0: Normal 1: Abnormality 2: Probably yes	0	2	0.528	0.526
8	thalach	Measures the heartbeat rate	91 different values	71	202	149.64	22.905

(continued)

Table 2. (*continued*)

S. No.	Name	Description	Possible values	Min	Max	Mean	Standard deviation
9	Exchange	Include exercise at location	{0, 1} 0: No 1: Yes	0	1	0.327	0.47
10	old peak	Depression caused due to exercise in units of mm	40 different values	0	6.2	1.04	1.61
11	Slope	Slope value obtained at the peak point of the exercise	{0, 1, 2} 0: Upslope 1: Flat Slope 2: Down Slope	0	2	1.399	0.616
12	CA	Number of major vessels affected	{0, 1, 2, 3, 4}	0	4	0.729	1.023
13	Thal	Measures the portion that is unable to detect thallium	{0, 1, 2, 3} 0: normal 1: fixed 2: reversible 3: Abnormal	0	3	2.314	0.612
14	Target	Class Label	{No, Yes}	–	–	–	–

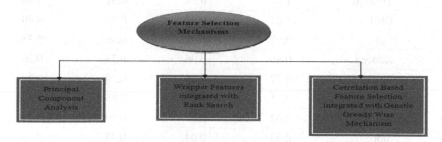

Fig. 3. Classification of feature selection mechanisms

combinations of attributes based on the Eigen Vector values, and it considers only the top attributes with good explained_variance_ratio_, which measures the variance between the attributes. The results are illustrated in Table 3.

(b) Wrapper Selection based on Ranking: Table x has selected the first 12 attributes as informative and removed "thal" attribute. However, still, the reduced attributes contain non-informative attributes. So as a next step, the model implements a wrapper mechanism, which constructs a set of sub-set features based on the ranking mechanism. This

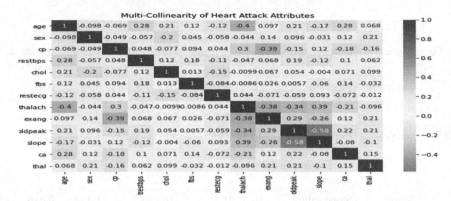

Fig. 4. Correlation matrix for heart disease dataset

method performs an exhaustive search as 2** a number of attributes times as follows, as shown in Fig. 5.

Table 3. Explained Variance using PCA

S. No.	Attribute name	Eigen value	Proportion	Cumulative	Rank
1	Age	2.76	0.21	0.21	0.78
2	Sex	1.53	0.11	0.33	0.66
3	CP	1.22	0.09	0.42	0.57
4	Trestbps	1.81	0.09	0.51	0.48
5	Chol	1.02	0.07	0.59	0.40
6	Fbs	0.97	0.07	0.66	0.33
7	Restecg	0.86	0.06	0.73	0.26
8	Thali	0.77	0.05	0.79	0.20
9	Exchange	0.71	0.05	0.85	0.14
10	old peak	0.62	0.04	0.89	0.10
11	Slope	0.53	0.04	0.93	0.06
12	CA	0.42	0.03	0.97	0.02
13	Thal	0.07	0.00	1.00	0.00

The method searches in both forward and backward directions to find the best node values. The searching mechanism stops based on the termination condition. In the proposed algorithm, the condition is mentioned as "−1". The System to find the global optimum solution rather than the local solution, the termination condition is continuously updated based on the search valley till the threshold value is greater than 1. The obtained results are shown in Table 4.

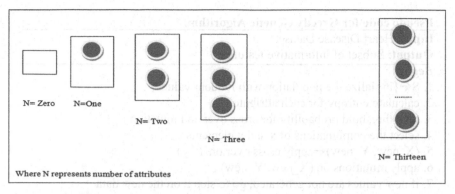

Fig. 5. Attribute selection mechanism using wrapper method

(c) Greedy Genetic Algorithm: The major advantage of implementing a genetic algorithm lies in its adaptiveness to the environment in which it is running. The model starts with a null set and slowly converges all the attributes based on their threshold values and population size to construct a complete feature set. It is a pure iterative method in which two operators, cross over and mutation, are applied to the population set for each iteration in order to obtain a better optimal subset than the previous iteration. The System has considered the cross-over rate as "0.6" and mutation rate as "0.033" in the proposed algorithm. The cross-over operator combines elements of different subsets to generate a unique subset, and mutation tries to either remove or add an element to the feature subset as defined in the below pseudo code. This algorithm has selected the top 7 attributes as informative, i.e., CP, thalach, exang, old peak, slope, CA, thal.

Table 4. Selected attributes using wrapper methods

Attribute no	Attribute name	Rank	Folds with accuracy
13	Thal	0.2127	10 (100%)
3	CP	0.2013	10 (100%)
12	CA	0.1617	8 (80%)
10	Old peak	0.1585	7 (70%)
9	Exchange	0.1422	7 (70%)
8	Thali	0.1297	5 (50%)
11	Slope	0.1157	3 (30%)

| **Pseudo code for Greedy Genetic Algorithm:** |
| **Input:** Heart Disease Dataset |
| **Output:** Subset of informative features |
| *Begin* |
| 1. S← {initialize the population with random values} |
| 2. calculate entropy for each attribute |
| 3. set a threshold probability for cross over and mutation |
| 4. select the combinations of x and y elements |
| 5. (X_new, Y_new)←apply cross over on (x,y) |
| 6. apply mutations on (X_new, Y_new) |
| 7. if new values are not generated, go to step 2 on the new data |
| *End* |

4 Proposed Methodology

The multi layer perceptron is implemented in the suggested system, which is based on the properties of the evolutionary algorithm. To classify the patients, the neural network is enhanced with multiple layers and a bias value. The System to minimize the error rate, the weights are adjusted using Eq. (3)

$$New_{Weight} = old_{weight} + l_{rate} * (original\_value - predicted\_value) + bias \quad (3)$$

The proposed model assumes a standard learning rate, l_{rate} as a parameter for constructing the model and improves the learning rate at each epoch. To adjust the weights of the neuron, the difference between the original and forecasted value is computed as "error rate". Later, these adjusted weights are normalized using bias values. Out of 8 layers designed, 6 are hidden layers, one is input and another is output. Every input is routed via every unit of every layer in these layers, which is described by dense functionality. The MLP design is well-known for the activation function it contains, which conducts affine transformations to reduce complicated activities into simple linear ones. As a result, precise systems can be developed in logarithmic time. The model's overall architecture is depicted in Fig. 6.

The back propagation defined for this function is a crucial factor to adjust the weights, and it has defined few conditions like learning rate as "0.3", momentum as "0.2"; all the instances are divided into a batch size of 100 with epoch size as "20". The results are represented in Table 5.

5 Experimental Results

The proposed algorithm has compared the previous models mentioned in the literature survey and presented in Table 6.

From Fig. 7, it is a clear view that all the metrics of evaluation are good in terms of the proposed algorithm, and the second-best model can be considered as J48, which is a type of tree-based classifier. On X-axis, the evaluation metrics are mentioned, and

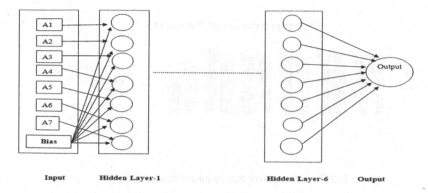

Input   Hidden Layer-1   Hidden Layer-6   Output

Fig. 6. 8- Layered architecture of MLP

Table 5. Weights of neurons in each layer

	Input	Hidden-1	Hidden-2	Hidden-3	Hidden-4	Hidden-5	Hidden-6	Output
N1	6.96	6.96	3.98	0.07	0.30	0.54	4.95	−1.58
N2	7.57	7.57	2.94	1.70	2.47	1.38	4.33	4.64
N3	6.20	6.20	0.73	3.13	3.40	7.79	5.40	0.02
N4	9.89	9.89	2.07	0.04	9.25	0.73	0.10	0.68
N5	8.80	8.80	1.43	1.73	0.89	2.60	3.10	1.24
N6	6.78	6.77	4.58	1.34	4.72	1.48	2.35	0.68
N7	9.12	9.12	0.12	3.96	3.91	5.62	1.50	0.88

Table 6. Comparative analysis on results obtained

Algorithm	Accuracy	Recall	Precision	F1-Score	AUC	Kappa
Naïve Bayesian	84.1	84.2	84.4	84.0	90.0	67.7
Decision tree	86.1	86.1	86.3	86.1	92.6	71.8
J48	93.7	93.7	93.7	93.7	97.2	87.35
ADABOOST	84.1	84.2	84.2	84.2	93.1	68.1
8-layered MLP	97.02	97.0	97.1	97.0	97.8	94.0

on the y-axis, the percentage of measurement with an interval of 20 units is mentioned. The computations of evaluation metrics are discussed in the below section based on the confusion matrix illustrated in Table 7.

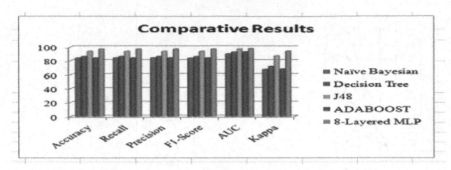

Fig. 7. Comparative results on evaluation metrics

(i) Accuracy: The value obtained by treating the summation of the correctly classified elements, as percentage of total elements in the data which is illustrated in (4)

$$Accuracy\_8\_layered\_MLP = \frac{TP\_Heart\_Attack + TN\_Non\_Heart\_Attack}{Total\ Elements}$$

$$= \frac{158 + 136}{303} = \mathbf{97.02\%} \tag{4}$$

Table 7. 8-Layered perceptron confusion matrix on heart disease

Actual values				
Predicted values		Yes (Heart_Attack)	No (Non_Heart_Attack)	
Yes (Heart_Attack)		158 (TP_Heart_Attack)	7 (FP_Heart_Attack)	165
No (Non_Heart_Attack)		2 (FN_Non_Heart_Attack)	136 (TN_Non_Heart_Attack)	138
		160	143	303

(ii) Many Researchers and others feel Recall and precision are the same, but there is a slight difference in their computations. Precision represents the fraction of the records that are considered to be positive from the correct predictions and is illustrated in (5), whereas Recall represents the fraction of actual positive records that can be predicted true, is illustrated in (6)

$$Precision\_8\_layered\_MLP = \frac{TP\_Heart\_Attack}{TP\_Heart\_Attack + FP\_Heart\_Attack}$$

$$= \frac{158}{158 + 7} = 95.7\% \tag{5}$$

$$Recall\_8\_layered\_MLP = \frac{TP\_Heart\_Attack}{TP\_Heart\_Attack + FN\_Non\_Heart\_Attack}$$

$$= \frac{158}{158 + 2} = 98.75\% \tag{6}$$

6 Conclusion

Since a few years, death rates from cardiac arrest have been rising year after year, regardless of human factors. A person's life can be saved by detecting a heart attack early. This research proposes an automated model employing ANN approaches for early heart attack prediction, with an accuracy of 97.02%. This model's main advantage is that it assesses the impact of each characteristic on the class label and adjusts the weight parameters based on the present occurrence in the testing data. When compared to ensemble techniques, the time it takes to develop this model is a little longer. As a result, in future research, researchers will be able to discover the adaptive nonlinear function and embed them in hyper-tuned systems.

References

1. Kumar, N.K., Sindhu, G.S., Prashanthi, D.K., Sulthana, A.S.: Analysis and prediction of cardio vascular disease using machine learning classifiers. In: 2020 6th International Conference on Advanced Computing and Communication Systems (ICACCS) (2020). https://doi.org/10.1109/icaccs48705.2020.9074183
2. Motarwar, P., Duraphe, A., Suganya, G., Premalatha, M.: Cognitive approach for heart disease prediction using machine learning. In: 2020 International Conference on Emerging Trends in Information Technology and Engineering (IC-ETITE) (2020). https://doi.org/10.1109/ic-etite47903.2020.242
3. Barik, S., Mohanty, S., Rout, D., Mohanty, S., Patra, A.K., Mishra, A.K.: Heart disease prediction using machine learning techniques. In: Pradhan, G., Morris, S., Nayak, N. (eds.) Advances in Electrical Control and Signal Systems. LNEE, vol. 665, pp. 879–888. Springer, Singapore (2020). https://doi.org/10.1007/978-981-15-5262-5_67
4. Diwakar, M., Tripathi, A., Joshi, K., Memoria, M., Singh, P., Kumar, N.: Latest trends on heart disease prediction using machine learning and image fusion. Mater. Today: Proc. **37**, 3213–3218 (2021). https://doi.org/10.1016/j.matpr.2020.09.078
5. Saw, M., Saxena, T., Kaithwas, S., Yadav, R., Lal, N.: Estimation of prediction for getting heart disease using logistic regression model of machine learning. In: 2020 International Conference on Computer Communication and Informatics (ICCCI) (2020). https://doi.org/10.1109/iccci48352.2020.9104210
6. Wang, M., Yao, X., Chen, Y.: An imbalanced-data processing algorithm for the prediction of heart attack in stroke patients. IEEE Access **9**, 25394–25404 (2021). https://doi.org/10.1109/access.2021.3057693
7. Nourmohammadi-Khiarak, J., Feizi-Derakhshi, M.-R., Behrouzi, K., Mazaheri, S., Zamani-Harghalani, Y., Tayebi, R.M.: New hybrid method for heart disease diagnosis utilizing optimization algorithm in feature selection. Heal. Technol. **10**(3), 667–678 (2019). https://doi.org/10.1007/s12553-019-00396-3
8. Alarsan, F.I., Younes, M.: Analysis and classification of heart diseases using heartbeat features and machine learning algorithms. J. Big Data **6**(1), 1–15 (2019). https://doi.org/10.1186/s40537-019-0244-x

9. Detrano, R., et al.: International application of a new probability algorithm for the diagnosis of coronary artery disease. Am. J. Cardiol. **64**(5), 304–310 (1989)
10. Gudadhe, M., Wankhade, K., Dongre, S.: Decision support system for heart disease based on support vector machine and artificial neural network. In: Proceedings of International Conference on Computer and Communication Technology (ICCCT), pp. 741–745 (2010)
11. Kahramanli, H., Allahverdi, N.: Design of a hybrid system for the diabetes and heart diseases. Expert Syst. Appl. **35**(1–2), 82–89 (2008)
12. Das, R., Turkoglu, I., Sengur, A.: 'Effective diagnosis of heart disease through neural networks ensembles.' Expert Syst. Appl. **36**(4), 7675–7680 (2009)
13. Jabbar, M.A., Deekshatulu, B., Chandra, P.: Classification of heart disease using artificial neural network and feature subset selection. Glob. J. Comput. Sci. Technol. Neural Artif. Intell. **13**(3), 4–8 (2013)
14. Palaniappan, S., Awang, R.: Intelligent heart disease prediction system using data mining techniques. In: Proceedings of IEEE/ACS International Conference on Computer Systems and Applications, pp. 108–115 (2008)
15. Heart Disease Dataset Link. https://www.kaggle.com/cherngs/heart-disease-cleveland-uci

Calculation Method of Economical Mode of Integrated Electrical Power System

Vladislav Kuchanskyy[1], Sree Lakshmi Gundebommu[2(✉)], S. Harivardhagini[2],
Petro Vasko[3], Olena Rubanenko[4], and Iryna Hunko[4]

[1] The Institute of Electrodynamics of the National Academy of Sciences of Ukraine, Kiev,
Ukraine
[2] CVR College of Engineering, Hyderabad, India
s_sreelakshmi@yahoo.com, harivardhagini@cvr.ac.in
[3] Institute of Renewable Energy of Ukraine, Kiev, Ukraine
[4] Vinnitsya National Technical University, Vinnitsya, Ukraine
{olenarubanenko,iryna_hunko}@ukr.net

Abstract. In the process of substantiating the development of a bulk electrical
network (BEN) of electric power systems (EPS), a set of the most economical
options for its development is formed, their technical and economic comparison
and the choice of the best solution for subsequent detailed design, construction
and commissioning of network facilities. Taking into account the territorial and
temporal aspect for managing the development of EPS, two main tasks are distinguished, which are solved sequentially. The methodological approach to solving
the problem of optimizing the development of the main electrical network of EPS
is proposed. The main idea of which is the joint use of linear streaming model of
network development and structural model of EPS with the aim of forming set
of the most rational options development of the main electrical network. Satisfying the restrictions on the limiting conditions static stability transmitted power
in EPS sections, allows you to more fully take into account while optimizing the
development of the electrical network, the conditions for its future functioning.

Keywords: Corona discharge power losses · Deep voltage regulation ·
Controlled reactive power compensation · Minimizing criterion · Parametrical
and structural optimization methods

1 Introduction

With the development of the industrial sector of the national economy and the sphere
of consumer services in cities and industrial centers are experiencing a steady increase
in electricity consumption, which, together with the need to maintain or increase the
reliability of power supply and the quality of electricity, increases the load on power
systems. Further development of power systems is to increase the capacity of power
transmission lines, modernization of power facilities, improvement of relay protection
and emergency control systems. The complication of energy systems those favored by

© The Author(s), under exclusive license to Springer Nature Switzerland AG 2022
A. Kumar et al. (Eds.): ICAIDS 2021, CCIS 1673, pp. 321–335, 2022.
https://doi.org/10.1007/978-3-031-21385-4_27

high-density power consumption (primarily in megalopolises), requires the development and introduction of new methods of emergency management [1–5].

One of the most important qualities of power systems controllability - the ability to vary widely in real time, power flows in the lines and current loads of equipment. This allows, with on the one hand, significantly increase their throughput and economic efficiency of power systems operation, optimally distributing power flows along lines and equipment in operation, on the other hand, to increase their reliability, providing fast redistribution of power flows in post-emergency modes. Power flow control methods and increasing the controllability of power systems are today the subject of numerous scientific studies. One of the main problems of organizing operational management power flows are large volumes computational operations required for the correct choice of the values of the parameters of the regulating devices, which does not allow find a solution in real time in complex power systems [6–9].

This article proposes a method for optimizing power fluxes in steady-state modes of power systems, based on the presentation of the characteristics of the power system-operating mode in the form of simple theoretically substantiated functions of the network parameters. At the presence in the power system of one or more control devices, using these functions, you can establish a relationship between their adjustable parameters and the characteristics of the mode. Accordingly, by mathematical analysis of these connections, it is possible to determine the optimal values of the parameters of the control devices that provide the best mode according to the selected criteria the work of the power system. The method is universal, applicable to power systems of any complexity and configuration, and also provides a search for optimal parameters in real time. He can also be applied for optimal control actively adaptive devices [4–8], which allow in a wide range to regulate the flow of power in the power system [10–13].

2   The Problem of Mathematical Modeling of Stationary Modes of Electrical Systems in Generalized Statement

This chapter reflects the results of the practical implementation of the above theoretical provisions and methodological principles of accounting for multimodality in solving problems of optimal compensation of reactive loads of electrical energy distribution systems. The algorithms and programs developed on their basis for calculating and analyzing operating modes, their integral characteristics, the optimal choice of compensating devices reflect certain aspects of the practical solution of this problem. Below are the algorithms and software developments for stochastic and deterministic calculation of the integral characteristics of the PC modes and the optimal compensation of reactive power in the electric power systems.

The initial basic part of the considered algorithms for calculating the integral characteristics and optimal compensation of reactive power are the algorithms for calculating the steady-state (stationary) EPS modes. This task has been most thoroughly worked out and brought to a high theoretical level and broad practical implementation by the work of many generations of domestic and foreign researchers and practitioners of the second half of the twentieth century, and as a scientific problem formulated back in the 50s, in general, it should be considered and stated as resolved. The foundations of the construction and development of the methodology for calculating steady-state regimes are presented in numerous sources, in particular [14–20], which are far from exhaustive lists of even the main significant works. However, the creation a new mathematical apparatus and a practical tool for solving the problems of the functioning and development of electric power system formulated in many edges is based on theoretical groundwork, individual experience and practical skills (including programming) of a specific developer. Some aspects of solving this problem, including in complex algorithms calculation, analysis, and optimization of electrical modes are reflected in the following main works [21–29].

The formulation of the essence of this task is briefly presented below:

where [Y] is the matrix of proper and mutual nodal conductivities, the order of which for a network of N nodes is equal to $n = N - 1$; [U], [J] are vectors of columns of nodal voltages and driving currents of order n. If the complex elements of Eqs. (1) are divided lay down on real and imaginary components

$$[Y] = [G] + j[B], \tag{1}$$

$$[\dot{U}] = [U_a] + j[U_r], \tag{2}$$

$$[J] = [J_a] + j[J_r]$$

then from equations in complex form (1) we can go over to the system of 2nd equations with real numbers

$$\begin{bmatrix} G & -B \\ B & G \end{bmatrix} \cdot \begin{bmatrix} U_a \\ U_r \end{bmatrix} = \begin{bmatrix} J_a \\ J_r \end{bmatrix} \tag{3}$$

In Eqs. (1), the matrix Y consists of four blocks of size $n \times n$, elements of which are active G and reactive B conductivity nodes and branches of the network. Rearranging elements and equations so that the balance equations for active and reactive currents in (2) for all network nodes were written in pairs, we obtain a system of equations with a matrix of coefficients Y, consisting of blocks of the second-order 2×2 [30–40]:

$$\begin{bmatrix} g_{11} & -b_{11} & g_{12} & -b_{12} & \dots & g_{1n} & -b_{1n} \\ b_{11} & g_{11} & b_{12} & g_{12} & \dots & b_{1n} & g_{1n} \\ g_{21} & -b_{21} & g_{22} & -b_{22} & \dots & g_{2n} & -b_{2n} \\ b_{21} & g_{21} & b_{22} & g_{22} & \dots & b_{2n} & g_{2n} \\ \dots & \dots & \dots & \dots & & & \\ g_{n1} & -b_{n1} & g_{n2} & -b_{n2} & \dots & g_{nm} & -b_{nm} \\ b_{n1} & g_{n1} & b_{n2} & g_{n2} & \dots & b_{nm} & g_{nm} \end{bmatrix} \times \begin{bmatrix} U_{a1} \\ U_{r1} \\ U_{a2} \\ U_{r2} \\ \dots \\ U_{an} \\ U_m \end{bmatrix} = \begin{bmatrix} J_{a1} \\ J_{r1} \\ J_{a2} \\ J_{r2} \\ \dots \\ J_{an} \\ J_m \end{bmatrix} \tag{4}$$

This form of writing the nodal equations, as will be seen from what follows, is preferable. Simulation of symmetric operating modes (model 2) is performed on a single-phase equivalent of a three-phase network based on nodal equations in the form of a power balance. Nodal equations in the form of power balance have the form [21, 22]:

$$\overline{U}_1(Y_{11}U_1 - Y_{12}U_2 - \dots - Y_{1n}U_n) = \overline{S}_1 + \overline{U}_1 Y_1 U$$

$$\overline{U}_2(Y_{21}U_1 - Y_{22}U_2 - \ldots - Y_{2n}U_n) = \overline{S}_2 + \overline{U}_2 Y_2 U$$

$$\ldots\ldots\ldots\ldots\ldots\ldots\ldots\ldots\ldots\ldots\ldots\ldots\ldots\ldots\ldots\ldots\ldots\ldots\ldots$$

$$\overline{U}_1(Y_{n1}U_1 - Y_{n2}U_2 - \ldots - Y_{nm}U_n) = \overline{S}_n + \overline{U}_n Y_n U \qquad (5)$$

are nonlinear and their solution is possible only by iterative methods. To solve nonlinear nodal equations in form of power balance (6) predominant Newton's method finds application. Solution for this is found as a result of successive approximations, at each step of the iterative process a linearized system is compiled and solved equations for corrections to moduli and angles voltage vectors [U] at network nodes

$$\begin{bmatrix} \frac{\partial \Delta P}{\partial U} & \frac{\partial \Delta P}{\partial \delta} \\ \frac{\partial \Delta Q}{\partial U} & \frac{\partial \Delta Q}{\partial \delta} \end{bmatrix} \cdot \begin{bmatrix} \Delta U \\ \Delta \delta \end{bmatrix} = \begin{bmatrix} \Delta P \\ \Delta Q \end{bmatrix} \qquad (6)$$

where $\begin{bmatrix} \frac{\partial \Delta P}{\partial U} & \frac{\partial \Delta P}{\partial \delta} \\ \frac{\partial \Delta Q}{\partial U} & \frac{\partial \Delta Q}{\partial \delta} \end{bmatrix}$ Jacobi matrix consisting of four blocks $\frac{\partial \Delta P}{\partial \delta}$, $\frac{\partial \Delta P}{\partial U}$, $\frac{\partial \Delta Q}{\partial \delta}$, $\frac{\partial \Delta Q}{\partial U}$, the elements of which are the partial derivatives of the imbalances of active P and reactive Q of the power in the nodes by the modules U and angles δ of the nodal voltages; ΔU, $\Delta \delta$ are corrections to modules and angles of nodal stresses. Having rearranged the unknown equations similarly to the previous one, (6) can be represented in the form [39–49]:

$$\begin{bmatrix} a_{11} & -b_{11} & a_{12} & -b_{12} & \ldots & a_{1n} & -b_{1n} \\ c_{11} & d_{11} & c_{12} & d_{12} & \ldots & c_{1n} & d_{1n} \\ a_{21} & -b_{21} & a_{22} & -b_{22} & \ldots & a_{2n} & -b_{2n} \\ c_{21} & d_{21} & c_{22} & d_{22} & \ldots & c_{2n} & d_{2n} \\ \ldots & & \ldots & & \ldots & \ldots \\ a_{n1} & -b_{n1} & a_{n2} & -b_{n2} & \ldots & a_{nm} & -b_{nm} \\ c_{n1} & d_{n1} & c_{n2} & d_{n2} & \ldots & c_{nm} & d_{nm} \end{bmatrix} \times \begin{bmatrix} \Delta \delta_1 \\ \Delta U_1 \\ \Delta \delta_2 \\ \Delta U_2 \\ \ldots \\ \Delta \delta_n \\ \Delta U_n \end{bmatrix} = \begin{bmatrix} \Delta P_1 \\ \Delta Q_1 \\ \Delta P_2 \\ \Delta Q_2 \\ \ldots \\ \Delta P_n \\ \Delta Q_n \end{bmatrix} \qquad (7)$$

where $a_{ij} = \frac{\partial \Delta P_j}{\partial \delta_j}$; $b_{ij} = \frac{\partial \Delta P_j}{\partial U_j}$; $c_{ij} = \frac{\partial \Delta Q_i}{\partial \delta_j}$; $d_{ij} = \frac{\partial \Delta Q_i}{\partial U_j}$.

Equations (7), as well as (4), differ in that the coefficient matrices in them consist of blocks of size 2 × 2, and the columns of unknown and given values contain pairwise values related to one node. Linear nodal equations in phase coordinates (model 3) for the analysis of asymmetric modes are obtained for the given EMF (electric motive force) of the generators according to phases and representation of loads of three-phase units (symmetrical and asymmetrical) constants conductivity matrices. Simulation problem at the same time it comes down to drawing up and solving system 3 × n equations of balance of currents of three-phase nodes

$$\begin{bmatrix} Y_{11}^F & Y_{12}^F & \ldots & Y_{1n}^F \\ Y_{21}^F & Y_{22}^F & \ldots & Y_{2n}^F \\ \ldots & \ldots & \ldots & \ldots \\ Y_{n1}^F & Y_{n2}^F & \ldots & Y_{nm}^F \end{bmatrix} \cdot \begin{bmatrix} U_1^F \\ U_2^F \\ \ldots \\ U_n^F \end{bmatrix} = \begin{bmatrix} J_1^F \\ J_2^F \\ \ldots \\ J_n^F \end{bmatrix} \qquad (8)$$

where Y_{ii}^F, Y_{ij}^F - intrinsic and mutual conductivities three-phase nodes, blocks of 3 × 3; U_i^F, J_i^F – on voltage and setting currents of three-phase units. Nonlinear models in asymmetric modes (model 4) are based on the formation of nodal power balance equations for each of the phases of the three-phase network in phase coordinates and their solution by iterative methods. If, at the same time, at each step of the iterative process, the load nodes (symmetric and asymmetric) to represent constant conductivities $[Y] = \text{const}$ or nonlinear current sources $[J]$, then the linearized equations at the step will have the same form as Eqs. (8). In a linear network model (when specifying loads constant phase resistances) phase voltages in network nodes in the considered asymmetric mode are determined by a single solution of the Eqs. (8), in a nonlinear model (for given powers, consumed and generated in the network nodes) phase voltages are specified during the iterative process up to as long as the sum of the powers of the three phases in each node the network will not be equal to the specified value [30–40] .

Thus, the proposed modifications of the nodal equations of the electrical network in the form of balance currents and powers provide the ability to represent any equations of the electrical network in steady modes - normal (6), emergency (3), in phase coordinates (7) - in a single, unified block-matrix form, characteristic which features are as follows: - matrixes of coefficients of any of the considered systems of equations consist of blocks and differ in the sizes of these blocks ($2 \times 2, 3 \times 3, 6 \times 6$); - elements of vectors of given values and unknowns are also grouped into blocks of 2 or 3, containing values related to one node networks; - the number of blocks in the matrix and vectors of given and sought values is equal to the number of independent nodes n of the simulated network. When using the proposed unified, common for all modeling problems, stationary regimes of the block-matrix form of writing equations, the algorithm for solving equations with matrices block structure, differing only in size blocks.

Since in a real electrical network, every one of the nodes is connected only with two or three neighboring ones, and there are no direct connections with the rest of the nodes, the graph of a three-phase electrical network is characterized by weakly connected, and for matrices - a block structure with a large number of zero blocks. In recent years, more and more factorization methods are widely used - a group of methods that allow you to get the reverse matrix in implicit form (in the form of a product of matrix factors, to some extent preserving weak filling). As a method of obtaining inverse matrices in the form of a product of matrix factors, which can be developed for application to weakly filled matrices of a block structure, a method of decomposition of the original matrix A of order n into n matrix factors is adopted, also having a weak filling [4]. The proposed block factorization method [4] is a generalization of methods for factorizing matrices with real coefficients on the weakly filled to develop efficient algorithms for solving nodal Eqs. (3)–(7) of electrical systems with any asymmetry in phase coordinates. Bringing all the four models highlighted above to a unified form allows, first, to unify computational procedures their formation and decision, and, secondly, to include them into a single generalized, basic model (M1) of electrical systems in stationary modes.

3 Parametric Optimization of the Operation Modes of the Main Electrical Network According to the Criterion of Active Power Losses

Substituting (10) in (3), we make sure that with optimal voltage regulation at the beginning of the power transmission, the no-load losses are equal to the short-circuit losses.

Total losses of active power in power transmission with such regulation are (11–16). In case of absent CSR will be (14–15). In case of installing CSR will be (15–16).

Let us single out two components of active power losses associated with the flow of reactive power. On the one hand, this is a part of the short-circuit losses, proportional to the square of the reactive power and therefore always positive, on the other hand, it is the component of losses from the transfer of reactive power, which, depending on the combination of the signs of the quantities Q and $G \cdot X - B \cdot R + \frac{B_{Re\,ac} \cdot n \cdot G \cdot A - B \cdot G \cdot A3}{2} + B_{Re\,ac} \cdot n \cdot R$), can both increase and decrease the total losses active power. The presence of these two components makes it possible reducing active power losses by optimizing the reactive power mode in long-distance power transmission.

The optimal value of reactive power at the beginning of the transmission is determined under the condition that the partial derivative of the form $\partial \Delta P / \partial Q$.

As follows from expression (2), the optimal reactive power does not depend on the active power transmitted through the line, but is determined only by the voltage and power transmission parameters. Calculations show that the coefficient of losses of active power of a short circuit is always positive, and the coefficient of losses from the transfer of reactive power according to the conditions of the start of transmission ash is always negative. Therefore, the optimal value of reactive power will always be positive, that is, according to the conditions for minimizing active power losses, it is advisable to implement the drain of a part of the charging power of the line into the transmission system.

By solving together Eqs. (9–16), it is possible to obtain the values of the voltage levels and reactive power at the beginning of the transmission with the joint regulation of the voltage and reactive power in the transmission.

$$U_1 = \sqrt[4]{(P^2 + Q^2)\frac{8 \cdot (\frac{G \cdot X^2}{2} - \frac{B \cdot R \cdot X}{2} + R)}{G \cdot (B^2 \cdot X^2 - 8 \cdot B \cdot X + G^2 \cdot X^2 + 8)}} \tag{9}$$

$$U_1 = \sqrt[4]{(P^2 + Q^2)\frac{4(R(2 - A2 + A7) + GX^2)}{G(A5 + A7(A7 - 2A8) + A6 + 8(A7 + 1 - A8))}} \tag{10}$$

$$\Delta P_{im} = \sqrt{(P^2 + Q^2)\frac{G(\frac{GX^2}{2} - \frac{BRX}{2} + R)(B^2X^2 - 8BX + G^2X^2 + 8)}{8}} \tag{11}$$

$$\Delta P_{sc} = \sqrt{(P^2 + Q^2)\frac{G(\frac{GX^2}{2} - \frac{BRX}{2} + R) \cdot (B^2X^2 - 8BX + G^2X^2 + 8)}{8}} \tag{12}$$

$$\Delta P_{Sc} = \sqrt{(P^2 + Q^2) \frac{G \cdot (2 \cdot R + G \cdot X^2 - B \cdot R \cdot X + B_{reac} \cdot R \cdot X)}{16}}$$
$$\times \sqrt{\frac{(B^2 \cdot X^2 - 2 \cdot B \cdot B_{reac} \cdot X^2 - 8 \cdot B \cdot X + B_{reac}^2 \cdot X^2 + 8 \cdot B_{reac} \cdot X + G^2 \cdot X^2 + 8)}{16}} \tag{13}$$

The total losses of active power with such voltage regulation are (15).

$$\Delta P_U = 2\sqrt{(P^2 + Q^2) \frac{G \cdot (\frac{G \cdot X^2}{2} - \frac{B \cdot R \cdot X}{2} + R) \cdot (B^2 \cdot X^2 - 8 \cdot B \cdot X + G^2 \cdot X^2 + 8)}{8}} - \frac{G \cdot (G \cdot A + 4 \cdot R)}{2} \cdot P$$
$$+ (G \cdot X - B \cdot R + \frac{B_{Re\,ac} \cdot n \cdot G \cdot A - B \cdot G \cdot A3}{2} + B_{Re\,ac} \cdot n \cdot R) \cdot Q \tag{14}$$

$$Q = -U^2 \left(\frac{12 B_{Re\,ac} R + 30GX - B_{Re\,ac} GR^2 + 8B_{Re\,ac}^2 RX + 7G^2 RX - 7B_{Re\,ac} RX}{4R + 2GX^2 - 2BRX + 2B_{Re\,ac} RX} - \frac{7B_{Re\,ac}}{2} \right) \tag{15}$$

Total power losses in the network are determined by the expression:

$$\Delta S_{\sum} = \sum_i S_{iN} - \sum_S S_S + Y_{BP} \cdot U_{BP}^2 \tag{16}$$

where $\sum_i S_{iN}$ is the sum of the total capacities of the beginnings of all lines departing from the BP (balancing point); S_S is the total power of the reduced loads of all points of the circuit network; Y_{BP} is the conductivity of the BP, which is transferred to the BP buses in the process of preparing the calculation scheme of the network.

The sum of the total capacities of the beginnings of all lines departing from the BP:

$$\Sigma S_{iH} = S_{01} + S_{05} + S_{07} + S_{08} + 0.5 \cdot (\Delta S_{01z} + \Delta S_{05z} + \Delta S_{07z} + \Delta S_{08z})$$
$$= 30.303 - j22.355 + 23.628 - j18.545 + 25.996$$
$$- j18.468 + 21.099 - j14.629 + 0.5 \cdot (0.202 - j0.674 + 0.258$$
$$- j0.859 + 0.144 - j0.478 + 0.302 - j0.516)$$
$$= 101.478 - j75.259 \quad [\text{MVAr}].$$

Power losses in equivalent conductivity applied to the BP:

$$\Delta S_{BP} = 0,5 \cdot (_{01} +_{05} +_{07} +_{08}) \cdot U_{BP}^2$$
$$= 0.5 \cdot (j39.76 + j79.53 + j39.76 + j59.1) \cdot 10^{-6} \cdot 121^2 = j1.597 \quad [\text{MVAr}].$$

The sum of the given values of power points:

$$\sum S_S = S_{red1} + S_{red2} + S_{red3} + S_{red4} + S_{red5} + S_{red6} + S_{red7} + S_{red8} + S_{red9}$$
$$= 6.053 - j4.902 + 12.077 - j8.913 + 9.065$$
$$- j7.304 + 8.064 - j6.486 + 12.097 - j9.109 + 14.088$$
$$- j10.535 + 12.074 - j9.632 + 17.107 - j13.128$$
$$= + 9.065 - j7.304 = 99.691 - j77.313 \quad [\text{MVAr}]$$

Total power losses:

$$\Delta S_{\Sigma} = \sum_i S_{iN} - \sum_S S_S + Y_{BP} \cdot U_{BP}^2 = 101.478 - j75.259 - 99.694$$

$$+ j77.313 + j1,597 = 1.787 + j3.651 \quad [MVAr]$$

The results of the calculation of the mode of operation of the network in the first iteration are shown in Fig. 1.

The first iteration of the calculation is complete. Let's move on to the second iteration.

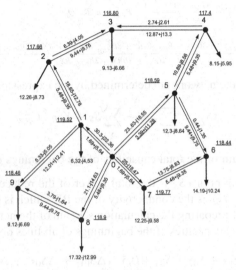

Fig. 1. The results of calculating the mode of operation of the network on the first iteration

The second iteration the second iteration is performed similarly. The results of calculating the parameters of the network substitution scheme for the second iteration, are summarized in the Table 1 and Table 2.

The voltage mode on the second iteration is determined by the resulting flow distribution in the same way as on the first.

$$U_{01end} = 119.541 \ [kV]; \qquad U_{01middle} = 120.273 \ [kV];$$

$$U_{05end} = 118.615 \ [kV]; \qquad U_{05middle} = 119.813 \ [kV];$$

$$U_{07end} = 119.782 \ [kV]; \qquad U_{07middle} = 120.392 \ [kV];$$

$$U_{08end} = 118.901 \ [kV]; \qquad U_{08middle} = 119.955 \ [kV];$$

$$U_{12end} = 117.687 \ [kV]; \qquad U_{12middle} = 118.617 \ [kV];$$

Table 1. Flow distribution from power losses in a closed network circuit

Branch	Flow distribution from power losses in a closed network circuit, MVAr	Resulting flow S_{rez}, MVAr
0–1	0.488+j1.6	30,268−j22,023
0–5	0.372+j1.261	23.623−j18.235
0–7	0.204+j0.82	25.957−j18.206
0–8	0.161+j0.599	21.068−j14.574
1–2	0.161+j0.856	18.622−j12.602
2–3	−0.006+j0.58	6.378−j3.965
3–4	0.062+j0.161	−2.743+j2.598
4–5	0.141+j0.799	−10.886+j8.446
5–6	0.05−j0.257	0.459−j1.698
6–7	0.051+j0.64	−13.73+j8.753
8–9	−0.019+j0.344	3.78−j1.701
9–1	0.097+j0.099	−5.362+j5.161

Table 2. Power losses in the points of the scheme

Network diagram item	Power losses in the points of the scheme ΔS_{1aux}, MVAr	Power in the points of the scheme S_{jrez}, MVAr
1	0.23+j0.642	6.284−j4.26
2	0.167+j0.276	12.244−j8.637
3	0.055+j0.741	9.12−j6.563
4	0.08+j0.639	8.143−j5.848
5	0.181+j0.719	12.278−j8.39
6	0.101+j0.383	14.189−j10.152
7	0.152+j0.18	12.226−j9.452
8	0.18+j0.256	17.287−j12.872
9	0.077+j0.443	9.142−j6.861

$$U_{23end} = 116.844 \ [kV]; \qquad U_{23middle} = 117.266 \ [kV];$$

$$U_{34end} = 117.44 \ [kV]; \qquad U_{34middle} = 117.142 \ [kV];$$

$$U_{45end} = 117.44 \ [kV]; \qquad U_{45middle} = 18.029 \ [kV];$$

$$U_{56end} = 118.463 \ [kV]; \qquad U_{56middle} = 118.539 \ [kV];$$

$$U_{67end} = 118.463 \ [kV]; \qquad U_{67middle} = 118.539 \ [kV];$$

$$U_{67end} = 119.782 \ [kV]; \qquad U_{67middle} = 119.124 \ [kV];$$

$$U_{89end} = 118.461 \ [kV]; \qquad U_{89middle} = 118.681 \ [kV];$$

$$U_{91end} = 118.461 \ [kV]; \qquad U_{91middle} = 119.002 \ [kV];$$

The total loss of capacity in the network is determined in the same way as in the first iteration.

The sum of the total capacities of the beginnings of all lines departing from the BP:

$$\sum S_{iH} = S_{01} + S_{05} + S_{07} + S_{08} + 0.5 \cdot (\Delta S_{01z} + \Delta S_{05z} + \Delta S_{07z} + \Delta S_{08z})$$
$$= 30.268 - j22.023 + 23.623 - j18.235 + 25.957$$
$$- j18.206 + 21.068 - j14.574 + 0.5 \cdot (0.166 - j0.553$$
$$+ 0.213 - j0.709 + 0.119 - j0.396 + 0.251 - j0.428)$$
$$= 101.29 - j74.08 \ [MVAr]$$

Power losses in equivalent conductivity applied to the BP (balancing point): $\Delta S_{BP} = j1.597$.

The sum of the given values of power points:

$$\sum S_S = 99.691 - j77.313 \ [MVAr]$$

Total   power   losses:
$$\Delta S_{\sum} = \sum_i S_{iN} - \sum_S S_S + Y_{BP} \cdot U_{BP}^2 = 101.29 - j74.08 - 99.691 + j77.313$$

$$+ j1.597 = 1.6 + j4.83 \ [MVAr]$$

The results of the calculation of the mode of operation of the network in the second iteration are shown in Fig. 2. The second iteration of the calculation is complete. Let's move on to the third iteration.

The third iteration is performed similarly, in order to satisfy the specified accuracy of the calculation B = 0.01 kV. The results of the calculation of the mode of operation of the network on the third iteration are shown in Fig. 3.

$$\Delta S_{\sum} = 1.589 + j4.861 \ [MVAr],$$

Since the maximum difference between the values of the voltage on the second and third iterations are:

$$\left| U_{23k}^{(3)} - U_{23k}^{(2)} \right| = |116.84377 - 116.84454| = 0.00077 \ [kV] < \varepsilon = 0.01 \ [kV],$$

Then the iterative process can end.

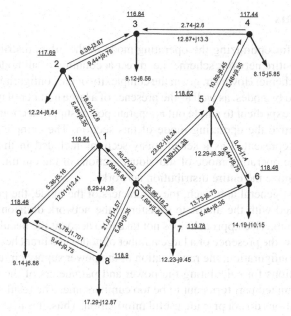

Fig. 2. The results of calculating the mode of operation of the network in the second iteration

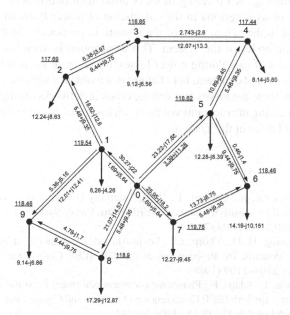

Fig. 3. The results of calculating the mode of operation of the network on the third iteration

4 Conclusions

The best option for optimizing the operating mode of the urban distribution system is to optimize the entire network scheme, i.e. direct accounting of all nodes and branches included in the scheme. However, given the complexity of the configuration, a significant change in the load by nodes, as well as the presence of a large number of network division points, it is more expedient to single out a separate power supply section in the complete circuit and optimize the operating mode of this section. The complete power supply scheme can be represented as a set of many sections included in this scheme, thus, by optimizing the operating mode of individual sections of the circuit, it is possible to achieve and optimize the entire distribution network.

With the most general approach, the parameters of the mode, the power in the system, are calculated with the alternate transfer of the network division point to all the nodes of the system. This approach does not take into account the peculiarities of urban networks, namely: the presence of a large number of nodes and branches, the complexity of the network configuration, the ramification of the power supply circuit. When all the necessary conditions for calculating the power and parameters of the operating mode are met, the calculated part turns out to be too cumbersome. The results obtained in the course of calculations do not provide useful information. Thus, it is necessary to develop an algorithm for allocating an optimized section in order to simplify and accelerate the processes of optimizing the operating mode of urban distribution networks.

The presence of assumptions in the calculation of power flows in the system that do not correspond to the actual state of the system, in particular, the constancy of the voltage level in the nodes of the system. This assumption is intended to simplify and speed up the process of calculating power losses, however, in a real urban scheme, the voltage at the nodes is not constant, but changes in accordance with the load value of the nodes. In addition, there are losses and voltage drops in networks during the distribution of electricity. Not taking into account voltage level losses leads to additional errors when calculating power losses in the system.

References

1. Flatabo, N., Ognedal, R., Carlsen, T.: Voltage stability condition in a power transmission system calculated by sensitivity methods. IEEE Trans. Power Syst. **5**(4), 1286–1293 (1990). https://doi.org/10.1109/59.99379
2. Dobson, I., Chiang, H.-D., Thorp, J.S., Fekih-Ahmed, L.: A model of voltage collapse in electric power systems. In: Proceedings of the 27th IEEE Control and Decision Theory Conference, pp. 2104–2109 (1988)
3. Mili, L., Baldwin, T., Adapa, R.: Phasor measurement placement for voltage stability analysis of power systems. In: 29th IEEE Conference on Decision and Control, vol. 6, pp. 3033–3038 (1990). https://doi.org/10.1109/CDC.1990.203341
4. Schlueter, R.A., Hu, I., Chang, M.W., Lo, J.C., Costi, A.: Methods for determining proximity to voltage collapse. In: 1990 IEEE Winter Meeting, 4–9 February 1990
5. Begovic, M.M., Phadke, A.G.: Voltage stability assessment through measurement of a reduced state vector. IEEE Trans. Power Syst. **PWRS-5**(1), 198–203 (1990)
6. Stankovic, A., Ilic, M., Maratukulam, D.: Recent results in secondary voltage control of power systems. In: 1990 IEEE Winter Meeting, 4–9 February 1990

7. Lagonotte, P., Sabonnadiére, J.C., Léost, J.Y., Paul, J.P.: Structural analysis of the electrical system: application to secondary voltage control in France. IEEE Trans. Power Syst. **4**(2), 479–486 (1989)
8. Begovic, M.M., Ostojic, D.R.: Determination of critical zones for voltage instability in power systems. In: Proceedings of the 29th IEEE Conference on Decision and Control, 5–7 December 1990
9. Scott, B.: Review of load-flow calculation methods. Proc. IEEE **62**(7), 916–929 (1974)
10. Davoudi, M.: Effects of phasor measurement unit on correlation of WLS state estimation results. In: 2016 21st Conference on Electrical Power Distribution Networks Conference (EPDC), pp. 142–146 (2016)
11. Baldwin, T.L., Mili, L., Phadke, A.G.: Dynamic ward equivalents for transient stability analysis. IEEE Trans. Power Syst. **9**(1), 59–67 (1994)
12. Vallakati, R., Mukherjee, A., Ranganathan, P.: Preserving observability in synchrophasors using Optimal Redundancy Criteria (ORC). In: DC Microgrids (ICDCM) 2015 IEEE First International Conference on, pp. 69–74 (2015)
13. Prabhakar, P., Kumar, A.: Voltage stability assessment using Phasor measurement technology. In: 2014 IEEE 6th India International Conference on Power Electronics (IICPE), pp. 1–6 (2014)
14. Ertürk, B., Göl, M.: Binary integer programming based PMU placement in the presence of conventional measurements. In: 2016 IEEE PES Innovative Smart Grid Technologies Conference Europe (ISGT-Europe), pp. 1–6 (2016)
15. Shukla, S., Mili, L.: A hierarchical decentralized coordinated voltage instability detection scheme for SVC. In: 2015 North American Power Symposium (NAPS), pp. 1–6 (2015)
16. Song, Y., Ma, S., Wu, L., Wang, Q., He, H.: PMU placement based on power system characteristics. In: International Conference on Sustainable Power Generation and Supply 2009, SUPERGEN 2009, pp. 1–6 (2009)
17. Seshadri Sravan Kumar, V., Thukaram, D.: Approach for multistage placement of phasor measurement units based on stability criteria. IEEE Trans. Power Syst. **31**(4), 2714–2725 (2016)
18. Xue, A., Liu, R., Li, M., Chow, J.H., Bi, T., Yu, T., Pu, T.: On-line voltage stability index based on the voltage equation of transmission lines. Gener. Transm. Distrib. IET **10**(14), 3441–3448 (2016)
19. Kuchanskyy, V.V.: The prevention measure of resonance overvoltges in extra high voltage transmission lines. In: 2017 IEEE First Ukraine Conference on Electrical and Computer Engineering (UKRCON), pp.436–441 (2017). https://doi.org/10.1109/UKRCON.2017.810 0529
20. Kuchanskyy, V.V.: Application of controlled shunt reactors for suppression abnormal resonance overvoltages in assymetric modes. In: 2019 IEEE 6th International Conference on Energy Smart Systems (ESS), pp.122–125 (2019). https://doi.org/10.1109/ESS.2019.876 4196
21. Kuchanskyy, V., Zaitsev, I.O.: Corona discharge power losses measurement systems in extra high voltage transmissions lines. In: 2020 IEEE 7th International Conference on Energy Smart Systems (ESS), Kyiv, Ukraine, pp. 48–53 (2020). https://doi.org/10.1109/ESS50319.2020.9160088
22. Kuchanskyy, V., Malakhatka, D., Ihor, B.: Application of reactive power compensation devices for increasing efficiency of bulk electrical power systems. In: 2020 IEEE 7th International Conference on Energy Smart Systems (ESS), Kyiv, Ukraine, pp. 83–86 (2020). https://doi.org/10.1109/ESS50319.2020.9160072
23. Tuhay, Yu.I., Kuchansky, V.V., Tuhay, I.Yu.: The using of controlled devices for the compensation of charging power on EHV power lines in electric networks. Tech. Electrodyn. (1), 53–56 (2021)

24. Kuznetsov, V., Tugay, Y., Kuchanskyy, V.: Overvoltages in open-phase mode. Tekh. Elektrodyn. **2**, 40–41 (2012)
25. Kuznetsov, V., Tugay, Y., Kuchanskyy, V.: Influence of corona discharge on the internal ovevoltages in highway electrical networks. Tekh. Elektrodyn. **6**, 55–60 (2017)
26. Kuchanskyy, V.: Criteria of resonance overvoltages occurrence in abnormal conditions of extra high voltage transmission lines. Visnyk naukovykh prats Vinnytskoho Nastionalnoho Tekhnichnoho Universytetu **4**, 51–54 (2016)
27. Blinov, I., Zaitsev, I.O., Kuchanskyy, V.V.: Problems, methods and means of monitoring power losses in overhead transmission lines. In: Babak, V., Isaienko, V., Zaporozhets, A. (eds.) Systems, Decision and Control in Energy I. SSDC, vol. 298, pp. 123–136. Springer, Cham (2020). https://doi.org/10.1007/978-3-030-48583-2_8
28. Kuznetsov, V.G., Tugay, Y.I., Kuchansky, V.V., Likhovid, Y.G., Melnichuk, V.A.: Resonant overvoltages in non-sinusoidal mode of the main electric network. Elektroteh. Elektromeh. **2**, 69–73 (2018)
29. Hunko, I., Kuchanskyi, V., Nesterko, A., Rubanenko, O.: Modes of Electrical Systems and Grids with Renewable Energy Sources, p. 184. LAMBERT Academic Publishing (2019). ISBN 978-613-9-8895-3
30. Kuchanskyy, V.: Olena Rubanenko Influence assesment of autotransformer remanent flux on resonance overvoltage UPB Scientific Bulletin. Ser. C: Electr. Eng. **82**(3), 233–250 (2020)
31. Kuchanskyy, V., Satyam, P., Rubanenko, O., Hunko, I.: Measures and technical means for increasing efficiency and reliability of extra high voltage transmission lines. Przegląd Elektrotech. **2020**(11), 135–141 (2020). https://doi.org/10.15199/48.2020.03.27
32. Gundebommu, S.L., Hunko, I., Rubanenko, O., Kuchanskyy, V.: Assessment of the power quality in electric networks with wind power plants. In: 2020 IEEE 7th International Conference on Energy Smart Systems (ESS), pp. 190–194 (2020). https://doi.org/10.1109/ESS 50319.2020.9160231
33. Kuchanskyy, V.: Influence of transmission line wire transposition on asymmetry levels and power transfer capability. In: 2020 IEEE Congreso Bienal de Argentina (ARGENCON), pp. 1–8 (2020). https://doi.org/10.1109/ARGENCON49523.2020.9505391
34. Kuchanskyy, V., Rubanenko, O., Hunko, I.: Autoparametric self-excitation of even harmonics in extra high voltage transmission lines. In: 2021 IEEE PES/IAS PowerAfrica, pp. 1–5 (2021). https://doi.org/10.1109/PowerAfrica52236.2021.9543263
35. Kuchanskyy, V., Zaitsev, I., Bajaj, M., Rubanenko, O., Hunko, I.: Method for calculation controlled compensating devices parameters extra high voltage power lines. In: 2021 IEEE 3rd Ukraine Conference on Electrical and Computer Engineering (UKRCON), pp. 385–390 (2021). https://doi.org/10.1109/UKRCON53503.2021.9575432
36. Rajalakshmi, P., Rathinakumar, M.: A comparison of transmission line voltage stability indices. In: 2016 2nd International Conference on Advances in Electrical Electronics Information Communication and Bio-Informatics (AEEICB), pp. 44–48 (2016)
37. Dong, X., Ding, Y., Zhao, P., Wang, C., Wang, Y., Sun, H.: Power flow calculation considering power exchange control for multi-area interconnection power networks. In: 2016 IEEE Industry Applications Society Annual Meeting, pp. 1–7 (2016)
38. Zhong, Q., Zhang, Y., Zhang, J., Wu, Z.: Voltage sensitivity analysis in voltage support of the china southern power grid. In: International Conference on Power System Technology 2006, PowerCon 2006, pp. 1–6 (2006)
39. Wang, X., Sun, H., Zhang, B., Wu, W., Guo, Q.: Real-time local voltage stability monitoring based on PMU and recursive least square method with variable forgetting factors. In: 2012 IEEE Innovative Smart Grid Technologies - Asia (ISGT Asia), pp. 1–5 (2012)
40. Conti, S., Raiti, S., Vagliasindi, G.: Voltage sensitivity analysis in radial MV distribution networks using constant current models. In: 2010 IEEE International Symposium on Industrial Electronics (ISIE), pp. 2548–2554 (2010)

41. Garcia, P.A.N., Pereira, J.L.R., Carneiro, S., da Costa, V.M., Martins, N.: Three-phase power flow calculations using the current injection method. IEEE Trans. Power Syst. **15**(2), 508–514 (2000). https://doi.org/10.1109/59.867133
42. Nguyen, H.L.: Newton–Raphson method in complex form. IEEE Trans. Power Syst. **12**(3), 1355–1359 (1997)
43. Cheng, C.S., Shirmohammadi, D.: A three-phase power flow method for real-time distribution system analysis. IEEE Trans. Power Syst. **10**(2), 671–679 (1995)
44. Martí, J.R., Ahmadi, H., Bashualdo, L.: Linear power-flow formulation based on a voltage-dependent load model. IEEE Trans. Power Delivery **28**(3), 1682–1690 (2013)
45. Schneider, K.P., Fuller, J.C., Chassin, D.P.: Multi-state load models for distribution system analysis. IEEE Trans. Power Syst. **26**(4), 2425–2433 (2011)
46. Therrien, F., Kocar, I., Jatskevich, J.: A unified distribution system state estimator using the concept of augmented matrices. IEEE Trans. Power Syst. **28**(3), 3390–3400 (2013)
47. de Araujo, L.R., Penido, D.R.R., Carneiro, S., Pereira, J.L.R.: A study of neutral conductors and grounding impacts on the load-flow solutions of unbalanced distribution systems. IEEE Trans. Power Syst. **31**(5), 3684–3692 (2016)
48. Ahmadi, H., Martı, J.R., von Meier, A.: A linear power flow formulation for three-phase distribution systems. IEEE Trans. Power Systems **31**(6), 5012–5021 (2016)
49. Montenegro, D., Ramos, G.A., Bacha, S.: A-diakoptics for the multicore sequential-time simulation of microgrids within large distribution systems. IEEE Trans. Smart Grid **8**(3), 1211–1219 (2017)

Testing and Integration Method Utilization for Restricted Software Development

Ahmed J. Obaid[1]([✉]), Azmi Shawkat Abdulbaqi[2], and Hayder Sabeeh Hadi[3]

[1] Faculty of Computer Science and Mathematics, University of Kufa, Kufa, Iraq
ahmedj.aljanaby@uokufa.edu.iq
[2] College of Computer Science and Information Technology, University of Anbar, Ramadi, Iraq
azmi_msc@uoanbar.edu.iq
[3] College of Nursing, University of Kufa, Kufa, Iraq
hayders.jabar@uokufa.edu.iq

Abstract. Restricted Software refers to any software programs or items that are subject to a licensing fee or royalty owing to a third party licensor if they are licensed, whether now or in the future. Eliminating software development limitations through software integration and testing is critical to distinguishing fully between the constraints we face through software development testing and integration, as methods are intertwined. This procedure reduces the constraints faced by the programmer during testing and integration for error-free debugging exercises. The checking protocol and integration process, on the other hand, can be segregated into multiple modules or subroutines before combining to make it easier to work with error-free software applications and testify to their compliance with client requirements. Therefore, using the sub-routines test is to ensure error-free software application also allows the checking of the software program line by line in other to detect errors that will flag off or get displayed on the screen.

Keywords: Software · Testing · Integration · Modules · Sub-routine · Procedure

1 Introduction

Restricted Software refers to software that is included in the Transferred Business Materials but is subject to terms or limits imposed by a technology licensor or other suppliers, and that needs approval before being disclosed or assigned to third parties. Software evaluation is an inspection to notify the customer of the consistency of the product or service tested. Software trials should provide reliable unbiased results that allow customers to identify and assess the risks involved in developing and implementing software applications [1]. The software application evaluation process is to detect the discrepancies between input and output; it is also to measure the quality rate of the software product. Software testing should be performed during the course of development. Software testing, in other words, is a method of validation and evaluation during development [2]. Not all defects within the program are fully identified by testing. The application package provides instead a critique or comparison of the state and the actions of the

© The Author(s), under exclusive license to Springer Nature Switzerland AG 2022
A. Kumar et al. (Eds.): ICAIDS 2021, CCIS 1673, pp. 336–347, 2022.
https://doi.org/10.1007/978-3-031-21385-4_28

application package that allows the user to detect the error. Specifications, comparable models, variations of the previous product; inferences about the consumer desired, required requirements [3]. In 1956, the software program was integrated without checking the module application kit, which did not enable the tester or user to freely perform debugging. However; from 1957–1978, the bulk debugging exercise of the software application was demonstrations again and its fail to debug effectively, which has made the software application package not to meets the client specification [4]. The failure of some IT projects is shocking to those who understand the complex and dynamic nature of the software development industry. In order to survive in this continuous innovative and progressive change, you must keep pace with the times. Not only can smart business people use software development services, but we can also weigh the pros and cons of each technology. It is estimated that by 2021, global IT spending will reach $40.18 billion, and these statistics are based on Statista's results from 2005 to 2021.

Every investor aims to achieve a high return on investment. The software industry can provide a lot of things, and you need to learn how to get its benefits. Enhance our daily application with the times. Likewise, we need to let go of organizing our business according to the latest trends. There are no other ways to survive in the fierce competition in the IT industry and Software development (Fig. 1).

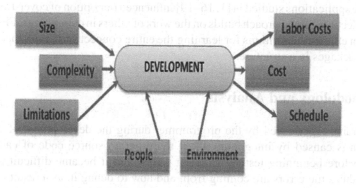

Fig. 1. Software development constraints

The paper organized as follows; Sect. 2, introduced Literature Review. Section 3, presented Methodology and Analysis. Section 10, viewed Method for the evaluation and identification of tests constraints. And finally, Sect. 12, the Conclusion.

Restricted software enables you to restrict access to particular apps for certain users or groups of users. For example, you could wish to ban all users from using a peer-to-peer file sharing software, limit access to popular administrative services to just IT employees, or prevent users from using a software beta version. A restricted software record must be created for each software that you wish to limit. This enables you to define which users are subject to the restriction and what occurs when they launch the application. You may, for example, terminate the restricted process, remove the software, and even show the user a message.

2 Literature Review

Our study is related to the topic of software upgrades, which has gotten a lot of coverage in the community [5–8, 10].

Since certain open-source devices, such as operating systems, are designed from kits, there have been some functional alternatives for downloading them in the past. These approaches look for a vast number of kits that can be installed together. Most of them use SAT solvers or pseudo-boolean optimizations [5, 6, 10] to solve the problem, or they learn greedy algorithms [7]. Also contests for discovering SAT solver-based solutions that optimize the number of installable packages has been held as part of the EU research project Mancoosi [11]. The authors of [9] also looked into the capabilities of MILP solvers for dealing with the upgradeability issue, and found that pseudo-boolean optimizations improved the results. All of the strategies presume that the dependencies and contradictions are understood, that the packages are installable, and that they are free of defects. By studying the true structure of the dependency's matrix, our solution complements current approaches. Another similar research field is the use of checks to find glitches in applications [12–15]. They're used to find an undetermined number of glitches. However, since our concern is based on packet dependencies, harmonic algorithms designed to detect errors cannot be immediately available, necessitating adjustments. The applications studied in [1, 16–19] influenced our option of cover-free families for test collection. Our approach builds on the work of others in computing CFFs [20–22], resulting in efficient algorithms for learning the entire connections graph that describes software packages in a structure.

3 Methodology and Analysis

The constraint experienced by the programmer during the development of a software application is caused by integrating all of the program source code of each module together before beginning testing to detect errors, and it became difficult to identify which modules the errors are coming from and how to debug it, as a result of the bulk testing method used during the execution process, which results in the programmer failing to meet the client specification. Hence; the primary purpose of testing software program is to know if the program is error free or not, if errors are detected then it should be debugged or corrected. Program software testing consists of examining the behavior of the program source code during execution process toward meeting the specifications. Since the software development is a team work and each module of the software application can be developed by one person or an organization, before integrating it together in other to achieve the set goal. Therefore; there is a need for each developer to test its module of software program to confirm the source code and to ensure that any error detected during the process be debug or corrected, to make the software program error free and meet it specification. Criteria for debugging the software quality include correctness, comprehensiveness and confidentiality of the source code of the application, as well as technical specifications such as capacity and reliability, performance, portability, maintenance and usability. The dynamic analysis of the software source code, is the data use to test the software program and to confirm if it has met the required specification before it being integrated. The emphasis is to achieve the error free testing capacity of the Software source code to verification and validation.

3.1 Verification (Vr)

IS the operation of testing the software application to see whether it truly expresses it consistency and meet its specification [6].

3.2 Validation (Vd)

IS the process to confirm the software application if it has met the specified requirement by the user for effective implementation [7].

3.3 Bottom-Up Testing (BuT)

This process is used to integrate the module-by-module procedures testing of the program source code before compiling it together for the development of a complete computer software application that are errors free and meet the client specification [8]. It enhances the degree of satisfaction and efficiency of actualizing the easier method use to eliminate the constraints face during testing and integration of program software [9].

3.4 Integration Testing (InT)

This method involves the interface mixture and interaction of the app's integral feature model and the optimized architectural design to confirm that the program complies with the user/client specification. As a result, each information technology platform has a target audience; for example, video game software has a different target audience than financial institution software [1]. The software application develop can be accessed through the end user to determine the acceptability of the product and to confirm its errors free and easier access to it operational technique. One may need to determine if it's user friendly before recommending the software application to the general society for patronage [10].

3.5 Redundant-Test Detector (RTD)

This test tool produces a wide range of test inputs that show the various sequences of the interface system during a module test. However, a substantial part of this procedure for the execution of input values argues for the entity states of the receiver. This process is to confirm the test being carried out on others module input values for the development of quality software product [12].

3.6 Non-Redundant-Test Generator (NRTG)

This process is to avoid generating redundant-tests that will not be used to explore the actual symbolic object state of receiver space for normal program software execution. One should check the module testing tool that will continue to its concrete state. Furthermore; help in controlling the complex data structures test for effective execution [13].

3.7 Visual Testing (VT)

The goal of VT is to allow developers to analyze and evaluate if a data test has met the specifications of the program and whether or not a functional test has succeeded. Visual evaluation approaches need increased contact between testers and developers because the tests can be used to offer accurate reports and reviews on a display on user activities from those interested in the implementation process [14].

4 Software, Applications, and Systems with Restrictions

Prior to 2004, language education used a lot of restricted language learning apps and platforms. Due to the limitations of digital technology at the time, and not because of a lack of understanding about teaching techniques or ideas, these software or systems had highly restricted functionalities. Repetition and rapid pre-stored feedback are the emphasis of restricted applications. Multiple choice and reassembling things are two of the most common tasks in restricted language learning systems. These programs compare the learner's responses. Restricted language learning methods aren't interactive, and they don't encourage sharing or cooperation [15, 16].

5 Warranty on Software

We can guarantee instantiations of a certain kind of software once we have a certification system in place. The law of product liability is founded on two kinds of warranties: explicit and implicit. The legal profession is starting to debate the applicability of this categorization approach to the US software sector. A licensor of software (or his employees) may construct an explicit guarantee in numerous ways, according to the recently accepted draft of the Uniform Commercial Information Transactions Act [17, 18]:

(1) An statement of fact or promise made by the licensor to its licensees in any way relating to the information and becoming part of the basis of the contract generates an explicit guarantee that the information to be given under the agreement must adhere to the affirmation or promise. (2) Any description of the information included in the basis of the contract generates an explicit assurance that the information will match the description. (3) Any sample, model, or demonstration of a final product made part of the basis of the agreement creates an express warranty that the performance of the information must reasonably conform to the performance of the sample, model, or demonstration, taking into account any differences that would appear to a reasonable person in the licensee's position between the sample, model, or demonstration and the information as it will be used [19, 20].

6 Limitations of SW Testing

Limitation is a concept that restricts something's scope. Testing does have certain drawbacks that should be considered in order to create fair expectations for its advantages. Despite being the most widely used verification method, software testing has the following drawbacks [21]:

1. Testing may be used to demonstrate the existence of mistakes, but it cannot be used to demonstrate their absence. It can only detect flaws or mistakes that are already known. It offers no indication of any problems that have yet to be discovered. It is impossible to ensure that the system under test is error-free throughout testing [22, 23].
2. When we have to choose between "releasing the product with errors to meet the deadline" and "releasing the product late, compromising the deadline," testing is useless.
3. Testing cannot prove that a product works well in all conditions; it can only prove that it does not work properly in certain conditions
4. Software testing does not assist in identifying the fundamental causes of fault insertion in the first place. Locating the fundamental causes of failures may aid in the prevention of future fault injection [24, 25].

7 End of SW Testing

Software testing is a continuous process that may carry on indefinitely but must come to a halt at some point. Testing is, in reality, a trade-off between cost, time, and quality. The amount of time spent testing should be proportional to the potential implications of software faults. The following are some of the probable reasons for testing to be discontinued [26]:

1. The software's risk is within accepted limits.
2. Code/functionality/requirements coverage reaches a specified point.
3. Budgetary and schedule constraints.

8 Innovatively Test a Software

Except in the most simple instances, testing everything (all combinations of inputs and preconditions) is impossible. It is difficult to test a program enough to ensure the absence of all faults. Instead of exhaustive testing, we employ risks and priorities to concentrate testing efforts more on suspected parts as contrasted to less suspected and seldom encountered components [27].

9 SW Testing Evaluating

We should have some sort of criterion for determining whether or not a test is successful. If just a few test cases are run, the test oracle (human or mechanical agent that determines if the SW behaved appropriately on a particular test) might be a tester who inspects and decides what circumstances constitute a test run successful [28–31]. When there are a large number of test cases, automated oracles must be used to decide if the tests passed or failed without the need for manual involvement. Test effectiveness is a solid metric for evaluating a test case (number of errors it uncovers in a given amount of time) [32, 33] (Fig. 2).

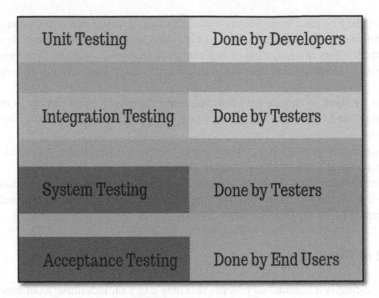

Fig. 2. SW testing levels

10 Method for the Evaluation and Identification of Tests Constraints

The best method used to eliminate the constraints experiences during testing and integration is sub routines programming format, to carry out the test and to avoid the traditional way of testing and integration technique. Therefore; sub-routines test used is to ensure error-free software which is easier to work with and meet the client specifications. Furthermore; it also allows the checking of the software program line by line in other to detect errors that will flag off or get displayed on screen. The line code where the error occurs allows the debugging/correction of that error to take place effectively without necessary starting all over the processes again [1, 12]. However; the combination of module-by-module method with code coverage method allow the update quality of debugging program source code to view the errors on screen during the execution processes and to accept the commands from keyboard to debugged the errors line by line until its complete the lifecycle of the system. As shown in the figure below (Fig. 3):

Test adequacy provides stopping rules for the tester to determine the correct step to follow in satisfying the testing requirement before carrying out the test using module by module method to achieve quality output that will meet the specification of the software [13, 20, 21]. Therefore; after successfully debugging the errors generated by input variables through the tools and the rules provided by test adequacy, it will now be easier to integrate all the modules together to make it a complete software application with errors-free that satisfy the client or user. Result/Discussion: The test engineer took the code coverage test result as an input variable to configure the process used in executing the program software line by line in order to detect the errors and generate a report for proper documentation [14]. Test abstractor: It's received the report generated from the test

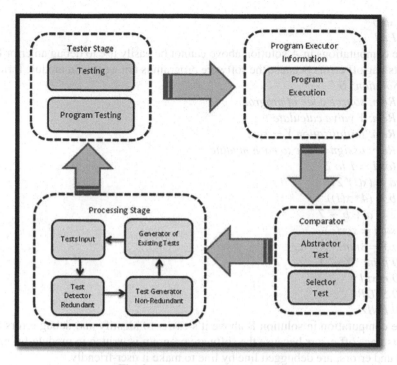

Fig. 3. System lifecycle structure

engineer during the testing of the software program and to know the actual technique used to the interface and abstract the errors for easier debugging. Program-spectra comparator: This method compares the different procedure used in testing the program source code that will actualize the errors free outputs, before integrating the program together to develop a complete software application that will meet the specification for accuracy and simplicity throughout the execution processes. The tool enhances the programmer to edit its program effectively.

Example: write a computer program to solve for the valve y from the equation below [1, 12]:

$$Y = \sqrt{x^2 + 4x - 7} \qquad (1)$$

where x equal to 1, 2

1. Solution: A
05 Rem: source code of program
10 Rem: Y valve calculate
15 Rem: Y = 0 initialization of Y
20 for I = 1 to 2 25 Z = sqr (x(I)^2) + (4 * x(I) − 7)
30 Y = sqr(Z)
35 print "Y=" Y
40 next I

45 Stop
50 End

The computations in A solution above cannot be easily use to debug an error freely when its flag off errors because the software program is not written in module format. 2.

2. *Solution: B*
10 Rem: source code of program
20 Rem: Y valve calculate
30 Rem: initialization Y = sum
40 Rem: assign a, b, c to each module
50 for I = 1 to 2
60 a = (x(I)^2)
70 b = (4* x(I))
80 c = a + b − 7
90 sum = sqr(c)
110 Y = sum
120 print "Y=" Y
130 next I
140 STOP
150 END.

The computation in solution B above it's easier to identify and debug errors freely when its flags off errors because the software program is written in module-by-module format and errors, are debugged line by line to make it user-friendly.

11   Integration Mechanism

All integrated project support environments provide some degree of mechanistic support for configuration management as a key tool service. However, this support is mostly rudimentary and is often created haphazardly depending on the authors of integrated Project Support Environments' assessment of the configuration management mechanisms that integrated project support environments tools are expected to need. The least common denominator approach was often utilized by designers of integrated project support environments since there is minimal consensus across tools for configuration management. As a result, many integrated project support environments only offered version control support inside/top mechanisms of the storage of data since all tools need some kind of version control for the data generated/utilized.

There is no comprehension of the semantics of the data objects at this stage. The benefit of this is that regardless of the kind of data, it can all be versioned using the same mechanism. However, it also has the drawback of making it impossible to include into the mechanisms a comprehension of the insert, remove and update the semantics of different kinds of data elements.

Integrated project support environments frameworks give just minimal configuration management mechanisms. The integrated project support environments customizer must now integrate configuration management ending-user services. This may be a complex and challenging process. Developing configuration management ending-user services in all integrated project support environments frameworks requires extending the data schema and creating new operators to access the new schema structures.

Tools from integrated project support environments can make utilize configuration management services by implementing the novel operators defined for data manipulation, or by making use of the structures of data described in the schema of data that make utilize of the fundamental data manipulation operators provided by the integrated project support environment when implementing.

A selection of configuration management ending-user services is offered by populated integrated project support environments. The implemented services assume a certain utilization pattern and are not easily extensible to different usage patterns. The notion of a contract, which represents a work item that is to be tracked and controlled, is crucial. A contract is a very basic notion that may theoretically be utilized in a variety of ways to support various processes of software development. However, in reality, only a few methods may be utilized contracts due to the installation of configuration management ending-user services. For instance, it was anticipated that a single person would manage each contract. Each contract has its own database as a consequence, and there are no capabilities for several users to access a database at once. Similar to this, no mechanisms for quick data transferring from one contract to another while carrying out a contract were given since it was never anticipated that this would be necessary.

12 Conclusion

The programmer should always give priority to testing the software program source code in the module-by-module format before integrating the entire program modules together for easier development of an error-free software application package that will meet the client specification. The combination of the module-by-module method with the code coverage method allows to be viewed the errors on-screen during the execution processes and to accept the commands from the keyboard to debug the errors line by line until its complete the lifecycle. Therefore; the difference between existing testing and integration software method is the independent technique used in detecting an error. The future directions for software development are AI-assisted development, RPA; Progressive Web Applications (PWA), Continuous Integration and Delivery; Digital Transformation; Catalysts, Low-Code Development; virtual reality VR and augmented reality AR; Blockchain; Artificial intelligence Apps; Internet of Things IoT.

References

1. Bshouty, N.H., Gabizon, A.: Almost optimal coverfree families. In: CIAC, pp. 140–151 (2017)
2. Ben-Basat, R., Goldstein, M., Segall, I.: Learning software constraints via installation attempts. CoRR, vol. abs/1804.08902 (2018). http://arxiv.org/abs/1804
3. Abbas, A., Siddiqui, I.F., Lee, S.U.J., Bashir, A.K.: Binary pattern for nested cardinality constraints for software product line of IoT-based feature models. IEEE Access 5, 3971–3980 (2017)
4. Czepa, C., Tran, H., Zdun, U., Kim, T.T.T., Weiss, E., Ruhsam, C.: On the understandability of semantic constraints for behavioral software architecture compliance: a controlled experiment. In: 2017 IEEE International Conference on Software Architecture (ICSA), pp. 155–164. IEEE (2017, April)

5. Mancinelli, F., Boender, J., di Cosmo, R., Vouillon, J., Durak, B., Leroy, X., Treinen, R.: Managing the complexity of large free and open-source package-based software distributions. In: ACM ASE (2006)
6. Di Cosmo, R., Boender, J.: Using strong conflicts to detect quality issues in component-based complex systems. In: ACM ISEC (2010)
7. Modelling and resolving software dependencies (2005). https://people.debian.org/dburrows/model.pdf
8. Trezentos, P., Lynce, I., Oliveira, A.L.: Aptpbo: solving the software dependency problem using pseudo-boolean optimization. In: ACM ASE (2010)
9. Michel, C., Rueher, M.: Handling software upgradeability problems with MILP solvers. In: LoCoCo (2010)
10. Tucker, C., Shuffelton, D., Jhala, R., Lerner, S.: Opium: optimal package install/uninstall manager. In: ICSE 2007
11. The mancoosi project (2017). http://mancoosi.org/papers/
12. Martínez, C., Moura, L., Panario, D., Stevens, B.: Locating errors using elas, covering arrays, and adaptive testing algorithms. SIAM J. Discret. Math. (2009)
13. Aldaco, A., Colbourn, C., Syrotiuk, V.: Locating arrays: a new experimental design for screening complex engineered systems. In: ACM OS Rev. (2015)
14. Segall, I., Tzoref-Brill, R.: Feedback-driven combinatorial test design and execution. In: SYSTOR (2015)
15. Yilmaz, C., Dumlu, E., Cohen, M.B., Porter, A.: Reducing masking effects in combinatorial interaction testing: a feedback driven adaptive approach. IEEE Trans. Softw. Eng. (2014)
16. Hwang, F., Sós, V.: Non-adaptive hypergeometric group testing. Studia Sci. Math. Hungar 22 (1987)
17. Berger, T., Levenshtein, V.: Application of coverfree codes and combinatorial designs to two-stage testing. In: Electronic Notes in Discrete Mathematics (2001)
18. Chor, B., Fiat, A., Naor, M.: Tracing traitors. In: Desmedt, Y.G. (ed.) CRYPTO 1994. LNCS, vol. 839, pp. 257–270. Springer, Heidelberg (1994). https://doi.org/10.1007/3-540-48658-5_25
19. Yamada, S., Hanaoka, G., Kunihiro, N.: Two Dimensional Representation of Cover Free Families and Its Applications: Short Signatures and More (2012)
20. Obaid, A.J.: Wireless sensor network (WSN) routing optimization via the implementation of fuzzy ant colony (FACO) algorithm: towards enhanced energy conservation. In: Kumar, R., Mishra, B.K., Pattnaik, P.K. (eds.) Next Generation of Internet of Things. LNNS, vol. 201, pp. 413–424. Springer, Singapore (2021). https://doi.org/10.1007/978-981-16-0666-3_33
21. Ibrahim, K., Obaid, A.: Fraud usage detection in internet users based on log data. Int. J. Nonlin. Anal. Appl. 12(2), 2179–2188 (2021). https://doi.org/10.22075/ijnaa.2021.5367
22. Jones, E.L.: Grading student programs – a software testing. In: Proceedings of the Fourteenth Annual Consortium for Computing Sciences in Colleges (2000)
23. Miller, Howden, W.E.: Tutorial, Software Testing & Validation Techniques. IEEE Computer Society Press (1981). [6] Ian Somerville, Software Engineering. Addison-Wesley (2001)
24. Bach, J.: Exploratory Testing Explained, v.1.3 4/16/03. [8] Bentley, J.E., Wachovia Bank, Charlotte NC, Software Testing Fundamentals—Concepts, Roles, and Terminology, SUGI 30
25. Myers, G.J.: The Art of Software Testing, Wiley, New York, c1979. ISBN:0471043281
26. Jenkins, N.: A Software Testing Primer (2008)
27. Sestoft, P.: Systematic software testing, Version 2 (2008)
28. Istaq, S., et al.: Debugging, advanced debugging and runtime analysis. Int. J. Comput. Sci. Eng. 2(2), 246–249 (2010)
29. Kumar, A.: Design of secure image fusion technique using cloud for privacy-preserving and copyright protection. Int. J. Cloud Appl. Comput. (IJCAC) 9(3), 22–36 (2019)

30. Kumar, A., Zhang, Z.J., Lyu, H.: Object detection in real time based on improved single shot multi-box detector algorithm. EURASIP J. Wirel. Commun. Netw. **2020**(1), 1–18 (2020). https://doi.org/10.1186/s13638-020-01826-x
31. Kumar, A.: A review on implementation of digital image watermarking techniques using LSB and DWT. In: Third International Conference on Information and Communication Technology for Sustainable Development (ICT4SD 2018), held during August 30–31, 2018 at Hotel Vivanta by Taj, Goa, India
32. Pfleeger, S.L.: Software Engineering, Theory and Practice. Pearson Education (2001)
33. Farooq, S.U., Quadri, S.M.K.: Effectiveness of software testing techniques on a measurement scale. Orient. J. Comput. Sci. Technol. **3**(1), 109–113 (2010)

Brain MRI Noise Reduction Using Convolutional Autoencoder

B. Nageshwar Rao[1]([⊠]) and D. Lakshmi Sreenivasa Reddy[2]

[1] Department of CSE, UCE (A), OU, Hyderabad, Telangana, India
[2] Department of IT, CBIT (A), Hyderabad, Telangana, India
`dlsrinivasareddy_it@cbit.ac.in`

Abstract. The Magnetic resonance imaging (MRI) machine will add random artifacts like intensity inhomogeneity, Gaussian noise, and Rician noise, while the image acquisition process. Due to hardware imperfection (magnetic fields, etc.), body motion during scanning, thermal noise, weak signal intensity (which causes low signal-to-noise ratio), etc. noises are present in the image. It is very difficult to diagnose of brain disorder if the MR image is corrected by Rician noise. In the past two decades, various algorithms have been proposed with different noise reduction performances. Recently machine learning and deep learning architectures outperform most of the conventional denoising algorithms. The Convolutional Neural Network (CNN) based residual learning architectures are showing promising performance in MRI noise reduction. The proposed algorithm makes use of convolutional neural network-based rician noise reduction using Augmented Autoencoder architecture, which increases the denoising performance with boosted MR image sample size. In particular, batch normalization and residual learning are applied to enhance noise reduction performance. To validate the proposed research work, tested two sets of MRI data from the Kaggle database. The proposed augmented autoencoder produced promising results at high rician noise levels and showed better performance over state of art deep learning architectures. The performance is measured in terms of Mean square error, Peak Signal to Noise Ratio, and Structural Similarity Index Measurements.

Keywords: Augmented autoencoder · CNN · MRI · Residual learning · Rician noise

1 Introduction

The most popular technique used in the medical field is medical imaging. Here without penetrating the human body internal organs can be viewed. Denoising, registration, reconstruction, segmentation, and compression are done by using medical image processing. To solve the problem of medical imaging, over the years various effective algorithms are formulated. In medical images, noise occurs mainly due to two phases of acquisition and transmission [1]. During the acquisition phase, noise occurs in images for two reasons. Wherein first, due to susceptible thermal noise and statistical randomness in the emission of photons, image acquisition devices induce noise in images. In second reason, due to physiological interference, it is difficult to progress the physiological processes of patient inability. So, diagnosis and obtaining useful information from images it's very difficult for doctors. Noise in the images is unavoidable and therefore noise removal is imperious, to improve the quality of the images doctors use these images to make an accurate diagnosis [2]. One of the main principal problems is Noise and artifact reduction, which are naturally solved with reconstruction techniques. Many approaches are there to address such problems which are proposed by various researchers, none of them is considered these artifacts. The method to approach is advanced filtering methods or retrospective correction that take advantage of deep learning. In high-dimensional spaces and non-linear problems, the most powerful algorithm is the deep learning-based algorithm, so it's useful for feature extraction and image noise reduction [3].

For automatic computer and visual inspection analysis most commonly we use MRI image reconstructed size. In mathematical form it can be expressed in the magnitude of the MRI signal is the square root of the sum of the squares of two independent Gaussian variables which follows Rician distribution [4]. In low intensity (dark) areas magnitude of Rician distribution leads to Rayleigh distribution and in high intensity (bright) areas it leads to Gaussian distribution. In dark image regions average pixel intensities are increased it leads to decrease in image contrast noise. Because of the signal-dependent mean of Rician noise, both the scaling coefficients and wavelet of a noisy MRI image are biased estimates of their noise-free counterparts.

At present, signal-to-noise ratio of MRI machine depends majorly on magnetic fields system strength. The SNR is low in Philips/Siemens Intera MRI 1.5T which are low field systems which is used to improve the quality of image by average. So that scan time increased expensive. To improve the SNR from 1.5T to 3.0T magnetic field strength is increased and it leads to high-frequency inhomogeneity artifacts. As cost increases because for noise reduction high power supply devices are required to increase super conducting effect [5]. The result shows the strength of practical application which new method increase the SNR, this reduce the scan time in low magnetic field scanners. To limit the impact of above mitigate manufactures developing a new technique named parallel magnetic resonance imaging (pMRI) in current modalities that can accelerate MRI scans using multi-channel coil array [6]. High acceleration factor (R) is enhanced in pMRI reconstructed noise images, this can be done by improving the quality and noise reduction of the pMRI image. Dynamic imaging protocols and multi-echo sequences is widely used in clinically in whole-body applications. Reconstruction algorithm and development of a robust denoising filter algorithm is used to increase SNR and image resolution. SNR has different methods based on single image, a pair of images, or a series of many images [7]. Based on two ROIs in a single image (i.e., image background (air, outside the imaged object) and tissue of interest), SNR measurements is done by using two methods standard deviation of the background intensity and mean value of the background intensity. We refer to these two region methods as SNR standard deviation and SNR mean, respectively.

The corrupted brain MRI has been faithfully reconstructed with Deep Learning autoencoder [8]. The reducing noise or an artifact is further applied in data augmentation, disease detection, or data acquisition for improvement. Similarly, with the disease-free neuroimaging data, we can train auto-encoder. For the absence of illness, we define a distribution (normal) range for the neuroanatomical variability with the potential purpose of removing noise or occurrence of diseases. Once trained, the autoencoder will encode all the input images and reconstruct them without any noise. The autoencoder does not remove any type of noise in paint lesions because it is treated like a denoise or an image-filler. It cannot reconstruct MRI without the reduced noise. It doesn't know how to reconstruct from noise because it is trained under target images like clean and control MRI. Therefore, in latent space, once the MRI is encoded, then the decoder can reconstruct a clean and control MRI. The rest of this research work is organized as shown, second part discusses the literature review of MR Image noise reduction using deep learning architectures. The third Section introduces about proposed augmented autoencoder. The fourth Section explains the simulation results with different databases and validation strategies, finally, the fifth Section presents our concluding remarks on the proposed method.

2 Literature Review on MR Image Denoising

The extensive investigation of MR image denoising is needed because of Rician noise, and intensity inhomogeneity (Bias Field), Therefore, point of reference to modified investigation, positive advances are needed to cause the images to show up more comparable and these means are ordinarily assigned to pre-processing. Ordinary pre-processing steps for underlying brain MRI incorporate the accompanying key steps. Registration is the process of primary arrangement of the images to a typical fundamental space. The enrolment in normalizing the MR images into a standard key space, like MNI (ICBM) [9], DICOM, and NIFTI. The registration will adjust the images of various formats to a standard format. The T1 sequence and T2 sequence are acquired with multi-channel representation. From the MRI machine whatever the metadata acquired it will consist of several artifacts like Partiality field, Skull, and Rician noise. In Partiality field/ Bias Field correction, the revision of diverged images varieties is present because of the magnetic field inhomogeneity. The process of taking of skull image from MR and focusing on intracranial tissues is known as skull stripping. The most widely used techniques are Robex, BET and SPM [10]. The most commonly selected methodology is N4ITK Partiality field /bias field modification. Which is used in the ITK brain image simulator tool [11].In reference [12], by using 2-D entropy maximization, a grayscale image is segmented. In Reference [13], for image denoising and segmentation, the most commonly used technique named variance minimization Introduced local statistics in the formulation of the energy function. In Reference [14], for image denoising to select multilevel threshold, it proposed an algorithm named as golden search minimization algorithms, hill-clustering technique, and linear minimax approximation algorithm computed a multi-threshold value.

In Reference [15] by using two entropy functions it implements image denoising. The two entropy functions are entropy region and entropy layout. In Reference [16] to eliminate non-cerebral tissue in an image of T1-weighted MRI commonly used method is skull stripping. In Reference [17] multi-threshold and multi-objective particle swarm optimization (MOPSO) techniques are used for image denoising and segmentation. In Reference [18], MRI images by using clustered-based MOPSO algorithm it separate the tumor part images. To produce the non-dominated solutions here two fitness functions-KFECSB and AWGLAC are used. In Reference [19], by using elitist learning technique, to balance convergence and diversity most significant parameters are the leading party, self-adaptive criteria, and disruptive operator with a Gaussian mutation. The author Wang. G et al. [20] proposed "Impacts of skull stripping on the construction of 3D-T1-weighted imaging-based brain structural network in full-term neonates" developed a Brain extraction tool that performs automatic brain extraction from MRI images. Kidoh M et. al [21] demonstrated an algorithm titled "Deep Learning-Based Noise Reduction for Brain MR Imaging: Tests on Phantoms and Healthy Volunteers". This method employs Convolutional Neural Networks (CNN) for MR image de-noising along with classification. Intensity Normalization is a procedure to adjust the intensity level of all images into a standard or reference scale based. e.g., somewhere in the range of 0 and 4095. Nyul et al. proposed an algorithm, which utilizes a piecewise direct adjusting of image intensities into an implication scale. It is one of the most famous standardization approaches, which regards deep learning systems, processing z-scores. From the image, it consists of all pixels where it extracts the mean image intensity and partitions of pixels by the standard deviation of intensities, which is another popular standardization approach. The MRI is corrupted by Rician noise, which is image-dependent and registered from both real and imaginary images. The Rician noise makes image-based critical estimation is troublesome. The Non-Local Means (NLM) [22] channel has been demonstrated to be effective against added additives.

3   Proposed Methodology

Reducing outliers or noise or missing values must increase the accuracy of the class detection method. Assuming that the total data set D is the collection of individual data points D_i, then this relationship can be formulated as for a total of n observations,

$$D = \sum_i^n D_i \tag{1}$$

Since the accumulated data are primarily extracted from the MR images at this point, each data point or observation is a combination of different MR image initial parameters such as image contrast (C), pixel density (PD), and the position of the objects (OP). This can be formulated as:

$$D_i =< C, PD, OP > \tag{2}$$

Even though the contract, the pixel density, and the object position are belonging to the collection here that are extracted from the MR image data. With the advent of deep learning, the new techniques for these pre-processing strategies are single-scale CNN, denoising with DNN [23] auto-encoders, and generative adversarial network (GAN)-based architectures. Among all of these techniques, auto-encoders are best for noise suppression from brain MR images. Autoencoder is an unsupervised machine learning algorithm that uses a back-propagation algorithm [24]. From the other models, it uses pre-trained layers and applied transfer learning to form encoder and decoder. With the help of appropriate dimensionality and sparsity constraints, the autoencoder can learn data projections that are most important than principal component analysis (PCA) or other deep learning techniques.

In this Fig. 1 the autoencoder aims to convert inputs into outputs with fewer errors and it can represent a linear and non-linear transformation in coding processes. The major parts of the Autoencoder implementation are encoder, code (or bottleneck), and decoder.

• Encoder: It converts the original high-dimension input into the low-dimensional code (with reduced dimension). The modified input is the output that is lower in size than the original input.
• Code: It feeds the compressed input to the decoder and it acts as a bridge between encoder and decoder.
• Decoder: The decoder block re-establishes the information from the code, it is the loss reconstruction of the original MR image.

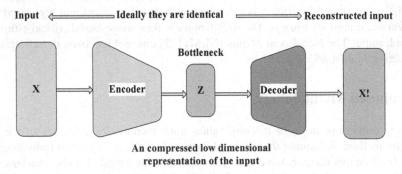

Fig. 1. Autoencoder model architecture [16]

In this proposed model, an encoder function is denoted as $g_\emptyset$ characterized with $\emptyset$, and a decoder function is represented as f_θ characterized with θ. The low-dimensional code learned for input x in the code (bottleneck) layer is $z = g_\emptyset(x)$ and the re-establish input is $x^i = f_\theta(g_\emptyset(x))$. There are two different ways to assess the difference between vectors. The first one is cross-entropy when the activation function is sigmoid or as basic as MSE loss:

$$\cos tfunctionL(\theta, \phi) = \frac{1}{n} \sum_{i=1}^{n} [x - f_\theta(g_\phi(x^i))]^2 \tag{3}$$

The boundaries (θ, ϕ) are learned together to get output through a re-establish information test, which is the same as the original information, $x \approx f_\theta(g_\emptyset(x))$. Since the autoencoder learns the respectability from pre-trained layers from another model, there is a possibility of "overfitting" when there are more network boundaries than the number of input data points. To solve this overfitting problem we develop the robust, Augmented Autoencoder for noise reduction. The input is partially corrupted by adding

Ricin noise or concealing a few upsides of the information vector in a stochastic manner, $\tilde{x}\, M_D\left(\tilde{x}/x\right)\tilde{x}M_D\left(\tilde{x}/x\right)$ then, the augmented autoencoder will be prepared to recover the original input from the corrupted sequence.

$$\tilde{x}^i\,\mathcal{M}_D\tilde{x}^i|x^i \tag{4}$$

$$Loss = L(\theta,\emptyset) = \frac{1}{n}\sum_{i=1}^{n}[x^{(i)} - f_\theta(g_\emptyset(\tilde{x}^i))]^2 \tag{5}$$

where $\mathcal{M}_D$ characterizes the true data pixel intensities to the noisy pixel intensities. To correct the halfway-destroyed input, the de-noise autoencoder has to notice and include the connection between the measurements of the contribution to determine missing parts. For a high dimensional contribution with high repetition, similar to images, the model will likely rely on evidence accumulated from a combination of many information measurements to restore the noise anomaly rather than overfitting a measurement. This develops a decent facility for learning robust inherent representation.

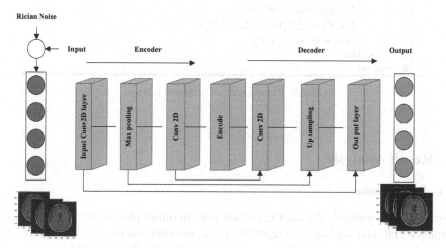

Fig. 2. Proposed augmented autoencoder based DCNN architecture

Figure 2 shows the block diagram of the extended autoencoder with the basic three components encoder, code, and decoder. The encoder partially destroys the input MR image and displays it as x-vector, and code or bottleneck leads this sparse display to the decoder.

The proposed Augmented Autoencoder Denoising algorithm is applied to Kaggle dataset. The input data is represented with x^i and trained with noisy data set with $\tilde{X}$ and it automatically reconstructs the original image from the distorted MR image data set of the brain with the aid of the proposed pre-trained CNN loss function $L(x,\hat{X})$ which is based on the augmented autoencoder. The MRI images are recorded with the aid of a DICOM viewer. From the experiment result, Axial T2 view images are taken. These experiments were performed on a 1.5-T MRI imaging machine so that it provides the pathology of the disease. The image consists of layer thickness is 5 mm and resolution are 256 x 256. The distance between the two layers is 1.5 mm (Fig. 3).

Algorithm Augmented Autoencoder Denoising
1: AAD Training $(e, b, x, c, 1, \theta)$
2:    $x^i = [x_1, x_2 \ldots x_n] \in R^{n*m}$ *is the matrix representation input image* , $x_i \in [0,1]^m (1 \leq i \leq m)$
3:    *t is the no of epochs*
4:    *b is the expected batches*
5:    *l is the learning rate*
6:    *n is the noise corrupted level*
7:    $g(.)$ *Encoder in terms of* $\emptyset$
8:    $f(.)$ *The decoder in terms of* θ
9:    $\theta = \{W, b, b_n\}$ *where* $W \in R^{n*d}, b \in R^d, b \in R^d, b_n \in R^d$ *are AAD Parameters*
10:      **for** 0 to t **do**
11:        **for** 0 to b **do**
12:          $\tilde{X} = getNoisyImage(x, n)$
13:          $s = sigmoid(\tilde{X} * W + b)$
14:          $\hat{X} = sigmoid(s * W^T + b)$
15:          $L(x, \hat{X}) = \frac{1}{n}\sum_{i=1}^{n}[x^{(i)} - f_\theta(g_\emptyset(\hat{X}^i))]^2$
16:          $Cost = mean(L(x, \hat{X}))$
17:        **end for**
18:      **end for**

Fig. 3. Pseudo code of proposed method

4   Result Analysis

4.1   Rician Noise

Image noise is probably the most important issue in image processing. Numerous techniques for eliminating Gaussian repetitive noise, motivational noise, Poisson noise, and multiplicative noise have been proposed over the years [25]. Because MRI is widespread, people constantly worry about another compelling noise, the Rician noise. The image corrupted by Rician noise can be indicated numerically by

$$y = \sqrt{x + n_1^2 + n_2^2} \qquad (6)$$

where x is the input image and n_1, n_2 $N(0, \sigma^2)$. We will likely track down the unexplained true image x from the debased image y as well as could be expected.

4.2   Performance Parameters

Based on performance metrics quality of the denoising filter is classified. Those are defined as follows.

4.2.1 Mean Square Error (MSE)

One available method of estimating this similarity is to quantify an error signal by removing the test signal from the reference and then calculating the normal energy of the error signal. The mean square error (MSE) is the least difficult and is the most commonly used to estimate image quality.

$$MSE = \frac{1}{MN} \sum_{i=1}^{M} \sum_{j=1}^{N} (x(i,j) - j(i,j))^2 \tag{7}$$

4.2.2 Peak Signal to Noise Ratio (PSNR)

It consists of two images that are original and distorted. PSNR values can be determined by separating these two images.it is calculated by using the following formula.

$$PSNR = 10 \log_{10}(\frac{R^2}{MSE}) \tag{8}$$

R is the maximum deviation of the input image data type. If the input is an 8-bit unsigned integer data type, then R is 255, and so on.

4.2.3 Structural Similarity Index Measurements (SSIM)

The difference to various techniques that are then referred to, for example, MSE or PSNR, is that these methods estimate the highest error, on the other hand, SSIM is a judgment-based model that regards image falsification as a change in the primary information seen and at the same time critical perception miracles united. Including both luminance obfuscation and the terms used to hide contrasts. Fundamental information consists of pixels which have strong intermediate conditions, especially if they are spatially close to one another. These conditions convey critical information about the layout of the items in the visual scene.

$$SSIM\,(x,y) = \frac{(2\mu_x\mu_y + c_1)(2\sigma + c_2)}{(\mu_x^2 + \mu_x^2 + c_1)(\sigma_x^2 + \sigma_y^2 + c_2)} \tag{9}$$

The test results in the analysis contain both synthetic and real patient data. The synthetic MR images come from the Brain Web database [26] and the Kaggle database [27]. The synthetic PD-weighted T1 and T2 MR images are recorded with and without noise. Each MR image of the brain is produced with a resolution of. Recorded and the encoding intensity is 256 digital bins. Rician noise is varied according to σ value variation and $\sigma = 0$ is without noise, which is taken as the ground truth image for validation of results. Different levels of Rician noise (percent %) are added to the MR images. The dataset is comprised of clinical MRI accumulated from the Kaggle dataset.

To train the model, we took an MRI image of 255 × 255 into account. This image expands to 544 × 544. This is shown in Fig. 4. The Rician noise was added to the MR image of the brain at an interval of 2%. The augmented autoencoder-based DCNN

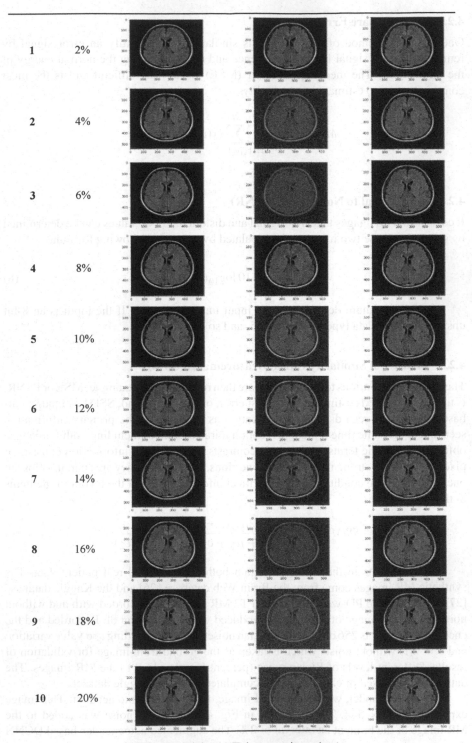

1	2%
2	4%
3	6%
4	8%
5	10%
6	12%
7	14%
8	16%
9	18%
10	20%

Fig. 4. T1 weighted MR image noise reduction

method is applied to the noisy image. The results obtained with the proposed method at 2% Rician noise are MSE = 0.0011, SSIM = 0.9357 and PSNR = 39.91.

Table 1 shows the proposed training model architecture of the Augmented Autoencoder-based DCNN with input, an output layer, and parameter specifications. The architecture consists of an image input layer with the specification (544, 544, 1), 2D convolution layer (Conv10) with the specification (544, 544, 16), 2D upscaling with (1088, 1088, 16), again a 2D Convolution layer with (1088, 1088, 1) and a 2D max pooling layer with (544, 544, 1). Table 2 shows the epoch loss function variation when training input images at 2% and 20% Rician noise and the associated graphs are shown in Fig. 4.

Table 1. Train model architecture of augmented autoencoder based DCNN

Layer type	Output layer	Parameter
input_1 (input layers)	(None, 544, 544, 1)	0
Conv10 (Conv2D)	(None, 544, 544, 16)	160
upsample5 (UpSampling2D)	(None, 1088, 1088, 16)	0
Conv1 (Conv2D)	(None, 1088, 1088, 1)	145
pool1 (MaxPooling2D)	(None, 544, 544, 1)	0

From this table to train the total parameters are 305, trainable parameters are 305 and non-trainable parameters are 0.

Table 2. Epochs Vs Loss function at 2% and 20% Rician noise

Epochs	Time	Loss	Epochs	Time	Loss
1	5 s 686 ms	1.5945	1	1 s 733 ms	2.2008
2	4 s 537 ms	0.6125	2	0 s 39 ms	2.1737
3	4 s 539 ms	0.5193	3	0 s 39 ms	2.1193
4	4 s 545 ms	0.4683	4	0 s 41 ms	2.0360
5	4 s 546 ms	0.4408	5	0 s 35 ms	1.8966
6	4 s 551 ms	0.4256	6	0 s 35 ms	1.6885
7	4 s 557 ms	0.4135	7	0 s 35 ms	1.4096
8	4 s 559 ms	0.4045	8	0 s 41 ms	1.0402
9	5 s 564 ms	0.4037	9	0 s 36 ms	0.8192
10	5 s 571 ms	0.4010	10	0 s 36 ms	0.6894
11	5 s 577 ms	0.3997	11	0 s 33 ms	0.6232

(continued)

Table 2. (*continued*)

Epochs	Time	Loss	Epochs	Time	Loss
12	5 s 579 ms	0.3983	12	0 s 39 ms	0.5818
13	5 s 583 ms	0.3971	13	0 s 30 ms	0.5558
14	5 s 588 ms	0.3954	14	0 s 35 ms	0.5377
15	5 s 597 ms	0.3945	15	0 s 31 ms	0.5240
16	5 s 601 ms	0.3939	16	0 s 33 ms	0.5127
17	5 s 608 ms	0.3934	17	0 s 36 ms	0.5031
18	5 s 614 ms	0.3930	18	0 s 31 ms	0.4945
19	5 s 617 ms	0.3928	19	0 s 30 ms	0.4868
20	5 s 621 ms	0.3926	20	0 s 33 ms	0.4798

Table 3. Performance measurements of the proposed method in terms of MSE, SSIM, and PSNR

Noise level	MSE	SSIM	PSNR
2%	0.0011	0.93576	39.91
4%	0.0099	0.93113	39.14
6%	0.0122	0.87218	38.88
8%	0.0135	0.83411	38.17
10%	0.0155	0.82449	37.42
12%	0.0213	0.80250	37.00
14%	0.0245	0.78088	36.32
16%	0.0249	0.74707	36.01
18%	0.0307	0.73702	34.19
20%	0.0430	0.62684	32.36

Table 3 shows the results obtained with the proposed method on T1-weighted MRI images. As the Rician noise variance increases, the PSNR decreases.

Figure 4 contains simulated results from T1-weighted brain MRI images. The simulated MRT image is available with a slice thickness of 1 mm to 9 mm; in the proposed method, we have taken the slice thickness of 2 mm into account. The variance intensity level of the ricin noise from 0% to 20% and the variance level of the bias field from 0% to 40%. The MRT data shown in the figure are cut in the axial plane. Table 3 shows the results obtained with the proposed method on T1-weighted MRI images. As the Rician noise variance increases, the PSNR decreases.

From this table to calculate the time and loss function at 2% to 20%, to train the 20 epochs of rician noise.

Table 4. The PSNR comparison with state-of-the-art methods

Noise level	ADF [28]	LMMSE [29]	TV [30]	PSNLM [31]	Proposed
2%	33.33	36.38	36.87	37.60	**39.91**
4%	27.48	32.41	33.19	33.93	**39.01**
6%	24.19	30.50	30.30	31.78	**38.88**
8%	21.86	28.32	28.53	30.12	**38.17**
10%	20.64	27.01	27.21	29.14	**37.42**
12%	19.42	25.48	25.63	27.93	**37.00**
14%	18.74	25.38	25.18	26.92	**36.32**
16%	17.86	24.45	24.69	26.13	**36.01**
18%	17.86	23.16	23.36	25.34	**34.19**
20%	16.91	22.34	22.40	24.52	**32.36**

Table 4 and Fig. 5 show the comparison results. The PSNR value was obtained with different Rician noise variance levels in 2% steps (2% to 20%). From Table 4 it can be seen that the proposed methods for noise suppression according to Rician are relatively good compared to Anisotropic Diffusion Filter (ADF), Linear Minimum Mean Square Error (LMMSE), and Total Variation Minimization (TV) Pre-Smoothing Nonlocal Mean (PSNLM.).

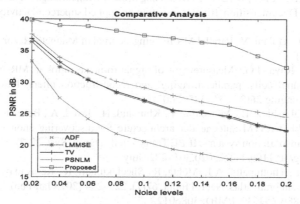

Fig. 5. Comparative Results

The results obtained for the proposed method using Jupiter python3.7 in Intel (R) Core (TM) i5–9500 CPU@3.00 GHz.

5 Conclusion

In this research work, we developed a DCNN based on Augmented Autoencoder for efficient brain MRI Rician noise suppression. In particular, batch normalization and residual learning are used to improve noise reduction performance. To validate the proposed methodology, extensive simulations are carried out with benchmark MRI data from the Kaggle database and real-time data sets. Performance is measured using Mean Square Error (MSE), Structural Similarity Index Measure (SSIM), and Peak Signal-to-Noise Ratio (PSNR). The results obtained with the proposed method at 2% Rician noise are MSE = 0.0011, SSIM = 0.9357 and PSNR = 39.91. Our advanced autoencoder can achieve promising results at high Rician noise levels and performs better than state-of-the-art deep learning architectures. Our future research will depend on extending this advanced autoencoder architecture for the classification of brain MRI tumors by increasing the noise reduction performance. The proposed scheme can be applied to reduce the Rician noise in MR images and it can also extend to the analysis of the brain tumor.

References

1. Anjanappa, C., Sheshadri, H.S.: Denoising of Rician noise in Magnitude MRI Images using wavelet shrinkage and fusion method. IOSR Journal of VLSI and Signal Processing (IOSR-JVSP) **6**(5), pp. 54–63, Ver. II (Sep. - Oct. 2016). e-ISSN: 2319 – 4200, p-ISSN No. : 2319 – 4197
2. Benjamin, Y.M.K.: Impulse noise reduction in brain magnetic resonance imaging using fuzzy filters. World Academy of Science, Engineering and Technology (2011)
3. Toprak, A.: Impulse noise reduction in medical images with the use of switch mode fuzzy adaptive median filter. Digital signal **17**, 711–723 (2007)
4. He, L., Greenshields, I.R.: A nonlocal maximum likelihood estimation method for Rician noise reduction in MR images. IEEE Trans Med Imaging **28**, 165–172 (2009)
5. Xu, L., Wang, C., Chen, W., Liu, X.: Denoising Multi-Channel Images in Parallel MRI by Low Rank Matrix Decomposition. IEEE transaction on applied superconductivity **24**(5), (October 2014)
6. Deshmane, A., Gulani, V.: Parallel MR imaging. Journal of Magnetic Resonance Imaging **36**, 55–72 (2012)
7. Dietrich, O., Raya, J.G.: Measurement of signal-to-noise ratios in MR images: influence of multi-channel coils, parallel imaging, and reconstruction filters. Journal of Magnetic Resonance Imaging **26**(2), 375–385 (2007)
8. Ashraf, J., Bakhshi, A.D., Moustafa, N., Khurshid, H., Javed, A., Beheshti, A.: Novel deep learning-enabled LSTM autoencoder architecture for discovering anomalous events from intelligent transportation systems. IEEE Trans. Intell. Transp. Syst. **22**(7), 4507–4518 (2021). https://doi.org/10.1109/TITS.2020.3017882. July
9. Sivaswamy, J., Thottupattu, A.J., Mehta, R., Sheelakumari, R., Kesavadas, C.: Construction of Indian human brain atlas. Neurol India. **67**(1), 229–234 (2019 Jan-Feb). https://doi.org/10.4103/0028-3886.253639. PMID: 30860125
10. Palumbo, L., et al.: Evaluation of the intra- and inter-method agreement of brain MRI segmentation software packages: a comparison between SPM12 and FreeSurfer v6.0". Physica Medica **64**, 261–272 (2019). ISSN 1120-1797
11. Gaillochet, M., Tezcan, K.C., Konukoglu, E.: Joint Reconstruction and Bias Field Correction for Undersampled MR Imaging. In: Martel, A.L., et al. (eds.) MICCAI 2020. LNCS, vol. 12262, pp. 44–52. Springer, Cham (2020). https://doi.org/10.1007/978-3-030-59713-9_5
12. Dhieb, M., Masmoudi, S., Oud, M.B.M., Arfia, F.B.: 2-D Entropy Image Segmentation on Thresholding Based on Particle Swarm Optimization (PSO). In: 1st International Conference on Advanced Technologies for Signal and Image processing (ATSIP), pp. 143–147 (2014). https://doi.org/10.1109/ATSIP.2014.6834594

13. Chen, B., Zou, Q.-H., Li, Y.: A new image segmentation model with local statistical characters based on variance minimization. Appl. Math. Model. **39**(12), 3227–3235 (2014)
14. Zhang, X., et al.: Multilevel filtering image denoising algorithm based on edge information fusion. In: Sixteenth National Conference on Laser Technology and Optoelectronics, 2021, p. 119070. Shanghai, China (2021). https://doi.org/10.1117/12.2601816
15. Zhang, H., Fritts, J., Goldman, S.: An entropy-based objective evaluation method for image segmentation. In: Proc. SPIE-Storage and Retrieval Methods and Application for Watershed Transform Multimedia, pp. 38–49 (2004)
16. Hahn, H.K., et al.: The Skull stripping Problem in MRI solved by a Single 3D. In: Proc. MICCAI, LNCS, pp 134–143. Springer, Berlin (2000)
17. Maryam, H., Mustapha, A., Younes, J.: A multilevel thresholding method for image segmentation based on multiobjective particle swarm optimization. International Conference on wireless technologies, Embedded and Intelligent systems (WITS), pp. 1–6 (2017). https://doi.org/10.1109/WITS.2017.7934620
18. Pham, T.X., Siarry, P., Oulhadj, H.: A multi-objective optimization approach for brain MRI segmentation using fuzzy entropy clustering and region-based active contour methods. Magn. Reson. Imaging **61**, 41–65 (2019)
19. Coello Coello, C.A., González Brambila, S., Figueroa Gamboa, J., Castillo Tapia, M.G., Hernández Gómez, R.: Evolutionary multiobjective optimization: open research areas and some challenges lying ahead. Complex & Intelligent Systems **6**(2), 221–236 (2019). https://doi.org/10.1007/s40747-019-0113-4
20. Wang, G., et al.: Impacts of skull stripping on construction of three-dimensional T1-weighted imaging-based brain structural network in full-term neonates. BioMed Eng OnLine **19**, 41 (2020). https://doi.org/10.1186/s12938-020-00785-0
21. Kidoh, M., et al.: Deep learning based noise reduction for brain MR imaging: tests on phantoms and healthy volunteers. Magn Reson Med Sci. **19**(3), 195–206 (2020 Aug 3). https://doi.org/10.2463/mrms.mp.2019-0018. Epub 2019 Sep 4. PMID: 31484849; PMCID: PMC7553817
22. Heo, Y.-C., Kim, K., Lee, Y.: Image Denoising Using Non-Local Means (NLM) Approach in Magnetic Resonance (MR) Imaging: A Systematic Review. Appl Aci. **10**, 7028 (2020). https://doi.org/10.3390/app10207028
23. Yasuda, M., Koizumi, Y., Saito, S., Uematsu, H., Imoto, K.: Sound Event Localization Based on Sound Intensity Vector Refined by Dnn-Based Denoising and Source Separation. ICASSP 2020 - 2020 IEEE International Conference on Acoustics, Speech and Signal Processing (ICASSP), pp. 651–655 (2020). https://doi.org/10.1109/ICASSP40776.2020.9054462
24. Nageshwar Rao, B., Laxmi Srinivasa Reddy, D., Bhaskar, G.: Thyroid Diagnosis Using Multilayer Perceptron. In: Satapathy, S.C., Raju, K.S., Shyamala, K., Krishna, D.R., Favorskaya, M.N. (eds.) ICETE 2019. LAIS, vol. 3, pp. 452–459. Springer, Cham (2020). https://doi.org/10.1007/978-3-030-24322-7_56
25. Lu, J., Tian, J., Shen, L., Jiang, Q., Zeng, X., Zou, Y.: Rician Noise Removal via a Learned Dictionary. Mathematical Problems in Engineering vol. 2019, Article ID 8535206, p. 13 (2019). https://doi.org/10.1155/2019/8535206
26. Kwan, R.K.-S., Evans, A.C., Pike, G.B.: MRI simulation-based evaluation of image-processing and classification methods. IEEE Transactions on Medical Imaging **18**(11), 1085–97 (Nov 1999)
27. Mohammed, E., Hassaan, M., Amin, S., Ebied, H.M.: Brain Tumor Segmentation: A Comparative Analysis. In: Hassanien, A.E., et al. (eds.) AICV 2021. AISC, vol. 1377, pp. 505–514. Springer, Cham (2021). https://doi.org/10.1007/978-3-030-76346-6_46
28. Yang, J., Fan, J., Ai, D., Zhou, S., Tang, S., Wang, Y.: Brain MR image denoising for Rician noise using pre-smooth non-local means filter. Biomed Eng Online **14**, 2 (2015). Published 2015 Jan 9. https://doi.org/10.1186/1475-925X-14-2

29. Aja-Fernandez, S., Alberola-Lopez, C., Westin, C.F.: Noise and signal estimation in magnitude MRI and Rician distributed images: a LMMSE approach. IEEE Trans Image Process. **17**(8), 1383–1398 (2008)
30. Getreuer, P., Tong, M., Vese, L.A.: A variational model for the restoration of MR images corrupted by blur and rician noise. Advances in Visual Computing, Lecture Notes in Computer Science **6938**, 686–698 (2011)
31. Foi, A.: Noise estimation and removal in mr imaging: The variance-stabilization approach. In: Biomedical Imaging:From Nano to Macro, 2011 IEEE International Symposium on. IEEE, 1809–14 (2011)

An Efficient Mobility Aware Scheduling Algorithm

Pankaj Sharma[✉][iD] and P. K. Gupta[iD]

Department of Computer Science and Engineering, Jaypee University of Information Technology, Waknaghat, India
pankajuppal.22@gmail.com, pkgupta@ieee.org

Abstract. In this new era of computing, stakeholders are moving towards IoT devices, supporting the seamless accessibility of service for IoT devices and applications becomes a critical challenge, particularly in an environment that does not rely on the centralized Cloud-based management system to support the interaction between the mobile users and Fog nodes. To support the excellent accessibility of Fog, mobile applications. In this paper, a mobility aware framework and algorithm is presented. The proposed framework consists of several IoT Devices and fog nodes that ensures the seamless accessibility of fog services to the mobile IoT device. In the experimentation's, we have considered the QoS parameters like execution time, Network bandwidth. Obtained simulation results represents that the proposed algorithms provides uninterrupted service to the various IoT devices.

Keywords: Mobility · Mapper · Fog computing · Scheduling algorithm · IoT

1 Introduction

The incredible development in smart devices has resulted in the proliferation of IoT devices [3]. These devices can be fixed or portable and generate a large stream of data with massive processing and storage requirements. Consequently, these IoT devices support the utilization of centralized Cloud Computing based systems for further processing of captured data at the back-end [6,7] . The computational requirements of these devices get increase as the communication and computation potential of wearable and smart devices persistently improve. One of the important facets of this new epoch of computing is that data creation and utilization are mainly distributed at the network's edges [2]. Moreover, the centralized cloud computing infrastructure along with its network connection is not compatible with huge amount of data from the edge. In this perspective, data management and computing models that strengthens the growing demand for computing capability at the network edge, are the main concern in research. Most of the application processing in the centralized cloud data centre does not consider user mobility locations; execution of an application can occurs at numerous geographically dispersed data centres [1]. Fog computing is the computational model that resolve the above issue and also known as computing at the cloud edge. Fog Computing also termed as "Edge Computing" exploit the network edge [11] where smart devices, mobile devices etc so called IoT are considered as shown in Fig. 1. Vehicular networks, IoT with fog environments are instances of this distributed computing sculpt which influences the edge capacity nearer to data production [12]. Data creation and utilization can occur at different times and locations. According to this perspective, various applications can have diverse needs, particularly response time. At the edge of network in distributed computing system, execution of data might be retained nearer to the end-user. As a result, it may reduce the network causing traffic to data centres and improve the overall response time of the applications; as an outcome of this, network latency might be low [25].

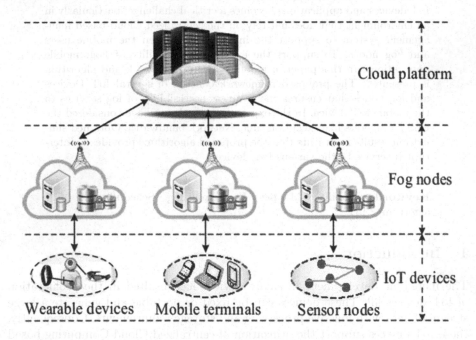

Fig. 1. IoT -Fog framework [10,15] .

Numerous resource scheduling algorithms across fog and edge computing environment has been proposed in the recent years [4,8,17]. All of these schemes based on the aspect how services can be mapped to mobile devices, edge resource. In this paper, a mobility aware framework and algorithm is proposed to overcome the various performance related issue. Here, we have considered the QoS parameters like execution time, Network bandwidth and appraise the allocation policy. The proposed framework consists of several IoT Devices and fog nodes which utilises fog for its real-time mobile applications. These mobile applications faces the novel issue of providing the seamless accessibility of Fog services to the mobile IoT device. Whenever the tasks originate from ubiquitous mobile applications Fog computing tackles the issue of mobility, where the data sources are moving objects.

The rest of the paper is prepared in the given order. Section 2 contains the correlated works on mobility aware scheduling strategy, and Sect. 3 provides the proposed framework. Section 4 provides the detailed result analysis. Finally, Sect. 5 concludes this work.

2 Related Work

Luiz et al. (2017) [1] have presented the scheduling issues and challenges that arise due to user mobility in the hierarchical environment of the fog-cloud system. They have considered the various user mobility scenarios at the edges based on their requirements. Varshney et al. (2019) [20] have discussed several studies in cloud computing about resource allocation and resource availability on the basis of QoS requirements. Singh et al. (2017) [18] provided some challenges regarding full usage of healthcare in cloud computing. This paper discusses about a survey whcich was conducted among 320 urban and rural Indian hospitals. It was concluded that many hospitals were opting for the utilisation of cloud computing technology. Saini et al. (2011) [14] presented a semantic similarity measure, which considers each term as a phrase or single word. The weights allotted to each term is given on the basis of its semantic importance. The authors have used this measure in combination with other standard similarity measure as Jaccard and cosine. Further to optimise the weights the genetic algorithm (GA) has been used.

Muhammad et al. (2018) [24] focuses on the issue of mobility in the fog computing environment. The authors have identified the proximity in a dynamic environment by measuring out the mobility factors. Jingrong wang et al. (2018) [25] have predicted system information uncertainties by implementing the mobility management technique based on Q learning. In this technique, mobile user equipment monitors the task delay and aquires the optimal mobility management strategy with the help of trials and errors. The obtained simulated results represent that the proposed schemes handle uncertainties better than the traditional schemes.

S Ghosh et al. (2019) [6] have presented the mobility-based fog, cloud, and edge-based real-time scenarios. This work analyses the spatiotemporal mobility data with the appropriate information. It sets up a machine-learning algorithm to predict the location of the real-time mobile users. The buildup Spatio-temporal information of the mobile users is represented using the probabilistic graphical model. The obtained experimental results for the proposed mobility prediction algorithm scores 93% accuracy, minimises the delay and less power consumption by 23–26% and 37–41% respectively, as compared to the existing mobility-aware task delegation system.

Wenhan et al. (2020) [25] explored the problem of offloading decisions and resource allocation by one base station among multiple users. The authors have proposed a heuristic mobility aware offloading algorithm (HMAOA) to achieve the optimal arrangement. Experimental results demonstrate that the proposed scheme achieves offloading performance with high efficiency. Sharma P et al. (2021') [16] have described an adaptive service placement model in fog computing environment. In this work a QoS service allocation framework has been projected. Within the fog nodes the allocation of service requests is ensured with the help of proposed framework. The efficient node can be detected by analyzing the performance parameters of fog node i.e average response time and execution cost. Service allocation has been done by using hybrid bee mutation method . Performance analysis of the proposed service placement method has been conducted based on different performance parameters like average response time, cost effectiveness, throughput, and several other metrics. The comparison of the proposed model is done with exiting genetic based algorithm. Varshney et al. (2020) [21] have presented a model for service placement in fog computing environment. The author have considered CPU cycle, processing speed, maximum latency, storage and network bandwidth. The results showed the improved efficiency of the Fog network.

Mukherjee et al. (2019) [13] projected a prototype based on two fold for solving (i) mobility issue of mobile devices, since these devices are moving with different speeds , (ii) job placement was very complicated when the location of mobile device always changed. All these problems has been resolved via a technique which utilises remote cloud server by the mobile devices for task execution. In case the connection gets interrupted between a mobile device and server, a message sent by the server, in order to reconnect the device in form of a push notification to the server. To rectify the location issue, migration of virtual machine concept has been adopted. The suggested task reduces the power consumption by 30–63 %. The results are attained using a mobile device with different speeds inside and outside the proposed environment. Kanupriya et al. (2021) [23] have proposed and implemented rank-based mobility aware scheduling algorithms which ranks teh resources on the basis of related information. The algorithm was implemented on the MobFogSim and compared with Distance-based scheduling technique. The obtained results show the rank-based scheduling algorithm outperforms the Distance-based scheduling technique. Varshney et al. (2021) [22] proposed a resource management approach by using AHP technique. This technique helps in managing the Fog resources on a priority basis. Tanissia D et al. (2021) [5] presented a model to identify the future locations of IoT objects, integrating migration and mobility information. The proposed work examines the service placement problem in the fog environment to minimize energy consumption as an optimization problem and improve the Quality of Services (QoS). The authors proposed a location history-based mobility model (HTM) to detect the IoT mobile nodes future locations. Later, presented a framework consisting of Mobility-aware Genetic Algorithm (MGA) for services migrations and online strategies for IoT services placement.

3   Proposed Methodology

A fog network is composed of Fog middleware that consists of several IoT Devices and fog nodes. Here, each fog node is in control of a specific coverage area and a set of fog nodes forms a location area (LA). A tier partition concept has been implemented that improves the granularity of location description [19]. A tier is a subset of a fog node and the service area of each tier consists of n number of mobile nodes which are controlled by the concerned middleware at the centre of all the tiers. Here, the role of mediator is performed by the middleware between the mobile nodes and fog nodes. This work proposes a proactive approach for Fog computing, which supports process migration and proactive Fog service discovery using Hidden Markov Model. Figure 1 shows the proposed mobility aware system framework.

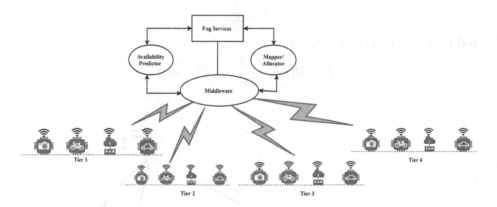

Fig. 2. Proposed mobility aware system framework.

3.1   Physical Availability Prediction

The random variable P1(t) represents the hidden state at time t, and the random variable P2(t) corresponds to the location visited at time t (with P2(t) $\in$ P21, P22). There also exist some conditional dependencies between these random variables P1(t) and P2 (t). Here, the the hidden variable P1(t) conditional probability distribution at time t, relies on the hidden variable P(t -1) value. Whereas, the value of the observed location P2(t) relies on the hidden variable P1(t); at time t. We have to calculate these probabilities for a given observation sequence.

Presented equations are centered and set on a separate line.

$$P(2) = \sum P(2|1)P(1) \tag{1}$$

where, P1 is a hidden variable, i.e. previous location of user P1= P(11),P(12), P(13), and P2 is the current location of the user, visited at time t, and denoted

by P2= <P(21), P(22), P(23),âĂę..>. Training of HMM means output sequence P1 is given, and we have to find the best set of output probabilities and state transition. On the basis of the movement type of the mobile device Md, the physical availability is predicted. The movement type helps to find the movement direction. HMM, model prediction helps to locate the position of the Mobile device Md in the near future. The type of movement is predicted on the basis of the movement direction of Md to the Fn. Here, we have considered two different types of movements i.e., a movement towards Fd, and a move apart from Fd. On the basis of Hidden Markov Model the movement type is predicted, i.e. the mobile resource current location depends on its previous location. The locations of Md are found with the help of GPS, that is assumed to be a part of the Fog layer. The distance between Md and the Fd is calculated using the Haversine formula. Where D is computed as the previous distance to Md.
Presented equations are set on a separate line and centered.

$$D = R\alpha \tag{2}$$

and R is the radius and distance

$$D = R(sin^{-1}\frac{d}{2R^2}\sqrt{4R^2 - d^2}) \tag{3}$$

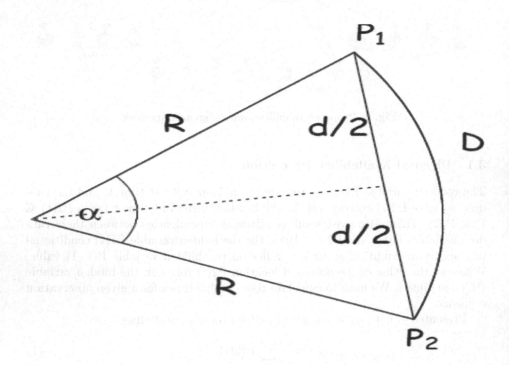

Fig. 3. Physical availability prediction.

Shown Equations are set on a separate line and centered.

$$Mobility = (P1 - P2)/Timetaken from P1 to P2 \tag{4}$$

$$Physical Availability = Fog node coverage area - P2/Mobility \tag{5}$$

$$Physical Availability Factor = Physical Availability/tier resident time \tag{6}$$

3.2 Mapper and Allocator

The mapping process performs mapping processes like task requirement, system state and mobile user identification. Mapping the system's fog node id makes the mobile user identification. Mapping takes place by representing the task requirement with the dynamically predicted mobile user location. In case, the mobile user requirements are satisfied, the availability of the fog node or resource is sent to the allocator function. Resource states are also taken into considerations that consist of running and queuing requests at a given time. Attributes are defined to represent appropriately compared resource states. To include the scheduling information the scheduling policies need to be placed into the state attributes which are reflected by policy attributes. Three important attributes information are known as the candidate policy attributes for resource states, i.e. requests in execution, request in mobile queue user, and remaining requests. This job credential information is frequently used to predict the fog node's status. Fundamentally, the algorithm allocates the job to fog nodes based on computational power in descending order, such as it allocates more powerful machines first among the other fog nodes in middleware. If the number of fog node is equal to no. of resource required, then optimal allocation takes place. However, some tiers might not have enough available fog nodes. In this case, the proposed algorithm revert back to the last level where by including one more fog node would result into more number of available resources as required. After the optimal allocation is completed the system allocates resource and utilises minimum available resource instead of maximum to another round of allocation.

Table 1. Resource state parameter.

Abbreviations	State Attribute	Calculations
ReqExecution	Categorized number of running requests	X=nYi
QueueReq	Categorized number of the queue request	X=nQi
ReqRunRemain	Categorized sum of remaining processor Xtime of running job	X=\sum remaint (j)XCPU(j)

4   Results and Discussion

The Proposed mobility aware framework was simulated on iFogsim [9]. The simulation tool, iFogsim can be applied on various platforms such as Windows and Linux with other configurations like 8 GB memory, Dual core intel processor with frequency of 1.87 GHz. This section shows evaluation done for the proposed mobility aware scheduling algorithm in a fog computing environment and performed various simulations using iFogSim. Here, we have considered the various parameters like execution time, Network bandwidth and appraise the allocation policy based on QoS parameters.

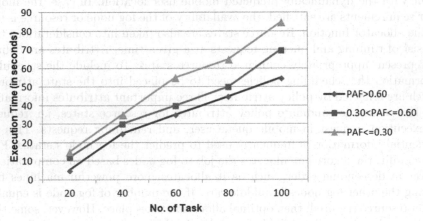

Fig. 4. Analysis of physical availability factor.

As shown in Fig. 4, The experiment was conducted to investigate the effects of physical availability of mobile devices on execution time.the execution time increases with respect to decreases in the physical availability factor. The proposed mobility aware framework has also been appraised using different performance metrics based on its recitation. The proposed framework considers the four fog devices that provide performances.

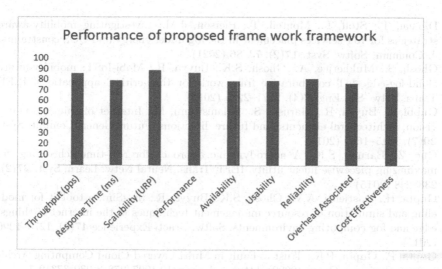

Fig. 5. Performance of various parameters based on proposed algorithm.

5 Conclusion

In this paper, a Mobility aware scheduling policy is proposed for predicting the mobile node location and allocating the mobile users requests to the fog devices. The proposed framework makes use of fog computing to improve the various QoS parameters like execution time, Network bandwidth and appraise the allocation policy. The physical availability prediction uses the movement type, movement pattern and movement direction of the fog node. The experiment results have depicted the consequence of physical availability on execution time, usability, reliability, and overall effectiveness of the proposed system. We have obtained the average overhead for the proposed framework is 76.6%, which is equivalent to cost-effectiveness of 73.4%.In future, a more efficient mobility aware scheduling algorithm and service placement algorithms will also be adopt to handle the requests from the more heterogeneous and geographically dispersed environment.

References

1. Bittencourt, L.F., Diaz-Montes, J., Buyya, R., Rana, O.F., Parashar, M.: Mobility-aware application scheduling in Fog computing. IEEE Cloud Comput. 4(2), 26–35 (2017)
2. Brogi, A., Forti, S., Ibrahim, A.: Deploying fog applications: how much does it cost, by the way? Small 1(2), 20 (2018)
3. Chiang, M., Zhang, T.: Fog and IoT: an overview of research opportunities. IEEE Internet Things J. 3(6), 854–864 (2016)
4. Dastjerdi, A.V., Gupta, H., Calheiros, R.N., Ghosh, S.K., Buyya, R.: Fog computing: principles, architectures, and applications. In: Internet of things, pp. 61–75. Elsevier (2016)

5. Djemai, T., Stolf, P., Monteil, T., Pierson, J.M.: Investigating mobility-aware strategies for IoT services placement in the fog under energy and QOS constraints. J. Commun. Softw. Syst. **17**(2), 73–86 (2021)
6. Ghosh, S., Mukherjee, A., Ghosh, S.K., Buyya, R.: Mobi-IoST: mobility-aware cloud-fog-edge-IoT collaborative framework for time-critical applications. IEEE Trans. Netw. Sci. Eng. **7**(4), 2271–2285 (2019)
7. Gubbi, J., Buyya, R., Marusic, S., Palaniswami, M.: Internet of things (IoT): a vision, architectural elements, and future directions. Futur. Gener. Comput. Syst. **29**(7), 1645–1660 (2013)
8. Guo, Z., Baruah, S.K.: A neurodynamic approach for real-time scheduling via maximizing piecewise linear utility. IEEE Trans. Neural Netw. Learn. Syst. **27**(2), 238–248 (2015)
9. Gupta, H., Dastjerdi, A.V., Ghosh, S.K., Buyya, R.: iFogSim: a toolkit for modeling and simulation of resource management techniques in the internet of things, edge and fog computing environments. Softw. Pract. Experience **47**(9), 1275–1296 (2017)
10. Gupta, P., Gupta, P.K.: Trust & Fault in Multi Layered Cloud Computing Architecture. Springer, Cham (2020). https://doi.org/10.1007/978-3-030-37319-1
11. Khan, W.Z., Ahmed, E., Hakak, S., Yaqoob, I., Ahmed, A.: Edge computing: a survey. Futur. Gener. Comput. Syst. **97**, 219–235 (2019)
12. Liu, X.y., Wu, M.Y.: Vehicular CPS: an application of IoT in vehicular networks. Jisuanji Yingyong/ J. Comput. Appl. **32**(4), 900–904 (2012)
13. Mukherjee, A., Roy, D.G., De, D.: Mobility-aware task delegation model in mobile cloud computing. J. Supercomput. **75**(1), 314–339 (2019). https://doi.org/10.1007/s11227-018-02729-x
14. Saini, M., Sharma, D., Gupta, P.K.: Enhancing information retrieval efficiency using semantic-based-combined-similarity-measure. In: 2011 International Conference on Image Information Processing, pp. 1–4 (2011). https://doi.org/10.1109/ICIIP.2011.6108982
15. Sharma, P., Gupta, P.: QoS-aware CR-BM-based hybrid framework to improve the fault tolerance of fog devices. J. Appl. Res. Technol. **19**(1), 66–76 (2021)
16. Sharma, P., Gupta, P.K.: An adaptive service placement framework in fog computing environment. In: Singh, M., Tyagi, V., Gupta, P.K., Flusser, J., Ören, T., Sonawane, V.R. (eds.) ICACDS 2021. CCIS, vol. 1440, pp. 729–738. Springer, Cham (2021). https://doi.org/10.1007/978-3-030-81462-5_64
17. Singh, J., Betha, S., Mangipudi, B., Auluck, N.: Contention aware energy efficient scheduling on heterogeneous multiprocessors. IEEE Trans. Parallel Distrib. Syst. **26**(5), 1251–1264 (2014)
18. Singh, M., Gupta, P.K., Srivastava, V.M.: Key challenges in implementing cloud computing in Indian healthcare industry. In: 2017 Pattern Recognition Association of South Africa and Robotics and Mechatronics (PRASA-RobMech), pp. 162–167 (2017). https://doi.org/10.1109/RoboMech.2017.8261141
19. Vaithiya, S.S., Bhanu, S.M.S.: Zone based job scheduling in mobile grid environment. Int. J. Grid Comput. Appl. (IJGCA) **3**(2), 3205 (2012)
20. Varshney, S., Sandhu, R., Gupta, P.K.: QoS based resource provisioning in cloud computing environment: a technical survey. In: Singh, M., Gupta, P.K., Tyagi, V., Flusser, J., Ören, T., Kashyap, R. (eds.) ICACDS 2019. CCIS, vol. 1046, pp. 711–723. Springer, Singapore (2019). https://doi.org/10.1007/978-981-13-9942-8_66
21. Varshney, S., Sandhu, R., Gupta, P.: QoE-based multi-criteria decision making for resource provisioning in fog computing using AHP technique. Int. J. Knowl. Syst. Sci. (IJKSS) **11**(4), 17–30 (2020)

22. Varshney, S., Sandhu, R., Gupta, P.: QoE-based resource management of applications in the fog computing environment using AHP technique. In: 2021 6th International Conference on Signal Processing, Computing and Control (ISPCC), pp. 669–673. IEEE (2021)
23. Verma, K., Kumar, A., Islam, M.S.U., Kanwar, T., Bhushan, M.: Rank based mobility-aware scheduling in fog computing. Inf. Med. Unlocked **24**, 100619 (2021)
24. Waqas, M., Niu, Y., Ahmed, M., Li, Y., Jin, D., Han, Z.: Mobility-aware fog computing in dynamic environments: understandings and implementation. IEEE Access **7**, 38867–38879 (2018)
25. Zhan, W., Luo, C., Min, G., Wang, C., Zhu, Q., Duan, H.: Mobility-aware multi-user offloading optimization for mobile edge computing. IEEE Trans. Veh. Technol. **69**(3), 3341–3356 (2020)

Data Science

Cloud-Based E-Learning: Development of Conceptual Model for Adaptive E-Learning Ecosystem Based on Cloud Computing Infrastructure

Ashraf Alam^(✉) (iD)

Indian Institute of Technology Kharagpur, Kharagpur, India
ashraf_alam@kgpian.iitkgp.ac.in

Abstract. The purpose of this article is to discuss researches done on the efficacy of cloud computing in e-learning. It summarises the present state of cloud-based e-learning and the consequences for educators. Thus, the article begins with an overview of e-learning and cloud computing architectures and a discussion of their key characteristics. The article discusses the potential challenges associated with implementing e-learning systems. The benefits of cloud computing are promoted as a possible solution to these issues. Additionally, there are answers to problems that arise when e-learning makes use of cloud computing, as well as an overview of the most commonly used architectural design patterns of cloud-based e-learning. Additionally, the challenges associated with implementing cloud-based e-learning systems and potential solutions are discussed. This article further proposes a paradigmatic model for cloud-based e-learning. The model is created using Diffusion of Innovation and Fit-Viability model, along with factors influencing information culture. The principal objective of the proposed model is to discover the most important variables that influence cloud computing for the purpose of improving e-learning.

Keywords: Educational technology · Cloud-based e-learning · Information culture · Diffusion of innovation · Fit-Viability model · E-learning · Cloud computing

1 Introduction

Cloud computing has had a profound effect on computer industry, driving technological progress [1]. With the advent of cloud computing, programmes that were previously delivered via the Internet have undergone significant modifications [2]. Organizations may use this technology to provide services via the Internet. It is a computer architecture that enables users to pay for access to hardware and software resources through a network [3]. Cloud Computing is currently gaining immense popularity, and is a generic term that refers to shared use of virtual resources by several businesses at a facility that distributes computer services [4].

© The Author(s), under exclusive license to Springer Nature Switzerland AG 2022
A. Kumar et al. (Eds.): ICAIDS 2021, CCIS 1673, pp. 377–391, 2022.
https://doi.org/10.1007/978-3-031-21385-4_31

Cloud computing may benefit applications with a graphical user interface and server-side applications that are difficult to develop on top of conventional computers and networks [5]. Cloud computing's simplicity, economics, and scalability allow companies to manage their IT infrastructure and administration at a lower cost, without compromising their operations. Due to increased software and hardware requirements of traditional computer systems, they are much more complicated than cloud computing platforms [5]. E-learning is a new kind of distant education that makes use of the internet as its platform. With so many software developers and suppliers devoted to cloud computing's application in education, especially e-learning, cloud computing's popularity has skyrocketed [6] (Fig. 1).

Fig. 1. Features and benefits of cloud computing

Electronic learning has had a major impact on how students study and instructors educate. E-learning activities are a synthesis of many media activities in which students may get lectures, notes, audio, images, and animations from their professors or instructors [7]. Implementing an e-learning system may be time consuming and costly if significant hardware and software resources are needed. Today's society gives immense importance to education and learning. Without a sound education, no one can live a fulfilling life or achieve success. Online education is the most efficient and cost-effective method of instruction [8]. An e-learning project may include online learner communities, educational content developers, and content experts, in addition to a range of instructional formats. To maintain the present speed of the e-learning system, cloud computing must be used in conjunction with newest multimedia and communication technologies [9]. As a result, cloud computing is an excellent alternative for academic organisations and institutions who lack the resources necessary to run their learning systems.

2   The Implications of Cloud Computing for E-Learning

The technological advances in modern information and communication (ICT) technologies heralded a period of unprecedented societal upheaval at the turn of the twentieth century. IT has fundamentally altered and impacted the relationships between diverse stakeholders working within the same economic sector [10]. Cloud computing has emerged as a cutting-edge technology in recent years, accelerating the pace of educational innovation. Electronic education is one strategy for bridging the divide between traditional and intelligent education (e-learning). The Internet has significantly altered how people learn and train in the field of education. Thus, cloud computing seems to be the optimal solution for sustaining the functioning of the e-learning system while incorporating cutting-edge multimedia and communication technologies [11].

Cloud computing is an excellent method for academic institutions and other resource-constrained organisations to host and run online learning systems. Cloud-based e-learning has gained widespread acceptance as a viable alternative to more conventional forms of e-learning. Additionally, information technology is seen as a necessary and efficient component of everyday life and has emerged as the defining characteristic of modern society [12]. Given the ubiquitous use of computers in businesses, homes, and educational institutions, as well as the rapid development of technology, there is tremendous potential to promote and create new learning cultures.

By integrating and linking disparate technologies such as cloud computing and grid computing, it is possible to fully integrate and connect the physical environment, information space, and human civilization [13]. For example, cloud computing enable customers to seek expertise, knowledge, and talent from experts regardless of their physical location. The importance of the internet as a facilitator of data interchange and information transmission has increased in recent years, because it is simple to use both for pleasure and for business. Businesses have been compelled to adapt to technological advancements for decades. This is due to the rapid advancement of ICTs, which is most noticeable in educational institutions. As a result, they must strengthen their capacity for developing learning systems and updating instructional models [14]. Due to the fact that these companies were compelled to change their technology in order to comply with

Architecture Layer	Architecture Block	(Yang, 2011)	(Wang and Huang, 2011)	(Liu and Chen, 2010)
Service Offering	Software Services	E-Learning System	Course Management	Google Apps
	Platform Services			Google Apps Engine
	Infrastructure Services			Google Machine Instance
	Other Services			
Operational Management	User	Schools and Learners	User Management	
	Quality		Management System	
	Security	Security and Identity	Security System	Security Management
	Administration			
	Services	Service Engine, Monitor, and Scheduler		Service Management
	Resource		Resource Management	Data Management
Infrastructure Management	Interface Infrastructure	Notebook, Mobile, and PC		
	Functional Infrastructure	Middleware and Virtual Machine	Virtual Server, Database, and Storage	Memory, Storage, and I/O virtualization
	Physical Infrastructure	Storage	Server, Storage, and Network	Storage and Server

Fig. 2. Understanding architecture layer in connection to E-Learning

regulatory standards, improving their capacity to create learning systems and update teaching models is critical (Fig. 2).

Learning may occur when members of a *community of practise* engage in highly participative activities. The term *"situated learning"* refers to a continuous and cyclical process in which each context of action generates new meaning. This does not imply that the learner creates a collection of mental representations or self-contained structures during the process [7]. Cloud computing is the infrastructure of the future for e-learning. Cloud-based e-learning is a term that refers to the incorporation of cloud computing technology into the e-learning sector, in which all required IT resources are used for e-learning [8] (Fig. 3).

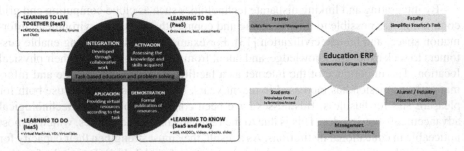

Fig. 3. Task-based education and problem solving

The current study analyses in brief the efficacy of e-learning services in the classroom and how cloud computing will play a significant role in the future of formal and non-formal education. While incorporating cloud computing into e-learning services has many advantages, there are certain risks and challenges to consider, including cost, bandwidth, security, user concept, forms, and methods, as well as management duties and resources. Due to the virtualization of these resources, educational businesses, students, and institutions may also lease them. Cloud computing's autonomous, cost-effective, flexible, and reliable infrastructure enables the creation of an e-learning ecosystem.

Educational institutions that utilise cloud-based learning must first establish the necessary networking systems and infrastructure to connect users of cloud technologies to the Internet efficiently [1]. Cloud computing has gained popularity in a number of fields, including education and training, due to some of its distinguishing features. Cloud computing has been enabled by improving pro-gramme designs, quickly developing technological standards, and ubiquitous Internet use [3]. Google anticipates a massive migration of services and soft-ware to the cloud. The ease with which businesses may use the cloud model's economic advantages shows cloud computing's fast development.

In contrast to previous academic studies, we are today controlled by the eco-nomic paradigm that enables the cloud to flourish [5]. This is a major departure from prior academic researches. Cloud provides significant benefits for IT businesses because it eliminates the need to invest in and maintain basic IT equipment. This allows them to focus on innovation while improving the eco-nomic value of their services. Cloud computing, due to its broad use, is now widely considered as one of the most significant information technology developments of the last decade [6, 7]. It is a huge network infrastructure construct-ed with the aid of data centres. E-learning refers to a distributed and open environment for learning via participation and activity that is facilitated by the use of information technology infrastructures [8, 9].

E-learning has been recognised as a critical component of long-term organisational performance and as a major indicator of an organization's efficiency, creative capability, and potential to grow in a competitive environment characterised by globalisation, growing complexity, and rapid change [1, 2]. It has established itself as the new paradigm in modern education, fundamentally altering our conception of learning. E-learning has enabled numerous higher education advancements. In a user-friendly environment, teachers may quickly update study materials and add multimedia content [5].

Electronic learning as a method highlights the variety of instructional materials accessible to instructors and allows teachers to evaluate and enhance their own content. Additionally, technological advancements have pushed the educational sector toward a more popular model of online education [6, 7]. Higher educational institutions, particularly colleges and universities, are increasingly adopting eLearning platforms for training and delivery, and web-based education has made considerable strides in recent years. Cloud computing and related concepts such as mobile cloud computing have altered the educational environment in recent years as a result of e-learning technologies [8–11].

Mobile technologies, authoring tools, digital instructional games, and virtual simulations are only some of the advancements in e-learning technology [5]. The adoption of digital classrooms and the promotion of learner-cantered training have created a need for pedagogical design and transformation to suit the requirements of current staff who encourage 21st century skill development via domain knowledge acquisition. Additionally, asynchronous e-learning systems enable users to access and learn from educational resources such as lecture videos and complete assignments at their convenience, rather than at predetermined times and locations [3, 4]. Students may study at their own speed and from any location using e-learning, which is distinct from traditional classroom instruction.

Variables influencing the quality of e-learning systems include content support, course design, social support, teacher characteristics, student characteristics, course assessment, and technical issues. As demand for information technology and associated infrastructure increases, educational institutions confront a slew of new challenges. Cloud computing, which is built on well-known information technology platforms such as the internet and virtualization, offers a reliable option for such businesses' software, storage, and infrastructure needs. Through the virtualization of e-learning technology, businesses, students, and educational institutions may now rent computer resources [5].

The components of cloud-based e-learning architecture may be classified on a number of levels. The infrastructure layer is made up of a collection of scalable and dynamic physical hosts. On the second layer, a standardised interface is accessible to all e-learning developers. At the system level, resource management guarantees the independence of hardware and software resources. The service layer includes a variety of well-known cloud services. Cloud computing services include cloud-based and platform-based software services [6, 7]. Along with administrative and assessment functions, the application layer provides collaboration capabilities such as a virtual lab and the ability to share and create content.

A cloud-based e-learning architecture is a subfield of cloud computing that focuses on e-learning systems for the education sector. Students and educational institutions may lease virtualized education resources for e-learning from cloud providers, which they can then rent to other students and educational institutions. A five-tier architecture for cloud-based e-learning architecture includes: business application layer; server layer; administrative layer; software layer; hardware layer; and network layer [8–10]. The hardware resource layer is responsible for managing the computer's fundamental components, such as the CPU and physical memory. This layer of eLearning development is critical to the overall system design. A software resource layer is constructed and supplied with assistance of middleware and operating systems. Software developers have a plethora of choices for developing e-learning system applications.

Cloud-based apps may be integrated into the services of software firms. It may be used by cloud users to compute the outcomes of many applications. Customers may choose from a number of services to get access to various cloud resources, including infrastructure, hardware, and software [1–3]. The business application layer is not cloud-based and thus does not correspond to a cloud-based e-learning architecture. It outlines the development of many e-learning components and serves as the primary business case for e-learning. Business apps primarily assist administrative educational activities such as teacher evaluation and platform development, as well as content distribution and production [3, 4].

A cloud-based e-learning approach can also be utilised in conjunction with a mobile device as an alternative to traditional e-learning deployments. Building structures and physical amenities are examples of physical infrastructure. Additionally, storage servers and networking equipment are covered. Also included are architecture-enabled infrastructures such as virtual repositories, virtual machines, and cloud platforms [5]. The application layer is the third level of the e-learning architecture. It is where user interactions such as synchronous and asynchronous chatting or debate occur. Users get access to cloud-based e-learning materials through the access layer. This work makes use of the multi-channel access idea, which enables users to access a variety of accessible services through a number of presentation models, including desktop programmes and mobile applications [6–8, 14].

The idea expands the device types that can connect to the cloud-based e-learning service. At the top of the stack are the service layer, cloud management systems, virtualized environment, and physical hardware. The surface is the layer that is most closely related to the physical layer. To augment the capabilities of the physical infrastructure, a private cloud architecture is developed on top of it. This architecture has two computer pools: one for hypervisor servers and another for thin client PCs, both of which are utilised for educational purposes [8–11]. Through a web browser, all services and host systems may be managed and monitored, and real-time data about the virtual infrastructure, such as access rights, configuration and alarms, and storage capabilities and performance, can be shown.

Physical layers outperform virtualized layers in terms of performance. A hypervisor is required if one wants to share a single hardware host across several operating systems. The hypervisor is in charge of managing the resources and CPUs on the host. It enables interoperability across virtual machines and therefore distributes the resources needed by each operating system. This service layer is responsible for delivering the software necessary for cloud clients to access SaaS and PaaS services. This layer is referred to as the cloud interface layer, since it serves as the cloud's main point of external interaction [1–4].

Virtual PCs are used in this instance to install software packages chosen by teachers and organisers. A novel online learning architecture based on a private cloud that students, teachers, and administrators could all use concurrently would include five systems to analyse demand: online communication, virtual laboratories, educational resources, online learning, and education management [3, 4]. Public clouds were included as a backup option after the advent of the private cloud concept in the education sector. The present public cloud infrastructure is always available.

Additionally, it offers six different benefits to consumers, including pricing, storage, computer skills, virtualization, individualised learning, and collaboration. Each course is designed and administered around a virtual theme, which includes the use of experimental partners, online learning communities, and virtual hardware resources [5]. Data and processing are spread over a vast number of distributed computers as a consequence of the architecture. A significant benefit of cloud-based e-learning is the ability to provide costly software on high-performance processors to distant institutions and students who have minimal resources [6, 7, 14].

3 Technological Contestations and Methodological Provisions for Rendering in Cloud-Based E-Learning

Customers can facilitate resource grouping to support multiple customers in heterogeneous networks; and unreliability, as demonstrated by features such as on-demand self-service, which enables customers to easily facilitate without interaction; deliberate and measured service, which enables organisations to self-fund; and on-the-job self-service, which enables customers to easily facilitate without interaction [4, 8].

It is founded on cognitive science principles and is an excellent method for students to participate in successful multimedia learning through electronic education materials. E-learning is a time-efficient and cost-effective way of learning that also takes care of user's comfort and the organization's profit margin [2, 5, 11].

Among the direct and positive effects of e-learning on pupils include improvement of learner-to-teacher ratio on a national and global scale; assisting pupils in learning about a certain programme or subject in a simplified way. Additionally, long-term data and information retention is improved. There will be no out-of-pocket costs on travelling to learning centres. Demand for e-learning thus continues to grow exponentially and is unlikely to slow down in the near future [3, 7].

4 Vantages of Cloud Computing Adoption for E-Learning Solutions

Many educational institutions lack the resources and infrastructure necessary to operate or install an e-learning system. Certain versions of BlackBoard and MOODLE's basic applications, as well as their e-learning tools, are available through cloud-based services. At all levels of education, e-learning is extensively utilised for a variety of reasons, including in-house education, academic courses, and corporate training [1, 4, 7]. Cloud-based e-learning systems provide many advantages over on-premises e-learning systems. Some of which include: the price is competitive, software updates are completed in a matter of seconds, added layer of security for cloud-based e-learning systems, enhances overall performance and productivity of employees, enables real-time collaboration amongst distant team members, revised version is more compatible with document types, no in-house IT assistance is needed, and assists in retaining current employees [8, 11, 12].

There are many benefits for students as well. Pupils can enrol in online distance learning (ODL) programmes. They can send students activities, projects, and tasks from home, can seek feedback and take examinations at the comfort of their home. Several advantages for educators include: content management, communication with pupils via forums, test preparation, evaluation of tests, grading of students' homework or assignments, projects, and sending of feedback are all included in benefits of e-learning [5, 6, 13].

5 Theories of New Technology Adoption

5.1 Fit-Viability Model

To address the problem of technological acceptability, a new paradigm of technology adoption, the Fit-Viability model, has been created. Tjan [12] created a model based on Goodhue and Thompson's Task-Technology Fit (TTF) paradigm [13]. In 2001, Fit-Viability theory was established to determine how effectively companies utilised the Internet (ecommerce). Fit evaluates the new technologies in terms of their compatibility with a company's core capabilities, structures, values, and culture. According to this idea, viability evaluates the potential for wealth creation inherent in creative applications, as well as the related human and capital requirements [3, 11, 12]. Fit criteria are developed by evaluating organisational, economic, and information technology infrastructure components, while DOI theory is utilised to create a variety of basic viability indicators.

5.2 Diffusion of Innovation Theory

The Diffusion of Innovation Theory (DOI) was developed and published in Rogers [11], a book named Diffusion of Innovation. The book contains 508 articles on dissemination research that describe how individuals and organisations acquire ideas. According to Rogers, four critical elements that contribute to the diffusion of innovation are creativity, communication channels, time, and the presence of a social structure. The DOI model [5, 9, 11], which incorporates five critical innovation characteristics - relative benefit, compatibility, complexity, testability, and observability - affects an organization's or individual's decision to accept or reject an idea. We examined the effects of relative advantage, compatibility, and complexity on the adoption of E-Learning Cloud

Computing in higher educational institutions, as well as the factors associated with the Fit-Viability model and the information culture, on the three most important factors influencing innovation identified by Tornatzky and Klein [6].

5.3 Information Culture Factors

The Information Culture [6, 10, 12] is described by Davenport and Prusak as behaviour patterns and attitudes that reflect an organization's approach to information. Organizational culture is often cited as a determinant in the success or failure of an information system's (IS) implementation. According to Mukred and colleagues, the evolution of information systems is dependent on the development of an information culture. Additionally, the absence of an information culture in organisations is a significant impediment to the development of information systems. The research examined the four information behaviours and values of integrity, formality, control, and proactiveness as variables influencing cloud-based e-learning in higher education institutions [5, 8, 11].

5.4 Conceptual Model and Research Hypothesis

The main aim of this study is to develop a model of higher education institutions' usage of cloud-based e-learning technologies, with a focus on the internal organisational factors that impact its adoption. Based on the approach outlined in this study, the researchers look forward to finding internal organisational factors that contribute to the fast adoption of cloud-based e-learning in higher education institutions. The proposed research paradigm is based on the Information Culture [1, 6, 8], Diffusion of Innovation Theory [3, 6, 13], and Fit-Viability Model [3, 12].

Numerous studies have been conducted in this area to establish a link between fitness models and the adoption of new information technologies. For example, Liang et al. [2, 5, 13] examined the adoption of mobile devices at work using the Fit-Viability paradigm. Another study examined the impact of cloud computing on government-owned businesses as an alternative to providing electronic government services and developed a research model based on Diffusion of Innovation Theory and Fit-Viability Model [3, 5, 8, 12]. According to their findings, it seems that it is critical to weigh both essential and feasible factors when making an educated decision on cloud computing in an eGovernment setting. Recent studies have identified and classified variables in three dimensions by integrating cloud-based e-learning and technological characteristics.

The proposed conceptual model is developed and classified in three dimensions. It discusses how cloud-based e-learning is compatible with the unique requirements of higher education institutions as defined by Fit-Viability Model. The findings show that the fit metric evaluates how well new applications fit inside the organization's core capabilities, structure, values, and culture. The effectiveness of cloud-based eLearning may be quantified using Rogers' DOI principles of relative advantage, complexity, and compatibility. The DOI hypothesis states that a development's relative worth is greater than that of its predecessors (Fig. 4).

Cloud-based e-learning enables higher education institutions to increase their data storage capacity and to provide students with access to any app or broadband internet from any device and location [4, 7]. The complexity of how difficult it is to utilise

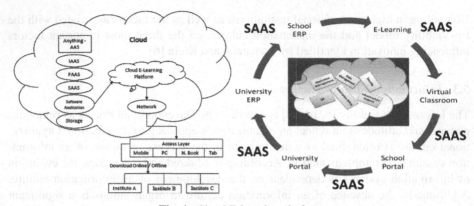

Fig. 4. Cloud E-learning platform

or acquire innovation and substantially reduces obstacles for educational institutions and information technology executives, making cloud-based electronic training platforms ideal for providing high-quality academic services. Second, compatibility refers to the degree to which continuous development is compatible with prospective adopters' current ideas, needs, and experiences. Compatibility refers to the degree to which a continuous development is connected to the values, needs, and experiences of future users [3, 5, 7]. When it comes to transferring different interfaces and data to the cloud, the pro-posed model shows the compatibility of technology and its appropriateness for higher education institutions.

Additionally, viability is critical, since it is utilised to determine if new applications are required and capable of delivering value. It encompasses the many components that contribute to the promotion of e-learning cloud computing technology in higher educational institutions due to the benefits it provides in terms of improved decision-making, cost savings, and IT availability. The decision-making process reveals management's attitude toward the necessary technology, as well as their level of support and commitment to its adoption. Decision-making is a critical element in viability [3, 6, 10, 14] (Fig. 5).

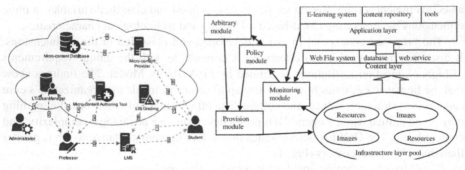

Fig. 5. Cloud-based E-learning model

This characteristic may show an increase in decision-making ability prior to the implementation of cloud-based e-learning in institutions of higher education. Cost reduction is related to the financial and human resources required by science and technology organisations to deploy and manage cloud computing. Adoption of a cloud-based learning management system is another critical factor in determining the feasibility of eLearning-based Cloud Computing in higher educational institutions and the accompanying cost reductions connected with internet access and data storage through the cloud [1, 6, 12–14]. The third characteristic of viability is IT readiness, which refers to the degree to which cloud computing is successfully prepared for IT and human resource requirements.

Before higher educational institutions embrace cloud computing, this proposed model should demonstrate the viability and readiness for the safe adoption of higher education institutions and cloud computing technology. The suggested conceptual model's second component is information culture, which focuses on qualities such as information integrity, formality, control, and responsiveness. As a result, cloud-based E-learning is widely recognised in higher educational institutions, which contributes substantially to the model's adoption. "Information integrity" refers to the reliability and trustworthiness of data in cloud computing technologies as well as the correction of errors or concerns regarding student or employee security [4, 7, 8, 14].

Information formality refers to the deliberate dependence on regulated data rather than uncontrolled data and shows the management and reactivation of data formality after the introduction of cloud computing technologies by higher educational organisations. This method enables users to rapidly discover solutions to a wide range of academic issues, which is cited as a reason for cloud adoption in higher educational institutions. Information control is synonymous with data control and refers to specific techniques of data usage that are designed to avoid or encourage certain behaviours. "Data control" and "information control" are mutually exclusive concepts. Decision-makers may monitor and control operational maneuvers by using data collected from a variety of sources [5, 6, 12–14].

These skills are necessary for successfully completing large contracts and resolving a wide range of business problems. In essence, these control systems are concerned with the exercise that is directly linked to the association's execution [4, 7]. As such, it provides as a mechanism for achieving the intended behaviours and achievements of the business while avoiding inappropriate behaviour. Information control is based on negative data management concepts and establishes boundaries for situations that may result in inappropriate conduct, thus avoiding erroneous behaviour and promoting the company's intended behaviour and success [6, 13, 14]. As a result of the fast changes and fluctuations, proactive data refers to a frame of mind that enables the rapid selection and application of fresh data in a business sector, resulting in rapid functional and managerial development (Fig. 6).

Proactive data is data collected prior to a business's requirements being fulfilled. Proactivity in global development necessitates the ability to foresee and recognise specific expected situations, such as forward and reverse data flow; the condition and capacity for comprehension are all components of proactivity and the capacity to react to what has been taught [2, 5, 14]. Data confidence too shall have an effect on data proactiveness.

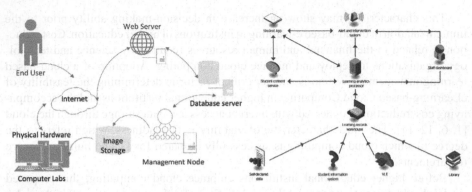

Fig. 6. Learning analytics, learning warehouse, and interconnections in cloud-based E-learning model

We propose a paradigmatic model for cloud-based e-learning guided by the following hypothesis, which are based on aforementioned conceptual framework model.

1. Cloud computing's relative benefit has an advantageous impact on its appropriateness for HEIs computing needs, resulting in a greater willingness to adopt cloud-based e-learning.
2. Decision-makers have a favourable impact on the feasibility of cloud computing and the acceptance of cloud computing based on e-learning in higher education institutions.
3. Information will benefit the proactive usage of cloud-based e-learning in higher education institutions.
4. Information formality will facilitate higher education institutions' adoption of cloud computing for e-learning.
5. Ensuring the integrity of data would assist higher education institutions in adopting cloud computing-based e-learning.
6. The practicality of cloud computing has an effect on higher educational institutions' ambitions for cloud-based e-learning.
7. IT readiness improves the perceived usefulness of cloud computing, which is essential for cloud computing to be used for e-learning in higher education institutions.
8. Cost reductions have an economic effect on the viability and acceptability of cloud computing in e-learning institutions.
9. The need of ensuring cloud computing is task-consistent for HEIs that utilise cloud computing to help with e-learning.
10. Compatibility plays a role in determining if cloud computing is suitable for meeting the computing needs of universities (HEIs) that use cloud-based e-learning.
11. Given the complexity of cloud computing, it is inappropriate for meeting the computing needs of higher education institutions for cloud computing based on e-learning.

6 Concluding Remarks and Future Work

Cloud computing enables on-demand, ubiquitous access to a diverse set of resources that may be rapidly made available to a service provider with little participation or administrative work. Cloud computing includes a number of distinguishing characteristics, including resource availability at any time and from any location, resource billing based on predefined use metrics, and remote access to computer resources without contacting the service provider. It is gaining considerable popularity in business sector, and has had a significant impact on the evolution of e-learning (Fig. 7).

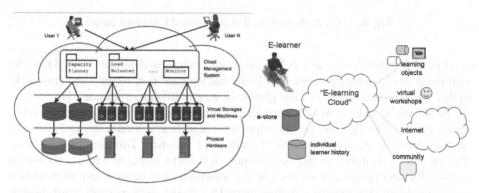

Fig. 7. Capacity planner, load balancer in cloud-based E-learning model

All of the following factors contribute to the success of e-learning: cloud quality, cloud features, institution development, and user readiness. By eliminating the requirement for IT companies to invest in basic infrastructure, the cloud provides substantial advantages. As a result, companies can concentrate entirely on business innovation and value generation via their services. Because cloud payment systems, e-learning systems, and cloud integration are widely used, resources such as network access, processing, and storage may be scaled up and modified at a cheaper cost, avoiding the need for new hardware and software for the creation of educational programmes. Cloud computing may also be used to improve the software, platform, and infrastructure of e-learning systems, resulting in cost savings. The need for highly skilled technicians and the maintenance of high-end computers has also been eliminated, since e-learning programmes run on the service provider's infrastructure (Fig. 8).

Cloud-based e-learning is being pushed as a legitimate and trustworthy way of teaching by a growing number of companies and educational organisations. The growing number of e-learning solutions that are being used in a variety of ways and that allow people to find and gain knowledge helps and profits everyone. All of the critical and pertinent data that various organizations/institutions provide may be shared through a network or cloud when cloud computing is used for e-learning. Cloud-based e-learning systems are much faster, cheaper, and more efficient than on-premises e-learning systems, as well as significantly safer. Users do not need cloud-based e-learning or high-end equipment or software to see or share data and hardware with other participants; all they

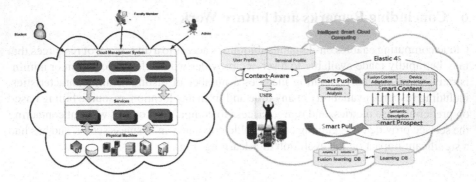

Fig. 8. Smart push, smart pull in cloud-based E-learning model

need is an Internet connection. All cloud-based systems undoubtedly have flaws. We examined several contemporary technologies and weighed their benefits and drawbacks in this article, concluding that some platforms are too difficult to operate.

In this study, we have also developed a new conceptual e-learning paradigm based on universities' extensive use of cloud computing. The technique used in this study is based on two generally accepted theories of technology adoption: Diffusion of Innovation Theory and Fit-Viability Model. Additionally, it includes issues related to information culture. Eleven hypotheses have been developed to demonstrate the role of fit in relation to technological characteristics derived from DOI theory, such as relative advantages, compatibility, and complications, as well as organisational, economic, and infrastructure factors, such as decision support (including cost reduction) and IT readiness (including network readiness). The study method proposed is based on empirical validation of concepts gleaned from a range of information technology research studies conducted at different organisational levels. As a consequence, before they can be used, the model's proposed structures must be validated in an experimental setting. The next stage in this study would be to collect data from various institutions of higher learning in order to verify the research model's hypothesis.

References

1. Rahhali, M., Oughdir, L., Jedidi, Y., Lahmadi, Y., El Khattabi, M.Z.: E-learning Recommendation System Based on Cloud Computing. In: Bennani, S., Lakhrissi, Y., Khaissidi, G., Mansouri, A., Khamlichi, Y. (eds.) WITS 2020. LNEE, vol. 745, pp. 89–99. Springer, Singapore (2022). https://doi.org/10.1007/978-981-33-6893-4_9
2. AlAjmi, Q., Arshah, R.A., Kamaludin, A., Al-Sharafi, M.A.: Developing an Instrument for Cloud-Based E-Learning Adoption: Higher Education Institutions Perspective. In: Advances in Computer, Communication and Computational Sciences, pp. 671–681. Springer, Singapore (2021)
3. Sharma, V., Singh, A.K., Raj, M.: Conceptual Online Education Using E-Learning Platform of Cloud Computing. In: Suma, V., Bouhmala, N., Wang, H. (eds.) Evolutionary Computing and Mobile Sustainable Networks. LNDECT, vol. 53, pp. 991–997. Springer, Singapore (2021). https://doi.org/10.1007/978-981-15-5258-8_91

4. Zaguia, A., Ameyed, D., Daadaa, Y.: Integrating modalities into context aware elearning system using cloud computing. In: 2021 International Conference of Women in Data Science at Taif University (WiDSTaif), pp. 1–6. IEEE (2021 March)
5. Jedidi, Y., Ibriz, A., Benslimane, M., Tmimi, M., Rahhali, M.: Predicting Student's Performance Based on Cloud Computing. In: WITS 2020, pp. 113–123. Springer, Singapore (2022)
6. Surameery, N.M.S., Shakor, M.Y.: CBES: Cloud Based Learning management System for Educational Institutions. In: 2021 3rd East Indonesia Conference on Computer and Information Technology (EIConCIT), pp. 270–275. IEEE (2021 April)
7. Thavi, R.R., Narwane, V.S., Jhaveri, R.H., Raut, R.D.: To determine the critical factors for the adoption of cloud computing in the educational sector in developing countries–a fuzzy DEMATEL approach. Kybernetes (2021)
8. Udhayakumar, S., Nandhini, D.U., Chandrasekaran, S.: Trusted cooperative e-learning service deployment model in multi-cloud environment. In: Inventive Communication and Computational Technologies, pp. 527–535. Springer, Singapore (2021)
9. Xiong, L., Li, M.: Behavioral modeling based on cloud computing and target user recommendation for English cloud classroom. Microprocess. Microsyst. **80**, 103587 (2021)
10. Al-Sharafi, M.A., AlAjmi, Q., Al-Emran, M., Qasem, Y.A., Aldheleai, Y.M.: Cloud computing adoption in higher education: an integrated theoretical model. Recent Advances in Technology Acceptance Models and Theories, 191–209 (2021)
11. Tenorio-Sepúlveda, G.C., Muñoz-Ortiz, K.D.P., Nova-Nova, C.A., Ramírez-Montoya, M.S.: Diagnostic instrument of the level of competencies in Cloud Computing for teachers in Education 4.0. In: Working Conference on Virtual Enterprises, pp. 665–673. Springer, Cham (2021 November)
12. Gupta, A., Mazumdar, B.D., Mishra, M., Shinde, P.P., Srivastava, S., Deepak, A.: Role of cloud computing in management and education. Materials Today: Proceedings (2021)
13. Sandhu, I.K., Malhotra, M., Randhawa, P.R.: A review of trust and security concerns in cloud computing adoption intention in the higher education sector: research in progress. Impacts and Challenges of Cloud Business Intelligence, 1–12 (2021)
14. Wu, W., Plakhtii, A.: E-learning based on cloud computing. International Journal of Emerging Technologies in Learning 16(10) (2021)

Performance of Secure Data Deduplication Framework in Cloud Services

Rajesh Banala[1](✉), Vicky Nair[1], and P. Nagaraj[2]

[1] TKR College of Engineering and Technology, Meerpet, India
rajesh.banala@gmail.com
[2] Osmania University, Hyderabad, India

Abstract. Data Deduplication makes it convenient to utilize the available disk space efficiently and proves as a solution for preventing data redundancy. Deduplication process allows only a unique set of data to be stored in the storage and all other copies are pointed towards connecting pointers that point towards unique data. In this work we propose a novel deduplication technique that focuses on preserving client privacy. The suggested method uses an effective deduplication algorithm which splits the input file into small units which get encrypted by the client using a secure hash function along with a chunk algorithm. In this technique the user constructs one index tree with hash values of the small units and encrypts them using asymmetric search encryption technique. The index tree assists the CSP in searching index structure and also restores the requested units. According to the suggested method, it enables the CSP to run deduplication without requiring the client's plain texts or decryption key.

1 Introduction

The use of internet and its integration with other applications has led to a huge surge of data. The efficient storage of data on cloud has become very efficient with the use of deduplication systems. Data deduplication is a technique that helps in tracking as well as removing duplicate copies of data in storage space. By implementing data deduplication techniques, storage utilization can be improved significantly thereby reducing the cost of storage. The key issue that has to be addressed by cloud computing is data privacy and security. The major highlight of using Deduplication system is that it reduces the storage [3] by only maintaining a single physical copy. All the rest duplicate copies of data are removed from the system. Deduplication techniques are generally used to reduce storage space of servers. In order to prevent unauthorized data access and duplicate data creation on cloud, encryption technique is employed, which encrypts the data before storing on cloud server. The process of test inline deduction is used to identify the eradication code of text. This enhances the backup system to deliver better. The system is tested against documents varying from 1 KB – 100 MB in size. Cloud services retain only one copy of the data that enables them to remove redundant duplicate data from their storage. The deduplication process increases the system storage and retrieval management. The increase in data has made secure deduplication system a high priority objective on the cloud. The system with high faster access, better storage management and accessible on low bandwidth are in demand. The deduplication systems have efficiently managed the storage requirements on the cloud.

Deduplication services in cloud aid the customer to lower their storage space and end up by paying less for storage. It is one of the major gains of data deduplication in cloud storage systems. Reduction in storage sizes aids the cloud service providers with reduce storage sizes in extremely big systems. The cost of saving of energy consumption also aids the vendors dealing with large storage systems. Data is very dynamic in cloud systems. Some chunk of data is accessed very frequently in a particular time period and multiple updating take place at a particular time period. The rest or major portion of the data in cloud remains unused for larger time period. Some dataset and data are accessed more frequently than other datasets and data. The primary goal of data deduplication strategy is to increase the system storage efficiency along with reduction in storage space. The dynamic behavior of data makes it necessary for the system to have a dynamic deduplication strategy in place. The user might use some data for some time period and the same data might not be accessed at all in different time period. The static approach faces faults when immediate change is observed in used data. This is overcome by using the dynamic approach of data deduplication.

The outcome of test results indicate in a positive manner that with less data capacity, the information recovery is better in the current structure [8].The proposed system MUSE was tested along with similar types of deduplication schemes. The results give a better indication that MUSE has better optimization in terms of Input Output performance/space-cost. The system provides better deduplication service to cloud systems enabled with deduplication [9]. The other advantages of using the dedupication services of MUSE are less time for dedulication, Handles the metadata itself along with the computation of hash for security. It results in reduction in comparing VM disk images [10]. The deduplication system can have multiple access from user. The data must remain secure even if cross user reference to the data is made. The privacy and security of data both in the cloud and during access are a high priority for deduplication systems. The data that are in demand and accessed very frequently need to be provided to the user at a faster rate. This is done by reducing the security of data to a medium level of security and increasing the storage management and bandwidth access of the data. On the other hand the data that are not accessed very frequently are termed as not popular data and are provided with high security access. Cloud system provide data on demand at faster rate with negligible delay in lower bandwidth systems. The data being accessed from multiple sources has made it necessary retain the ownership of the data to the rightful owner. In deduplication system where multiple data access are made, the system should provide high data security and ownership of the data should never change, unless approved by the real owner of the system.

The contribution of this article is a data deduplication scheme along with two algorithms that help improve the efficiency of the storage system along with fault tolerance. The rest of the article contains literature review in Sect. 2. The system architecture and framework of deduplication is detailed in Sect. 3. Section 4 highlights the client perceptions of deduplication systems. Section 5 gives the conclusion and followed with discussions.

2 Literature Review

Leesakul et al. [15] conducted a study on dynamic data deduplication in cloud storage and proposed a dynamic deduplication method that increases the storage efficiency and keeps the fault tolerance level in check. The proposed system changes the QoS with change in the dynamic number of copies of chunk data. The scalability problem faced by cloud systems handling data deduplication was successfully addressed. Pooranian et al. [19] in their study revealed how the data check for duplicate files in the cloud could reveal the binary information of the data and help attackers to launch an attack on the system. Data check can reveal the existence of duplicate copy of data. The method proposed by them was RAndom REsponse (RARE), the system would request two chunks of data to the dedupication chunk against one and the dedupication cloud would response back with the gains while keeping the security information of binary intact. Harnik et al. [20] highlight the potential risk involved in cross user deduplication process. They have successfully implemented a system that closes the backdoor access to the data in cross user systems. The method helps to enforce high security to data even in low bandwidth systems making it safer to use cross user systems in cloud deduplication systems. Stanek et al. [11] proposed a method to provide security to the data on the cloud. The encryption system provides high priority security to less accessed data and would provide less security to data that are accessed very frequently. The balance of low security is matched by providing better storage management and accessibility in low bandwidths. Yan et al. [13] discussed about the access of encrypted data on the deduplication system in cloud. Kim et al. [14] discuss the various techniques available for deduplication and to secure the data on the cloud. Reddy et al. proposed a method to ensure the ownership of the data in the cloud. The tradeoff is made with high data security and optimization of the data on the storage in the cloud. The authors follow the principle of providing high data security to least accessed data and low security to very popular data. The ownership of the data at any level or stage does not change. Ne et al. discuss about the various deduplication data protocols used in cloud systems. The proposed private data deduplication protocols is proposed and checked with two party computations. Shin et al. [12] discuss about secure data deduplication system for cloud systems. The risk and types of attack that can take place on the deduplication system are highlighted. Armknecht et al. [21] propose a storage solution. The system is called ClearBox. The system checks for copy of the data available in the cloud. The data in encrypted form is appended with the user data. The user can check and see the storage space that is occupied by the earlier data in the storage. Kumar et al. [22–24] proposed an object detection method for blind people.

3 Architecture and Deduplication Framework for Cloud

In Fig. 1 the cloud Cloud Service Provider (CSP) provides the data deduplication service to the user. The two proposed algorithms are Asymmetric Extremum (AE) chunking algorithm and Rapid Asymmetric Maximum (RAM) chucking algorithm. The AE divides the data into smaller chunks. A chunk is a small unit of data. System to system the size of the chunk varies based on the storage system management and the reliability of CSP

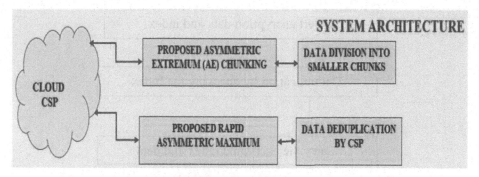

Fig. 1. Architecture

to provide services. The fault tolerance of the system is low. The second AE performs the data deduplication services insight with the criteria of the CSP. The tradeoff between the storage management system and data security of the data is made and highlighted at RAM. The detailed explanation of AE and RAM along with pseudocode of the procedure is provided in Sect. 3.2.

In this paper, a novel secure deduplication technique for cloud is proposed that focuses on preserving client privacy. It can ensure the privacy of the data in the cloud storage and can allow the CSP to conduct deduplication of data with safeguarding privacy and integrity of client data [4]. The design of the aforementioned framework rely on several algorithms as follows. First, the Asymmetric Extremum (AE) chunking algorithm [1] is used to perform the file (data) division into smaller units (chunks). Second, Rapid Asymmetric Maximum (RAM) chucking algorithm [1] is used to allow the Cloud Service Provider (CSP) to perform the data deduplication. It is also meant to provide data privacy against the CSP or any malicious user. Third, an indexing scheme is designed to generate an index of the encrypted file chunks for fast search purposes by the CSP. Fourth, an asymmetric searchable encryption scheme [2] is used for encrypting the generated index of the deduplicated data.

3.1 Client Perception

In this situation a client needs to upload a number of records to the cloud. The client will find through downloading the user request to his device. This request will then create an encrypted master key which will be taken closest from the CSP as it will be stored nearby on the client device. This process will have 3 parts. They are Data processor, DataVerifier and DataFinder: The data processor gets invoked when the client uploads information to the cloud. The Data processor consists of five components. They are File chunking component, the Chunk Encryption component, the Index Generation component, the Index Encryption component and the Data and the Index (Fig. 2).

Data verifier gets started when the user intends to confirm the reliability of data. It uses the client's master key to connect with cloud storage provider to be sure of the reliability of data stored in the cloud (Fig. 3).

Data Finder gets activated if the user intends to recover information stored in the cloud. It generates tokens that consist of ChunkIds to the files which user intends to

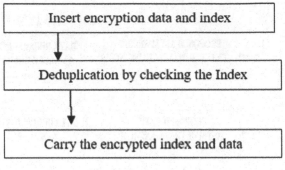

Fig. 2. Data processor

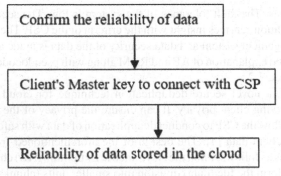

Fig. 3. Data verifier

recover. The CSP obtains the tokens which then explores the encrypted index for the Chunk Ids. After finding the Chunk Ids, CSP will recover them along with metadata from the index and return to the client. The client will use his private key for decrypting every chunk and recreate the data.

3.2 Chunk Modules of AE and RAM Chunking Algorithms in CSP

The process of information process analysis, generates a file window. The data bytes are placed in the window. The end point in the window will point where the highest value data or bytes are placed. The end points will be fixed at end if the highest value bytes are at the end of window. In the same manner shift the window by a single byte forward and continue till every end point and chunk data and files are identified. During the data stream analysis process, file window can be placed after the end point or at the initial point. If from the window a byte value with less the collection of all byte value contained in the window is passed, the corresponding byte contains the end point, if not continue to red and replicate the values of byte till all the chunks and end points are not identified.

The data window remains in a fixed state during the process of reading data flow. The cut-off is set where the max value of bytes is found in the data window. If cut-off points to window end if max value of bytes is at the end, if not shift the data window

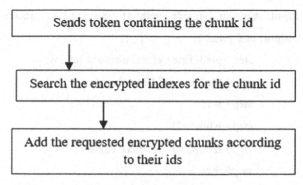

Fig. 4. Data finder

by single byte forward. The entire process is iterated again until the identification of chunks and cut-off points in data stream has been made. Figure 5 gives the process of AE algorithm and Fig. 6 gives the pseudocode AE algorithm.

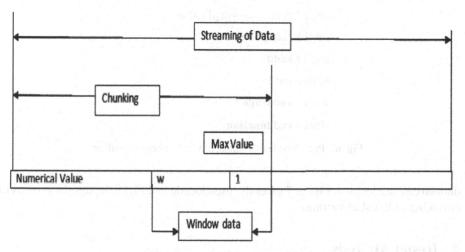

Fig. 5. Process of AE algorithm

The data window remains in a fixed state during the process of reading data flow. The cut-off is set where the max value of bytes is found in the data window. If cut-off points to window end if max value of bytes is at the end, if not shift the data window by single byte forward. The entire process is iterated again until the identification of chunks and cut-off points in data stream has been made. Figure 4 gives the pseudocode and the process of AE algorithm.

The position of the data stream during the reading process is either set at the starting point or at the end of last cut-off point. The cut-off point is set to the byte value that contains lesser than the all byte values if read out of the window else continue to iterate the process to read byte values and locate chunks and cut-off points contained in the

input: string str, left side lenght of the string l: stream are

output: end point 1:

    step1:predefine values: window size, w;

    step2:**function** AE Chuncking(str,l)

    step3:i=1;

    step4:**while**(i<l)

    step5:**if** str[i].value<=max.value

    step6:**than**

    step7:**if**i=max.position+w

    step8:**than**

    step9:**return**i

    step10:**endif**

    step11:**else**

    step12:max.value=str[i].value

    step13:max.position=i

    step14:**endif**

    step15:i=i+1

    step16:**end while**

    step17:**end function**

Fig. 6. Pseudocode of proposed AE chunking algorithm

data stream are located. Figure 7 gives the pseudocode and Fig. 8 depicts the process of chunking of RAM algorithm.

4   Result Analysis

The two algorithms were checked with data downloaded from different clouds. The data were of different sizes and from different storage management systems. The data were divided into five datasets namely dataset 1 to dataset 5. The sizes of the data varied from 0.8×10^9 to 1.9×10^9. Experiment analysis showed that the combination of two algorithms AE and RAM improve the data deduplication of the data stored in cloud. The reliability of the data and storage management both increase with reduction in fault tolerance of the system. The data chunks of the dataset are considered as the entire data of the cloud could not be made available for experiment. Table 1 gives the dataset fir the chunk algorithms.

Algorithm 2:Rapid Asymmetric Maximum Chuncking

input: string str, left side lenght of the string l:

output: end point 1:

    step1:predefine values: window size, w;

    step2:**function** RAM Chuncking(str,l)

    step3:i=1;

    step4:**while**(i<l)

    step5:**if** str[i].value>=max.value

    step6:**than**

    step7:**if**i>w

    step8:**than**

    step9:**return**i

    step10:**endif**

    step11:max.value=str[i].value

    step12:max.position=i

    step13:**endif**

Fig. 7. Pseudocode of RAM

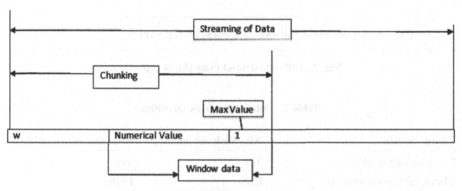

Fig. 8. Process of RAM

4.1 Chunk Modules of AE and RAM Chunking Algorithms in CSP

Table 1 gives the dataset used for chunk algorithm. The selection of experimental data involves two problems associated with real documents. The first being the algorithm might have some sort of special effects on selected data which might indicate to inconsistent conclusions during the comparison stage. The second reason being only a few documents can be selected for the experimental analysis. The reason being that of the quantity and variety of documents being very high. It now becomes extremely difficult to judge the performance of the algorithm based on limited scope of the experimental documents. During the experimental stage the authors selected the datasets based

Table 1. Dataset for chunk algorithms

Dataset	Size	Algorithm
Dataset 1	1.9×10^9	AE and RAM chunk
Dataset 2	1.5×10^9	AE and RAM chunk
Dataset 3	1.2×10^9	AE and RAM chunk
Dataset 4	1×10^9	AE and RAM chunk
Dataset 5	0.8×10^9	AE and RAM chunk

on random generation of file that increase files non-particularity property highlighting randomness of the experimental data (Fig. 9, Table 2).

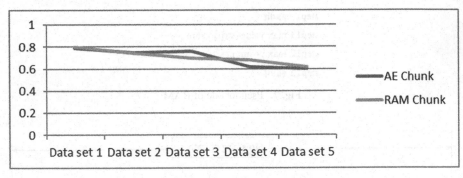

Fig. 9. Different dataset using chunk algorithm

Table 2. Dataset for chunk algorithms

Chunk module	AE chunk end point	RAM chunk end point
File chunking module	Yes	Yes
Chunk encryption module	High	High
Index generation module	Low	High
Index encryption module	Yes	Yes
Data and index encoding module	Yes	Yes

In the proposed method, the deduplication process is divided into five parts. The first part divides the input files into smaller fragments. In the second part encryption of these small fragments is done using a secure hash algorithm and block encryption algorithm. In the third part, an index of these encrypted units is created. The fourth part index that is created is encrypted using an asymmetric searchable encryption method. The cloud storage provider will use the encrypted index for searching the information. In the fifth part, encoding and arranging metadata of the index and information is done.

The experimental results of two algorithms along with the chunking results of size distribution are discussed in the following section. We have used two individual files to test the chunking process. Here there are two algorithms that act on the experimental file generated at random. The results include all the chunks for each algorithm. The size distribution of the chunks is obtained by same length. Figure 10 shows the performance of the chunk.

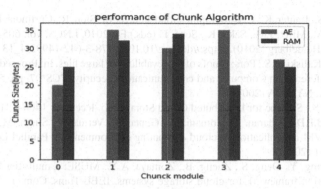

Fig. 10. Different dataset using chunk algorithm

5 Conclusion

Deduplication techniques are very useful in eliminating duplicate copies and avoid redundancy of data thus, saving storage space and improving bandwidth. The security and privacy issues are issues to be considered. The suggested method uses a fusion of current techniques to deal with security problems that arise during deduplication. In the proposed method, the deduplication process is divided into five parts. The first part divides the input files into smaller fragments. Block encryption algorithm and a hash algorithm are used to perform encryption of fragments in the second part. The generation of the index of encryption units takes place in the third part. The asymmetric searchable encryption process is used for encrypting the index in the fourth part. The cloud storage provider will use the encrypted index for searching the information. In the fifth part, encoding and arranging metadata of the index and information is done. Based on the performance of applied chunk modules, Chunk encryption module has high AE chunk end point and RAM chunk end point whereas, Index generation module has low AE chunk end point and High RAM chunk end point.

References

1. Zhang, C., Qi, D., Li, W., Guo, J.: Function of content defined chunking algorithms in incremental synchronization. IEEE Access **8**, 5316–5330 (2020)
2. Rashid, F.: A secure data deduplication framework for cloud environments. In: Tenth Annual Conference Privacy, Security Trust (PST 2012), Paris, France (2012)

3. Eshghi, K., Tang, H.K.: A framework for analyzing and improving content basedchunking algorithms. In: Int. Enterp. Technol. Lab. Lab. Palo Alto (2005)
4. Wang, C., Qin, Z.-G., Peng, J., Wang, J.: A novel encryption scheme for datadeduplication system. In: 2010 International Conference on Communications, Circuits and Systems (ICCCAS), pp. 265–269 (2010)
5. Thwel, T.T., Thein, N.L.: An efficient indexing mechanism for data deduplication. In: 2009 International Conference on the Current Trends in Information Technology (CTIT), pp. 1–5 (2009)
6. Kamara, S., Lauter, K.: Cryptographic cloud storage. In: Sion, R., Curtmola, R., Dietrich, S., Kiayias, A., Miret, J.M., Sako, K., Sebé, F. (eds.) FC 2010. LNCS, vol. 6054, pp. 136–149. Springer, Heidelberg (2010). https://doi.org/10.1007/978-3-642-14992-4_13
7. Juels, A., Kaliski, B.S.: Pors: proofs of retrievability for large files. In: Proceedings of the 14th ACM conference on Computer and communications security, CCS'07. pp. 584–597. ACM, New York, NY, USA (2007)
8. Chavhan, S.: Scheme for Distributed Cloud Storage. no. Icces, pp. 1406–1410 (2020)
9. Comput, J.P.D., Saharan, S., Somani, G., Gupta, G., Verma, R., Singh, M.: QuickDedup: Efficient VM deduplication in cloud computing environments. J. Parallel Distrib. Comput. **139**, 18–31 (2020)
10. Yin, J., Tang, Y., Deng, S., Zheng, B., Zomaya, A.Y.: MUSE: a multi-tierd and sla-driven deduplication framework for cloud storage systems. IEEE Trans. Comput. **70**(5), 759–774 (2021)
11. Stanek, J., Sorniotti, A., Androulaki, E., Kencl, L.: A secure data deduplication scheme for cloud storage. In: Christin, N., Safavi-Naini, R. (eds.) FC 2014. LNCS, vol. 8437, pp. 99–118. Springer, Heidelberg (2014). https://doi.org/10.1007/978-3-662-45472-5_8
12. Shin, Y., Koo, D., Hur, J.: A survey of secure data deduplication schemes for cloud storage systems. ACM Comput. Surv. **49**(4), 1–38 (2017). https://doi.org/10.1145/3017428
13. Fu, Y., Xiao, N., Jiang, H., Hu, G., Chen, W.: Application-aware big data deduplication in cloud environment. IEEE Trans. Cloud Comput. **7**(4), 921–934 (2019). https://doi.org/10.1109/TCC.2017.2710043
14. Kim, W., Lee, I.: Survey on data deduplication in cloud storageenvironments. J. Inform. Process. Syst. **17**(3), 658–673 (2021). https://doi.org/10.3745/JIPS.03.0160
15. Leesakul, W., Townend, P., Xu, J.: Dynamic data deduplication in cloud storage. In: 2014 IEEE 8th International Symposium on Service Oriented System Engineering, pp. 320–325. Oxford, United Kingdom (2014). https://doi.org/10.1109/SOSE.2014.46
16. Yan, Z., Wang, M., Li, Y., Vasilakos, A.V.: Encrypted data management with deduplication in cloud computing. IEEE Cloud Comput. **3**(2), 28–35 (2016). https://doi.org/10.1109/MCC.2016.29
17. Reddy, B., Rao, M.: Filter based data deduplication in cloud storage using dynamic perfect hash functions. Int. J. Simul. Syst,. Sci. Technol. **19**, 8.1-8.8 (2018). https://doi.org/10.5013/IJSSST.a.19.04.08
18. Ng, W.K., Wen, Y., Zhu, Y.: Private data deduplication protocols in cloud storage. In: SAC, pp. 441–446 (2012)
19. Pooranian, Z., Chen, K.-C., Yu, C.-M., Conti, M.: RARE: Defeating side channels based on data-deduplication in cloud storage. In: IEEE INFOCOM 2018 - IEEE Conference on Computer Communications Workshops (INFOCOM WKSHPS), pp. 444–449. Honolulu, HI (2018). https://doi.org/10.1109/INFCOMW.2018.8406888
20. Harnik, D., Pinkas, B., Shulman-Peleg, A.: Side channels in cloud services: deduplication in cloud storage. IEEE Secur. Priv. **8**, 40–47 (2010). https://doi.org/10.1109/MSP.2010.187

21. Armknecht, F., Bohli, J.-M., Karame, G.O., Youssef, F.: Transparent data deduplication in the cloud. In: Proceedings of the 22nd ACM SIGSAC Conference on Computer and Communications Security, Denver Colorado USA, pp. 886–900 (2015). https://doi.org/10.1145/2810103.2813630

22. Kumar, A.: Design of secure image fusion technique using cloud for privacy-preserving and copyright protection. Int. J. Cloud Appl. Comput. **9**(3), 22–36 (2019)

23. Kumar, A., Zhang, Z.J., Lyu, H.: Object detection in real time based on improved single shot multi-box detector algorithm. EURASIP J. Wirel. Commun. Netw. **2020**(1), 1–18 (2020). https://doi.org/10.1186/s13638-020-01826-x

24. Kumar, A.: A review on implementation of digital image watermarking techniques using LSB and DWT. In: The Third International Conference on Information and Communication Technology for Sustainable Development (ICT4SD 2018), Hotel Vivanta by Taj, GOA, INDIA, 30–31 Aug 2018

A Comprehensive Study on Eucalyptus, Open Stack and Cloud Stack

S. Saisree[1](✉) and S. Shitharth[2]

[1] Department of Computer Science, Vardhaman College of Engineering, Hyderabad, India
ssaisree841@gmail.com
[2] Department of Computer Science, KebriDehar University, KebriDehar, Ethiopia

Abstract. Cloud computing remains the discussing topic in the field of deploying applications, data storage, improvising operational efficiency, cost savings, and high performance. Incremented storage capacity and automation suppleness, flexibility, and scalability are the key factors in cloud computing. Choosing an appropriate cloud platform can be very difficult and every platform can have advantages and disadvantages. So, in our research, we are comparing the attributes of open stack and cloud stack. This platform comparison intends to compare the efficiency and usage of the cloud platforms. Then, the eucalyptus, cloud stack, and open stack come under the cloud platform to perform efficiently with high scalability. These platforms can go hybrid with AWS to develop applications. The comparison between this cloud platforms is to summarize the scalability and services. Eucalyptus, open stack, and cloud stack are all reopen-source cloud computing software platforms and this paper heavily focuses on their pros and cons in terms of efficiency, storage, and usage parameters. Conservation of user data should be more cost-efficient in the cloud and these tools comparison would highly assist the users to have an eagle view over the major cloud computing platforms.

Keywords: Eucalyptus · Cloud tools · Open stack · Cloud stack

1 Introduction

Cloud is a parallel and computing framework comprising of a collection of interconnected and virtualized computers. Those are powerfully provisioned and displayed as computing resources. The appearance of hardware-related costs, adaptability, and high fault resilience, so your choice will depend on your budget, business, and compliance needs. There are different types of cloud-like public, private, community, and hybrid cloud. The public cloud is the cheapest way to conduct cloud investigation, as the infrastructure costs are split among cloud inhabitants. It is recommended to utilize an open cloud (Aceto et al. 2012, 2013) to handle huge information workloads, store tremendous information sets, and use such imaginative advances as machine learning, artificial intelligence, etc. [1, 2]. To permit assembly of such specific needs (Andreozzi et al. 2005; Guide 2009), a private cloud is physically found either at your possess data center or at the cloud provider's site with hardware and software committed to your company exclusively. In analogy, to build and manage the things we would require different tools to ensure the comfort of the things we choose to do and ensuring no threats (Shitharth 2017) [5]. The motivation of this work is to conduct a detailed analysis of the primary cloud tools like eucalyptus, cloud stack, and open stack by using various performance measures. The major objectives of this research are as follows:

To compare the performance and efficiency of various cloud platforms such as eucalyptus, cloud stack, and open stack based on the measures of increased scalability and services.

To investigate the advantages and disadvantages of these cloud platforms with the use of storage and usage parameters.

To analyse the working nature and operating principles of these platforms, a separate architecture and interfacing illustrations are presented with its components.

To conduct an extensive comparative analysis among these platforms for selecting the most optimal one by using the measures of active community and usage of cloud.

The remaining sections of this paper are structuralized as follows: Sect. 2 describes the architecture model and elements of Eucalyptus cloud platform with its corresponding features. Section 3 presents the interior and external architectures with its working components of cloud stack platform. Consequently, Sect. 4 presents the open stack cloud architecture with its appropriate elements and communication strategies. Section 5 investigates the usage of all these cloud platforms, and Sect. 6 validates the performance results of all cloud platforms by using various measures. At last, Sect. 7 summarizes the obtainments of the entire paper with the future scope.

(Bystrov et al. 2020) intended to validate the performance of heterogeneous clouds based on the factors of overhead, computational speed and energy consumption. The main intention of this paper was to provide the most suitable solution for solving the bi-objective optimization problems by using the linear scalarization method. (Ventre et al. 2018) aimed to design a flexible framework for efficiently processing various open stack distributions using the open source platform. The main focus of this work was to improve the automation status of processing the applications with reduced deployment time consumption. In addition to that, the virtual cloud orchestration model was deployed in this work, where the distribution support has been assessed based on the parameters of network support, packages installation, architecture setup, and software utilization. (Karuppasamy 2021) suggested an enhanced VM allocation mechanism for solving the optimization problems by predicting the unique solutions with increased energy efficiency. (Pericherla 2020) recommended the open stack cloud platform for an efficient allocation of host resources, where the key parameters like memory utilization, processing speed, and disk I/O have been validated. Also, the open stack model could be deployed for managing the resources on cloud in an effective way.

2 Eucalyptus Architecture

Eucalyptus systems were composed to commercialize eucalyptus software. Eucalyptus is a paid and open-source platform for building Amazon web services with private and hybrid cloud environments. Eucalyptus is an elastic utility computing architecture for relating your programs to utilizable systems. Eucalyptus comes up with a single user interface so that the users can forecast the resources accessible within a private cloud. It is also appliance the standard AWS (Bala and Chana 2012) [6]. There are two versions in the eucalyptus open core enterprise edition and open-source edition it can operate with the both Linux distribution and Microsoft windows. It pools together subsisting virtualized infrastructure to engender cloud resources for IAAS cloud service (Barth 2008; Bellavista et al. 2012) [7]. It is designed to be easy and install for a research setting's it can very easy to modify and extend (Benedict 2013). In this cloud platform of eucalyptus can be easily deployed and maintained, but there is no need for a modification for an underlying infrastructure. Eucalyptus isn't perfectly open-source, but it utilizes a predominant procedure called open center that puts most of the code out there in open source but keeps a few of the bits compiled thereby endorsing eucalyptus to alter for those additional treats.

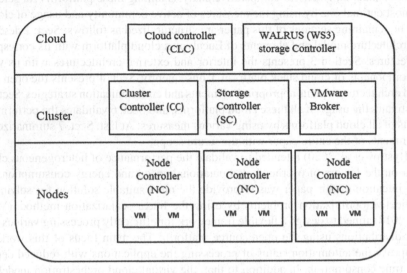

Fig. 1. Eucalyptus architecture

In Fig. 1, the eucalyptus architecture is explained Eucalyptus has components, including node control, VM broker, storage controller, and cloud controller. Eucalyptus is an open software tool that is used to build a cloud platform in few minutes and this cloud platform is introduced for the purpose of enterprise usage. This platform is uniquely accommodated for hybrid clouds so that it can support all the virtualization platforms. At present, it is an active and growing ecosystem for a partner, researchers, developers, and customers. Most widely deployed software platform for the assertion IAAS cloud. It is utilized to build private, public, and hybrid clouds. Eucalyptus provides APIs to be utilized with the web accommodations to cope up with the injective authorization of resources utilized in the private cloud (Bonev and Ilieva 2012) [10]. The interfacing components of Eucalyptus architecture model is shown in Fig. 2.

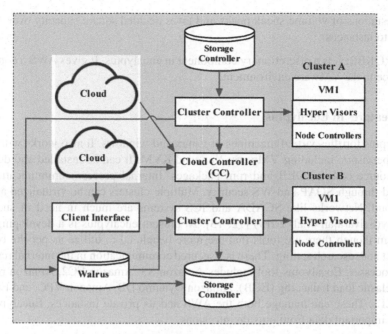

Fig. 2. Eucalyptus interface

2.1 Components of Eucalyptus Cloud

CLOUD CONTROLLER (CLC): As explained in Fig. 2, the client interface interacts with the cloud. The cloud controller acts as the front end of the whole environment. It provides Amazon EC2/S3 congruent web services interface for client instruments and also communicates with the rest of the component's eucalyptus infrastructure (Shitharth and Winston 2016) [11].

CLUSTER CONTROLLER (CC): The Cluster controller manages the node controllers and is dependable for sending and managing the occurrence for them. It also communicates with the node controller and cloud controller. The Cloud controller manages the network of occurrences that are running beneath certain sorts of network nodes that can access eucalyptus.

WALRUS: This is often another java program in eucalyptus that's comparable to AWS S3 capacity. And moreover, it contains pictures, volumes, and depictions comparable to AWS.

NODE CONTROLLER (NC): The node controller keeps up the life cycle of the event running on each node. The node controller communicates with the system, hypervisor, and with cluster controller at the same time.

STORAGE CONTROLLER (SC): It may be a C program that can have a virtual machine occurrence. It is at the slightest level in eucalyptus cloud. It downloads pictures from walrus and makes an occurrence for computing prerequisites in the cloud. It permits the manifestations of volume sneak peaks and gives decided square capacity over AOC or ISCSI to instances.

VMBROKER: It is a discretionary component in eucalyptus. It gives AWS a congruous interface to the VMware environment.

2.2 Features in Eucalyptus

Eucalyptus fortifies virtual machines of Linux and windows. It also works with multiple hypervisors, including VMware, Xen, and KVM. It can be installed and deployed from source code or DEB and rpm packages. Internal process communications are secured through SOAP and WS security. Multiple clusters can be virtualized as a single cloud. Networks like SCADA and ICS systems are much in need of such high security(Selvarajan et al. 2019) [12, 13]. At present eucalyptus is a developing cloud platform though there are tools that are more beneficial to utilize as per the business product and research setting. There is a secured communication in the internal resources and processes. Eucalyptus tool includes Amazon S3, Amazon EC2, Amazon route53, AWS elastic load balancing (ECB), Amazon Dynamo DB, Amazon VPC, and Eucalyptus CLI's. These can manage both the AWS and its private instances. Eucalyptus can secure important data from outside intrusions.

3 Cloud Stack

Cloud stack is open-source management for appliances of cloud services. It utilizes subsisting hypervisors to facilitate cloud handling products like cloud stack as a service solution that distributes certain infrastructure as a hosted service(Cardellini and Iannucci 2012) [14]. Figure 3 and Fig. 4 show the cloud stack's internal and external architecture. It avails developers to engender multi-tenant, multifarious cloud services and scale cloud projects. It can additionally be utilized by businesses that want to provide their private cloud and hybrid cloud service on-premise. Cloud stack permits the programmed deployment and administration of cloud engineering, so that it can effortlessly be coordinated with other computer programs. It utilizes subsisting hypervisors stage for virtualization, such as KVM, VMware VSphere, counting ESXi and Vcenter and xen server/XCP (Celesti et al. 2010) [15].

Cloud stack internal and external Architecture communications done through internally and normal network. It manages storage, network, compute nodes. Cloud stack allocates virtual machines to individual servers. Each cluster utilizes to host the virtual machines from primary storage. And stores the templates snapshots of virtual machine in secondary storage. Pods are a selection of hardware that is configured to form a cluster. A cluster is a group of identical hosts running a common hypervisor. A zone consists of one or more pods and secondary storage that are shared by all pods in the zone. The supervisor server on the internal network is used to manage the entire network. VM Creator is used to create virtual machines. The storage server used to store snapshots. There is no separate network for communication.

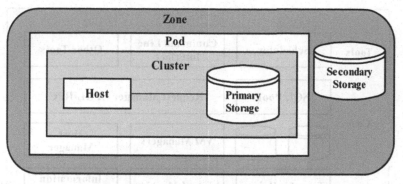

Fig. 3. Cloud stack interior architecture

Cloud Stack Architecture

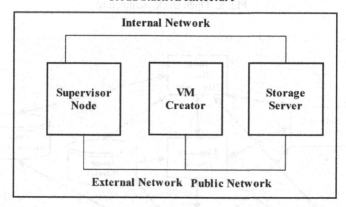

Fig. 4. Cloud stack external architecture

4 Open Stack

Open stack is an open-source private cloud platform designed to manage the distributed computations, networks and storage resources in the data centers. This implies that anybody can get the source code, make any change or alternations, they require, and openly share these changes back out to the community at expansive. In principle, open stack aggregates physical resources into one immensely colossal pool and allocates virtual resources out of this to clients who can request them on-demand through a self-service portal or application programming interface (API's) but open stack itself does not handle virtualization (Chen et al. 2011) [16]. Instead, it leverages the subsisting virtualization technologies. Subsequently, open stack is more homogenous to a wrapper around conventional virtualization instruments, empowering cloud- native capabilities. All of this information is overseen through APIs with a common verification component. Figure 5 showopen stack architecture involves tools, core and drivers.

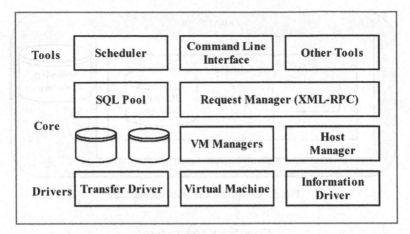

Fig. 5. Open stack architecture

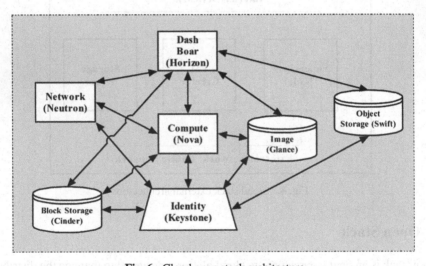

Fig. 6. Cloud open stack architecture

4.1 Open Stack Components

Open stack is competent to supply all over service models, but in practice it is generally sent with infrastructure as a service, where virtual machines (VMs) and other resources (Client interface, Capacity, Compute and Checking) are made accessible to clients. Figure 6 shows how open stack o communicate with each other (Chen and Zhao 2012; Cheng et al. 2009) [17, 18]. The open stack platform is comprised of interrelated components that can control differing, multi vendor equipment pools of computing, capacity and organizing resources all through a data center. Open stack permit administration through a web based dashboard or through CLI commands or Relaxing web services.

4.2 Open Stack Communication

Open stack can't be specifically introduced on equipment. It requires working frameworks which support virtualization within the back-end (Cirstoiu et al. 2007) [19]. Figure 7 depicts the communication structure of open stack cloud platform, where its management networking model has been illustrated with the components of computer node, network node and controller node. At present, Ubuntu (KVM), red-hat undertaking Linux (KVM), prophet Linux (Xen), prophet Solaris (Zones), Microsoft hyper-v, VMware ESXi bolsters open stack cloud stage. That's why open stack is the key choice of numerous sorts of organization of benefit suppliers looking offer cloud computing services on standard equipment, to companies looking to send private cloud, to huge undertakings sending a worldwide cloud arrangement over different landmass. Rack space and HP are advertising open cloud through open stack cloud platform (Comuzzi et al. 2009) [20].

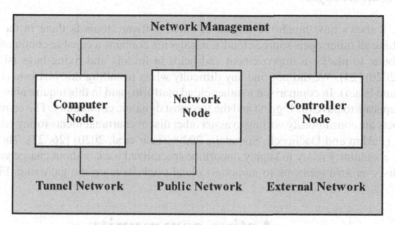

Fig. 7. Open stack communication

4.3 Open Stack Architecture

Open stack may be a cloud computing stage that controls the expansive number of computes hubs, capacity, and organizing resources all through a datacenter, all overseen through a dashboard (Horizon) that gives directors control whereas enabling their clients to arrangement resources through a web interface (Merlino et al. 2019). Open stack gives an infrastructure- as- a- service (IAAS) arrangement through a set of interrelated administrations.

5 Usage of Platforms

Eucalyptus is an open-source computer program framework in cloud computing and that is utilized to implement clusters within the cloud computing stage. It makes the public, private and hybrid cloud. And it permits a client to make them possess data center in a private cloud and utilize its functionalities to numerous other organizations (Lee and Kim 2018) [21]. Cloud stack has a few kinds of highlights such as storage independent computers and admins to make security zones over locals. This makes them idealize for day-to-day use and resource accessibility. It is additionally culminating for centralized administration and enormous versatility. Cloud stack is user friendly whereas open stack is not a user friendly. It faces trouble since establishment and engineering method and it still require a part of time to convey. In installation process it requires extra information before it can legitimately be utilized. And it generally unused platform and it needs a huge community base and isn't supported by the industry. It could be refined item with an overwhelming client selection (Melo et al. 2017) [22]. Table 1 shows how the cloud tools are compared based on security, Installation, scalability, usage and market spread.

6 Result Analysis

Figure 8 shows how much the impact of cloud software tools is there in the industries. Like all other open-source cloud's, eucalyptus contains a capable community that contributes to platform improvement and helps in finding and fixing bugs (Butkiene et al. 2020) [23]. We did not find any difficulty while installing this platform (Husain, Zaki, and Islam). In comparison to other cloud platform, said in this inquire about; open stack appears to have the biggest and the foremost dynamic community. The community members are continuously willing to assist other discover arrangements to any emerging issues (Pokhra and Dadheech; Suryateja, 2020; Tissir et al. 2020) [26, 27]. There's an online community ready to supply opportune specialized back without charge you'll be able discover arrangements to numerous cloud stack issue on the gathering. Figure 9

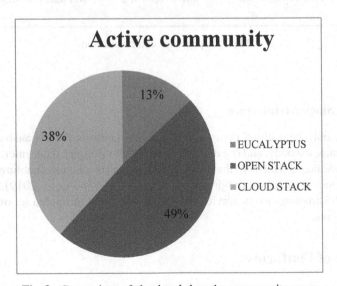

Fig. 8. Comparison of cloud tools based on community usage

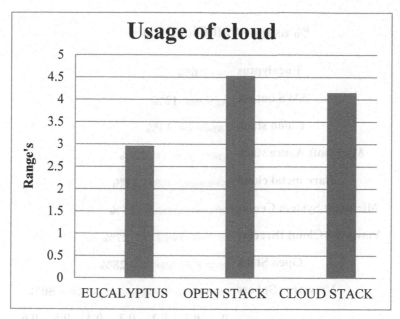

Fig. 9. Comparison of cloud tools based on usage

illustrates the usage of different cloud platforms such as Eucalyptus, open stack, and cloud stack with respect to its value of range.

The usage of open stack is more than the other Eucalyptus and cloud stack because it has more VM's and strong security and scalability and also it is good in disk I/O operations. Even in security purpose eucalyptus is very high and easy to deploy as a hybrid cloud. It makes it simple to provide cloud computing, a bit like AWS, from inside your information center (Gaikwad, et al. 2017; Sriupsa et al. 2020) [25]. Figure 10 represents the usage of various cloud tools in terms of percentage, where the usage has been assessed based on its efficiency, operating characteristics, and simplicity.

Figure 10 Represents that how much rate the users are utilizing cloud tools. There are 3.6 billion users are projected to get to cloud computing services. In that Eucalyptus users are 6% everyday using of eucalyptus tool is developing and its an effective stage to work. Cloud stack has 14% of users, open stack has 28% of the users.

User POV Comparison

From the view of the cloud builder, open cloud means that the hub or the community of the open-source software is endeavor status and backed by an expansive number of systems commercially, without having the need for installation, a seller can move forward conveyance. Precisely where users and innovation buyers can access the openness of the project. From the users' perspective, it is stated that these cloud platforms provide various benefits to the end users with reduced cost consumption, better maintenance, and optimal processing speed. Also, it provides the constant support to the users with authenticated security and safety measures.

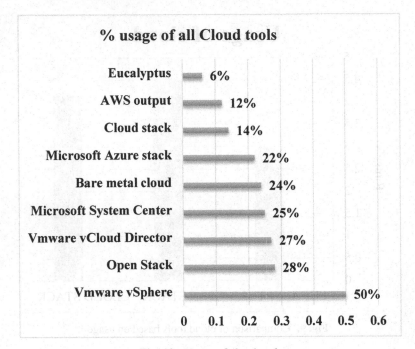

Fig. 10. Usage of cloud tools

Table 1. Comparison of cloud tools based on user point of view

User POV comparison			
	Eucalyptus	Open stack	Cloud stack
API eco system	Amazon API	Open stack API	Amazon API
Product readiness	Business ready and benefits with constant support from developers	No. It is only accessible via any of the various vendor specific stacks	Business ready and benefits with constant support from developers
Developer POV comparison			
Development model	Public development	Public development	Public development
Developer engagement	Contributor license agreement	Contributor license agreement	Contributor license agreement
Governance model	Benevolent	Foundation	Technical meritocracy

API Environment: States, whether the program is supporting a compelling standard with a wide ecosystem(Bhushan et al. 2018) [28].

Product readiness: Makes a difference in selecting the proper market, according to the backed utilize. Development model: Makes a difference in stating what the public needs.

Developer engagement: Makes a difference in expressing the sum of external help within the improvement process.

Governance Model: Makes a difference in expressing how roadmap decisions are made. Table 2 illustrates the different types of cloud properties with its virtualization and provision models, which includes the parameters of applications, interfaces, management abilities, distributed nature of cloud, internal architecture model, enterprise capabilities, and data center integration. Typically, the datacenter virtualization has been mainly used in the cloud for increasing the amount of data storage with reduced cost consumption. Also, it provides the major benefits of better maintenance, minimal downtime, optimal storage, and reduced resource consumption. Moreover, the provisioning is described as the process of delivering the valid services to the customers by using the established cloud platforms. In this analysis, the type of virtualization and infrastructure provisioning has been described with respect to the distinct properties of cloud.

Table 2. Comparison based on cloud properties

	Datacenter virtualization	Infrastructure provision
Applications	Multitier software programs established in the conventional, enterprise way	Re-architected software programs that are compatible in the cloud criterion
Interfaces	Feature rich API's and an administration portal	Simple cloud API's and self-service
Management capabilities	Comprehensive maintenance of virtual and physical resources	Easy maintenance of virtual resources while hiding the basic infrastructure
Cloud distribution	Mostly private	Mostly public
Internal design	Bottom-up design determined by the maintenance of datacenter complexity	Top-down design determined by the efficient execution of cloud interfaces
Enterprise capabilities	High accessibility, defect tolerance, duplication and arrangement done on the condition by the cloud management platform	For the most part found and fabricate into the applications
Datacenter integration	Simple to show into any existing framework environment and it impact on any IT investments	Built on modern, homogeneous object infrastructure

Datacenter Virtualization

Data center virtualization encompasses a wide extend of instruments, innovations and forms an information center to function and give administration on top of the virtualization layer or the technology. Utilizing data center virtualization, an existing or a standard information center office can be utilized to provide hosting to host numerous virtualized data centers on the same physical framework.

Infrastructure Provisioning: Companies may utilize cloud sellers like AWS to set up a foundation as code frameworks that permit them to seek after their objectives in this sort of preoccupied environment. Groups are capable of provisioning and keeping up frameworks beyond any doubt that they are flexible, sufficient to remain valuable for occasion, utilizing S3 buckets and a protest capacity show, rather than setting up physical plates in an equipment foundation on premises [30].

7 Conclusion

This paper presents the study on analyzing the performance of three different cloud platforms such as eucalyptus, cloud stack and open stack, which are exceptionally prevalent cloud resources. For this assessment, the operating characteristics and elements of all platforms have been analyzed with its corresponding architecture illustrations. Typically, these cloud platforms are more beneficial for both cloud users as well as organizational sectors using the cloud model, because which delivers the advantages of easy maintenance, high security, adaptability, and reduced cost consumption. Also, all models following some unique principles and operating characteristics for improving the quality of services. So, it is not clearly stated that which is superior to other models without analyzing the clear purpose of its utilization. Since in the present cloud environment finding out where the actual data of user resides is still a tedious task. Also, the best recommendations to the end-users and service providers of cloud are, the cloud platforms offer an ensured security, privacy, consumes minimal cost for functioning. In addition to that, these platforms are more flexible in nature and is more suitable for managing and controlling the operations based on the requirements. Moreover we feel that community initiatives towards eucalyptus, cloud stack and open stack. Eucalyptus also makes an good option than cloud stack, open stack. Cloud stack bothers composing of multiple servers. For open stack need to install separately to configure the Projects.

In future, an in depth analysis would be done more on data scheduling and data replication in cloud tool environment.

References

1. Aceto, G., Botta, A., de Donato, W., Pescapè, A.: Cloud monitoring: definitions, issues and future directions. In: 2012 IEEE 1st International Conference on Cloud Networking (CLOUDNET), pp. 63–67 (2012)
2. Aceto, G., Botta, A., De Donato, W., Pescapè, A.: Cloud monitoring: a survey. Comput. Netw. **57**(9), 2093–2115 (2013)
3. Andreozzi, S., et al.: GridICE: a monitoring service for Grid systems. Futur. Gener. Comput. Syst. **21**(4), 559–571 (2005)

4. Bala, A., Chana, I.: Fault tolerance-challenges, techniques and implementation in cloud computing. Int. J. Comput. Sci. Issues **9**(1), 288 (2012)
5. Barth, W.: Nagios: System and Network Monitoring. No Starch Press (2008)
6. Bellavista, P., Carella, G., Foschini, L., Magedanz, T., Schreiner, F., Campowsky, K.: QoS-aware elastic cloud brokering for IMS infrastructures. In: 2012 IEEE Symposium on Computers and Communications (ISCC), pp. 000157–000160 (2012)
7. Benedict, S.: Performance issues and performance analysis tools for HPC cloud applications: a survey. Computing **95**(2), 89–108 (2013)
8. Bhushan, S.B., Reddy, P., Subramanian, D.V., Gao, X.: Systematic survey on evolution of cloud architectures. Int. J. Auton. Adapt. Commun. Syst. **11**(1), 14–38 (2018)
9. Bonev, B., Ilieva, S.: Monitoring Java based SOA applications. In: Proceedings of the 13th International Conference on Computer Systems and Technologies (CompSysTech '12). Association for Computing Machinery, pp. 155–162. New York, NY, USA (2012)
10. Butkiene, R., Karpovic, J., Sabaliauskas, R., Sriupsa, L., Vaitkunas, M., Vilutis, G.: Survey of open-source clouds capabilities extension. In: Lopata, A., Butkienė, R., Gudonienė, D., Sukackė, V. (eds.) ICIST 2020. CCIS, vol. 1283, pp. 3–13. Springer, Cham (2020). https://doi.org/10.1007/978-3-030-59506-7_1
11. Bystrov, O., et al.: Performance evaluation of parallel haemodynamic computations on heterogeneous clouds. Compu. Informatics: Special issue: Providing Comput. Solutions Exascale Challenges **39**(4), 695–723 (2020)
12. Cardellini, V., Iannucci, S.: Designing a flexible and modular architecture for a private cloud: a case study. In: Proceedings of the 6th international workshop on Virtualization Technologies in Distributed Computing Date (VTDC'12), pp. 37–44. Association for Computing Machinery, New York, NY, USA (2012)
13. Celesti, A., Tusa, F., Villari, M., Puliafito, A.: How to enhance cloud architectures to enable cross-federation. In: 2010 IEEE 3rd International Conference on Cloud Computing, pp. 337–345 (2010)
14. Chen, D., Zhao, H.: Data security and privacy protection issues in cloud computing. In: 2012 International Conference on Computer Science and Electronics Engineering, pp. 647–651 (2012)
15. Chen, J., Childress, R., Mcintosh, I., Africa, G., Sitaramayya, A.: A service management architecture component model. In: 2011 7th International Conference on Network and Service Management, pp. 1–4 (2011)
16. Cheng, X., Shi, Y., Li, Q.: A multi-tenant oriented performance monitoring, detecting and scheduling architecture based on SLA. In: 2009 Joint Conferences on Pervasive Computing (JCPC), pp. 599–604 (2009)
17. Cirstoiu, C.C., Grigoras, C.C., Betev, L.L., Costan, A.A., Legrand, I.C.: Monitoring, accounting and automated decision support for the alice experiment based on the MonALISA framework. In: Proceedings of the 2007 workshop on Grid monitoring (GMW'07). Association for Computing Machinery, pp. 39–44. New York, NY, USA (2007)
18. Comuzzi, M., Kotsokalis, C., Spanoudakis, G., Yahyapour, R.: Establishing and monitoring SLAs in complex service based systems. In: 2009 IEEE International Conference on Web Services, pp. 783–790 (2009)
19. Gaikwad, C., Churi, B., Patil, K., Tatwadarshi, P.N.: Providing storage as a service on cloud using OpenStack. In: 2017 International Conference on Innovations in Information, Embedded and Communication Systems (ICIIECS), pp. 1–4 (2017)
20. Guide, D.: Amazon CloudWatch (2009)
21. Husain, A., Zaki, M., Islam, S.: Performance evaluation of private clouds: openstack vs eucalyptus. Int. J. Distrib. Cloud Comput. **6**, 29–36 (2018)
22. Karuppasamy, M.: Energy aware on demand VM allocation for a green cloud environment. Ann. Rom. Soc. Cell Biol. **25**, 9705–9709 (2021)

23. Lee, K., Kim, K.: A performance evaluation of a geo-spatial image processing service based on open source PaaS cloud computing using cloud foundry on OpenStack. Remote Sens. **10**(8), 1274 (2018)
24. Melo, C., Araujo, J., Alves, V., Maciel, P.R.M.: Investigation of software aging effects on the OpenStack cloud computing platform. J. Softw. **12**(2), 125–137 (2017)
25. Merlino, G., Dautov, R., Distefano, S., Bruneo, D.: Enabling workload engineering in edge, fog, and cloud computing through OpenStack-based middleware. ACM Trans. Internet Technol. **19**(2), 1–22 (2019)
26. Pericherla, S.: Analysis of host resources utilization by openstack in ubuntu environment. Emerg. Sci. J. **4**(6), 466–492 (2020)
27. Pokhra, S., Dadheech, S.: Relative assessment of open source software for cloud computing platform: the stack war. Pacific Univ. J. Sci. Technol. 51, 4–30
28. Selvarajan, S., Shaik, M., Ameerjohn, S., Kannan, S.: Mining of intrusion attack in SCADA network using clustering and genetically seeded flora-based optimal classification algorithm. IET Inf. Secur. **14**(1), 1–11 (2019)
29. Shitharth, S.: An enhanced optimization based algorithm for intrusion detection in SCADA network. Comput. Secur. **70**, 16–26 (2017)
30. Shitharth, S., Winston, D.P.: A new probablistic relavancy classification (PRC) based intrusion detection system (IDS) for SCADA network. J. Electr. Eng. **16**(3), 278–288 (2016)
31. Butkiene, R., Karpovic, J., Sabaliauskas, R., Sriupsa, L., Vaitkunas, M., Vilutis, G.: Survey of open-source clouds capabilities extension. In: Lopata, A., Butkienė, R., Gudonienė, D., Sukackė, V. (eds.) ICIST 2020. CCIS, vol. 1283, pp. 3–13. Springer, Cham (2020). https://doi.org/10.1007/978-3-030-59506-7_1
32. Suryateja, P.S.: Experimental analysis of OpenStack effect on host resources utilization. In: Khanna, A., Gupta, D., Bhattacharyya, S., Snasel, V., Platos, J., Hassanien, A.E. (eds.) International Conference on Innovative Computing and Communications. AISC, vol. 1059, pp. 11–19. Springer, Singapore (2020). https://doi.org/10.1007/978-981-15-0324-5_2
33. Tissir, N., ElKafhali, S., Aboutabit, N.: How much your cloud management platform is secure? OpenStack use case. In: Ben Ahmed, M., Karaş, İR., Santos, D., Sergeyeva, O., Boudhir, A.A. (eds.) SCA 2020. LNNS, vol. 183, pp. 1117–1129. Springer, Cham (2021). https://doi.org/10.1007/978-3-030-66840-2_85
34. Ventre, P.L., et al.: On the fly orchestration of unikernels: Tuning and performance evaluation of virtual infrastructure managers. IEEE Trans. Cloud Comput. **9**, 710–723 (2018)

Cloud Security by LZW Technique and Fast Searching by Genetic Data Clustering

Amit Kumar Jha(✉) and Megha Kamble

Department Computer Science Engineering, LNCT University, Bhopal, India
amitkumarjha40@gmail.com

Abstract. Digital text content is unstructured in nature as each document writer as its own flow of delivering thoughts. This nature of data leads to searching and retrieval issue for the cloud service providers. Many of researcher get motivated to proposed different approaches for fast retrieval. This paper has developed a model that can provide a secured data storage technique with relevant fetching. Input text data is preprocessing to transform into appropriate format and pass through the LZW technique to encode input data for security. This transformed data was analyzed to get the appropriate cluster. Clustering was done by the firefly genetic algorithm where each document act as firefly. As per patterns similarity from the transformed data, documents were clustered by estimating a fitness value. Experimental work was done on dataset obtained from international journal. It was obtained that the proposed LZWFDS (LZW Firefly Document Searching) improved the relevancy and reduce computational time as compared to other comparing algorithms.

Keywords: Information retrieval · Cloud computing · Data security · LZW · Genetic algorithm

1 Introduction

In recent years, the nature and volume of data have been impacted by technological advances, posing a serious difficulty for data management and retrieval approaches. Almost every element of our life has been transformed by information communication. Data, once thought to be an impossible dream, has now come true, allowing computers to understand and communicate with humans while processing their thoughts.

Most text databases store semistructured data, which is material that is neither totally unstructured nor completely structured. A document, for example, might have a few structured fields like title, authors, publication date, and category, but also some entirely unstructured text components like abstract and contents [1]. In contemporary database research, there have been numerous studies on the modelling and implementation of semi structured data. In addition, strategies for retrieving information, such as text indexing approaches, have been developed to deal with unstructured documents. For the ever-increasing volumes of text data, traditional information retrieval approaches are becoming inadequate.

A. Kumar et al. (Eds.): ICAIDS 2021, CCIS 1673, pp. 419–429, 2022.
https://doi.org/10.1007/978-3-031-21385-4_34

The organising and retrieval of information from large database collections is concerned with information retrieval [2, 3].

It deals with information retrieval, as well as the representation, storage, and organisation of knowledge. Information retrieval is concerned with search operations in which a user must identify a subset of information among a big amount of knowledge that is relevant to his information demand. "Finding relevant information or a document that satisfies user information needs" is the main purpose of an information retrieval system (IRS) [4]. IRSs often use processes like indexing, filtering, and searching to achieve this purpose. The three processes listed above are the fundamentals of information retrieval. In indexing, documents are described in a summary fashion.

Because cloud storage divides data into fixed-size parts, there is a requirement for a reliable and efficient fault tolerance solution that can ensure that even if a plurality of slices is lost, relying on the remaining slices may also restore file integrity [5]. Figures 1 and 2 depict a data security schematic diagram based on cloud storage. Because the essential technology of data security in cloud storage is a broad topic with numerous facets, it is vital to explain the paper's main content. There has been a lot of research into data security in cloud storage, cloud storage in access control, and so on.

2   Review of the Literature

Perform document clustering utilizing supplemental information in addition to the material in [7] paper to get clusters with improved purity. This research also identifies the usage of such supplemental data for clustering in applications involving different file formats such as audio, image, video, and so on. If the extra information linked with pure content is noisy, the clustering performance may suffer. Taking this into account, this research employs a partitioning-based clustering technique as well as a probabilistic model.

Cluster-based Retrieval with Pattern Mining is a revolutionary cluster-based information retrieval approach described in [8]. (CRPM). Various clustering and pattern mining methods are combined in this strategy. To begin, it creates clusters of things that are similar in nature. To reduce the number of shared terms across clusters of items, three clustering techniques based on k-means, DBSCAN (Density-based spatial clustering of applications with noise), and Spectral are proposed. Second, each cluster is subjected to frequent and high-utility pattern mining methods in order to extract the pattern bases. Finally, for each query, the clusters of items are ranked. Two ranking strategies are proposed in this context: I Score Pattern Computing (SPC), which computes a score representing the similarity between a user query and a cluster; and ii) Weighted Terms in Clusters (WTC), which computes a weight for each term and uses the relevant terms to compute the score between a user query and each cluster. Unexpected user inquiries are also dealt with using irrelevant information gathered from the pattern bases.

In [9] authors provides text document categorization utilizing two clustering algorithms, K-means and K-means++, with a comparison to determine which approach is optimal for categorising text documents. Pre-processing is also introduced in this project, which comprises tokenization, stop-word elimination, and stemming. It also entails calculating Tf-Idf. The impact of the three distance/similarity measurements

(Cosine Similarity, Jaccard coefficient, and Euclidean distance) on the outcomes of both clustering algorithms (K-means and K-means++ is also assessed. The evaluation dataset comprises of 600 text pieces from three different categories in India: festivals, sports, and tourism. Our findings suggest that employing the K-Means++ clustering algorithm with the Cosine Similarity measure to categorise text articles produces better results.

The security and energy consumption of medical electronic health record (EHR) data transmission and storage between cloud server and IoT device users are the subject of the [10] study. By integrating a safe energy-saving communication scheme and encryption algorithm to the existing medical cloud model, this work creates a secure energy-saving communication and encrypted storage model. This paper proposes the MedGreen communication authentication technique, which is based on an elliptic curve and a bilinear pair. The approach allows the two communication parties to complete key establishment and identity authentication in only one conversation, successfully balancing the key centre and user resource overhead and preventing the Man-in-the-Middle attack. This paper presents MedSecrecy, a secure data storage algorithm based on Huffman compression and RC4 that aims to address the features of large repetition and high sensitivity of medical data.

Describe the system architecture, data distribution technique, and retrieval system that this effort has created in [11]. For effective retrieval and indexing of data for crawling, a convolutional neural network (CNN) is used to classify text documents. An API-based micro-service architecture is used to disseminate and retrieve information depending on the identifying key. The system provides a platform for extracting knowledge and channeling data for use by the company, as well as allowing support centres to provide on-demand services.

Limitation: In above research papers it was found that security of cloud data need to improved with user login steps. Further retrieval of data as per user query is also need be enhanced as searching of relevant information from large data is taken process. In order to resolve all identified issues paper has proposed a model that improve searching and security both.

3 Proposed Work

Cloud services attract many platform, but security of data and storage in structured form depends on data architecture. This paper has proposed a LZWFDS (LZW Firefly Document Searching) model where LZW protect input data from any unauthorized user reading and Firefly provide structure for searching relevant data. Whole model steps were shown in Fig. 1 where each block describe the work efficiently. Further document searching steps were shown in Fig. 2. For storage of data LZW compression encrypt data store compressed information as well.

Pre-Processing: Text file was transform into set of word vectors Wv where each word is store in separate position. Document file may have different size of text word vector as per content. In this step space is remove from the Wv, as it was assume that all position word or special character have space separator. Each word was transform into its ASCII number range of 0 to 255. This transformation increase the security of content. Each row in the Am have 16 position to store character ASCII number, for short words position have default value 0. So set of Wv is now set of Am (ASCII matrix).

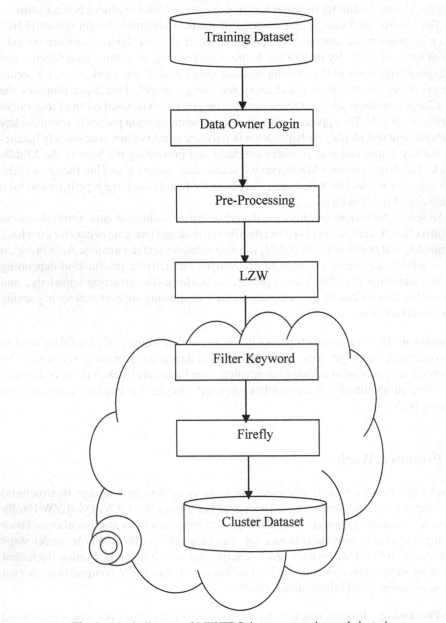

Fig. 1. Block diagram of LZWFDS document storing and clustering.

LZW Compression
LZW reduces the data storage size with security as encoded information store on cloud, hence encoded data need keys to get exact information. LZW dynamically creates a secret code for the word sequence without any prior information. Data recovery is also lossless as whole data generate at reviever end without high detail of secret code, as at receiver side secret codes were recreate.

step 1. Character specific table is created for encoding
step 2. S = character first letter
step 3. WHILE last character left in sentence

    a. C = last input character
    b. IF S + C is in the ST (string table)

        i. S = S + C

    c. ELSE

        i. Output the code for S
        ii. Add S + C to the string table
        iii. S = C

step 4. END WHILE
step 5. Output code for Input string

Filter Keyword: In order to improve the cloud performance retrieval relevancy need to be improved. For this clustering of encrypted data need to done at cloud side, this was performed by applying Frog Leaping Algorithm. Each row in Em is representing a word but some words are important act as keyword in the document, so as per frequency such words are filter. Stop words are identified by encrypted Sw dictionary. So rows having similar set of numbers are actually same word and counting of such word was done to get term frequency Tf [12].

Terms which have minimum number of counts are filter as keyword Fk from the document and rest words are not taken in frog leaping algorithm for document representation.

Module 2: Feature Selection
In this module input feature vector LZW operated BOW were used to cluster words document class. Genetic Data Clustering reduces the data retrieval time, as clustered data access is more relevant and fast. Genetic algorithm performs this work.

Generate Path Population
Assume some chromosome set that are the combination of different document BOW. So chromosome have p number of words $Ch = \{W_1, W_2, \dots . W_p\}$. All words in chromosome

should have unique set of means $W_1 \cap W_2 \cap W_m = $ Null.. Now population is set of probable solution hence $F_f = \{Ch_1, Ch_2, Ch_3 ....Ch_p\}$.

$$F_f \leftarrow Generate\_Population(n, m)$$

Fitness Function

Firefly searching ability was evaluate by fitness function. Distance between cluster center Fkc and non cluster center Fk were summed. Summation of this difference is fitness value of the frog. Equation 2 shows the fitness evaluation formula.

$$F_{v,f} = \sum_1^d Min_{c=1}^c (F_{kc} - F_k) \tag{2}$$

In above equation d is number of documents for clustering.

Light Intensity of Pattern

Calculation of this was done by estimating the total presence of important words available in document [15]. So as per pattern presence in dataset intensity value was set.

$$I_p = N_r \times e^{-\tau r}$$

where I_p is intensity of Nth node. While τ is constant value range between 0–1 and r is random number vary from 0–1 for each pattern.

Crossover

In this work population F_f chromosome values were modified by best chromosome path. As per fitness value best path was select in the population. Best solution change other set of solutions by replacing node in the path randomly. This crossover generate other set of solution which evaluate and compared with previous fitness value to update the population in the model for next iteration.

Now check fitness value of this new solution Ccnew, let its fitness value is better as compared to previous one than this Ccnew is insert into population. In similar fashion if Ccnew fitness value is lower than previous solution exist. Hence new updated population is

In similar fashion other set of chromosomes were modified, here it is possible that modification of chromosome were done at more than one place.

Update Population

Once population get new chromosome than it need to filter with best solution sets. Hence fitness value of each were evaluate and the top p solutions from the new set are filter. Once population get update than as per iteration fitness, light intensity and crossover again start. If iteration over than best available solution from the population is consider as final cluster center of the document sets.

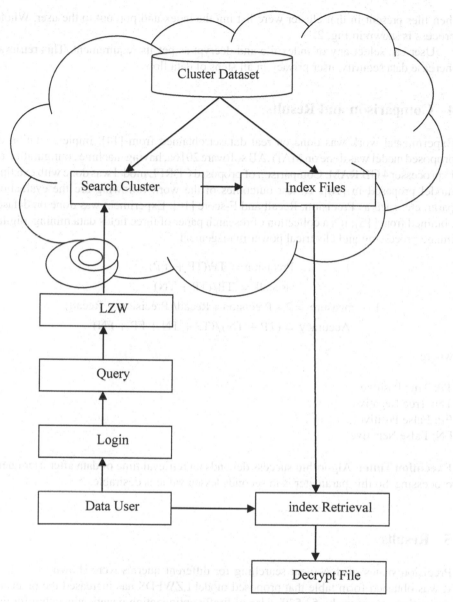

Fig. 2. Document retrieval by data user.

Document Retrieval

Data user login to access its data owner document files. This paper has provides security of user query as well, as text query send to server in LZW format. For encryption data owner keys were used. As per data user query each word is transform into numeric values. These transformed or encrypted words were match with cluster center keywords to get the desired cluster data. Once cluster center highly matching keywords are found then files present in that cluster were list inn the index and pop out to the user. Whole process is shown in Fig. 2.

User can select any of index file and decrypt as per its requirement. This retrieval increase data security, user privacy in all steps of data flow.

4   Comparison and Results

Experimental work was done on real dataset obtained from [14]. Implementation of proposed model was done on MATLAB software 2016a, having machine configuration of I3 processor 4 GB RAM. Comparison of proposed CDRFL model was done with existing model proposed in [16]. To test outcomes of the work following are the evaluation parameter such as Precision, Recall and F-score [16]. Experiment was done on dataset obtained from [15], it's a collection of research paper of three fields data mining, digital image processing and electrical power management.

$$Precision = TP/(TP + FP)$$
$$Recall = TP/(TP + TN)$$
$$F - measure = 2 * Precision * Recall/(Precision + Recall)$$
$$Accuracy = (TP + TN)/(TP + TN + FP + FN)$$

where

TP: True Positive
TN: True Negative
FP: False Positive
FN: False Negative

Execution Time: Algorithm success depends on retrieval time of data after user query processing. So this parameter is in seconds lessen value is desirable.

5   Results

Precision values of document searching for different queries were shown in Table 1. It was obtained form table that proposed model LZWFDS has increased the precision evaluation parameter by 53.53%. Use of firefly optimization genetic algorithm for text data clustering increases this relevance parameter as per different query set.

Table 1. Precision value based comparison of document retrieval.

User query	LZWFDS	FMRMS [16]
Query 1	0.888889	0.421053
Query 2	0.6	0.368421
Query 3	0.6	0.315789
Query 4	0.888889	0.421053
Query 5	0.866667	0.315789
Query 6	0.8	0.315789

Table 2. Recall value based comparison of document retrieval.

User Query	LZWFDS	FMRMS [16]
Query 1	1	0.470588
Query 2	0. 692308	0.388889
Query 3	0.692308	0.333333
Query 4	1	0.388889
Query 5	1	0.333333
Query 6	0.8	0.352941

Table 2 shows different query set recall values output, it was obtained that proposed LZWFDS has increase the parameter value by an average 0.52, as compared to comparing algorithm FMRMS. Use of LZW encryption method for data security with firefly clustering algorithm has increase the algorithm output. It was obtained that proposed model has search the text document by passing query in LZW format. This increases the privacy of the model as well.

Table 3. F-measure value based comparison of document retrieval.

User Query	LZWFDS	FMRMS [16]
Query 1	0.941176	0.444444
Query 2	0. 642857	0.378378
Query 3	0.642857	0.333333
Query 4	0.941176	0.444444
Query 5	0.928571	0.324324
Query 6	0.8	0.333333

F-measure values of document searching for different queries were shown in Table 3. It was obtained form table that proposed model LZWFDS has increased the F-measure evaluation parameter by 55.75%. Use of firefly optimization genetic algorithm for text data clustering increases this relevance parameter as per different query set.

Table 4. Accuracy value based comparison of document retrieval.

User Query	LZWFDS	FMRMS [16]
Query 1	0.9375	0.444444
Query 2	0.642857	0.361111
Query 3	0.642857	0.305556
Query 4	0.9375	0.444444
Query 5	0.928571	0.305556
Query 6	0.785714	0.333333

Table 4 shows different query set accuracy values output, it was obtained that proposed LZWFDS has increase the parameter value by an average 0.4467, as compared to comparing algorithm FMRMS. Use of LZW encryption method for data security with firefly clustering algorithm has increase the algorithm output. It was obtained that proposed model has search the text document by passing query in LZW format. This increases the privacy of the model as well (Table 5).

Table 5. Execution time based comparison of document retrieval.

User Query	LZWFDS	FMRMS[16]
Query 1	2.17855	3.9527
Query 2	2.01488	3.4529
Query 3	1.62288	3.288
Query 4	2.59085	2.9892
Query 5	2.43107	3.778
Query 6	2.1041	3.0892

Use of LZW algorithm for searching data and storing information on cloud reduces the comparing time of the model by 37.02% as compared to FMRMS algorithm. As keys are depend on set of characters so hard number of steps are required to get information relevancy score for indexing of document as per query.

6   Conclusion

Text data is good source to collect for various application and knowledge sharing. Many of cloud services provide storage but retrieval of such set of documents depends on data architecture. This paper has proposed a text clustering model for storing data in LZW encrypted format. This encryption increases the data security with privacy of search as well. In this paper research papers of different fields were used in the work for experimental purpose. It was obtained form the result section that proposed model has increase the relevancy of searching by 53.5% increase in precision value. As the same time accuracy of the model was also enhanced. In future it is desired to further reduce the time of work by use of pipeline technique for execution of algorithm.

References

1. Qin, J., et al.: An encrypted image retrieval method based on harris corner optimization and LSH in cloud computing. IEEE Access **7**, 24626–24633 (2019)
2. Sang, Y., Zhang, Q., Zhang, K., Wang, D., Yuan, Q., Liu, H.: Fuzzy keywords-driven public sports resource allocation strategies retrieval with privacy-preservation. IEEE Access **8**, 195980–195988 (2020)
3. Oppermann, M., Kincaid, R., Munzner, T.: Vizcommender: computing text-based similarity in visualization repositories for content-based recommendations. IEEE Trans. Visual Comput. Graphics **27**(2), 495–505 (2021)
4. Li, Y., Yu, Y., Yang, B., Min, G., Wu, H.: Privacy preserving cloud data auditing with efficient key update. Future Gener. Comput. Syst. **78**, 789–798 (2018). https://doi.org/10.1016/j.fut ure.2016.09.003
5. Han, J., Li, Y., Chen, W.: A Lightweight and privacy-preserving public cloud auditing scheme without bilinear pairings in smart cities. Comput. Stan. Interfaces **62**, 84–97 (2019). https://doi.org/10.1016/j.csi.2018.08.004
6. Li, J., Ma, J., Miao, Y., Yang, R., Liu, X., Choo, K.-K.R.: Practical multi-keyword ranked search with access control over encrypted cloud data. IEEE Trans. Cloud Comput. **10**(3), 2005–2019 (2022)
7. Kalyanasundaram, C., Ahire, S., Jain, G., Jain, S.: Text clustering for information retrieval system using supplementary information. Int. J. Comput. Sci. Inform. Technol. **6**(2), 1613–1615 (2015)
8. Djenouri, Y., Belhadi, A., Djenouri, D., Lin, J.-W.: Cluster-based information retrieval using pattern mining. Appl. Intell. **51**(4), 1888–1903 (2020). https://doi.org/10.1007/s10489-020-01922-x
9. Anand Shetkar, A., Fernandes, S.: Text categorization of documents using K-Means and K-Means++ clustering algorithm. Int. J. Recent Innov. Trends Comput. Commun. 4(6), 485–489 (2016)
10. Zhang, J., Liu, H., Ni, L.: A secure energy-saving communication and encrypted storage model based on RC4 for EHR. IEEE Access **8**, 38995–39012 (2020)
11. Chiranjeevi, H., Manjula, K.S.: An text document retrieval system for university support service on a high performance distributed information system. In: 2019 IEEE 4th International Conference on Cloud Computing and Big Data Analysis (ICCCBDA) (2019)
12. Zhang, W., Jiao, C., Zhou, Q., Liu, Y., Xu, T.: Gender-based deep learning firefly optimization method for test data generation. Comput. Intell. Neurosci. **2021**, 8056225 (2021)
13. Yang, X.-S.: Introduction to Algorithms for Data Mining and Machine Learning, pp. 45–65. Academic Press (2019)
14. Tao, X., et al.: Developing shuffled frog-leaping algorithm (SFLA) method to solve power load-constrained TCRTO problems in civil engineering. Adv. Civil Eng. **2019**, 1404636 (2019)
15. Dataset: https://ijsret.com/2017/12/14/computer-science/

Document Summarization Model Using Modified Pagerank Algorithm

S. Sai Satyanarayana Reddy[1]([✉]), Chithram Deeven Kumar[2], Sreekanth Reddy Pisati[2], and Rama Devi Kolli[3]

[1] Sreyas Institute of Engineering and Technology, Hyderabad 500068, India
saisn90@gmail.com
[2] Department of Computer Science and Engineering, Sreyas Institute of Engineering and Technology, Hyderabad 500068, India
[3] Department of Computer Science & Engineering (AIML), Sreyas Institute of Engineering and Technology, Hyderabad 500068, India

Abstract. Document summarization refers to the writing of huge documents in a precise and short manner without losing the vital information. Automatic summarization of documents is important due to the fact that it consumes less time, less biased compared with human summarizations and the selection process can be made easier using these document summarization methods. Advanced natural language processing techniques are utilized to interpret the text and providing summarizations. In this research, a pagerank-based document summarization model is implemented to effectively summarize the document. Initially, the documents are collected and all the documents present in various formats are converted into text format and summarized using the modified pagerank algorithm. The experimentation results are analyzed using Rouge-N and Rouge-L with F1 measure, precision and recall and the results shows that the proposed model works more efficient than the existing methods with an f1 measure of 76.85%.

Keywords: Document summarization · Natural language processing · Pagerank · Cosine similarity · Summary

1   First Section

Emerging growth in the aspects of daily life by the influence of technologies promotes the outrageous usage of smart phones and other gadgets. This provides a massive data in the form of texts or any other format which is difficult to summarize manually, hence automatic text summarization is enabled utilizing various techniques and methodologies [4]. Text summarization is the process of minimizing the texts by extracting the important information from the original data and provides the user a brief summary, for further proceedings [1]. Information overloading problem could be greatly reduced using this summarization techniques which reduces the length of the sentence without change in their original conception. Hence the document summarization can be considered as a data reduction process for the quick accessibility by the user. Automatic text summarizations are less biased when contrasted with human summaries and it provides great

A. Kumar et al. (Eds.): ICAIDS 2021, CCIS 1673, pp. 430–439, 2022.
https://doi.org/10.1007/978-3-031-21385-4_35

significance in the question answering systems and it also reduces the consumption of time. Reading the summaries will greatly reduce the time and helps in choosing the necessary documents according to their needs [2]. The summarization also has an influence in decision making relying upon the information attained from the social platforms [4]. Underneath NTCIR, the text summarization challenge is initiated in Japan that aimed to collect the repository that consists of training and test samples for the document summarization. The dataset are provided to researchers who studies large scale assessment in single and multiple document summarizations [12]. Kumar et al. proposed an object detection method using SSMD algorithm [13–19].

The Text Summarization Challenge (TSC) task under the NTCIR (NIINACSIS Test Collection for IR Systems) project started in 2000 in Japan. DUC and TSC both aim to compile standard training and test collections that can be shared among researchers and to provide common and large scale evaluations in single and multiple document summarization for their participants. Text summarization is available mainly based on the English language and researchers are focusing on introducing this document summarization in various languages. As an initiative Arabic text summarization is performed due to the fact that the people availing Arabic language is quite larger that is around 5 million [1]. Depending upon the documents the text summarization is classified into single and multiple documents and relying on the type of sentences it is categorized into extractive and abstractive summary [4, 6]. Summarization is carried mainly using two approaches namely supervised and unsupervised learning techniques. The supervised learning summarize the document more efficiently but it requires large amount of data, contrarily the unsupervised methods avails statistical and linguistic features for summarization but it doesn't focus on other important properties in the sentence [2]. The application of this summarization are not only limited with social media sectors but also it is useful in marketing, political campaign and various other sectors. It can be also used to limit the search results with precise and significant content in search engines and keyword direct subscription in news. The effective summarization helps to gain the trust of individuals based on their searches [3]. The commonly used algorithm for the effective summarization is pagerank algorithm that assigns ranks to the words or documents or websites.

The main aim of the research is to summarize the document to enable the composed contents of the document to the user. Initially, the documents are collected from the repository of BBC news classification. Around 2225 articles are present in the dataset that are categorized into five sections. It contains the document that consists of the information collected from the environments, such as business, sports, politics, entertainment and technology. The data collected are preprocessed by the process of conversion, stemming, and stopword removal. The document present in the pdf format are converted into text format for the ease of use of machine and then the words are minimized by utilizing stopword removal and finally the stemming process is carried in the preprocessing stage. From the preprocessed data, the important features are extracted using the TF-IDF vector and similarity measure modeled through hybridizing the similarity measures. The ranks are assigned to the words and the similar sentence present in the documents is grouped. At last, the summarized content is attained. The significant contribution of the research is as follows:

- The documents are effectively summarized using modified page rank algorithm, which is developed through implementing the hybrid similarity measure, such as Manhattan, cosine and Bhattacharya measures.
- The analysis of the modified pagerank algorithm is done based on the measures, such as precision, F1 measure and recall that reflected that the performance of summarizer is greatly improved while summarizing the document.

The rest of the paper is organized as: Sect. 2 summarizes the review of the research, methodology is discussed in Sect. 3, results are detailed in Sect. 4 and finally, Sect. 5 concludes the research.

2 Motivation

The following section gives the perspective of introducing the proposed document summarization model by evaluating the advantages and disadvantages of the previous methods.

2.1 Literature Review

Reda Elbarougy *et al.* [1] introduced a graph based system for the text summarization of Arabic language which performed well and improved the precision of the summarization but due to the complexity in the Arabic language still it should be enhanced. MudasirMohd *et al.* [2] recommended a distributional semantic model that automatically captures the semantics in the text and provided high quality summarizations. Although it summarize the data well it needs a huge amount of training data and computational time. Xingxing Zhang *et al.* [3] presented a method to pre-train the hierarchical bidirectional transformers that train the model with better performance but the pitfall is that the architecture of the model could be further enhanced. Samira Ghodratnama *et al.* [4] established the technique ExDoS, which utilizes both supervised and non-supervised learning algorithms that has the capability to measure the significance of the features but the drawback is that it lacks coherence when compared with human summarizations. Danqing Wang *et al.* [5] suggested a heterogeneous graph based neural network that has the ability to initiate a complex relationship between the sentences.

2.2 Challenges

- It is a challenging task to extract the significant and necessary information from the texts that covers the whole concept [5].
- Training of complex neural network models with inaccurate binary labels is a challenging task [3].
- There is a huge amount of unstructured data which are difficult to analyze and providing the data in a coherent and cohesive manner without redundancy is also a strenuous task [4].
- There is a need for excess amount of labeled training data that are quite difficult to create and expensive [2].

3 Proposed Document Summarization Model Using Modified pagerank Algorithm

Summaries are necessary to decrease the time consumption of an individual. Whenever there is a need for the particular document the summaries will help to select the document precisely without large effort. The most common algorithm used for the effective summarization is the pagerank algorithm. The document summarization is performed using the BBC news classification dataset, where the documents are initially converted into text format and then the preprocessing techniques are performed. Stopword removal and stemming are utilized here and the TF-IDF and cosine similarity measures are extracted using the feature extraction techniques and then the weights are assigned to the words and grouping of similar sentences are performed using the pagerank algorithm and finally the summarization of the document are obtained. The schematic representation of the document summarization is shown in Fig. 1.

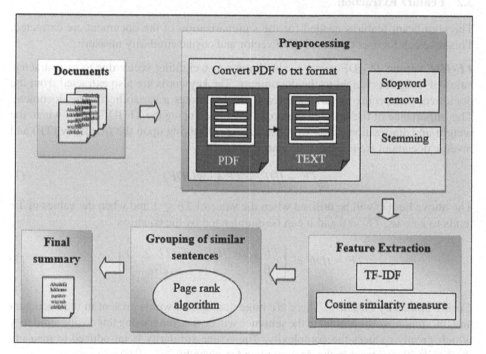

Fig. 1. Systematic representation of Document summarization model

3.1 Preprocessing of Data

The preprocessing is the step that converts the raw data to usable format for the model. The cleaning of the text data and filtering of the unwanted noises takes place in the preprocessing. The initial step performed in the preprocessing stage is conversion of the

PDF document into text format. Furthermore, it is filtered using the stopword removal method and stemming process.

Stopword Removal

The document consists of abundance of words which increases the complexity. To deal with more significant information the low level information carrying words are removed. Certain keywords present in the sentence such as the, as, about, for and so on. These words are removed from the sentence in order to reduce the complexity of the sentence.

Stemming

The process of converting the words present in the document to their original form is known as stemming. Stemming is the process of detection and conversion of the words to its root form. The stemming factor is used because it minimizes the number of distinct words in the document that enhances the frequency term calculations.

3.2 Feature Extraction

The significant features needed for the summarization of the document are extracted. This research focuses on the TF-IDF vector and cosine similarity measure.

TF-IDF vector: TF-IDF vector is also known as weighting vector due to its characteristics of assigning weight to the documents. The keywords are also extracted from the document thet occurs in variant classes which initiates a variability in the document. The importance of the selected feature is calculated using the TF-IDF vector where the weight and digitization of the words are assigned relying upon the frequency (TF) and inverse document frequency (IDF) and is given by

$$TF - IDF = TF * \log(IDF) \tag{1}$$

The above Eq. (1) will be utilized when the value of $TF \geq 1$ and when the values of TF tends to zero *ie.*, $TF = 0$ and it can be enumerated by the equation

$$TF - IDF = \begin{Bmatrix} TF * \log(IDF); & if & (TF \geq 1) \\ 0 & ; & else \end{Bmatrix} \tag{2}$$

Cosine similarity measure: There are huge numbers of words present in the document and the similar words present in the sentence will be measured using this cosine similarity which greatly reduces the complexity. The cosine similarity is introduced to measure the similarities present in the document and is given by

$$Cosine\ similarity = \frac{\sum_{p=1}^{q} TF - IDF(z_{mp}) * TF - IDF(z_{nq})}{\sqrt{\sum_{p=1}^{q} TF - IDF(z_{mp})^2} * \sqrt{\sum_{p=1}^{q} TF - IDF(z_{nq})^2}} \tag{3}$$

where,

$$TF(z) = \left(\frac{O_z}{T}\right) \tag{4}$$

$$IDF(z) = \log\left(\frac{O_z}{T}\right) \tag{5}$$

Here TF represents the term frequency which is obtained by dividing the number of times the word z occurs to the total number of terms in the document. z denotes the word present in the sentence, q notifies the number of similar words and p notifies the offset of the similar words.

3.3 Modified Pagerank Algorithm for Document Summarization

The modified pagerank algorithm is used to determine the probability of the number of users accessing a particular document through link. The modified pagerank has the capability to dwell with the collection of documents of any size. In the beginning of the computational processes, the distribution occurs evenly. To compute the theoretical true value, the modified pagerank algorithm consumes huge number of iterations. The nouns present in the sentence plays a significant role in extracting the summary of the document. The functions of modified pagerank algorithm are: i) The replacement of pages with sentences are performed, ii) The weight of the edges present in the document is also taken into account, and iii) Number of nouns present in the sentence is considered as the initial rank of the sentence. The new rank node is calculated by using the formula.

$$EHR(u) = (1 - v) + v * \sum_{f=1}^{t} Pagerank(d_f) * p(u, d_f) \tag{6}$$

where, u represents the new rank node, $Page\ rank(d_f)$ denotes the present rank of the sentence, $p(u, d_f)$ represents the weight of the edge connected to the sentences, which refers to the similarity measures, which is determined using the cosine similarity and the whole factors are divided by the number of remaining sentences present in the document represented by $(t - 1)$. Normally, the cosine similarity is used with the pagerank algorithm, but the modified pagerank algorithm uses the hybrid similarity measure designed through hybridizing the cosine similarity, Bhattacharya similarity, and Manhattan similarity.

$$p(u, d_f) = \lfloor p_{man}, p_{cos}, p_{bhat} \rfloor \tag{7}$$

During the initialization, each and every variable is assigned to be 1. For the further classifications, the probability is assigned between 0 and 1. The modified pagerank value of any document or webpage can be expressed using,

$$Page\ rank)z) = \frac{\sum page\ rank(y)}{L(y)} \tag{8}$$

Here, $page\ rank\ (y)$ represents the rank assigned to the documents for every page and $L(y)$ represents the number of times the link is utilized.

3.4 Summary Extraction

Relying upon the final rank, the step nodes are sorted, and the sentences are extracted one another until, it reaches the compression ratio. If the selected sentence and other sentence are overlapped then, the sentence is neglected in order to prevent redundancy.

4 Results and Discussion

The document summarization is performed using the page rank method and the results are depicted in a detailed manner is as follows.

4.1 Dataset Description

The dataset utilized for the document summarization is the BBC news classification which consists of around 2225 articles, that are categorized into five different sections and the section includes business, entertainment, sports, politics and technology. The dataset is split into training and testing and the training dataset consists of 1490 and the testing dataset consists of 735 labels.

4.2 Parameter Metrics

The parameters utilized for representing the improvement in the proposed summarization model are Rouge-N and Rouge-L and under both these parameters the F1 measure, precision, recall are calculated.

4.2.1 Rouge-N & Rouge-L

The overlapping of the N-grams is called the rouge. N-grams refer to the contagious sentence in the given document. Rouge-N refers to the overlap of unigram or bigram present in the system during summarization and Rouge-L refers to the longest common sequence that deals with the structure of the sentence and naturally identifies the longest sentence present in it.

F1 measure: F1 measure is the correctness of the test accuracy rate and it can be derived from the parameters precision and recall and is given by

$$F1measure = \frac{2TP}{2TP + FP + FN} \qquad (9)$$

Precision: Precision measures the quality of the proposed document summarization method and is given by

$$\Pr ecision = \frac{TP}{TP + FP} \qquad (10)$$

Recall: The measure of the true positives that are correctly recalled and are given by

$$Recall = \frac{TP}{TP + FN} \qquad (11)$$

4.3 Experimental Setup

The process of document summarization is implemented in the python software and the system configuration is windows 10 with python 3.7.6 version.

4.4 Comparative Methods

The methods used for the comparison are Textrank [8], Lexrank [9], Latent semantic Indexing [10], LDA-based document summarization [11] and is compared with the proposed page rank-based document summarization.

Comparative analysis using Rouge-N

The comparative analysis is performed for the proposed document summarization model and the values of F1 measure, precision and recall are shown in Fig. 2. The value of f1 measure for the methods Textrank, Lexrank, Latent semantic Indexing, LDA-based document summarization and the proposed page rank based document summarization are depicted as 0.695, 0.698, 0.712, 0.721, 0.768 respectively while using 25 documents. Similarly the precision rate of the methods Textrank, Lexrank, Latent semantic Indexing, LDA-based document summarization and the proposed page rank based document summarization are given by 0.634, 0.641, 0.690, 0.699, and 0.708 respectively. The recall rate of the methods Textrank, Lexrank, Latent semantic Indexing, LDA-based document summarization and the proposed page rank based document summarization while using 25 documents are 0.655, 0.675, 0.675, 0.716, and 0.757 respectively.

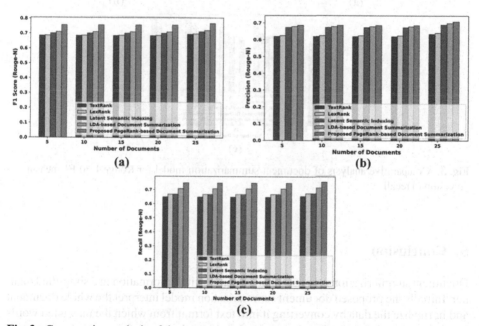

Fig. 2. Comparative analysis of document summarization model for Rouge-N a) F1 measure b) precision c) recall

Comparative analysis using Rouge-L

Here the comparisons are made based on the rouge-N and the values of f1 measure, precision and recall are measured shown in Fig. 3. The f1 measure of the methods Textrank, Lexrank, Latent semantic Indexing, LDA-based document summarization and the proposed page rank based document summarization experimenting with 25 documents gives the values 0.641, 0.643, 0.658, 0.667, 0.713 respectively. Likewise the precision rate of the methods Textrank, Lexrank, Latent semantic Indexing, LDA-based document summarization are given by 0.591, 0.596, 0.645, 0.651, 0.658 respectively and finally the recall rate of the methods Textrank, Lexrank, Latent semantic Indexing, LDA-based document summarization are given as 0.518, 0.538, 0.538, 0.578, 0.618 respectively while using 25 documents.

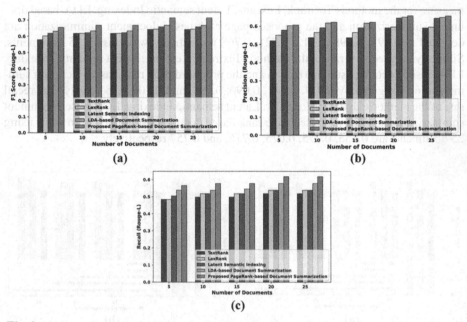

Fig. 3. Comparative analysis of document summarization model for Rouge-L a) F1 measure b) precision c) recall

5   Conclusion

Document summarizations are useful in extracting vital information in a simplified manner. Initially the proposed document summarization model interpret the whole document and normalize the data by converting it into text format from which the unwanted words are removed and the words are converted from to their root form and the important features are extracted using TF-IDF vector. Using the proposed modified pagerank algorithm, the weights are assigned to the words and the summaries of the documents are obtained. The proposed method is analyzed using the Rouge-N and Rouge-L parameters that consist of metrics f1 measure, precision and recall and the analysis shows that the proposed method works in coherent manner compared with the existing methods. While using Rouge-N, the values attained for f1 measure is 0.768, precision is 0.708, and recall is 0.757. Similarly, for the Rouge-L method, the f1 measure is 0.713, precision rate is 0.658, and recall rate is 0.618, which shows that the proposed method works more effective than the existing methods.

References

1. Elbarougy, R., Gamal, B., Akram, E.K.: Extractive Arabic text summarization using modified PageRank algorithm. Egyptian Inform. J. **21**(2), 73–81 (2020)
2. Mohd, M., Jan, R., Shah, M.: Text document summarization using word embedding. Expert Syst. Appl. **143**, 112958 (2020)
3. Zhang, X., Furu, W., Ming, Z.: HIBERT: Document level pre-training of hierarchical bidirectional transformers for document summarization. arXiv preprint arXiv:1905.06566 (2019)
4. Ghodratnama, S., Beheshti, A., Zakershahrak, M., Sobhanmanesh, F.: Extractive document summarization based on dynamic feature space mapping. IEEE Access **8**, 139084–139095 (2020)
5. Wang, D., Pengfei, L., Yining, Z., Xipeng, Q., Xuanjing, H.: Heterogeneous graph neural networks for extractive document summarization. arXiv preprint arXiv:2004.12393 (2020)
6. Shahrak, M.Z., Shahriar, M., Hamid, S.: Middle east user navigation in online social networks and interactions in e-commerce an analogy. Adv. Comput. Sci.: an Int. J. **3**(2), 32–36 (2014)
7. https://www.kaggle.com/c/learn-ai-bbc
8. Mihalcea, R., Paul, T.: Textrank: Bringing order into text. In: Proceedings of the 2004 Conference on Empirical Methods in Natural Language Processing, pp. 404–411 (2004)
9. Erkan, G., Radev, D.R.: Lexrank: Graph-based lexical centrality as salience in text summarization. J. Artif. Intell. Res. **22**, 457–479 (2004)
10. Hofmann, T.: Probabilistic latent semantic indexing. In: Proceedings of the 22nd Annual International ACM SIGIR Conference on Research and Development in Information Retrieval, pp. 50–57 (2014)
11. Gao, D., Li, W., Ouyang, Y., Zhang, R.: LDA-based topic formation and topic-sentence reinforcement for graph-based multi-document summarization. In: Hou, Y., Nie, J.-Y., Sun, L., Wang, B., Zhang, P. (eds.) AIRS 2012. LNCS, vol. 7675, pp. 376–385. Springer, Heidelberg (2012). https://doi.org/10.1007/978-3-642-35341-3_33
12. Lin, C.-Y., Eduard, H.: From single to multi-document summaryzation. In: Proceedings of the 40th annual meeting of the association for computational linguistics, pp. 457–464 (2002)
13. Sai Satyanarayana Reddy, S., Kumar, A.: Edge detection and enhancement of color images based on bilateral filtering method using K-means clustering algorithm. In: Tuba, M., Akashe, S., Joshi, A. (eds.) ICT Systems and Sustainability. AISC, vol. 1077, pp. 151–159. Springer, Singapore (2020). https://doi.org/10.1007/978-981-15-0936-0_14
14. Kumar, A., Satyanarayana Reddy, S. (eds.): Advancements in Security and Privacy Initiatives for Multimedia Images. IGI Global, Hershey, PA (2021)
15. Kumar, A., Ghrera, S.P., Tyagi, V.: Implementation of wavelet based modified buyer-seller watermarking protocol (BSWP). Wseas Trans. Signal Process. **10**, 212–220 (2014)
16. Kumar, A.: Design of secure image fusion technique using cloud for privacy-preserving and copyright protection. Int. J. Cloud Appl. Comput. **9**(3), 22–36 (2019)
17. Kumar, A., Srivastava, S.: Object detection system based on convolution neural networks using single shot multi-box detector. Procedia Comput. Sci. **171**, 2610–2617 (2020)
18. Kumar, A., Zhang, Z.J., Lyu, H.: Object detection in real time based on improved single shot multi-box detector algorithm. EURASIP J. Wireless Commun. Networking **2020**(1), 1–18 (2020)
19. Fatima, S.A., Kumar, A., Pratap, A., Raoof, S.S.: Object recognition and detection in remote sensing images: a comparative study. In: 2020 International Conference on Artificial Intelligence and Signal Processing (AISP), pp. 1–5 (2020)

Architects Companion: Simulation of Visual Impairments for Architectural Purposes

Gaurish Garg(✉) 📵, Aditya Makhija📵, Nikunj Madan📵, Vaibhav Vij📵,
Gaurav Mathur📵, and Shivendra Shivani📵

Thapar Institute of Engineering and Technology, Patiala 147004, India
gaurish_garg@outlook.com

Abstract. Augmented Reality (AR) refers to merging of a live view of the physical, real world with context-sensitive, computer-generated images to create a mixed reality. The Augmented Reality based system for architects and designers aids the architect in designing the product according to the needs of the people affected with visual impairments. The conditions that the simulator will simulate are Glaucoma, Cataract and Macular Degeneration. The architects can see their digital edition of the 3D model from the perspective of visual impairment so that they can modify the model as per the needs of visually impaired. The proposed algorithm is that the user will first point to a QR code which contains the link of the 3D object which will be augmented on another Image target and can be seen from the perspective of visually impaired.

Keywords: Glaucoma · Cataract · Macular degeneration · Augmented reality · Virtual reality · Mixed reality · Architect · Models · Simulation · Visually impaired

1 Introduction

1.1 Overview of the Paper and Challenges Faced

Augmented Reality (AR) refers to the merging of a live view of the physical, real world with context-sensitive, computer-generated images to create a mixed reality [1]. Whereas, Virtual Reality (VR) is an interactive simulation tool that simulates a full-scale immersive environment [2]. The Virtual Reality based system for architects and designers aids the architect in designing the product according to the needs of the people affected with visual impairments. The architects can see their digital edition of the 3D model from the perspective of visual impairment so that they can modify the model as per the needs of visually impaired.

In general, the objects designed are not optimized for people that are visually impaired. For example, if we take a design of a building. Visually impaired customers need architects to anticipate how they will see that particular object or building in this case. The conditions that the simulator will simulate are Glaucoma, Cataract and Macular Degeneration. The proposed algorithm is that the user will first point to a QR code

A. Kumar et al. (Eds.): ICAIDS 2021, CCIS 1673, pp. 440–451, 2022.
https://doi.org/10.1007/978-3-031-21385-4_36

which contains the link of the 3D object which will be augmented on another Image target and can be seen from the perspective of visually impaired.

The major challenges faced were in runtime object import in both the handheld and AR Cardboard variants.

2 Literature Survey

2.1 Virtual Reality Helmet

In one of the papers, which uses virtual reality helmet, following findings were observed [2]. Virtual Reality has been used as a modern visualization device to create a practical Virtual Environment for engineers or architects. In architecture projects for grown-up people, designers can instinctively recognize the positions of the aged through the use of this technology. Virtual reality applications withinside the sector continues to provide result design and have now no longer been carried out in the design development because of the constraints of organized situations of Virtual Reality. The performance and usefulness of the simulator may be estimated with actual tasks. Here they display a visually weakened old people simulator, and the performance and use of it may be based on the actual tasks [2].

2.2 Wearable See-Through Display

In another paper that uses wearable see through display for immersive simulation of visual impairments, following findings were observed [3]. Replication of vision defects may cause higher expertise in the way healthy sighted people to know how people with visual weakening understand the surrounding around them. A person observes the 3-Dimensional image which surrounds the user and analyses the serviceableness and success of the device instead of the usage of a smartphone primarily based totally simulator. It is a wearable display device that allows fast availability. of an extensive perspective digital digicam on a head-hooked-up show to generate a see-via stereoscopic illustration that makes numerous sorts and ranges of visual weakening [3].

2.3 Emagin Z800 3DVisor

Another paper that uses virtual imaging and virtual reality helmet proposes A device that offers a precise replication of the visually impaired [4]. Using digital generated imaging, strong sighted can practice unique visible impairments like central and peripheral ring scotoma, cataract, diabetic retinopathy and glaucoma. The device includes a V.R. helmet that submerges the person in a computer-managed situation. The most important goals of this paper are to teach a strong vision about low-sighted [4].

2.4 Simulation of Eye Diseases in a Virtual Environment

In another paper, Virtual Reality was used to create a visual impairment resulting from various eye diseases. Virtual Reality is being utilized in medical exercise and education. Virtual Reality is used to enhance the visible constancy of the simulated objects [5].

Virtual Reality's first character communicating nature gives mechanisms for imaginings that aren't gifted in other mediums, including video, print, or film. This virtual system has been formed so that those visual complications may be replicated in an acquainted situation. A digital photomask is used to simulate glaucoma. Diplopia is copied via way of means of presenting wrong observing guidelines inside the digital environment. Macular degeneration is created by distorting the imperative location of the simulated environment [5].

2.5 XREye

Another paper features XREye to help in visual impairments experience, representing a set of medically knowledgeable simulations in eye-tracked X.R. of numerous mutual situations that affect visible notion like refractive errors (presbyopia, hyperopia, and myopia), age-related macular degeneration (wet and dry), and cornea disease [6]. These simulations require a Virtual Reality or video–see-thru Augmented Reality and also can be experienced while viewing all-around images. Applicants experiencing the demonstrator will experience simulated visual impairments [6] (Table 1).

Table 1. Literature survey

Reference	Technology Used	Eye Tracking	Diseases Simulated	Voice Instruction	Pre-defined Objects	Runtime Object Import	Citation
Developing a visually impaired older people Virtual Reality (VR) simulator to apply VR in the aged living design workflow	Virtual Reality Helmet	Yes	Glaucoma, Macular-degeneration, Cataract, Color-Blindness,	No	Yes	No	[2]
Immersive Simulation of Visual Impairments Using a Wearable See-through Display	Wearable See-through display	Yes	Glaucoma, Macular-degeneration, Cataract, Diabetic, Retinopathy, Retinitis Pigmentosa	No	No	No	[3]
Simulation of Vision Impairment with Virtual Imaging	Virtual Reality Helmet, Emagin Z800 3DVisor	No	Glaucoma, diabetic, retinopathy, Cataract, central and peripheral ring scotoma	No	Yes	No	[4]
Simulation of eye diseases in a virtual environment	Virtual Reality Helmet	No	Glaucoma, Age-related macular degeneration (AMD), Diplopia	No	Yes	Yes	[5]

(continued)

Table 1. (*continued*)

XREye: Simulating Visual Impairments in Eye-Tracked XR	VR or video–see-through AR, Pupil Labs 200Hz binocular eye tracker	Yes	Refractive errors (myopia, hyperopia, and presbyopia), Cornea disease, Age-related macular Degeneration (AMD)	No	No	No	[6]
Our Accomplished Model-1	Handheld Device	No	Glaucoma, Macular-degeneration, Cataract	No	Yes	Yes	NA
Our Accomplished Model-2	AR Cardboard	No		Yes	Yes	No	
Our Proposed Model	AR Cardboard	No		Yes	Yes	Yes	

3 Methods and Models

For simulation of visual impairments like Glaucoma, Cataract and Macular Degeneration, the following tools and technology were used for the target platforms: Android Handheld Device and Augmented Reality Cardboard (Phone + Viewer) (Table 2).

Table 2. Tools and technologies

	App for Handheld Device	App for Augmented Reality Cardboard
Unity Version	2020.3.18f1	2018.4.3
Augmented Reality SDK	Vuforia 10.1.4	Vuforia 8.3 (inbuilt)
Other SDK	Lean Touch for Pinch, Scaling and Rotation	PingAK9's Speech to Text SDK for voice instructions
Pinch to Zoom	Yes	No
Voice Instructions	No	Yes
Predefined Objects	Yes	Yes
Runtime Object Import	Proposed	Proposed (Minimal Touch maybe Required)

For simulation of these visual impairments, different filters were used and rendered with User Interface Sprite Renderer.

3.1 Simulation of Glaucoma

Glaucoma is a visual impairment that corresponds to the loss of peripheral vision. A person can see what's in the centre of their field of view, but their peripheral field of view gets blocked. For simulation of Glaucoma, a vignette-like PNG image, transparent in the centre and black at the boundaries, was used. This image was then placed in the canvas and could be toggled on or off by voice instruction "Glaucoma" for the Augmented Reality Cardboard App and by using touch for the handheld device app (Figs. 2, 3, 4 and 5).

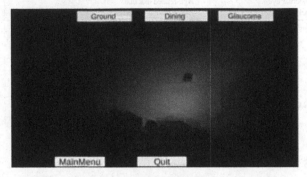

Fig. 1. Simulation of glaucoma in handheld device

Fig. 2. Simulation of glaucoma in AR cardboard

3.2 Simulation of Macular Degeneration

Macular Degeneration is a visual impairment that corresponds to the loss of central vision. In this, the person's peripheral vision is normal, but their central vision gets blocked. Macular Degeneration is just the inverse of Glaucoma. For simulation of Macular Degeneration, a reverse vignette-like PNG image was used with black in the centre and transparent at the sides. This image was then placed in the canvas and could be toggled on or off by voice instructions like "Macular" or "Macular Degeneration" for the Augmented Reality Cardboard app. For the handheld device app, it could be toggled only with touch.

3.3 Simulation of Cataract

A cataract is the cloudiness of the lens, and the lens becomes slowly opaque. Different types of simulations were used for the voice-controlled Augmented Reality app, and the handheld Augmented Reality app. A particle system was used for the handheld device,

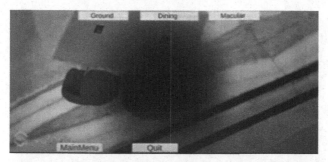

Fig. 3. Simulation of macular degeneration in handheld device

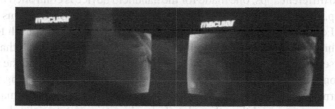

Fig. 4. Simulation of macular degeneration in AR cardboard

a ground fog asset from unity's particle system pack. A PNG image, cloudy at some pixels, was used as a canvas overlay image with a sprite renderer for the Augmented Reality Cardboard app. However, the ground fog asset worked better and accurately than the PNG mage due to different resolutions. In the handheld Augmented Reality App, the disease was toggled on or off by touch. For the Augmented Reality Cardboard app, the condition could be toggled with voice instruction "Cataract". However, it is not difficult to change the method of cataract implementation in Augmented Reality Cardboard by making the ground fog asset the child of the AR camera and adjusting accordingly.

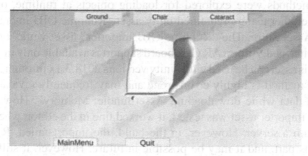

Fig. 5. Simulation of cataract in handheld device

Fig. 6. Simulation of cataract in AR cardboard

3.4   Method of Control

For these two different apps, one made for the handheld device is controlled by touch, and the other app, made for Augmented Reality Cardboard, gives instructions using voice commands. For voice commands, PingAK9's Text to Speech and Speech to Text SDK was used. This SDK was used in combination with Vuforia SDK such that the person wearing the see-through AR Cardboard looked into an image target and the microphone was turned on, and the app listened to the voice commands. On speaking the name of visual impairment, the corresponding filter was turned on among Glaucoma, Cataract or Macular Degeneration, and then the related visual impairment was simulated. Another method is to use Android Native Dialogs and Functions Plugin from the asset store which provides a feature for speech recognition. However, simultaneous simulation of multiple diseases is not yet supported.

3.5   Predefined Objects and Runtime Object Import

Both of the apps, developed for the handheld device or AR cardboard, support predefined objects. However, there will be cases when the architect needs to import 3D objects at runtime. Currently, if an architect has to view their model in the real world with visual impairments, the developer needs to access the object, which is not always possible (Figs. 7 and 8).

Different methods were explored for loading objects at runtime, one using asset bundles and the other using predefined unity asset "Runtime OBJ importer", available on the Unity Asset Store. The "Runtime OBJ Importer" asset works only with Unity 2018.3.1 or higher, and Vuforia AR Cardboard support is available only in Unity 2018.4.3 or lower. So, this asset can be used with Unity versions 2018.3.1x through 2018.4.3x. The Asset Bundles method is highly error-prone and may frequently give an error "Failed to decompress data while downloading AssetBundle: Memory". However, when the runtime object importer asset was tested, it worked fine in the editor, wherein the object was loaded from a server. However, in the build, the import failed. Research is still going on in this part, and it may be possible in future. However, it still works fine in the Unity Editor. On building the app by tweaking the following settings, it successfully loads an object from a server in the app at runtime. For the runtime object import to work properly, these settings need to be tweaked. Edit > Project setting > Graphics > Always Included Shaders > Size += 1 > Standard (Specular) and requiring internet access. The only disadvantage is that it makes the build slower.

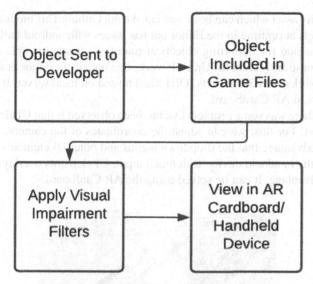

Fig. 7. Existing methods

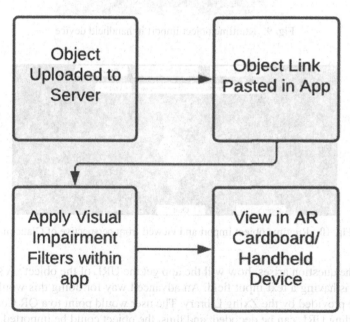

Fig. 8. Proposed solution

Another method for importing the object at runtime by loading GLTF or GLB objects in Unity from a web server using DownloadHandlerFile class and local file caching. GLTF and GLB files make use of JSON to allow easy uploading and downloading of files. The prerequisites for using this method are JSON.Net library from Unity Asset Store and GLTFUtility asset which can be downloaded from Github. This method successfully loads the models at runtime in the Editor but has issues with android build.

Another method for importing objects at runtime is using AsimpL Asynchronous Importer and run-time Loader for Unity. It works fine both in the editor as well as android build. It also works with 3D objects (OBJ files) hosted on local server. It would help in loading objects in AR Cardboard.

However, there was some problem that has been observed is that UI elements overlay on the viewport. For this, we can adjust the coordinates of the camera. But that leads to another disadvantage that the dropdown menus and other UI elements become unresponsive. For the handheld device with touch input, UI elements overlay would always remain a disadvantage. It can be solved using the AR Cardboard.

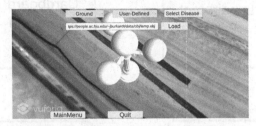

Fig. 9. Runtime object import in handheld device

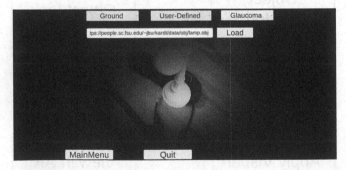

Fig. 10. Runtime object import and viewed from perspective of Glaucoma

Now the question arises, how will the app get the URL of the object? A straightforward way is having a text input field. An advanced way for doing this would be using a QR code provided by the Zxing Library. The user would point to a QR Code, and the corresponding URL can be decoded, and thus, the object could be imported.

The optimum solution for simulating the visually impaired would be as follows. Firstly, the Unity Version to be used should be 2018.4.3 for enabling AR Cardboard build and using its inbuilt Vuforia SDK. Next, have a QR Code reader plugin (Zxing Library) and Text to Speech and Speech to Text plugin (PingAK9 SDK) in the project. The workflow for the user experience would be that first, and the users would point onto an image target that enables the microphone. They will choose the visual impairment using voice instruction. Then they would point towards a QR Code that contains the link, and thus the corresponding 3D model can be made the child of an image target using scripting and Unity Event System. Once the model is imported, it can be viewed on an image target of which it is made the child. Another solution is to get the object link before wearing the cardboard.

3.6 Detailed Solution and Steps

The optimum solution for simulating the visually impaired would be as follows. Firstly, the Unity Version to be used should be 2018.4.3 for enabling AR Cardboard build and using its inbuilt Vuforia SDK and support for stereoscopic view. Now to read QR Code from AR Camera, we need to get a Texture2D from the camera view in the script. This can be done using render textures. Once the Texture2D is obtained, it can be used for decoding text from QR Code. This text or object link in the QR Code can be used to load objects at runtime using AsimpL Asynchronous Importer and run-time Loader. Then voice instructions can be given to toggle the simulation of diseases like Cataract, Glaucoma and Macular Degeneration.

The basic workflow would be as follows. First the user will point to a QR Code to register the link. Then the user would point to an image target (let it be image target A) to enable loading of the object at runtime and enable the object to be augmented with image target B, which would be used for enabling the voice instruction. The object is now registered for augmentation with image target B. Then the user will point to image target B to enable voice instruction. Once the voice instruction is enabled, user can speak the name of the disease (cataract, glaucoma or macular degeneration) and simulate the same. The user can view the object at runtime from the perspective of the visually impaired as augmented on image target B. The complete algorithm is indicated below.

Start

Step 1.   User points to QR Code
Step 2.   System Registers QR Code text in a public and static variable "link".
Step 3.   The user then points to an image target A to enable loading of object at runtime
Step 4.   Check if link is valid. If it is not valid, then give error and go to step 3. If link is valid, go to step 5.
Step 5.   The system loads object from "link" at runtime and sets it for augmentation with image target B
Step 6.   The user then points to image target B.
Step 7.   Either user can see the object from the perspective of healthy sighted or the user can give voice commands. For voice commands, go to Step 8.
Step 8.   Check if voice command is valid or not. If the command is not valid, then system gives error and go to step 7. If the command is valid, go to Step 9.
Step 9.   The user can see the object from the perspective of visually impaired (Table 3).

End

Table 3. Summary of tools used

	For handheld device	For AR Cardboard
Unity Version	2020.3.18f1 or later	2018.4.3
Augmented Reality SDK	Vuforia 10.1.4 or later	Vuforia 8.3 (inbuilt)
Special Touch Gestures	Lean Touch asset from Unity's asset store	Not applicable
QR Code Scanning	Not required as link can be pasted in app with touch	Using Zxing Library
Runtime OBJ Import	Runtime OBJ Importer from Unity's Asset Store or AsimpL (Asynchronous Loader and Importer)	Runtime OBJ Importer from Unity's Asset Store or AsimpL (Asynchronous Loader and Importer)
Voice Instructions	Not required as interaction would be with touch	PingAK9's speech to text and text to speech SDK
Diseases simulated	Cataract, Glaucoma and Macular Degeneration	Cataract, Glaucoma and Macular Degeneration

4 Result and Discussion

The Augmented Reality based system for architects and designers aids the architect in designing the product according to the needs of the people affected with visual impairments. The architects can see their digital edition of the 3D model from the perspective of the visual impaired so that they can modify the model as per their needs. Generally, the objects designed are not optimized for people that are suffering from some kind of visually handicap.

For simulation of visual impairments like Glaucoma, Cataract and Macular Degeneration, the following tools and technology were used for the target platforms: Android Handheld Device and Augmented Reality Cardboard (Phone + Viewer).

For simulation of these visual impairments, A particle system was used for simulation of cataract for the handheld device, a ground fog asset from unity's particle system pack, and various filters were used and rendered with User Interface Sprite Renderer for the Augmented Reality Cardboard app.

The app made for the handheld devices is controlled by touch, while the other app, made for Augmented Reality Cardboard, accepts voice commands as instructions (using speech to text SDK). On speaking the name of visual impairment, the corresponding overlay is turned on among Glaucoma, Cataract or Macular Degeneration, and then the related visual impairment was simulated. This helps the architects to visualize the perspective of their clients and help them design with the necessary workarounds.

Both of the apps, developed for the handheld device or AR cardboard, support predefined objects as well as runtime object import. The workflow for the user experience would be that first, and the users would point onto an image target that enables the microphone. They will choose the visual impairment using voice instruction. Then they would point towards a QR Code which contains the URL, and thus the corresponding

3D model can be made the child of an image target using scripting and Unity Event System. Once the model is imported, it can be viewed on an image target of which it is made the child. Another solution is to get the object link, and importing it into the scene before wearing the cardboard.

The main disadvantage of AR Cardboard is that user can't freely rotate the object by pinching.

As of now, the app features simulation of Glaucoma, Macular Degeneration and Cataract in both the handheld variant and the AR Cardboard variant enabled by voice instructions with runtime object import as a feature in handheld variant and proposed in AR Cardboard variant as indicated in Fig. 1 through Fig. 6 and Fig. 9 and Fig. 10.

5   Conclusion and Future Scope

The app is a simulator used by architects by enabling them to visualize how people affected with visual impairments like Glaucoma, Cataract and Macular Degeneration view their models. The app has some premade objects as well as an option for the architects to import its own objects or models at run time suing object links. The main aim of the app is to make the architect see what the visually impaired see and how they see the various objects and models made by the architects. This helps the architects make their models compatible for the visually impaired as architects could view the digital edition of their models from the perspective of visually impaired through this app. The future work for the app shall support voice commands along with importing 3D models at runtime and can be viewed in Augmented Reality. This project can be extended to Virtual Reality wherein architects could visualize the 3D plan of the house the design, from the perspective of visually impaired.

References

1. Furht, B.: Handbook of Augmented Reality. Springer Science & Business Media (2011)
2. Zhang, Y., Codinhoto, R.: Developing a visually impaired older people Virtual Reality (VR) simulator to apply VR in the aged living design workflow. In: 24th International Conference Information Visualisation (IV), pp. 226–235 (2020)
3. Ates, H.C., Fiannaca, A.J., Folmer, E.: Immersive simulation of visual impairments using a wearable see-through display. In: Proceedings of the 16th international ACM SIGACCESS conference on Computers & accessibility, pp. 225–228 (2015)
4. Velazquez, R.: Simulation of vision impairment with virtual imaging. In: Pan American Health Care Exchanges (PAHCE), p. 1 (2013)
5. Ai, Z., et al.: Simulation of eye diseases in a virtual environment. In: Proceedings of the 33rd Annual Hawaii International Conference on System Sciences, pp. 1–5 (2000)
6. Krösl, K., Elvezio, C., Hürbe, M., Karst, S., Feiner. S., Wimmer, M.: XREye: Simulating Visual Impairments in Eye-Tracked XR. In: 2020 IEEE Conference on Virtual Reality and 3D User Interfaces Abstracts and Workshops (VRW), pp. 830–831 (2020)

Classification Models for Autism Spectrum Disorder

Vincent Peter C. Magboo$^{(\boxtimes)}$ and Ma. Sheila A. Magboo

Department of Physical Sciences and Mathematics, University of the Philippines Manila,
Manila, Philippines
{vcmagboo,mamagboo}@up.edu.ph

Abstract. Autism spectrum disorder (ASD) is a neurodevelopmental disorder affecting all age groups. A diagnosis of ASD require an exhaustive and time-consuming evaluation by a health professional. There are no diagnostic tests that can quickly detect ASD. Several machine learning models (logistic regression, k-nearest neighbors, Naïve Bayes, support vector machine, decision trees, random forest, AdaBoost, XGBoost and deep neural network) were applied to publicly available ASD child, adolescent, and adult datasets. In the child dataset, the best performing models were obtained by AdaBoost, support vector machine, and logistic regression with 95–99% accuracy while logistic regression, random forest, and support vector machine were the best performing models for the adolescent dataset with 95–100% accuracy. AdaBoost, support vector machine, and logistic regression gave an excellent performance for the adult dataset with 99–100% accuracy. Our findings are promising and comparable to other studies in the literature. Our results have generated useful insights in the development of automated models that are faster and with high reliability which can be of use to health practitioners in the diagnosis of autism across age groups. Together with early and prompt assessment, particularly in cases of limited number of trained professionals, tools aided with machine learning can potentially reduce the number of patients required to undergo the lengthy, multistep process to get an official diagnosis. As a result, early intervention efforts ensure the best quality of care for our patients.

Keywords: Autism · Machine learning · Deep neural network · AdaBoost · XGBoost · SVM · kNN · Logistic regression · Random forest · Naïve Bayes · Decision tree

1 Introduction

Autism Spectrum Disorder (ASD) is a neurodevelopmental disorder characterized by challenges in social communication and interaction, restricted interests, and repetitive behavior [1]. According to the Center for Disease Control and Prevention Autism and Developmental Disabilities Monitoring Network (ADDM), about 1 in 44 children has been diagnosed with ASD, occurring in all racial, ethnic, and socioeconomic groups, and four times more common among boys than girls [2]. While beginning symptoms are often

© The Author(s), under exclusive license to Springer Nature Switzerland AG 2022
A. Kumar et al. (Eds.): ICAIDS 2021, CCIS 1673, pp. 452–464, 2022.
https://doi.org/10.1007/978-3-031-21385-4_37

observed by parents or caregivers during infancy stage, they become more prominent in the early childhood period and usually persisting till adolescence and adulthood. As such, diagnosis of ASD can be made during infancy, childhood, adolescence and even adulthood [3]. Depending on the severity, patients with ASD maybe functionally independent or may need constant care or round the clock assistance. To make a diagnosis of ASD, an extensive and lengthy evaluation by psychologists is done using numerous tools such as Autism Diagnostic Interview Revised (ADI-R) and Autism Diagnostic Observation Schedule Revised (ADOS-R) [4]. It is important to assess the child for ASD in the early stages so that early intervention can be proposed, thus improving the quality of life of the patient. It is in this area of early diagnosis where machine learning can be utilized, thus enhancing the whole diagnostic process leading to institution of the much-needed therapy.

2 Literature Review

In the study by Omar et al., tree-based predictive models (decision tree, random forest and merged random forest) were compared to assess for ASD. Merged random forest appeared to be the highest performing classifier with an accuracy rate of more than 92% on child, adolescent and adult datasets taken from University of California Irvine Machine Learning Repository [3]. Raj and Masood studied several models (Naïve Bayes (NB), Support Vector Machine (SVM), Logistic Regression (LR), KNN and Convolutional Neural Network (CNN)) for predicting ASD in children, adolescents, and adults [5]. Results showed CNN-based prediction models with the highest prediction performance with accuracy of 99.53%, 98.30%, 96.88% for ASD for Adult, Children, and Adolescents, respectively. Vakadkar et al. [4] applied SVM, Random Forest Classifier (RFC), NB, LR and KNN to child dataset with LR having the highest accuracy of 97%. In [6], several machine learning models namely: SVM, KNN, Random Forest (RF), NB, Stochastic gradient descent (SGD), AdaBoost, and CN2 Rule Induction were also applied to the 4 ASD UCI ML repository datasets. The best performing models were SGD in the adult dataset, RF in the adolescent dataset, SGD in the child dataset and AdaBoost in the toddler dataset, with an accuracy of 99.7%, 97.2%, 99.6% and 99.8%, respectively. Sharif and Khan applied a machine learning based framework for automatic detection of ASD using features extracted from corpus callosum and intracranial brain volume. The authors used a Convolutional Neural Networks (CNN) via the transfer learning approach (VGG16) for classification of ASD with satisfactory accuracy results and have also claimed a reduction of complexity of the model through a selection of the most significant features with discriminative capabilities [7].

Mohanty et al., applied a Deep Neural Network Prediction and Classification (DNNPC) model after a dimension reduction via diffusion mapping to the ASD UCI ML child dataset [8]. Their results generated good accuracy and sensitivity rates and concluded that metrics could be further improved by the addition of more layers in the neural network model. In [9], authors applied different machine learning models following a 10-fold cross validation (SVM, KNN, DT, RF and Discriminant Analysis) and dimensionality reduction with principal component analysis on the ASD UCI ML toddler dataset. All performance metrics generated more than 90% result despite the unbalanced nature of the toddler dataset. Lu and Perkowski analyzed the facial images of East Asia ASD Children Facial Image Dataset (East Asian Dataset) and Kaggle Autism Facial Dataset (Kaggle Dataset) through a VGG16 transfer learning-based deep learning with 95% accuracy and F1 scores [10]. Erkan and Thanh also applied various machine learning models (SVM, RF, and KNN) to the ASD UCI ML child, adolescent, and adult datasets with very high accuracy results particularly of the RF model [11]. In another study by Gardner-Hoag et al., authors applied k-means clustering and multiple linear regression to identify types of autism spectrum disorder based on engagement in different challenging behaviors and evaluate differences in treatment response between groups [12]. Their findings indicate that self-injurious behavior and aggression were prevalent among participants with the worst treatment response, indicating that interventions targeting these behaviors are warranted and highlighting the potential use of unsupervised machine learning models to identify types of autism spectrum disorder. In [13], various classifiers (artificial neural network (ANN), recurrent neural network, DT, extreme learning machine, gradient boost, KNN, LR, NB RF, SVM and XGBoost) were applied on ASD Kaggle and UCI machine learning repository toddler, child, and adolescent datasets. Their results show LR with the best performance to detect autism.

Our objective is to predict if a patient has autism spectrum disorder using a variety of machine learning classification algorithms namely: Logistic Regression (LR), Naive Bayes (NB), k-Nearest Neighbor (KNN), Support Vector Machine (SVM), Decision Tree (DT), Random Forest (RF), AdaBoost, XGBoost, and Deep Neural Network (DNN) evaluated on publicly available Autism datasets. Performance metrics include accuracy, precision, recall, specificity and F1 score. Confusion matrices were also obtained.

3 Methodology

The study shall be performed in several stages. The first step is the loading of the dataset. This is to be followed by pre-processing steps which include: (1) data cleaning for inconsistent data (2) application of imputation technique for missing data (3) dataset normalization and (4) application of random oversampling for handling data imbalance. The next step is to apply a variety of machine learning algorithms to be followed by assessment of its performance.

3.1 Dataset Description

Like the studies reported in the literature, we used the ASD University of Califonia Irvine Machine Learning Repository child, adolescent, and adult datasets [14–16]. The attributes with their description are shown in Table 1 while the profile is seen in Table 2. We take note of the child dataset as a balanced dataset while the adolescent and adult datasets show imbalance. The datasets are based on the AQ-10 screening tool which is used to ascertain whether an individual requires comprehensive autism assessment. For each of the AQ-10 categories (child: 4–11 years, adolescent: 12–16 years, adult: 18-year-old and above), it has 10 screening test questions that can easily be completed within a short period of time, and results would guide if a user would need extensive autism assessment. The questions are extracted uniformly from five different sections: attention to detail, attention switching, communication, imagination, and social interaction [3].

Table 1. Description of attributes of ASD

Attribute	Type	Description
Age	Number	Years
Sex	String	Male or Female
Ethnicity	String	List of common ethnicities in text format
Born with jaundice	Boolean (Yes or No)	Whether the case was born with jaundice
Family member with PDD (Pervasive Development Disorder)	Boolean (Yes or No)	Whether any immediate family member has a PDD
Who is completing the test	String	Parent, self, caregiver, etc.
Country of Residence	String	List of Countries in text format
Use the screening app before	Boolean (Yes or No)	Whether the use has used a screening app
Screening method Type (A1–A10)	Binary (0, 1)	Answer to the question based on screening method used (AQ–10)
Screening score	Integer	Final score based on the screening method
Age Description	String	Age description pertaining to the method
Class/ASD	Boolean (Yes or No)	Class Description

Table 2. Descriptive profile of the three ASD datasets

ASD datasets	Number of instances	Male:female ratio	Age (mean ± std dev)	With ASD/Without ASD
Child	292	208:84	6.00 ± 0.45	141 (48%)/151 (52%)
Adolescent	104	50:54	14.00 ± 1.56	63 (61%)/41(39%)
Adult	703	367:336	29.00 ± 9.70	514 (73%)/189 (27%)

3.2 Pre-processing Steps

To prepare the dataset for machine learning, we started with data cleaning and applied pre-processing methods. We dropped the variables - screening score and age description, which were deemed unimportant to make an ASD classification. As most of the fields of the dataset are reported as strings, we converted these fields to categorical labels. A few missing age values (four for child dataset and two for adult dataset) were imputed using the mean imputation. Also, one record in the adult dataset was dropped due to unbelievable age of 383 years. Missing ethnicity values were replaced by "others" while the missing "who completed the test" were reencoded as "not mentioned". Feature scaling with normalization using the StandardScaler function of scikit-learn library was also applied so that all numeric attribute values range between [0,1]. To handle the imbalance for adolescent and adult datasets, we applied random oversampling method. The machine learning pipeline for this study is seen in Fig. 1.

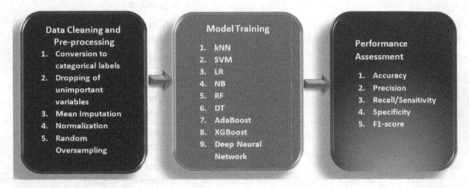

Fig. 1. Machine learning pipeline for autism classification

3.3 Machine Learning Models

Each dataset was split into 30% testing and 70% training. 10-fold cross validation was also applied. The training set was further divided into 80% training and 20% validation. Python 3.8 and its various machine learning libraries (scikit-learn, keras, tensorflow, pandas, Matplotlib, seaborn, and NumPy) were used in this experiment.

Logistic Regression (LR). Logistic Regression predicts a binary outcome variable using a set of independent variables. It uses a logistic function to map probabilities to discrete classes to generate an output in the range of 0 to 1. A probability falling over a certain threshold is then classified as falling into one or the other category [4, 5, 13, 17, 18].

K-Nearest Neighbors (KNN). KNN is a form of a lazy, non-parametric supervised classification model based on the notion that points that are near to one another must be similar. The k nearest neighbors of a point is determined by minimizing a similarity measure usually, the Euclidean distance, with the unlabeled object then classified either by majority voting (the predominant class in the neighborhood) or by a weighted majority, where a greater weight is given to points closer to the unlabeled object [4, 6, 9, 11, 13, 17–19].

Naïve Bayes (NB). Naïve Bayes is a supervised probabilistic classifier using the Bayes Theorem. This method assumes that each input variable is strongly independent of the other variables. Classification of one characteristic within a class has no bearing on the classification of another characteristic [4–6, 13, 17, 19]. However, it only works well with limited number of features. Moreover, there is a high bias when there is a small amount of data [4].

Support Vector Machine (SVM). SVM is a commonly used machine learning algorithm in classification and regression. Each record is plotted as a point on an n-dimensional space with N number of features in the dataset. The main goal is to find the best hyperplane that can separate the classes well, maximizing the distance between the point nearest it and the hyperplane [4–6, 9, 11, 13, 17, 19]. In this study, the best parameters were obtained with a linear kernel.

Decision Tree (DT). DT, a supervised classification algorithm with tree like structure, in which a decision is done by the root of the tree using a few attributes. It selects the highest gain in these attributes in each step of the decision. A decision tree makes decisions by splitting nodes into sub-nodes where each leaf in the tree is labeled with a class or probability distribution over the classes. This procedure stops when only homogeneous nodes are left [3, 13, 17, 20].

Random Forest (RF). RF uses a combination of decision trees similar to an ensemble classifier. A bootstrap technique is applied to each tree from the training dataset. Given a data input, each tree makes a prediction. RF prediction is the class with the highest votes. Thus, the prediction performance is better as compared to a vote of an individual decision tree [3, 4, 6, 9, 11, 13, 17].

AdaBoost. AdaBoost uses a collection of stumps consisting of a decision tree with one root node and two leaves coupled with a feedback system. The stump uses a selected feature to make a decision wherein the mistakes are passed on to the next stump. The weights of misclassified samples in the training set are subsequently increased in each iteration. AdaBoost hence puts more weight on difficult to classify instances and fewer weights on those it has already classified correctly. Thus, it can generate better performance by combining weak classifiers into a single strong classifier. However, AdaBoost is less vulnerable to overfitting compared to other learning algorithms [6, 17, 21–23].

XGBoost. XGBoost is an integrated model based on scalable tree boosting system which uses a gradient boost framework designed for speed and to maximize performance. It assumes that the existent relationship between the input and output variables is not always linear. It is also easier to interpret the results like that of random forests, but its predictive accuracy is higher than random forests when trained properly with the corresponding hyperparameters [13, 17, 24, 25].

Deep Neural Network (DNN). Deep learning, a specific field of machine learning inspired by information processing in human brain, uses a data model with a complex structure combining distinct non-linear transformations. A deep neural network consists of one input layer, several hidden layers responsible for extracting important features from input data and one output layer [5, 8, 26–29]. In our study, we use a simple deep feed forward model that use only the dense or the fully connected layers with an Adam optimizer, and a categorical cross-entropy loss.

4 Results and Discussion

The performance metrics of the 9 ML models for each of the datasets are shown in Table 3. The best performing models for the child dataset were AdaBoost, SVM, and LR with equally superior accuracy rates (95%-99%), precision (95–100%), sensitivity (92–100%), specificity (96–100%), and F-scores (96–99%). RF and XGBoost have also acceptable performance metric results. Likewise, it is also evident that NB and kNN performed rather poorly for this dataset. For the adolescent dataset, the best combination of performance metrics was given by the LR, RF, and SVM with excellent performance metrics of 90–100%. Additionally, AdaBoost and XGBoost also provided good performance. On the other hand, NB and kNN obtained very poor prediction performance. The optimum result for the adult dataset was garnered by AdaBoost, SVM and LR with 99–100% in all performance metrics. DT, RF, XGBoost and DNN have also superior performance metrics ranging from 95–99%. Similarly with the child and adolescent datasets, NB has a very poor performance metrics, particularly in the specificity rate while kNN has a satisfactory performance. Across all datasets, LR and SVM have excellent performance while kNN and NB were not good models for autism prediction.

Table 4 highlights the confusion matrix of the best performing models for each dataset. Comparative performance of best machine learning models across datasets is shown in Fig. 2. We also compared the effect of random oversampling to handle data imbalance in the adolescent and adult datasets as highlighted in Tables 5 and 6. Overall, there is general improvement of the metrics when random oversampling is applied to our datasets with the exception of XGBoost for adolescent dataset. This highlights the importance of addressing the data imbalance to obtain a more reliable diagnostic performance of the models.

Our results are comparable with the other studies [3–6, 8, 11, 27, 29] in the literature with respect to the performance metrics across all datasets. These findings suggest the feasibility of applying the ML models to generate a screening diagnosis of ASD with acceptable results. The clinical utility of this study is even more highlighted with models that can provide faster, more accessible and with high reliability to help clinicians screen for neurodevelopmental disorders like autism. This is more prominently seen in children where an early diagnosis and consequently prompt intervention efforts can make a significant impact in improving behavior, skills, and language development. This research, thus, provided useful insights in the development of an automated model that can assist medical practitioners in detecting autism spectrum disorders across age groups.

Table 3. Performance metrics for the autism dataset

ML Model	Dataset	Accuracy	Precision	Recall (Sensitivity)	Specificity	F-score
LR	Child	0.95	0.95	0.95	0.96	0.95
	Adolescent	1.00	1.00	1.00	1.00	1.00
	Adult	1.00	0.99	1.00	0.99	1.00
kNN	Child	0.68	0.58	0.92	0.51	0.71
	Adolescent	0.76	0.70	0.89	0.65	0.78
	Adult	0.92	0.88	0.98	0.86	0.93
NB	Child	0.49	0.45	1.00	0.90	0.62
	Adolescent	0.63	0.57	0.89	0.40	0.70
	Adult	0.57	0.54	1.00	0.12	0.70
SVM	Child	0.97	1.00	0.92	1.00	0.96
	Adolescent	0.95	0.90	1.00	0.90	0.95
	Adult	1.00	1.00	1.00	1.00	1.00
DT	Child	0.82	0.71	0.95	0.73	0.81
	Adolescent	0.84	0.88	0.78	0.90	0.82
	Adult	0.95	0.96	0.96	0.95	0.96
RF	Child	0.92	0.88	0.95	0.90	0.91
	Adolescent	0.95	0.94	0.94	0.95	0.94
	Adult	0.97	0.96	0.99	0.95	0.97
AdaBoost	Child	0.99	0.97	1.00	0.98	0.99
	Adolescent	0.92	1.00	0.83	1.00	0.91
	Adult	1.00	1.00	1.00	1.00	1.00
XGBoost	Child	0.92	0.86	0.97	0.88	0.91
	Adolescent	0.92	0.94	0.89	0.95	0.91
	Adult	0.99	0.98	0.99	0.98	0.99
DNN	Child	0.91	0.85	0.95	0.88	0.90
	Adolescent	0.84	0.77	0.94	0.75	0.85
	Adult	0.98	0.98	0.97	0.98	0.98

Table 4. Confusion matrix of the best performing ML models

Dataset	AdaBoost	SVM	LR	RF
Child	[[50 1] [0 37]]	[[51 0] [3 34]]	[[49 2] [2 35]]	
Adolescent		[[18 2] [0 18]]	[[20 0] [0 18]]	[[19 1] [1 17]]
Adult	[[151 0] [0 158]]	[[151 0] [0 158]]	[[150 1] [0 158]]	

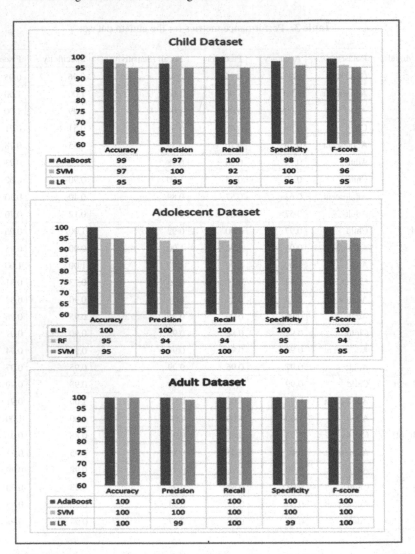

Fig. 2. Performance metrics of best models for autism classification across datasets

Table 5. Performance metrics with/without Random Oversampling (RO) in adolescents

Metric	LR	kNN	NB	SVM	DT	RF	AdaBoost	XGBoost	DNN
Accuracy - No RO	0.88	0.75	0.62	0.88	0.72	0.91	0.88	0.97	0.78
Accuracy with RO	1.00	0.76	0.63	0.95	0.84	0.95	0.92	0.92	0.84

(*continued*)

Table 5. (*continued*)

Metric	LR	kNN	NB	SVM	DT	RF	AdaBoost	XGBoost	DNN
Precision -No RO	0.94	0.75	0.64	1.00	0.82	0.90	1.00	1.00	0.88
Precision with RO	1.00	0.70	0.57	0.90	0.88	0.94	1.00	0.94	0.77
Recall – No RO	0.85	0.90	0.90	0.80	0.70	0.95	0.80	0.95	0.75
Recall with RO	1.00	0.89	0.89	1.00	0.78	0.94	0.83	0.89	0.94
Specificity - No RO	0.92	0.50	0.17	1.00	0.75	0.83	1.00	1.00	0.83
Specificity with RO	1.00	0.65	0.40	0.90	0.90	0.95	1.00	0.95	0.75
F-score – No RO	0.89	0.82	0.75	0.89	0.76	0.93	0.89	0.97	0.81
F-score with RO	1.00	0.78	0.70	0.95	0.82	0.94	0.91	0.91	0.85

Table 6. Performance metrics with/without Random Oversampling (RO) in adults

Metric	LR	kNN	NB	SVM	DT	RF	AdaBoost	XGBoost	DNN
Accuracy - No RO	0.96	0.84	0.36	0.97	0.91	0.97	1.00	0.96	0.93
Accuracy with RO	1.00	0.92	0.57	1.00	0.95	0.97	1.00	0.99	0.98
Precision -No RO	0.95	0.84	0.32	0.98	0.83	0.95	1.00	0.92	0.89
Precision with RO	0.99	0.88	0.54	1.00	0.96	0.96	1.00	0.98	0.98
Recall – No RO	0.91	0.59	0.97	0.92	0.86	0.94	0.98	0.95	0.88
Recall with RO	1.00	0.98	1.00	1.00	0.96	0.99	1.00	0.99	0.97
Specificity - No RO	0.98	0.95	1.00	0.99	0.93	0.98	1.00	0.97	0.95
Specificity with RO	0.99	0.86	0.10	1.00	0.95	0.95	1.00	0.98	0.98
F-score – No RO	0.93	0.70	0.48	0.95	0.85	0.94	0.99	0.94	0.88
F-score with RO	1.00	0.93	0.70	1.00	0.96	0.97	1.00	0.99	0.98

5 Conclusion

Autism Spectrum Disorder is a neurodevelopmental disorder afflicting all age groups. Several machine learning models were applied to publicly available ASD child, adolescent, and adult datasets. In the child dataset, the best performing models were obtained by with AdaBoost, support vector machine, and logistic regression with a 95–99% accuracy while logistic regression, random forest, and support vector machine were the best performing models for the adolescent dataset with an accuracy of 95–100%. AdaBoost, support vector machine, and logistic regression gave an excellent performance for the adult dataset with 99–100% accuracy. Overall, there is a general improvement on the performance metrics when random oversampling is applied on the adolescent and adult datasets, highlighting the necessity of addressing the data imbalance to generate a more reliable diagnostic performance of the models. The primary limitation of our research is that we used small datasets. This is because of unavailability of large and open source ASD datasets.

Future enhancement of this study should focus on inclusion of feature selection techniques, feature importance of attributes and other tools in explainable AI for better understanding of the models by health professionals. Additionally, machine learning models could also be applied to mixed type of datasets which combines symptomatology with neuroimaging features seen in functional magnetic resonance imaging or with genetic data in the hope of achieving excellent diagnostic accuracy. Nonetheless, our findings are promising and have generated useful insights in the development of automated models that are faster and with high reliability which can be of use to health practitioners in the diagnosis of autism across age groups. Together with early and prompt assessment, particularly in cases of limited number of trained professionals, tools aided with machine learning can potentially reduce the number of patients required to undergo the lengthy, multistep process to get an official diagnosis. As a result, early intervention efforts and treatment ensure the best quality of care for our patients.

References

1. American Psychiatric Association Homepage, https://www.psychiatry.org/patients-families/autism/what-is-autism-spectrum-disorder. Acessed 21 Dec 2021
2. Center for Disease Control and Prevention Homepage, https://www.cdc.gov/ncbddd/autism/data.html. Accessed 21 Dec 2021
3. Omar, K.S., Islam, M.N., Khan, N.S.: Chapter 9 - Exploring tree-based machine learning methods to predict autism spectrum disorder. In: Neural Engineering Techniques for Autism Spectrum Disorder, vol (1), pp 165–183. Academic Press (2021). https://doi.org/10.1016/B978-0-12-822822-7.00009-0
4. Vakadkar, K., Purkayastha, D., Krishnan, D.: Detection of autism spectrum disorder in children using machine learning techniques. SN Computer Science 2(5), 1–9 (2021). https://doi.org/10.1007/s42979-021-00776-5
5. Raj, S., Masood, S.: Analysis and detection of autism spectrum disorder using machine learning techniques. Procedia Computer Science 167, 994–1004 (2020). https://doi.org/10.1016/j.procs.2020.03.399
6. Sujatha, R., Aarthy, S.L., Chatterjee, J.M., Alaboudi, A., Jhanjhi, N.: A machine learning way to classify autism spectrum disorder. Int. J. Emerging Technolo. Learn. (iJET) 16(06), 182–200 (2021). https://doi.org/10.3991/ijet.v16i06.19559
7. Sharif, H., Khan, R.A.: A novel machine learning based framework for detection of autism spectrum disorder (ASD). Applied Artificial Intelligence, 1–33 (2021). https://doi.org/10.1080/08839514.2021.2004655
8. Mohanty, A.S., Parida, P., Patra, K.C.: ASD Classification for children using deep neural network. Global Transitions Proceedings 2(2), 461–466 (2021). https://doi.org/10.1016/j.gltp.2021.08.042
9. Mohanty, A.S., Patra, K.C., Parida, P.: Toddler ASD classification using machine learning techniques. Int. J. Online and Biomedical Eng. (iJOE) 17(07), 156–171 (2021). https://doi.org/10.3991/ijoe.v17i07.23497
10. Lu, A., Perkowski, M.: Deep learning approach for screening autism spectrum disorder in children with facial images and analysis of ethnoracial factors in model development and application. Brain Sci. 11(11), 1446 (2021). https://doi.org/10.3390/brainsci11111446

11. Erkan, U., Thanh, N.H.D.: Autism spectrum disorder detection with machine learning methods. Current Psychiatry Research and Reviews **15**(4), 297–308 (2019). https://doi.org/10.2174/2666082215666191111121115

12. Gardner-Hoag, J., Novack, M., Parlett-Pelleriti, C., Stevens, E., Dixon, D., Linstead, E.: Unsupervised machine learning for identifying challenging behavior profiles to explore cluster-based treatment efficacy in children with autism spectrum disorder: retrospective data analysis study. JMIR Med Inform **9**(6), e27793 (2021). https://medinform.jmir.org/2021/6/e27793

13. Akter, T., Khan, M.I., Ali, M.H., Satu, M.S., Uddin, M.J., Moni, M.A.: Improved machine learning based classification model for early autism detection. In: 2nd International Conference on Robotics, Electrical and Signal Processing Techniques (ICREST), pp. 742–747. IEEE, Dhaka Bangladesh (2021). https://doi.org/10.1109/ICREST51555.2021.9331013

14. Thabtah, F.F.: Autistic Spectrum Disorder Screening Data for Adult. https://archive.ics.uci.edu/ml/machine-learning-databases/00426/ last accessed 14 November 2021

15. Thabtah, F.F.: Autistic Spectrum Disorder Screening Data for children. https://archive.ics.uci.edu/ml/machine-learning-databases/00419/ last accessed 14 November 2021

16. Thabtah, F.F.: Autistic Spectrum Disorder Screening Data for Adolescent. https://archive.ics.uci.edu/ml/machine-learning-databases/00420/ last accessed 4 November 2021

17. Magboo, V.C., Magboo, M.S.: Machine learning classifiers on breast cancer recurrences. In: Watrobski, J., Salabun, W., Toro, C., Zanni-Merk, C., Howlett, R., Jain, L. (eds.) 25th International Conference on Knowledge-Based and Intelligent Information & Engineering System 2021, Procedia Computer Science, vol 192, pp. 2742–2752. Elsevier, Warsaw, Poland (2021). https://doi.org/10.1016/j.procs.2021.09.044

18. Jumaa, N.S., Salman, A.D., al-hamdani, R.: The autism spectrum disorder classification based on machine learning techniques. Journal of Xi'an University of Architecture & Technology **12**(5), 575–583 (2020)

19. Lopez, K.M., Magboo, M.S.: A Clinical Decision Support Tool to Detect Invasive Ductal Carcinoma in Histopathological Images Using Support Vector Machines, Naïve-Bayes, and K-Nearest Neighbor Classifiers. In: Tallón-Ballesteros, A., Chen, C.H. (eds.) International Conference on Machine Learning and Intelligent Systems (MLIS 2020), Frontiers in Artificial Intelligence and Applications, vol. 332. IOS Press, Seoul, South Korea. (2020). https://doi.org/10.3233/FAIA200765

20. Zhao, Z., Tang, H., Zhang, X., Qu, X., Hu, X., Lu, J.: Classification of children with autism and typical development using eye-tracking data from face-to-face conversations: machine learning model development and performance evaluation. J. Med. Internet Res. **23**(8), e29328 (2021). https://doi.org/10.2196/29328

21. Stella, M., Kumar, S.: Prediction and Comparison using AdaBoost and ML Algorithms with Autistic Children Dataset., Kumar, S.: Prediction and Comparison using AdaBoost and ML Algorithms with Autistic Children Dataset. Int. J. Eng. Res. Technol. **9**(7), 133–136 (2020). https://doi.org/10.17577/IJERTV9IS070091

22. Kruthi, C.H., Tejashwini, H.N., Poojitha, G.S., Shreelakshmi, H.S., Shobha Chandra, K.: Detection of autism spectrum disorder using machine learning. Int. J. Sci. Res. Eng. Trends **7**(4), 2267–2271 (2020). https://ijsret.com/wp-content/uploads/2021/07/IJSRET_V7_issue4_524.pdf

23. Rabbi, M.F., Hasan, S.M.M., Champa, A.I., Zaman, M.A.: A Convolutional Neural Network Model for Early-Stage Detection of Autism Spectrum Disorder. In: 2021 International Conference on Information and Communication Technology for Sustainable Development (ICICT4SD), pp. 110–114. IEEE, Dhaka Bangladesh (2021). https://doi.org/10.1109/ICICT4SD50815.2021.9397020

24. Chakraborty, S., Bhattacharya, S.: Application of XGBoost Algorithm as a Predictive Tool in a CNC Turning Process. Reports in Mechanical Engineering **2**(1), 190–201 (2021). https://doi.org/10.31181/rme2001021901b

25. Raju, N.V.G., Madhavi, K., Kumar, G.S., Reddy, G.V., Latha, K., Sushma, K.L.: Prognostication of Autism Spectrum Disorder (ASD) using Supervised Machine Learning Models. Int. J. Eng. Adv. Technol. (IJEAT) **8**(4), 1028–1032 (2019). https://www.ijeat.org/wp-content/uploads/papers/v8i4/D6547048419.pdf

26. Saleh, A.Y., Chern, L.H.: Autism spectrum disorder classification using deep learning. Int. J. Online and Biomedi. Eng. (iJOE) **17**(08), 103–114 (2021). https://doi.org/10.3991/ijoe.v17i08.24603

27. Mohanty, A.S., Parida, P., Patra, K.C.: Identification of autism spectrum disorder using deep neural network. In: First International Conference on Advances in Smart Sensor, Signal Processing and Communication Technology (ICASSCT 2021) Journal of Physics: Conference Series, 1921 (2021). https://doi.org/10.1088/1742-6596/1921/1/012006

28. Eslami, T., Almuqhim, F., Raiker, J.S., Saeed, F.: Machine learning methods for diagnosing autism spectrum disorder and attention- deficit/hyperactivity disorder using functional and structural MRI: a survey. Front. Neuroinform. **14**, 575999 (2021). https://doi.org/10.3389/fninf.2020.575999

29. Mohanty, A.S., Parida, P., Patra, K.: ASD classification in adolescent and adult utilizing deep neural network. In: Proceedings of the 3rd International Conference on Integrated Intelligent Computing Communication & Security (ICIIC 2021), pp 202–210. Atlantis Highlights in Computer Sciences, volume 4. Atlantis Press, Bangalore, India (2021). https://doi.org/10.2991/ahis.k.210913.025

Life Prediction of Underwater Electroacoustic Sensor Using Data-Driven Approach

Vineeth P. Ramachandran[1]([✉]), V. P. Pranavam[2], and Pramod Sreedharan[2]

[1] DRDO Young Scientists' Laboratory for Smart Materials, Hyderabad, India
prvineeth.dysl-sm@gov.in
[2] Department of Mechanical Engineering, Amrita Vishwa Vidyapeetham, Amritapuri, India

Abstract. Underwater electroacoustic sensors used for marine application and underwater pipeline inspection degrade over time due to water ingress through the water-proof polymer encapsulation. The degradation of the sensor can be assessed by measuring the insulation resistance due to the leakage resistance added by polymer over a long time. An experimental study is conducted on a sensor dipped in a sea water bath, measuring insulation resistance in regular intervals of time. The data is analysed using a deep learning algorithm for predicting the end-of-life of the sensor. A type of Recurrent Neural Network (RNN) called Long Short-Term Memory (LSTM) is employed to study the degradation pattern of the sensor, as LSTM-RNN can efficiently learn the long-term dependence of degradation data. The actual end of life of the sensor measured experimentally is compared with that obtained using LSTM-RNN for verification of the model. Main advantage of this study is, this methodology does not require disassembly of sensor from the system to make decisions on maintenance or replacement.

Keywords: Underwater electroacoustic sensor · Deep learning · End-of-life · Long short-term memory

1 Introduction

1.1 Underwater Electroacoustic Sensor

Underwater Electroacoustic sensors are commonly used in military and non-military marine applications, inspection of submarine pipe lines, dams, Autonomous Underwater Vehicles (AUV), Remote Operated Vehicle (ROV) and other studies related to seismology and marine organisms (Fig. 1).

For electroacoustic transduction in these sensors, dielectric smart materials such as piezoelectric materials are typically used. Such smart materials are suitably encapsulated using rubber polymer to make it water tight for underwater application. The life of the sensor is majorly contributed by the strength of rubber encapsulation, which in turn depends on exposure to degradation agents. The detrimental effect of moisture absorption by rubber may affect the material by swelling of the material, reduction in the glass transition temperature of resin and reduction in mechanical properties which

A. Kumar et al. (Eds.): ICAIDS 2021, CCIS 1673, pp. 465–475, 2022.
https://doi.org/10.1007/978-3-031-21385-4_38

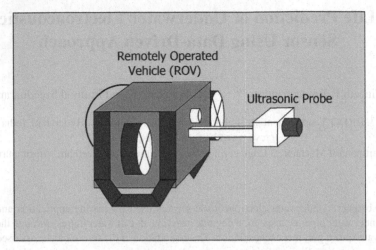

Fig. 1. Schematic of an ROV used for inspection of underwater pipelines, dam etc.

in turn will result in performance degradation in sea over a time. This performance degradation is marked by the drop in sensitivity of the sensor. The dependence of the insulation resistance and capacitance of the piezoelectric material on the sensitivity was studied by Ramesh *et al.* [1] and derived an empirical equation for sensitivity of the sensor. For an un-loaded sensor (not connected to pre-amplifier and having negligible cable capacitance) the sensitivity (M) at low frequencies is given by [1],

$$M = g_{31}a\frac{(C_1 + C_0)}{C_1}\frac{\omega C_0 R_i}{\sqrt{1 + (\omega C_0 R_i)^2}} \tag{1}$$

where g_{31} is the piezoelectric coefficient; a is the mean radius of the Piezoelectric Cylinder; C_0 and C_1 are the dielectric capacitance of piezoelectric element and modal compliance respectively; ω is the frequency far below the resonance of piezoelectric cylinder; R_i is the insulation resistance across the terminals of the sensor.

The dependence of sensitivity on R_i and C_0 from Eqn. [1] is plotted in Fig. 2 below.

It can be easily observed in Fig. 2 that the sensitivity of the sensor drops drastically below a cut-off value of insulation resistance ($R_{cut-off}$) at all capacitance values marking the end of life of sensor. This cut-off value is often called as threshold value of insulation resistance in this paper.

1.2 Prognostic Approaches

Prognosis [2] is the process of estimating the time at which a component fails to perform its intended functionality. Prognostic techniques aim to estimate the Remaining Useful Life (RUL) of the component using the data obtained from sensors or other means.

Prognostic approaches are classified into three, i.e.; (1) data-driven, (2) physics based and (3) hybrid approach [2, 3], as in Fig. 3.

Data-driven approach uses previously obtained data to identify current degradation state of the component and to predict the future performance of the component. The

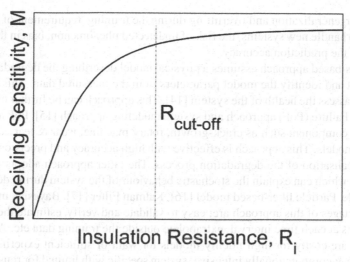

Fig. 2. Dependence of M on insulation resistance (R_i) frequencies far below resonance, showing a cut-off value of R_i

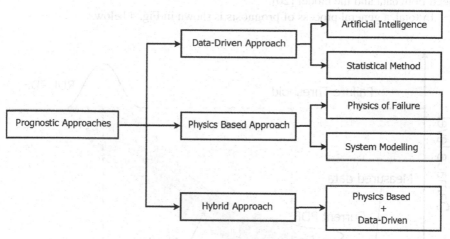

Fig. 3. Classification of prognostics

data-driven approach is further classified into Artificial Intelligence (AI) approach and statistical approach [4]. The AI approach includes regression, Neural Network (NN) [5], fuzzy logic [6], swarm intelligence (SI), and ant colony; the statistical approach includes the Gaussian process (GP) regression [7], support vector machine [8], least squares regression [9], the gamma process [10], the Wiener processes [11], hidden Markov model [12], Bayesian network (BN), proportional hazard model etc. All the above models can establish the relationship between degradation state and time and hence come with a low cost of implementation [13]. Further, the algorithms can handle high dimensional noisy data by transforming to low dimensional data. The demerits such as, the overgeneralization and overfitting during the training, requirement of large data, inability to handle new systems, the risk of undetected phenomenon, bias in the data etc. may affect the prediction accuracy.

Physics-based approach assumes a physical model describing the degradation of the component and identify the model parameters from the measured data. This model can be used to assess the health of the system [14]. This approach can be further classified as Physics of Failure (PoF) approach and system modeling approach [15]. PoF approach is specific to component such as crack-growth, rotary machine, wear & tear, and electro-chemical models. This approach is effective with high accuracy and precision due to the physical realisation of the degradation process. The latter approach adopts a model of the system which can explain the stochastic behaviour of the system during degradation, for example, Particle filter-based model [16], Kalman Filter [17], Bayesian method [18] etc. Advantages of this approach are; easy to validate and verify, estimate the dynamics of the states at each time interval, extrapolate outside the training data etc. At the same time, they are costly for high fidelity models for want of sufficient experiments, time consuming & computationally intensive, system specific with limited for reusability etc.

Hybrid approaches combine both the above methods [19], and hence eliminate the drawbacks of physics based and data-driven approaches while gain their merits. But they need both data and the model [20].

In total, a general process of prognosis is shown in Fig. 4 below.

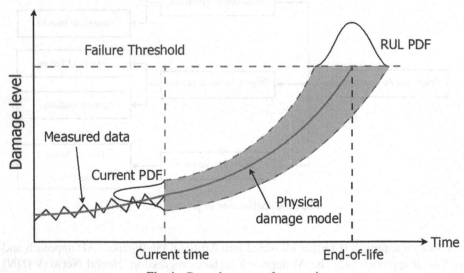

Fig. 4. General process of prognosis

In subsection below, life prediction of components/systems using different data driven approaches reported in literatures is explained.

1.2.1 Literature Survey on Data-Driven Prognostic Approach

Data-driven prognostic approaches are typically used to check the Remaining Useful Life (RUL) of system/components. For this case the data is in the form of multiple multivariate time series. Chui *et al.* [21] used a type of Recurrent Neural Network (RNN) called Long Short-Term Memory (LSTM) for long-term prediction of RUL of Turbofan Engine [21]. This improved the Root Mean Square Error (RMSE) by 6.07–14.72% when compared with standalone RNN and LSTM. Zhang *et al.* [22] used LSTM-RNN to learn the capacity degradation trajectories of lithium-ion batteries. This deep learning approach was able to effectively capture the underlying long-term dependencies of battery capacities, and to predict the RUL. A bidirectional handshaking LSTM for RUL prediction is reported by Elsheikh *et al.* [23], wherein the given sequence of observations is processed in the forward direction through several LSTM cells producing a summary vector and also in the in reverse order through another set of LSTM cells ending up with another summary vector. The advantages of this method, as reported, is that LSTM network will have more insights about the trend of the sequence in both directions and also allows the learning process to be collaborative in both directions. Ahmadzadeh *et al.* [24] used Artificial Neural Network (ANN) for predicting RUL of grinding mill liners, and the results proved 90% accuracy. But ANN requires large amount of data for training the network. Che *et al.* [25] proposed a model combining Deep Belief Network (DBN) and LSTM for RUL estimation of aircraft. They reported that when dealing with multivariate time series of aircraft, the proposed model has more accurate prediction than traditional models. Qiu *et al.* [26] proposed an ensemble RUL prediction method comprising Support Vector Regression (SVR), Genetic Algorithm (GA) and Weibull proportional hazards model (WPHM) and validated by a bearing run to failure experiment. Results show that the minimum RMSE, MAE, and MAPE appear in SVR, indicating SVR is the most suitable method in pseudo-operation information prediction. To the best of our knowledge, there is no study so far conducted or reported to predict the degradation of underwater electroacoustic sensors using time series data. It is very important to predict the performance of such sensor with time to reduce equipment downtime and unnecessary maintenance checks. We have used deep learning algorithm such as RNN for this study. Since the conventional RNN is useful for short-term prediction, LSTM-RNN is used here for long-term prediction [21]. The architecture of LSTM and its advantage for time sequence prediction are explained in the subsequent sections below.

2 Data Collection Procedure

Since the sensor is expected to work in sea water and the degradation is mainly contributed by generation of conducting paths across the electrodes of the dielectric piezoelectric material due to water ingress, an experimental study is conducted in the laboratory on a sensor dipped in sea water bath. Insulation resistance and capacitance of the sensor are measured over a time till it showed degradation behaviour. The schematic of the experimental set-up is shown in Fig. 5.

Capacitance and insulation resistance of the sensor are entered into the database in regular intervals of time till insulation resistance reaches $R_{cut-off}$. The features considered

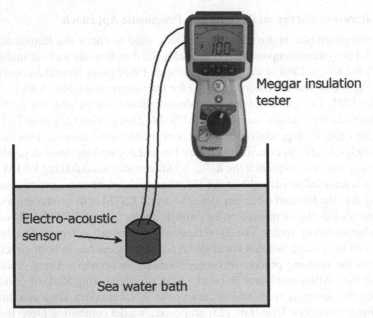

Fig. 5. Schematic of experimental set-up

for the present study are duration in number of days from beginning of test, insulation resistance and capacitance. The presented data set consists of multivariate time series containing 'no of days' as the time unit, along with readings on insulation resistance (R_i) and Capacitance (C_0) against each day. The sensor is assumed to start the test with unknown degrees of initial degradation and manufacturing variation.

3 LSTM Architecture

The LSTM, a special kind of RNN architecture was proposed [27, 28] to address the limitations in training the existing RNNs [29], such as the vanishing gradients (exponential decay of weight) or exploding gradients (blowing up of weight) in weight update procedure. They are capable of learning sequences of observations and hence suitable for forecasting time series events. The architecture of the LSTM is illustrated in Fig. 6 below.

In the figure x_t is the input at time t, c_{t-1} and h_{t-1} represent the prior cell state and prior hidden output respectively, whereas c_t and h_t represent the current cell state and current hidden output respectively.

$$i_t = \sigma(W_i x_t + H_t h_{t-1} + b_i) \tag{2}$$

$$o_t = \sigma(W_o x_t + H_o h_{t-1} + b_o) \tag{3}$$

$$f_t = \sigma(W_f x_t + H_f h_{t-1} + b_f) \tag{4}$$

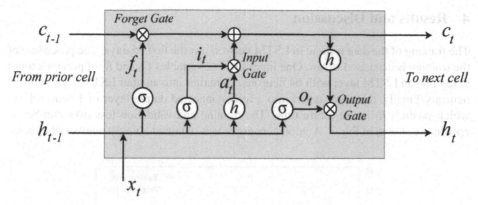

Fig. 6. The architecture of the LSTM cell

$$a_t = \tanh(W_a x_t + H_a h_{t-1} + b_a) \tag{5}$$

$$c_t = f_t \odot c_{t-1} + i_t \odot a_t \tag{6}$$

$$h_t = o_t \odot \tanh(c_t) \tag{7}$$

where W_* and H_* are the trainable weights; b_* is the trainable bias for each gating signal; the gate activations a_t, i_t, f_t, and o_t are the cell input, input gate, forget gate, and output gate respectively; σ and tanh denote the sigmoid function and tanh function respectively; $\odot$ is the element wise multiplication operator.

The forget gate takes h_{t-1} and x_t, and outputs f_t which decides whether to forget or retain c_{t-1} (previous state) of the LSTM. Next step involves decision on what to store in the current cell state. An input gate looks at h_{t-1} and x_t, and the output i_t after passing through the sigmoid layer decides what values to be updated. i_t is multiplied with a_t, an output obtained from h_{t-1} and x_t after passing through a hyperbolic tangent (tanh) layer, and added with the output of forget gate to update the cell state from c_{t-1} to c_t. At last, the output of the cell is to be decided. A sigmoid layer is run through h_{t-1} and x_t to determine which parts of the cell state are set to be the output. Thereafter, the cell state c_t is put through a hyperbolic tangent layer and multiplied with the output from previous operation to output relevant parts.

4   Results and Discussion

The training of the data is done in LSTM network for the first 65 days. The procedure of the training is discussed below. One input layer (2 variables C_0 and R_i of previous time) is fed into an LSTM layer with 64 neurons, thereafter into another LSTM layer with 32 neurons. Finally, this layer is fed into a fully connected output layer of 1 neuron [29], which predicts R_i in the future time. The training and validation loss over number of epochs are shown in Fig. 7. A good convergence is obtained after 50 number of epochs.

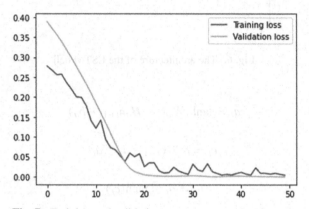

Fig. 7. Training and validation error over number of epochs

A failure is reported when the predicted value of R_i is lower than the threshold value as the sensitivity of the sensor reduces drastically below this threshold. In this study the threshold value of the sensor is fixed at 43 MΩ from the past sensitivity measurement data. The predicted results are compared with the actual data from the experiment till the end-of-life.

From Fig. 8(a) & (b) it can be observed that the LSTM- RNN can do early prediction as compared to the actual end-of-life and the error in prediction is only 9 days. From the prognostics point of view, early prediction is always better as it avoids the catastrophe resulting from the failure. Hence LSTM-RNN is proven to be a useful tool for data-driven prognosis of underwater electroacoustic sensor for applications mentioned in previous sections.

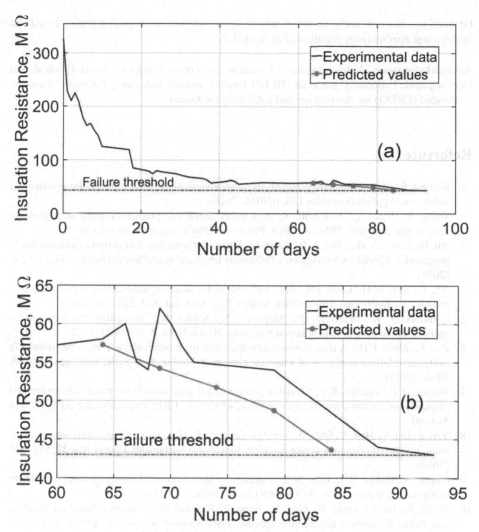

Fig. 8. (a) Comparison of experimental data and LSTM based prediction results; (b) detailed view near the end-of-life

5 Conclusions

In summary, we report for the first time a data-driven approach to do life prediction of underwater electroacoustic sensor. An experiment is conducted on a sensor in sea water bath measuring the critical parameter such as insulation resistance over several days till it reaches cut-off value. A data-driven prognosis of this sensor is done using LSTM-RNN, a type of recurrent neural network. The training of a LSTM-RNN is done using the data from first 65 days to predict the time at which the insulation resistance reaches the threshold value. The result shows that the LSTM-RNN predictor could do early life prediction with an error of 9 days as compared to the actual results. This predictor can be used to alarm an early failure warning for the replacement of the sensor in all the underwater applications mentioned in Sect. 1.1.

Acknowledgements. Vineeth wishes to express his sincere thanks to Naval Physical and Oceanographic Laboratory, Kochi and DRDO Young Scientists' Laboratory for Smart Materials, Hyderabad (DRDO) for carrying out and publishing the research.

References

1. Ramesh, R., et al.: Life prediction analysis on underwater acoustic sensors and its experimental validation. Applied Acoustics **158**, 107054 (2020)
2. Wang, Y., Zhao, Y., Addepalli, S.: Remaining useful life prediction using deep learning approaches: a review. TESConf 2019, Procedia Manufacturing **49**, 81–88 (2020)
3. An, D., Kim a, N.H., Choi. J.-H.: Practical options for selecting data-driven or physics-based prognostics algorithms with reviews. Reliability Engineering and System Safety **133**, 223–236 (2015)
4. An, D., Kim, N.H., Choi, J.H.: Practical options for selecting data-driven or physics-based prognostics algorithms with reviews. Reliab. Eng. Syst. Saf. **133**, 223–236 (2015)
5. Chakraborty, K., Mehrotra, K., Mohan, C.K., Ranka, S.: Forecasting the behavior of multivariate time series using neural networks. Neural Netw. **5**, 961–970 (1992)
6. Zio, E., Maio, F.D.: A data-driven fuzzy approach for predicting the remaining useful life in dynamic failure scenarios of a nuclear system. ReliabEng Syst SafReliabEngSystSaf **95**, 49–57 (2010)
7. Wilson, A.G., Adams, R.P.: Gaussian process covariance kernels for pattern discovery and extrapolation. arXiv preprint arXiv:1302.4245 (2013). URL: http://arxiv.org/pdf/1302.4245v3.pdf
8. Yan, J., Liu, Y., Han, S., Qiu, M.: Wind power grouping forecasts and its uncertainty analysis using optimized relevance vector machine. Renewable Sustainable Energy Rev **27**, 613–621 (2013)
9. Coppe, A., Haftka, R.T., Kim, N.H.: Uncertainty identification of damage growth parameters using nonlinear regression. AIAA J **49**(12), 2818–2821 (2011)
10. Wang, X., Balakrishnan, N., Gu,o B., Jiang, P.: Residual life estimation based on bivariate non-stationary gamma degradation process. J Stat Comput Simul 1–17 (2013). (ahead-of-print)
11. Si, X.S., Wang, W., Hu, C.H., Chen, M.Y., Zhou, D.H.: A wiener process-based degradation model with a recursive filter algorithm for remaining useful life estimation. Mech Syst Sig Process **35**(1–2), 219–237 (2013)
12. Liu, A., Dong, M., Peng, Y.: A novel method for online health prognosis of equipment based on hidden semi-Markov model using sequential Monte Carlo methods. Mech Syst Sig Process **32**, 331–348 (2012)
13. Vachtsevanos, G., Lewis, F., Roemer, M., Hess, A., Wu, B.: Intelligent Fault Diagnosis and Prognosis for Engineering Systems. Wiley, Hoboken, NJ, USA (2006)
14. Cubillo, A., Perinpanayagam, S., EsperonMiguez, M.: A review of physics-based models in prognostics: Application to gears and bearings of rotating machinery. Adv. Mech. Eng. **8**(8), 1–21 (2016)
15. Guo, J., Li, Z., Li, M.: A review on prognostics methods for engineering systems. IEEE Transactions on Reliability **69**(3) (September 2020)

16. Saidi, L., Ali, J.B., Bechhoefer, E., Benbouzid, M.: Particle filter-based prognostic approach for high-speed shaft bearing wind turbine progressive degradations. In: IECON 2017–43rd Annual Conference of the IEEE Industrial Electronics Society, pp. 8099–8104. IEEE (October 2017)
17. Tang, X., Xiao, M., Hu, B.: Application of kalman filter to model-based prognostics for solenoid valve. Soft. Comput. **24**(8), 5741–5753 (2020)
18. Kramer, S.C., Sorenson, H.W.: Bayesian parameter estimation. IEEE Trans. Autom. Control **33**(2), 217–222 (1988)
19. Liao, L., Köttig, F.: Review of hybrid prognostics approaches for remaining useful life prediction of engineered systems, and an application to battery life prediction. IEEE Trans Reliab **63**(1), 191–207 (2014)
20. Peel, L.: Data driven prognostics using a Kalman filter ensemble of neural network models. In: 2008 international conference on prognostics and health management, pp. 1–6. IEEE (October 2008)
21. Chui, K.T., Gupta, B.B., Vasant, P.: A genetic algorithm optimized RNN-LSTM model for remaining useful life prediction of turbofan engine. Electronics **10**(3), 285 (2021)
22. Zhang, Y., Xiong, R., He, H., Liu, Z.: A LSTM-RNN method for the lithuim-ion battery remaining useful life prediction. In: 2017 Prognostics and System Health Management Conference (PHM-Harbin), pp. 1–4. IEEE (July 2017)
23. Elsheikh, A., Yacout, S., Ouali, M.S.: Bidirectional handshaking LSTM for remaining useful life prediction. Neurocomputing **323**, 148–156 (2019)
24. Ahmadzadeh, F., Lundberg, J.: Remaining useful life prediction of grinding mill liners using an artificial neural network. Miner. Eng. **53**, 1–8 (2013)
25. Che, C., Wang, H., Fu, Q., Ni, X.: Combining multiple deep learning algorithms for prognostic and health management of aircraft. Aerosp. Sci. Technol. **94**, 105423 (2019)
26. Qiu, G., Gu, Y., Chen, J.: Selective health indicator for bearings ensemble remaining useful life prediction with genetic algorithm and Weibull proportional hazards model. Measurement **150**, 107097 (2020)
27. Hocheiter, S., Schmidhuber, J.U.R.: Long short-term memory. Neural comput **9**, 1735 (1997)
28. Gers, F., Schraudolph, N., Schmidhuber, J.: Learning precise timing with LSTM recurrent networks. J. Mach. Learn. Res. **3**, 115 143 (2002)
29. Hochreiter, S., Bengio, Y., Frasconi, P., Schmidhuber, J.: Gradient flow in recurrent nets: The difficulty of learning long-term dependencies. In: Kremer, S.C., Kolen, J.F. (eds.) A field guide to dynamical recurrent neural networks. IEEE Press (2001)

Smart Transportation and Evolutionary Algorithms: An Approach to Understand Vehicular Ad-Hoc Network

Rakesh Kumar Maram[1], V. A. Sankar Ponnapalli[1](✉),
and Harsha Vardan Maddiboyina[2]

[1] Department of Electronics and Communication Engineering, Sreyas Institute of Engineering and Technology, Hyderabad 500068, India
vadityasankar3@gmail.com
[2] R & D Department, Planet Sigma Embedded Systems Private Limited, Hyderabad 500068, India

Abstract. In the present world, With the increasing number of automobiles on the road in recent years, the number of accidents has increased massively. Traffic congestion is worsened by the large number of vehicles on the road. As a result, new technologies are critical in reducing road fatalities and improving traffic safety. Intelligent Transportation Systems (ITS) are a new technology that aims to improve road safety and traffic flow. ITS can be used for both safety and non-safety purposes. A variety of strategies are being used to construct smart transportation networks. The Vehicular Ad hoc Networks are the most important type (VANET). VANET is quickly becoming the most used ITS network. Vehicular Ad-Hoc Network (VANET) plays a vital role in the field of transportation. Smart and well-developed technologies such as wireless sensors, advanced communication systems, etc. were integrated with the VANETs to give better and highly secure communication to the vehicles to avoid traffic congestions, vehicular calamities, etc. In this paper, a study on VANETs based vehicular transportation system with different optimization techniques and algorithms were discussed. This paper also discussed about the security attacks which affect the VANETs and also discussed about the remedial acts to be taken to avoid these attacks. This review paper results that the safety and well secured transportation can be established by using VANETs and also gives the high accuracy by integrating Type-2 fuzzy with the VANETs methodology.

Keywords: VANETs · Optimization techniques · Security attacks · Smart transportation system · Traffic

1 Introduction

Because of enhancing the number of vehicles day by day, the vehicular calamities are increasing rapidly around the world. So, to minimize such types of scenarios a methodology was developed by integrating computing technology with wireless sensor networks

A. Kumar et al. (Eds.): ICAIDS 2021, CCIS 1673, pp. 476–489, 2022.
https://doi.org/10.1007/978-3-031-21385-4_39

to form a vehicular network. Such type of vehicular network is known as Vehicular Ad-Hoc Network (VANET). VANET is implemented by using the characteristics of a Mobile Ad-Hoc Network (MANET). It is a wireless network, based on one-to-one communication. In VANETs, vehicles communicate with each other within their vehicular network range [1]. Here the vehicles may communicate by using Vehicle-to-Vehicle (V-2-V) communication or through Vehicle-to-Infrastructure (V-2-I) communication. In V-2-I communication, infrastructure represents road side units (RSUs) [16] VANETs majorly utilize two types of messaging systems such as the beacon messaging system and the safety messaging system. In the beacon messaging system, the vehicles use to broadcast the live status of the self and surrounded vehicle information such as vehicle speed, position, etc. to other vehicles periodically. In the safety messaging system, the vehicles use to broadcast emergency information such as road accidents, traffic congestions, etc. to all other neighboring vehicles. Every vehicle is integrated with an on-board system (OBS) which is used to deliver the messages and also process the received messages using the controller in OBS and gives a better output to the user. This OBS communicates with the other OBS in neighboring vehicles as well as RSUs. This RSU enlarges the range of communication [1]. In VANETs, every vehicle can act as a host. Figure 1 shows the structure of VANETs.

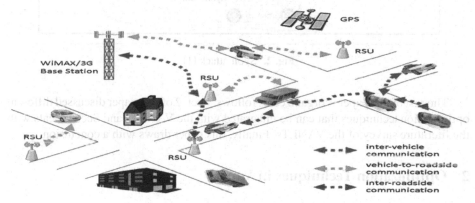

Fig. 1. Structure of VANETs [1].

Security attacks are the key challenges in VANETs. The major security attacks in VANETs are Denial of Service (DoS) attack, Sybil attack, Node Impersonation attack, Application attack, Timing attack, etc. In the DoS attack, the attacker tries to disrupt the communication network between the vehicles and RSUs and vice versa [17]. In the Sybil attack, the attacker manipulates the messaging system and sends the single message for multiple times or a single message to multiple users. Figure 2 shows the Sybil attack. In the Node Impersonation attack, the attacker tries to send incorrect messages to the neighboring vehicles. In the Application attack, the attacker tries to manipulate the authentic messages. In the Timing attack, the attacker generates the time delay between the messages. These security attacks in VANETs can be avoided by integrating the system with the following parameters such as authentication, confidentiality, privacy, integrity, and availability. Authentication plays a major role in avoiding the security attacks in VANETs. Every vehicle in the group will have a unique identity number for the identification. By using this identity number, the OBS validates the messages. In confidentiality, the user only needs to intelligible the messages that are posted by the other vehicles in the group. In integrity, the messages in the network cannot be manipulated by the attacker. In availability, the communication network should be obtainable to the OBS, although the attacker tries to attack the system. Even the privacy should be maintained by the system [3, 4, 18, 22, 23].

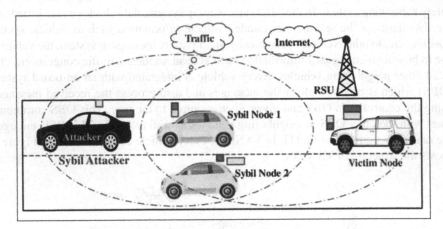

Fig. 2. Sybil attack [1].

The rest of this paper is organized as follows: Sect. 2 of this paper discussed different optimization techniques that can be integrated with the VANETs and Sect. 3 deals with the literature survey of the VANETs. Finally, this paper draws with a conclusion.

2   Optimization Techniques in Vanets

2.1   Neural Network

A neural network (NN) is a group of electronic neurons which are resemble to the neurons in the human brain [1]. This NN optimization technique (OT) is majorly used in artificial intelligence (AI) methodologies. The integration of NN with AI forms a new optimization technique known as Artificial Neural Network (ANN). This ANN methodology senses the input data and obtains the output by processing the data as a human brain. A simple ANN OT majorly contains three layers such as input, hidden, and output layers respectively. The input layer is a very initial layer to ANN. In this layer, the required inputs will be loaded and process the data to the successive layer of ANN. The hidden layer is a processing layer in ANN. In this layer, the developed algorithm will process the data and post the data to the followed layer. The output layer is the very final layer in ANN. In this layer, the outputs for the inputs will be obtained. This ANN OT is used in different real-time environments such as image processing, smart transportation system, medical fields, etc. Figure 3 shows a simple ANN structure.

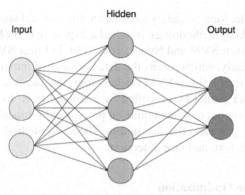

Fig. 3. A simple ANN structure [2].

2.2 Fuzzy Logic

Fuzzy Logic (FL) is a branch of mathematics, which is manipulated based on 'degree of truth' rather than the Boolean logic elements such as 'true or false'. True indicates '1' and false indicates '0'. It was initially implemented by Dr. Lofti Zadeh in 1960. FL is identical to the human brain thinking [1, 11]. It is majorly processed by using IF-THEN rules. To obtain the output, the input data should be processed by four different sectors in FL such as fuzzification, rule base, inference engine, and defuzzification. In the fuzzification process, the input data i.e., crisp data into fuzzy sets. This rule base contains the set of IF-THEN rules for making the decisions. Inference engine maps the fuzzy sets with the respected IF-THEN rules. Finally, the defuzzification process converts the fuzzy sets data into crisp data for the output. This defuzzification process can be implemented by using different methods. FL is majorly used in many AI applications. Figure 4 shows the structure of fuzzy logic.

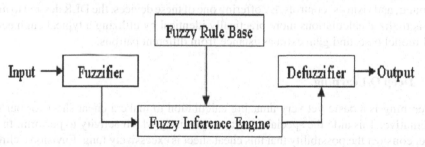

Fig. 4. Structure of fuzzy logic [11].

2.3 Support Vector Machine

Support Vector Machine (SVM) is a supervised learning methodology used to analyze the data by using classifications, outliers' detection, and regression analysis. It was developed by Vapnik at AT & T Laboratories [9]. The main objective of the SVM algorithm is to build the finest decision boundary to isolate n-dimensional spaces into classes. This type of decision-making methodology is called a hyperplane. SVM OT is divided into two types such as Linear SVM and Non-Linear SVM. In linear SVM methodology, the data is separated linearly, which means the data is classified into a couple of classes by using a straight line. In non-linear SVM methodology, the data is separated non-linearly, which means the data cannot be classified by a straight line. To obtain the output in SVM methodology, the input data should be processed by model training, prediction processes and finally generates the data output. The SVM methodology is majorly used for image processing, text, and face detection.

2.4 Particle Swarm Optimization

Particle Swarm Optimization (PSO) is a computational based stochastic OT developed by Dr. Eberhart and Dr. Kennedy in 1995, which was instigated by the nature of bird flocking or fish schooling [1, 9]. PSO solves the different optimization issues by learning from the current scenarios. PSO is set with a number of random solutions and then explore for optima by modernizing generations. PSO is utilized for solving the issues such as single and multi-objective optimization problems, constrained and unconstrained problems, and with the problems that are changing dynamically. The PSO is majorly used in the fields such as data mining, signal processing, telecommunication and power systems.

2.5 SUMO (Simulation of Urban Mobility)

SUMO's production began in the year 2000. Supporting the traffic research community with a tool with the potential to incorporate and test its own algorithms was the key reason for creating an open source, microscopic road traffic simulation. The device has no want for concerning all of the wanted matters for acquiring a whole visitors simulation including enforcing and/or putting in place techniques for handling avenue networks, demand, and visitors' controls. By offering one of these devices, the DLR desired to make the actualized calculations more practically identical by utilizing a typical engineering and model base, and gain extra assistance from different patrons.

2.6 Deep Q-Learning

Q-learning is a basic yet very amazing calculation to make a cheat sheet for our representative. This aide the specialist sort out precisely which activity to perform. In any case, consider the possibility that this cheat sheet is excessively long. Envision a climate with 10,000 states and 1,000 activities for every state. This would make a table of 10 million cells. Things will rapidly gain out of power. It is really evident that we can't derive the Q-estimation of new states from as of now investigated states. This presents two issues: First, the measure of memory needed to save and refresh that table would increment as the quantity of states increments. Second, the measure of time needed to investigate each state to make the necessary Q-table would be unreasonable.

2.7 Deep Q-Networks

In profound Q-learning, we utilize a neural organization to inexact the Q-esteem work. The state is given as the info and the Q-estimation of all potential activities is created as the yield. The correlation between Q-learning and profound Q-learning is brilliantly delineated beneath. All the previous experience is put away by the client in memory. The next activity is controlled by the most extreme yield of the Q-organization. The misfortune work here is mean squared blunder of the anticipated Q-esteem and the objective Q-esteem – Q*. This is fundamentally a relapse issue. Be that as it may, we don't have the foggiest idea about the objective or real incentive here as we are managing a support learning issue. Returning to the Q-esteem update condition got from the Bellman condition. The part in green addresses the objective. We can contend that it is anticipating its own worth, yet since R is the fair obvious prize, the organization will refresh its angle utilizing back engendering to at last meet.

3 Related Work

An emergency message detection system using VANETs was discussed by [21]. In this paper, an advanced messaging transmission protocol was developed for transmitting emergency messages to the vehicles using VANETS methodology. This messaging protocol was implemented by using neural network architecture. This method will broadcast the emergency messages to the selected vehicles based on the people's interest that are travelling in their respective vehicles and routes. This process mainly works on two bases. Initially, the emergency messages will be delivered based on the distribution and distance of the vehicles. And secondary it filters the messages whether they are real or fake. Figure 5 shows the architecture of this method.

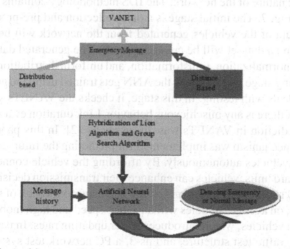

Fig. 5. Architecture of emergency message transmission protocol [21].

A neuro wav toward real time waveform design for VANETs using neural networks was discussed by [6]. In this paper, a methodology was developed to break out the noise interference in the RF section between the vehicles using VANETs. In this, a NeuroWav methodology was implemented using neural networks to minimize noise interference. It is a low sized, less weighted, and works with minimum power consumption. With the help of the neural network optimization technique, the NeuroWav method will have the capable of categorizing the input waveforms at a very high accuracy. By using this method VANETs can break out the RF noise for the communication between the cloud system and the vehicles. Figure 6 shows the VANETs in dynamic RF environment.

Fig. 6. VANETs in dynamic RF environment [6].

An intrusion detection system in autonomous vehicles to avoid security attacks was discussed by [2]. In this paper, an intrusion detection system (IDS) mechanism was developed using ANNs for the VANETs to determine vulnerable attacks such as the denial of service (DoS) attacks. The IDS mechanism detects the attack by using the data originated by the nature of the network. The IDS methodology contains majorly 3 stages as shown in the Fig. 7. The initial stage is a data collection and pre-processing stage. In this stage, the data of the vehicles generated from the network will be loaded into the NS2 simulator and a dataset will be created as a file. The generated dataset will be pre-processed using normalization, transformation, and uniform distribution. The secondary stage is the training stage. In this stage, the ANN gets trained using the generated dataset. The final stage deals with testing. In this stage, it checks the VANETs security and generates an alarm if there is any mischievous behavior. Link duration evaluation using NNs pedestal live prediction in VANETs was discussed by [2]. In this paper, a lightweight neural network mechanism was implemented for predicting the future mobility speed of the neighboring vehicles autonomously. By affording the vehicle connectivity information to the on-board units, vehicles can enhance their transmission decisions, next routers information, and route construction protocols. The major drawback of this method is, at the intersections, on average vehicles will have less speed and high mobility of vehicular data between the vehicles, which introduces fewer updating rates. In paper presents [12] SUMO, a street traffic test structure, and ns-3, a PC network test system, to develop a VANET. The vehicles in VANET move around the destined course moreover, trade TCP or UDP gatherings. Three unpremeditated managing checks are utilized for evaluating the showcase of the vehicle rate. The vehicles move at a speed of 30 km/s and 100 km/s.

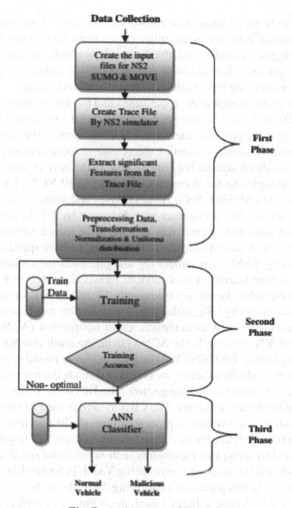

Fig. 7. Architecture of IDS [2].

The generation results show that DSDV multiplies incidental directing information to the association which oppositely impacts the bundle transport execution. AODV serves to convey pack at a reasonable rate as the bandwidth gave in the association. DSR shows the most observably awful throughput among the three counts in light of the fact that the controlling information kept up by the sending vehicle stales routinely and the sender needs to reproduce the invigorated course, which achieves the defilement of the group transport rate. Right when the vehicles move speedier, the typical throughput is decreased, and its standard deviation is extended. For example, when 3 S/R sets convey UDP bundles with AODV estimation and the driving rate goes up from 30 km/s to 100 km/s, the typical throughput downs to 10% and its standard scattering additions to 21% [12]. A cross authenticated clustering mechanism to avoid road accidents using VANET was discussed by [10]. In this paper, with the combination of cluster head mechanism and ANN a high-speed data transfer rate mechanism was implemented. This algorithm was assessed using the mean square error and packet delivery ratio. Because of the vehicles moving at the high speed, the data packets which are transmitting between the vehicles may get lost. Here the road side units (RSUs) collect the current status of the vehicles and process the information using the ANN technique.

This [5] work plans to look at the apparatuses and models required for the VANETs test work. VANETs are thought of the greatest examination zone for as far back as couple of years. According to the previous scientists, VANET empowers the vehicles to assemble a remote association however fabricating the remote associations and communicating with hubs continuously conditions is a difficult task. In this way various recreation stages are available for completing the correspondence part in VANETs, for example, NS-2, NS-3, OMNET++, GloMoSiM, SNS, JiST/SWANS, and some more. Traffic accident detection using random forest classifier was discussed by [9]. In this paper, a smart vehicular accident detection system was developed to reduce vehicular accidents in the traffic. This method collects the data information such as speed and co-ordinates of the vehicles using VANETs methodology and processes the collected data through the developed machine learning-based random forests algorithm and post the current traffic updates to the vehicular drivers incessantly. FL in VANET for autonomous crash notification was discussed by [20]. In this paper, a road safety mechanism was developed to reduce road accidents such as automatic crash notification (ACN) and congested road notification (CRN) system. In the ACN system, the crash severity of the vehicle is estimated by using binary, URGENCY algorithm, and fuzzy model systems. This binary system generates the vehicle calamity messages and sends the current status messages to all other vehicles to avoid traffic congestion. The URGENCY algorithm will predict the occurrence of vehicular accidents. The CRN system is used to know the severity of live traffic congestion. This system is processed through the two-level systems such as binary system and co-operative traffic congestion detection (CTCD) system. This CTCD system is processed by using two parameters such as vehicular speed and density.

Fuzzy group-based intersection control using VANETs for intelligent transportation was discussed by [7]. In this paper, for controlling the traffic at the intersection of roads, instead of using traffic lights, a fuzzy-based algorithm was developed. By using this algorithm, the vehicles are partitioned into small groups and into small lanes. Every group and lane is scheduled via wireless communication rather than the traffic lights control system. Here the vehicles are scheduled through VANETs which are integrated with the neuro-fuzzy network. An attack detection system in VANETs using neuro-fuzzy system was discussed by [13]. In this paper, an efficient information scattering approach is intended which augments the vehicle-to-vehicle accessibility as well as augments the quality of service between the source and the destination. VANETs majorly contain two entities such as access point and the vehicular network. In this method, initialize the collected vehicular data in the pre-processed stage and then apply the developed neuro-fuzzy optimized algorithm to detect vehicular attacks.

In-vehicle cognitive route decision using fuzzy modeling and artificial neural network was discussed by [23]. In this paper, a self-decision-making methodology was developed to select the best routes by the vehicles to reach their destinations using fuzzy and artificial neural network optimization techniques. Here the daily route map information will be stored in a cognitive memory element, which will be integrated with an on-board unit. Here the live position of the vehicle is received by the GPS or by the road side units to the vehicle. The received vehicular position data will be well organized before it is stored in the cognitive memory. The received information will be sent to the OBS for taking the decisions. Gridlock is a critical contemporary issue in various thickly populated metropolitan regions. Thusly, during the past a drawn-out period of time, various vehicle course structures are proposed for vehicles to show up at their complaints as quick as possible when traffic is involved. Regardless, it's definitely not an immaterial task to find an ideal game plan under a multifaceted city environment. In this paper, a novel DRL based vehicle coordinating improvement methodology is proposed to re-course vehicles to their protests in complex metropolitan transportation organizations. In unequivocal, we reproduce nine useful traffic circumstances, using SUMO and train significant neural association model, to investigate vehicle logically. The improved arrangement of a DQN configuration makes our answer generally suitable for progressing insightful vehicle course. Our DRL model has been exhibited effectively [27–30].

Bandwidth efficient FL aided broadcast for VANET was discussed by [15]. In this paper, a fuzzy logic based assisted intelligent receiver was developed to intend a bandwidth efficient VANET protocol. In this method, the vehicle will receive and validate the acknowledgment messages from the neighbor vehicles by using a set of potential forwarders mechanism. The implemented fuzzy logic-based algorithm decides whether a recipient vehicle is eligible to rebroadcast the messages. Here the vehicles broadcast the messages by using the distance-to-mean parameter. This method diminishes the number of rebroadcasting vehicles which pilots to saving the bandwidth.

A FBFOZBR protocol for VANET was discussed by [19]. In this paper, a protocol was developed to find out the short and easiest route for the vehicles in a short period of time under any circumstances. This protocol was developed by integrating three techniques such as zone-based routing (ZBR), bacterial foraging optimization (BFO), and FL. ZBR is used to increase the stability of the system. BFO detects the shortest route in a small amount of time. Fuzzy logic is used to knob the tentative conditions of VANETs. Initially, it partitioned the vehicles into different zones. Each zone data will be transfer to the fuzzy logic section. This section also determines different merit factors such as bandwidth, mobility, and link quality. Finally, the result of the fuzzy logic is processed to the developed BFO algorithm to set out a reliable route. A dynamic traffic light management system for the minimization of the red-light running marvel was discussed by [8]. In this paper, a methodology was developed to diminish the waiting time of the vehicles in the traffic queue at the traffic signals. In this method, a wireless sensor network was utilized to track the live traffic conditions and communicate with the system integrated with the traffic lights about the current traffic status dynamically. After receiving the data from the Reduces Function Devices (RDFs), it sends the respected data to the Full Function Devices (FFDs) and then it forwards the data to the First Pan Co-coordinator (FPC). The principal point of this paper is to introduce a brilliant answer for the issue of gridlock. This point is accomplished by refreshing the courses of the vehicles stranded in gridlock and re-directing them to the backup way to go driving eventually to the objective. We have contemplated the effect of gridlock brought about by any episode on the movement season of vehicles. Alongside it, different natural factors, for example, CO_2 outflow and the fuel utilization by the vehicles is additionally investigated and an examination is made depending on three distinct situations. The proposed re-steering system shows an effective decrease in the movement season of a crisis vehicle too. Precedence based multichannel MAC to assist the vulnerable applications in SCH intermission at RSU in V2I communication was discussed by [14].

In this paper, a novel precedence based multichannel system was developed to support the insecurity applications in V2I communication with the help of RSU. The medium access control assigns the service channels based on the priority of the divided groups. By utilizing the Markov chain model and simulation, it assesses the performance of the network and focus on the advantages of the innovative scheme under the influence of vehicles with a diverse number of vehicles. A tentative characterization of routing protocols in urban vehicular communication was discussed by [23]. In this paper, a steering convention was created to discuss the vehicles with one another. The created steering calculation at first chooses the best way by utilizing a convey and forward methodology and afterward it communicates the information on that way. The created calculation is then assessed with present day steering conventions dependent on various nature of administrations (QoS) boundaries, for example, throughput, postponement, and parcel conveyance proportion to assess the idea of the diverse directing conventions.

Fuzzy logic based VANETs, a review on smart transportation system was discussed by [17]. In this paper, different optimization techniques and several security attack issues in VANETs were explained. This paper explains some of the methodologies implemented at the intersection of roads to control traffic congestion and also explained some of the remedial actions to be taken to avoid vehicular security attacks using VANETs. The paper [25] work introduced a credible investigation of the believability of a RL way to deal with the issue of traffic signals transformation and the executives. The work has utilized a sensible furthermore, approved traffic test system to give a climate in which preparing and assessing a RL specialist. Two measurements for the prize of specialist' activities have been researched, explaining that a legitimate decryption of the application setting is simply as significant as the ability in the legitimate use of AI approaches for accomplishing appropriate outcomes. Future works are focused on additional improving accomplished results, yet in addition, inside a more drawn out term, at researching what would be the ramifications of presenting multiple RL specialists inside a street organization and what might be the possibility to facilitate their endeavors for accomplishing worldwide enhancements over neighborhood ones, and furthermore the ramifications on the vehicle populace, that could see the adjustment in the foundation furthermore, adjust thusly to abuse extra chances and conceivably nullifying the accomplished enhancements because of an extra traffic interest on the improved crossing points. It is significant to perform examinations along this profession to comprehend the believability, expected preferences or even unintended negative ramifications of the presentation in genuine this structure of self-versatile framework [25]. Vehicle network is a critical subsystem of metropolitan keen transportation, which comprises of Internet of Things. Vehicle area information, driving status and street data can be acquired. Productivity, wellbeing and solidness are the economic improvement objectives of the framework. Simultaneously, vehicle systems administration can likewise utilize sensors, GPS and other gadgets to completely see the inner and outer climate of vehicles, and use real-time correspondence intends to understand the data trade among individuals and hardware. Through transmission, stockpiling, examination and guidance conveyance on the network, the insightful checking, guideline and the board of drivers, vehicles and walkers can be finished, and oneself getting sorted out control activity arrangement of metropolitan clever traffic lights can be set up [26].

The general system of metropolitan shrewd traffic light self-sorting out control dependent on vehicle organizing in genuine climate, which comprises of two sections wise vehicle and traffic way estimation framework. The fundamental information and fringe data of vehicles are gained by OBU module, and the client's human-machine data trade and fundamental control are finished by remote correspondence gadget [26]. In the rush hour gridlock street estimation framework, RSU module gets all vehicle traffic information in restricted space through sensors and sends them to focal control along with outer information, for example, climate conditions, convergence boundaries and anomalous identification. The expert control unit controls the ongoing unique data of the principal assemblage of metropolitan traffic and the climate, and adequately finishes the control of all vehicles in this zone [26]. The T–S fluffy neural organization model continually develops during the preparation. In view of the information for testing the totally prepared organization, the T–S fluffy neural organization expectation measure is built up the normal objective yields of the smooth, general clog and exceptionally blocked conditions are 1, 2 and 3, individually. The T–S fluffy neural organization is tried by utilizing the test tests and the vehicle clog rating is resolved after the adjusting rule dependent on the organization yield esteem. The expectation brings about show great concurrence with the working conditions of the vehicle and features the great forecast capacity of the T–S fluffy neural organization. In this manner, the proposed T–S fluffy neural organization model exhibits a phenomenal execution in assessing and recognizing blockage conditions.

To improve the exactness of recognizing vehicle blockage conditions, the driving status of vehicles in five driving condition parts are inspected. Each part goes on for 20 s. On the off chance that the quantity of pieces of incredibly clogged conditions n1 = 3, at that point the vehicle driving conditions is viewed as exceptionally blocked. In the event that the quantity of sections of smooth conditions 2 n = 4, at that point the vehicle driving conditions are viewed as smooth. In the event that neither of these conditions is met, at that point the vehicle is supposed to be under a general blockage condition [26].

4 Conclusion

In this review paper, the nature of smart transportation with the integration of VANETs was discussed. Because of increasing vehicular calamities day-by-day, a drastic change taking place in the field of transportation to avoid such calamities. To avoid such scenarios different smart transportation techniques by using VANETs were discussed. The introduction segment deals with the VANETs and their security attacks and also elucidated the remedial acts to be taken in VANETs to avoid the real-time security attacks. Different optimization techniques were discussed in the optimization techniques segment. By integrating these optimization mechanisms with the VANETs, several transportation issues can be solved. In the third section, different VANET based smart transportation system with different optimization techniques was discussed. In a further study, this VANETs based transportation system can be implemented with the Type-2 fuzzy optimization technique to get even more accuracy in communication and security when compared with the methodologies discussed in Sect. 3.

References

1. Adhikary, K., Bhushan, S.: Recent techniques used for preventing DOS attacks in VANETs. In: 2017 International Conference on Computing, Communication and Automation (ICCCA), pp. 564–569. IEEE (May 2017)
2. Alheeti, K.M.A., Gruebler, A., McDonald-Maier, K.D.: An intrusion detection system against malicious attacks on the communication network of driverless cars. In: 2015 12th Annual IEEE Consumer Communications and Networking Conference (CCNC), pp. 916–921. IEEE (Jan 2015)
3. Alsharif, N., Aldubaikhy, K., Shen, X.S.: Link duration estimation using neural networks-based mobility prediction in vehicular networks. In: 2016 IEEE Canadian Conference on Electrical and Computer Engineering (CCECE), pp. 1–4. IEEE (May 2016)
4. Amiri, E., Hooshmand, R.: Improving AODV with TOPSIS algorithm and fuzzy logic in VANETs. In: 2019 27th Iranian Conference on Electrical Engineering (ICEE), pp. 1367–1372. IEEE (Apr 2019)
5. Bhatia, T.K., Ramachandran, R.K., Doss, R., Pan, L., A review of simulators used for VANETs: The case-study of vehicular mobility generators. In: 2020 7th International Conference on Signal Processing and Integrated Networks (SPIN), pp. 234–239. IEEE (Feb 2020)
6. Boubin, J., Jones, A.M., Bihl, T.: Neurowav: Toward real-time waveform design for vanets using neural networks. In: 2019 IEEE Vehicular Networking Conference (VNC), pp. 1–4. IEEE (Dec 2019)
7. Cheng, J., Wu, W., Cao, J., Li, K.: Fuzzy group-based intersection control via vehicular networks for smart transportations. IEEE Trans. Industr. Inf. 13(2), 751–758 (2016)
8. Collotta, M., Pau, G., Scatà, G., Campisi, T.: A dynamic traffic light management system based on wireless sensor networks for the reduction of the red-light running phenomenon. Transp. Telecommun. J. 15(1), 1–11 (2014)
9. Dogru, N., Subasi, A.: Traffic accident detection using random forest classifier. In: 2018 15th Learning and Technology Conference (L&T), pp. 40–45. IEEE (Feb 2018)
10. Dutta, C., Singhal, N.: A cross validated clustering technique to prevent road accidents in VANET. In: 2018 International Conference on System Modeling and Advancement in Research Trends (SMART), pp. 183–187. IEEE (Nov 2018)
11. Feyzi, A., Sattari-Naeini, V.: Application of fuzzy logic for selecting the route in AODV routing protocol for vehicular ad hoc networks. In: 2015 23rd Iranian Conference on Electrical Engineering, pp. 684–687. IEEE (May 2015)
12. Kang, S.S., Chae, Y.E., Yeon, S.: VANET routing algorithm performance comparison using ns-3 and SUMO. In: 2017 4th International Conference on Computer Applications and Information Processing Technology (CAIPT), pp. 1–5. IEEE (Aug 2017)
13. Kaur, J., Singh, T., Lakhwani, K.: An enhanced approach for attack detection in VANETs using adaptive neuro-fuzzy system. In: 2019 International Conference on Automation, Computational and Technology Management (ICACTM), pp. 191–197. IEEE (Apr 2019)
14. Le, D.T., Nguyen, T.G., Simonina, O., Buinevich, M., Vladyko, A.: A priority-based multichannel mac to support the non-safety applications in SCH interval at RSU in V2I communication. Transp. Telecommun. J. 19(4), 269–283 (2018)

15. Limouchi, E., Mahgoub, I.: BEFLAB: bandwidth efficient fuzzy logic-assisted broadcast for VANET. In: 2016 IEEE Symposium Series on Computational Intelligence (SSCI), pp. 1–8. IEEE (Dec 2016)
16. Liu, X., Yan, G.: Analytically modeling data dissemination in vehicular ad hoc networks. Ad Hoc Netw. **52**, 17–27 (2016)
17. Maddiboyina, H.V., Ponnapalli, V.S.: Fuzzy logic based VANETS: a review on smart transportation system. In: 2019 International Conference on Computer Communication and Informatics (ICCCI), pp. 1–4. IEEE (Jan 2019)
18. Malik, F., Khattak, H.A., Shah, M.A.: Evaluation of the impact of traffic congestion based on SUMO. In: 2019 25th International Conference on Automation and Computing (ICAC), pp. 1–5. IEEE (Sep 2019)
19. Mehta, K., Bajaj, P.R., Malik, L.G.: Fuzzy bacterial foraging optimization zone-based routing (FBFOZBR) protocol for VANET. In: 2016 International Conference on ICT in Business Industry & Government (ICTBIG), pp. 1–10. IEEE (Nov 2016)
20. Nassar, L., Karray, F.: Fuzzy logic in VANET context aware congested road and automatic crash notification. In: 2016 IEEE International Conference on Fuzzy Systems (FUZZ-IEEE), pp. 1031–1037. IEEE (July 2016)
21. Patil, P.: A Survey on emergency message transmission protocol in VANET with message type recognition: a modified neural network architecture. In: 2019 IEEE International Conference on Electrical, Computer and Communication Technologies (ICECCT), pp. 1–5. IEEE (Feb 2019)
22. Punia, D., Kumar, R.: Experimental characterization of routing protocols in urban vehicular communication. Transp. Telecommun. J. **20**(3), 229–241 (2019)
23. Saeed, Y., Ahmed, K., Zareei, M., Zeb, A., Vargas-Rosales, C., Awan, K.M.: In-vehicle cognitive route decision using fuzzy modeling and artificial neural network. IEEE Access **7**, 20262–20272 (2019)
24. Singh, J., Singh, K.: Advanced VANET information dissemination scheme using fuzzy logic. In: 2018 IEEE 8th annual computing and communication workshop and conference (CCWC), pp. 874–879. IEEE (Jan 2018)
25. Vidali, A., Crociani, L., Vizzari, G., Bandini, S.: A deep reinforcement learning approach to adaptive traffic lights management. In: WOA, pp. 42–50 (Jun 2019)
26. Xia, G., Zheng, Y., Tang, X., Sun, B., Wang, S.: Shift control of vehicle automatic transmission based on traffic congestion identification. Int. J. Veh. Auton. Syst. **15**(2), 131–151 (2020)
27. Zhang, J., El Kamel, A.: Virtual traffic simulation with neural network learned mobility model. Adv. Eng. Softw. **115**, 103–111 (2018)
28. Kumar, A.: Design of secure image fusion technique using cloud for privacy-preserving and copyright protection. Int. J. Cloud Appl. Comput. (IJCAC) **9**(3), 22–36 (2019)
29. Kumar, A., Zhang, Z.J., Lyu, H.: Object detection in real time based on improved single shot multi-box detector algorithm. EURASIP J. Wirel. Commun. Netw. **2020**(1), 1–18 (2020). https://doi.org/10.1186/s13638-020-01826-x
30. Kumar, A.: A review on implementation of digital image watermarking techniques using LSB and DWT. In: The Third International Conference on Information and Communication Technology for Sustainable Development (ICT4SD 2018), held during August 30–31, 2018 at Hotel Vivanta by Taj, GOA, INDIA

Blockchain and Climate Smart Agriculture Technologies in Agri-Food Security System

Viktoriia Vostriakova[1,2], M. Lakshmi Swarupa[3], Olena Rubanenko[2,4],
and Sree Lakshmi Gundebommu[3($\boxtimes$)]

[1] Vinnytsia National Agrarian University, Vinnytsia, Ukraine
[2] Vinnytsia National Technical University, Vinnytsia, Ukraine
[3] CVR College of Engineering, Hyderabad, India
swarupamalladi@cvr.ac.in, s_sreelakshmi@yahoo.com
[4] Institute of Renewable Energy of Ukraine, Kyev, Ukraine
olenarubanenko@ukr.net

Abstract. The most common risks in the agri-food security system (AFSS) are the lack of financial resources and unpredictability of natural and climate change. In our opinion, there can be identified three most significant barriers to saturation of the economic system of the agrarian sector with financial resources: inadequate institutional environment, impact of agricultural risks and high transaction costs. The aim of the paper to examines the blockchain technology applications of in agri-food supply chains, innovative finance, agricultural insurance, climat smart farming for both theoretical and practical perspectives. Features of the production process in agriculture and its complexity require careful analysis, assessment and development of the methods aimed to neutralize the specific and general risks and threats of agri-food security system. Blockchain technology allows tracking information in the food supply chain and, thus, improves food safety. It provides a secure way to store and manage data that facilitates the development and use of data-driven innovations for smart agriculture and smart index-based agricultural insurance. In addition, it can reduce transaction costs, which will help farmers' access markets and create new income streams.

Keywords: Blockchain · Agri-food security system · Climate smart agriculture technologies · Smart index-based agricultural insurance

1 Introduction

The biggest problem of the agrarian sector is inability to manage the effects of seasonal cash flow risks, which has serious consequences for the economic security of agriculture. On the one hand, dependence on seasonal production cycles leads to uneven distribution of income and changes in the liquidity of agricultural enterprises during the year, which creates additional threats to financial management and limits their ability to invest in production activities.

Global climate change, which leads to a decline in agricultural production, the problem of food and economic security in the world require a serious adaptation of agriculture

A. Kumar et al. (Eds.): ICAIDS 2021, CCIS 1673, pp. 490–504, 2022.
https://doi.org/10.1007/978-3-031-21385-4_40

to new conditions. Responding to the challenges, the former Ministry of Agrarian Policy, together with FAO, prepared a draft strategy for adapting Ukrainian agriculture to climate change, based on the reorientation of agricultural systems and creation of climate smart-adapted agriculture to ensure economic security of the agrarian sector [1]. In particular, FAO promotes the idea of "climate smart" agriculture (CSA) and forestry, which aims to increase their productivity while reducing greenhouse gas emissions and adapting to climate change. Considering potential threats to socio-economic development and agri-resource potential in particular, which are possible under climate change, there is an urgent problem of strengthening the adaptation of certain sectors of the national economy, including those in the agricultural sector, to climate change [2]. Also there are a lot of researches in the field of implementation blockchain technologies in CSA. For instance, Patil et al. [3] developed a "lightweight blockchain architecture for smart greenhouse farms", combining IoT sensors into a private local blockchain operated by a farmer. The introduction of a smart agriculture system based on blockchain and the Internet of Things was studied by Lin et al. [4], the basis of their model is a platform through which all participants in the supply chain can access data stored in the blockchain via smartphones.

The concept of Climate Smart Agriculture [5] is not another interpretation of the "Green Revolution". On the contrary, CSA has much in common with the concept of sustainable development. This means that adaptation to climate change does not require a revision of existing theories of sustainable development in the agrarian sector. In fact, CSA is based on the well-known technical framework used in sustainability approaches [6], e.g. sustainable agricultural development, sustainable intensification and ecosystem adaptation, which ensure CSA implementation in practice

Providing accurate and reliable information to agribusiness is becoming a determining factor in increasing productivity and sustainability. The introduction of information and communication technologies (ICT) significantly increases the efficiency of data collection, storage, analysis and use in agriculture [7], allows users to get up-to-date information and make informed management decisions easily [8]. A number of modern technologies used in agribusiness have been studied: soil sensing [9], mobile capabilities [10], and the Global Positioning System (GPS), which is used to map fields and precision farming [11] and blockchain technologies in supply chains [12].

2 Agri-Food Supply Chains

The concept of supply chain management includes economic activities (and therefore income, employment and profit generation) of intermediate suppliers and services (engineering, logistics, business services, etc.) and suppliers of resources (infrastructure, financial and human capital, regulatory environment and level of introduction of new technologies, including information and communication technologies).

Globalization processes growth and the increase of the competitive market environment have made longer and more complex. The main problems that arise in the agri-food supply chains include the following: traceability of operations, safety and quality of agri-food products, consumer confidence and inefficient management along the supply chain, which creates additional risks in both the economic and social sectors, as it directly affects people's health. However, blockchain technology implementation helps to build a transparent relationship between consumers and producers, strengthening trust in consumer products through detailed information about individual products and each transaction in the blockchain. From the producer's side blockchain helps to increase demand for products, strengthen competitiveness and make it more difficult to access the market for unscrupulous producers. Clarity and transparency of processes helps customers to overcome consumer concerns about food safety, quality and environmental friendliness [13]. In addition, the blockchain provides reliable and accurate information to regulators to ensure sound and effective regulatory action [14, 15]. The proposed strategy "Value Added Multiplier 2+" is a strategy based on the analysis of the value added chain developed by Michael Porter and creation of an agri-food integrated cluster-based hub (Fig. 1).

The strategy involves stimulation of participation and investment in economic activity of all agri-food value chain (AFVC) participants: enterprises and organizations of higher (research and development, certified seeds, high-yield varieties, farming systems), medium (processing, end use of value added) and lower (packaging, food safety, branding, target markets, IT) segments of the value chain. Thus, the first plus (or increase in value added) will occur due to the productivity improvement as a result of improving the system of supply of the means of production: supply of high-quality seeds, irrigation systems, fertilizers, mechanization, while the second plus (increase in value added) will be the result of expansion and deepening of economic functions in various strategic segments of the supply chain (see Fig. 1) with the help of blockchain technology.

Combination of the proposed strategy with mapping of weak links of the studied supply chains makes it possible to determine the priorities and sequence of organizational and investment measures, especially in terms of attracting relevant strategic foreign direct investment and/or technical assistance that can serve as a necessary technological and innovative component and will ensure access to foreign (external) markets. The development of integrated agri-food value chains in Ukraine should be concentrated in key sectors of the food industry of the cluster having the greatest unfulfilled potential for creation of the value added, e.g. fruit and vegetable industry, dairy and meat processing. Typically, in developed countries, AFVCs operate independently of each other, serving their domestic markets [16] mainly due to different strengths and competitive advantages of a particular AFVC.

Despite a significant economic impact of integrated AFVCs, several key issues (weaknesses) need to be addressed at the upper, middle and lower levels of AFVCs to ensure effective integration of AFVCs within sectoral production systems at the regional level. Firstly, at the highest level (agricultural production segment) of the value chain, there are numerous, unorganized farms that dominate in production of fruits, vegetables, milk, livestock and are characterized by a poorly organized production system and low productivity. At the middle level (processing), processing enterprises lack reliable suppliers of high quality fruits, vegetables, dairy products and livestock from farms.

They have to act situationally and establish cooperation with numerous and scattered farms. Most processing enterprises are small and medium-sized enterprises (SMEs), their vast majority are unorganized, which hinders specialization and agro-industrial agglomeration of the agrarian sector. SMEs use outdated equipment due to the lack of access to

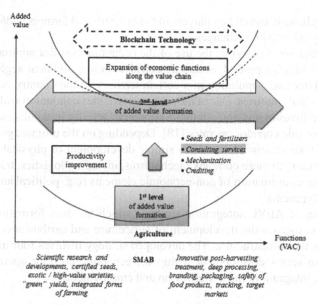

Fig. 1. Conceptual model of AFSS strengthening by agri-food value added chain (AFVC) "Value Added Multiplier 2+".* *Source: developed by the author

finance. Their products do not meet international standards for food safety and quality. In addition, there are no strong links between SME and domestic and foreign markets. At the lower level (marketing and distribution), there are no specialized regional shopping centers and logistics platforms for perishable products such as fruits, vegetables, meat and dairy products. Logistics infrastructure (e.g. refrigerated storage) and services (e.g. freight, forwarding services, etc.) for food transit are generally insufficient to cover available production volumes. These weaknesses in logistics, exacerbated by the lack of a reliable supply system, increase the transaction costs of transporting agricultural products and raw materials to the agri-food sector and reduce its profitability, which directly affects AFSS.

We have proposed several strategic solutions to address and overcome challenges in the formation of integrated AFVC. One of the strategies aims to ensure access to markets through public-private partnerships (PPPs). For example, in the course of such cooperation, public authorities of the appropriate level can provide land for long-term lease and provide subsidies and benefits, while the private sector can share the experience of doing business effectively. In addition, some forms of PPP can be useful, e.g. those in which the private and public sectors work together to create training programs for farmers that aim to increase productivity, product quality and yields, and therefore profitability [16].

Such integration of the main stakeholders of the agrarian sector in order to provide resources (new varieties of seeds, fertilizers and pesticides) to farmers and SMEs can stimulate the formation of SME clusters that will serve as satellites for large agricultural producers, wholesale and retail trade [16, 17]. This initiative will provide an opportunity to build strong links between key players in the industry and farmers and/or SMEs, thus addressing key mid-level challenges.

Another strategy is based on the use of the economic corridor approach to develop integrated AFVACs. In general, economic corridors belong to linear agglomerations of economic activity and population in a certain territory of the country or may develop between individual countries. One of the advantages of the economic corridor is its ability to attract more investments and stimulate economic activity in the district or region in which the economic corridor operates [18]. Depending on the ultimate goals, economic corridors can take various forms: from simple development of physical infrastructure (transport corridor) to more complex mechanisms, including logistics, trade facilitation policy and even coordination of non-economic elements (e.g. political and institutional capacity development).

Application of AFVC integration strategy, which involves formation of the economic corridor, focuses the development of agriculture and agribusiness around major investments in the infrastructure. The developed strategy involves four main directions of the agrarian sector development within the economic corridor operation (Fig. 2): infrastructure, integration, industrialization and employment.

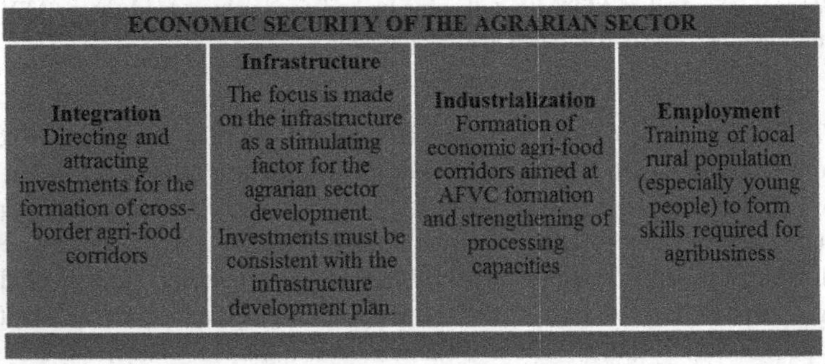

ECONOMIC SECURITY OF THE AGRARIAN SECTOR			
	Infrastructure		
Integration Directing and attracting investments for the formation of cross-border agri-food corridors	The focus is made on the infrastructure as a stimulating factor for the agrarian sector development. Investments must be consistent with the infrastructure development plan.	**Industrialization** Formation of economic agri-food corridors aimed at AFVC formation and strengthening of processing capacities	**Employment** Training of local rural population (especially young people) to form skills required for agribusiness

Fig. 2. Strategic components of economic corridor.* *Source: developed by the author

Implementation of the proposed strategy at the state level will improve the physical infrastructure and functioning of the markets in order to obtain the scale effect in the agrarian sector due to attracting investments in the agro-industrial complex within the territorial production systems of the region through the development of economic corridors. This involves the creation of value added networks within the agrarian sector, which will increase investment volumes and stimulate cross-border trade. Based on the theoretical generalizations on the main mechanisms of development of territorial-industrial production systems and integrated forms of management in accordance with the concept of integrated AFVC, it has been found that the development of integrated AFVC should be carried out using combined forms of integration to form a model of innovative ecosystem of the agrarian sector development. The developed concept of an open innovative ecosystem for the formation of integrated AFVC is presented in Fig. 3.

The proposed model of the innovative ecosystem of the agrarian sector development is based on the assumption that improvement of interaction within the ecosystem minimizes barriers to expanding production and increasing its efficiency, which in turn will strengthen economic security of the agrarian sector through the formation of integrated AFVC.

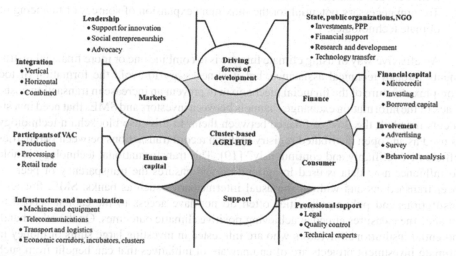

Fig. 3. Model of the innovative agrarian ecosystem on the basis of logistic integration.* *Source: developed by the author

In addition, the core of the proposed ecosystem is a coordination center – an agro-hub based on the relevant cluster working at the local level to ensure effective communication and provide specialized services including legal support, quality control expertise, consulting, etc.

3   Innovative Finance Mechanism in CSA

Considering the need to raise additional capital to address the challenges posed by climate change, a low level of funding for the agrarian sector development can only increase lack of funds. To ensure the access of SMEs to finance, barriers to agricultural lending need to be removed, which will direct the cash flows provided to finance climate technologies directly to farmers and SME. Financial resources aimed to find solutions to climate change can be used to build institutional links between financial institutions, on the one hand, and SME, on the other. Introduction of climate smart agriculture as an innovation and investment mechanism to provide AFSS is beneficial for the effective attraction of climate finance, which will contribute to achieving positive results in the process of adaptation to climate change, while providing significant economic and social impact. In order to work out the proposed mechanism, it is necessary to apply innovative ways of attracting additional capital to the agricultural sector both at the state level and in the private sector. In particular, it is necessary:

1. To use public-private partnership (PPP) and innovation and investment mechanisms to attract additional funding for implementation of CSA technologies, including concession agreements, to neutralize risks and help balance investment profiles according to the level of risk;
2. Identify effective tools for channeling climate finance to agriculture, providing direct links between financial institutions and SMEs;
3. To form necessary potential for the maximum expansion of sources of financing of climate technologies.

An effective way of using climate finance is to combine one or more financial instruments through technical assistance, but it is necessary to avoid the formation of too complex structure of the financial mechanism to prevent an increase in transaction costs. Lack of the information exchange channels between investors and SMEs that need investments may halt the flow of finance between them. In this case blockchain technology is used as an "open distributed registry that can record transactions between two parties efficiently, verifiably and continuously" [19]. This transformational technology is able to influence how data is used in agriculture and ensures the transparency of peer-to-peer transactions and without the usual intermediaries such as banks. SME, financial institutions and public authorities often do not have access to the capital needed to finance the measures aimed at achieving positive climatic outcomes. On the other hand, potential institutional investors who are interested in investing large sums of money in climate investment projects are often unaware of initiatives that can benefit from such investments.

Due to PPP in the field of climate-smart investments, it is possible to eliminate the problem of mismatch between the degree of risk and return on investments and the existing information asymmetry. Implementation of PPP-based cooperation practices is important for mapping national, regional and international CSA projects that require significant investments and pooling them into investment portfolios that include social, economic and environmentally sustainable investment projects. Another way to solve the problem of information asymmetry is to introduce the practice of PPP as a climate-smart investment (CSI) incubator. The proposed forms of PPP can provide brokerage services at the national level, accumulating small and medium-sized climate investment projects from SMEs and combining them into climate investment portfolios for financial institutions. We have developed two different models of climate investment, which include both concepts, but differ in the mechanism of operation.

Model 1 (Fig. 4) is based on the statement that the climate smart mechanism promoting investments on the basis of brokerage services (facilitator of the climate investment process – broker) provides for a commission for proving services on combining investors with relevant climate portfolios, while CSI incubators can combine relevant financial institutions with both certified climate investment portfolios and SMAB climate-change projects.

Model 2 (Fig. 5) assumes that climate investment brokers actually act as intermediaries, combining potential investors with climate investment projects of appropriate scale and developing appropriate multi-level capital structures for further participation in the process of managing investment assets.

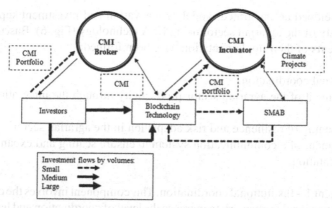

Fig. 4. Climate smart investments mechanism through brokerage services and blockchain.*
*Source: developed by the author. **Note: CMI – climate smart investments

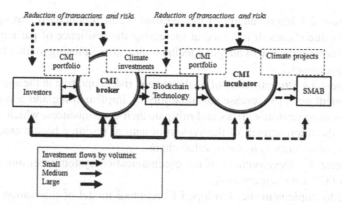

Fig. 5. Climate smart investment mechanism through intermediation and blockchain.* *Source·
author's development. Note: CSI – climate smart investments

Implementation of the developed model makes it possible to significantly reduce transaction costs and risks for investors and select those projects that will achieve positive results in the field of natural and climate technologies [20]. The models developed by us can be modified to provide a mechanism for simple and continuous communication between financial institutions (climate funds, institutional and investment funds, other financial institutions) and parties interested in climate investment in agriculture (financial institutions, SME, etc.) to strengthen economic security of the agrarian sector.

Blockchain technologies are also used to cover the risks of the agricultural sector, but they can be used in conjunction with an alternative index-based insurance system [21], where payments are calculated not at the same time as the insured event but according to the measured index [22, 23]. In order to strengthen economic security of the agrarian sector and neutralize natural and climatic risks in terms of adaptation to climate change, we have developed an integrated model of innovation and investment support of economic security of the agrarian sector using CSA technology (Fig. 6). Based on the goal set, components of their implementation have been formed:

1. Institutional coordination.
2. Improvement of the agrarian sector productivity through the integration into value chains.
3. Strengthening of resilience and risk adaptation in the agrarian sector.
4. Development of a communication system to ensure scaling and expansion of CSA implementation.

Component 1 – Institutional coordination. This component involves the creation of an inclusive institutional framework to increase the level of coordination and harmonization of climate smart technologies in the agrarian sector, as well as the development of a favorable legal and institutional environment for the implementation of CSA objectives as a whole.

Component 2 – Improvement of the agrarian sector productivity through the integration into value chains. It is aimed at increasing the resilience of participants in the value chain through the use of adaptive technologies, strengthening market linkages and integration processes.

Component 3 – Strengthening of resilience and risk adaptation in the agrarian sector. This component aims to increase sustainability by implementing and adapting appropriate measures to neutralize risks and mitigate their consequences, which will be possible due to the improvement of the system of natural resource base management and development of security systems in value chains.

Component 4 – Development of the communication system to ensure scaling and expanding of CSA implementation.

In order to implement the developed Conceptual model of innovation and investment support of economic security of agrarian sector development on the basis of CSA, it is necessary to carry out a number of preparatory measures. These include: activating stakeholders, prioritizing actions at both the national and regional levels, and mobilizing resources for their implementation. A necessary condition for the successful implementation of the proposed conceptual model is to strengthen the capacity of stakeholders in the field of CSA and to establish necessary links for implementation of the system at the national, regional and community levels.

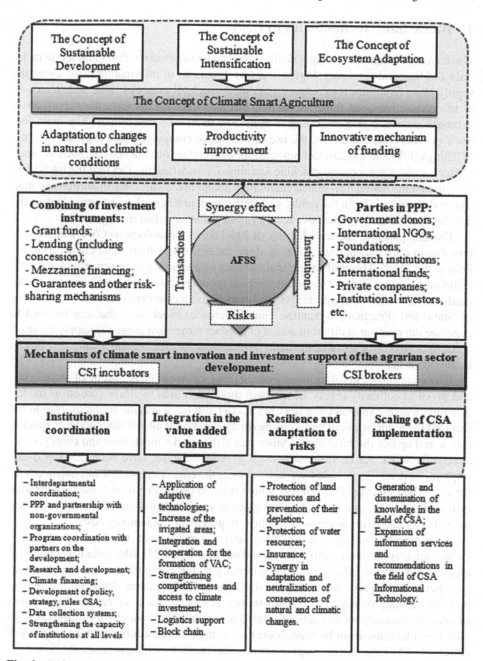

Fig. 6. An integrated model of innovation and investment support for AFSS on the CSA basis.*
*Source: developed by the author

4   Blockchain Technologies in CSA

The basis of the agri-food supply chain is formed by information flows about raw materials and financial resources. Figure 7 shows directions of information flows along the supply chain from inputs to outputs, passing through all stages of value added, as well as the reverse financial flow. All participants and stakeholders form the supply chain database and manage it according to their own needs and capabilities. The main features of Smart Agriculture are the use of innovative computer technology, the Internet of Things (IoT) and modern technologies for data collection and analysis, such as quadcopters, various sensors and machine learning. Considering the fact that the traditional system of information flow management may accept inaccurate data, distortion and misuse of data, especially in the public sector, the main problem of smart agriculture is the development of a comprehensive security system for easy data management.

For this purpose, the introduction of blockchain technology in CSA will make it possible to store data and information along the entire agri-food value chain "from the field to the table". This will ensure transparency and accuracy of information for supply chain participants. Figure 7 shows appropriate types (permissioned and permissionless), platforms (Ethereum or Hyperledger) and consensus mechanisms (Proof of Work / Proof of Stake and (Practical) Byzantine Fault Tolerance) blockchain that can be used to generate information at different stages of product movement along the supply chain. A consensus algorithm is one of the main mechanisms for creating and adding new blocks to the blockchain.

The main consensus algorithms include proof-of-work (PoW), proof-of-stake (PoS) and proof-of-authority (PoA). Blockchain most often uses the PoW consensus model, in which a node can create the next block after solving a specific problem. Due to the fact that the result of calculations can be easily checked, it allows other nodes to quickly check and update the blockchain. Since calculations take much time and energy, other alternative block verification methods, e.g. proof-of-stake, have been developed and implemented. Unlike proof-of-work, it replaces the energy consumed and overheads by the rate. The Delegated PoS (DPoS), which is based on the PoS model, uses a somewhat different approach, as nodes select delegates to verify calculations. Each algorithm has its own characteristics in terms of rewards, requirements and energy costs.

In a decentralized system, i.e. essentially a supply chain, blockchain technology creates an information security system, and not vice versa [24]. Blockchain technologies enable to distribute information flows directly to the computers of the supply chain members, which prevents the loss or distortion of information stored on the servers that are centrally managed by administrators. A blockchain is a database that consists of specific transactions and actions related to a particular product with timestamps. In addition, blockchain can be used to create a complex secure infrastructure for the IoT (Internet of Things) and to integrate other information technologies used in CSA.

Blockchain technologies provide opportunities for safe and stable storage of product information along the entire value chain, from pesticide residues in plant products to animal DNA. Introduction of modern blockchain technologies in AFVAC is still at the early stage of development due to high cost and the need to involve information technology. There are three main types of blockchain networks, each one having its own characteristics: consortium, private and public (Fig. 8).

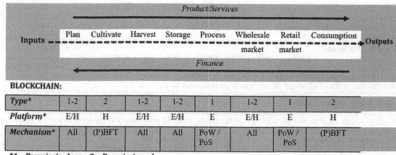

	Plan	Cultivate	Harvest	Storage	Process	Wholesale market	Retail market	Consumption
Type*	1-2	2	1-2	1-2	1	1-2	1	2
Platform*	E/H	H	E/H	E/H	E	E/H	E	H
Mechanism*	All	(P)BFT	All	All	PoW/PoS	All	PoW/PoS	(P)BFT

*1 – Permissionless; 2 – Permissioned

E – Etherium;   H – Hiperledger

PoW – Proof of Work;   PoS – Proof of Stake;   (P)BFT – Practical Byzantine Fault Tolerance

Fig. 7. Blockchain technologies in AFVC.

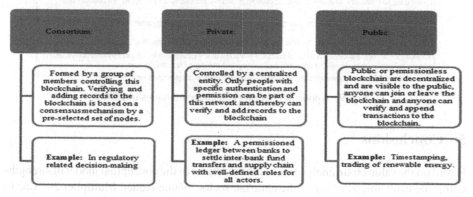

Fig. 8. Types of blockchain-networks in CSA

To understand the appropriateness of implementation of blockchain technologies in agriculture, it is necessary to consider the main areas of their application (Fig. 9).

In world practice, transactions based on blockchain technologies are tested in various sectors, including financial, logistics [20], energy [25–27] and government. Initially, blockchain technology was created to ensure decentralization of the financial system (along with cryptocurrencies). Nowadays, this technology is innovatively used in a wide range of operations, including AFVAC management, insurance, land registration by digital identifiers.

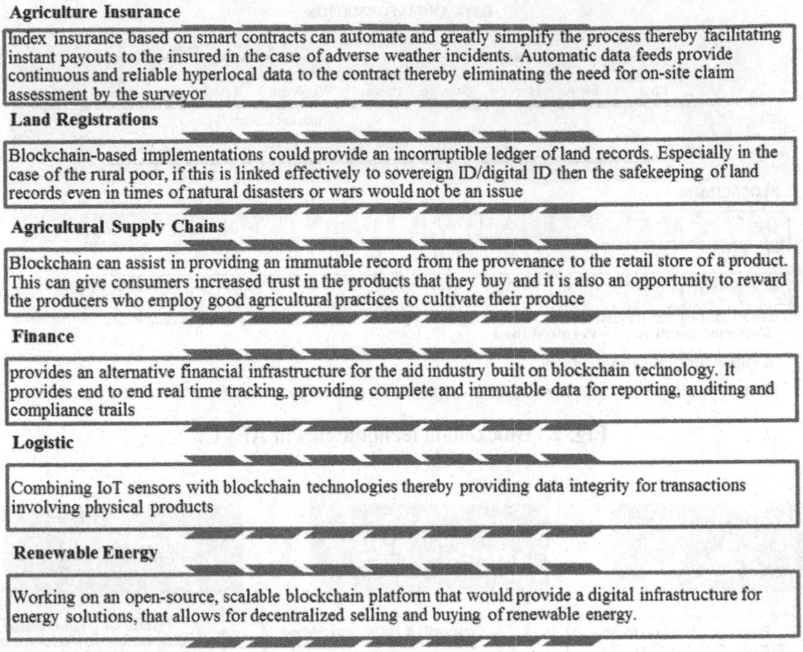

Agriculture Insurance

Index insurance based on smart contracts can automate and greatly simplify the process thereby facilitating instant payouts to the insured in the case of adverse weather incidents. Automatic data feeds provide continuous and reliable hyperlocal data to the contract thereby eliminating the need for on-site claim assessment by the surveyor

Land Registrations

Blockchain-based implementations could provide an incorruptible ledger of land records. Especially in the case of the rural poor, if this is linked effectively to sovereign ID/digital ID then the safekeeping of land records even in times of natural disasters or wars would not be an issue

Agricultural Supply Chains

Blockchain can assist in providing an immutable record from the provenance to the retail store of a product. This can give consumers increased trust in the products that they buy and it is also an opportunity to reward the producers who employ good agricultural practices to cultivate their produce

Finance

provides an alternative financial infrastructure for the aid industry built on blockchain technology. It provides end to end real time tracking, providing complete and immutable data for reporting, auditing and compliance trails

Logistic

Combining IoT sensors with blockchain technologies thereby providing data integrity for transactions involving physical products

Renewable Energy

Working on an open-source, scalable blockchain platform that would provide a digital infrastructure for energy solutions, that allows for decentralized selling and buying of renewable energy.

Fig. 9. Application of blockchain technologies in CSA.

5 Conclusions

Based on the value chain analysis, the author's vision of the conceptual model of strengthening the economic security of the agrarian sector "Value Added Multiplier 2+" due to the creation of an agri-food integrated cluster-based hub. Two level mechanism of the economic effect multiplication through the added value creation on the basis of increase of the productivity level (at the first level) and expansion of economic functions along the value chain thorough blockchain technology (at the second level) is substantiated. Combining the proposed concept with mapping the weak links of the studied supply chains will make it possible to determine the priority and sequence of organizational and investment measures to attract direct foreign investments and technical assistance to expand ISAF access to foreign markets.

Implementation of the proposed integrated approach will facilitate the emergence of links between agriculture, the manufacturing sector and the service sector in the future along the supply chain/value chain and the market. The proposed model of innovative ecosystem of the agrarian sector development is aimed at improving interaction within the ecosystem, which will minimize barriers that hinder the expansion of production and increase of its efficiency, which in its turn will strengthen economic security of agrarian sector through the formation of integrated AFVC.

Two different climate smart mechanisms have been developed to promote PPP investment: intermediation and brokerage services, which are aimed at providing conditions necessary for the creation and maintenance of innovation and investment ecosystem of the agrarian sector development, which will improve relations between financial institutions, on the one hand, and SME representatives, on the other, in the future. It is established that implementation of the proposed mechanisms will significantly reduce transaction costs, minimize risks for investors and form investment portfolios of projects that will maximize a positive impact in the field of climate technologies. To ensure an integrated and harmonious development of the agrarian sector in Ukraine, we have developed an integrated model of innovation and investment support of economic security of the agrarian sector, a distinctive feature of which is the implementation of CSA technologies to ensure sustainable development of the agrarian sector, a combination of investment instruments and PPP practices to attract foreign investment capital aimed at preventing climate change in the agrarian sector of the economy.

In order to ensure maximum efficiency of blockchain technologies in CSA, it is necessary to develop infrastructural support for such innovative technologies as the availability of a high quality information base, development of appropriate policies and regulations. Global trends in the introduction of blockchain technologies in traditional production processes and operations in most cases require additional costs, but it does not ensure significant benefits in the short term, but in the long run it enables to create a transparent, decentralized, secure transaction process and thus reduce transaction costs.

References

1. Kovalova, O.: Government portal. Ukrainian agriculture must become climate-adapted. https://www.kmu.gov.ua/news/ukrayinske-silske-gospodarstvo-maye-stati-klimatichno-ada ptovanim-olena-kovalova. Accessed 21 Jan 2022
2. Cooperation with the German-Ukrainian agri-political dialogue in the field of adaptation to climate change. https://mepr.gov.ua/news/34794.html. Accessed 21 Jan 2022
3. Patil, A.S., Tama, B.A., Park, Y., Rhee, K.-H.: A framework for blockchain based secure smart green house farming. In: Park, J.J., Loia, V., Yi, G., Sung, Y. (eds.) CUTE/CSA -2017. LNEE, vol. 474, pp. 1162–1167. Springer, Singapore (2018). https://doi.org/10.1007/978-981-10-7605-3_185
4. Lin, J., Shen, Z., Zhang, A., Chai, Y.: Blockchain and IoT based food traceability for smart agriculture. In: Proceedings of the 3rd International Conference on Crowd Science and Engineering, pp. 1–3. Association for Computing Machinery, New York, NY (2018)
5. Motashko, P., Panchulidze, K.: Agricultural insurance in the context of climate change. Agrosvit 10, 99–109 (2020)
6. Vostriakova, V.: The renewable energy sources contribution to sustainable economic growth. In: 2nd KhPI Week IEEE Proceedings on Advanced Technology (KhPIWeek), Ukraine, pp. 381–386 (2021)
7. Walter, A., Finger, R., Huber, R., Buchmann, N.: Opinion: smart farming is key to developing sustainable agriculture. Proc. Natl. Acad. Sci. U.S.A. 114, 6148–6150 (2017). https://doi.org/10.1073/pnas.1707462114
8. Kaddu, S., Haumba, E.N.: Promoting ICT based agricultural knowledge management for increased production by smallholder rural farmers in Uganda: a case of Communication and Information Technology for Agriculture and Rural Development (CITARD), Butaleja. In: Proceedings of the 22nd Standing Conference of Eastern, Central and Southern Africa Library and Information Associations, Butaleja, pp. 243–252 (2016)
9. Brown, M.E.: Satellite remote sensing in agriculture and food security assessment. Procedia Environ. 29, 307 (2015). https://doi.org/10.1016/j.proenv.2015.07.278

10. Kaske, D., Mvena, Z., Sife, A.: Mobile phone usage for accessing agricultural information in Southern Ethiopia. J. Agric. Food Inf. **19**, 284–298 (2018)
11. Yousefi, M.R., Razdari, A.M.: Application of GIS and GPS in precision agriculture (a review). Int. J. Adv. Biol. Biomed. **3**, 7–9 (2015)
12. Montecchi, M., Plangger, K., Etter, M.: It's real, trust me! Establishing supply chain provenance using blockchain. Bus. Horiz. **62**, 283–293 (2019)
13. Ge, L., et al.: Blockchain for Agriculture and Food: Findings from the Pilot Study. Wageningen Economic Research Report No. 2017-112. Wageningen Economic Research, Wageningen (2017)
14. Zhou, Q., Wang, Y., Fu, X.: Information asymmetry, blockchain and food safety. Res. China Mark. Superv. **11**, 53–56 (2016). https://doi.org/10.3390/ijerph15081627
15. Chen, W.: Administrative Rules and Regulations for the Introduction of Food Information Traceability in Blockchain. Ph.D. Thesis, Shanghai Normal University, Shanghai (2018)
16. Adriano, L.: Towards an Almaty–Bishkek Food Value Chain Cluster in the Almaty-Bishkek Economic Corridor. In: Presentation at the Second Meeting of the Joint Working Group on the Almaty–Bishkek Corridor Initiative Agreement. Central Asia Regional Economic Cooperation, Bengaluru (2015)
17. Son, D.: World economic forum's new vision for agriculture: the grow Asia Viet Nam case. In: Presentation at Enabling Agro Food Value Chain: A Capacity Building Workshop. Asian Development Bank Institute, Tokyo (2016)
18. Nogales, E.: Making Economic Corridors Work for the Agrarian Sector. Food and Agriculture Organization of the United Nations, Rome (2014)
19. Vostriakova, V., et al.: Optimization of agri-food supply Chain in a sustainable way using simulation modeling. Int. J. Comput. Sci. Netw. Secur. **21**, 245–256 (2021)
20. Iansiti, M., Lakhani, K.R.: The truth about blockchain. Harv. Bus. Rev. **95**, 118–127 (2017). https://doi.org/10.3390/s19153267
21. Turvey, C.G.: Weather derivatives for specific event risks in agriculture. Rev. Agric. Econ. **23**, 333–351 (2001). https://doi.org/10.1111/1467-9353.00065
22. Barnett, B.J., Mahul, O.: Weather index insurance for agriculture and rural areas in lower-income countries. Am. J. Agric. Econ. **89**, 1241–1247 (2007)
23. Barnett, B.J., Barrett, C.B., Skees, J.R.: Poverty traps and index-based risk transfer products. World Dev. **36**, 1766–1785 (2008)
24. IBM Institute for Business Value. Device Democracy: Saving the Future of the Internet of Things (2015)
25. Rubanenko, O., Hunko, I., Rubanenko, O., Rassõlkin, A.: Influence of solar power plants on 0.4 kV consumers. In: 60th International Scientific Conference IEEE on Power and Electrical Engineering of Riga Technical University (RTUCON), pp. 1–5 (2019)
26. Lakshmi, G.S., Rubanenko, O., Divya, G., Lavanya, V.: Distribution energy generation using renewable energy sources. In: 2020 IEEE India Council International Subsections Conference (INDISCON), pp. 108–113 (2020)
27. Belik, M.: Passive solar systems enhanced efficiency. Renewable Energy Power Qual. J. **17**, 235–239 (2019)

Using Symmetric Group to Generate Dynamic S-box

Kareem Abbas Alghurabi[1], Ahmed J. Obaid[2(✉)], Heyam K. Alkhayyat[3],
Yahya M. Abdulabbas[3], and Salah A. Albermany[2]

[1] University of Babylon, Babylon, Iraq
[2] Faculty of Computer Science and Mathematics, University of Kufa, Kufa, Iraq
{ahmedj.aljanaby, salah.albermany}@uokufa.edu.iq
[3] University of Kufa, Kufa, Iraq
hiyamk.hasan@uokufa.edu.iq

Abstract. The main purpose of utilizing s-box (static, or dynamic) is to encrypt data with/without decrypt cipher-data, s-box may be a public in the cipher method, but if it's private and included with steps of the cipher method, and depended it on the key cipher method. This work used the integer chaos data which are generated from the tent chaos map and symmetric group Sn in order to generate the private dynamic s-box between the sender and the receiver. An initial n × m s-box constructed by utilizing the random mixed between integer chaos sequence, and key method, with random element of symmetric group. The generation of s-box depend on the sequence I_{cs}, where I_{cs} generated from chaos sequence called Tent map is a simple linear function $T(x_n)$ such that to convert Tent chaos sequence x_1, x_2, ..., x_n to integer sequence $d_1, d_2, ..., d_n$. When the proposed method analyzed provide high randomness and high sensitivity to any simple changes of the initial used values.

Keywords: Chaos · S-box · Symmetric group

1 Introduction

Cryptography is commonly used to secure communication and data transmission over insecure networks through the use of cryptosystems. A cryptosystem is a set of cryptographic algorithms offering security facilities for maintaining more cover-ups. A substitution-box (S-box) is the lone component in a cryptosystem that gives rise to a nonlinear mapping between inputs and outputs, thus providing confusion in data. An S-box that possesses high nonlinearity and low linear and differential probability is considered cryptographically secure [1]. The s-box plays the vital role of creating confusion between the cipher text and secret key in any cryptosystem, and is the only nonlinear component in many block ciphers. Dynamic s-boxes, as compared to static, improve entropy of the system, hence leading to better resistance against linear and differential attacks [2, 3]. Tent map is a discrete-time piecewise-affine I/O characteristic curve, which

A. Kumar et al. (Eds.): ICAIDS 2021, CCIS 1673, pp. 505–517, 2022.
https://doi.org/10.1007/978-3-031-21385-4_41

is used for chaos-based applications, such as true random number generation [3].The tent map function T(x): (0, 1) → (0, 1), is given by [4, 5]:

$$x_{n+1} = T(x_n) = \{\mu x_n x_n < 0.5 \; \mu(1 - x_n) x_n \geq 0.5 \quad n = 1, 2, \ldots$$

where $3.6 < \mu < 4$ [6].The symmetric groups in abstract algebras are defined over any family of members. The basic some definitions regarding symmetric and alternating groups [6].

Definition 1.1: [7]

The symmetric group over a set S (denoted as S_n) is defined as follows:

- The elements of the group are permutations on, (i.e., bijective maps from **S** to itself).
- The binary operation (or product) of two permutations $\sigma, \tau : S \to S$ is the permutation $\sigma \circ \tau : S \to S$, i.e., the permutation given by $x \mapsto \sigma(\tau(x))$.
- The identity element of the group is the identity map of S.
- The inverse of a permutation σ is the permutation that sends each element $x \in S$ to the unique y such that $(y) = x$.

Definition 1.2: [8]

Let S_n be Symmetric group for any $g \in S_n$, we can write g as $\delta_1, \delta_2, \ldots, \delta_{c(g)}$ is the number of separate cycle factors with the 1-cycle of g and δ_j separate cycles of length α_1.

Definition 1.3: [1]

Let α be partition of n. We define $C^\alpha \subset S_n$ to be the set of all elements with cycle type $= \alpha(g) = (\alpha_1(g), \ldots, \alpha_{c(g)}(g))$. Also, C^α is denoted by S_n the number of conjugacy classes in $g \in C^\alpha$, if $C^\alpha(g)$ is denoted by $N_c(S_n)$.

2   Related Works

In [9] their goal was to specify the most appropriate chaos founded the entropy source by utilizing the optimization algorithms. This utilized entropy source in the construction of the substitution boxes (s-boxes), is essential cryptographic elementary. In the proposed work, the best initial conditions and discipline parameters have been specified for four different discrete time chaotic systems utilizing seven various famous noted optimization algorithms.

In [10] they proposed a construction of the S-box based a modern method which includes coset blueprint for the operation of a result of the modular group on the projective line over the finite field. This S-box has been assembled by chosen vertices of the closet blueprint in a private way. A useful transformation including Fibonacci sequence is also utilized in the choosing of the vertices of the closet diagram.

In [1] a cryptographing robust (8 × 8) S-boxes is constructed by implementation of the adjacency matrix on the Galois field GF (28). The compactness matrix is acquired identical to the closet blueprint for the operation of modular group PSL (2; Z) on a projective line PL (F7) over a finite field F7. The S-box tests prof the strength of the proposed S-boxes.

In [11] the chaotic logistic map, Mobius transformation and symmetric group S_{256} are utilized in order to construct the S-box for AES. The main idea behind the proposed work is to make the S-box more safe. LP, NL, DP, SAC, and BIC analyses applied. These analyses show that the proposed method is advantageous in the creation of high protection S-box to the known attacks.

In [12] a cryptographing robust bijective substitution-boxes is constructed by utilizing the chaotic map merits and the algebraic groups. The proposed work consists of two stages which are: the first stage in which the key-dependent dynamic S-boxes is generated by utilizing the chaotic heuristic search strategy and the second stage in which the S-boxes will evolved with the help of potent proposed algebraic group structures.

In [13] the proposed method is utilized in order to create the key abased changing (n x n) clone s-boxes which are having the similar algebraic features namely bijection, nonlinearity, the strict avalanche criterion (SAC), the output bits independence criterion (BIC) as of the original seed s-box. The proposed approach is established on the group action of symmetric group Sn and a subgroup S2n consequently on columns and rows of Boolean functions (GF(2^n) ! GF (2)) of s-box.

In [14] construction of dynamic S-boxes is proposed based on a contemporary and simple square polynomial conversion, the very first time, along with a prose affine conversion and a pioneering permutation approach. The proposed method erects a large number of the powerful S-boxes by implementing the minute changes in the parameters of conversion and permutation operations.

3   Generation n × m S-box

The s-box of size $n \times m$ define by

$$\alpha : \{0, 1\}^{nm)} \to Y$$

where

$$Y = \{A : A[a_{ij}] of\ n \times m, \quad a_{ij} \in \{0, 1\}^k, 2 \le k \le nm)\},$$

where if $D \in \{0, 1\}^k$, then D sequence of 0, and 1 of length k, $k \in N$, and each element in the matrix of the $n \times m$ s-box belong to Y, if the α is bijective function, then the input/output data corresponding just one only data. Let the size of data input x bits to the $n \times m$ s-box is $|D|$

$$|D| = (n) + (m) = (nm)$$

Suppose $|D_r| = \left\lfloor \frac{|D|}{2} \right\rfloor = \lceil (n) \rceil$, and $|D_c| = |D| - |D_r|$ then $n = 2^{|D_r|}$, and $m = 2^{|D_c|}$. The input data D of length $|D|$ bits, it will be divided into two parts, $log_2(n)$ bits for rows, and $log_2(m)$ bits for columns of $n \times m$ s-box.

Suppose that the two sequences I_D, and I_{cs} are distinct integer chaos sequence of size $n + m$, $2^{|D_r|} \times 2^{|D_c|}$, *with respectively* $2^{|D_r|} \times 2^{|D_c|}$, *withrespectively,,* such that

$$I_D = \{x_i : 1 \leq x_i \leq n+m, i = 1, 2, \ldots, n+m, x_i \in N\}$$

$$I_{cs} = \left\{x_i : 0 \leq x_i \leq 2^{(|D_r|+|D_c|)} - 1, i = 1, 2, \ldots, 2^{(|D_r|+|D_c|)}, x_i \in N\right\}$$

If $x, y \in I_D$, then $x \neq y$, also if $x, y \in I_{cs}$, then $x \neq y$.

If $D \in \left\{x : x \in \{0, 1\}^{n+m}\right\}$, where D(i) is a bit in the index i, then

$$D_r = \{x_i : x_i = D(I_D(i)), i = 1, \ldots, n\}$$

$$D_c = \{x_i : x_i = D(I_D(i+n)), i = 1, \ldots, m\}$$

Then

$$r = \sum_{i=0}^{n-1} x_i 2^i, \quad x_i \in D_r, i = 1, \ldots, n$$

$$c = \sum_{i=0}^{m-1} x_i 2^i, \quad x_i \in D_c, i = 1, \ldots, m$$

The output of s-box is $\alpha(r, c)$.

4   Tent Map Integer Sequence

The generation of s-box depend on the sequence I_{cs}, where I_{cs} generated from chaos sequence called Tent map is a simple linear function $T(x_n)$ such that to convert Tent chaos sequence $x_1, x_2, \ldots, x_n$ to integer sequence $d_1, d_2, \ldots, d_n$, by

$$if \; x_{j_k} = min^k \{x_i\}_1^n \Rightarrow d_k = j, \quad k = 1, \ldots, n, \quad 1 \leq j \leq n$$

where x_{j_k} *isminimumofsequence* $\{x_1, x_2, \ldots, x_n\}$ *without* $\left\{x_{j_1}, x_{j_2}, \ldots, x_{j_{k-1}}\right\}$
And $x_{j_1} = min^1 \{x_i\}_1^n = min\{x_i\}_1^n$, *and* $x_{j_n} = min^n \{x_i\}_1^n = \{x_i\}_1^n$.

Example 4.1: Suppose

$$x_1 = 0.4500, \quad x_2 = 0.8910, \quad x_3 = 0.2158, \quad x_4 = 0.4273,$$

$$x_5 = 0.8461, \; x_6 = 0.3047, \; x_7 = 0.6033, \; x_8 = 0.7854$$

Then

$$x_3 = x_{j_1} = 0.2158 \Rightarrow d_1 = 3, \quad x_6 = x_{j_{21}} = 0.3047 \Rightarrow d_2 = 6, x_4 = x_{j_3} =$$
$$0.4273 \Rightarrow d_3 = 4, x_1 = x_{j_4} = 0.4500 \Rightarrow d_4 = 1, x_7 = x_{j_5} = 0.6033 \Rightarrow d_5 = 7,$$
$$x_8 = x_{j_6} = 0.7854 \Rightarrow d_6 = 8, x_5 = x_{j_7} = 0.8461 \Rightarrow d_7 = 5, x_2 = x_{j_8} = 0.8461 \Rightarrow$$
$$d_8 = 2$$

Suppose the matrix S of size $n \times m$ corresponding to the s-box, the elements of s-box generated by AZA integer chaos

$$d_1, d_2, \ldots, d_{n \times m}$$

Such that

$$s(i, j) = d_{m(j-1)+i}$$

Or

$$if \ s(i, j) = d_k, \ then \ i = \left\lceil \frac{k}{m} \right\rceil, \ j = 1 + (k - 1) \mod (m)$$

5   Generate S-box from Symmetric Group

Suppose the $d_1, d_2, \ldots, d_{n \times m}$ are a permutation element of group S_{nm}, and corresponding to chaos number x, for example if nm = 6, and x = 0.7841, then

$$\lfloor x(nm)! \rfloor = \lfloor 0.7841 * 6! \rfloor = \lfloor 0.7841 * 720 \rfloor = 564$$

The number 564 corresponding to the permutation (542631), or

$$d_1 = 5, d_2 = 4, d_3 = 2, d_4 = 6, d_5 = 3, d_6 = 1$$

But 564 in binary of length $\lceil log_2(6!) \rceil = 10$ is 000110100.

Since each binary data corresponding to one permutation of size nm in S_{nm}. If the length of permutation n, then there are n! permutations on the set $p_n = \{1, 2, \ldots, n\}$, or denoted by S_n, where the set S_n is a symmetric group [7], we can classification S_n into n classes denoted by $S_{n-1}^{d_1}$, where $d_1 \in p_n$, on the set $p_{n-1}^{d_1} = p_n \backslash \{d_1\}$, also we can classification $S_{n-1}^{d_1}$ into n-1 classes denoted by $S_{n-2}^{d_2}$, $d_2 \in p_{n-1}^{d_1}$ on the set $p_{n-2}^{d_2} = p_{n-1}^{d_1} \backslash \{d_2\}$, and continue classification of S_n.

If $1 \leq x \leq n!$, and we want to determine the permutation corresponding to the number x by using the following [15]:

The initial set is $p_n = \{1, 2, \ldots, n\}$, $x \in \{1, 2, \ldots, n!\}$,

Set $p_n^{d_0} = p_n$, $x_1 = x$, $such \ that \ d_0 = 0$

$$y_i = \left\lceil \frac{x_i}{(n-i)!} \right\rceil$$
$$d_i = p_{n-i+1}^{d_{i-1}}(y_i)$$
$$p_{n-i}^{d_i} = p_{n-i+1}^{d_{i-1}} \backslash \{d_i\}$$
$$x_{i+1} = x_i - (y_i - 1)(n - i)!$$
$$i = 1, 2, \ldots, n$$

The permutation $d_1, d_2, \ldots, d_n$ corresponding to x.

Algorithm 5.1
Input   : n, x<=n!
Output: P vector of permutation corresponding to x.
Begin
$p_n = \{1, 2, \ldots, n\}$;
$p_n^{d_0} = p_n$;
$x_1 = x$;
$p_x = (\ )$;
for i=1 to n
$$y_i = \left\lceil \frac{x_i}{(n-i)!} \right\rceil;$$
$$d_i = p_{n-i+1}^{d_{i-1}}(y_i);$$
$$p_{n-i}^{d_i} = p_{n-i+1}^{d_{i-1}} \setminus \{d_i\};\ \ // \text{ delete } d_i \text{ from vector } p_{n-i+1}^{d_{i-1}}$$
add d_i to vector P;
$$x_{i+1} = x_i - (y_i - 1)(n-i)!;$$
end
end.

For example n = 4, and x = 15, then $p_4^0 = (1234)$, $x_1 = 15$

$$y_1 = \left\lceil \frac{x_1}{(n-1)!} \right\rceil = \left\lceil \frac{15}{3!} \right\rceil = 3, d_1 = p_4^0(3) = 3,$$
$$p_3^3 = p_4^0 \setminus \{3\} = (124)$$
$$P = (3)$$
$$x_2 = x_1 - (3-1)(4-1)! = 15 - 2*6 = 3$$
$$y_2 = \left\lceil \frac{x_2}{(n-2)!} \right\rceil = \left\lceil \frac{3}{2!} \right\rceil = 2, d_2 = p_3^3(2) = 2,$$
$$p_2^2 = p_3^3 \setminus \{2\} = (14)$$
$$P = (32)$$
$$x_3 = x_2 - (2-1)(4-2)! = 3 - 1*2 = 1$$
$$y_3 = \left\lceil \frac{x_3}{(n-3)!} \right\rceil = \left\lceil \frac{1}{1!} \right\rceil = 1, d_3 = p_2^2(1) = 1$$
$$p_1^1 = p_2^2 \setminus \{1\} = (4)$$
$$P = (321)$$
$$x_4 = x_3 - (1-1)(4-3)! = 1 - 0 = 1$$
$$y_4 = \left\lceil \frac{x_4}{(n-4)!} \right\rceil = \left\lceil \frac{1}{0!} \right\rceil = 1, d_4 = p_1^1(1) = 4$$
$$P = (3214)$$

Then the permutation is 3 2 1 4 corresponding to x = 15.

Example 5.1 Suppose $n \times m = 10 \times 12 = 120$, and $x_0 = 0.4177, x = \lfloor x_0 \times (nm)! \rfloor$, then the permutation in s-box is

51	15	92	26	41	118	30	47	100	71
	61	80							
110	69	65	114	20	66	88	96	82	9
	85	109							
76	35	63	57	89	36	94	10	112	106
	77	17							
62	22	46	79	105	39	53	37	98	81
	95	7							
111	16	78	119	14	43	86	48	115	64
	58	120							
101	102	104	50	1	52	74	68	32	108
	19	55							
25	113	59	33	116	67	28	93	23	49
	73	21							
31	97	54	83	29	12	107	34	40	45
	90	91							
11	27	70	5	60	2	3	6	56	84
	44	38							
75	4	42	99	24	72	117	13	87	18
	103	8							

Lemma 5.1

$$x = \sum_{i=1}^{n-1} \alpha_i(n-i)!$$

$\forall x, n \in Z^+$, and $1 \le x \le n! - 1$, $\exists \alpha_i \in Z^+, 0 \le \alpha_i \le (n-i)$, where $i = 1, 2, \ldots, n-1$.

Proof For $n \in Z^+$, *and* $1 \le x \le 5 = 3! - 1$, then

$$x = 1 : \alpha_{n-1} = 0, \alpha_{n-2} = 0, \ldots, \alpha_2 = 0, \alpha_1 = 1$$
$$x = 2 : \alpha_{n-1} = 0, \alpha_{n-2} = 0, \ldots, \alpha_2 = 1, \alpha_1 = 0$$
$$x = 3 : \alpha_{n-1} = 0, \alpha_{n-2} = 0, \ldots, \alpha_2 = 1, \alpha_1 = 1$$
$$x = 4 : \alpha_{n-1} = 0, \alpha_{n-2} = 0, \ldots, \alpha_2 = 2, \alpha_1 = 0$$
$$x = 5 : \alpha_{n-1} = 0, \alpha_{n-2} = 0, \ldots, \alpha_2 = 2, \alpha_1 = 1$$

$$\sum_{i=1}^{n-1} \alpha_i(n-i)! = \sum_{k=1}^{n-1} \alpha_k k! 0 \le \alpha_i \le (n-i) \quad 0 \le \alpha_k \le k$$

Suppose $k \in Z^+$, $\alpha_{k-1} \ne 0, k < n$, and $1 \le x \le k! - 1$ satisfy (5.1) such that $\alpha_{n-i} = 0, 1 \le i \le (n-k)$, then

$$x = \sum_{i=1}^{n-1} \alpha_i(n-i)! = \sum_{i=k-1}^{n-1} \alpha_i(n-i)!$$

To prove *for* $n \in Z^+$, *for* $\alpha_k \ne 0$ for interval $1 \le x \le (k+1)! - 1$, since in interval $1 \le x \le (k! - 1)$ satisfy (3.1) of size interval is k!-1, then *for* $k! \le x \le ((k+1)! - 1)$

have size $((k+1)! - 1) - k! + 1 = k\,k!$, but there are (k) of $\alpha_i = 0$, $i = 1, 2, \ldots, k$, and each $\alpha_{k+1} = 1, 2, \ldots, k$, have k!, then $(k+1)(k! - 1) + (k+1) = (k+1)k! = (k+1)!$, and also for k = n.

If $\alpha = \alpha_1 \alpha_2 \ldots \alpha_{n-1}$ is a permutation $\alpha \in \Sigma$ such that $0 \le \alpha_i \le (n-i)$, $i = 1, 2, \ldots, (n-1)$ the function $\rho : \Sigma \to S_n$.

Let $V_n = (12 \ldots n)$, and $P_0 = ()$, we can define

$$V_{i-1} = V_i \backslash V_i(\alpha_{n-i+1} + 1), i = n, n-1, \ldots, 2$$
$$V_0 = V_1 \backslash V_1(1)$$
$$P_i = P_{i-1} \| V_i(\alpha_{n-i+1} + 1), \, i = 1, 2, \ldots, n, \, such.that\, p_i \in S_i$$

where \ and \| denoted to difference operation, and concatenation operation with respectively.

Lemma 5.2

$$\sum_{i=1}^{n-1} (n-i)(n-i)! = n! - 1 \tag{5.2}$$

$\forall n \in Z^+$, and $n \ge 2$,

Proof The proof of (5.2) by induction, the first case, proves for n = 2, it's verifying.

To prove that for any $k \ge 2$, if (5.2) for n = k is holds, then (5.2) also holds for n = k + 1, then (5.2) satisfy for all $n \ge 2$.

Lemma 5.3. The function $\rho : \Sigma \to S_n$ is bijective function.

Proof Since by lemma 3.1 the size of $(\alpha_1 \alpha_2 \ldots \alpha_{n-1}) \in \Sigma$ is n!, and the order of symmetric group under the set S_n is n!, and each $\alpha \in \Sigma$ corresponding one element in S_n, then ρ is bijective function.

To apply the lemma 5.1 by use the following algorithm 5.2

Algorithm 5.2
Input   : $n \geq 1 ; 0 \leq x \leq n! - 1$
Output: p vector of permutation corresponding to x.
Begin
$V = \{ 1, 2, \dots, n\}$;
$p = ()$;
for j=1 to n

$$e(n - j + 1) = \left\lfloor \frac{(x \bmod (j+1)!)}{j!} \right\rfloor + 1;$$

end

for j=1 to n
      if j< n
         $d = V(e(j))$;
         $V = V \backslash e(j)$;
      else
         $d = V(1)$;
         $V = V \backslash V(1)$;
      end
$p(j) = d$;
end
end.

Apply above algorithm for x = 279, and n = 6, 7, 8

3	2	5	4	6	1		
1	4	3	6	5	7	2	
1	2	5	4	7	6	8	3

By apply example 3.1, n = 10, m = 12, and x0 = 0.4177, then.

51	15	92	26	41	118	30	49	38	47	57	36
105	58	86	24	115	97	78	46	93	91	59	3
40	56	65	10	96	111	68	8	48	50	95	44
114	28	66	1	81	55	5	23	63	104	12	120
71	54	94	109	100	35	87	76	89	77	25	61
84	16	113	117	19	2	108	90	39	79	34	101
80	22	112	37	9	88	4	69	82	106	27	13
72	102	60	21	75	29	62	31	32	98	42	7
53	20	70	73	85	45	119	83	52	103	67	11
107	74	6	116	33	18	43	110	14	17	64	99

6 Performance Analysis

To testing of the performance for each initial data collection x_i corresponding Sbox Ai, i = 1,2,...,t where t is a number of initial data. The similarity between two Sbox A, and B of size n × m is:

$$Sim(A, B) = \frac{\sum_i \sum_j S_{ij}}{nm}$$

Such that

$$S_{ij} = \{1\, a_{ij} = b_{ij}\, 0\, a_{ij} \neq b_{ij}$$

For example the two Sbox A,and B of size 5 · 5 corresponding the initial data 0.21, and 0.219, then the similarity is 0.04.

To analysis the Sboxes A1, A2,...,At corresponding with random sequence of initial values $x_1, x_2, ..., x_t$, then the *ratio* of difference Sboxes corresponding $x_1, x_2, ..., x_t$, define by the following equation

$$ratio = \frac{\sum_{i \neq j, i,j=1}^{t} Sim\beta(Ai, Aj)}{t^2}$$

where

$$Sim\beta(Ai, Aj) = \{0\, Sim(Ai, Aj) < \beta\, 1\, otherwise$$

Such that $0 < \beta < 0.5$. For example t = 9, x1 = 0.1,x2 = 0.2,...,x9 = 0.9,and β = 0.5, then *ratio* = 0.1358, and for t = 11, x1 = 0.1,x2 = 0.11,x3 = 0.13,....,x11 = 0.2, and β = 0.5, then *ratio* = 0.1405.

Suppose t = 99, x1 = 0.01,x2 = 0.02,...,x99 = 0.99, and β = 0.5, then *ratio* = 0.0299.

The following figure represented different between the S-box, and the sensitivity between them, where t = 198, X_1 = 0.001, $X_{i+1} = X_i + 0.005$, i = 1,2,...,t, and β = 0.5 then *ratio* = 0.0192 (Figs. 1 and 2 Table 1).

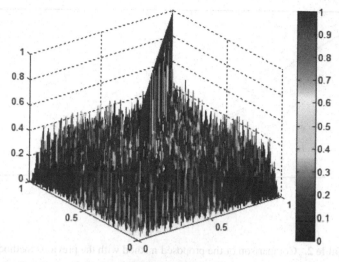

Fig. 1. Representation of the difference between the S-box, and the sensitivity

Table 1. The ratio of t values

β	Ratio		
	t = 99	t = 197	t = 981
0.1	0.3590	0.3673	0.3260
0.2	0.2897	0.2787	0.1805
0.3	0.1648	0.1595	0.0495
0.4	0.1019	0.0901	0.0214
0.5	0.0254	0.0163	0.0031
0.6	0.0115	0.0060	0.0012
0.7	0.0103	0.0051	0.0010

7 Comparison with Previous Works

In this section the proposed method will be compared with the related works that are related to this paper work in specific main features (Table 2).

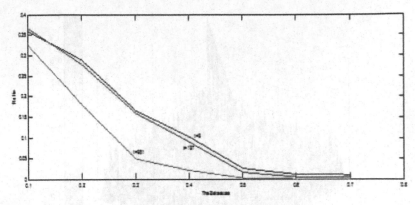

Fig. 2. The ratio of t values

Table 2. Comparison of the proposed method with the previous methods

The method	Speed feature	Dynamic generation of the S-box	Fixed S-box size	Using chaos map
[9]	Good	No	Yes	Yes
[10]	Good	No	Yes	No
[1]	Good	No	Yes	No
[11]	Good	No	Yes	Yes
[12]	Good	No	Yes	Yes
[13]	Good	Yes	No	No
[14]	Good	Yes	No	No
The proposed method	High	Yes	No	Yes

8 Conclusion

In this paper we construct secure and dynamic substation box (s-box). The basic idea to construct this s-box by using integer chaos tent map. The constructed s-box dimensions are (n*m) where n represent rows and m represent the columns. The method which is used in order to construct as follow: 1) the numbers will be converted to integer numbers, 2) generation of permutation sequences (length n*m) 3) then these sequences will be converted to matrix with n*m dimensions. The proposed method provides high randomness. Also, the proposed method provides high sensitivity to any simple changes in the initial values which enable to generate different Sbox in each simple change in the initial values. For example, the two Sbox A, and B of size 5 · 5 corresponding the initial data 0.21, and 0.219, then the similarity is 0.04 which means that the sensitivity very high to any simple change in the initial values. This feature gives the proposed method the ability to generate different and strong Sbox in every change of the used initial values.

References

1. Siddiqui, N., et al.: A highly nonlinear substitution-box (S-box) design using action of modular group on a projective line over a finite field. PLoS ONE **15**(11), e0241890 (2020). https://doi.org/10.1371/journal.pone.0241890
2. Easttom, C.: An Examination of in eciencies in key dependent variations of the rijndael S-Box. InElectrical Engineering (ICEE), Iranian Conference on 2018 May 8, pp. 1658–1663. IEEE
3. Singh, P.K., et al.: S-BOX Architecture. Springer (2019)
4. Nejati, H., et al.: A realizable modified tent map for true random number generation. Math. Ds. (2012)
5. Gora, P., et al.: On the significance of the tent map. Internat. J. Bifur. Chaos **13**(5) (2003)
6. Wildman, W.J., Russell, R.J.: Chaos: a mathematical introduction with philosophical reflections (1995)
7. Michael, D., Watts, M.A.: On characterizing pairs of permutations in determining their generated group. Directed by Dr. Greg Bell. **89** (2013)
8. Mahmood, S., et al.: Applications on new category of the symmetric groups. In:The 8th International Conference on Applied Science and Technology (ICAST 2020)
9. Tanyıldızı, E., et al.: A new chaotic S-box generation method using parameter optimization of one dimensional chaotic maps. IEEE (2017)
10. Shahzad, I., Mushtaq, Q., Razaq, A.: Construction of new S-Box using action of quotient of the modular group for multimedia security. Secur. Commun. Netw. **2019**, 1–13 (2019). https://doi.org/10.1155/2019/2847801
11. Iqtadar, H., et al.: Construction of S-Box based on chaotic map and algebraic structures. Symmetry **11**, 351 (2019)
12. Ahmad, M., Al-Solami, E., Alghamdi, A.M., Yousaf, M.A.: Bijective S-Boxes method using improved chaotic map-based heuristic search and algebraic group structures. IEEE Access **8**, 110397–110411 (2020). https://doi.org/10.1109/ACCESS.2020.3001868
13. Al-Dweik, A.Y., et al.: A novel method to generate key-dependent S boxes with identical algebraic properties. CS.CR (2021)
14. Amjad, H.Z., et al.: Dynamic S-Box design using a novel square polynomial transformation and permutation. IEEE Access **9** (2021)
15. Oabid, A.J., AlBermany, S., Alkaam, N.O.: Enhancement in S-Box of BRADG algorithm. In: Solanki, V.K., Hoang, M.K., Lu, Z.(, Pattnaik, P.K. (eds.) Intelligent Computing in Engineering. AISC, vol. 1125, pp. 737–745. Springer, Singapore (2020). https://doi.org/10.1007/978-981-15-2780-7_80

Wolf Algorithm Based Routing and Adamic Adar Trust for Secured IOT Network

Shailendra Kumar Tiwari[1]([✉]) and Praveen Kumar Mannepalli[2]

[1] Department of Computer Application, LNCT University, Bhopal, Madhya Pradesh, India
Shailendra.t86@gmail.com
[2] Department of Computer Science and Engineering, LNCT University, Bhopal, Madhya
Pradesh, India

Abstract. IoT network increases the utilization of the spectrum, by transferring data on blank channels. In order to reduce the robustness of the network from different attacks, many of researcher proposed various models. This paper has developed a secure routing technique to improved the spectrum utilization in IoT network. Routing of the packet was done by wolf genetic algorithm. IoT network is dynamic in nature hence genetic algorithm find good set of sequential node from sender device to receiver device. To identify malicious node in the network Adamic Adar trust value was estimate by the system. Neighbor relation was used in the function for the trust evaluation in virtual environment. Experiment was done on MATLAB platform and result shows that proposed model has increases the parameter values as compared to existing models.

Keywords: IoT netowrk · Genetic algorithm · Data security · Spectrum utilization · Trust based model

1 Introduction

The Internet of Things (IoT) is a critical stage in the evolution of the information age. Individuals, and even governments, are paying more attention to social information as it continues to develop. The Internet of Things is viewed as the next trillion-dollar market opportunity [1] due to massive market demand and vast development opportunities. Many governments throughout the world now place a high value on the Internet of Things.

The Internet of Things (IoT) is an open, intelligent system in which the majority of nodes are unmanaged and susceptible to malicious attacks [2]. In another approach, the external environment might harm IoT devices. For example, IoT nodes with a single function and low computer resources can easily infiltrated and turned into malevolent nodes that conduct internal attacks with legal status and pose serious security issues [3].

Multi-hop routing is used by all other nodes to send data to the data collection node [1, 2]. The security of data collecting, on the other hand, is a critical problem [4]. Many IoT devices can be joined to the network on their own because of the network's openness [5]. As a result, rogue IoT devices will obstruct conventional data collecting. The black

A. Kumar et al. (Eds.): ICAIDS 2021, CCIS 1673, pp. 518–529, 2022.
https://doi.org/10.1007/978-3-031-21385-4_42

hole attack [6] is the most common. Malicious nodes drop all packets forwarded by themselves in such an attack to destroy the data gathering [7]. The other is a sophisticated attack known as selective forwarding attack (SFA) [8]. Malicious nodes in SFA attacks do not simply discard data packets into a black hole, but rather selectively drop packets of selected nodes [8]. As a result, the wireless network has a certain packet loss rate. Malicious nodes can selectively drop some packets to avoid being identified, allowing them to launch assaults at a vital time to cause longer-term and more severe harm [8]. Data consistency is extremely important for data-driven applications. Insecure behaviours, such as data interception by malicious nodes, can result in packet loss, causing the control centre to make the wrong decision in the event of a data shortage, resulting in catastrophic losses.

Network assaults on the Internet of Things will not only inflict material harm, but also pose a threat to human life. As a result, developing a security plan for the IoT environment is very critical and important. In any IoT implementation, privacy, security, and trust are critical [2–5]. In IoT networks, trust can be divided into two categories: (1) trust in the interactions between network entities, and (2) trust in the network itself [4]. This research focuses on assessing an IoT node's trustworthiness, and in particular, techniques allowing a user to assess the trustworthiness of an IoT node's pass.

2 Related Work

Yu, Jia, and Tao devised a new quantitative method for assessing IoT trust. Integrity, Delay, Packet consistency, Repetition rate, and forwarding capacity were utilised to test the trustworthiness of a node in this approach. To synthesise and deduce trust, Shannon entropy and D-S theory are used to determine each and every trust factor [9].

In the Internet of Things, Hellaoui, Bouabdallah, and Koudil devised a trust adaptive security system (TAS-IoT). The trust evaluation in this approach is based on three factors: personal experience, observations, and recommendations. An evaluating node validates the authenticity of packets originating from the evaluated node under Own Experience. If the packet is authenticated, the node is trustworthy; otherwise, the node is malicious. Then, under suggestion, another neighbour node recommends the nodes' trustworthiness [10].

For the Internet of Things, D. Chen and G. Chang proposed a Trust and Reputation mode (TRM-IoT). End-to-end packet forwarding ratio (EPFR), Average Energy Consumption (AEC), and Packet Delivery Ratio were used to evaluate trust in this method (PDR). This method also assessed local and global trust, modelling them using a fuzzy reputation model [11].

M. Elkhodr and B. Alsinglawi introduced a new trust management solution that provides a trust establishment method among IoT communication devices, focusing on data provenance. This approach verifies the data's freshness, originality, traceability, and accuracy using data provenance [12].

ConTrust, a novel trust evaluation methodology based on everyday life inspiration, was proposed by V. Suryani, S. Sulistyo, and W. Widyawan. ConTrust evaluates trust based on two factors: historical reputation and present trust rating. The reputation based on history denotes previous object encounters. The nodes are categorised as Very Trusted,

Trusted, Very Untrusted, and Untrusted using a trust rating. ConTrust, on the other hand, did not pay attention to energy consumption at the node level [13].

V. M. Carolina and H. K. Joo [14] introduced a new trust management strategy to mitigate on-off assaults to a multiservice IoT. This approach analyses the behaviour of any node by using information collected from directly connected links between nodes [14, 15].

The defection of three insider assaults, black hole, sink hole, and wormhole, was studied by K. N. Ambili and J. Jose. For detection, a distributed trust management approach is proposed. The current trust score is compared to the previous trust score, and a decision is made whether or not to include or exclude a node [18].

Based on the Improved Bacterial Foraging Optimization (IBFO) method, P. K. Reddy and R.S. Babu proposed an Optimal Secure and Energy Aware Protocol (OSEAP) for IoT. The Fuzzy Cmeans method is used for clustering, while IBFO is used for cluster head selection in this approach. Group key distribution is also used to increase security. IBFO [19] is used to determine the best key pick.

3 Proposed Methodology

Whole work was divide into two section first was to generate the trust and other was to generate path. In first section a observation window was create to find the trust of the wireless nodes. Working steps of model is shown in Fig. 1. Second section finds the route from the source to destination in wireless network with an objective of optimizing the channel utilization.

Develop Virtual Region and Place Node Position
This work start with placement of N number of nodes and in an MxM region. In order to assume the initial stage of the network some energy need to be set for each node in the network [10, 11]. Each link between node have fix spectrum channel to communicate.

Observation Window: It's a centralized data storage in manage by fusion center where each transaction related information was maintain. Fusion center store node specific transaction count, successful transaction count, failed transaction count and transaction node ID. This bridge store data as per window. After completion of window trust value of the nodes were evaluate as per the trasaction behavior done by node in window. Wireless radio needs a fix size time. So in one window more than one node may initiate a transaction.

Adamic-Adar.
This is similar to Resource Allocation, but the denominator of the fraction is the log of the degree of the shared neighbor, rather than simply the degree [19].

$$Aa = \sum_{x \in a \cap b} \frac{1}{\log(d(x))} \tag{1}$$

where d(c) is the sum of the of the degrees of vertices adjacent to both a and b. d(x) is degree of x and y. Each node in the observation matrix has a trust value. This value

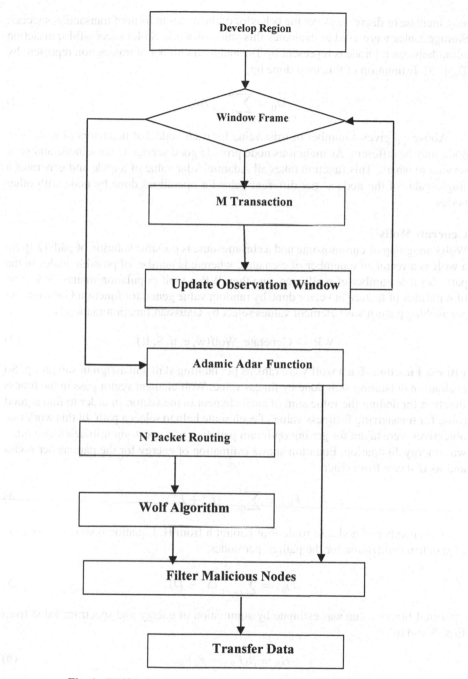

Fig. 1. Wolf and Adamic Adar based proposed model flow diagram.

may increase or decrease as per the behavior of the nodes in form of transaction success. Storage tables were used to evaluates this value of work. So let successful transaction count between i, j node is represent by Ts_{ij} and total number of transaction represent by Tt_{ij} [45]. Estimation of this trust done by:

$$D_{ij} = \sum_{i,j=1}^{n} Aa_{ij} \tag{2}$$

Above eq. gives n number of trust value for each node, but behaviors of node with node may be different. As malicious node provide good service to some node and poor service to others. This function takes all Adamic-Adar value of a node and generates a single value of the node as per different behavior operations done by node with other nodes.

Generate Wolfs

Wolfs are group of chromosome and a chromosome is possible solution of path [20]. So a wolf is a vector of e number of elements, where e is number of possible nodes in the path. So if w number of wolfs generate then WP is wolf population matrix. Selection of n number of feature in vector done by random value generator function Gaussian. As per weblog pattern wolf element values select by Gaussian function randomly.

$$WP \leftarrow Generate\_Wolf(w, e, n, S, R) \tag{3}$$

Fitness Function Each wolf were rank as per hunting skill and assign in sub group. So evaluation of hunting skill done by fitness value. Wolf element vector pass in the fitness function for finding the value sum of each element in the vector. In order to find a good route for transferring D fitness value of each route help to select a path. In this work two objectives were taken for getting optimum path first was spectrum utilization and other was energy dissipation. Equation shows estimation of energy for the path as per nodes and its distance from other.

$$F_{h,e} = \sum_{n=1}^{P'} (E_t^n + E_r^n) \tag{4}$$

P' is number of nodes in route P of habitat h from H. Equation 6 shows estimation of spectrum utilization for the path as per nodes.

$$F_{h,s} = \sum_{n=1}^{P'} (S^n - D) \tag{5}$$

Final fitness value was estimate by summation of energy and spectrum value from Eqs. 5 and 6.

$$H_h = \beta_1 F_{h,s} + \beta_2 F_{he} \tag{6}$$

where β_1 and β_2 are constant to normalize values at same scale because energy loss value is very low as compared to spectrum utilization.

This fitness H value is hunting parameter in the work to rank or assign a wolf in sub category of alpha, beta, delta and gamma. H is hunting skill value of wolf.

Update Wolf Position

Once H value obtain by fitness function then sort H in deseeding order and find wolf sub category. First sorted fitness value is consider as alpha wolf, then next m/3 consider as beta wolfs and next m/3 wolfs consider as delta wolfs [20, 21]. Position of each wolf were modified by the Eqs. 7, 8 and 9.

$$A = Pos - Ct * (Pos/Mt) * r - Pos - Ct * (Pos/Mt) \tag{7}$$

$$D_w = c. * (Delta\_Wolf - Alpha\_Wolf) \tag{8}$$

$$X_1 = Delta\_Wolf - A. * abs(D_w) \tag{9}$$

where Pos is position of wolf range{0,1,2,3} from Prey, c obtain by Pos*r and r is random number range from {1 to n}.

Similarly

$$D_w = c. * (Beta\_Wolf - Alpha\_Wolf) \tag{10}$$

$$X_2 = Beta\_Wolf - A. * abs(D) \tag{11}$$

$$X_3 = Alpha\_Wolf \tag{12}$$

Final position shifting value estimate by Eq. 12

$$X = \frac{x_1 + x_2 + x_3}{3} \tag{13}$$

Crossover Genetic algorithm success depends on change of chromosomes, hence as per X values number of random position value of wolfs were modified. This operation was not done in alpha wolf. In this step each wolf X number of positions were modified randomly as per alpha wolf element set. These wolf were further test for hunting skill and compared its hunting skill with parent wolf if child wolf has better values then remove parent otherwise parent will continue. After this step if maximum iteration steps occur then jump to filter feature block otherwise evaluate fitness value of each wolf.

New wolf fitness value is better than parent wolf then replace parent with new wolf in the population this is population updation in the work. After this population update perform same operation with other wolf in beta, delta and omega category. Once all wolf get update then check for iteration count if count is less than max iteration then jump to fitness value evaluation of updated population.

Hunting Rule After t number of iteration steps (fitness function, wolf position update, crossover) final wolf population pas through fitness function and best fitted wolf is consider as alpha wolf [21]. This wolf element nodes are predicted possible path to transfer data packet.

Filter Malicious Nodes Path generate by wolf algorithm is further scanned by the system to identify malicious node from the path. As per Adamic Adar trust value nodes having low value is consider as the malicious and other are consider as the real node. If path have malicious node then packet is not transfer on that path and it saves the spectrum and energy of the network.

4   Experiment and Results

Experimental work was done on MATLAB platform having machine of I3 processor and 4GB RAM. For comparison existing model proposed in SACR [22] was implement on MATLAB and run in same environment. To proof the dynamic adoptability of work experiment was done on different conditions, such as number of nodes, region size, packets movement [16, 17]. Evaluation parameters were taken from [23, 24].

Results

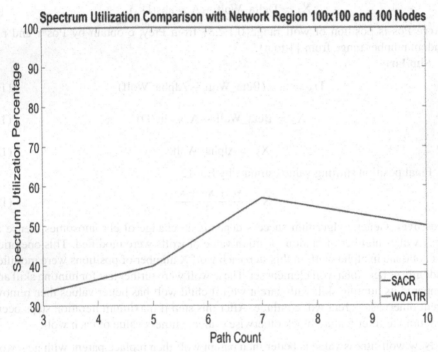

Fig. 2. Spectrum utilization based comparison of path count routing algorithms.

Table 1, Figs. 2 and 3 shows the spectrum utilization percentage of the IOT routing models. Table shows that WOATIR model is better as compared to SACR [22]. It was found that with increase of network area spectrum utilization get decreases. Impact of number of route in same set of nodes do not affect the spectrum utilization.

Table 1. Spectrum utilization percentage based comparison.

Nodes	Region	Route	SACR	WOATIR
100	100 × 100	3	33.27	99.8454
100	100 × 100	5	39.95	99.9767
100	100 × 100	7	57.04	99.9
100	100 × 100	10	49.95	99.8918
120	100 × 100	10	49.89	50.4988
140	100 × 100	10	79.7848	99.796
160	100 × 100	10	59.8529	99.8547
100	120 × 120	10	89.8519	99.843
100	140 × 140	10	69.8129	89.8121

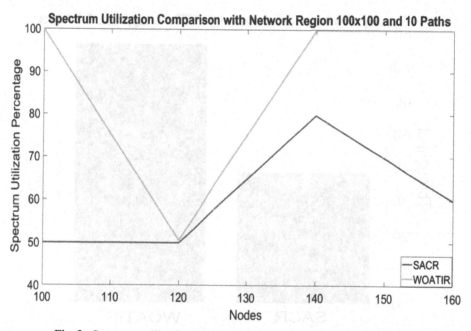

Fig. 3. Spectrum utilization based comparison of node routing algorithms.

Table 2 and Fig. 4 shows that throughput of the model proposed by this paper is more efficient as compared to SACR. Use of wolf genetic algorithm in the model for path node selection has increases the work efficiency. Alpha, Beta concept of wolf algorithm directly affect the node selection criteria of the work.

Table 2. Throughput (kbps) of cognitive routing based comparison.

Nodes	Region	Route	SACR	WOATIR
100	100 × 100	3	26.6152	79.9918
100	100 × 100	5	35.9528	95.9528
100	100 × 100	7	39.9371	82.8263
100	100 × 100	10	25.9734	73.98
120	100 × 100	10	23.9537	75.9421
140	100 × 100	10	51.87	69.8698
160	100 × 100	10	39.9202	79.9209
100	120 × 120	10	51.9087	57.911
100	140 × 140	10	47.885	67.8823

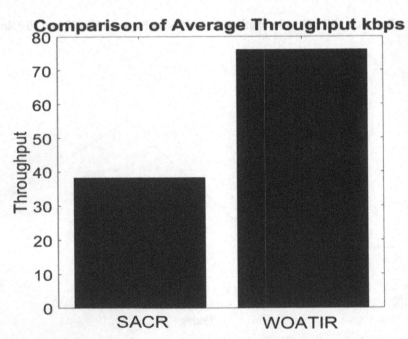

Fig. 4. Average throughput based comparison of routing models.

Table 3 shows that proposed model has reduced the transfer time of the work. Use of wolf algorithm has increased the work efficiency.

Table 4 and Fig. 5 shows that transfer time of the model proposed by this paper is more efficient as compared to SACR. Use of wolf genetic algorithm in the model for path node selection has increases the work efficiency. Alpha, Beta concept of wolf algorithm directly affect the node selection criteria of the work. It was found that with increase of

Table 3. Transfer Time (mile. Seconds) based comparison.

Nodes	Region	Route	SACR	WOATIR
100	100 × 100	3	123.2917	172.0667
100	100 × 100	5	112.8715	112.8515
100	100 × 100	7	127.0107	122.7
100	100 × 100	10	137.7569	135.0263
120	100 × 100	10	142.5933	134.2446
140	100 × 100	10	119.1397	117.3218
160	100 × 100	10	130.9862	130.9762
100	120 × 120	10	122.1779	118.0379
100	140 × 140	10	99.4546	98.4546

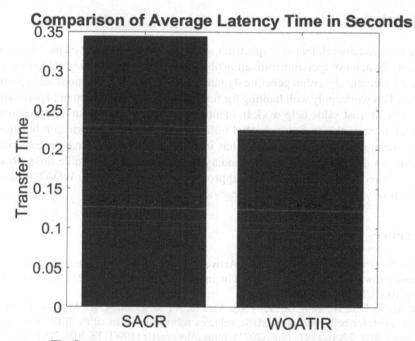

Fig. 5. Average transfer time based comparison of routing models.

network area spectrum utilization get decreases. Impact of number of route in same set of nodes do not affect the spectrum utilization.

Table 4. Latency Time (mile. Seconds) based comparison.

Nodes	Region	Route	SACR	WOATIR
100	100 × 100	3	0.5478	0.3397
100	100 × 100	5	0.4284	0.2295
100	100 × 100	7	0.3659	0.2189
100	100 × 100	10	0.3469	0.2734
120	100 × 100	10	0.3262	0.2279
140	100 × 100	10	0.2675	0.1765
160	100 × 100	10	0.3774	0.2224
100	120 × 120	10	0.1942	0.151
100	140 × 140	10	0.2405	0.1799

5 Conclusion

Wireless radio network increase spectrum as non-licensed users get chance to transfer there data. To achieve spectrum utilization objective genetic algorithm wolf Optimization was used. Genetic algorithm generate dynamic path as per node positions and spectrum channel. This work apply wolf hunting for finding end to end path. Further paper evaluate Adamic Adar trust value help work to identify malicious node and stop packet routing in malicious path, this increase channel utilization of the work. Hybrid combination of trust evaluation and routing algorithm has increases the IOT performance. Experiment was done on different number of secondary nodes for various possible links. Results were compared with previous existing approach and it was found that WOATIR has low transfer time values as compare to the previous approaches work.

References

1. Liu, Y., Dong, M., Ota, K., Liu, A.: ActiveTrust: secure and trustable routing in wireless sensor networks. IEEE Trans. Inform. Forensics Secur. **11**(9), 2013–2027 (2016). https://doi.org/10.1109/TIFS.2016.2570740
2. Wang, T., Luo, H., Zeng, X., Zhiyong, Y., Liu, A., Sangaiah, A. K.: Mobility based trust evaluation for heterogeneous electric vehicles network in smart cities. IEEE Trans. Intell. Transp. Syst. **22**(3), 1797–1806 (2021). https://doi.org/10.1109/TITS.2020.2997377
3. Wang, T., et al.: Privacy-enhanced data collection based on deep learning for internet of vehicles. IEEE Trans. Ind. Inform. **16**(10), 6663–6672 (2020)
4. Wang, H., Ma, S., Dai, H.N., Imran, M., Wang, T.: Blockchain-based data privacy management with nudge theory in open banking. Futur. Gener. Comput. Syst. **110**, 812–823 (2020)
5. Li, T., Liu, W., Wang, T., Zhao, M., Li, X., Ma, M.: Trust data collections via vehicles joint with unmanned aerial vehicles in the smart internet of things. Trans. Emerg. Telecommun. Technol. (2020)
6. Zhuo, C., Luo, S., Gan, H., Hu, J., Shi, Z.: Noise-aware DVFS for efficient transitions on battery-powered IoT devices. IEEE Trans. Comput. Aided Des. Integr. Circuits Syst. 2019 (2019)

7. Liu, A., Zheng, Z., Zhang, C., Chen, Z., Shen, X.: Secure and energy-efficient disjoint multi-path routing for WSNs. IEEE Trans. Veh. Technol. **61**(7), 3255–3265 (2012)
8. Xiao, B., Yu, B., Gao, C.: CHEMAS: identify suspect nodes in selective forwarding attacks. J. Parallel Distributed Comput. **67**(11), 1218–1230 (2007)
9. Yu, Y., Jia, Z., Tao, W., Xue, B., Lee, C.: An efficient trust evaluation scheme for node behavior detection in the internet of things. Wireless Pers. Commun. **93**(2), 571–587 (2017)
10. Hellaoui, H., Bouabdallah, A., Koudil, M.: TAS-IoT: trust-based adaptive security in the IoT. In: Proceedings of the 41st IEEE Conference on Local Computer Networks, Dubai UAE, pp. 599–602 (2016)
11. Chen, D., Chang, G., Sun, D., Li, J., Jia, J., Wang, X.: TRM-IoT: a trust management model based on fuzzy reputation for internet of things. Comput. Sci. Inf. Syst. **8**(4), 1207–1228 (2011)
12. Elkhodr, M., Alsinglawi, B.: Data provenance and trust establishment in the Internet of Things. Secur. Priv. 1–11 (2020)
13. Suryani, V., Sulistyo, S., Widyawan, W.: ConTrust: a trust model to enhance the privacy in internet of things. Int. J. Intell. Eng. Syst. **10**(3), 30–37 (2017)
14. Carolina, V.L.M., João, H.K.: Mitigating on-off attacks in the internet of things using a distributed trust management scheme. Int. J. of Distrib. Sens. Netw. 1–8 (2015)
15. Chae, Y., DiPippo, L.C., Sun, Y.L.: Trust management for defending on-off attacks. IEEE Trans. Parallel Distrib. Syst. **26**(4), 1178–1191 (2015)
16. Saied, Y.B., Olivereau, A., Zeghlache, D., Laurent, M.: Trust management system design for the Internet of Things: a context- aware and multi-service approach. Comput. Secur. **39**, 351–365 (2013)
17. Caminha, J., Perkusich, A., Perkusich, M.: A smart trust management method to detect on-off attacks in the internet of things. Secur. Commun. Netw. **2018**, 1–10 (2018). https://doi.org/10.1155/2018/6063456
18. Ambili, K.N., Jose, J.: Trust based Intrusion detection system to detect insider attacks in IoT systems. Inf. Sci. Appl., Cryptology ePrint (2019)
19. Adamic, L.A., Adar, E.: Friends and neighbors on the web. Soc. Netw. **25**(3), 211–230 (2003). https://doi.org/10.1016/S0378-8733(03)00009-1
20. Mirjalili, S., Mirjalili, S.M., Lewis, A.: Grey wolf optimizer. Adv. Eng. Softw. **69**, 46–61 (2014)
21. Abdo, M., Kamel, S., Ebeed, M., Yu, J, Jurado, F.: Solving non-smooth optimal power flow problems using a developed grey wolf optimizer. Energies (2018)
22. Rani, P., Kavita, Verma, S., Nguyen, G.N.: Mitigation of black hole and gray hole attack using swarm inspired algorithm with artificial neural network. IEEE Access (16 Jul 2020)
23. Mahapatra, S., Singh, A.: Application of IoT-based smart devices in health care using fog computing. In: Tanwar, S. (ed.) Fog Data Analytics for IoT Applications. SBD, vol. 76, pp. 263–278. Springer, Singapore (2020). https://doi.org/10.1007/978-981-15-6044-6_11

Using Convolution Networks to Remove Stripes Noise from Infrared Cloud Images

K. Chandana Sri[1], Y. Deepika[1], N. Radha[1], and Mahesh Kumar Singh[2(✉)]

[1] Department of ECE, Aditya Engineering College, Surampalem, India
radha.nainavarapu@aec.edu.in
[2] Accendere Knowledge Management Services, New Delhi, India
mahesh.singh@accendere.co.in

Abstract. To eliminate stripe noise from the single infaring image of a meteorological satellite, a new deep network design is being proposed. Existing methods of fixed modes for noise reduction can easily be exaggerated by the movement status of the sight and operating conditions of the image sensors, leading to smoothing belongings, ghosted, and slow conversion. We create an advanced neural network model with residual skipping connections in case of cascade-free single frame blind operation to resolve these issues. Furthermore, a common very well convolution unit is introduced to extract and fuse additional features over many scales to extract additional spatial information. In infrared imaging systems, stripe noise greatly degrades image quality. Continue to strike a balance between noise suppression, protection of information, and real-time precision, restricting their use in spectral imaging and signal processing, with existing striping algorithms. The suggested network can be trained and tested using a new set of infrared cloud photos from meteorological satellites. After these tests, it was discovered that the proposed technique recovered photographs with a similar level of quality and efficiency to other cutting-edge technologies. This paper presents a revolutionary deep-neural network of wavelets from a transformative domain. To tackle the problem perspectives which utilizes the intrinsic properties of stripe noise and additional information between different wavelets. The sub-bands coefficients are used to accurately estimate the noise at a low computational charge.

Keywords: Deep convolution neural networks · De-striping Convolutional network · Stripe noise removal · Fixed pattern noise reduction

1 Introduction

Remote sensing technology is used to detect and classify objects on earth based on satellite sensor-based technology. So, as a part of the secluded sensing technique, meteorological protectorate obscure image is extensively used to forecast for weather. Meteorology satellites collected cloud images that are classified into perceptible obscure descriptions and infrared obscure descriptions. Infrared images are produced by sensing the emitted radiation coming off of clouds. These can be used day and night time [1]. So, infrared obscure descriptions are more extensively used than visible cloud images.

© The Author(s), under exclusive license to Springer Nature Switzerland AG 2022
A. Kumar et al. (Eds.): ICAIDS 2021, CCIS 1673, pp. 530–539, 2022.
https://doi.org/10.1007/978-3-031-21385-4_43

Infrared images are mainly used in applications like military and inhabitant applications, counting remote sensing, visual tracking, imaging astronomy, IoT sensing, recognition for automatic targets, and video inspection. Due to conflicting responses of the dissimilar detector, the infrared cloud image combined with stripes noises. Hence, it is difficult to identify the structure of the cloud to predict weather [2]. To facilitate improving the eminence of infrared images, it is necessary to eliminate the stripe's noise [3].

For researchers working in the field of infrared imaging, stripe noise removal is a continuing problem. Striped noise in infrared images was reduced using least squares and gradient-domain directed filtering in this study [6]. An infrared image is smoothed using least-squares integrated with a bilateral filter to obtain high-frequency picture information. As a result, a gradient domain-guided filtering method is used to extract fine-grained texture information from vertical stripe noise in high-frequency photographs [8]. It's then subtracted from the noise image to produce a denoised version of it. According to the results of tests on publicly available datasets, the recommended method can achieve satisfactory results in terms of computing efficiency, denoising effect, and details [10].

Using a unique deep network architecture removes stripe noise from a single infrared cloud image captured by a weather satellite. Residual learning is used to reduce the mapping range between input and output, which improves de-striping performance and speeds up training [4, 5]. We used wider CNNs with more convolutions in the first part of our proposed network, which helps us learn similar pixel-distribution features from noisy images, inspired by wide inference networks. Local-global combination structures, which combine the representations of multiple layers, have been suggested as a way to improve performance even more [9]. We extend our rain-removal algorithm to remove rain streaks from single photos to improve it even more. We provide an infrared cloud image dataset from a new meteorological satellite to train and validate the proposed network. The results of the experiments show that the proposed method can achieve comparable restoration quality and computational efficiency to several existing methods [11].

Stripe noise is divided into two types, aperiodic stripes noise and periodic stripes noise. Aperiodic stripes noise is additional commonly occurred and hard to transaction, compared to periodic stripe noise [3]. To overcome this complication, deep network architecture was introduced. Till now, several methods were introduced to remove stripe noise. Now, let us examine the different approaches and contributions of this work. In the past few years, single-image de-stripping has become the standard approach. These approaches can be broadly divided into prior-based on two principal, statistical approaches, and deep learning approaches. Neural networks allow for state-of-of-the-the-the-art computer-art research. DNNs implement several complex structures made up of numerous layers called networks [4]. On the other hand, a larger number of network layers needs greater amounts of computation and memory. To minimize compute requirements of these networks, low-precision convolution networks are proposed [5].

The major ideas and achievements of the paper are recorded in the following statements:

1. Initiate a deep neural network to specifically learn the strip noise characteristics of the wavelet domain, which helps to measure the noise intensity and distribution accurately and responsibly.

2. "To correct the rendition of the images" means offering a regularize to eliminate and avoid distorting the strips of the model and isolate further noise detail.
3. The expansion of the wavelet can be used for analyzing the input image in quarter-sized coefficients, thereby increasing the calculation efficiency and simultaneously reducing the unwanted effects of high-separation effects.

When it comes to reducing the amount of stripe noise in a single infrared cloud image taken from a meteorological satellite, our deep network architecture outperforms the competition [9]. As mentioned in the proposed framework, a residual learning technique may be used to directly shorten the mapping range from input to output, which would speed up the training process and simultaneously improve the destroying performance of the system. For learning similar pixel-distribution properties from noisy images, we use broader CNNs with more convolutions, which are used in the second phase of the proposed network and inspired by wide inference networks. The authors offer a local-global combination structure model for the recovery of infrared cloud images' rich information, which integrates representations of various levels and numerous layers [8]. As a result of this model, the system will function even better. This research also proposes a novel approach to the problem of eliminating rain streaks from single images: a new method. There is also a bonus: a whole new collection of meteorological satellite infrared cloud image datasets for training and testing the proposed network. This method has been thoroughly studied and found to be more computationally efficient while still providing high-quality restoration at a lower cost than numerous other current state-of-the-art approaches [15].

All cumuliform clouds must be extracted from infrared satellite photos when studying cumuliform clouds. Only cumulonimbus clouds have been able to be extracted from the atmosphere using current methods. The cumuliform cloud cover over monsoon Asia is dominated by warm cumulus and cumulus congestus clouds, which make up a large portion of the total cumuliform cloud cover. These cumuliform clouds cannot be detected using a single brightness temperature (BT) extraction method [12]. Due to the difficulty in obtaining genuine aerial infrared cloud photos, we propose an effective method of creating cloud simulation data sets using a particle system and texture synthesis to alleviate the current data scarcity problem. To reduce the demand for genuine aerial photos by several orders of magnitude, our cloud segmentation is trained on our simulation image data set A reasonable segmentation result with 79.64% accuracy was obtained during testing on an actual photo dataset and is sufficient to meet the conditions for use [13]. Deep cloud segmentation network training is possible despite a lack of real-world images, and the cost of data gathering can be reduced using our strategy.

Atmospheric scientists rely on ground-based cloud imaging observations to classify different types of clouds. When it comes to classifying clouds, the use of infrared and visible light images is becoming increasingly common. However, they are only evaluated and compared separately in the current study, not simultaneously. For example, the information included in these two photographs is not fully utilized and integrated. Classification accuracy could be improved by making full use of the additional information offered by these two observations [11]. We have now created the first database that contains both types of cloud photos at the same temporal resolution. Cloud classification is discussed in the following section using a two-observation joint encoding technique for

LBP (local binary pattern) features. This technique encapsulates the distribution of LBP patterns in distinct observations, which represents the correlation between two observations, to implement cloud categorization. Experiments using this database show that compared to results based on a single observation, the suggested strategy is substantially more effective than the results based on the database [12].

This paper is structured in the following manner. In Sect. 2 literature review the development era of the Convolution Networks to Remove Stripes Noise from Infrared Cloud Images has been discussed. The proposed method for stripes noise detection techniques is discussed in Sect. 3. Result analysis is for stripes noise detection discussed in Sect. 4. In Sect. 5 conclusion of the Stripes, Noise from Infrared Cloud Images is discussed.

2 Literature Review

In 2020, Jongh lee and Young man proposed that it is accepted that infrared images have noise, which interferes with image quality. These images suffer from visible degradations because of their black-and-and-white method of presentation [6, 7]. Thus, therefore, the method for stripping down and restoring strip patterned images was created, which avoids any loss of information in the stripes [1]. Because of the low contrast infrared image property, processing does not produce large quantities of unwanted imagery [8]. A new stripping technique, known as deep convolution, is applied to photos to help remove FPN and to prevent image corruption [9].

In 2017, Jiao Chen and Hongwu Jiang introduced some methods to remove typical stripe noise. They presented the method of using FPGA implementation noise removal to clear up strip image data. The proposed approach, which is dependent on the most recent and most constant casement, is a similar algorithm, that will be implemented on an FPGA platform [11].

Near-infrared photographs are good for identifying night scenes and cloudy settings because they can recognize items in the absence of visible illumination. However, improving the resolution of infrared photographs is difficult due to the sensitivity of infrared images to their surroundings as well as thermal noise. There have been various approaches proposed for increasing the quality of infrared photos, including the standard super-resolution method. However, thanks to poor picture registration results caused by thick edges, which is a characteristic of thermal images, they were unable to acquire a satisfying outcome. As a result, the conventional super-resolution technique has been changed to eliminate the necessity for picture registration. The results of the testing revealed that the revised method delivers higher image resolution than the original method [5].

Sky and cloud photos from the ground Whole Sky Imagers are a cost-effective technique of acquiring data to better understand cloud cover and weather patterns. Because clouds have no obvious structure, producing successful cloud segmentation in these photographs is tough. Multiple algorithms exist in the literature that use various color models to achieve their objectives [16]. This work employs a systematic approach to offer a strategy for selecting color spaces and components for optimal segmentation of sky/cloud photos. For evaluation reasons, we employ principal component analysis and fuzzy clustering to determine the color components that are best appropriate for this activity [2].

Satellite images with cloudy pixels obscure the details of the Earth's surface. To achieve our goals, we devise a convolutional neural network-based cloud removal algorithm and a novel cloud synthesis model. Extracting cloud masks from satellite images as well as from sky photos with clouds is what we do. As a next step, we investigate the characteristics of real cloudy images and build up an accurate cloudy image synthesis model that takes these characteristics into account [14]. A hierarchical cloud removal network is trained on the synthetic cloudy images. The suggested technique successfully removes clouds from hazy satellite photos, and the results show that it is more accurate and faster than the currently used approaches. Convective cloud identification in meteorology relies heavily on thermal infrared photos, which may be gathered quickly [15]. There are several ways to identify and track clouds in satellite thermal-infrared images. The temperature-induced mean-based cloud motion prediction model is one of these models. But thus far it has only been used to track one cloud cluster at a given time. We are currently working to improve this model so that it may be used for future weather forecasting by tracking numerous cloud clusters [16].

DMSP OLS nighttime visible and infrared images are combined in this study using a standard set of imaging algorithms to improve cloud detection and recognition at night. Q is the quality measure we use to evaluate each algorithm's performance. Because of image fusion, fused photographs have a higher quality than individual visible and infrared images, and they have a far higher quality than individual nighttime visible images as a result of the process. The fused image has more cloud information than the original one [14]. Satellite images have long been a source of interest in atmospheric and environmental studies, but classification and analysis remain a difficult task. In this research, we present a new method for cloud type classification based on fuzzy logic. Previously, we used near-infrared images in addition to visible and infrared images as an extra input source. We can successfully improve the noise reduction procedure and the firsthand assessment of cloud presence height by taking into consideration cloud reflection and release characteristics. Fuzzy membership functions are used to arrive at the final categorization choice. These functions are designed to be flexible. Based on the experiment's findings, the proposed method is more efficient and accurate than the previous attempt, which primarily relied on infrared image characteristics [6].

Multiangle remote sensing gives a plethora of information for Earth and climate monitoring, such as the capacity to estimate cloud top heights using stereoscopic imaging, which enables cloud top height measurement. As technology progresses, the possibilities for designing spacecraft instrumentation that is sufficiently diverse to suit the needs of multiangle measurements are rising. The Infrared Spectral Imaging Radiometer, for example, was the first Earth-observing radiometer to use an uncooled microbolometer array detector as its image sensor and flew as part of the Space Shuttle Columbia's STS-85 mission in 1997 [3]. A method for calculating cloud-top height with a precision of 620 m has been created specifically for this flight's multispectral stereo readings, and the findings are compared to contemporaneous direct laser ranging measurements from the Shuttle Laser Altimeter. Mission STS-85 was the first space mission to use a mix of laser range and thermal infrared camera sensors for cloud distance assessment [4].

It is difficult to segment satellite photographs due to the intricacy of the processes shown within them. We developed a method for satellite infrared image segmentation based on an Ahuja approach that had previously been published but not widely used. Based on the similarities between the images, the previously described transform provides a pixel cohesion force field [6]. We discovered that the forces' convergence points create uniform region median lines, which we call uniform regions. Combining the information provided by the transform with a properly fitted segmentation algorithm yields a good region extraction. The classification of infrared photographs obtained over polar regions is a tough endeavor. The method that has been described takes advantage of the textural qualities of segments. The classification is done with the help of a neural network. The preliminary results are encouraging. It's expected that around 90 percent of the pixels are correctly detected [8].

To effectively predict precipitation amounts, meteorologists must be able to recognize and track mesoscale convective storms, as well as record their duration. It is feasible to discern between mesoscale convective systems and other systems using satellite infrared photography [5]. The temperature-induced mean-based cloud motion prediction model and the temperature-induced mean-based cloud motion prediction model are two existing methodologies for detecting and tracking cloud shapes using a succession of thermal infrared photographs. This method has previously been used to track individual cloud clusters, and then multiple cloud clusters at once. A temperature-induced mean-based cloud motion prediction model, which has been used in this work to track and predict cloud motion, has been used to monitor and project an entire convective system [7].

In 2018, Qianqian Yuan and Quang Zhang proposed hyperspectral image (HSI), it is essential to do extensive de-noising to help to boost the subsequent processing and application efficiency [12]. All proposed networks, regardless of the location or band, will get together the spatial and supernatural in order allocated to them. In the present manuscript, we proposed a profound erudition HSI denouncement technique by scholarship a non-linear back-to-back map among the deafening and clean HSIs with a deep spatially-spectral neural network [13]. In 2016, Yasmin Qian and Mingxia Bi proposed architecture to redesign the method to deal with background noise to make it more efficient [14].

3   Proposed Method for Stripes Noise Detection

Costly the contribution of ICSRN is an experiential stripe infrared images, as well as the degradation, is given when

$$Y = X + N \tag{1}$$

where 'Y' represents experiential stripe infrared cloud images and 'X' represents spotless infrared blur images. The expression 'N' represents the stripe constituent and inconsequential unsystematic noise. The detailed configuration is accessible and shown in Table 1. The system organization of this division can be articulated as

$$f_i = \sigma(W_i * f_i - 1 + b_i) \tag{2}$$

where 'i = 1,2,3......n' represent the whole number of the layer in this fraction, 'f0' is the contribution, '∗' indicate the complication procedure. '**W**' contained the weight and '**b**' bias, 'σ' is a rectification linear unit for non-linearity.

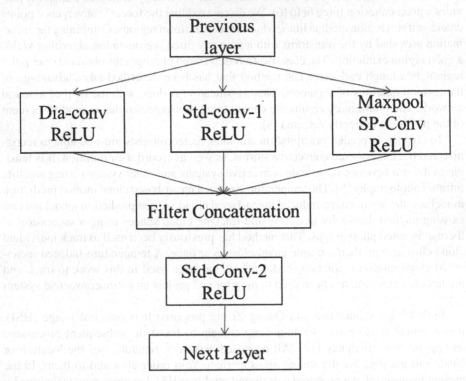

Fig. 1. The proposed method for detail architecture of CF-conv unit

Suggested that add a CF unit that handles multi-layer spatial attributes as in Fig. 1, dilation and subdivision (Dia-Conv) and sub-pixel are used to extract the common and very well skin texture. The convolution caused by expansion would cover the blind spots (Std-Conv) [16]. All the outputs of the convolution layer are applied to the Re-LU activation function, and the results are concatenated together into a single activation [15]. Finally, a constraint layer Std-Conv2 is added to fuse features and reduce feature and image duplication.

4 Results

ICSRN is a three-level de-striping train, i.e., α = 20, 25, 30. We set the size of the patch equivalent to 25 to 35. An increase in data is used to train the model by cropping 203496 patches with step 35. The stripe noise we add on aperiodic is much harder to treat because aperiodic stripe sound than regular stripe noise is almost entirely removable from distance sensing images.

Table 1. Detailed Configuration of ICSRN

Three main parts	Layers	Filters size	Filters number	Strides	Pads
Representation	Conv1	7×7	64	1	3
	Conv2	$64 \times 7 \times 7$	64	1	3
	Conv3	$64 \times 7 \times 7$	64	1	3
	Conv4	$64 \times 7 \times 7$	64	1	3
	Conv5	$64 \times 3 \times 3$	64	1	1
	Conv6	$64 \times 3 \times 3$	64	1	1
	Conv7	$64 \times 3 \times 3$	64	1	1
Local-global combination	Concat	Conv5 + Conv6 + Conv7			
	Conv8	$64 \times 3 \times 3$	64	1	1
Reconstruction	Conv9	$64 \times 3 \times 3$	1	1	1

Table 1 shows the detailed configuration of the CF-Convolution unit. Previous experiments show that the 3×3 sized filters are highly effective in enhancing feature quality and de-noising the use of image super-resolution Because it is smaller in size, the filter density of the CF-v unit must be lowered to $3\times$. Finally, to ensure the dimensions of all output features were identical, the device layer had zero padded (Table 2).

Table 2. The configurations of proposed Ms-Conv units

Layers	Layer type	Parameters	Filter number	Activation function	Strides
Max-pools	Max-pooling	Pooling Sizes = 2	–	–	4,4
Dia-convolution	Dilations Conv	Dilations Rates = 2	64	Re-LU	2,2
Std-convolution-1	Standards Conv	–	32	Re-LU	2,2
SP-convolution	Sub-pixels Conv	Subpixel Scales = 4	64	Re-LU	2,2

In this section, we'll show how CF-Conv and SCNA training leads to reduced noise in the validation package. This section contains various tests that employ the CF-Conv and SCNA training strategies to explore noise reduction capabilities.

5 Conclusion

These manuscripts, suggested a deep residual learning for neural networks processing to accelerate the training process while also improving efficiency when de-striping for satellite meteorological infrared images, both of which are accomplished utilizing large volume datasets. Instead of interface registration or motion parameter optimization, the proposed CNN-FPNR technique can be used to evaluate the frame/template reference radiation calibration parameters without the need for imperceptibility, which helps to simplify the single frame methods. When using a particular coarse fine convolution unit, the projected CNN models are able to select more targeted cross features to increase the precision of the discrimination. As well, we were able to demonstrate the possibility of extending ICSNR to a removal process where it can handle individual rain streaks in images. This was a real-world application of decomposing the existing problem into horizontal and vertical components.

Reference:s

1. Lee, J., Ro, Y.M.: Dual-branch structured de-striping convolution network using parametric noise model. IEEE Access **8**, 155519–155528 (2020)
2. Chen, J., Jiang, H.: The efficient-parallel stripe noise removal algorithm with low resource utilization is based on FPGA. In: 2017 IEEE 2nd International Conference on Signal and Image Processing (ICSIP), pp. 137–143. IEEE (2017)
3. Yuan, Q., Zhang, Q., Li, J., Shen, H., Zhang, L.: Hyperspectral image denoising employing a spatial–spectral deep residual convolutional neural network. IEEE Trans. Geosci. Remote Sens. **57**(2), 1205–1218 (2018)
4. Qian, Y., Bi, M., Tan, T., Yu, K.: Very deep convolutional neural networks for noise robust speech recognition. IEEE/ACM Trans. Audio, Speech, Lang. Process. **24**(12), 2263–2276 (2016)
5. Singh, M.K., Singh, A.K., Singh, N.: Multimedia analysis for disguised voice and classification efficiency. Multimed. Tools Appl. **78**(20), 29395–29411 (2018). https://doi.org/10.1007/s11042-018-6718-6
6. Guan, J., Lai, R., Xiong, A., Liu, Z., Gu, L.: Fixed pattern noise reduction for infrared images based on cascade residual attention CNN. Neurocomputing **377**, 301–313 (2020)
7. Singh, M.K., Singh, A.K., Singh, N.: Disguised voice with fast and slow speech and its acoustic analysis. Int. J. Pure Appl. Math **11**(14), 241–246 (2018)
8. Chang, Y., Chen, M., Yan, L., Zhao, X.L., Li, Y., Zhong, S.: Toward universal stripe removal via wavelet-based deep convolutional neural network. IEEE Trans. Geosci. Remote Sens. **58**(4), 2880–2897 (2019)
9. Singh, M.K., Singh, A.K., Singh, N.: Multimedia utilization of non-computerized disguised voice and acoustic similarity measurement. Multimed. Tools Appl. **79**(47–48), 35537–35552 (2019). https://doi.org/10.1007/s11042-019-08329-y
10. Padma, U., Jagadish, S., Singh, M.K.: Recognition of plant's leaf infection by image processing approach. Mate. Today: Proc. **53**, 914–917 (2021)
11. Satya, P.M., Jagadish, S., Satyanarayana, V., Singh, M.K.: Stripe noise removal from remote sensing images. In: 2021 6th International Conference on Signal Processing, Computing and Control (ISPCC), pp. 233–236. IEEE (2021)
12. Nandini, A., Kumar, R.A., Singh, M.K.: Circuits based on the memristor for fundamental operations. In: 2021 6th International Conference on Signal Processing, Computing and Control (ISPCC), pp. 251–255. IEEE (2021)
13. Anushka, R.L., Jagadish, S., Satyanarayana, V., Singh, M.K.: Lens less cameras for face detection and verification. In: 2021 6th International Conference on Signal Processing, Computing and Control (ISPCC), pp. 242–246. IEEE (2021)

14. Rakwatin, P., Takeuchi, W., Yasuoka, Y.: Restoration of Aqua MODIS band 6 using histogram matching and local least squares fitting. IEEE Trans. Geosci. Remote Sens. **47**(2), 613–627 (2008)
15. Singh, M., Nandan, D., Kumar, S.: Statistical analysis of lower and raised pitch voice signal and its efficiency calculation. Traitement du Signal **36**(5), 455–461 (2019)
16. Singh, M.K., Singh, A.K., Singh, N.: Acoustic comparison of electronics disguised voice using different semitones. Int. J. Eng. Technol. (UAE) **7**, 98 (2018). https://doi.org/10.14419/ijet.v7i2.16.11502

Correction to: Apple Leaf Diseases Detection System: A Review of the Different Segmentation and Deep Learning Methods

Anupam Bonkra, Ajit Noonia, and Amandeep Kaur

Correction to:
Chapter "Apple Leaf Diseases Detection System: A Review of the Different Segmentation and Deep Learning Methods" in: A. Kumar et al. (Eds.): *Artificial Intelligence and Data Science,* **CCIS 1673, https://doi.org/10.1007/978-3-031-21385-4_23**

In the originally published version of the chapter 23, the author affiliation information was not complete. The affiliation of the Author Amandeep Kaur has been changed to "Chitkara University Institute of Engineering and Technology, Chitkara University, Punjab, India".

The updated original version of this chapter can be found at
https://doi.org/10.1007/978-3-031-21385-4_23

Author Index

Abdulabbas, Yahya M. 505
Abdulbaqi, Azmi Shawkat 336
Acharya, B. Samirana 3
Ahmed, Kawsar 203, 215
Akhtar, Md. Amir Khusru 16
Akkineni, Haritha 135
Alam, Ashraf 377
Albermany, Salah A. 505
Alghurabi, Kareem Abbas 505
Ali, Md. Mamun 203, 215
Alkhayyat, Heyam K. 505

Banala, Rajesh 392
Bhardwaj, Sumit 181
Bisht, Shivani 52
Boda, Panna Lal 41
Bonkra, Anupam 263
Bui, Francis M. 203, 215

Chandana Sri, K. 530
Chatterjee, Rajesh Kumar 16

Deepank, G. 52
Deepika, Y. 530
Deshmukh, Vaishali M. 160
Durgam, Revathi 252

G, Surya Deepak 66
Gajjar, Nagendra 241
Gajjar, Ruchi 241
Garg, Gaurish 440
Grandhe, Padmaja 135
Gundebommu, Sree Lakshmi 321, 490
Gupta, P. K 169, 363
Gupta, Punit 181
Gupta, Ruchin 291
Gupta, Yogesh Kumar 279

Hadi, Hayder Sabeeh 336
Hanika, Ande 135
Harivardhagini, S. 321
Hossain, Md. Sazzad 215
Hossen, Md. Nazmul 203
Hunko, Iryna 321

Jethwa, Vipul 241
Jha, Amit Kumar 419
Jyothi, R. 52

K, Rohith Kumar 66
Kalyan, M. Pavan 89
Kamble, Megha 419
Kaur, Amandeep 263
Kishore, D. 89
Kolli, Rama Devi 430
Kuchanskyy, Vladislav 321
Kumar, Ashwani 191
Kumar, Boodidha Deepak 191
Kumar, Chithram Deeven 430
Kumar, Munish 77
Kumar, R. Anil 112

Lakshmi, P. V. S. 135

Madan, Nikunj 440
Maddiboyina, Harsha Vardan 476
Magboo, Ma. Sheila A. 452
Magboo, Vincent Peter C. 452
Makhija, Aditya 440
Manjunath, H. 227
Mannepalli, Praveen Kumar 518
Maram, Rakesh Kumar 476
Mathur, Gaurav 440
Mummadi, Akhilendranath 27

Nabi, Shaik Abdul 252
Nagaraj, P. 392
Nair, Vicky 392
Narayana, M. V. 144
Nayer, Md. 203, 215
Noonia, Ajit 263

Obaid, Ahmed J. 336, 505

Padmaja, D. Lakshmi 66
Pareek, Piyush Kumar 144
Pisati, Sreekanth Reddy 430
Ponnapalli, V. A. Sankar 476
Pradhan, Dinesh K. 16
Pranavam, V. P. 465

Radha, N.   530
Rahaman, Md. Abdur   203
Ramachandran, Vineeth P.   465
Ramadevi, Y.   41
Ramasubramanian, K.   3
Rani, Veenu   77
Rao, B. Nageshwar   348
Rao, S. Srinivasa   123
Rath, Subhashree   160
Reddy, D. Lakshmi Sreenivasa   348
Reddy, S. Sai Satyanarayana   191, 430
Reddy, Vudara Bhaskar   191
Rout, Ranjeet Kumar   306
Rubanenko, Olena   321, 490

S., Geetha Sree   160
S., Harshitha   160
Sadhwika, Rachamalla   27
Saisree, S.   404
Saravana Kumar, S.   227
Satyanarayana, V.   101
Saxena, Khushboo   279
Sharma, Pankaj   363
Shitharth, S.   27, 404
Shivani, Shivendra   440
Shovo, Mehedi Hassan   215
Singh, Bhupinder   77

Singh, Devanshu Kumar   181
Singh, Mahesh K.   89, 101, 112
Singh, Mahesh Kumar   530
Singh, Ria   181
Singh, Sandeep Kumar   291
Sowmya, G.   191
Sree, V. Navya   123
Sreedharan, Pramod   465
Sriharsha, G. K.   66
Subbalakshmi, Chatti   144
Sushma, K.   101
Swarupa, M. Lakshmi   490

Tandon, Righa   169
Tharun Raj, R.   52
Tiwari, Shailendra Kumar   518

Urmila, Sabbella   112

V., Shree Raksha   160
Vasko, Petro   321
Venkata Maha Lakshmi, N.   306
Verma, Aditya   52
Vij, Vaibhav   440
Vostriakova, Viktoriia   490

Yadav, B. Midhun Krishna   27